THE BLOOD BANKERS

Tales from the Global Underground Economy

by

James S. Henry

FOUR WALLS EIGHT WINDOWS
NEW YORK/LONDON

This book is dedicated to my family.

Published in the United States by:
Four Walls Eight Windows
39 West 14th Street, room 503
New York, NY 10011

Visit our website at http://www.4w8w.com

First printing October 2003

Library of Congress Cataloging-in-Publication Data

Henry, James S.
    The blood bankers : tales from the underground global economy / by
James S. Henry.
    p. cm.
Includes bibliographical references and index.
ISBN 1-56858-254-4 (cloth)
    1. Transnational crime 2. Globalization. I. Title.

HV6252.H45   2003
364.1'36—dc22   2003060223
                                                       CIP

10 9 8 7 6 5 4 3 2 1

Typesetting by Dr. Prepress, Inc.

Printed in the United States

TABLE OF CONTENTS

FOREWORD

by

FORMER SENATOR BILL BRADLEY

This year marks the twentieth anniversary of the so-called Third World "debt crisis" and the continuing development crisis that succeeded it, especially for the more than three billion people around the world who still subsist on less than two dollars per day. Until now, however, those of us who have been deeply concerned with problems of debt and development haven't had a critical account of what really happened. This eye-opening book, the product of Jim Henry's pathbreaking work as an investigative journalist over the past two decades, fills this gap. It brings us astonishing new insights about why these countries have remained poor for so long—despite the fact that so many of them have abundant human and natural resources.

As Jim Henry indicates, the key puzzle is based on the fact that from 1970 to 1982, First World banks loaned more than a trillion dollars to developing countries. Then, from the late 1980s through 2003, spurred on by free-market enthusiasts and institutions like the IMF and the World Bank, developing countries tried to absorb another $2.2 trillion in foreign capital, three-fourths of it in the form of private investment and bonds.

Unhappily, while a few countries were able to digest all this foreign capital and develop, many others failed to use it wisely. The result is that after thirty years of heavy investment and a decade of experiments with free trade, debt restructuring, and deregulation, we now face a situation where debt levels are higher than ever in many countries, and the gap between the living standards and technology levels of the world's richest and poorest countries—and the world's richest and poorest citizens—has increased dramatically. To fix this problem, we'll have to transcend both the simple-minded "big project" strategies of the 1970s and the equally-simplistic laissez-faire solutions of the 1990s.

This situation may come as a surprise to many First World residents, for whom the last decade of the twentieth century was a period of unprecedented prosperity. The Cold War came to an end, the world saw relative peace, unemployment fell to record lows, and vast fortunes were made overnight. Many of us trusted that market forces—globalization, liberalization, and privatization—would work similar miracles for developing countries, permitting them to substitute private trade and investment for debt and aid, and free markets for state intervention. In fact, conditions in large parts of the world did not improve—in many places they actually became worse.

Especially in the wake of September 11, ignorance or indifference to these realities are no longer luxuries that we can afford. Yet up to now the main First World response to 9/11 has been to strengthen our homeland security forces and deploy First World troops and law enforcement staff all over the globe, from Afghanistan and Iraq to Colombia and the Philippines. This is an understandable first response: September 11 was a shocking assault. But it is a profound mistake to believe that police and military alone will ever be a sufficient answer to the poverty, inequality, and injustice that breed much of today's extremism.

In fact, reliance on punitive responses alone may breed even more hostility. Remember, after September 11 when we were forced to ask ourselves the question: "Why do *they* hate us so much?" Of course there are many ideological and cultural factors, as well as long-standing political conflicts, that are responsible for this hostility. Most of the hijackers on September 11, after all, were from middle-class Saudi families, not from the worst neighborhoods in Cairo or Karachi. In many countries there is also a lingering antipathy that is the legacy of long-term colonial policies and racial or ethnic discrimination.

But if First Worlders really want to understand why many Third Worlders don't necessarily share our high opinions of ourselves—despite our military might, democratic institutions, and good intentions, not to mention the innumerable conferences that we sponsor on "sustainable development"—they might consider the stories in this book about the First World's *systemic* contributions to the problem of underdevelopment. Be warned, however—it is not a pretty picture.

This book reports on a series of first-hand investigations by Mr. Henry into the darker side of globalization and development. Each chapter stands alone as a separate detective story, with investigations that range from the looting of the Philippines by the Marcos clan to wasteful, corrupt lending practices in Venezuela, Brazil, Nicaragua, and Argentina, to the role that excessive debts played in the downfall of the Shah in Iran and Saddam's aggressive behavior in Iraq. All these tales share important common themes. One key theme is the dramatic growth of the global underground economy since the 1970s, as a kind of unsavory by-product of neoliberalism's long-sought triumph. That triumph brought the undeniable benefits of increased global economic integration and more open markets. But it also made it more difficult for individual nation-states, especially weaker ones, to control the most aggressive rats in the new global rat race.

Another key theme is the rise of a sophisticated global haven banking industry. This weakly regulated haven network now shelters hundreds of billions of dollars in ill-gotten gains that were generated by all sorts of dubious behavior, from bribery and tax evasion to drug dealing and arms trafficking. It has made a profound contribution to Third World underdevelopment. Yet First World authorities have so far been unable or unwilling to attack the expanding list of haven sinkholes for dirty money and control their circumvention of national laws—despite the fact that most of this money resides in First World banks.

Perhaps the most important theme explored in *The Blood Bankers* is a new perspective on the root causes of Third World underdevelopment and failed states. It has long been common for First World experts to blame development problems mainly on local anomalies in the developing countries themselves: wrongheaded policies, the absence of Western-style markets, supposedly higher levels of corruption and cronyism, and unfavorable climates or geography. But—as scandals like Enron and Worldcom have reminded us—cronyism and high-level chicanery are by no means peculiar to the Third World. Moreover, we will see from Jim Henry's investigations how the global haven network has contributed systematically to the looting of "submerging markets" all over the world, from Argentina, Brazil, Venezuela, Indonesia and the Philippines to Russia and Zimbabwe. Surprisingly, according to Jim Henry, most of the key players in the band were not shady Third World banks, but some of the world's most prestigious financial institutions—as tolerated by "regulators" like the US Treasury, the IMF, and the World Bank.

Overall, the patterns explored here raise serious questions about the First World's responsibility for the fact that so much development capital was either completely wasted or ended up in the pockets of the elites and their private bankers over the last thirty years. In the early 1960s, at a time when many Americans were enjoying the prosperity of John F. Kennedy's New Frontier, Michael Harrington's *The Other America* reminded us that one out of four Americans was stuck in grinding poverty, and that everyone had a stake in fixing that problem. That reminder, in turn, helped to mobilize a whole new "War on Poverty" in the US. That battle has by no means been won. But this book is a timely reminder of the urgent need to launch a broader effort, a new "War on Global Poverty" that takes stock of the costly lessons described here.

In the long run, military might and police power are no substitute for developing prosperous economies and democratic institutions for the vast majority of citizens, not just for "we happy few." This is not only essential for our own peace and securit; it also happens to be the right thing to do. *The Blood Bankers* demonstrates that we have our work cut out for us.

Bill Bradley
New York City
June 2003

INTRODUCTION:
WHERE THE MONEY WENT

It reminds me of the story of the eunuch in the harem. He studied everything, took careful notes, and asked lots of questions. But somehow he did
not quite grasp the essence of what was going on.

> —Professor Alex Gerschenkron, economic historian

But where has the money gone? What of the millions that the government
took in between 1922, the year in which El Barroso erupted and gushed its
heavy crude for nine days, sixty feet into the air . . . and 1938? Where are the
roads, the public works, the subsidized agricultural holdings, the mining
concessions, the hospitals, the Social Security programs? Why is the poor
peon so often lethargic with malaria, infected with syphilis, even sometimes
touched with leprosy? Why is he still using the fans of the moriche palm for
his insect-infested roof? Why is he wearing those ragged trousers, patched
with pieces from an old cement sack?

> —Clarence Horn, *Fortune Magazine*, March 1939

Let us face the uncomfortable truth. The model of development we are
accustomed to has been fruitful for the few, but flawed for the many. A path
to prosperity that ravages the environment and leaves a majority of
humankind behind in squalor will soon prove to be a dead-end road for
everyone.

> —Kofi Annan, UN Secretary General, World Summit on
> Sustainable Development, Johannesburg, September 2002

The invisible hand . . . is nowhere to be seen.

> —Indian economist, 1980s

*Niebla is a tiny Chilean fishing village on a cliff at the mouth of an estuary, four
hundred miles south of Santiago. To a newcomer, Niebla is picturesque and charming.
The harbor is filled with brightly colored fishing boats, and there is a seventeenth-cen-
tury Spanish fortress with stone towers and brass cannons. The women of the village
sell strings of shrimp and braided garlic under the palm trees near the beach. There are
few cars—a favorite form of local transportation is still the ox cart.*

But Niebla's most interesting feature lies two miles upstream along the river to Val-divia—a rusty old steamship, high and dry in the middle of a town plaza. The ship's unusual position dates back to May 22, 1960, when two earthquakes—9.5 on the Richter scale, the strongest ever recorded—suddenly struck Chile back-to-back early that Sunday morning. The quakes originated one hundred miles off shore, 180 feet below the ocean floor. By noon the resulting tsunami had caused the Pacific Ocean to recede from the shore, much faster and farther than the usual tides.[1]

Word of this event spread quickly, and the people of the village gathered along the shore to stare out in amazement at the retracting sea. The sea withdrew so quickly that it left little pools of water on the seabed, filled with stranded fish. To the hardworking villagers this was a dream come true—they marched out eagerly to scoop them up into baskets. Women and children, the mayor, and the parish priest all joined in. They offered a prayer of thanks to God for their good fortune.

Most people ignored the first faint rumble. A few thought they heard something and stared out at the ocean. All they could see was a thin dark edge on the horizon. Probably a storm. They turned back to work, wandering up to several hundred yards out from shore to fill their baskets.

Then the wind died down and the rumble grew louder. All of a sudden there was a shock of recognition, like the handshake of a corpse. People cried out, dropped their baskets, and scrambled back toward shore. But for hundreds it was too late. A few min-utes later a black wall of water 60 feet high, traveling 200 miles an hour, cascaded over the beach and the village. The grounded ship became a kind of memorial to their col-lective dream and awakening.[1]

This book is about another kind of unexpected catastrophe: the complete collapse of economic and political development in many parts of the devel-oping world since the 1980s. In many countries this has been accompanied by soaring unemployment and inflation; the bankruptcy of the public and private sectors; sharp increases in famine, malnutrition, disease, corruption, environmental damage, and social violence; and the revival of antidemocratic movements and terrorism.

At a time when many First Worlders, especially Americans, are asking, "Why do they hate us?" understanding the roots of this global development crisis may provide us with some answers.[2]

ORIGINS

This crisis was not the widely celebrated collapse of Soviet socialism. It originated for the most part in *market* economies and in the perverse rela-tionships that have come to exist between rich and poor countries in our new, mercilessly competitive global economic system.

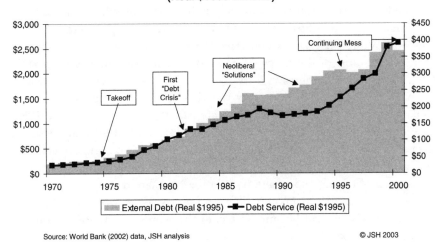

Chart I.1–Third World Foreign Debt and Debt Service, 1970–2000

Like the Chilean tidal wave, this crisis was preceded by very high hopes—at first, in the 1970s and early 1980s, when massive amounts of foreign debt first became available to developing countries, and again in the 1990s, when globalization, free trade, privatization, and foreign investment were widely expected to undo all the problems created by this debt.

The 1970s had been the heyday of the "big project" paradigm of economic development. Officials from institutions like the World Bank, the Inter-American Development Bank (IDB), the Asian Development Bank (ADB), and the US Agency for International Development (USAID) roamed the globe, making huge project loans and preaching the virtues of sophisticated development-planning techniques. In the wake of the collapse of the gold standard in August 1971 and the dramatic oil price rise of 1973, international capital markets became much more open. Most of the world's leading private banks and corporations joined in, flogging subsidized loans, construction projects, and equipment to the new markets that came to be known collectively as the "Third World." The superpowers of the day, the US and the Soviet Union also competed aggressively for client states in the Third World with unprecedented quantities of aid and arms.

This new level of First World involvement in Third World development was based on what had been, in hindsight, several decades of solid progress. During the so-called Golden Age of Development—from the late 1940s to the early 1970s, *before* Third World lending took off—conditions in many developing countries had improved.[3] Infant and maternal mortality, disease, and malnutrition declined; average life spans increased, per capita incomes rose, and the distribution of world income became somewhat more equal.[4]

Then the world's first global debt crisis hit developing countries hard in 1982–83. While First World countries recovered quickly and continued to forge ahead, most of the developing world lost an entire decade of growth. China and India—comprising forty-seven percent of the developing world's population—did better because they were less open to the vagaries of foreign banks, capital, and trade.[5] But for the other half of the Third World, the 1980s proved to be disastrous. By 1990, developing countries had accumulated more than $1.3 trillion in foreign debt, with little to show for it except huge white elephant projects, widespread corruption, and private elites that had learned to stash much of their liquid wealth back in the First World.[6]

In the 1990s, the disappointments were no less acute. Because of the debt crisis, foreign loans had become scarce; in the words of one former finance minister, "A banker is someone who lends you money when you don't need it." The Cold War's abrupt end in 1989–90 also reminded poor countries that foreign aid was not motivated by generosity alone. As the threat of "Communist subversion" subsided, so did the aid. The real value of foreign aid fell dramatically in the 1990s; by 2002, Europe, the US, and Japan were providing only $49 billion a year in aid to five billion people in developing countries, the lowest level of aid in a decade. This amounted to less than fifteen percent

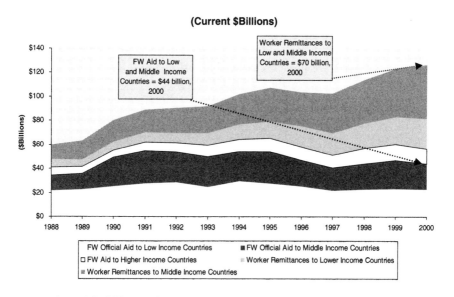

Source: WB, SIPRI data, JSH analysis

Chart I.2–Foreign Aid and Worker Remittances

of the $350 billion in subsidies paid to the First World's twelve million farmers each year, and less than ten percent of the First World's military budget.[7] It was also less than a third of the "0.7% of GDP" aid that rich countries had promised at the 1992 Earth Summit in Rio, considered the minimum required to meet their "millennium development" goals.[8] Furthermore, only forty percent of this official aid actually went to poor countries, a proportion that had also declined sharply since the 1970s. By the turn of the century, the US and Western Europe were all spending more on pet food, cosmetics, and weight loss programs each year than on foreign aid.[9]

Meanwhile, partly because of worsening conditions, there was a sharp increase in emigration from developing countries to the First World. The new "guest" workers remitted a large portion of their earnings to beleaguered families back home. In 2003, this *private* "foreign" aid exceeded $80 billion—four times the First World's entire aid budget for poor countries. Of course these remittances are also free from the "tying" requirements that encumber official aid, although they *are* subject to hefty First World taxes and transfer fees levied by Western Union, Citigroup, Wells Fargo, and other leading money-transfer agents.

Faced with this shortage of loans and foreign aid in the 1990s, development experts at the World Bank and the IMF invented a whole new policy paradigm—the so-called "Washington Consensus." The precise prescription varied from country to country, but it usually included the same basic ingredients: (1) rapid privatization of state enterprises; (2) a sharp reduction in government budgets—except for interest payments on foreign debt; (3) tough new anti-inflation measures, especially the maintenance of a strong currency; (4) the immediate removal of price supports, agricultural subsidies, price caps for public services, and restrictions on imports; (5) the rapid opening of capital markets to foreign capital, whether or not there were adequate security laws, bank regulations, or tax enforcers in place; (6) rigid enforcement of First World patents and copyrights; and (7) the relaxation of minimum wage laws and trade union rights. Overall, so far as developing countries was concerned, this "new" neoliberal approach placed greater reliance on unfettered free markets than at any time since the nineteenth century.

Throughout the 1990s, leading Western economists, bankers, politicians, and mainstream journalists righteously lambasted developing countries that departed from this *sauve qui peut* model, and the "global policy cops" at the IMF and the World Bank often conditioned aid and debt relief on its adoption. When it came to taking their own medicine, however, most First World countries passed. They were fortunate enough not to depend on debt relief or foreign aid. So despite all their rhetoric about free markets, when their own farmers, steel producers, textile manufacturers, and other influential industries

	1970	1982	1990	2000
All Developing Countries (n= 155)				
Population (Billions)	2.63	3.75	4.37	5.11
Gross Foreign Debt($B)	$70	$772	$1,423	$2,356
Net Foreign Reserves ($B)	$10	$113	$167	$701
Net Foreign Debt ($B)	**$60**	**$659**	**$1,257**	**$1,655**
Gross National Income ($B)	$677	$2,922	$4,061	$5,951
Household Consumption ($B)	$443	$1,806	$2,452	$3,666
Total Foreign Debt/ GNI (%)	10%	26%	35%	40%
Net Debt/ Gross Nat Income(%)	**9%**	**23%**	**31%**	**28%**
Net Debt/ Person ($95)	$66	$203	$320	$338
Total Debt Service ($)	$9	$115	$156	$375
Annual Debt Service/ GNI (%)	**1.3%**	**3.9%**	**3.8%**	**6.3%**
Health Spending/ GDP	-	3.5% (e)	4.8%	5.6% (e)
Net Foreign Direct Investment/ GDP	0.48%	0.55%	0.6%	2.8%
Annual Debt Service/ Person ($)	$3.39	$30.81	$35.62	$73.47
Ave. Consumption Per Person ($)	$169	$482	$562	$717
"Debt Days"/Person/Year	**7**	**23**	**23**	**37**
Source: World Bank WDI Online data (2002), JSH analysis © JSH 2002				
*"Low income" countries = <$755 per capita gross national income, 2000				
*"Middle income" countries = $755- $9265 per capita gross national income, 2000				

Table I.1–Increasing Foreign Debt Burdens

were threatened by competition, they often reverted to protectionism, maintaining high barriers to Third World farm exports and immigrants and hefty export credits. They also insisted on punitive drug laws, whose enforcement costs weighed heavily on many developing countries.

At the same time, First World banks, companies, and governments also fostered the rise of a new, highly efficient global haven banking network that came to facilitate capital flight, money laundering, privatization rip-offs, and corruption on an unprecedented scale, making it harder than ever for developing countries to tax and regulate global companies or their own fleet-footed elites. In the spirit of the times, suggestion that this network might be taxed or regulated, much less outlawed, were regarded by many First World policy makers as an outrageous, or at least impractical, intrusion on market freedom.

As for the developing countries that were forced to undergo the neoliberal bloodletting cure, even true believers admitted that it might have harsh effects in the "short run" by boosting foreign competition, inequality, unemployment, speculative capital flows, human capital flight, the costs of food, energy, and medicine, and corruption all at once. But its advocates were certain that it would also quickly lead to increased investment, growth, and employment, just as advocates of the "big projects" paradigm had been in the 1970s. If necessary, "social protection mechanisms" could be used to compensate those harmed by the "short-term" impacts—although these somehow never quite got enacted.[10]

This increased growth, in turn, would supposedly lead not only to higher profits, but to better living standards for everyone. The privatization of state assets would supposedly increase competition, reduce debt, improve efficiency, and equalize the distribution of wealth. Global poverty would supposedly decline without any need for messy wealth redistributions. Long-standing ethnic conflicts would be smoothed over by a New Era of Good Feeling. Class distinctions would be blurred. The world's peasant farmers—more than seventy percent of the population in many countries—would finally learn to stop loving their olive trees and embrace the brave, new, globalized paradise of the Lexus and the Internet.[11]

The more progressive members of the business and development intelligentsia also believed that this globalization paradigm would produce enough extra growth to take care of all the environmental concerns that had been so badly neglected during the big-project heyday of the 1970s. In the 1990s, "sustainable development" became the new mantra for the world's seventy-five thousand development professionals employed at multilateral institutions, and the more than one hundred thousand employees of nongovernmental institutions (NGOs).[12] The UN and the World Bank joined hands with companies like Shell, BP, and IBM to sponsor more than two dozen conferences on the subject. These jamborees, held in colorful places like Paris, Copenhagen, Beijing, and Bali, gathered tens of thousands of officials, NGOs, and journalists, cost hundreds of millions of dollars, and yielded long-winded statements supporting a long list of "Millennium Development Goals"—like the reduction of global poverty, infant mortality, malnutrition, and other quantifiable maladies.

These goals shared several characteristics. First, none of them had any teeth—unlike the World Trade Organization (WTO), which since 1995 has been empowered to crack down on countries that violate their commitments to free trade and intellectual property. Second, the goals were set so far in the future—2015 to 2020—that no policy makers risked being embarrassed if they were not met. Third, they skirted contentious issues like the distribution of wealth; the role of banks and multinationals in dubious projects, capital flight and corruption; the role of drug companies in vaccine research; the role of tobacco companies in cigarette smuggling; and the questionable behavior of particular officials and corporations—many of whom were, after all, attending these conferences. Finally, the goals' endorsers were in the enviable position of having no budgetary responsibility whatsoever. In the event, First World governments did not even come close to providing the *extra* $60 to $100 billion per year that Oxfam and the World Bank estimated it would cost to realize all these goals.

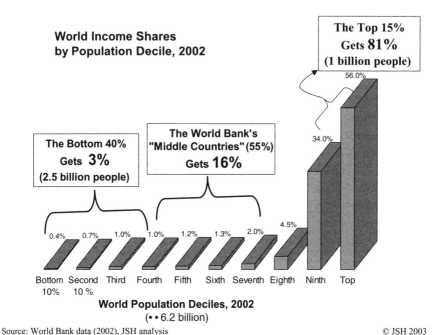

Chart I.3–World Distributional Realities

Against the backdrop of sharp aid cutbacks, minimal debt relief, and mounting Third World hardships, this spectacle of lavish development summits was surreal, like inviting the world's poor to dinner and serving them *pictures* of food.

THE LEGACY

It has not taken long to reveal the fundamental contradictions between all this high-minded goal setting and the neoliberal paradigm's fundamentally "*brutalitarian*" model. As the latest development spectacle, the 2002 UN's World Summit on Sustainable Development in Johannesburg, underscored, for most developing countries, the "lost decade" of the 1980s was succeeded only by a decade of failed promises in the 1990s. In particular:

(1) Receding Goals. Only a few short years after the "Millennium Development Goals" (MDG) were declared, the world has already fallen behind or given up completely on most of them. The best-known goal—halving the proportion of people subsisting on less than one dollar per day by the year 2015—is not likely to be met, except perhaps in China. Originally, in 1990, the World Bank predicted that the number of people below this arbitrary poverty

line would drop from 1.125 billion in 1985 to 825 million by 2000. But in 2001, the World Bank reported that the absolute number had remained at 1.124 billion. There are also serious conceptual problems with the World Bank's whole approach to measuring global poverty: It appears to substantially understate the size of the problem.[13] It is also clear that, at current course and speed, even the modest goal of providing at least two dollars per day per person will be hard to attain for at least *half* the world's population by 2015, unless there are huge increases in aid and debt relief, plus sharp reductions in First World trade barriers and farm subsidies. All the other MDGs have also slipped badly behind schedule.[14]

(2) The Fourth World. Badly wounded in the 1980s, many of the world's poorest countries in the 1990s completely fell apart. The forty-nine countries labeled the world's "least developed" by the UN now account for eleven percent of the world's population, but just one-half percent of its income. From 1980 to 2000, their real per capita incomes—which average well below one dollar per day—barely increased, their share of world income declined, and their share of world trade fell by half.[15] Many of these countries are now best described as *war zones.* If one minimal definition of victory for the world's development strategy is that it provides hope for the very poorest of the poor, by this standard, it is very hard to make this track record look like an achievement.

(3) "Submerging" Markets. Even among "middle-income" developing countries, the story of the last decade is one of deep disappointment. Some countries, like Chile, Peru, Mexico, Thailand, Indonesia, and

	World Pop	Share of Population (%)						Share of World Income (%)				
	2000 (MM)	1960	1970	1980	1990	2000	2025	1960	1970	1980	1990	2000
China	1263	22%	22%	22%	22%	21%	19.4%	0.9%	0.7%	0.8%	1.5%	3.1%
India	1016	14%	15%	16%	16%	17%	17.2%	1.0%	0.8%	0.8%	1.0%	1.4%
Poorest 49 (UN)	660	8%	8%	9%	10%	11%	13.6%	0.55%	0.57%	0.59%	0.52%	0.57%
Other dev.countries	2169	33%	34%	35%	36%	36%	36.8%	13.5%	13.6%	15.7%	14.5%	13.7%
• Non China/India DCs	2829	41%	43%	44%	45%	47%	50.4%	14.1%	14.2%	16.3%	15.0%	14.2%
High income countries	950	22%	21%	19%	17%	16%	13.0%	84.0%	84.3%	82.1%	82.4%	81.3%
> Of which: US	282	6%	6%	5%	5%	5%	4.1%	30.2%	25.8%	24.6%	24.8%	26.4%
World Total	6058	3021	3677	4430	5253	6058	8348	100%	100%	100%	100%	100%

	World Pop	Real Income per Capita ($1995)						Average Growth Rate, Per Capita Income (%)				
	2000 (MM)	1960	1970	1980	1990	2000	2025	1960-70	1970-80	1980-90	1990-2000	1960-2000
China	1263	$112	$120	$168	$349	$824	na	0.7%	3.4%	7.6%	9.0%	5.1%
India	1016	$183	$211	$226	$323	$459	na	1.5%	0.7%	3.6%	3.6%	2.3%
Poorest 49 (UN)	660	$177	$246	$284	$264	$293	na	3.3%	1.4%	-0.7%	1.1%	1.3%
Other dev.countries	2169	$1,063	$1,459	$1,987	$2,044	$2,151	na	3.2%	3.1%	0.3%	0.5%	1.8%
• Non China/India DCs	2829	$889	$1,218	$1,634	$1,658	$1,718	na	3.2%	2.8%	0.1%	0.6%	1.7%
High income countries	950	$9,779	$14,934	$19,265	$24,547	$29,193	na	4.3%	2.6%	2.5%	1.7%	2.8%
> Of which: US	282	$13,155	$16,893	$21,001	$26,141	$31,996	na	2.5%	2.2%	2.2%	2.0%	2.2%
World Total	6058	$2,609	$3,656	$4,385	$5,013	$5,630	na	3.4%	1.8%	1.3%	1.2%	1.9%

© JSH 2002 Source: World Bank (2002) and UNCTAD (2002) data, JSH analysis

Table I.2–Thirty Years of Bank-Led Economic Development

Argentina, were early adopters of the neoliberal model, and managed to steal a march on their competitors for a while. In the early 1990s, they were briefly described as "emerging markets" and "Asian tigers" by First World officials, bankers, and mainstream journalists. These days, one seldom hears such terms. Many of the benefits of their neoliberal experiments proved to be fleeting, while the costs—slower growth, increased competition, inequality, and corruption—have persisted into the long run.

Indeed, as of 2003, former "Asian tigers" like Thailand and Indonesia, which threw their banking systems wide open to dollar loans, are still suffering greatly from the 1997–98 Asian debacle. They've learned the hard way about the lethal effects of unsupervised foreign loans, wide-open capital markets, and "crony" banking.[16] As of 2003, countries like Argentina, Indonesia, and Turkey, which were all IMF poster boys for neoliberal reform in the early 1990s, were in the throes of deep social crises, struggling to service their debts, preserve democracy, and figure out what happened to all the billions of dollars missing from their banking systems.

The long-term consequences of such failed country strategies are striking. At the end of World War II, for example, the Philippines's real per capita income was within striking distance of Japan's. In 1960, Argentina's per capita income was the same as Ireland's and Italy's, and greater than Spain's. Venezuela's was greater than Hong Kong's or Portugal's. Of course, at the individual country level, a myriad of factors contributed to these countries' subsequent regressions. But as a group, they have suffered greatly not only from inept domestic leaders, but also from far too much "openness" to foreign banks, flight bankers, and US-educated neoliberal economists.

By ignoring the *political* consequences of the neoliberal agenda, its supporters may have outsmarted themselves, actually undermining the prospects for economic reform and democracy, and indirectly *raising* barriers to trade, capital, and immigration. Neoliberal policies are now under fierce attack, not only from fringe radicals in Seattle and Florence, but in almost all leading former "emerging markets," including Argentina, Bolivia, Brazil, Columbia, Ecuador, Indonesia, Kenya, Mexico, Malaysia, Peru, the Philippines, Poland, Russia, South Africa, Thailand, Turkey, and Venezuela. Fueled by economic discontent, populist leaders have gained power in Argentina (Kirchner), Brazil (Lula), Bolivia (Evo Morales), Venezuela (Chavez), Peru (Toledo), Ecuador (Lucio Gutierrez), Russia, Turkey, and Indonesia. Populist leaders are also spearheading new Islamic movements in Nigeria, Egypt, Pakistan, and other Middle Eastern countries. The Third World neoliberal movement of the 1980s and 1990s now appears to have stalled, in large measure due to these hard-

Consumption/Day ($)	People (Billions)	%	Income ($Trillions)	%	Ave Income Per Year ($)
<$1	2.51	41%	1.06	3%	$422
$1<$2.50	2.16	35%	2.70	9%	$1,246
<$2.50 Day	4.67	76%	3.75	12%	$803
$2.50<$8	0.50	8%	2.29	7%	$4,553
>$8	1.0	16%	25.12	81%	$26,282
Total	6.13	100%	31.16	100%	$5,081

Source: World Bank (2002) data, JSH analysis   © JSH 2003

Table. I.3–Distributional Realities

ships and disappointments. Opinion polls and visa applications in countries like Russia, the Philippines, Argentina, Ecuador, South Africa, Guatemala, Nicaragua, and Venezuela indicate that many people have become frustrated with neoliberal democracy and are trying to emigrate.[17]

(4) Soaring Inequality. Meanwhile, the last few decades have brought extraordinary prosperity to the First World, especially its elites. One result is that the gap between the living standards of the world's richest and poorest citizens is now greater than at any other time in modern history.[18] The First World now accounts for just sixteen percent of the world's population, but receives more than *eighty-one* percent of its income. While this is slightly below the share it commanded in the 1970s, this is only because of the progress made since then by relatively non-neoliberal, debt-averse China and India. Even after the stock market decline of 2000–02, the world's top 497 billionaires were still worth more than $1.5 trillion—more than the entire imputed wealth of the world's 600 million poorest citizens.[19]

Rising inequality is an important anomaly for conventional economics to explain, because it predicts that competitive markets and free trade should lead to the convergence of global income and wealth levels over time, not their divergence. Indeed, one standard utilitarian defense for inequality is that it eventually "floats all boats." However, the fact is that there is simply no evidence of a positive relationship between the kind of extreme inequality that we have recently seen and reductions in poverty. Indeed, just the opposite is true—living standards have fallen farthest precisely in places, like post-Soviet Russia, where inequality has increased the most.

Overall, the neoliberal paradigm has turned out to be even more disappointing than the big project paradigm that preceded it. Far from reducing poverty and inequality, it has exacerbated them. Far from encouraging First and Third World countries to collaborate on free trade, it has proliferated regional antagonisms and trading blocks. Far from leaving extra room to take care of the environment, education, health, and public order, it has crowded them out. Far from leading to privatizations that improve efficiency and competition, it has produced a series of giveaways and land grabs that have made Third World markets less competitive, while making their elites richer than ever. Far from fostering institutional development and the rule of law, the neoliberal model has systematically undermined them. Debt dependence has not been reduced, but prolonged. Growth and development have not been made sustainable, but even slower and less stable.

All told, by the dawn of the twenty-first century, after thirty years of development strategies that were designed in Washington DC, New York, London, Frankfurt, Paris, and Tokyo, and trillions of dollars in foreign loans, aid, and investment, more than half of the world's population still finds daily life a struggle, surviving on less than two dollars a day, about the same level of real income they had thirty years ago. More than two billion people still lack access to basic amenities like electricity, clean water, sanitation, land titles, police and fire protection, and paved roads, let alone their own phones, bank accounts, medical care, or Internet access. Despite years of rhetoric about debt relief, dozens of structural adjustment plans (Baker Plans, Mizakawa Plans, Brady Bonds, Rubin Plans, Summers Plans, and HIPC Plans), the real value of Third World debt and the absolute burden of servicing it have continued to grow— to the point where the total now exceeds $1.7 trillion.[20] The cost of servicing this debt exceeds $375 billion a year—more than all Third World spending on health or education, nearly ten times their foreign aid receipts, and more than twice what they have recently received in foreign direct investment.[21]

This debt service burden now amounts to thirty-seven days per year of consumption for every man, woman, and child in the Third World, an even

(Median Real Per Capita Income Growth Rates, By Period)

	1960-70	1970-80	1980-90	90-2001	70-2001
A. Developing Countries (n=155)					
Median Growth Rate (%)	3.3	3.1	0.9	1.5	1.9
Variance (%)	1.9	1.6	1.3	1.9	2.1
Risk/Reward Ratio	59%	53%	140%	122%	108%
B. High Income Counties (n=31)					
	1960-70	1970-80	1980-90	90-2001	70-2000
Median Growth Rate (%)	3.9	3.0	2.6	1.9	2.4
Variance (%)	0.5	4.1	1.7	0.7	2.3
Risk/Reward Ratio	14%	139%	67%	35%	95%

Source: World Bank (2003) data, JSH analysis   © JSH 2003

Table I.4–Lower Growth Rates

greater per capita burden than it was in the 1980s. And all this goes to service debts that in many cases have *less than nothing* to show for them.

In short, even if developing countries continue to reform their economies, it may be decades before capital, aid, and advice are ever as abundant as they were in the last thirty years. Yet in country after country, there is little to show for all the resources already consumed. After all these costly experiments with Western development models, there is virtually *no* example to date of any country that has pursued either the "big project paradigm" or the neoliberal development paradigm and emerged with a developed economy, much less a liberal democracy. But there are plenty of countries that have ended up as virtual basketcases by taking these half-baked, quasi-religious paradigms too seriously.

THE PUZZLE

So how did thirty years of greatly expanded international lending, investment, aid, and official development efforts end up producing such a fiasco? Where did all the money actually go? And what can we do, if anything, to undo the damage that has been done?

There is no shortage of armchair analyses of the so-called "Third World debt crisis," or the globalization crisis that succeeded it and continues to this day. The 1980s debt crisis became visible as early as August 1982, when Mexico, Argentina, and twenty-six other countries suddenly rescheduled their debts at once. Our disappointments with globalization have been a popular subject for economists and policy makers at least since the Mexico crunch of January 1995, as amplified by the East Asian and Russian crises in 1997–98, and the crisis in Turkey, Ecuador, Bolivia, Argentina, Venezuela, and many other countries since then.

But until now there has been no detailed account of the *structural roots* of this prolonged development crisis. Among orthodox economists, the conventional wisdom is still that it originated in a combination of unpredictable shocks and Third World policies that were either corrupt or just plain stupid, on top of factors like bad geographic and climatic luck.[22] In other words, the standard explanation of Third World backwardness is a slightly more sophisticated version of the same "blame-the-victim" ideology that ruling elites have used for centuries to explain poverty and wealth—a combination of "tough luck" and "their own damn fault."

For example, the conventional view of the 1980s debt crisis is that, in response to the 1973 oil price rise, Western banks recycled oil deposits from the Middle East back to the Third World, lending to finance oil imports and development projects. Independently, a huge new tidal wave of capital flight sprang up alongside all this lending. Then an unfortunate combination of events—rising interest rates, recession, and the 1982 Malvinas War—supposedly took everyone by surprise. In this version of the crisis, no one was responsible. There were no villains or victims, just innocent bystanders. Like the Chilean tidal wave, it was a natural catastrophe.

Similarly, in the case of the more recent debacles in submerging markets like Indonesia and Thailand, the official story is that these resulted almost entirely from Third World mistakes and local market imperfections—poorly designed bank regulations, faulty accounting, inexplicable failures to privatize and liberalize fast enough, and indigenous "corruption, cronyism, and collusion" ("KKN," as it is known in Indonesia). The notion that there might be serious problems with the development paradigms themselves, that Western banks, investors, policymakers, and the structure of international capital markets might have aggravated the situation, or that they might have taught local elites a thing or two about "clever chicanery," has received much less attention. While numerous critics of globalization have recently emerged, including a few prominent economists and investors and a rising tide of mass protestors, much of this criticism has dealt in generalities, lacking the gory investigative details needed to drive the critique home.

The fact is that the conventional portrait of the global development crisis is an economist's fairy tale. It leaves out all the blood and guts of what really happened—all the payoffs, corrupt privatizations, fraudulent loans, intentionally wasteful projects, black market "round-trip" transfers, arms deals, insider information, and the behind-the-scenes operation of the global haven banking network that facilitated this behavior. It ignores the fact that in the mid-1970s, and again in the mid-1990s, there were repeated warnings of deep trouble—yet irresponsible overlending, poorly conceived projects and privatizations, the outright looting of central bank reserves, and massive capital flight continued right under the noses of Western bankers and officials. The conventional explanation begs the question of why some developing countries and banks got into so much more trouble than others, and why certain bankers, investors, and officials got rich. The conventional story focuses too much on uncontrollable shocks to the system and skates far too quickly over the structure of that system itself.

Most importantly, the official story of shocks, surprises, and indigenous corruption ignores the pivotal role that was often played by sophisticated First World banks and multinationals, aided by governments and local elites—first in pressing developing countries to overborrow, then in pressing them to overservice their debts, honor overpriced privatization contracts, and liberalize and privatize far too quickly. Many of these players were also aggressively recruiting flight capital and investment deals from these very same countries, teaching their clients the basics on how to launder, plunder, and conceal.

The conventional fairy tale glosses over many key questions. What really became of all the loans and investments? Why did foreign banks lend so much money to these governments, even while their private banking arms knew full well that they were financing massive capital flight? Who ended up owning all the juicy assets? How much did the IMF and the World Bank know about all these shenanigans, and why didn't they do more to stop them?

It is not easy to give precise answers to such questions; studying the global underground economy is an exercise in night vision, not double-entry accounting. One actually has to get up out of the armchair and do some investigative reporting. But then the patterns that become visible turn out to be full of villains and victims.

Unfortunately, it has taken years to uncover the truth about such matters, and we've really only begun to scratch the surface. In the last decade, bits and pieces of the "dirty debt" story have become more accessible. The demise of kleptocracies like those of Abacha, Andres Perez, Collor, Duvalier, Marcos, Mobuto, Milosevic, Salinas, Suharto, and Stroessner focused attention on the billions they managed to steal and stash abroad. The collapse of leading money-laundering banks like BCCI and BNL, and corrupt regimes in Mexico, Argentina, Turkey, and Indonesia demonstrated the risks that corrupt banking poses to the entire global financial system.

However, partly because this kind of investigative research is so difficult, there are only a few rather armchair-ish studies of the global underground economy and the "real-economique" of underdevelopment. These have also usually treated the subjects of irresponsible lending, wasteful projects, capital flight, corruption, money laundering, and havens separately. In fact, they go hand in hand. The rise of Third World lending in the 1970s and 1980s laid the foundations for a global haven network that now shelters the wealth of the world's most venal citizens. The corruption that this network facilitated was just a special case of a much more general phenomenon—the export of vast quantities of capital and tax-free incomes by the elites of poor countries, even as their countries were incurring vast debts and struggling to service them. Individual kleptocratic regimes and evil dictators come and go, but this sophisticated transnational system remains more vibrant than ever.

THE GLOBAL HAVEN NETWORK

Indeed, one of our key themes is the maturation of this haven network in the last thirty years, coincident with the rise of global lending, the liberalization of capital markets, and the development crisis. Of course "private banking" is hardly new. Except for electronic transfers and airplanes, most of its paraphernalia—secret accounts, shell companies, black market exchanges, mis-invoicing, back-to-back loans, and backdated transactions—were very important early innovations in the history of capitalism. They helped to bring "mattress money" out into the open so that it could be productively invested.

For decades these tools were underutilized. Then, from the 1970s through the 1990s, their use expanded tremendously under the impact of the greatest torrent of loose lending in history. This torrent, driven by a coalition of influential interests that included leading Western banks, equipment vendors, and construction companies—plus their allies among aid donors, export finance agencies, multilateral institutions, and local elites—drove a hole in developing country defenses against overborrowing. And that, in turn, created a source of structural instability and depressed demand in the world economy that continues to this day.

It is possible to estimate the volume and composition of the flight capital that was financed by all this lending. Our own estimates rely on a combination of statistical methods and interviews with more than a hundred private bankers and wealthy clients. They reveal that at least *half* the funds borrowed by the largest "debtor" countries flowed right out the back door, usually the same year or even the same month that the loans arrived. For the developing world as a whole, this amounted to a huge "Marshall Plan" *in reverse*.

The corresponding *stock* of unrecorded foreign wealth owned by Third World elites is even larger than these outflows, since the outflows were typically invested in tax havens, where—unlike the earnings of low-income "guest workers"—they were permitted to accumulate tax-free interest, dividends, and capital gains. Estimates show that by the 1990s, there was already enough of this anonymous Third World "flight wealth" on hand in Europe and the US that the income it generated would have been able to service the *entire* Third World debt—if only it had been subjected to a modest global tax. By the late 1990s, the market value of private wealth accumulated outside Third World countries by their resident elites totaled at least $1.5 trillion to $1.7 trillion—almost equal to the face value of all Third World debt, net of reserves. As one Federal Reserve official chuckled at the time, "The problem is not that these countries don't have any assets. The problem is, they're all in Miami."

Most of the resulting flight wealth—defined as foreign capital whose true ownership is concealed—ended up in just a handful of First World havens. Their identity may be surprising to those who usually associate "tax havens" and money laundering with obscure nameplate banks in sultry tropical paradises. BCCI's exceptional case notwithstanding, shady banks have never really been very important in the flight market—most rich people don't trust them. Rather, Third World decapitalization has taken place with the active aid of preeminent global financial institutions, including Citigroup, JPMorgan Chase (Chemical MHT), UBS, Barclays, Credit Suisse First Boston, ABN-AMRO Merrill Lynch, ING Bank, The Bank of New York, American Express Bank, and about two dozen other leading Swiss, British, Dutch, French, German, and Austrian banks. These august, centuries-old institutions led the way in knowingly facilitating these perverse capital flows. In fact, despite their reputations "as lenders," many of these institutions have actually been *net borrowers* from poor countries for most of the last thirty years. International private banking—a large share of which involved Third World elites—became one of their most profitable lines of business.

Because their own leading banks were so successful at profiting from Third World grief, the US, the UK, and Switzerland also actually became—despite their reputations as major capital providers and aid donors—*net debtors* with respect to the Third World over the last thirty years. So it is misleading to speak of a "Third World debt crisis"—for developing countries, it has really been an *asset crisis*, while for key First World countries and their banks, it was an incredibly profitable *global bleed-out*.

The upshot is that the ownership of Third Wealth onshore and offshore wealth is now even more concentrated than it was before the debt crisis in the 1980s and the privatization wave of the 1990s. Depending on the country, the top one percent of households now accounts for seventy-five to ninety percent of all private financial wealth and real estate. We are not talking about millions of diligent middle-class savers. These are the seven hundred members of the Rio Country Club, the one thousand top landowners of Argentina, El Salvador's *catorce*, the fifty top families of Caracas, the three hundred top families of Mexico City, and so on. These are not people who merely observe the rules of the game. When a minister builds a dam, nationalizes a private company or its debts, privatizes a state enterprise, floats a currency, or manipulates tax provisions, these folks have the inside track. This is not to say that there are no new self-made Third World elites, or that the top tier is limited to capitalists; there are also quite a few politicians, generals, diplomats, union bosses, and even a bishop or cardinal or two.

But the overall system is beautifully symbiotic. On the one hand, flight havens provide an ideal way to launder loot. On the other hand, over time, corruption, insider deals, and the inequalities they generate encourage still more disinvestment and emigration. For people living in these countries, of course, the incentives to engage in money laundering and tax evasion are often so powerful that it is quixotic not to do so. At the macroeconomic level, however, the results are terribly destructive. Conventional explanations of capital flight, overborrowing, and mismanaged privatizations, which focus on technical policy errors and the exogenous "riskiness" of Third World markets, ignore these systemic factors. They also ignore the international community's collective responsibility for perpetuating a system that encourages noneconomic lending, tax evasion, flight-prone speculative investments, and perverse privatizations.

The widespread myth, shared by neoliberals and radicals alike, that individual countries can pursue "development" on their own without tackling these deformations in the world system, is responsible for many of our current woes. Under the prevailing rules of the game, developing countries are put to a hard choice. One option is to follow the "successes" of China, Pinochet's Chile, Fujimori's Peru, and one-party Singapore, maintaining repressive political controls while liberalizing their economies. The other is to throw caution to the wind and become hostage to the demands of fickle electorates and speculative capital. This is not a choice that leads to balanced development.

Other key ingredients in the "money trail" puzzle, in addition to capital flight, were wasteful projects and arms purchases.[23] Hundreds of billions of Third World loans were devoted to nonproductive projects and corruption. Many of these debt-financed projects also had harmful long-term consequences. In some cases, the chicanery took place on a purely local level. But what is most striking are the recurrent global patterns—overpricing, rigged bids, endless delays, loans to front companies with close ties to the government, investments in dubious technologies, "public" projects undertaken for private motives, and private debts assumed by the state. Over and over again, we see the handiwork of the very same international banks, contractors, equipment vendors and export credit agencies, which grew fat while the countries grew poorer. These were not ideological errors—regimes of different ideological hues proved equally vulnerable. Nor were they due to random policy mistakes or purely indigenous corruption. A sophisticated *transnational system* of influential institutions contrived to produce similar mistakes over and over again, in every region of the world. Corruption has always existed, but without this global system, the abuses simply could not have been generalized on such a massive scale.

Recently, some of the leading players in the global haven industry, Citigroup and JPMorgan Chase, had also applied their "haveneering" skills to help clients like Enron, Worldcom, and Global Crossing use Panama and Cayman shell companies to conceal billions in off-balance-sheet loans from their stockholders. When this scandal finally surfaced in 2001–02, the resulting bankruptcies cost First World investors several hundred billion dollars. Analysts who had not followed the history of these banks in the Third World were shocked . . . shocked! Those who knew them better were just reminded that "character is destiny" and that "what goes around, comes around." As one wise business colleague of mine once said, "The problem with a rat race is, even if you win, you are still a rat."

The *official* story of the global development crisis leaves out all this dirty laundry. At best, it reduces the subject to a series of sanitized asides about the importance of transparency and good governance. Meanwhile, the one-two punch of the debt/flight boom and the neoliberal fiasco that succeeded it has been to undermine the role and capacities of the state in developing countries, creating a larger global underground economy than ever before.

My emphasis on this darker side of globalization is not meant to imply that every banker was a briber, or every public official a crook. But dirty money, bad banking, money laundering, and self-seeking chicanery were not merely *incidental* to the development crisis. As a governor of the Bank for International Settlements admitted privately in the late 1980s, "If Latin America's corrupt politicians simply gave back all the money they've stolen from their own countries, the debt problem could be solved."[24] And most of that thievery could not have occurred without the active assistance of leading First World banks, contractors, vendors, multilateral lenders, advisors, and governments. This was not a natural catastrophe, but a *man-made* one. For the developing world to overcome it, it is not only the developing world that will have to be "reformed."

Today, despite decades of official development efforts and trillions in foreign loans, bonds, and investments, the vast majority of the world's residents are still living on the very borderline of existence. Yet most of the "developing countries" they inhabit are not really poor at all, in terms of natural resources, technical know-how, or raw human talent. This is the central contradiction that this book seeks to explain.

Some have searched for the explanation among the natural disadvantages of climate, pestilence, and topography that many of these countries experience. Some have pointed toward cultural deficiencies—for example, the purported lack of trust outside the family in some countries, or an unusual propensity for corruption at all levels of society in others. Some have invoked the *deus ex machina* of "policy errors" like overvalued exchange rates, excessive borrowing, and weak securities laws, as if these were uncaused causes and as if policy were made in a disinterested vacuum. Still others have emphasized other misfortunes that developing countries have been subject to—like the 1970's oil crisis, the HIV/AIDS epidemic in Africa, Indonesia's bad luck in having Thailand as a neighbor when its currency plummeted in July 1997, and so on.

These efforts are reminiscent of economic historian Alex Gerschenkron's remark about the eunuch in the harem—"He studied everything, took careful notes, and asked lots of questions. But somehow he did not quite grasp the *essence* of what was going on." From a slight distance, what is missing from all these explanations is the profound contribution that First World countries and their global agents have played, not only in the last thirty years, but for much longer, in tolerating, contributing to, and profiting from the immiseration that surrounds them.

If one really looks objectively at why countries like the Philippines, Guatemala, Indonesia, the Congo, South Africa, Argentina, Venezuela, Nicaragua, Brazil, Mexico, Haiti, and India have ended up as they have in the world economy, one cannot ignore the negative influence of First World corporations, governments, and financial institutions. As a rule, the closer and more unequal those relationships have been, the worse things have turned out for developing countries.

The developing world is now in its deepest crisis since a half century. The First World, now so preoccupied with its own security, needs to place these security concerns and the "global war on terrorism" in the context of this even more fundamental global war—on underdevelopment. The world is simply too interdependent for us to ignore this other war any longer. Forest fires in the Amazon or Kalimantan set by poor people who are clearing land because they can't find jobs threaten the world's air supply. Epidemics left untreated in Africa or Russia threaten to create drug-resistant diseases that might sweep the planet. The hatred bred by the real "weapons of mass destruction"—outrageous poverty and inequality—are only a plane or a boat ride away in Port-au-Prince, Jakarta, Cairo, Kabul, and Karachi.

At the end of World War I, John Maynard Keynes wrote a seminal book about the Allies' failure to deal rationally with the reparations they imposed on Germany, as well as their own debt overhang. In 1920, he warned of the dire consequences of continuing to enforce these short-sighted claims:

> We shall never be able to move again, unless we can free our limits of these paper shackles. A general bonfire is so great a necessity that unless we can make of it an orderly and good-tempered affair in which no serious injustice is done to anyone, it will, when it comes at last, grow into a conflagration.[25]

More than eighty years later, we now understand that the Allies' failure to transcend their self-righteous rage and assist Germany's revival with relief, debt, and aid after World War I contributed mightily to Hitler' rise and the coming of World War II. We also realize that one key obstacle to debt relief in that period was the fact that a handful of major banks, notably JPMorgan, was deeply vested in the issue. After World War II, of course, we tried to follow Keynes's advice with respect to Germany—he was a prime force for the creation of the "International Bank for Reconstruction and Development," the forerunner of the World Bank, at Bretton Woods in 1944. Liberals and conservatives alike also claimed to have learned "the lessons of Munich"—the importance of standing up to aggressive dictators.

More recently, however, we seem to have forgotten Keynes's advice and the other lesson of Munich—about the relationship between security and development, and the social conditions that foster wars and dictators in the first place.

The first step is understanding. Today, most First Worlders are living in a bubble. Only twenty percent of Americans have passports, just twenty-one percent of non-Hispanic Americans speak a second language, and less than a fifth of adults have ever traveled abroad. A poll taken in late 2002 showed that only thirteen percent of 18–24 year olds in the US could find Iraq on a map, fourteen percent could find Israel, thirty-one percent could find the UK, forty-two percent could find Japan, and only two-thirds could even find the Pacific Ocean.[26] This kind of ignorance is not just unfortunate. It is dangerous. It is especially menacing to the citizens of the Third World, because the First World now has more political, economic, and military hegemony than ever before. It is also a menace to ourselves, because if this power is not used wisely, a growing portion of the Third World will simply disappear into "the Fourth World," a vast, impoverished, hostile labor camp without many visitors, investors, or prospects for growth. And that, in turn, will only heighten our insecurities and raise the drawbridge even higher.

Those who wish to alter these current trends toward immiserization and anti-development may choose to put their faith in the global economy, free trade, investment, technology and entrepreneurship if they like. But as this book documents in detail, these market-based nostrums have not been sufficient. To go beyond them, people will need to invest in their *own* globalization, their own practical education about how the world really works.

This kind of education is not available in a university economics course. People need to understand why political parties, the police, the military, the media, the courts, and the church are often so unresponsive to popular demands, even in nominal "democracies," why senior officials, banks, corporations, and elites continue to prefer monster projects to schools and clinics; why the courts rarely enforce the law against people of means, let alone global companies like Freeport McMoran or Citigroup; why the radical liberalization of global capital markets and trade has taken precedence over the enforcement of tax codes, labor laws, health codes, securities laws, environmental laws, education rights, pension reform, and property rights for ordinary people; and why the poor are subject to unavoidable excise taxes, even as the elites are encouraged to invest tax-free, at home and abroad.

They also need to ask why developed and developing countries alike, after fifty years of malpractice, still permit First World bankers, corporations, and investors to engage in business practices in the Third World that would be grossly illegal back home; why the anti-foreign bribery statutes of the US and the OECD countries are so underenforced; why undocumented capital is recruited aggressively from developing countries while undocumented labor is increasingly harassed; and why the huge proportion of the Third World's multi-trillion dollar debt that was contracted illegally and spent on failed projects and elite bank accounts deserves to be *serviced at all*.

But first of all, they may want to start with the question of where the money went. This book may help them find it.

CHAPTER ONE

DEBT ELEPHANTS

In the carnival days from 1922 to 1929, when money was easy, many bankers forsook the dignified, aloof attitude traditional of bankers and became, in reality, high pressure salesmen of money. They carried on a cutthroat competition against their fellow bankers, and once they obtained the business, endeavored to urge larger loans on the borrowing countries.
—Francis White, US assistant secretary of state for Latin America, 1930[1]

We know a great deal about who the poor are, where they are, and how they live. We understand what keeps them poor and what must be done to improve their lives.
—Barber Conable, World Bank president, 1990

All these projects are either finished or given up, so it's not worthwhile to speak about these dams. We are not politicians, and we have to look for work. . . .
—senior executive, Lahmeyer International/RWE AG, 1999

One major piece of the puzzle about where all the money loaned to developing countries went, in addition to capital flight, involved wasteful projects. Many of these projects were started in the 1970s and 1980s, but they had long-term effects—not only providing a fountain of corruption, capital flight, and continuing environmental damage, but also laying the foundations for the 1990s privatization boom, when many governments found themselves trying to sell these elephants back to the private sector, or at least clean up after them. To understand the foundations of the development crisis and the prolonged consequences of these widespread "mistakes," we'll examine a cross section of such projects in different countries and then draw some general conclusions.

Almost everywhere one goes to research the history of the development crisis, one hears a similar tale:

An official visits his friend, an official of another country, who has an impressive estate, fancy cars, and a collection of polo ponies. "Confidentially, how did you get so rich?" the first official asks. "I will show you," says

the second. He takes his friend on a drive to a huge dam. "See that project? Fifty percent." Later, the second was visiting the first, who had an even
more impressive estate. "Confidentially, how did you get so rich?" the second asks. "I will show you," says the first. They take a drive to a river where
a major dam was supposed to have been built. "You see that dam?" the first
official says, pointing to the completely unobstructed river. "*One hundred
percent.*"

As Brazil's Finance Minister Mario Enrique Simonsen once remarked, there
were many cases in which such "one hundred percent commissions" might
actually have been *less* wasteful than the monstrosities that were in fact constructed. The development crisis is not an abstraction—the carnage is everywhere.

BRAZIL'S PHARAOHS

To illustrate this point, we'll start with Simonsen's own Brazil, the world's
fifth largest country, accounting for at least forty percent of South America's
economic activity. Brazil, the Third World's largest borrower in the 1970s, had
an unusual number of "pharaohnic" projects. It is also a fascinating case study
because its networks of influence and corruption were absolutely Byzantine,
and for most of the 1990s, neoliberals ruled the roost. One of them, Fernando
Collor, was booted out of the presidency in October 1992 after just two years
in office for corruption—the proceeds of which were laundered with the
help of several Miami private bankers. The other, Fernando Henrique Cardoso, was a French-speaking political economy professor from the University
of Sao Paulo, a supposed Social Democrat. After winning the 1994 election,
he developed a taste for power and took a sharp rightward turn, implementing a "strong *reis*" policy that stifled inflation and growth, slashed tariffs, and
barriers to foreign investment, and ordained the world's largest privatization
program—partly to clean up all the debt elephants, but mainly to secure
another term in office.

After all this, today Brazil still remains the Third World's largest debtor.
Indeed, it is now paying more debt service, as a share of national income, than
it did at the height of the 1980s debt crisis! It also has to generate even more
income to pay dividends to a hungry new crop of foreign investors. In 2002,
after all its "reforms of the 1990s," Brazil still needed a $30 billion IMF bailout
to prevent it from following Argentina into default. And it is hardly out of the
woods. In late 2002 it elected Luis ("Lula") Ignacio da Silva as president, a
bearded leftist metal worker from Pernambuco in Brazil's Northeast. Lula had
been running for president since 1989. He was finally elected on his fourth
try because most Brazilians had become completely fed up with thirty years

of corruption, rising debts, and grand neoliberal experiments. So how did all this come to pass? In a nutshell, as Lula said during his campaign, "The elite failed in the art of governing our country."

In the 1970s, Brazil believed it had every right to become a First World country as quickly as possible. What it did become was the world's largest and most profitable Third World banking market, with more than one hundred public projects in the energy, transport, and telephone sectors. By 1990, more than twenty-five percent of its $120 billion foreign debt was derived from projects in the energy sector alone. With First World export credit agencies, banks, equipment suppliers, and influential local contractors and politicians falling all over themselves for a piece of these projects, mundane concerns like profitability, the cost of capital, and project risk went by the boards—anticipating the First World's Internet boom in the late 1990s, when almost anyone with a business plan could get his startup funded.

After 1979, when the easy money began to dry up, Brazil got caught out. Many of its hastily conceived, capital-intensive projects turned out to be poorly designed and way behind schedule. Other projects might have been economic if they had been permitted to charge reasonable prices for their services, but politically-influential consumers of electricity, transportation, and telephone services in Brazil were used to subsidized prices. Beneath the surface, there was a whole fabric of corruption—commissions on loans, kickbacks on contracts, overpriced bids awarded without competition, nepotism, contributions to political campaigns—which lubricated the whole system. This yielded a whole herd of "debt elephants," a huge overhang of unserviceable debts, and a structural shortage of public services that continues to this day.

If Brazil had been Enron, it would have been allowed to declare bankruptcy. But international bankers had discovered the best thing of all about developing countries: unlike private debtors, they are not allowed to declare bankruptcy. Indeed, if they try to default on their debts, powerful global institutions like the IMF *exist* to bail out the banks and pressure the countries to pay.

• Eighty miles west of Rio de Janeiro, on a site the locals call *Itaorna* ("bad stone"), are Brazil's three costly attempts to build nuclear power plants. The contract for Angra I, a 626-megawatt plant, was awarded to Westinghouse and Bechtel in 1970, funded by export credits from the US Export-Import ("EXIM") Bank. It was supposed to cost $320 million and be ready by 1975. In reality, it cost $2.1 billion and wasn't in commercial operation until 1983. Then it developed the nasty habit of turning itself on and off—earning the nickname "firefly." Angra I is still in operation, but it suffers from repeated equipment failures. In May 2000, thousands of gallons of radioactive seawater leaked from the plant, a fact that Brazil's nuclear power authorities neglected to reveal for four months. Similar malfunctioning nuclear plants were built by Westinghouse and funded by EXIM Bank loans in the Philippines, Spain, Sweden and Yugoslavia.[2]

The construction of Angra II, a 1,229-megawatt nuclear plant, was started in late 1975 by Norberto Odebrecht, the owner of what has since become Brazil's largest construction company. For some reason Odebrecht, which had no previous experience with nuclear plants, got the bid without competition. At the time, that didn't seem to matter, because Odebrecht was able to rely on technology from the German company Siemens, plus generous loans from Deutsche Bank and HERMES, the German export development bank. It also had very close ties to General Ernesto Geisel, Brazil's unelected German-speaking president in the mid-1970s, who became president of an Odebrecht subsidiary after he retired from office. Angra II was to be the first of eight nuclear plants built by Siemens for Electrobras, Brazil's state-owned electricity monopoly, under the terms of the "Agreement of the Century" that Geisel concluded with the Germans in 1975.[3]

SIEMENS
Energieerzeugung

All these plants were supposed to be finished by 1990. Angra II was supposed to cost $1.6 billion and be operational by 1983. In fact, it only went live *twenty-six years* later, in July 2001, at a total cost of more than $10 billion—excluding the opportunity costs of Rio's severe electricity shortages all those years. One of the key problems was indeed "bad stone." Built without solid foundations, at a location that had suffered one earthquake in 1961 and another in 1976, Angra II became known as the world's only "sliding" nuclear power plant.[4] Angra II also set records not only for its delays, but also for its total cost—as one leading Brazilian engineer remarked, "If you divide $10 billion by 1,300 megawatts, you come up with the price of diamonds or cocaine, not energy."[5]

Nor was this the end of the story. Angra III, another 1,229-megawatt nuclear plant that was financed by the Germans and built by the politically influential Odebrecht, using the same aging "pressure water reactor" technology as Angra II, was supposed to cost $1 billion. It was started in 1986, then "mothballed" for fifteen years, after $2 billion had been spent finishing just thirty percent of it. In the interim, Siemens sold its nuclear subsidiary to the French—Germany's Green Party increased its political influence, and the country's leaders decided to close their own nuclear plants and stopped financing new ones abroad. Nuclear plants were also explicitly excluded from the "Clean Development" provisions of the 1997 Kyoto Protocol on Climate Change.[6]

But Angra is a problem that won't go away. The most recent twist involved Russia's prime minister, who visited Brazil in December 2001, offering export credits to finance a project in which Minatom, Russia's nuclear supplier—together with Siemens and the French nuclear supplier Framatome—would take over the completion of Angra III and the modernization of Angras I and II. However, in 2002, faced with a new debt crisis and the prospect of Angra III needing another six years and (at least) $1.7 billion to reach the finish line, Cardoso punted the decision about what to do with Angra III to the next president. During his 2002 campaign, in a speech to Brazil's military, Lula assured them of his nationalism by calling for the revival of a $100 million project to develop one nuclear submarine. But da Silva should pay careful attention to recent trends with respect to nuclear power. For example, in early 2003, Great Britain's privatized nuclear power generator, British Nuclear, was on the brink of bankruptcy, and the UK government was faced with having to lend the company $1.1 billion and renationalize the whole industry. He should also pay attention to the World Bank economists who have—to their credit—been uniformly against nuclear power in developing countries. Indeed, one of the few beneficial effects of the debt crisis was that it made nuclear power plants clearly unaffordable, although players like Westinghouse, Mitsubishi, and Framatome are still lobbying developing countries very hard to revive the industry.

Of course if any country ever needed nuclear power, it was not Brazil. After all, it has the world's greatest hydroelectric potential—more than 215-gigawatts, less than a third of which is developed. It also has huge potential for wind, biomass, and solar energy, and more efficient electricity transmission and utilization, as well as undeveloped oil and natural gas reserves. With all this, one would have expected Brazil to have rejected the nuclear power option long ago.

But, Brazil's nuclear plants generated thousands of soft jobs for Brazil's military, which ran the country's nuclear power program from its creation in 1969 to 1985, by which time Nucleabras employed nineteen thousand such timeservers. The nuclear industry also generated payoffs and campaign contributions from construction companies to leading generals and politicians. Until Cardoso finally signed the Nuclear Non-Proliferation Treaty in 1998, Brazil was even developing its own plutonium processing facilities and nuclear submarines, and was running a miniature nuclear arms race against Argentina's military!

Brazil's military also enjoyed the fact that, for a time, their nuclear endeavors generated commercial opportunities. In the 1980s Brazil became one of the Third World's top arms exporters. Its top customer was none other than Iraq's Saddam Hussein. In addition to huge quantities of tanks, airplanes, and jeeps, at least until 1990, Brazil secretly supplied Saddam Hussein with thousands of kilos of uranium yellow cake, in addition to expertise on fuel reprocessing and missiles. When Saddam invaded Kuwait in 1990, a twenty-nine-person team under Brazil's "Werner von Braun," Dr. Hugo de Oliveira Piva, was actually still in Baghdad, helping Iraq develop long-range missiles. Dr. Piva had been a director of Brazil's Aerospace Technology Center, leading a program to convert its Sonda IV sounding rocket into a nuclear-capable long range missile. In the late 1980s he led a team of Brazilian engineers that worked with Iraq to develop two three-stage, 1000-mile ballistic missiles, the Al Abid and Tammuz, using Scud motors for the first two stages, and a new Brazilian-designed third stage. The 48-ton Al Abid was reportedly close to completion by the time of the invasion, just five years after Iraq had initiated its long-range missile program—a record pace that only Brazil's assistance can explain. This revelation figured in the Bush adminstration's Fall 2002 assessment that Saddam Hussein might not be far away from possessing enough plutonium to assemble a nuclear weapon—a combination of German centrifuges, stockpiles of Brazilian "yellow cake," and the lethal skills of a few former Nucleobras experts. As we'll see later, one of the key companies involved in this dubious Iraq-Brazil arms trade was financed by dirty deals made by JPMorgan's senior vice president for Latin America.[7]

In retrospect, the notion of subsidizing the export of nuclear power with cheap loans to Third World countries all over the planet was probably not one of the finest hours for either First World development experts or national security specialists. After all, even First World countries have had trouble mastering the safety and security hazards, capital costs, and toxic wastes of nuclear power—to the point where no new nuclear plants have been ordered in North America and Western Europe in twenty-five years. For developing countries with relatively weak safety standards and environmental laws, unstable economies, deep national rivalries, weak export controls, lawless militaries, and capital shortages, it seems especially risky. Of course having nuclear plants isn't *sufficient* for producing nuclear weapons. However, except for China and North Korea, every Third World country that has tried to acquire them has started with nuclear power plants. In Brazil's case, its transition to democracy in the 1980s may have saved us from nuclear proliferation in Latin America *and* perhaps Iraq. But Brazil itself has been paying a hefty price since then for this particularly nasty debt elephant.

• Unfortunately, Brazil was not that much better at managing large hydro projects. For example, Balbina, a 250-megawatt hydro dam on the River Uatami near Manaus, in the middle of the Amazon river basin, was designed for Eletronorte—the federal power company in the Amazon—by Andrade Gutierrez, another influential Brazilian construction firm. Quite coincidentally, Andrade Gutierrez also built a house in Terasopolis for President/General Geisel and an equestrian center in Brasilia for his successor, President João Figueiredo. Balbina's five turbines were supplied by French company Neyrpic and financed with French export credits. Coincidentally, former French prime minister Giscard d'Estaing's family reportedly owned a stake in the company, and his cousin headed France's export credit agency.[8]

Originally priced at $383 million, Balbina's actual price tag turned out to exceed $800 million. Even if it had worked as advertised, that would have made Balbina's electricity the most expensive in Brazil, up to that point. But Balbina was so poorly designed that when its artificial lake started filling up in 1987, the water just kept on spreading. Eventually it flooded more than two thousand square miles, including an Indian reserve. The inhabitants—the Waimiri and Atroari tribes—had to be relocated by force. The lake was also not logged beforehand, so it became impossible to navigate because of all the submerged trees. At least a dozen exotic animal and fish species were wiped out, and the lake will not be habitable by fish or wildlife any time soon because of all the acid gas produced by rotting trees. Indeed, the rotting trees produce three million tons of methane each year, up to 28 times the output of greenhouse gases from an equivalent coal-fired power plant.[9] In 1988, Electronorte also discovered that Lago de Balbina's water level was so low that the lake would never reach its designed output unless another $700 million was spent to dam yet another river and destroy another Indian reserve. So the dam's output is now just 112 megawatts, half the original design, and less than one-sixteenth the power of the Tucurui hydro dam, which flooded two hundred fewer square miles.[10]

• Itaipu is located near Iguacu Falls, near Brazil's meeting point with Paraguay and Argentina. With 12,500-megawatts of capacity, it is one of the world's largest hydro dams (at least until China's massive Three Gorges becomes operational sometime in the next decade with 18,200-megawatts of power). Each of Itaipu's eighteen turbines generates more power than Angra I's entire output, and is large enough to contain a symphony orchestra. Jointly designed by Brazil and Paraguay, during the days when General Alfredo Stroessner still ran Paraguay and the military ran Brazil, Itaipu was a carnival of corruption. As one contractor recalled:

This was our most profitable project *ever*. Sebastian Camargo saw it coming about 1970, so he "made friends" with General Stroessner. Originally the bid went to Andrade, then Stroessner went to General Geisel and said, "You're hurting my good friend Sebastian Camargo." So a new bid was made and the contract went to a consortium of Camargo, Andrade, Mendes Junior, and Odebrecht....The bids were on a unit cost basis—so much per yard of rock, of earth, and so forth. The difference in cost between stone and earth was five to one, and since nobody knew the composition of the site, we played games with what kind of work was done....There was also lots of graft on the Paraguayan side—we had to contribute to Stroessner's Coronado Party at every turn.

Itaipu was conceived in the early 1970s—the original 1972 price tag was estimated at $3.6 billion. Construction started in 1975 and was supposed to take five years. In fact, it took almost three years just to carve a 1.3-mile-long, 300-foot-deep, 490-foot-wide diversion channel to shift the course of the Parana River, the world's seventh largest river, before dam construction could begin. More than forty-two thousand people had to be evicted to make way for the dam's 135,000-hectare reservoir. Many were resettled in Amazonia, with unhappy consequences for themselves as well as for the indigenous Amazonians. When Itaipu was finally completed in 1991, the actual cost was more than $21 billion, adding $8 billion to Brazil's foreign debt. A former Paraguayan minister of energy described it as "possibly the largest fraud in the history of capitalism." The dam produces sixty times as much power as Paraguay consumes and sells the surplus to Brazil, at prices that, at Brazil's insistence, have often been below cost. As a result, the binational commission that manages Itaipu now has a $4.2 billion debt of its own.

Among the key contractors involved in the project were the Swedish-Swiss company ABB/Alstom, France's Dumez, Germany's Siemens, which supplied eight of the dam's eighteen turbines, Brazil's construction firms Andrade Gutierrez and Odebrecht, and Paraguay's engineering company Conempa SA, which was also involved in the infamous Yacyreta Dam project. At the time, Conempa was headed by Juan Carlos Wasmosy, who later served as Paraguay's first elected president in thirty-four years from 1993 to 1998. In a politically charged case in 1994, one of Wasmosy's opponents in the 1993 election, Ricardo Canese, was found guilty of criminal slander and sentenced to two months in jail for accusing President Wasmosy of having made his fortune by facilitating huge Itaipu kickbacks to former dictator Alfredo Stroessner. Turning the tables, Canese became energy minister in the next government, and in 2002, Wasmosy was sentenced to four years in jail for diverting $40 million from a social welfare institute to one of his private banks. In 2001, the newspaper *La Nación* also published documents which allegedly showed that he had accumulated up to $700 million in Cayman Island accounts during his six years in office. As of 2003, that is still being investigated.[11]

• Tucurui, the Amazon's first power dam, is located two hundred miles south of Belem on the Toncatins River. Work on the 4,200-megawatt dam began in 1976. Camargo Correa, yet another politically influential Brazilian construction firm, was selected to do the job, despite the fact that its bid was high-cost, because President Geisel wanted to help Camargo recover from its huge losses on the Guri Dam in Venezuela. ABB/Alstom was also a key supplier to this dam. Tucurui's first phase was finished in 1984 at a cost of $6 billion, four times the original cost projection of $1.4 billion. One former project manager for Camargo at Tucurui explained: "All our experience had been in the south—we didn't know a thing about building dams in the Amazon. But projects like this one were awarded on 'political' grounds, and then you negotiated the costs."[12] As an investigation by Brazil's Congress later discovered in the mid-1990s, twenty to thirty percent "overpricing" by government contractors on these dam projects was the rule of thumb. And there were many other irregularities. In 1983, in the *Relatorio Saraiva* scandal, a leading French banker charged that Brazil's minister, Antonio Delfim Neto, had demanded a huge bribe to get the project approved, while he was in charge of what became known as Brazil's "ten percent embassy" in Paris.[13]

Tucurui also proved to be another ecological disaster. In March 1980, the Tocantins River came within inches of overflowing the dam. The sea backed up because of the river's reduced outflow, creating massive salinization damage. Mosquitoes multiplied in the new reservoir, and fisheries complained that the river's fish stocks were badly depleted. The dam also displaced twenty-four thousand people, including several indigenous groups that virtually disappeared. Like Balbina, Tucurui also submerged an entire forest. The resulting acid gases from the trees corroded the turbines. Capemi, a private company owned by Brazilian military officers and financed by a $100 million foreign loan from Lazard Frere, Banque Nacional de Paris, and American Express, had been set up to log the lake. But Amazon hardwoods proved to be so hard that ordinary saws couldn't cut them, so Capemi went broke and the money disappeared. As for Tucurui's electricity, Brazil agreed to sell a third of it below cost to two aluminum projects that were located downstream in Belem: Alumar, a joint venture of Camargo, Correa, Alcoa, and Shell, and a Japanese consortium. These sweetheart deals meant that Eletronorte, already burdened by a $2.3 billion foreign debt, lost three hundred dollars for every ton of aluminum produced.[14] Finally, when Eletronorte completed the dam's $1.5 billion second phase in the 1990s, adding eleven new turbines to create another 4,000-megawatts of capacity, it discovered that the dam would operate far below capacity during the dry season because there was too little reservoir storage upstream.[15]

• In early 1979, when the first signs of another oil price shock appeared in the wake of the Iran hostage crisis, Brazil's economy minister Antonio Delfim Neto was desperate to keep Brazil's foreign borrowing spree rolling. With the help of his bankers, especially JPMorgan's Tony Gebauer, he contrived a novel scheme. Brazil would launch several new power projects, not because of their individual merits, but to generate billions more in supplier credits—courtesy of foreign equipment vendors like GE and Siemens and their government supporters, export credit agencies like the US EXIM Bank and Germany's HERMES. He asked his powerful friend, Paulo Maluf, the governor of Sao Paulo State, to help out. Maluf was happy to do so. Big construction projects were an opportunity to hand out lucrative contracts to powerful *empreteiros* like Camargo Correa, influential engineering firms like Sao Paulo's THEMAG, and equipment vendors, who, in turn, could be quite appreciative with campaign contributions and other amenities.[16]

Maluf promptly ordered four new hydro dams, plus a new canal and a hairbrained scheme to explore for oil in Sao Paulo State.[17] The prime borrower would be CESP, Sao Paulo's state-owned electricity company. One of these projects was a new 1,815-megawatt hydro dam to be built at Porto Primavera on the Parana River, on Sao Paulo's border with Mato Grosso do Sul, the home of the Pantenal, one of the world's most remarkable ecological reserves. Its prime contractors would be Camargo Correa and THEMAG. The dam's original design estimated it would cost $1.5 billion, including interest, and be completed by 1987.[18] Construction began in June 1980.

More than twenty years later, the dam—now called "Engenheiro Sérgio Motta," after a former communications minister—is still not finished. In February 1999, Porto Primavera was inaugurated with just sixty-five percent of its designed capacity, at an estimated cost of $10 billion.[19] At the earliest, the dam will be finished by 2004. CESP is now bankrupt, saddled with $4 billion in foreign debts, due mainly to these six projects, plus several billion more in legal liabilities. All this debt has foiled Brazil's repeated attempts to privatize CESP. Not surprisingly, there is little demand for a debt-ridden company that produces the most expensive electricity in Brazil and faces dozens of lawsuits from environmentalists, displaced farmers and Indians, unpaid creditors, and the State of Sao Paulo itself.[20]

But, as in the case of Balbina, Porto Primavera's greatest costs were not financial. It created a reservoir that flooded 1,400 square miles, an area larger than Itaipu's reservoir, even though Porto Primavera produces less than ten percent of Itaipu's energy. According to environmental experts, the dam has drowned 77 river islands and 118 archaeological sites, destroying wetlands that contain thousands of animal and plant species, including endangered species like the spotted jaguar and the jacaré crocodile. It also displaced six thousand farmers, ceramics workers (the area has unusual clays), and fishermen. The dam was constructed with no fish ladders, so species like the dourado and the pacu are unable to swim upstream to breed. As a result, fishing on the river has declined by eighty percent. It has also forced some of last remaining members of an Indian tribe, the Xavante, off their lands. Overall, while there are more than 140 competitors for this title, Porto Primavera is certainly in the running for Brazil's worst dam project ever.[21]

• The $600 million Transamazonica Highway was started in 1970 by the Medici government and financed by the World Bank's largest foreign loan up to that point. It was part of the military's strategy to reduce pressure on landowners in southern Brazil—in President Medici's words, "To bring men without land to land without men." But the jungle soon overgrew the road, and it was also flooded by the Tucurui Dam's lake—a case of debt elephants at war with each other. Interestingly, one key motivation for the construction of this and other roads in the Amazon was to gain access to uranium deposits that Brazil's planning elite believed it might use in its own nuclear plants—or export to all the others built around the world.

• In 1981, the World Bank loaned Brazil $445 million to help finance the $1.5 billion Polonoreste project, which set out to build a nine hundred-mile highway from Cuiba—the capital of Mata Grosso—to Porto Velho, in the remote Amazon state of Rondonia, on the border with Bolivia. The World Bank approved the loan despite serious objections from its own economists and several outside consultants. When the road was finished in 1985, more than thirteen thousand land-hungry colonists per month—five hundred thousand by 1991—poured into Rondonia, accompanied by corporate farmers, who acquired huge forest tracts and burned them to the ground to get tax breaks. Deforestation increased tenfold; in just four years an area the size of Wisconsin was deforested, disrupting the lives of the Nambicuara tribe and setting the stage for conflicts among land-hungry peasants, Indians, and ranchers that still continue. The colonialists also discovered, to their surprise, that the region had some of the world's most fragile soils. But over the next decade, backed by continuing government subsidies for logging and cattle ranching, the deforestation continued. In 2001, for example, logging and fires reportedly destroyed 6,095 square miles of the Amazon, an area about half the size of Belgium. At current cutting rates, we are headed for a disaster that will have impacts far beyond Brazil: more than forty percent of the Amazon will be deforested or heavily degraded by 2020.[22]

• The Ferrovia do Aço, a railroad from Minas Gerais to Volta Redonda, which was started in 1975, was supposed to cost $1.2 billion. By 1996, when Brazil privatized its rail network, the project had consumed $2.1 billion in government loans and was still unfinished. President Jose Sarney also spent

$2.4 billion on his favorite railroad, Ferrovia Norte Sul, when he was in office during the late 1980s, to connect his home state of Maranhao with the remote state of Goias—"the railroad from no place to nowhere," as one observer put it. A key *empreteiro* involved in both projects, Murilio Mendes, was a member of Sarney's "kitchen cabinet." In 1987, one week before Norte Sul's contractors were to be selected by sealed bid, *Folha de Sao Paulo* published a list of eighteen preselected winners, including Mendes' company.[23]

• By the late 1980s, the foreign debts of Siderbrás, Brazil's state-owned steel company, totaled $11 billion, and many of its projects were losing money. For example, a $500 million steel mill in Tubarao was built in the wrong place and was designed to use charcoal, a steel-making technology not commonly used since nineteenth-century England. The Acominas steel project near Belo Horizonte consumed $1.1 billion to build one of the world's largest blast furnaces, to make structural steel for US-style high-rise buildings. Unfortunately few Brazilian contractors knew how to build US-style high-rise buildings, and the furnace never worked properly. In the state of Para, another railroad was constructed with a $300 million World Bank loan to connect the Carajas iron-ore project to the ocean. Twenty-two pig iron factories were built next to the railroad. Each one consumed five thousand acres of Amazon forest per year. (Because of the soil's delicacy there has never been a successful Amazon reforestation project.) Brazil sold the iron to auto companies like Volkswagen and Ford at prices sixty percent below world levels—a case of these auto companies literally driving away with the forest.[24]

In the 1990s, in an attempt to get out from under these burdens, Brazil swung to the other extreme, abolishing Siderbrás in 1990 and privatizing all its operating companies for $9.4 billion. This seemed like a good idea at the time. Not only had the sector compiled a huge foreign debt, but its operating losses in 1990 alone were $2.2 billion. In 1994, however, one year after privatization, the companies made $1 billion in net profits—leading many to wonder whether the government should have tried to restructure the enterprise itself. On closer inspection, the rapid improvement was due to a combination of luck and special help to the new owners with price controls and debt relief. But the sector had been poorly managed for so long that it was easy for privatization advocates to claim a victory.[25]

• In 1975, under the influence of its powerful sugar lobby, Brazil launched a multi-billion dollar effort to make gasohol, a gasoline substitute, from sugar cane and corn. Then sugar prices plummeted, bankrupting many cane farmers and sharply increasing the program's cost. But by the time Brazil's 450 distilleries were ready to supply alcohol in the late 1980s, prices had recovered, and it had become more profitable to export sugar than to make gasohol. To satisfy industrial interests, Brazil also set prices for public services, electricity and gasoline far below cost. As a result, most state-owned enterprises realized negative returns throughout the 1980s. This stimulated energy demand and added to the government deficit. Meanwhile, Petrobras, Brazil's state oil company, took its time with the search for oil—the rich Campos basin, discovered in the early 1960s, wasn't even drilled until 1983, and still remains underdeveloped.

• Brazil's many other wasteful projects include Complexo Pedra do Carvalo, a Bahian water treatment plant that was supposed to cost $85 million and ended up costing $800 million; Sonegran do Sao Paulo, a sanitation facility so overbuilt that it could handle twenty times the city's actual sewage; the Rio-Niteroi Bridge, a $400 million boondoggle funded by Banque Rothschild that collapsed while under construction and suffered a fifty percent cost overrun; the $150 million Regional Labor Court of Sao Paulo, a construction project approved by President Cardoso in 1996, after which $80 million disappeared, reportedly into the hands of politicians and judges; the $3.9 billion Belo Monte hydro dam on the River Xingu in the state of Para, which has been on-and-off again for ten years, has already cost twice its original budget, and would flood another 270 square miles of agricultural land and forest; and the $2 billion dollar Sudene and Sudam development bureaus for the Amazon region, which were abolished by Cardoso in 2001 after it was determined that most of the money had been diverted into private pockets.[26]

AFTER THE CARNIVAL

So where did Brazil end up after all these pharaohnic projects—not to mention 135 others that we don't have time to examine? First, in the energy sector, by the millennium the country was really in trouble. Not only were many key projects late and over budget, but Brazil had also become dependent on large hydro dams and nuclear power plants for ninety-five percent of its power. Whenever a drought hit, as it did in 2001, the government had to introduce rationing to slash power consumption by more than twenty percent. To avoid future shortages, Brazil will need more than thirty-five thousand megawatts of new capacity—a forty percent increase—in the next decade. It is not clear where the extra money for all this will come from, especially given the country's debt burden. As we'll explore further in Chapter V, responsibility for this fiasco goes to a self-serving coalition of foreign bankers, equipment vendors, and government officials.

By 2003, Brazil still owed more than $237 billion of foreign debt, more than any other developing country—more than all of Sub-Saharan Africa. Servicing it costs $63 billion a year, a whopping eleven percent of national income—the same share that Brazil spends on all health care and public education combined, and an even greater share than it paid during the 1980s debt crisis. Up to half of this is traceable directly or indirectly to misguided projects.

And this mess existed *even after* Brazil mounted the world's largest privatization program in the 1990s, when the neoliberal administrations of Fernando Collor and Fernando Henrique Cardoso sold off 119 state-owned enterprises and other assets to foreign and domestic private investors for $103 billion.

But privatization was not really about cleaning up after the debt elephants, reforming the economy, or democratizing Brazil's extraordinarily unequal distribution of wealth. Rather, it was mainly about selling off the state's crown jewels. This financed a (temporarily) strong currency, kept the IMF happy, and, most importantly, profited the elite—just as in the 1970s, when loans had provided opportunists like Delfim Neto.

In this case, the candy was not big projects, but the very best public assets: valuable cellular and tollroad concessions; Telebras, Brazil's telephone system, which was sold for just $19 billion in 1998; and CVRD, the world's largest mining company, which had little debt, no subsidies, and generated $600 million in profits in 1997, the year before it was privatized for just $3.5 billion. These assets were sold, not in public offerings, but in "controlled packages" at private auctions—an approach that was later revealed to have been riddled with corruption. And the main beneficiaries included key government officials, foreign banks like Citigroup, FleetBoston, CreditSuisse, and JPMorgan Chase, foreign investors like Enron, Worldcom, Bell South, Telecom Italia, and Telefonica, domestic investors like Bradesco, Globo, Odebrecht, and Andrade Gutierrez. They also included Banco Opportunity, the Rio investment bank that managed money for George Soros, Citibank, and the family of Antonio Carlos Magalhaes, who was the president of Brazil's Senate and the country's most powerful "kingmaker" until he was forced to resign for spying on his colleagues in 2001. For a time, these investors took advantage of the opening to buy up many of Brazil's finest private companies. As one leading Brazilian magazine commented, "The history of capitalism has seen very few transfers of control as intense as this over a short period of time."

Unfortunately, the privatization boom ended almost as badly as the debt boom before it. As time went by, there were fewer easily sold assets on offer, and financial crises in distant places like Indonesia and Russia, plus several major corruption scandals involving the privatization, made investors increasingly nervous about Brazil. So higher and higher real interest rates—twenty-seven percent in 1998—were needed to keep the dollars coming in and prevent the reis from plummeting. However, high real rates and the increasingly overvalued currency stifled economic growth and encouraged increased foreign borrowing. The incredible interest costs also swelled the government's budget deficit.

Eventually this whole neoliberal edifice fell like a house of cards. In August 1998, soon after Russia's devaluation, investors began to speculate that Brazil would also have to devalue. They made this a self-fulfilling prophecy by taking advantage of Brazil's new liberal capital markets to take their money out of the country. In the second half of 1998, the volume of flight capital exceeded the volume of direct foreign investment brought in by privatization. Reserves were shrinking and the current account deficit was mounting. In January 1999, despite a $42 billion IMF loan, Cardoso was forced to float the *reis*, and its value sank by more than sixty percent in two months.

At the end of Cardoso's pseudoreforms, Brazil ended up with slower growth, rising unemployment, a huge budget deficit, ballooning foreign and domestic debts, a growing stock of unfunded pension fund liabilities, rising inflation, corruption on a scale that made Delfim Neto's generation envious, and greater inequality among Brazil's social classes than ever, with some of its finest public assets now in the hands of its venal elite. In August 2002, Brazil needed yet another $30 billion IMF bailout to prevent it from following Argentina into the tank. In October 2002, the country finally elected da Silva—an outright opponent of neoliberal policies. In short, by postponing issues like the need for devaluation, real reform of the domestic economy, and greater attention to social justice, privatization played the same role foreign loans had in the 1970s and early 1980s. In a sense, it was the largest white elephant of all.

While Brazil had an unusual number of debt elephants, other developing countries also had a few herds of their own. In the 1970s, the Philippines built a $2.3 billion, 620-megawatt Westinghouse nuclear power plant at scenic Morong on the Bataan Peninsula just thirty miles from Manila. The plant was within twenty-five miles of three earthquake fault lines and less than five miles from two active volcanoes, Natib and Pinatubo, which erupted in 1991.

The Philippines National Power Corporation had started the project in 1973, its largest power plan ever, as part of a national plan to build 6 nuclear plants, in order to cut dependence on oil and satisfy the islands' fast-growing demand for electricity. In early 1974, GE submitted a proposal to build two 620 MW plants for $700 million. Then Westinghouse suddenly jumped in. Its Philippine distributor got in touch with one of Marcos' golf partners, Herminio T. Disini, whose wife was Imelda's governess and first-cousin.[38a1]

In May 1974, after making all these arrangements, Westinghouse presented a cursory "proposal" of its own that had a $500 million price tag for two 626 MW plants. The proposal made lots of promises, which were subject to lots of qualifications:

(Our) proposed approach can result in an overall saving of time of two to three years. . . . . A great advantage to the Philippines is the number of overseas turnkey plants in this size range that Westinghouse is managing. Plants similar to the one we propose are being undertaken in Brazil, Yugoslavia, Korea, Italy, Sweden, and Switzerland. We estimate that your cost for two turnkey type 626 MW electric plants will be $500 million, or $650 million, including fuel and transmission lines. . . . The estimate is subject to: . . . . . . final determination scope . . . escalation . . . evaluation of site data . . . establishment of a final project schedule . . . and development of plant layouts.

Despite the vague and open-ended nature of this proposal, in May 1974 Marcos ordered NPC's general manager to accept it. The astonished GE executives got the news from Marcos's personal secretary in late June.[38a4] Only then, however, did real negotiations begin. By September 1974 Westinghouse's bid was up to $695 million; by February 1976, when the contract was actually signed, the price was $722 million for just one plant, plus another $387 million of interest and escalation cost. By 1992, including interest on the debt, the direct cost was more than $2.5 billion, for a "Three Mile Island-type" plant with more than 4000 design errors that even a Marcos-appointed commission would conclude was unsafe to operate.

Citibank used similar inducements to become the project's agent bank, while William J. Casey, the Rogers & Wells partner who headed the US EXIM Bank from 1974 to 1976, overruled his own staff at EXIM and approved the project. This was the bank's biggest financing project until Indonesia's Paiton project in the 1990s, part of more than $7.7 billion that EXIM devoted to promoting nuclear power around the world. Casey returned to Rogers & Wells in 1976–80, ran the Reagan-Bush campaign from February to November 1980, and then became Reagan's CIA Director from January 1981 to December 1986. Later on, it turned out that Casey's former law firm, Rogers & Wells, had worked on numerous Marcos investments, and that one of Casey's closest friends and clients, fellow OSS veteran John M. Shaheen—also later a veteran of the Iran-Contra arms deals—had partnered with Marcos in a curious Hong Kong bank.[27] And Marcos himself later alleged—with some degree of support from Reagan's 1984 campaign manager Ed Rollins, along with evidence discovered at Malacanang Palace after the dictator's demise—that he had contributed millions of dollars in illegal cash contributions to Reagan's presidential campaigns in 1980 and 1984. So far, investigators have not produced the "smoking documents" needed to corroborate these allegations. But given the high-level bribery scandals across the political spectrum that have recently surfaced in countries like Germany, France, Japan, and Italy, it is not out of the question that Marcos might have found takers for a few "foreign bribes" of his own to key US supporters in both major parties.

The Bataan nuclear plant was finished in 1985, but it has been postponed for safety and cost reasons ever since, with $80 million of uranium sitting nearby in storage. It is the largest single-line item in the Philippines's $50 billion foreign debt, costing taxpayers more than $170,000 a day in interest—$1.2 billion in total as of 2003.

The plant also became the subject of a prolonged lawsuit between the Philippines and Westinghouse. Westinghouse argued successfully that, despite making the payoffs, it was not guilty of violating the US Foreign Corrupt Practices Act because corruption in the Philippines had reached the point where such payoffs were considered "normal business practices." In October 1995, the hard-pressed Philippine government agreed to a $100 million out-of-court settlement with Westinghouse that freed the company from any liability for the plant, allowed it back into the country, and continued the government's obligation to service the debt. In 1994, President Fidel Ramos announced plans to convert the Bataan plant to a combined-cycle gas-fired plant, but that would have cost $600 million, so it was not implemented. As of 2003 the government was still trying to figure out what to do with the plant.

Meanwhile, largely because of the dearth of electricity caused by the Bataan nuclear fiasco, Manila experienced acute electricity shortages in the early 1990s. But in this new era of privatization, rather than build new plants, the National Power Corporation (Napacor) decided to rely on the private sector. Over the next decade, it signed forty-eight contracts with private independent power producers (IPPs). Written "under the influence," these turned out to be boondoggles for the IPPs and another disaster for the government. They obligated Napacor to pay the full cost of IPP capacity whether or not it was actually used. By 2003, these one-sided deals had cost the country more than $14 billion, and the Philippines had the world's most costly electricity. While most of these dubious "power privatization" deals were signed under President Ramos in 1992–98, the outrages have continued—including a questionable $470 million hydro project awarded to an obscure Argentine firm by President Gloria Macagapal-Arroyo, just four days after she took power in 2001. A comment by Manila's INS newspaper provided a nice summary: "The Power Purchase Agreement is our payment for a huge amount of electricity that we actually do not use. In other words, the PPA is like a huge vacuum cleaner. It sucks."[28]

Another key beneficiary of the Philippines' IPP program, while it lasted, was Enron, the now-bankrupt US energy giant. In 1993–94, Enron obtained $106 million in foreign loans and risk insurance from two government agencies, the Asian Development Bank and the US Overseas Private Investment Corporation, for two Philippine power plants, and lucrative "take or pay" contracts with Napacor. This was achieved with special help from US ambassador Frank Wisner Jr., who later joined Enron's Board in October 1997, after working hard to get these Philippine plants and the $2.9 billion Dabhol "independent power" plant for Enron in India. One of the Enron contracts with the Philippines was so one-sided that it caused Napacor's entire board to resign in protest when it was signed in 1993.[29]

• Autopistas Urbanas, a highway that transects Buenos Aires, was built by Argentina's military government from 1976 to 1982 at a cost of more than $1 billion—four times the original bid. About $300 million of this came from a syndicate led by Libra Bank—a consortium partly owned by Chase, whose chairman, David Rockefeller, and Chase's private banking group, had close ties to the junta. In 1978, Argentina hosted the World Cup, and its admirals, who controlled that year's "World Cup concession," borrowed $700 million to refurbish every soccer stadium in the city. The junta also got US banks like Chase and Morgan, and even major British banks like Lloyds, to finance the arms buildup that culminated in the 1982 Malvinas War between Argentina and the UK. During the military's six-year reign, Argentina's foreign debt increased from $7.8 billion to $43.6 billion.

Argentina also had many wasteful power projects, the crown prince of which was Yacyreta, a 2,760-megawatt hydro dam built with Paraguay on the Parana River. Financed by loans from the World Bank and the IDB, the dam was originally devised in a 1973 agreement between Paraguay's dictator, General Alfredo Stroessner, and Argentina's Juan Perón. It was estimated to cost $1.6 billion and be completed by 1989. As of 2003, it has actually cost $11.5 billion, not including $1.2 billion of electricity that might have been sold had it been available. The dam is still only sixty percent finished. The electricity it generates costs more than three times international averages, and the project needs up to $2 billion to reach the 3,700-megawatt size required to be economic. The project is also fighting a swarm of legal actions from eighty thousand displaced locals, environmental activists, and unpaid contractors. In 2001, Paraguay's government put out a bid for cheaper power from other sources, despite the fact that it is a half-owner of Yacyreta. A 1994 study by the World Commission on Dams estimated that the project had lost at least $6 billion to outright corruption. Even Argentina's president Carlos Menem called it a "monument to corruption." World Bank president James Wolfensohn conceded that it was "a rather sad case."

For contractors and vendors, however, Yacyreta was a feeding frenzy. The prime contractor was the Italian construction giant Impregilo SPa, owned by the Fiat Group, a twenty-one percent share in Eriday, the ten-company consortium that built the dam. Also involved were Italy's Ansaldo, Japan's Mitsubishi, Hitachi, and Toshiba, GE Canada, Germany's Siemens/Voith and Lahmeyer International/RWE AG, the French-German contractor Dumez, Harza, Argentina's IMPSA and Cometarsa, and Paraguay's Conempa SA, which was also involved in Itaipu. In 1999, the Entidad Binacional Yacyreta (EBY) that contracted the project rejected claims from these contractors for an additional billion dollars, which they said was due to unwarranted delays. In 1998, three turbines had to be replaced when cracks appeared, costing $5 million. In May 1999, four more of the project's twenty turbines failed completely. A World Bank Performance Audit Report found that Argentina's power demand had only grown 2 percent a year during the 1990s, not the 8–10 percent envisioned by Yacyreta's planners. It concluded that "Yacyreta was not a least-cost solution to expanded power supply and its relevance to the country's priorities was negligible. On several occasions, the Bank had good cause for stopping the project before the major civil works were too advanced." Especially after Argentina's deep economic crisis of 2001–03, including its default on all private lending in January 2002 and its default on all IMF and World Bank loans in October–December 2002—the entire project now looks like a complete write-off. EBY has expressed interest in privatizing the project, but there have been no takers.[30]

• In Peru's arid southwest region, one of the world's driest deserts, the massive Majes-Siguey irrigation project was conceived by the radical military junta of General Juan Velasco Alvarado and General Francisco Morales Bermúdez, which ruled Peru from 1968 to 1980. Huge dams were constructed across the Apurimac and Colca Rivers, and 60 miles of tunnels and 250 miles of service roads were constructed. After thirty years and $2 billion, 150,000 acres have been irrigated, but it is clear that this capital and water-intensive approach to agricultural reform made little sense. The growth of agricultural productivity in this region has remained modest. And despite the regime's rhetoric about "agrarian reform," the project's benefits went mainly to the top three percent of landowners, who still control seventy-seven percent of Peru's arable land. The twenty-seven percent of Peru's population who still depend on small farms for their living have received very little of such aid.[31]

• At Parque Central, in downtown Caracas, near the Belles Artes metro station, there is no park. Instead, there are some of Latin America's tallest eyesores—two fifty-six-story office and condominium towers that were constructed in the 1970s and 1980s. Financed by a $100 million foreign loan to Centro Simon Bolivar, a corrupt government agency, the project started in 1966 and was only completed in 1984. Its designers hoped to create a modern, elegant cultural oasis to revitalize the city's center. Today it is occupied mainly by government offices, with only a handful of its twenty-four elevators working on any given day. The area has become a run-down Mecca for homeless people, skateboarders, and other urban proles. The nearby bunkerlike Complejo Cultural Teresa Carreño took ten years to build and cost $500 million, five times the original bid. The unfinished Oliva Lara tunnel, built under a mountain that caved in, cost even more. In the 1970s, President Carlos Andres Perez felt so flush with loans and oil that he ordered every public toilet in Venezuela to hire an attendant. He even used foreign loans to purchase a $40 million high-rise building *in downtown Miami*. Carlos Andres Perez's disastrous terms as Venezuela's president from 1974 to 1979 and again from 1989 to 1993, when he was finally removed from office for corruption, laid the foundations for the political turmoil that continues to this day. It also helps to explain why the country now has a lower real per capita income than it did in 1960.[32]

• Among Mexico's many white elephants is a $2 billion Canadian-designed nuclear plant, Laguna Verde, located seventy miles north of Veracruz. Designed with GE reactors and built with US EXIM bank loans, it took eleven years to complete. But the real problem with Laguna Verde was not the delay—since it started operating in 1987, there have been more than sixty accidents, and it has earned the nickname "Chernobyl on the Gulf". There are also four underutilized ports at Las Truchas, Altamira, Ostion, and Salinacruz that cost $4 billion; an unattractive water fountain on Mexico City's Paseo de la Reforma that was built with a $100 million Citibank loan; a petrochemical complex at Cangrejera that was designed by the British company ICI and proved too hazardous to use; and the underutilized $2.4 billion second stage of the La Truchas steel mill.

• Bolivians may have one of the lowest per capita incomes in Latin America, but one thing they do not lack is the lavish four-lane, 6.2 mile, $140 million highway that connects downtown La Paz to its international airport. Funded by the IDB, this was one of the world's most expensive roads per mile. The Bolivian Air Force also used foreign loans to buy ten C-130 cargo planes from the US military, more than any other Latin American country. In the late 1980s, these planes made many suspicious, unregistered flights to Miami.[33]

• Honduras's three hundred-megawatt El Cajon Dam is the largest dam in Central America and one of the tallest in the world at 768 feet, 36 feet taller than the Hoover Dam. It was built in the early 1980s on the Humuya River in the north-central part of the country, funded with $800 million from the World Bank and the IDB. About 4,700 people lost their homes and arable land on the flat river bottom, the best area to farm. Little compensation was provided by the government. With land ownership already highly concentrated and most campesinos unable to provide legal titles, the dam further concentrated the ownership of the best land and forced campesinos to clear surrounding hillsides, which increased erosion and silting. The reservoir has seldom reached more than half of its designed capacity, except in November

1998, when Hurricane Mitch struck. As a result, Honduras has suffered repeated energy shortages. Fiat's Impregilo SA was also the main contractor on this project.[34]

• Partly because of its unusual openness to US banks, Panama got stuck with more than its share of debt elephants. These included the $100 million Vandam bridge, which provided a $4 million bonus to a former president; an $80 million cement plant whose output cost three times as much as cement imported from Costa Rica; a $100 million copper mine that never worked; and a $700 million hydro dam that is too small and functions erratically. General Omar Torrijos, the country's populist dictator in the 1970s, even used foreign funds to finance—a buffalo farm! Best of all, however, was the second-hand sugar mill that Torrijos imported from Louisiana. The mill was so old that when it was disassembled for export, there were public protests—many New Orleans residents considered it a landmark!

• Lest we think that "state capitalism" and public sector spending were the sole routes to "dirty debt" troubles, we need to examine closely the case of General Augusto Pinochet's right-wing dictatorship, which ruled Chile from 1973 to 1989 under the spell of Milton Friedman. Friedman espoused an especially virulent strain of neoliberal *sauve qui peut* doctrine. As a result of his influence, Chile was inoculated against most of the public sector spending excesses that plagued so many other developing countries. However, the Chicago neoliberals substituted their own excesses, especially a strange combination of monetary policies that used exchange rate targets to control inflation. While this stifled inflation, it also stifled growth and encouraged excessive foreign borrowing *by the private sector*. In 1982–83, these policies culminated in a devaluation that caused most of the country's leading private banks to fail. Under pressure from foreign banks, Chile's right-wing military junta then nationalized all the private debt, converting it into what then became the second-highest per capita public foreign debt in Latin America. And since the private banks, which all failed and had to be taken over by the government, owned a huge share of Chile's entire private sector, that meant the Pinochet government also ended up owning a huge share of Chile's private sector. Later on, the Pinochet government received widespread praise in the Western media for implementing one of the developing world's first large scale privatization programs. No one bothered to recall why Chile's government had so many assets to privatize in the first place, nor why the government's largest asset—the copper mines—remained firmly in state hands. In the end, the Boys from Chicago outsmarted themselves, pioneering what some economists called "the Chicago road to socialism."

• Guatemala's Pueblo Viejo-Quixal project, or the Chixoy Dam, is an example of a debt project that not only wasted money and time, but human lives as well. In 1975, the Instituto Nacional de Electrificación (INDE)—

Guatemala's state-owned power monopoly—undertook to redress the country's energy problems by building a three hundred-megawatt hydroelectric dam in Baja Verapaz, four miles downstream from a Mayan village called Río Negro. The project had been designed by a consortium of consultants from the US, West Germany and Switzerland, and financed by foreign loans from the IDB ($175 million), the World Bank ($127 million), and $10 million in foreign aid from Italy, whose contractor, Impregilo, became the prime contractor. Other key players were Germany's Lahmeyer/RWE and Hochtief, both owned by the powerful RWE AG (one of Germany's top five companies, with key minority holdings by Deutsche Bank and Dresdner Bank). The original 1974 price tag for the dam proposed by the Lahmeyer/RWE-led LAMI consortium was $270 million. It was also supposed to be finished by 1981 and save Guatemala $30-$40 million a year in imported oil. This was just one of 527 such "dam loans," totaling $58 billion, that the World Bank handed out by the mid-1990s, financing 604 dams in 93 developing countries. All this was part of its long-term strategy to provide developing countries with cheap hydroelectric power.

From an economic standpoint, like many of these Third World dams, Chixoy proved to be a disaster. It was constructed between 1976 and 1985 at a cost of $1.2 billion, five times the original estimate. Corruption played a key role in the cost overruns. As Rafael Bolaños, dean of the School of Civil Engineering at Guatemala's San Carlos University, commented, "[Chixoy] was the biggest gold mine the crooked generals ever had." According to one estimate, the corruption exceeded $350 million.

The project was also plagued by foul-ups and design flaws. Construction had to be halted for fifteen months in 1976 after an earthquake, and in September 1983, when one of the dam's main tunnels collapsed. The repairs took two more years. Even after the dam resumed operation in November 1985, it had repeated maintenance problems and low capacity utilization. Electricity prices in Guatemala actually rose faster after its construction. Chixoy was also supposed to have a useful life of 50–200 years, but its reservoir is silting up so fast that it may require massive dredging as soon as 2005. Finally, the dam is also having harmful effects on fish and other wildlife, and boosting the incidence of diseases like malaria and dengue fever.

Overall, as the World Bank's own project review of Chixoy concluded in 1991, "The project experienced significant cost and time overruns and very reduced benefits." In 1996, World Bank president James Wolfensohn conceded that Chixoy had been "a very weak project on technical and economic grounds." As of 2002, this debt elephant alone accounted for more than ten percent of Guatemala's $4.6 billion foreign debt.

However, Chixoy's most important problems may have involved human rights, not economics. From 1978 to 1986, Guatemala was ruled by a blood-thirsty junta directed by Fernando Romeo Lucas Garcia (1978–82), General Efrain Rios Montt (1982–83), and General Oscar Mejia Victores (1983–86). In the early 1980s, with the tacit support of the Reagan administration, this group of US-trained uniformed savages began to systematically annihilate Mayan villages that they feared might be sympathetic to left-wing guerrillas. The result was a lopsided "civil war" that a UN-backed Truth Commission later concluded claimed at least two hundred thousand civilian lives—about two percent of the country's population. More than eighty-three percent of the victims were Mayan. While three percent of the murders were attributed to the guerrillas, the Commission concluded that ninety-three percent had been murdered by the army and its death squads, which had conducted no less than 626 massacres against Mayan villages. In addition, up to 1.5 million people were displaced. The Commission aptly described this "policy" as geno-cide.

For the 790 Achi-speaking Mayan inhabitants of Río Negro and many others in surrounding villages, this was not an abstraction. They were among the seventy-five thousand Achi-speaking Mayans in the central region deemed hostile by the military. Their people had lived there for at least 1,200 years, but apparently this did not matter to INDE, the project consultants, the World Bank, or the IDB, none of which bothered to consult them about the dam's location or resettlement. When these Mayans resisted INDE's offers to relocate, they discovered that they now faced two powerful enemies: not only the army, but also the coalition of INDE officials, international contractors, and IDB and World Bank financiers—all of whom, for their own reasons, wanted the dam built at any cost.

For three years prior to the flooding of Chixoy's thirty-one-mile reser-voir in January 1983, INDE pursued an increasingly harsh approach to per-suading the Río Negro villagers to relocate to the Guatemalan Army's "model villages." This was later singled out by the 1999 UN Commission as one of the country's clearest examples of outright genocide, the result not only of army policy but also "the hydro-electric project . . . and the resistance of the Río Negro community to be removed from their land." A 1996 investigation by the NGO Witness for Peace said that eyewitnesses recalled that the army had used trucks from the dam's leading contractor, and it concluded that "the Río Negro victims died because they blocked the 'progress' of the Chixoy Project." Corruption may have also played a role. According to the NGO, many villagers believed that INDE officials supported violent tactics in order to pocket their resettlement compensation.

In any case, Río Negro soon became a butcher shop. In July 1980, two community leaders who traveled to the Chixoy Dam to negotiate with INDE were mutilated. In late 1981 and 1982, the pace of the brutality quickened. Eyewitnesses later recalled brutal scenes from five massacres in Río Negro that year. During the first, in March 1982, 70 women and 107 children were murdered in cold blood by the army. Jaime, a Guatemalan Indian male from Río Negro who had been ten years old at the time, recalled the scene:

> I remember one woman, a soldier jumped up and kicked her in the back. He must have broken her spine, because she tried to get up, but her legs wouldn't move. Then he smashed her skull with his rifle. [They] were tying ropes around the children's ankles and swinging them, smashing their heads and bodies into rocks and trees.[35]

Another episode, in September 1992, involved the nearby village of Agua Fria:

> On the 14th of September, 1982, at about 7 AM, Civilian Defense Patrollers from the village of Xococ, Rabinal, Baja Verapaz accompanied by the national army and military commissioners, arrived at the hamlet of Agua Fría, Municipality of Chicamán, Department of El Quiché, where they rounded up all the men, women, and children from Agua Fría and Xococ for a meeting. The meeting took place in a house in the hamlet of Agua Fría, which was being used as a school. Once all the people were together, the soldiers riddled them with bullets using a variety of firearms, as well using grenades. They killed a total of approximately ninety-two people. Afterwards, they doused the bodies with petrol and burned them as well as their houses, where they people had been living. They robbed livestock, poultry, swine and anything else of value. . . .[36]

From February 1982 to September 1982, according to the UN Commission, death squads and the military killed at least 440 people in Río Negro alone—more than half its inhabitants. In the adjacent department of Rabinal, the death toll was estimated at 4,000–5,000. Under this reign of terror, about 3,400 survivors from the basin area finally agreed to take up residence in Pacux, an INDE resettlement near the town of Rabinal. Most of them remain there today, in dire poverty.

Meanwhile, General Lucas Garcia retired to Venezuela after his ouster. Rios Montt stayed on in Guatemala, founding a new conservative party, the Republican Front (FRG). In 1999 his party swept both the Congressional elections and the Presidency, installing his protégé, Alfredo Portillo, as the new

President in January 2000. After three years, his administration had earned the distinction, as one Guatemalan newspaper put it, of being "one of the most corrupt in the history of this Central American country; even the Bush Administration's Ambassador refused to attend Portillo's annual speech to Congress. Rios Montt became president of the National Congress, with immunity from prosecution. For the time being he rested on his laurels—a graduate of Fort Benning's School of the Americas and an ordained minister in California-based Gospel Outreach's Guatemala Verbo evangelical Church. He was also a man whom former US Assistant Secretary of State Thomas Enders had once praised for hi "effective counter-insurgency," and Ronald Reagan had once called "a man of great personal integrity," "totally dedicated to democracy," someone who Amnesty International had given "a bum rap." By 2003, he was running for President, arguing successfully before Guatemala's stacked Supreme Court that a constitutional provision barring him from running was a violation of his "human rights."

So where were the World Bank, the IDB, and the international contractors during all this? After all, the banks were footing the bill for the dam and presumably had some influence. According to a recent study by the Woodrow Wilson School, they had representatives on the ground who "either knew or had reason to know" about the intimidation used by INDE and the military to relocate the Mayans. Yet there is no record of any complaints registered by either institution. Just as the violence was escalating, the IDB advanced the project another $70 million in November 1981, and the World Bank loaned it another $45 million in 1985.

In this regard, it may be helpful to recall the legal definition of several criminal offenses in civilized countries. A key element of "accessory to murder" is to intentionally aid, abet, or counsel murderers, before or after the fact, even if one is absent when the killing is done. "Involuntary manslaughter" is the intentional disregard of a duty to provide reasonable care or aid to a victim, which results in that person's death. "Negligent homicide" is the neglection of duty to exercise reasonable care that results in death, even if unintended. As applied at Nuremberg and by the newly created International Criminal Court that has been ratified by more than ninety countries, including all OECD countries except the US, there are also several categories of "crimes against humanity" that may be relevant here. These include the crimes of "genocide"—an "act or omission committed with intent to destroy, in whole or in part, an identifiable group of persons," and "crimes against humanity"—"murder, extermination, enslavement, deportation, imprisonment, torture, sexual violence, persecution or any other inhumane act or omission committed against any civilian population."[37]

Finally in July 1996, after Witness for Peace published a detailed report on the Rio Negro Massacre that was based on eyewitness interviews, the World Bank conducted its own investigation. It found that not only had the Mayans at Río Negro never been adequately consulted, resettled, or compensated for the taking of their land, but that more than half of them had been slaughtered. However, the World Bank referred all requests for additional compensation to INDE, which had gone broke by then and was privatized in 1998, and to a local Fund for National Development. In a casual remark over a conference lunch with the IMF's acting managing director Stanley Fischer and American University's president Ben Ladner, the World Bank's president Wolfensohn revealed by accident—when he failed to notice that his microphone was on—his own skepticism about the Río Negro victims' claims:

> Wolfensohn: It's all *ad hominem*, it's all, ah, they've brought in an indigenous person who was displaced in 1975 and whose family has been ruined, and they'll then blame us for the problems of Guatemala. And we'll say that there was a civil war for thirty-two years and . . . this probably had nothing to do with the project. . . . And now there's another Chixoy Indian coming, saying well, we appreciated what you did, but now we want reparations and damages. And so they've got an Indian here who's very keen to do it. . . . These indigenous people, I'm not suggesting they didn't have problems, but they're also very smart. So they come up, and they think, "It's a pretty good way to make a few bucks."
> Fischer: "And you can't say anything about the victims, you know, it's . . ."
> Ladner: "No, it's off limits."[38]

Meanwhile, Lahmeyer/RWE, Hochtief, and the LAMI consortium were also involved in Guatemala's aborted $1.25 billion 450-megawatt Chulac Dam. According to a former INDE president, the military was so eager to cash in on the project that construction was started in 1981, even before INDE had signed off on the project and before feasibility studies were complete. In 1982, however, after spending $137 million on two tunnels, it was discovered that the underlying rock was too weak to support the dam, so work was halted.[39]

• Joseph Mobutu, a former officer in the Belgian Army, seized power with CIA help in 1960 and became the Congo/Zaire's president-for-life in 1965. In 1972 he changed his name to "Mobutu Sese Seko Kuku Ngbendu wa za Banga" (the all-powerful warrior who, because of endurance and will to win, goes from conquest to conquest leaving fire in his wake). He also announced his ambitious "Objective 1980"—more of a wish list than an economic plan, which included plans for new ports, copper and oil refineries, and an aluminum foundry. Foreign bankers swarmed in like piranha at a cattle-crossing. By the early 1980s, there were not many completed projects, but the country did have Africa's largest foreign debt at that point, about $5 billion.

Then copper prices crashed, and Zaire was stuck with numerous debt elephants.

One of these was the twenty-story, French-designed Kinshasa World Trade Center. Regrettably, it was designed without windows that could open and an air-conditioning system too weak to manage the Congo's intense heat. The largest debt elephant was the $1.1 billion Inga Shaba power project. This called for stringing the world's longest transmission line across 1,700 miles of dense jungle from the Inga Dam at the mouth of the Congo to Shaba province, where the country's copper reserves were. Financed by Citibank and several other banks with US EXIM Bank guarantees, designed by Morris-Knudsen, supplied by GE and ASEA, constructed by Sadelmi, and "produced" with the help of US. CIA station chief Lawrence Devlin, General Thomas Hayes, and US ambassadors Sheldon Vance and Deane Hinton, the project's original cost estimate was $275 million. But it was riddled with corruption, and its principal "beneficiaries" were the president-for-life's huge extended family. Completed in 1983 at a cost of more than $1.2 billion, it has never used more than a fifth of its capacity.

By 1997, when Mobutu was finally tossed out, his personal wealth was estimated at more than $4 billion. He had helped himself and his family to three palaces in Zaire, luxury mansions in Switzerland, Morocco, South Africa, France, Belgium, Spain, and Portugal, a fleet of jumbo jets, one of the world's largest supermarkets, five hundred British double-decker buses, and his own steel mill. The wine collection at his castle in Portugal alone was valued at $2.3 million.[40]

• Following the Brasilia model, Nigeria's new capital, Abuja, was planted in the center of the country—in the middle of nowhere—by General Murtala Muhammed in 1976. By 1983, there was just one hotel, an airport, and a sewage system, all costing $4 billion. The city was officially opened in 1991, but construction continues to this day, after more than $30 billion—including $500 million for a sports stadium alone. Nigerians tell a story in which God is asked whether the Nigerians will ever see Abuja's benefits. God replies, "Not in my lifetime!" At Ajaokuta, on the River Niger, a $400 million steel plant also sits idle, a hapless combination of Russian technology, French loans, and multinational graft. As of 2003, another $560 million was needed to finish this steel mill and another one, Delta Steel. The World Bank recommended against putting another penny into both these projects. Although Nigeria is one of the world's top ten oil and gas producers, it has to import all its iron ore from Brazil. Today, despite its ample oil wealth, Nigeria boasts the largest foreign debt in Africa—$34 billion.[41]

In 1985, Kenya invited bids for the 155-meter-high Turkwell Gorge Dam in the Elgeyo-Marakwet district of northern Kenya. However, according to a report by courageous Kenyan journalist, Edward Abuor, who later had to flee the country for his own safety, the companies that won the initial bid refused to pay a $5 million bribe. The charge was sensitive, because Energy Minister Nicolas Biwott was also a member of the Elgeyo-Marakwet Kalenjin tribe and a very close advisor and business partner of fellow-Kalenjin President Daniel Arap Moi, the venal autocrat who ruled the country from 1978 until January 2003. Biwott cancelled the contract and re-let it without a competitive tender. This time, it went to a consortium led by France's Spie Batignoles, Sogreah, and GEC Alsthom; Norconsult; and the UK's Knight Piesold, which served as overall design consultant for the dam from 1986 to 1993. The dam's $300 million price tag was financed with loans from a consortium of French banks led by Banque de l'Union Europeenne, with additional financing from COFACE, the French export credit agency and the UK's ECGD.

On January 24, 1986, Kenya's finance minister George Saitoti signed a new contract with this consortium. In March 1986, Achim Kratz, the EC's commissioner to Kenya, wrote a memo about the Turkwell Gorge Dam that was later leaked to *The Financial Times*. It identified several problems with the project:

> [The contract price was] more than double the amount Kenya's government would have had to pay for the project based on an international competitive tender. . . . The Kenyan government officials who are involved in the project are fully aware of the disadvantages of the French deal . . . but they nevertheless accepted it because of high personal advantages. While Kenyan politicians and top civil servants form an alliance with foreigners to take billions in hard currency abroad while knowing that the country is dying for lack of foreign exchange, for the import of medicine and other essentials, that is an outright war against one's own country and people. . . .[42]

When these reports appeared, the Kenyan press was even more blunt: It proclaimed the dam "a stinking scandal" and "the whitest of white elephants." Partly as a result of this scandal, foreign aid to Kenya's entire energy sector was frozen from 1989 to 1996. Indeed, from 1997 to July 2000, and again from December 2000 to 2003, more than $1 billion in aid from the World Bank, the IMF, and other Western donors was suspended because of concerns about "official corruption" and Kenya's failure to pass antigraft legislation.[43] In 2002, Kenya ranked 96 out of 102 countries on Transparency International's annual corruption rankings.

Meanwhile, in February 1990, Minister Biwott was briefly detained, then released, in connection with an investigation of the murder of Kenya's foreign minister Robert Ouko, who had disappeared from his farm soon after returning from a quick "private visit" to the US with Moi and Biwott on February 2–4, 1990. Ouko's burned, mutilated body was found close to his farm two weeks later. The crime was never solved. But in 1997, Smith Hempstone, US ambassador to Kenya from 1989 to 1993 and a close friend of George H. W. Bush, published a memoir in which he speculated, based on "statements of those closely associated with the Ouko case," that "the most likely scenario" was that Moi had lost his temper at Ouko, and had personally beaten him into unconsciousness at the State House. According to Hempstone's scenario, Moi had him tortured until he was "a bloody mess." Then Biwott—"the most feared and hated man in Kenya, who was alleged to collect a shilling on every gallon of petroleum imported into Kenya, and to have made tens of millions of dollars in kickbacks on the Turkwell Gorge dam"—allegedly "shot [Ouko] twice in the head." The motive? Hempstone wasn't sure. But he recalled receiving a photo from a former chief of protocol for the State Department in 1991, showing a smiling President Bush shaking hands with Minister Ouko on the White House steps. Moi, in contrast, had only been granted a meeting with an assistant secretary of state on that trip to Washington, DC.[44]

The FT had a slightly different angle: It reported that Ouko had "clashed with Biwott during a trip to the US over foreign accounts Biwott and other government ministers held in other countries."[45] In 1991, John Troon, a detective from Scotland Yard who investigated the case, told a Kenyan judicial commission Mr. Biwott was a prime suspect.[46] In July 2001, Moi and Biwott sued Hempstone for libel in Kenya's High Court, alleging that the charges brought their reputations "public odium, scandal and contempt."[47]

Biwott also had run-ins with private bankers at Citibank and in Switzerland. In June 1991, Terry Davidson, managing director of Citibank's Nairobi branch, was warned by Biwott's employee to "be prepared for strange car accidents . . ." after he tried to collect on $14 million in loans to Biwott's companies. The loans were reportedly secured by $11.2 million in loans against Biwott's Swiss accounts. The *New York Times* reported that Biwott, one of Kenya's richest men, "had amassed large interests in construction, petroleum distribution, aviation, and property," and that he owned "hundreds of millions of dollars, chiefly in offshore holdings."[48]

Biwott resigned from the energy ministry post after his arrest, but he remained in parliament. After Moi was "reelected" in 1997, he continued to serve in the cabinet. Saitoti, a former math professor, served as finance minister until 1993, and on and off as vice president until August 2002. In May 2000, both Biwott and Saitoti were named by a Kenyan parliamentary anti-corruption committee on a "list of shame," but were later removed at the request of Moi's party. In December 2002, Moi's reign of power came to an end, when the opposition party's presidential candidate Mwai Kibaki defeated Moi's designated successor by sixty-three percent to thirty percent.

Meanwhile, the Turkwell dam itself was another failure. It was completed by February 1991, but the reservoir was only one quarter full by the time Moi officially opened the hydro plant in October 1993. Throughout the 1990s,

Turkwell consistently operated below its designed capacity, and the country experienced recurrent power shortages. In 1999–2000, when Kenya was struck by one of its worst droughts ever, hydro-dependent Nairobi had to institute daily power blackouts. For the 3.3 million rural Kenyans facing starvation at that point, power was not their primary concern. But after twenty-four years of brutality and kleptocracy, they were eager to survive just to have a chance to vote the *mijizi* (thieves) out of office.[49]

• Next to China's gargantuan Three Gorges Dam, Lesotho's Highland Water Project (LHWP) is the world's second largest water transfer project and Africa's largest dam project ever. In the finest traditions of hubristic engineering, the design called for a thirty-year effort to build five big dams and a hydro plant in Lesotho's Maluti Mountains, eventually diverting nearly half of the water—two billion cubic meters a year—from the Orange River (known in Lesotho as the "Senqunyane River" basin) through 125 miles of tunnels to the Vaal Dam near Johannesburg. The basic concept, which dates back to the 1930s, was simple. Lesotho, an otherwise tiny, poor, landlocked, mountainous kingdom, is known as "The Kingdom in the Sky," the only country in the world whose entire territory is higher than one thousand meters. It also is entirely surrounded by, and dependent upon, its wealthy neighbor, South Africa. Most of its 2.2 million people work either as subsistence farmers or as migrants in South Africa, which provides jobs for half of Lesotho's labor force. In addition to its surplus labor, one of Lesotho's few natural resources is the abundant rainfall that its mountains receive each summer. Johannesburg's mines and other industries, on the other hand, account for sixty percent of South Africa's economy, and need a steady supply of water and energy, as well as cheap labor.

In South Africa's view, all this provided the basis for a win–win deal. LHWP was designed by South African-trained engineers in the 1970s and jointly approved by the two countries in 1986. Until 1994, South Africa was still an apartheid state, ruled by whites, who comprised just fourteen percent of its population. Lesotho was ruled by a military regime that South Africa had installed only a few months before the LHWP agreement.

These antidemocratic roots did not worry the global development industry very much at the time. Indeed, as we've seen, this industry and its financial supporters actually seem to thrive in situations where popular concerns like resettlement, land ownership, the pricing of natural resources and electricity, erosion, and environmental matters are subordinated to the priorities of the ruling elite. This may be one key reason why there is a strong negative correlation between "big projects" and democratic development.

In any case, those who structured LHWP's finances also did not worry very much about the fact that they were violating international sanctions against apartheid. Charted WestLB's merchant bankers consulted with the World Bank and got approval to make Lesotho the $8 billion project's official borrower—with South Africa kicking back debt service and royalties under the table to a London trust. This, in effect, "laundered" LHWP, opening the door to a hog's breakfast for multilateral lenders, private banks, equipment vendors, and contractors who didn't care whether the project undermined apartheid or quenched its thirst forever. Soon, Lesotho's official foreign debt was soaring, from $200 million in 1986 to $625 million by 1994, when apartheid gave way to the new South Africa.

With Lesotho fronting for South Africa, the multibillion dollar project attracted the support of many leading development funders, including the World Bank, the CDC, the EIB, the EDF, the AFDB, the UK's EGCD, France's COFACE, Italy's SACE, and Germany's HERMES. Germany, France, and the UK also provided bilateral aid—an indirect way of channeling subsidies to their own contractors. The private banks that signed up to deliver (government-backed) loans to the project included France's BNP and Credit Lyonnais, Germany's Dresdner Bank and KFW, and the UK's Hill Samuel, plus all five top South African Banks. And the contractors and suppliers included many of those that we've already met in other Third World fiascos—ABB, Impregilo, Lahmeyer/RWE, Sogreah, Hochtief, Spie Batignolles, Dumez, Knight Piesold, GEC Alstom, GE, and Zublin; Germany's Diwi Consulting; France's Coyne et Bellier, Campenon Bernard, and Bouygues; the UK's Sir Alex Gibb, Kier, Stirling, Kvaerner, Mott McDonald, and Balfour Beatty; Canada's Acres International; and South Africa's own Concor and LTA.

Two decades later, as of 2003, this bevy of contractors had finished the Katse and Muela Dams and fifty-three miles of tunnels, at a total cost of $2.5 billion. The Mohale Dam is due in a year, for an additional $1 billion, followed by the Mashai Dam in 2008 and the final Tsoelike Dam in 2017. The total cost is supposed to be $8 billion by 2020—though we already know how much such cost predictions are worth.

Unfortunately, LHWP has also hit a few snags. To begin with, the people of Lesotho are having second thoughts about parting with so much of their water on such one-sided terms. There have also been some other nasty side effects. In January 1996, the sheer weight of Katse Dam's reservoir helped to cause earthquakes that shook many nearby villages. In September 1996, 2,300 workers at Muela Dam were fired for striking illegally, protesting harsh working conditions and wage discrimination. Contractors like Balfour Beatty called in the police and five workers at their camp were shot dead, with thirty injured. In 1998, partly to deter a possible military coup, but also to remind Lesotho that this was the New South Africa's largest infrastructure investment, South Africa invaded Lesotho, killed sixty-six people, and "restored order." The *Johannesburg Star* later reported that protecting the dam had been one of the invasion's primary concerns. There have also been more than the usual litany of environmental, distributional, and social problems associated with LHWP—with many complaints from dam critics about the displacement of twenty-four thousand people, inadequate compensation for resettlement, and increased erosion.[50]

Most interestingly, LHWP has made history in the field of penalties for global corruption. The US has had the Foreign Corrupt Practices Act (FCPA) on its books since 1977. This statute has provided US officials with more than one opportunity to lecture their European and Asian counterparts on the importance of taking a strong stand against Third World corruption. But actually enforcing this statute has never been a priority for any administration. There have only been thirty-four US criminal prosecutions under the FCPA in thirty-six years, the median fine levied on twenty-eight convicted corporations has been a mere $50,000, and only three out of twelve convicted business bribers ever did jail time—a total of thirty-four months for all three. So far there has only been one sizeable fine: $21.8 million levied on Lockheed in 1994, for paying bribes to win Egyptian defense contracts.

Nevertheless, in the late 1990s, responding to incessant American whining that global competitiveness was *suffering* because of this statute, thirty OECD countries adopted a new treaty that increased penalties for First World companies that bribe foreign officials. Organizations like Transparency International, backed by corporate and government supporters, started to publish a "corruption index," an annual ranking that claimed to identify the world's "most corrupt" countries—all of which turned out to be developing countries. The World Bank also adopted new guidelines on corruption that were supposed to crack down on contractor/vendor bribery. At the Annual World Bank Meetings in Washington, DC on October 1996, President James Wolfensohn declared: "The Bank Group will not tolerate corruption in the programs that we support, and we are taking steps to ensure that our own activities continue to meet the highest standards of probity."[51] Despite these new laws, indices, and declarations, until the LHWP graft case exploded in 1999, there had been very little actual enforcement of such rules against bribery, especially against the leading members of the global development industry. This is partly because it is often hard to follow the money trail through the global haven thicket. However, even tiny Lesotho was able to break through Swiss and Panamanian banking secrecy in less than two years and make a winning case against some of the world's largest contractors.

The more important obstacle is that, when push comes to shove, many First World countries and multilateral donors have been reluctant to enforce such rules against bribers, as opposed to "corrupt" local officials. They are concerned not only with alienating influential political supporters, but also with disrupting the progress of particularly big projects. They are also concerned that if they really looked hard at what has been going on around them, the revelations might be hard to handle. For example, the very first global auditor that Wolfensohn hired in 1996 as part of his new "spot audit" effort to get tough on corruption—Switzerland's Société Générale de Surveillance (SGS)—was revealed just a year later to have paid more than $9 million in bribes by way of British Virgin Island companies, Swiss lawyers, and UBS bank accounts to Pakistan's former president Benazir Bhutto and her husband Ali Zardari, as well as to other intermediaries, in order to win a lucrative Pakistani government contract for customs inspection services in 1994.

In July 1999, Lesotho charged the former CEO of the Lesotho Highlands Project, Masupha Sole, with receiving more than $2.5 million in bribes by way of Swiss accounts, from all the key contractors involved in LHWP's first three dams. With the help of Durban lawyers, Lesotho managed to track down precisely who had paid the bribes and where the money went. The astonishing indictment listed the contractors and the amounts they had paid:

- Zublin: $444, 466, plus its share of $57,269 paid by LHPC and LHPC-Chantiers's $63,959
- Impregilo: $250,000, plus its share of $733,404 paid by the HWV consortium
- Acres International: $260,000
- Spie Batignolles: $119,393, plus its share of LHPC's $57,269 and LHPC-Chantiers's $63,959
- Dumez: $82,422
- ABB: $40, 410
- Sogreah: $13,578, plus its share of LHPC-Chantiers's $63,959
- Lahmeyer/RWE: $8,674
- Diwi: $2,439
- Balfour Beatty: its share of LHPC's $57,269 and LHPC-Chantiers's $63,959
- LTA: its share of LHPC's $57,269 and LHPC-Chantiers's $63,959
- Hochtief: its share of $733,404 paid by the HWV consortium
- Bouygues: its share of $733,404 paid by the HWV consortium
- Keir International: its share of $733,404 paid by the HWV consortium
- Stirling International: its share of $733,404 paid by the HWV consortium
- Concor: its share of $733,404 paid by the HWV consortium
- Sir Alex Gibb: its share of the LHPC-Chantiers's $63,959
- Coyne & Bellier: its share of the LHPC-Chantiers's $63,959
- Knight Piesold: its share of the LHPC-Chantiers's $63,959

In August 1999, Lesotho also decided to prosecute fourteen of these companies, plus three French and South African intermediaries that had helped to "escort" the bribes to their final destinations.

A Canadian-trained engineer, Sole had been Lesotho's highest-paid public official when he was put on leave in 1995, pending the investigation's outcome. He had worked as a director in Lesotho's Department of Water, Lands, and Energy until October 1986, when he was appointed the first CEO of the Lesotho Highlands Development Authority, the project's contracting agent. In this capacity, he supervised all project tenders. Everything proceeded quietly until a new minister of natural resources hired Ernst and Young to audit LHDA's account in 1994. The audit turned up discrepancies. Further investigation revealed that Sole had received large transfers to his Johannesburg bank accounts from accounts in his name at three Swiss banks—Union Bancaire Prive and Banque MultiCommercial in Geneva, and UBS in Zurich.

Furthermore, Swiss authorities who decided to help Lesotho, found that at least fourteen companies had made deposits to these accounts by way of two Panama shell companies and other accounts in the Channel Islands, set up by one of Panama's leading law firms, Morgan y Morgan.[52] This "havenneering" structure was surprisingly crude. It neglected to add extra layers upstream to conceal the payers' identities, and had also made the gross mistake of setting up Swiss accounts in Sole's name.

In any case, except for ABB, whose CEO admitted knowing about "problems" in Lesotho since at least 1987 and agreed to cooperate with the authorities, all these contractors vehemently protested their innocence. They were probably worried that the World Bank and other development banks might ban them from the annual $7–10 billion in loans and credits that they still distribute each year to Third World projects.

In May 2002, after a yearlong trial, Sole was convicted on eleven counts of bribery and two counts of fraud in Lesotho's High Court, and sentenced to eighteen years in prison. The court concluded that he had taken payments from international contractors in exchange for "furthering their private interests."[53] In March 1991, for example, one month before a $250 million contract was signed with one of the two key consortia in the case, the consortium paid him more than $1.2 million.

Sole's conviction set the stage for prosecuting the companies in question and blacklisting them from bidding on World Bank and other development contracts. In October 2002, after a seven-month trial, the first contractor tried—the Canadian engineering firm Acres International—was found guilty of bribing Sole and fined $2.2 million.[54] As of 2003, Lahmeyer/RWE AG and Spie Batignolles, of Chixoy and Turkwell fame, and Balfour Beatty, which has also faced corruption allegations in Singapore and Malaysia, were still facing trials. This is an historic case. As Lesotho's attorney general explained, "The attitude has always been that Africans are corrupt. We want rich world corporations and countries to acknowledge their role. We are telling them that it is no longer business as usual."[55]

One might have thought that the World Bank, for all of its recent rhetoric about "transparency," would have responded quickly to this case. However, in February 2002, it made its real priorities clear. Eager to get on with LHWP, the World Bank reported that its own internal investigation had dismissed bribery claims against all fourteen contractors for lack of evidence. It refused to blacklist any of them. It also presented a new, narrower interpretation of its own rules. According to this, companies would only be blacklisted if it were shown that bribes actually used World Bank money, or were related to a portion of a project directly funded by the Bank. Since contract payments are fungible, this opens a very wide loophole indeed.

As of 2003, after more than three years of court hearings, the World Bank's "Ineligible List" still contains none of the LHWP contractors, and *no* major international contractors, vendors, or banks. Evidently, the World Bank faces intense pressure from leading First World countries—its "shareholders"—to maintain key contractor eligibility, and to see that the big projects that it finances move along. Indeed, in Lesotho's case, leaked correspondence between the World Bank and Lesotho's government showed that the World Bank knew all about the Sole investigation as early as 1994. Its reaction? World Bank officials expressed concern to Lesotho's authorities that by suspending Sole, they might slow the project down.[56]

LARGER PATTERNS—THE FABRIC OF INTERESTS

Unfortunately, this is just a partial census of debt elephants. For the interested reader, there are hundreds more that deserve to be examined closely. There are also many new ones under way, including one that may turn out to be the most monstrous debt elephant ever: China's Three Gorges Dam project, a $75 billion, twenty-year project that will displace up 2 million people, create a 375-mile reservoir, bury three million tons of refuse and toxic waste, and provide untold corruption possibilities for Chinese officials.

This state communist daydream, originally conceived by Mao Zedong in the 1960s, is being financed in part with the help of bonds underwritten and issued by such leading capitalist bankers as Morgan Stanley, Goldman Sachs, CFSB, Nomura, IBJ, and Merrill Lynch, plus equipment finance from German, Japanese, French, Brazilian, Canadian, Norwegian, Swedish, and Swiss export credit agencies. The World Bank has also issued soft loans to finance the enormous resettlements required. Acre International, the Toronto-based

engineering firm that we met in Lesotho, did a $14 million "feasibility stud-
ies" for the dam in 1985–88, a study that was widely panned by other independent experts. To its credit, the US government has so far resisted the temp-
tation to provide any financial support for the dam, although some US
contractors and equipment vendors are involved. In the words of one US
Bureau of Reclamation spokesperson: "Large-scale, water retention dam projects are not environmentally or economically feasible. We wouldn't support
such a project in the US, so it would be incongruous for us to support such
a project in another country."[57] Would that such wisdom were more generally applied.

All told, about forty-five thousand large dams were built around the
world in the twentieth century, at a total cost of more than $2 trillion and a
"displacement" total of 40–50 million people. The World Commission on
Dams, established by the World Bank and the World Conservation Union in
1998 to examine this one category of development spending, estimates that
worldwide construction peaked in the 1970s, at 5,400 new large dams per
year, and is now less than 2,000 per year. However, countries are still spending at least $32–46 billion a year on new dams.[58] There are also thousands of
other infrastructure projects: power plants, pipelines, roads, airports, ports, rail
systems, irrigation projects, flood control, and sanitation systems. All told, in
the last decade, developing countries have devoted more than a trillion dollars to such new infrastructure projects. Clearly such investments are vital to
their futures, and it is crucial that they be well managed.

Unfortunately, most of this spending to date was funded by foreign loans
that were not, in fact, well managed. The World Bank alone has provided more
than $90 billion to finance 620 dam-only projects and 910 other projects that
included dams in more than ninety-two countries. The Bank has also spent at
least three times this amount on other infrastructure projects.[59] In addition,
other multilateral lenders like the ADB and the IDB, and leading First World
export credit agencies ("ECAs") like the US EXIM Bank, the UK's ECGD,
and Germany's HERMES, have provided hundreds of billions for infrastructure.

In this chapter, a *prima facie* case has been made for the contention that
much of this First World-financed big project spending has involved significant waste and corruption, as well as significant environmental and social
damage. In theory, perhaps, even great big dams might be justified, assuming
we really take into account their substantial social and environmental side
effects. However, the proof is in the pudding. The long-term track record of
large, foreign debt-financed dams and other big projects has been nothing
short of a *global disgrace*. This conclusion is supported by many other recent
studies, with larger samples. For example, the WCD's study of eighty-one

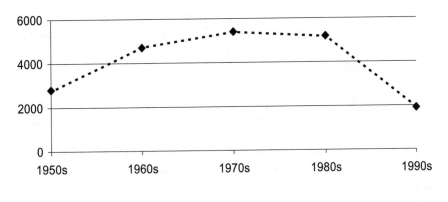

Ave. Number of New Dams Per Year

Source: WCD data (2002); JSH analysis   © JSH 2003

Chart 1.1–Global Big Dam Market

large dams found that seventy-three percent exceeded their budgets, and thirty percent overshot by more than fifty percent. And that was only the financial cost. If we also take into account the displaced and undercompensated people, the lost species, damaged aquifers and forests, methane pollution, increased corruption, and the high opportunity costs of the resulting excessive debts, these "cost overruns" would be much higher. There are several *systemic pathologies* that help to explain this recurrent pattern.

THE GLOBAL SYSTEM OF CORRUPTION AND IMPUNITY

On the demand side, especially in the cases of impoverished countries with outright dictatorships or fledgling democracies, weak legal systems, and limited resources, the sheer amount of capital at stake in these projects provides huge temptations to officials and contractors alike. In fact, as we saw in the case of Brazil, many projects are *never intended* to make economic sense—that is almost beside the point.

Since most of the loans flow through a handful of First World institutions, however, one might have thought that, in principle, strict global standards for project selection and management might be mandated by the industry or, at least, by the World Bank and other big lenders. It should also be possible to insist on accounting controls that prevent gross diversions—for example, by requiring companies to "publish what you pay," or disburse only against performance, backed up by independent audits.[60]

In practice, however, as the examples of Casey's US EXIM Bank and the World Bank in Lesotho showed, the real problems are not technical. And the driving forces are often self-enrichment and patronage rather than accounting rules! Perhaps we should expect that Third World countries would have difficulty prosecuting international companies or even their own officials for bribery and malpractice, though Lesotho is an interesting exception. In fact, many developing countries are now beginning to tackle the problem of impunity head-on.

First World countries, however, have the necessary legal and investigative resources. But they have so far been reluctant to lay down enforceable international standards for business conduct in the Third World, much less enforce existing bribery and money laundering statutes against their own contractors and banks.

Why is this? It is partly because the cases are far-flung, hard to investigate, and—from a prosecutor's standpoint—rather thankless. The "victims" are the residents of countries that most Americans, for example, can't even locate. It is also because "this is the real world, " and some First World countries apparently believe that their own companies are so disadvantaged that they need to pay bribes in order to compete. They have been willing to expose *competitor* bribery if it helps them win bids and keeps underutilized intelligence agencies busy, but aggressively pursuing their own contractors is a no-win proposition. We should also not neglect the fact that many First World "bribers" also make fat campaign contributions back home.

In short, the notion that everyone might be better off if laws against corruption were rigorously enforced remains, in practice, a nice theory, because of this global system of mutually reinforcing self-interests.

The other important reality is that there is a whole army of sophisticated First World private bankers that basically makes its living by helping the wealthy elite at home and abroad shelter their loot, no questions asked—"know your customer" regulations and because it refers back to "army" statutes notwithstanding. In economic terms, given the huge potential rewards, low expected costs of concealment, and modest expected penalties, the real surprise may be that Third World projects actually get built at all.

A GLOBAL SYSTEM FOR AVOIDING ACCOUNTABILITY

Another key influence has to do with the fact that especially in projects financed by foreign government-backed loans, there is often no one in charge or accountable for the overall results of a project. Contractors, equipment vendors, and private banks naturally try to arrange things so that they will get paid whether or not "risky" Third World projects are ever completed. As we

(81 Large Dams, 1990s)

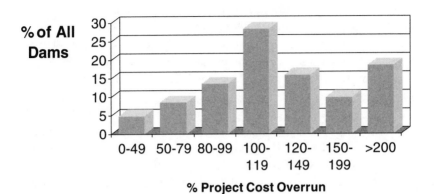

% Project Cost Overrun

Source: WCD data (2002), 81 dam samples; JSH analysis   © JSH 2003

Chart 1.2–Average Cost Overruns

saw in Lesotho, there are often so many different vendors involved that opportunities for finger pointing abound. Meanwhile, developing countries get stuck with the debts, whether or not projects pay off, while foreign lenders like export credit agencies score points with their supporters—big exporters, banks, and their political clients—just for generating exports, whether or not projects make good use of them.

Therefore, while any given project mishap may be due to local fortuities, design errors, malfeasance, or incompetence, the overall global patterns revealed here are too striking to ignore. Everywhere one sees the same kinds of misbehavior and the same global players. This supports the notion that what we really have is a deeply entrenched, transnational system of interests and influence that profits from committing the same mistakes.

This conclusion is also consistent with the recent trends in Third World project finance. In the last decade, an increasing share of infrastructure investment has been financed by a combination of private sector participation and loans from export credit agencies. In the 1990s, for example, more than $680 billion of Third World infrastructure had some degree of private sector involvement—a sharp increase from the 1980s.[61]

At the same time, especially since 1995, support for monster "hard asset" loans at the World Bank and other multilateral lenders has slowed dramatically, and they have shifted more than two-thirds of their portfolios to soft assets like public administration, education, and health. This is partly due to all the flack multilaterals have taken for their numerous failed big dam projects.

Development critics who enjoy beating up on the World Bank should be careful about what they wish for. There is much more to the development crisis than well-meaning institutions struggling to get things right. As we're already beginning to understand, there is a powerful fabric of interests at work in all these matters. And one consequence of this network is that all these changes in multilateral lending behavior may not improve things one iota. Indeed, in many ways, the world may be worse off now that the World Bank is withdrawing into its soft-asset shell.

After all, the global development industry—the giant contractors, engineering firms, equipment vendors, investment banks and commercial banks, and their attendant armies of lawyers, accountants, and other intermediaries—has not gone away. It has been working overtime to catch the privatization wave and turn from the World Bank and other multilaterals to the more primitive political arena at the ECAs, where they have recently obtained billions in government-backed loans and billions more in "political risk" insurance for dubious projects all over the world.

Even as the role of multilaterals in development finance has declined in the last decade, the role of the ECAs has been expanding. The export credit agencies of the US, Japan, France, Germany, the UK, and other OECD countries now average $60–70 billion a year in new foreign loans, loan guarantees, and political risk insurance—more than three times the World Bank's annual lending. Almost all of this goes to support a handful of giant contractors, exporters and banks, mainly for projects in "middle-income" developing countries.[62]

In 2000, eighty-six percent of the US EXIM Bank's $7.7 billion in new foreign export credits and guarantees went to just ten politically influential US companies, including Enron, Halliburton, GE, Boeing, Bechtel, United Technologies, Schlumberger, and Raytheon. In the 1990s, EXIM loaned Enron—whose senior officials were major contributors to both the Democratic and the Republican Parties—more than $673 million for projects in India, Turkey, the Philippines, and Venezuela. This included $304 million for Frank Wisner, Jr.'s dubious Dabhol plant in India, which the World Bank had refused to finance because it was not "economically viable." After endless disputes with the Indian government, the plant was closed in May 2001, sticking EXIM with an unpaid project loan of $175 million.

Enron also managed to obtain $385 million in EXIM loans for power projects that it controlled in Turkey and Venezuela, essentially to finance purchases from *itself*. In light of subsequent revelations about Enron's cooked bookkeeping, government auditors were forced to look more closely at these self-dealings. As of 2003, Enron still owed EXIM at least $454 million.

Nor was Enron the only politically well-connected US multinational to receive huge EXIM credits to support its foreign sales. Another key beneficiary was Texas-based oil services company Halliburton, whose CEO from 1995 to 2000 was future Vice President Richard Cheney. Halliburton had managed to obtain about $72 million in EXIM financing during the early 1990s, but with the help of Cheney's Washington, DC connections, this really exploded to more than $890 million in guaranteed loans and credits during his tenure as CEO. Some of these loans financed Halliburton service exports to rather strange places. For example, in the late 1990s, with the help of Clinton's Secretary of State Albright, Halliburton received $87 million in EXIM credits and $90 million in loan guarantees to support its oil service operations in Angola, whose pseudo-leftist MPLA government was up to its eyeballs in arms traffic, repression, and the diversion of billions in oil revenues to offshore accounts. In 2000 alone, Cheney's last year as CEO before he moved to Washington, DC, the company received $120 million in EXIM export credits. In May 2002, the SEC announced that Halliburton was under investigation for misstating its costs on overseas construction jobs financed by these credits.[63]

There have been many other recent EXIM bank financings that are questionable on environmental, social, and economic grounds. As we saw in the Philippines and Brazil, the US EXIM bank had a long history of financing doubtful nuclear projects in developing countries. And it has also recently financed many other questionable power plants. For example, its 1997 $374 million loan to the 2,100-megawatt Yanching coal-fired plant in Shanxi province, China, will fund a plant that will produce more than 14.1 million tons of greenhouse gases each year. It was also involved in funding the dubious Paiton power complex in Indonesia.[64]

Given EXIM's miserable track record on such projects, its marginal impact on overall American exports (<1.5%), the fact that most of its benefits have gone to a handful of giant banks and corporations, and to dictatorial regimes like China and Suharto's Indonesia, not to mention its lack of attention to environmental, social, and anticorruption issues, many free-market conservatives expected President George W. Bush to sharply downsize, or even eliminate, the US EXIM Bank when he took office in 2001. Indeed, his very first budget proposal to Congress called for a twenty-five percent reduction in EXIM's funding, with support from the Cato Institute and other conservatives, who argued that the Bank was an outrageous example of "corporate welfare," and that its loans to "Communist" China and Angola were especially offensive.

Apparently this captured the attention of the Fortune 500 lobbyists, as well as Vice President Cheney. In June 2002, Bush signed a new four-year authorization for the EXIM Bank that raised its authorized lending level from $80 billion to $100 billion. In 2002, EXIM authorized $10.1 billion in new loans, credit guarantees and risk insurance, nearly as much as the World Bank's entire IBRD "hard money" loan budget.[65]

Overall, therefore, the World Bank, other multilateral lenders, and the IMF certainly have more work to do to fight corruption, pay closer attention to environmental and social concerns, and be more open and democratic about their procedures. But compared with ECAs like the US EXIM Bank, these multilateral institutions are paragons of virtue. It is very important for development critics to avoid fighting the last war. Many ECAs, while officially "public" institutions, are basically just captive subsidiaries of the global *anti-development* industry. Indeed, some, like the UK's EGCD, have recently been privatized, and are no longer subject to even minimal independent citizen review. The credits they provide often have little to do with Third World development and everything to do with paying back corporate interests for the contributions, careers, and other benefits they have bestowed on First World political leaders.

Thus it is not easy to separate the continuing problems of debt, corruption, and democracy in the Third World from the complementary problems of debt, corruption, and democracy *in the First World*.

Together, these agencies and their political supporters are helping to write the next chapter in the ongoing story of First and Third World crony capitalism, by financing a whole new generation of Third World debt elephants that, technically speaking, are "private" projects that don't require any "country loans" at all.

CHAPTER TWO

PHILIPPINE MONEY FLIES

Ali Baba has departed but the Forty Thieves still remain. . . .
—Jaime Cardinal Sin of Manilla,
after Ferdinand and Imelda Marcos fled the country

It was very easy to put in money there. But it was impossible to take it
out....
—Imelda Marcos, on her relationship with Swiss banks,
London Channel Four documentary, 1994

We love your adherence to democratic principles and democratic process. . . .
—Vice President George Bush, toast to President Marcos, Manila 1981

Marcos has lifted everything else around here—he might as well lift martial
law.
—Marcos opponent, 1981

If you repudiate your debts, it will cause you *immense* suffering.
—Citibank chairman John Reed in his Manila speech, 1986

I turned off one of Manila's sweltering streets and found myself in a private trop-ical forest compound the size of a whole city block. At the end of a long row of banyan trees was a huge, stylish, glass and mahogany house that was barely visible from the road outside. I welcomed the respite from the claustrophobic traffic, but the two machine gun-toting guards made me nervous—unlike the rest of the Philippines's troubled econ-omy, the market for security guards was booming. My host "Keo," a member of one of Manila's first families, had retained a whole private army to protect his plantations and homes from the growing number of rebels, bandits, and desperately poor people.

Keo's family came to Manila from Spain in the eighteenth century and prospered on the basis of propitious investments in land, sugar, and lumber. For generations, his family had watched corrupt officials come and go. As Keo says, corruption was the Philippines's "national sport" long before Ferdinand E. Marcos declared martial law in 1972.

But Marcos, a Philippine-trained lawyer with a dubious war record, was a virtual Leonardo when it came to the mechanical engineering of corruption. He erected a colos-

sal pyramid of thievery that gave him a piece of almost everything the government touched, from arms purchases and import quotas to power plants and dams, the special taxes levied on thousands of coconut farmers, the repatriated earnings of Filipino maids, and even student loans. One US AID officer I interviewed estimated that in 1985, the regime's last year, his staff spent seventy percent of its time just trying to prevent Ferdinand and his cronies from ripping their programs off.[1] Even the oldest landed families, which had generally disdained the upstart lawyer and his beauty queen wife, had to cut deals in order to survive. By the end of his twenty-one-year reign in February 1986, Marcos had become so expensive that very few members of the Philippines' elite beyond his closest cronies were sorry to see him go.

This is not to say that the Philippines's elite eagerly embraced popular demands for land reform, social spending, or debt repudiation, or that they necessarily even supported Corazon Aquino's moderate Yellow Revolution. On the contrary, in the decades after Marcos's demise, many have come to feel a kind of strange nostalgia for his strong-armed rule. In 2003, the question quietly spoken in many of Manila's best neighborhoods is, "Where's young Ferdinand, now that we really need him?"

To survive in these conditions, my host, an expert on rice farming, also became a self-taught expert on personal security systems, small arms, and influence peddling. Back in the good old days, Imelda had threatened to build a highway through Keo's private forest, and "something had to be done" to prevent it. There have also been a few more hungry bureaucratic mouths to feed since then—Marcos's departure hardly ended corruption in the Philippines, or the global private banking system that supports it. But Keo's expertise has its uses: I've asked him to help me through the overgrown, unmarked backwaters of the Philippines's underground economy, and solve a few puzzles. . . .

THE FESTIVAL

As part of her effort to make Manila a cultural capital, Imelda Marcos sponsored the Philippines's first International Film Festival in 1981. This was just one of her many odd, extravagant projects, which included the Lung Center, the Heart Center, the Culture Complex, the International Convention Center, a fish farm, a floating casino, and fourteen new first-class hotels that were built especially for the World Bank's 1976 Annual Meetings. The Film Center was even more ambitious than the projects that preceded it. Imelda Marcos wanted it to become a venue for the first "Asian Cannes," a film event that would attract luminaries from all over the world to her hometown each year. She hired Henry C. Rogers, a leading Los Angeles agent, to promote its twelve-day first edition, and she and her eldest daughter Imee sent out more than four thousand invitations.

With only six months to go, Imelda suddenly decided to hold the event in a striking new auditorium—an eight-story, $21.3 million replica of the Parthenon, complete with marble porticoes and statues, constructed next to the ocean on land that had been reclaimed from Manila Bay. Unfortunately, Imelda's ambitious design and the short timetable strained Philippine construction skills to the breaking point. Huge blocks of marble had to be imported from Italy and shaped by laborers who had little experience working with marble. In November 1981, with just two months to go, the project was way behind schedule, and the eight thousand construction workers were sweating night and day to catch up.

Suddenly there was a terrible accident—two floors of the building collapsed, burying two dozen workers under tons of rubble. Church and union leaders appealed to Imelda Marcos to halt work, so their bodies could be recovered. But she insisted on pressing ahead. Her project managers simply ordered the bodies to be covered over with cement.

On January 18, 1982, Imelda Marcos's new Manila Film Center was finished just in time. The jack hammers were still pounding and there was dust in the air as President Marcos gave the dedication speech. That evening, more than 1,600 members of the Philippines's elite and 300 foreign dignitaries jammed into the new hall, dressed to the "nines" in black ties and evening gowns. Imelda Marcos held center stage in a stunning white terno with a two-foot long diamond necklace, giant diamond teardrop earrings, and three diamond bracelets. She was surrounded by all her favorite celebrities—including George Hamilton, Peter Ustinov, Jeremy Irons, Pia Zadora, Michael York, Priscilla Presley, Charlotte Ford, Adnan Khashoggi, Jack Valenti, and Doris Buchanan Duke, the US tobacco heiress. They dined on cows that had been roasted on open spits and bottles of Dom Perignon. Then there was a spectacular fireworks festival, which featured a medieval pageant and a parade of beauty queens, native dancers, and religious floats with bejeweled figures of the Madonna and the Baby Jesus. Finally, they turned to the films—with Henry C. Rogers's help, and plenty of seed money, Imelda Marcos had managed to attract 179 new movies from thirty-nine countries, including first-rank entries like *Body Heat* and *Gallipoli*.

What no one had quite planned for, however, was that this particular evening was unusually warm and humid. And, of course, cement is porous. So Imelda Marcos's great embarrassment and the dismay of her guests, the opening was also attended by what several guests later recalled as an "enormous cloud" of black flies. All evening long they swarmed about the very center of the hall, close to the place where the workers' bodies had been interred two months earlier.

Unfortunately, Imelda Marcos's Film Festival was a financial debacle—it cost nearly $100 million, but produced very little revenue. After one more installment in 1983, which featured pornography, it was cancelled for good. In 1987, President Corazon ("Cory") Aquino's new government placed a small plaque on the Film Center in honor of the workers who had died racing to complete it on time.[2]

THE TREASURE HUNT

Of all the debt story's dirty linen, none has tougher stains than the tale of Ferdinand and Imelda Marcos, the globe-trotting couple who ruled the Philippines with iron fists and open pockets from 1965 to 1986, and whose family members, cronies, and sympathizers still exert tremendous political and economic influence there. There is already a huge amount of literature on their seemingly insatiable appetites for real estate, bank deposits, pianos, gold, paintings, jewelry, and their rather gauche version of high fashion: Until Imelda Marcos's return to the Philippines in 1991, Malacanang Palace maintained an exhibit of 1,220 pairs of shoes, 300 bras, 500 gowns, and 200 girdles. The family's total wealth remains uncertain, partly because they were so adept at hiding it, and partly because blood bankers in Switzerland, Panama, Liechtenstein, Luxembourg, London, B.I, and the US still help keep their secrets. But clearly they were among the world's greatest flight capitalists ever.[3]

The hunt for the Marcos treasure preoccupied Ferdinand Marcos's immediate successor, Corazon Aquino. Indeed, her very first official act as president, on February 28, 1986, was to establish a Presidential Commission on Good Government (PCGG) to track down the assets of the dictator and his cronies. At the time, everyone in her government believed that this would be relatively simple. After all, Ferdinand Marcos clearly had billions tucked away—everyone said so. In March 1986, the Philippines's solicitor general estimated that he had squirreled away at least $5–10 billion in more than thirteen countries, including $3.5 billion in Switzerland alone.

In the aftermath of Marcos's downfall, there was also a groundswell of international sympathy for Aquino's "Yellow Revolution" and the long-suffering Filipino people, thousands of whom had been murdered by the Marcos regime. The PCGG rather naively expected to win cooperation even from Marcos's staunch former allies like the US, and relatively airtight havens like Switzerland and Liechtenstein.

The "Conjugal Dictatorship" had also left behind tons of documents. While Marcos's minions at Malacanang Palace had worn out four giant paper shredders in their last few weeks before fleeing to Hawaii, the opposition still found abandoned records that identifed seventeen Liechtenstein foundations and sixty Swiss and Hong Kong bank accounts—including twenty-six at Credit Suisse, eleven at Standard Chartered, nineteen at Swiss Bank Corp, six at Paribas, two at Bankers Trust, three at Bank Hoffman, and one each at Lombard-Odier and Edmond Safra's Trade Development Bank. US Customs had also seized other papers when Marcos arrived in Honolulu, although many of these are still being withheld on "national security" grounds to this day.[4]

Unfortunately, there were no current bank statements for any of the identified accounts. To a haven expert, there were also glaring omissions—like the absence of even one single account at UBS, Switzerland's largest bank; at any of the "elite private" Swiss banks, other than Lombard Odier; at HSBC, Hong Kong's largest bank; or at any leading US banks, other than Bankers Trust. It also appeared that there were no Swiss "Form B" appointments, which had been commonly used until 1992 by the clients of Swiss banks who had really dirty money to hide.[5]

However, the Malacanang records did at least give Aquino's PCGG a running start. Moving at what would later seem like lightning speed, in April 1986, the PCGG filed a formal request for mutual assistance with the Swiss Federal Office, retained its own lawyers in Geneva, Zurich, and Lugano, and assembled a hundred-page criminal brief against Marcos that detailed all the identified foundations and accounts.[6] Based in part on this request, Swiss authorities agreed to escrow $356 million in nine of the sixty identified accounts owned by five of the seventeen identified Marcos-controlled foundations. According to the inscrutable Swiss, only these nine accounts, which were all at Credit Suisse and SBC, held any money—all of the other accounts and foundations noted in the PCGG brief were either defunct or empty. Furthermore, the Swiss were also unable to locate any other Marcos accounts or trusts whatsoever. And Credit Suisse and SBC would continue to earn fees for managing the escrowed money, pending a Philippines trial to determine the rightful owners of the funds.

This was a little disappointing. However, on the whole, the Aquino government was satisfied with its early progress on the treasure trail. By the end of 1986, the PCGG had secured the Swiss asset freeze, commenced more than thirty-five lawsuits to recover other properties, and sequestered Marcos's holding in several large Philippines companies, including the major brewery San Miguel and the long-distance telephone company PLDT. The first PCGG chairman, Senator Jovita Salonga, was optimistic that billions of dollars in Marcos loot would soon be returned—perhaps even soon enough to help reduce the country's $30 billion foreign debt.

Seventeen years and eight more PCGG chairpersons later, however, this treasure hunt, like most other such postdictatorship quests, has turned out to be quixotic. The PCCG did manage to locate another $867 million in gold and cash in six Hong Kong banks, plus homes in London, Rome, and Geneva, and $200 million worth of property in Hawaii, New York, New Jersey, Texas, Mississippi, Nevada, and California. There was also Charlie Chaplin's mansion in Beverly Hills, which George Hamilton bought in 1981 for $1.5 million, refinanced with a $4 million Imelda Marcos loan in 1983, and sold for $6.5 million to Imelda Marcos's frontman Adman Khashoggi in 1986; the California Overseas Bank, a $30 million bank in Beverly Hills; three condos in San Francisco; an estate in Honolulu, a thirteen-acre farm in Princeton; the $6 million (now $30 million) "Lindenmere" estate on Long Island, three suites in the Olympic Towers, a six-story townhouse and four skyscrapers in Manhattan; and Houston's "Galleria," which Marcos had developed with help from the law firm of Robert Strauss, Jimmy Carter's campaign manager. Investigators also found another $200 million in real estate, jewelry, art, antiques and securities in the Philippines.

Unfortunately, the ownership of most of these assets is still being hotly contested.[7] Even the original $356 million that was frozen by the Swiss in 1986—which is now worth $678 million, including interest—was not surrendered to Philippine government control until July 2003, when the Philippine Supreme Court finally ruled that these funds must have been "ill-gotten." Another hundred million that may belong to other Marcos cronies has also been frozen, but this will also take years to recover. The Zurich DA's office recently even unblocked some of these crony assets.[8] Most of the law suits filed in 1986 to recover other assets are still pending. Overall, it turns out that if the loot is large enough, leading havens like Switzerland, Liechenstein, and the US as well as the court systems in developing countries, are much more scrupulous about returning stolen property than about receiving, protecting, and concealing it in the first place.[9]

Meanwhile, the PCGG's asset recovery efforts have consumed vast resources, time, and attention. They may have inspired as much corruption as they have deterred, by stimulating some of the investigators and their political bosses to seek private deals with the Marcos clan, and to tout bogus claims of "found" assets.

The case has also provided a steady income stream for PCGG bureaucrats, high-priced attorneys, and innumerable Marcos minions—like the Manila law firm of Senator Juan Ponce Enrile, Marcos's former defense secretary; Bruno de Preux, former president of the Geneva Bar Association, who allegedly placed up to $1.3 billion in Marcos assets in accounts under his son's name in the early 1990s; the numerous US attorneys for the Marcos family, including Gerry Spence and James Linn; New York attorneys Sullivan & Cromwell, which represent UBS; the Zurich office of KPMG, the global accounting firm, which was recently accused of transferring $400 million of Marcos's money to an obscure Credit Suisse subsidiary in Liechtenstein on the very eve of the Swiss asset freeze; the uncle of Liechtenstein's constitutional monarch Prince Hans-Adam II, Prince Constantin, who was reportedly rewarded for turning a blind eye to these midnight shenanigans by the KPMG; and the prolific Liechstenstein attorney "Professor Dr. Dr." Herbert Batliner, whose other distinguished dry-cleaning clients have reportedly included Colombian and Ecudorian drug dealers, Saudi Arabia's King Fahd, Marc Rich, Zaire's Mobutu, former President Habibie of Indonesia, Brazilian soccer officials, former German President Helmut Kohl, and selected members of the Russian mafia.[10]

As of 2003, less than $2 billion in Marcos and crony-owned assets had been positively identified by the PCGG, far below its expectations seventeen years earlier. Less than half of this has actually been transferred to the Philippine government, and none of it has been paid to Marcos's thousands of human rights victims.[11] The Marcos clan has also been able to recover many of the assets that were seized by the PCGG, and there is also evidence that huge assets still remain under their control, or the control of their cronies and private bankers.[12] Given this track record, which is typical of such private banking asset recovery operations, there are growing demands for the PCGG's abolition.

THE PIE

It is not easy to estimate how much loot has fallen through the the cracks, though the number is very large. Another piece of circumstantial evidence was Ferdinand Marcos's own abortive 1988 offer to trade $5 billion for immunity from prosecution and the right to return home. President Aquino's response was, "Send the $5 billion, then we'll talk." He refused. In August 1988, Adnan Khashoggi also offered to buy $5 billion of Philippine foreign debt for $1 billion if Marcos got immunity—the world's first "debt-for-dictator" swap.[13] But Aquino also rejected that offer, and Marcos died a man without a country in Honolulu.

Another indicator of Marcos's wealth may be the controversial claims of Reiner Jacobi, an Australian private eye, former PCGG contractor, and by some accounts, a complete charlatan.[14] According to Jacobi, another Liechtenstein foundation, Sandy Anstalt, was supposedly created in the 1960s, in trust for Marcos's youngest daughter, Irene Marcos-Araneta. He claims that as of July 1998, this trust still held $13.2 billion in a gold account at UBS in

Zurich.[15] Based on these assertions, several PCGG officials made inquiries to the Swiss authorities, and the Philippine Senate held rather inconclusive hearings.

Like many other aspects of the Marcos treasure hunt, this particular story turns out to be a tangled thicket of rival claims. In many ways, that is the key point: once the private banking industry gets its hands on a huge stash of illicit wealth, most of it is usually lost forever. Of course, Jacobi is hardly disinterested. He and his partners/investors stand to collect a ten percent finders' fee if his story holds up and the Philippines honors his purported contract. UBS, Swiss authorities, and even the PCGG's own (former) Swiss attorney have all disputed the alleged UBS account's existence and importance. Of course, UBS is also not disinterested. If it ever admits to having undisclosed Marcos accounts as late as 1998, it could be prosecuted for money laundering, even under Swiss law.[16] In this regard, the track record of Swiss banks—and UBS in particular—with respect to the assets of World War II Holocaust victims is not an encouraging precedent.[17]

In February 2001, Ms. Marcos-Araneta and her husband "Greggy" Araneta reportedly traveled to Germany, opened several accounts at Deutsche Bank in Dusseldorf, and faxed UBS in Zurich, instructing it to transfer over any assets in the Sandy Anstalt account or any others belonging to them. This transaction was never completed. But it appears to support Jacobi's account—unless, of course, the Aranetas themselves were the dupes of an elaborate scam.[18]

By now, any assets that were ever deposited into this alleged account or any others in Switzerland have probably long since been moved elsewhere.[19] Consistent with the hallowed "Holocaust-victims" tradition of Swiss private banking, the Marcos family might well have lost control over much of the loot that it entrusted to pinstriped privateers. Nevertheless, this purported stash is at least consistent with other evidence that we have on the sheer size of Marcos's looting—much more so than the PCGG's own pathetic recoveries.

The best estimates of Marcos family wealth may be based on Imelda Marcos's own bragging just two months after the Philippines Supreme Court reversed her twelve-year criminal sentence in late 1998. In an unguarded moment with a local newspaper, she boasted that her family still owned more than $800 million in undisclosed assets in Switzerland, and that her family had entrusted 500 billion pesos ($12.8 billion, at prevailing exchange rates) of other corporate assets to cronies who held them as trustees for her family. In Imelda Marcos's own words:

> We practically own eveything in the Philippines, from electricity, telecommunications, airplanes, banking, beer and tobacco, newspaper publishing, television stations, shipping, oil, mining, hotels, and health resorts, down to

coconut mills, small firearms, real estate and insurance. . . . We will take back everything that the trustees held on behalf of Ferdinand Marcos, including those that they have sold and surrendered to the government. . . . I have evidence that these trustees, who eventually turned their backs on us and became untrusted, can never ever dispute.[20]

Among the companies that Imelda Marcos claimed as Marcos family property were PLDT, the Philippines's main telephone company, with a 1998 market cap of $3.2 billion; San Miguel, the Philippines's largest food and beverage company, worth $2.4 billion; Meralco, Manila's main electricity distributor, worth $1.2 billion; Manila Bulletin Publishing, publishers of the Philippines's daily newspaper and a weekly magazine, worth $104 million; UCPB, one of the Philippines's top ten banks, with $2.5 billion in assets; Allied Bank, another leading commercial bank, officially owned by Lucio Tan, and worth $2.2 billion; Fortune Tobacco, another Tan company, the country's largest cigarette manufacturer; and Asia Brewery, the Philippines's second largest brewery, also officially owned by Tan. In addition to Tan, the other leading cronies on her list of "trustees" were Eduardo ("Danding") Cojuangco, Ramon Cojuangco, his son Antonio, Herminio Disini, Rolando Gapud, Jose Yao Campos, and Roberto Benedicto.

Of course, Imelda Marcos may have had personal motives for overstating such claims in public. At the time, she was trying to persuade President Joseph Estrada to form an alliance, pursue these assets together, and divvy up the proceeds. Later, after Estrada fell, she and her family tried to take back all these statements. They pleaded "penniless," for example, when the Philippine government tried to enforce a 1999 tax court judgment and when it came time to pay up on a $150 million settlement for the 9,939 Filipino victims of her husband's human rights policies, won by them in a 1995 US lawsuit.[21] Of course, all of the alleged cronies who were still alive disputed her claims vociferously.

However, her interview may actually have not been that far off the mark. As the PCGG has long asserted, the cronies played a crucial role in the enrichment of Ferdinand and Imelda Marcos. It may now be a certain rough justice that places her in the position, near the end of her life, of being ripped off by her "friends."

SOURCES

Whatever the precise scale of Marcos's loot, even the PCCG's initial estimates established a fortune that was pretty hard to explain on the basis of Marcos's official 110,000 peso per year salary as president. In 1966, after one year in office, Ferdinand Marcos estimated his net worth to be a mere

$30,000. So precisely how did he and Imelda Marcos manage to accumulate billions of dollars and squirrel them abroad? The Philippines, after all, was not Angola, Mexico, Nigeria, Iran, Russia, Indonesia, or Venezuela—there was no steady stream of oil revenues that could be diverted into private pockets and offshore accounts. While Marcos certainly helped himself to a share of most investments and trade deals around the country and to government concessions, he was only in power sixteen years, his wife had expensive tastes, and $10 billion or more was a great deal of money, especially in that economy. So how did he pull it off?

There has been little careful research on this basic question. There has been a great deal of loose talk about Marcos's role as "Mr. Ten Percent" in public works projects, his diversions from foreign aid, taxes on coconuts, sugar, and gambling, his purported theft of the country's gold reserves, and his own favorite cover story, the supposed discovery of General Yamashita's World War II gold hoard—which was later parlayed by the US in the late 1980s into a cover story that provided General John Singlaub an excuse to wander the islands, recruiting right-wing vigilantes.[22] There have also been several court cases and investigations that have provided a great deal of evidence about Marcos's particular crimes.[23]

But far too little attention has been paid to the witting, systematic role of foreign banks in Marcos's rapid ascent to fame and fortune, and the specific role of the global haven banking system, which fostered the accumulation of massive public foreign debts side by side with the accumulation of massive, illicit, foreign private assets.

From this angle, Ferdinand and Imelda Marcos's case was just one of the more extreme special cases of the general dirty debt/flight story. As sensational as their record-setting venality was, it is important to see them in context of this pervasive global system, because, to a great extent, that system still exists. As Jaime Cardinal Sin of Manila said after Ferdinand and Imelda Marcos fled the country: "Ali Baba has departed, but the Forty Thieves still remain." The Marcos family may or may not succeed in restoring its position; after all, the family has many enemies and even more "former friends." Given the country's critical situation, however, as well as its continuing strategic importance, there may be plenty of demand for "young Ferdinands" yet to come.

The Philippines also presents an important enigma to development historians. After all, it long enjoyed the closest relationships with the US, Japan, the World Bank, the IMF, and the ADB of any other Asian country. The loans provided by multilateral institutions and export credit agencies accounted for more than a fifth of the Philippines's foreign debt by 1986. Under Marcos, the Philippines was one of the IMF's most compliant clients, with eighteen standby programs in twenty-five years and one of the highest levels of IMF funding in the world. After World War II, the Philippines also achieved one of Asia's highest per capita levels of foreign private bank lending and foreign investment. The country is incredibly rich in natural resources—as one geological survey in the late 1980s concluded, "The Philippines is far more densely mineralized than Australia. . . ."[24] Indeed, it has far more natural resources than Japan, Korea, or Taiwan. In the seventeenth century, long before Japan opened up to trade, Spanish galleons were crossing the Pacific laden with Mexican silver to exchange for Philippine products. Right after World War II, the Philippines's income level was second only to Japan's among Asian countries, its manufacturing sector was twice the size of Korea's as a share of national income, and its literacy rate was as high as any Asian country's. Yet by the late 1980s, the Philippines had become Asia's basketcase, a poster child for underdevelopment and inequality, with one of the largest continuing armed insurgencies in Asia—a status that it still retains to this day. So, what happened?

To tackle this puzzle and also understand how Marcos managed to procure so much wealth in such a short time, it is not sufficient to look only at the history of "the Conjugal Dictatorship." Some historians might argue, on the other hand, that we should really head all the way back to the 1890s, when the US first conquered the country, betrayed and slaughtered its rebel allies several times over, and implemented a kind of proxy colonialism with support from the local elites. However, a more proximate cause for the Philippines's misfortune can be located later, in the fateful choices made—and evaded—during a critical period right after World War II.

So let us return for a moment to Asia during the mid-1940s and examine why social revolutions were made in some countries and not others—not only by communists and the Red Army, but by the US Army, its "supreme commander," and an obscure US Army lieutenant named Beplat.

YAMASHITA'S REAL GOLD—MACARTHUR & BEPLAT

Major wars are often decisive turning points in the development of whole regions. Many historians have written about the impact that the US-backed Marshall Plan had on Western Europe after World War II. Far less attention has been paid to what might be called the "MacArthur Plan," which was implemented with much less money, but much more profound structural consequences, throughout East Asia from 1946 to 1952. For reasons of their own, the Americans who guided these interventions turned out to be much kinder to the ruling elites in the Philippines than in Japan, Korea, and Taiwan.

In October 1945, Tokyo lay in ruins, half of it leveled by US firebombs. The streets were clogged with debris, industry was at a complete standstill, and there was an acute shortage of food, water, and clothing for the city's four million inhabitants. Tokyo was overcrowded with the US Army's Occupation Force, commanded by General Douglas MacArthur. But it was almost devoid of young women. Their parents had feared for their virtue at the hands of the GIs and sent them to the countryside.[25]

The Japanese soon learned they had little to fear from most Americans— this would turn out to be one of the most tranquil and magnanimous foreign occupations ever, certainly by comparison with Japan's own brutal occupations of China, the Philippines, or Korea. That is not to say the Japanese elite all got off lightly. MacArthur seized the opportunity to introduce an unprecedented "social democratic" revolution from above.

Among the well-meaning Americans to arrive in Tokyo that October was Tristan E. Beplat, a thirty-three-year-old first lieutenant from New York City. He'd been assigned to Tokyo because he had a combination of skills that was very rare at the time—he spoke Japanese and had been trained as a banker. In the mid-1930s, Beplat had traded foreign exchange at JW Seligman, a leading Wall Street investment bank. In 1937, he moved to Manufacturers Trust, the forerunner of MHT (which would eventually be digested by JPMorgan Chase), and in 1940, to The Bank of New York, where he ran its Foreign Exchange Department. In 1944, he was drafted into officers' school and spent six months at Professor Edwin Reischauer's famous Japanese language and culture program at Harvard. From there, Beplat was sent straight to Tokyo, to head MacArthur's twenty-person "Money and Banking Branch." That put him, fresh out of Wall Street and Harvard, in charge of restructuring Japan's entire banking industry.

At that point, General MacArthur, supreme commander of the Allied Powers, headed the military government that would rule Japan until 1952. He still believed that Japan's society badly needed restructuring. Before the war, Japan had been a highly stratified autocratic capitalist society, with land ownership dominated by a tiny group of absentee landowners, and three-quarters of industry and banking controlled by just eleven private groups, the *zaibatsu*.[26] Since Japan's industrialization began in the 1880s, the country had achieved a respectable but hardly exceptional real annual average growth rate of just 2–3 percent a year, and a savings rate that averaged just 17 percent of national income.[27] Many factors contributed to this middling performance, but the most important ones were institutional: the country's rigid social structure, noncompetitive, cartelized industries, and regressive land tenure system inhibited savings, labor mobility, and the adoption of new technologies. On the eve of World War II, except for its military might, Japan was hardly a First World country—its per capita income level was well below that of the US, Western Europe, and even Argentina, Venezuela, and Chile.[28]

MacArthur's initial aim was to democratize and demilitarize this rather bureaucratic, authoritarian society, and, along the way, create a role model that might serve as an alternative to the Communist land redistributions that were beginning to sweep through China, on the road to Mao's ultimate defeat of Chiang Kai Shek in 1949. Beplat's job was to determine the fate of Japan's five most powerful banks, owned by the *zaibatsu*. All of them had financed and profited greatly from Japan's war effort, so there was strong sentiment on MacArthur's staff for scattering them to the winds.[29] The Antitrust Branch, influenced by New Deal progressive liberals like Rexford G. Tugwell and A. A. Berle Jr., advocated breaking them up geographically, as in Germany. There, the big banks were divided in three after the war, one part for each of the three regions controlled by the noncommunist Allies, the US, the UK, and France.

In Japan there was only one Allied power, and Beplat was strongly opposed to geographical dismemberment. He saw his main task as restoring Japan's capital market to working order:

> It made no sense to break up the Japanese banks geographically, because the economic regions were all different. You didn't want a fragmented banking system if you wanted to get the economy growing again. . . . My long-term policy was sort of to make Japan what it has become today.[30]

At first this was distinctly a minority viewpoint. Throughout 1946–47, there was an intense debate—as Beplat's wife recalls, "Tris had to fight tooth and nail against the New Dealers" who favored dismemberment and even more punitive social reforms. As the Occupation dragged on, however, Beplat's position drew strength from the perceived threat of growing Communist movements in China, Greece, Eastern Europe, Vietnam, and North Korea. As the Western Allies and the Russians became increasingly suspicious of each other, MacArthur's priorities shifted from reforming Japan's society to rebuilding its economy.[31] In late 1947, Beplat convinced MacArthur to let him chair a five-man commission to finally resolve the banking structure question. In April 1948, this commission finally decided to let all the *zaibatsu* banks survive. The only significant change was that their number was increased from five to twelve, to stimulate competition.

In striking contrast to many other developing countries, therefore, and largely for reasons of contemporary US foreign policy, a strong core of domestic banks was permitted to retain control over Japan's financial markets. Foreign banks like Citibank, Chase, and Bank of America were permitted to obtain licenses for Tokyo offices, but they weren't allowed to own deposit-taking foreign branches until Morgan opened a tiny one in 1965. Even then, there were many restrictions on their ability to offer foreign loans and recruit private assets. In effect, the US placed strong limits on "free capital markets," in order to strengthen its strategically vital new ward.

Meanwhile, leveraging the military government's extensive powers, Beplat helped to modernize many other key aspects of Japan's financial system. He reorganized the Yokohama Specie Bank, which specialized in foreign exchange, changing its name to The Bank of Tokyo—a name that it still uses to this day. He arranged a $100 million US loan that kicked off Japan's first postwar export boom, in cotton textiles. He also organized a nationwide savings campaign, giving speeches all over the country to encourage the Japanese to save more so they could finance their own recovery. Unlike Germany, there was no support for a Marshall Plan for Japan, partly because there was less of a threat from the Left. Since US banks weren't allowed to lend there, domestic savings had to do the job.

As Beplat later recalled, one key objective was to develop a strong industrial export base, and US authorities intervened strongly in capital and currency markets to do that:

> We wanted them on our side politically. The country had been destroyed by the war and devastated by hunger and inflation. [To stimulate exports,] we estimated that ninety percent of exports could be competitive at a rate of three hundred yen per dollar, and that some were even lucrative at two hundred. But we didn't want to err on something so important, so we finally set the rate at 360. To get exports started, we also got a bank loan to buy cotton supplies in California, and we sent commercial missions to the Philippines, Indonesia, and Brazil, to get other supplies.[32]

Despite the slowdown in social reform brought about by the Cold War, up to July 1948, when Beplat left MacArthur's staff, the US military had indeed presided over a sweeping program of social restructuring. With the help of leading social scientists like Harvard's Talcott Parsons and Reischauer, MacArthur had implemented basic institutional reforms, designing a new constitution that provided for a two-house parliamentary system, a bill of rights, an independent judiciary, legal trade unions, and a decentralized system of municipal government. Thousands of Japanese militarists were purged, imprisoned, and rehabilitated, the military was limited to "self-defense" forces and one percent of national income, and the heretofore-divine emperor was forced to admit in public that he was just a man. For the first time, women were allowed to vote, own property, and attend school. Education was made compulsory. A capital levy was exacted from the upper classes to redistribute wealth, and the *zaibatsu*'s dominance over industry was reduced.

Furthermore, under the leadership of Wolfgang Ladejinsky, a progressive Russian-born agronomist and advisor to the US Department of Agriculture, and his aide Robert S. Hardie, the US Army implemented a very rigorous, popular land reform program in Japan. Ladejinsky drafted the land reform bill that was adopted by the Japanese Diet (Japan's parliament), on October 21, 1946. This limited individual farms to a maximum of three hectares in most of the country, redistributed more than five million acres with little compensation for landlords, and virtually abolished tenant farming.[33] Similar land reform measures were also implemented with US support by Chiang Kai Shek's right-wing Kuo-Ming-Tang regime in Taiwan and Syngman Rhee's autocratic regime in South Korea, for reasons that were hardly selfless, but got the job done.[34] By the mid-1950s, the pattern of land ownership in all three of these future "Asian tigers" had been fundamentally altered with help from these American "revolutionaries."[35] As Ladejinsky later wrote, they had achieved their politico-economic purpose, stealing "communist thunder" and producing a class structure that supported a more stable, democratic government. In Ladejinsky's words: "Agrarian reform is a precondition for economic, social, political and technological changes, without which democracy in Asia has no bright future. . . ."[36]

Although it is impossible to measure precisely the effects of all these changes, there is little doubt that they made a crucial and often-ignored contribution to these all countries' subsequent growth paths and their "export-led" takeoffs. Agricultural productivity increased, as small-scale farming became more intensive and savings and investment by the former tenants accelerated. Increased rural incomes provided stronger home markets for domestic industry and sped up technological progress. Savings and growth rates increased sharply. The rise of a conservative class of small, land-owning farmers enhanced political stability.[37] The emancipation of women—still far from complete to this day, but at least accelerated by MacArthur's reforms—not only struck a blow for social justice, but also provided a new source of heretofore-underutilitized human capital for industry. And Japan's economic strategy shifted from agriculture toward manufacturing as the main source of growth.

On the other hand, to a great extent because of Beplat's influence, MacArthur spared the *zaibatsu* banks from dismemberment. This helps to explain why, more than fifty years later, the same basic banks that dominated pre-war Japan still do so today—although in the last decade they have consolidated significantly, under the impact of Japan's own prolonged domestic debt crisis.

At that point, starting in the late 1980s and early 1990s, Beplat's relatively closed Japanese banking system finally caught up with itself. The incestuous ties that Japan's "city" banks had fostered with industry, construction companies, and political leaders, got them all into deep trouble. They financed a huge speculative "asset bubble" in real estate, and when that bubble burst, their crony connections prevented them from writing down the loans fast enough to save the whole economy from a prolonged process of deflation and slow growth. As a result, all the leading Japanese banks are now saddled with trillions of dollars in unproductive loans that will take at least until 2006 to burn off.[38]

Until the 1990s, however, Beplat's system at least permitted Japan to develop almost entirely free of foreign debt, foreign aid, and foreign investment—as did Taiwan and, to a lesser extent, South Korea, where foreign investment and foreign loans were even more tightly controlled and, indeed, commercial banks were ultimately nationalized.[39] The strength and independence of these countries' domestic banking systems contributed greatly to their dynamism from the 1950s to the late 1980s. If, at that point, they had been able to open up the banking systems, carefully become more competitive and less incestuous, many of the excesses of the last decade might have been avoided.

In any case, the postwar reforms in Japan, Korea, and Taiwan were surely some of the world's most successful "social revolutions" ever—certainly by comparsion with the results achieved later on by First World development experts and economic advisors in places like post-Soviet Russia and most other developing countries that followed the simple-minded neoliberal path. And this success, in turn, was due in no small part to the forthright focus on institutional development, the driving threat of radical revolutions in Korea and China, and the firm use of state power by these otherwise "conservative" US soldiers.

HE SHALL RETURN

Beplat not only had the catbird seat for Japan's postwar reconstruction, he also got an inside look at the restoration of the *status quo ante bellum* in the Philippines and Ferdinand Marcos's rise to power.

At the war's end, MHT's only foreign office was in London. In October 1948, Beplat rejoined the bank and opened its first Asian office in Tokyo as the head of its new Far East department. His focus was "correspondent banking": clearing checks, supplying short-term credits, and managing reserves for other banks. Beplat's best customers turned out to be the very same large Japanese banks whose survival he had earlier insured. He took an energetic approach to this market, cultivating strong personal relationships with local bankers, launching a program to teach them how to handle foreign exchange and letters of credit, and helping his wife organize the first US college scholarship program for Japan. This personal approach proved invaluable. As one Asian banker explained, "I prefer to do business with Beplat—I don't do business with a computer, I do business with my friends."[40]

Beplat also called on other Asian countries aggressively. He was one of the few bankers to visit Seoul during the Korean War (by hitching a ride on a military plane), and he was also among the first to call on Taiwan, Thailand, Indonesia, and Singapore. By 1952, MHT's clientele stretched from Bombay to Manila, and Beplat had become its youngest VP ever.

In 1949, he visited the Philippines for the first time. It presented a strong contrast to the other "Asian tigers." Manila had been as devastated by the war as Tokyo, and even after 1946, when the Philippines achieved nominal independence, the country was also subject to almost as much US influence—all four of its presidents in the late 1940s and 1950s got substantial covert assistance from the CIA.[41] Land ownership was even more concentrated than in Japan—sugar, tobacco, and coconut plantations were dominated by just forty families. And most of them—including the father of Benigno Aquino, who would later become Marcos's main political opponent—had been Japanese collaborators.[42]

But Douglas MacArthur was simply not prepared to make a social revolution in what amounted to be his own hometown. Since 1898, the Philippines had been a virtual US colony. Ironically enough, unlike Japan, the Philippines had never really been a feudal society, and while land ownership was already pretty concentrated when the US arrived, the most important land holdings belonged to the Catholic Church. Rather than support the widespread distribution of these holdings, however, the US permitted them to be sold off to a handful of elite families in the Christian community, mainly of Spanish origin.

Over the next few decades, this local elite developed very close ties with US companies and officials, including MacArthur's own family. His father, General Arthur A. MacArthur, had been the islands' governor-general, in charge of brutally suppressing Aguinaldo's peasant rebellion in 1899–1902.[43] Douglas MacArthur grew up in Manila; he was a close friend of Philippine presidents Manuel Quezon and Sergio Osmeña, the former speaker of the Philippine Assembly from 1907 to 1920, who had perfected the spoils system long before Ferdinand Marcos: "Nobody could join the government without a letter from him. . . . He perfected the kami-kami, tayo-tayo [we and us] of Philippine politics."[44] Two of Douglas MacArthur's closest advisors were Andres Soriano, a wealthy landowner and brewer, and Brigadier General Courtney Whitney, the "fiercely anti-union" lawyer who represented many of Manila's business interests and commanded a rightist militia. Many of his other pals were from *ilustrado* (illustrious) families, like the Elizaldes, Ayalas, and Sorianos. In the 1930s, Douglas MacArthur became a military advisor to the Philippine government, in charge of putting down another peasant rebellion. He was not about to upset his friends in the Philippine elite with confiscatory land reform.

So, General Douglas MacArthur treated the Philippines very differently from Japan. A new constitution was promulgated in 1946, but the US tolerated rampant electoral fraud in the 1946 and 1949 elections and used bribery to help its preferred candidates win.[45] MacArthur purged a few blatant Japanese sympathizers from the government, but he freed five thousand other collaborators, restoring their jobs and property. He even rehabilitated one of the most notorious ones, the landlord and attorney Manual A. Roxas, issued him a pardon for his wartime crimes, and got him elected president. On the other hand, the peasant-based Hukbalahap guerillas, who had fought hard against the Japanese, became his archenemies.

Meanwhile, far from making the economy independent, the Bell Act of 1946—drafted by the US Congress and virtually imposed on the Philippines as a condition of independence—abolished all tariffs on US imports, pegged the peso to the dollar, prohibited the Philippines from manufacturing or selling any products that might "come into substantial competition" with US-made goods, required that the Philippine constitution be revised to grant US citizens and corporations equal access to Philippine minerals, forests and other natural resources, and lifted all restrictions on financial flows between the US and the Philippines.[46] The US also retained effective sovereignty over dozens of military bases under the terms of this "independence," which officially commenced, oddly enough, on July 4, 1946.

As for land reform, nothing was done about it until a new Huks rebellion took off in 1946, partly in response to the harsh Bell Act conditions, which the country's first president Manuel A. Roxas—the attorney for the sugar interests and Japanese collaborator—accepted. Ramon Magsay, a US-backed defense minister and presidential candidate, made vague promises about land reform in his 1950 election campaign, and in 1952 Robert S. Hardie, Wolfgang Ladejinsky's protégé in Japan, even visited Manila and drafted a land reform law along Japanese lines. But it was never implemented. Instead, the US preferred to pursue a military strategy. The rebellion was temporarily quelled by the Philippine military, directed by the CIA's Colonel Edward G. Lansdale, who later applied his experiences in the Philippines to the development of the US "counterinsurgency" strategy in Vietnam. Robert S. Hardie's proposals for land reform in the Philippines were quietly shelved in 1953 after he was denounced by the landed families, and in 1954, Wolfgang Ladejinsky was fired as a "security risk" by President Eisenhower's secretary of agriculture.[47]

Later, Beplat and other US bankers financed all the Philippines's largest sugar and coconut barons, including the Cojuangcos, Aquinos, Elizaldes, and Lopezes. They got special quotas for the US market, generous World Bank loans, and US AID grants for irrigation, power projects, and other capital-intensive rural projects. Ladejinsky's hard-won lessons were forgotten. And the World Bank/IMF's own low-wage "export crop" model of agricultural development also forgot the role that land reform and small-scale rice and corn production had played in the successful social transformations of Japan, Taiwan, and Korea.

The resulting long-term alliance between the US government and the Philippine elite had profound consequences. For example, the "import substitution" policy that many development economists eventually came to deplore by the late 1980s had previously been pursued by all the "Asian tigers" in the 1950s. What really hurt the Philippines was that it continued this policy long after countries like Japan, Taiwan, and Korea switched to a strategy of export-led growth, based on manufacturing for global markets. To explain this inertia, we need to invoke the persistent influence of the Philippine local elite, backed by US power, interests, and, of course, wide-open foreign banking.

The Philippines's persistent long-term problems of competitiveness and dependence on foreign debt were thus directly related to the problem of land. The elite found it almost too easy to enjoy the sweet life simply by exporting sugar, copper, abaca, and other cash commodities. Partly because of the Bell Act, the only manufacturing done was for the local market. But this market was small to begin with, and the highly unequal class system helped to keep it that way. For decades, in turn, this provincial local industry lacked the scale and technical depth needed to compete abroad, except in low-skilled industries like electronics assembly. The Philippine elite also acquired a strong appetite for imports—US luxury goods, cars and trucks, fertilizer, trade finance, machinery, education at US schools, foreign vacations, medical care, fashions, and bank accounts. The result was a stunted form of capitalist development, a schizophrenic combination of import substitution and foreign dominance. By the 1980s, of the top thousand Philippine companies, 334 foreign-owned ones still accounted for fifty-five percent of total sales. And the country was left wide open to profit repatriation, foreign loans, and flight. The contrast with Japan's growth path and economic structure could not have been greater.

The whole character of the Philippine state in turn was shaped by the agro-industrial elite's precarious situation. Surrounded by a sea of property-less, uneducated peasants, as well as by the growth of radical peasant-based movements in other Southeast Asian countries that also lacked land reform, like Indonesia and Vietnam, the elite's primary need was security. It came to rely on the US as a defender against the perceived "Communist threat" at home and abroad—just as the Philippine elite had also relied on the Japanese against the Huks. The growing peasant problem, in turn, fed US perceptions of a Vietnam-like security threat and encouraged the US to provide generous amounts of military and economic assistance, while it turned its back on labor unions, peasant cooperatives, land reform, and free elections. In 1946–50, the Philippines received more than $2 billion in US aid. In this respect, too, the contrast with Japan's MacArthur Plan, which had relied on institutional reform rather than doles and loans, could not be stronger.

With weak legal institutions and democratic checks and balances, the Philippines's immature security state soon became bloated and corrupt. The narrow class system, rampant corruption, and peasant unrest fostered a capital exodus. From the early 1950s on, not long after foreign bankers like Tris Beplat started calling, capital flight began to trickle out. The Philippine elite's central dilemma was that, given its position, it needed the security state to preserve order, yet in the hands of a ruthless autocrat like Marcos, this whole state security apparatus could easily became exploitative. To understand the origins of the Philippines's development problem, its continuing debt/flight problem, and its exceptional status in Asia, it is crucial for us to acknowledge this central contradiction. At its root were the fateful choices made more than forty years ago by US generals, bankers, and their cronies in the Philippine elite, long before Ferdinand Marcos ever courted his "Rose of Tacloban."

OLD FRIENDS

Unlike Japan, with the Philippine economy wide open to foreign capital, there were almost no domestic banks for Tris Beplat to call on when he first arrived in Manila in 1949. The market was already dominated by Citibank, Bank of America, Lloyds, and Standard Chartered—all of which had opened full branches before the war. Fortunately for MHT, the country was just organizing its first Central Bank. So Beplat called on its new governor, Manual Cuadernos, and offered some timely advice on the basis of his Japanese experience. Unlike Japan, where the strong domestic private banks were MHT's largest clients, the Central Bank and other government agencies soon came to play that role in the Philippines.

On his first visit, Beplat also called on José "Pepe" Cojuangco, head of the Philippine Bank of Commerce (PCB), the islands' only locally owned bank at that point, established in 1938. Cojuangco was another happy find. His family owned the country's richest sugar and tobacco plantations in Tarlac Province ninety miles north of Manila, and Pepe's brother Ramon Cojuangco later became a key owner in PLDT, the Philippine Long Distance Telephone Company. In the 1970s, his brother Eduardo Cojuangco would become the islands' coconut czar and acquire the United Coconut Planters Bank (UCPB). He would also be Ferdinand ("Bong Bong") Marcos Jr.'s godfather, and one of Marcos's richest allies. After 1986, Eduardo Cojuangco continued to represent the Marcos faction in the Philippines and sponsored at least one failed coup attempt against Corazon Aquino.

In 1960, José Cojuangco's assistant, José B. ("Jobo") Fernandez, founded an important bank of his own, Far East Bank and Trust (FEBTC). By the 1980s it was the islands' fastest growing bank. Fernandez served as governor of the Central Bank from 1984 to 1990. And José's son Pedro, who ran PCB after he died, became one of Beplat's best friends. Finally, in 1954, Corazon ("Cory") Cojuangco, José's daughter and Fernandez's cousin, married a rich young politician named Benigno ("Ninoy") Aquino Jr., whose family owned much of the southern half of Tarlac. Benigno Aquino would become Ferdinand Marcos's main rival. When Benigno Aquino was assassinated by Marcos's henchmen in August 1983, Corazon Cojuangco inherited his role as leader of the moderate opposition. When Ferdinand Marcos was ousted in February 1986, she became president.

In any case, Tris Beplat returned to Japan from this very first visit to Manila with a whole lifetime's portfolio of influential friends, plus the country's two most important financial institutions as clients. He continued to strengthen these relationships throughout the 1950s, aided by Dwight Allen, an ex-marine who had parachuted into the Philippines in 1944 on MacArthur's "I will return" campaign, and joined MHT in Tokyo in 1952. Beplat returned to New York in 1955 to become MHT's senior vice president for the Far East, but he continued to visit the Philippines at least twice a year. In 1961, MHT's Dwight Allen opened a Manila office. Between them, Beplat and Allen knew every Philippine president and every Central Bank governor personally. In the early 1960s, Beplat often dined with President Diosdado Macapagal, who introduced him in 1962 to Ferdinand Marcos, a bright young lawyer-turned-senator from the Nacionalista Party. That began a friendship that lasted until the dictator's death in 1989.

In 1965, the year Marcos was elected president, the country's entire foreign debt was only $577 million. By February 1970, it exceeded $2 billion, and the Philippines was in the middle of its first deep payment crisis. Gregorio S. Licaros, Central Bank governer, asked Beplat to organize its very first IMF "standby" loan. He recalled the response:

> I knew trouble was coming because I had talked it over with the previous Central Bank governor. They had huge debts, and they were so low on cash they had to pledge all their gold to get a $20 million loan. Then Licaros took over. I knew him ever since he ran the Industrial Bank. He went to New

York and was unable to raise any money. "None of the banks even want to see me," he told me. It took me four months to raise $300 million. We got the IMF to pledge that it would not come down hard, and we got Caltex to delay payments for its oil shipments to the Philippines for a year. I was right in the middle. It really helped that I had been out there, knew all the players, and had confidence in the country.[48]

Because of Beplat's crusading role in organizing this loan, Marcos awarded him a "Golden Heart," the Philippines' highest decoration, in 1972. Marshall Green, former US ambassador to Indonesia and Richard Nixon's assistant secretary of state for the Far East, described Beplat as "the only banker I know who behaves like a statesman."[49] His efforts also established MHT as the Central Bank's lead bank. As the Philippines' director of external debt said, "We have a special relationship with MHT. . . . It started before 1970 when we experienced the exchange crisis; then we found out who our real friends were."[50] During Marcos's twenty-one-year rule, MHT raised more than $5 billion for the Central Bank, financing all fifteen of its annual Consolidated Foreign Borrower Programs (CFBPs).

One of MHT's first big Central Bank loans was a $50 million syndication in 1972. It came by way of Edmond Safra, the founder of Geneva's Trade Development Bank (TDB). Safra, a Lebanese-Brazilian private banker who had little lending experience at that point, got the nod to assemble the loan because Governor Licaros had all his private accounts at TDB.[51] MHT, TDB's main correspondent, had helped it go public, so Safra returned the favor.

To fund such loans, Beplat and his successors provided more than $2.4 billion in MHT loans. They also leaned on their old Japanese connections. Relations between Japan and the Philippines had been cool until the 1970s, but with the help of Beplat's diplomacy, the leading Japanese banks entered the Manila market aggressively. In the Central Bank's $465 million first consolidated foreign-borrowing program in 1978, led by MHT, the Bank of Tokyo contributed $62 million, compared with MHT's own $25 million. By 1986, the Bank of Tokyo, Daiwa, Fuji, Mitsubishi, and the other leading Japanese banks had loaned the Philippines Central Bank $775 million, while Japan's Overseas Export Credit Fund had added another $614 million. Together, MHT and "Japan Inc." funded almost all of the Philippine Central Bank's $6 billion debt which mostly ended up in private pockets.

In any case, the circle was now complete. Having saved the Japanese banks from dismemberment and then recruited them to become MHT's correspondents in Japan in the late 1940s, Beplat now persuaded them to finance his Philippine friends. In the 1970s and early 1980s, Japanese loans and investments in the Philippines surged. In addition to the Central Bank loans, from

1970 to 1986, Japanese lenders provided $4.7 billion to other Philippine gov-
ernment entities and $830 million to private companies. Another $1.4 billion
came by way of the ADB, where Japan had great influence. This lending was
not only due to Beplat's influence. At the time, Ferdinand Marcos looked like
a pretty safe bet. He had powerful US friends, the economy was growing fast
enough, and the country was viewed as a source of low-cost commodities,
labor, and durable goods orders. But it was Beplat who made many of the crucial introductions. For Marcos and his cronies, Beplat's friendship may have
been the real "Yamashita gold."

Given MHT's role, it is not surprising that Beplat became one of Ferdinand Marcos's closest personal advisors. Even after he retired from MHT in
1974, he continued to advise the president personally. Marcos's personal papers
contain many letters from Beplat about matters like elections and the economy.[52] Throughout the 1970s, he and his wife, as well as Harry Pangburne, the
head of MHT's Private Banking Department, were often invited to Imelda
Marcos's New York parties. When Imee Marcos attended Princeton in the
1970s, Beplat's real estate broker located a thirteen-acre farm for her, and
Beplat personally served as the property's trustee.[53] When other Marcos associates like José Campos and Fay Roa Jimenez, Imelda Marcos's personal secretary, an unindicted coconspirator in Imelda Marcos's 1989 New York trial,
sought to hide $80 million in deposits, MHT's Harry Pangburne helped
out.[54] MHT also made more than $112 million in government-guaranteed
loans to the private sector, especially to Eduardo Cojuangco's companies.
When the country got in trouble in the mid-1980s, it was MHT senior vice
president David Pflug who was handpicked by Marcos to chair the Advisory
Committee of Foreign Banks, in charge of restructuring the Philippines foreign debt.

The "Golden Heart" was not Beplat's only Asian award. In 1975, the
Emperor of Japan awarded him the "Order of the Sacred Treasure, Second
Class," Japan's highest honor for a foreigner, for "services to the Japanese
economy." Other recipients of this honor have included Paul Volcker and
Ronald Reagan. Daiwa Bank, one of the Japanese banks that lent most heavily to the Philippines, also made Beplat a director. He was also a member of
the Council of Foreign Relations from 1984 until his death in 1997.

In the course of his life, Tris Beplat thus had the unique opportunity to
participate in the radical transformations of two key Asian societies. These
transformations had profoundly different outcomes. In one case, a vanquished
foe was forced through a sweeping set of institutional reforms and ended up
with one of the world's most vigorous democratic capitalist economies. In the
other case, a collaborating elite was treated with kid gloves by its "ally," which
provided the country with record levels of foreign finance, military aid, and

technical advice about "economic development." That country wound up almost bankrupt and abysmally poor, with a weak, underskilled economy, an unstable democracy, rampant corruption, massive inequalities, capital flight, a huge parasitic foreign debt, and—ironically—the largest amount of *Japanese* loans, aid, and investments of any country in Asia.

THE BEST SYSTEM OF ALL

In the 1980s, the Philippines was often described—as US Treasury Secretary James Baker did in 1985 and World Bank President Barber Conable did again in 1989—as a "heavily indebted" country. In fact by most aggregate measures, the country's debt was not any heavier than that of its neighbors, and certainly much lighter than that of many Latin American countries.[55] Nor do the raw numbers indicate that the Philippines was too "dependent" on foreign finance, or that its overall investment rate was too low. From 1974 to 1982, it was comparable to Korea in both respects. The *efficiency* with which all this capital was used, however, was quite another matter—the Philippines's incremental capital-output ratio was twice as high as Korea's. As in many other countries, the real problem was not so much overborrowing per se, but the question of what was done with the money. As usual, there has been no rigorous audit of the debt. Our first exhibit concerns Beplat's favorite customer, the Philippine Central Bank, which accounted for more than a quarter of the Philippine foreign debt by the time Marcos left office.

It may seem surprising, but debt mismanagement was perhaps the one problem that banks like the IMF and the World Bank never expected to find in the Philippines. Indeed, until 1983, it was regarded as one of the world's *best* debt managers. In 1971, the Philippine Central Bank set up a statistical system to monitor public-sector debt, which the World Bank described as "the best in Asia" and adopted as a model for other countries.[56] It was the only country in the world with a legal limit on debt service—a maximum of twenty percent of export earnings. It was also one of the few that tried to control all private foreign borrowing. Under the CFBP, the Central Bank took charge of all foreign borrowing, arranging jumbo loans and dividing them up. By 1983, the Central Bank had borrowed $4.2 billion under this program, most of it through MHT.

There was also no shortage of technical experts to administer all these controls. President Marcos adored US-educated technocrats—six of his top ministers in the 1980s were Harvard graduates. Dr. Jaime C. Laya, Central Bank governor from 1981 to 1984, had a PhD in finance from Stanford. Cesar Virata, finance minister and prime minister, had a Wharton MBA. Roberto Ongpin, minister of industry and Jaime Ongpin's brother, Corazon Aquino's first finance minister, had a Harvard MBA, as did Placido Mapa Jr., planning minister and manager of the Philippine National Bank, the largest state-owned bank. Several of Marcos's top officials were also partners in the leading Manila accounting firm of SyCip, Gorres, Velayo (SGV & Co.). And even if all these experts and controls failed, the economy supposedly being monitored closely by the IMF's full-time resident advisor, Kamel Sieber, who had his own suite right inside the Central Bank. So what could possibly go wrong?

In June 1983, a team of bankers and economists from two leading New York banks felt compelled to travel twelve thousand miles to Manila. Late June is not the best time of year to visit. It is typhoon season, when pollution and traffic are more obnoxious than usual, and there is also the usual dangers of floods, earthquakes, and volcanic eruptions. But the bankers felt they had to ask the Philippine Central Bank a few tough questions. Paul H. Mayers, head of Chemical Bank's Asia/Middle East Division, and David L. Pflug, Beplat's successor as MHT's Asian point man, suggested the visit. By the spring of 1983, they sensed that an economic typhoon was brewing.

On the surface, the Marcos regime had not really fared too badly in the 1970s. Overall growth averaged six percent, while manufacturing grew at eight percent, investment at seven percent, and exports at ten percent, even though inflation stayed low. Out in the rice paddies, the US-funded "Green Revolution" boosted farm productivity by five percent a year. All this apparent "growth" had helped persuade the Philippines's foreign creditors to keep Marcos's balls in the air for more than a decade. In retrospect, however, this growth had a false bottom. Manufacturing growth took place behind high protectionist barriers, which yielded noncompetitive local firms, distorted prices, and, ironically enough, the continued dominance of foreign companies. The growth of exports was based on traditional raw commodities like sugar, coconuts, copper, and gold, as well as the overexploitation of tropical rain forests and fisheries. The growth in investment depended on a steady stream of foreign capital and loans. Export agriculture also depended heavily on a form of capital-and-fertilizer-intensive technology that was close to its natural limits. And the main beneficiaries of all this were just a handful of agro-industrialists who thrived on insider deals, government subsidies, and protected markets.

In the early 1980s, the shallowness of this strategy suddenly became clear under the pressure of external shocks. The 1979 oil shock added $750 million to the islands' energy bill, while rising world interest rates in 1980–82 boosted debt service by more than $250 million. The terms of trade for commodities like sugar and coconuts, which accounted for two-thirds of exports, fell by twenty-five percent. The 1982 debt crunch in Latin America also led First World banks to cut back on their loans to Asia. The US, Japan, and the UK—the Philippines's main markets—entered deep recessions all at once.

Korea, Taiwan, and Japan weathered this tough environment well and kept growing. But the Philippine economy fell apart. Under pressure from domestic interest groups to maintain a strong peso, low taxes and interest rates, the Central Bank borrowed heavily abroad, financing the peso's appreciation. That stimulated imports and capital flight, which consumed nearly half of all new foreign loans from 1976 to 1982. By one estimate, more than sixty percent of export earnings were parked offshore.[57] Jaime Ongpin summarized the situation well: "Every successful businessman, lawyer, accountant, doctor and dentist I know has some form of cash that he began to squirrel abroad after Marcos declared martial law and frightened every Filipino who had anything to lose."[58]

In 1982, the trade deficit and the government deficit both soared out of control. By early 1983, pressure on the peso was so strong that Ferdinand Marcos cynically ordered thousands of the ordinary Filipinos working abroad—mostly maids and construction workers—to repatriate half their earnings, on pain of losing their passports.[59] Meanwhile, his secret police organized the country's top five "Binondo black market" dealers into a cartel, forcing them to buy and sell dollars at rates that were dictated by the government. That created another $400 million arbitrage opportunity for his friends.[60]

Capital flight was fed by growing political uncertainty. In the aftermath of Benigno Aquino's 1977 imprisonment and the rigged 1978 National Assembly elections, journalists around the world began to call the Philippines the "Pacific powder keg."[61] In December 1980, a World Bank study concluded that Ferdinand Marcos's position was "precarious." Then, defying all warnings, in June 1981, Marcos awarded himself another six-year term with a commanding eighty-six percent of the "vote." He proclaimed the beginning of a "New Republic" and an end to martial law. But very few were fooled—the same martial law measures remained in effect. Throughout 1982, reports circulated that his health was failing, that he was losing control to Imelda Marcos and the generals, and that he was smuggling huge quantities of cash and gold abroad. There was also mounting repression in rural areas. By 1983, even his closest foreign allies, like the CIA's William J. Casey, were becoming concerned.

As early as January 1981, MHT had had trouble completing a $200 million syndicated loan for the Philippine Central Bank.[62] MHT's own exposure to the Philippines peaked at $650 million in June 1982 and then fell to $450 million by 1983. But it was reluctant to stop lending entirely for fear of precipitating a panic.[63] In January 1983, MHT assembled a $300 million loan for the Central Bank, its last "voluntary" syndication. As one senior MHT banker later recalled, that loan was very controversial within the bank: "Our share was only $20 million, but there were many heated arguments. Some bankers had dealt with these guys a long time; they kept saying the Philippines was different. We just didn't want that world to end."[64]

Other US banks soon began to curtail their Philippine credits. In April 1983, with the country's reserves almost gone, the government started secret talks with the IMF, seeking yet another standby loan. In late April 1983, Chemical Bank's Mayers suggested to "Gabby" Singson, the Central Bank's deputy director, that his two most trusted creditors should take a discrete look at the Central Bank's books to see if a debt rescheduling could be avoided. Singson passed the idea on to Dr. Jaime Laya, the Central Bank's governor, who agreed on the condition that only MHT and Chemical be involved. He felt they could be trusted, since they had both worked with the Central Bank for so long.

On June 20, 1983, three economists and two bankers from Chemical and MHT, including its chief economist, arrived at the Central Bank on a highly secretive mission. They found an IMF Country Mission already there. They also discovered that when they asked for information, they met stiff resistance. As one of the auditing team members later recalled, "We had to keep asking for certain tables." Eventually the bankers hauled out the ultimate weapon: "Look, we're your largest creditors. Show us the books or we'll pull all your credit lines. *Today.*"

It turns out that there was good reason for the lack of cooperation—"the best system in Asia" had a lot to hide.

One Central Bank secret became public in late 1983, in the wake of Benigno Aquino's "one-gun salute" assassination at Manila Airport on August 12. In September 1983, Jaime Laya and Prime Minister Virata met privately with bankers at the IMF Annual Meeting in Washington, DC. Dr. Laya startled them by blurting out that "we might have to think about a debt rescheduling." In October, Dr. Laya, Virata, and Imelda Marcos's brother, US ambassador Benjamin ("Kokoy") Romualdez, met the Advisory Committee of Banks in New York, and Dr. Laya announced that the Philippines was suspending debt service. He explained that the Aquino assassination had triggered a capital outflow of more than $1 billion, draining reserves. Surprisingly, the Advisory Committee gave Dr. Laya a standing ovation. They still had supreme confidence in Fedinand's technocrats.

Only three days later, the Advisory Committee's chairman got a tense phone call from the Central Bank. It seemed that Dr. Laya had made a little misstatement—the country's foreign reserves were not $1.4 billion, but less than $400 million. The Advisory Committee immediately dispatched a Morgan vice president and two other senior bankers to Manila to clear things up. One of them later recalled what they found:

I spent a week going through every one of the Central Bank's foreign
exchange contracts for the past year. I happened to notice one that went
unsettled way back in April, so we checked all the other contracts . . . and
then we knew—the Central Bank had been lying to us all year about its
reserves. [65]

As it turned out, in the fall of 1982, the Philippine Central Bank had started
inflating its foreign reserve estimates to cover up the growing crisis and com-
ply with IMF targets for reserve levels. Several schemes had been used. The
most important was that the Philippine National Bank's London office borrowed funds for one day at the end of each month and then secretly reloaned
them to the Central Bank. The average overstatement was $600 million. By
mid-1983, it exceeded $1 billion. So Dr. Laya had been lying—the "$1 billion
flight drain" really had been missing all year long.

The Morgan banker also discovered that the Philippine foreign debt was
not $18 billion, as widely assumed, but at least $24.6 billion. Despite all the
fancy debt measurement systems, the country had completely lost track of its
short-term foreign debt. Except for the numerical horseplay they induced,
the IMF's fancy economic planning targets had been completely meaning-
less. [66] At first, the visiting team of bankers kept the findings secret. They did-
n't want to upset the debt rescheduling talks, and, quite frankly, they were a
little nervous:

After all, we knew the IMF was going to be mad as hell. President Marcos
would be embarrassed, and heads were going to roll. And this was Manila.
So our imaginations worked overtime—I'd say there was actual physical fear.
The day we found out, we made plane reservations to go home—on separate planes. [67]

On November 1, 1983, this team met Pflug and Taylor in Manila, who flew
directly to see IMF managing director Jacques Delarosier in Washington, DC.
All of them were deeply embarrassed, especially Delarosier. After all, since the
1950s the IMF had maintained a closer relationship with the Philippines than
almost any other developing country, and Dr. Laya's inflated numbers had
undermined a very carefully crafted IMF "structural adjustment" program.
Delarosier immediately fired his resident expert, Kamel Sieber, and ordered his
own auditors to Manila. A week later, he met Pflug and Taylor at the first-class
lounge at Kennedy Airport. He told them his auditors had uncovered many
other distortions. The situation was unworkable; he was recalling his Country
Mission and delaying the disbursement of the $630 million standby loan,
pending a complete "independent" audit of the Philippine Central Bank.

Marcos's top officials didn't lose much stride, however. In January 1984,
Marcos appointed the scrupulous Dr. Laya to be minister of education and

chairman of PNB. His replacement at the Central Bank was Jose B. Fernandez, Jose Cojuangco's protègè, who was not only a close friend of both Marcos and Beplat, but also the majority owner of FEBTC, in which Chemical and Mitsui Bank both had minority interests. And who was chosen by the IMF to do the "independent" audit? None other than Dr. Laya's own accounting firm, SGV & Co.

The audit was finished in just a few weeks. It has never been released. A Central Bank spokesman said at the time that it "found all translations dealing with foreign exchange to be normal and legitimate." The IMF and the foreign banks accepted this whitewash and reopened their debt restructuring negotiations. In late November 1984, the banks, under Pflug's leadership, advanced the Marcos government another $925 million. This was added to the country's outstanding debt and immediately used to pay overdue interest.

Despite this diplomatic settlement, the episode left a lot of bad feelings. As one banker later recalled:

> In all our banks' boardrooms people had been saying, "The Philippine numbers may look bad, but Marcos has a first-rate team." Then it turned out that his team had been lying through its teeth. We felt let down. And it threw suspicion on everything. If the Central Bank was capable of doing that, what else might it do?[68]

Years later, PCGG investigators discovered that the Philippine Central Bank had indeed been highly versatile. For example, it secretly spent $200 million on pro-Marcos candidates for National Congress in the May 1984 elections, and it minted thirty-seven million fifty-centavo coins with the name of a Philippine eagle species intentionally misspelled so that it would immediately became a collectors' item for insiders.

There was also the little matter of the missing gold. In December 1982, the Central Bank's official gold reserves had been 1.9 million ounces; by the end of 1983, they were just 0.3 million ounces, a 50-ton difference that was worth at least $660 million.[69] Asked to explain this disparity in 1986, Central Bank officials explained that there had been some "routine" gold sales to make up for capital flight.[70] But why liquidate gold stocks at such a sensitive time rather than borrow against them? A few PCCG investigators noted the coincidence between the size of the "missing gold" and the reserves overstatement. They also found evidence of many rather unorthodox gold shipments:[71]

- In September 1983, a Korean Air flight bound for Zurich ran off the end of a Manila runway. The KAL pilot reported that the mishap occurred "because of the weight of the gold."

- In October 1983, a Boeing 707 was chartered to fly from Manila by way of Hong Kong and Karachi to Zurich, carrying "flowers." These were shipped under a diplomatic airway bill that prevented searches by customs authorities. The plane nearly crashed in the South China Sea, reportedly because it was overloaded with gold.
- On September 9, 1983, two weeks after Benigno Aquino's assassination, 247 four hundred-ounce gold bars, worth $39 million at the time, were secretly flown from Manila to London on a KLM cargo plane, and consigned for sale to Morgan Bank. The customs declaration stated falsely that the shipment was of "no commercial value." The proceeds were deposited at Morgan and Citicorp, then wired elsewhere.[72]
- In late 1985, the Central Bank sold 8.4 tons of gold and 8.2 tons of silver with help from Drexel Burnham, which deposited $94 million in the Bank's accounts at the New York Federal Reserve. In December 1985, three months before Marcos fell, these funds were disbursed to MHT, Citibank, Bankers Trust, Bank of Boston, First Chicago, Chase, Natwest, Morgan, and then on to Swiss and Luxembourgian banks.[73]

There were also many other reports of large-scale gold deals during this period.[74] One of the most interesting involved a US attorney, Richard Hirschfield, who had extensive discussions with Marcos in 1987 in Hawaii, under the guise of helping him buy arms. Hirschfield taped the discussions and later testified before Congress. On the tapes, Marcos said that he planned to retake the Philippines with an invasion financed by "plenty of Central Bank gold" that he had stashed away.[75] He claimed it had been resmelted to look like Japanese war gold, and that some had already been sold through Hong Kong. According to Hirschfield:

> Marcos tried to persuade us that he had enough money to mount the overthrow. He showed me a list of accounts at the Hong Kong branches of Citibank, BCCI, and California Overseas Bank. Because his assets were frozen by lawsuits, he had to live on "loans" from these accounts, which were officially controlled by other people. He showed me transfers involving millions of dollars—for example, payments to his Washington law firm by way of Citibank-Hong Kong.[76]

THE POISONING

By far, the most important discovery about the Central Bank's misbehavior, however, was actually made way back in June 1983, at the initial "friendly private audit" by the bankers from MHT and Chemical. Until now, its results have not been disclosed. This long-lasting secrecy is a tribute to the discretion

of these bankers, their bosses, and the US Federal Reserve and National Security Agency, all of which were fully informed of the audit's findings. One key
participant, one of the bankers who made the trip, later recalled what happened:

> We arrived in Manila on a sticky Monday in late June and went straight to
> the Central Bank. After a little arm twisting, I was escorted to a room where
> bookkeeping entries for all the Banks' loan receipts were kept. I don't think
> they realized what I was looking for, but since my bank, MHT, had handled
> most of the Central Bank's syndications I had a record of all our disburse-
> ments to the Central Bank, with the precise dates and amounts of the loans.
> You see, you couldn't get a complete picture with just one side of the story.
> You had to have both sides. And for that one week I had it.
>
> So I sat in a hot, little room at the Central Bank, added up what the
> Central Bank showed it had received from us on its books, and compared it
> with our disbursements.
>
> And nearly $5 billion was just not there! I mean, it had just not come
> into the country! It had been disbursed by us, but it was completely miss-
> ing from the Central Bank's books!
>
> It turned out that most of these loans had been disbursed to account
> numbers assigned to Philippine OBUs (offshore banking units) or other pri-
> vate companies. Apparently what happened was, the Central Bank gave
> MHT the account numbers, and we never questioned whether they were
> Central Bank accounts—we just wired the loans to them. And then they dis-
> appeared offshore.
>
> I realized this toward the end of the week, and it was a real shock. But
> by then I think that some people at the Central Bank must have guessed
> what I was on to. One banker I was with left that Friday, but I stayed over
> until Saturday morning. I was rushing to catch my plane, and I got this big
> breakfast in my hotel room, "courtesy of management." Fortunately, I only
> had time to grab a bite of toast. By the time I reached Tokyo I was sick, and
> then on the flight home I went into convulsions and spent three days in a
> Vancouver hospital recovering from what the doctors said was "an unknown
> toxin."
>
> When I got back, I wrote a thorough report about all this to my bosses
> at MHT. I also told the New York Fed and a friend at the NSC. But appar-
> ently they just kept it to themselves. So the Philippines is still servicing all
> those Central Bank loans.
>
> You see, I think there were just too many powerful interests involved
> for them to do anything about it. The US.government had supported Mar-
> cos, and banks like mine, we just wanted to get paid. But my bank did at
> least agree that I would never have to set foot in the Philippines again. . . .
>
> People wonder how Marcos made his money. I think this was one big
> way. Maybe in ten or twenty years they'll release my memos to the Federal
> Reserve, and you can write the whole story then. . . .[77]

When I first heard this banker's tale, I found it pretty incredible, although he had a very credible reputation in the New York banking industry and all his confirmable dates and travel plans checked out. But the gap in the Central Bank's books was tantalizingly difficult to confirm at first. Of the four other bankers who also went on this June 1983 trip, one refused to talk. A second confirmed many of the details, but claimed that he personally had lacked access to the loan disbursement records. A third erroneously recalled that his team had stumbled on to Dr. Laya's "missing reserves" scandal.[78]

But it was clear that something very important had turned up in Manila that week in June 1983. Just one week later, Harry Taylor, MHT's vice chairman and senior international lending officer, arrived to see President Marcos in person. There was also a sharp clash between IMF observer Sieber and Governor Laya at a meeting where a blackboard was broken. An officer from Chemical Bank on the trip briefed US ambassador Michael H. Armacost, and US Secretary of State George Schultz also paid a personal call on Marcos at the end of June.[79]

CONFIRMATION

Two years after I first heard this story, on a visit to Manila, I managed to obtain a Central Bank computer printout of all the Philippine foreign loans by borrower and lender, as of 1986. In 1987, the Central Bank had dumped this two thousand-page printout, the so-called "Jobo Report," on the National Congress, where it had since gathered dust. With help from friends like "Keo," however, I was able to identify most of the crony companies that had obtained Central Bank loans. The analysis strongly supported the banker's story.

In particular, the Jobo Report itemized more than $6 billion of Philippine government-guaranteed loans that had passed through Marcos's Central Bank and were later assumed by the Aquino government. These included $4.9 billion in syndicated loans that had been disbursed by MHT, as the Central Bank's agent. Of those, $4.2 billion had been lent under the Consolidated Foreign Borrower Program. There was also another $809 million in "Paris Club" export credits to private companies. Unfortunately, the Jobo Report only identified a few of the loan recipients by name. But the recipients of 796 loans, totalling $855 million, were listed. More than three-quarters of them—$624 million—went to companies that were controlled by Marcos and his closest associates.[80] For example:

• Benguet Mining Corporation, the country's largest mining company, received $43 million from the Central Bank. Sixty percent of Benguet was secretly owned by Imelda Marcos's brother, Romualdez.[81] Jaime Ongpin was Benguet's president for sixteen years. When the Marcos interest in Benguet became public in 1987, he committed suicide. Companies controlled by Romualdez also received $142.3 million, including $123 million by way of MHT and the Central Bank.

- Lucio C. Tan was one of Ferdinand Marcos's closest cronies, the Chairman of the later-sequestered Allied Banking Corporation, the Philippines's fourth largest bank, and a defendant in a fifty billion peso suit filed by the PCCG. Tan's companies received $51 million in MHT-Central Bank loans.
- Eduardo Cojuangco, Ferdinand Marcos Jr.'s godfather, the largest sugar landlord in the South, the head of Marcos's Coconut Authority, and Corazon Cojuangco's first cousin, owned companies that received $201 million, including $141.6 million from the Central Bank. Companies owned by his brother Ramon Cojuangco also received $30.9 million.
- Roberto Benedicto, Marcos's law school classmate and fraternity brother at the University of the Philippines, his 1965 campaign chairman, ambassador to Japan, and a signatory on Marcos's accounts at Credit Suisse, owned companies that received $42.9 million from the Central Bank, plus $705 million in other guaranteed loans.
- Companies belonging directly to Marcos or his family, like Security Bank and Trust, Erectors Inc., and Pamplona Redwood, received $83 million from the Central Bank and another $223 million from other government agencies. A bank run by Minister of Planning Placido Mapa Jr. received $51 million from the Central Bank. A satellite company run by Minister of Defense Juan Ponce Enrile received $29 million.
- Other members of the president's inner circle like Herminio Disini, Roberto Cuenca, Bienvinido Tantoco, Roberto Villafuerte, Hans Menzi, Enrique Zobel de Ayala, and Salvador Laurel received $93 million.
- Jose B. Fernandez, the Central Bank's governor, owned companies that received more than $180 million in government-assumed loans, including $12 million from the Central Bank. In 1981, his bank, FEBTC, also acquired eighty-seven percent of the Private Development Corporation of the Philippines (PDCP), which made loans to industry. PDCP's chairman was Roberto T. Villanueva, the first head of Corazon Aquino's industrial restructuring program. Its president was Vicente R. Jayme, Jaime Ongpin's successor as finance minister. On PDCP's board was John Gokongwei Jr., who owned CFC Corporation, Universal Robina, and Litton Mills. There was also Carlos Palanca Jr., chairman of Insular

Lumber, the Philippines's largest mahagony exporter and Lepanto Consolidated Mining, a leading copper producer. Another PDCP board member was Gerardo Sicat, Marcos's planning minister who later joined the World Bank. PDCP also had strong relations with creditors; for example, the ADB loaned it $86 million and the World Bank added $83 million. The Central Bank loaned $3.5 million, plus $9 million to FEBTC. The Central Bank loaned Gokongwei's CFC, Universal Robina, and Litton Mills $40.2 million. Lepanto received $12 million.

So in 1986, when President Corazon Aquino's economy ministers, Jose B. Fernandez, Jaime Ongpin, Vincente Jayme, and Roberto Villanueva sat down with the Philippines's foreign creditors to discuss how the government should deal with the bitter legacy of the huge Marcos foreign debt, they were not exactly disinterested parties.

All told, Philippine Central Bank documents show that Marcos and his cronies, including these Aquino officials, received at least $3.58 billion of identifiable government-swallowed foreign loans:

Companies Controlled by:

• Roberto Benedicto	$747.6 million
• Marcos family members	$726.5
• Roberto Cuenca	$676.9
• Herminio Disini	$258.4
• Eduardo Cojuangco	$201.2
• Jose B. Fernandez	$180.0
• Benjamin Romualdez	$150.4
• Manual Elizalde Jr.	$104.1
• Jose de Venecia	$71.4
• Lucio C. Tan	$51.8
• Placido Mapa Jr.	$50.6
• Ramon Cojuangco	$30.9
• Ricardo Silverio	$30.6
• Juan Ponce Enrile	$28.6
• Vicente Chiudian	$15.6
• Roberto Villafuerte	$15.2
• Bienvenido Tantoco	$6.0
• Salvador Laurel	$5.8
• Other Marcos allies:	$134.4
TOTAL:	$3.58 billion

Furthermore, this list omits many loans that couldn't be attributed to particular companies. This includes another *$3.5 billion* of Central Bank relending. For reasons that may now be clear, the Aquino government never really vigorously investigated these loans, or tried to recover them.

In March 1989, Dr. Laya was arrested in Miami by the FBI and charged in connection with the indictments of Ferdinand and Imelda Marcos by New York District Attorney Rudolph Giuliani on racketeering charges. But in July 1990, Ferdinand and Imelda Marcos were acquitted—in large measure simply because the jury thought the Philippine government should be prosecuting these people for their crimes, not the US. But senior officials in the post-Marcos government had no intention of trying their elite friends in the *ancien régime*. And the role of US and Swiss banks in all these shenanigans, as well as the loans that disappeared from the Central Bank in the accounts of Marcos and his cronies, were never even considered by the New York grand jury. The much larger racketeering case—involving the collusion that continues to this day among the Filipino elite, their foreign creditors, private bankers, and their allies in the US, Japanese, and other First World governments—has never been tried before any jury.

CITI'S PLAIN MANILA BANKING

Ferdinand and Imelda Marcos's bounty of pocketed funds did not all pass through intermediaries like Benedicto and the Central Bank. Some of it traveled much more directly. One disturbing example involved Citibank.

Citibank's Manila branch had been established at the turn of the century by the International Banking Corporation, which Citi acquired in 1921. By the end of World War II, it was the islands' largest domestic bank. Citibank's future chairman Walter Wriston served in the Philippines during World War II and got to know Marcos personally: "He was a real hero, I knew him there," Wriston later recalled. "One day these guys are heroes, the next day they're out."[82] Wriston's predecessor as Citibank's CEO, George Moore, also knew Marcos well. He had headed the Philippine-American Society in the late 1960s. By 1985, Citi's local bank in Manila had a $1.8 billion loan portfolio.

Unlike MHT, most of Citi-Manila's portfolio consisted of loans to the private sector. A notable exception involved the nuclear power plant on the Bataan Peninsula sixty miles west of Manila. This was an entirely US operation. Westinghouse was the prime contractor; Burns & Roe was the lead engineering firm; and the US EXIM Bank, Citibank, American Express, and MHT were the main financiers.

There were only a few problems. One problem was that the plant was so poorly designed that it soon became one of the Philippines's leading safety hazards and "debt elephants." It has also provided the occasion for several extraordinary payoffs. As noted, Westinghouse and the other contractors paid off one of Marcos's closest cronies to get the job and then overpriced it by several hundred million dollars, which made it one of the world's most expensive power plants at the time.

The other untold story about the plant involves its bankers. Arguably, this was more important than the hardware payoffs—after all, "no loans, no power plant." It had two parts. The first involved getting the US EXIM Bank to finance the plant with $277.2 million in public credits, plus a guarantee for a $256.6 million syndicated private bank loan and $90 million in interest. EXIM was accustomed to financing big-ticket exports for its influential corporate clients. In the 1970s, two-thirds of its credits went to just seven US companies: GE, Westinghouse, Boeing, Lockheed, McDonnell Douglas, Combustion Engineering, and AT&T. But the Bataan Nuclear Plant was its largest loan ever, consuming half its lending authority in 1975. Both the US Embassy and EXIM's staff had recommended against the deal on economic grounds.

In November 1975, the EXIM staff members were overruled by their boss, William J. Casey, after he visited President Marcos in Manila. A month later, Casey left EXIM to return to his law practice at Rogers and Wells in New York. In 1981, when he was appointed to head the CIA by President Reagan, Casey submitted a list of his Rogers & Wells clients to the US Senate. One of them turned out to be a San Francisco company that was owned by a Marcos front man, Herminio T. Disini.[83] Casey, his close friends, and his boss Ronald Reagan also had many other curious connections to the Marcos clan—many of which remain under tight wrap in US national security archives and the Reagan Presidential Library.

The other crucial piece of the Bataan financing story involved the project's syndication. The bank that became the syndicate's lead agent stood to collect a nice $2.3 million fee, in addition to interest. (In the mid-1970s, that was still considered a lot of money.) So when MHT's syndicators in London got wind of the deal in 1973, they dove for it. So did American Express Bank's Cordell Hull Jr., the son of a former secretary of state and a good friend of Casey's. As of 1975, Hull was certain that he had the Bataan deal in the bag. Then, as another banker who was deeply involved in the deal recalled, "Suddenly this guy from Citibank's London syndication unit swooped down, saw Disini, and just grabbed it." Two *New York Times* reporters later tracked down the Citibanker, and, according to them, he admitted paying off Disini. In February 1976, a thirty-bank syndicate, with Citibank as its agent and led by Citi,

American Express Bank, and MHT, made the loan. AEB and MHT each contributed $19 million, while Citi provided $16 million, for a return on a "deal equity" of more than 150 percent. Unfortunately, the *New York Times* never printed their own reporters' discoveries about this aspect of Citibank's involvement in the plant.[84]

This was by no means the only case of abusive Citibanking in the Philippines. For example, in the early 1980s, Citi's country manager was Rafael B. Buenaventura, whose brother Cesar ran Shell Oil's subsidiary and was also a member of Marcos's Monetary Board. In 1983, Citi-Manila suddenly switched its funding from its head office in New York to Manila's interbank market. This had two benefits. First, it reduced Citibank's share of new money assessments in the debt talks. Second, amazingly, the Philippines also became liable for part of Citi-Manila's own "foreign debt." One disgruntled Japanese banker recalled what happened:

> Somehow Citibank saw that 1983 rescheduling coming—the Monetary Board probably got advance warning of the repayment freeze. So Citi started borrowing heavily from offshore banking units like Bank of Tokyo's. We just said to ourselves "Citibank risk!" and loaned them whatever they asked. Then the Philippines froze payments, and we turned to Citi-New York for repayment. They said, "Sorry, boys—Philippine risk!" We're talking about $500 million. Nice day's work![85]

After Marcos tumbled, responsibility for private-sector debts like this one became a key issue in the country's debt negotiations. In October 1986, John Reed, Citibank's chairman at the time, addressed the American Chamber of Commerce in the Philippines in Manila and warned the Aquino government baldly: "If you repudiate your debts, it will cause you *immense* suffering."[86]

Evidently Corazon Aquino got the message: Her 1987 rescheduling agreement with the banks provided that $34 million of Citi-Manila's debt to itself (Citibank-New York) was assumed by the Philippines. She also assumed about $30 million of Central Bank loans to the Bank of the Philippine Islands, which was twenty-percent owned by JPMorgan, plus $210 million of debts borrowed by Central Bank governor Fernandez's own FEBTC Bank, one-quarter owned by Chemical and Mitsui.[87] So here we have the ultimate role reversal in the Third World debt story—for purposes of this bailout, Citibank, JPMorgan, Chemical, and Mitsui all became "debtor countries."

CREDIT SUISSE'S BITTER PILL

Yet another inside job involved Credit Suisse-First Boston (CSFB). In June 1981, CSFB syndicated a $17 million loan to Asia Reliability Co. Inc.

(ARCI), a company created in 1980 and owned by several Marcos front organizations, including Imelda Marcos's Ministry of Human Settlements. ARCI also got $8 million from Security Bank and Trust, a Hong Kong bank secretly owned by President Marcos.[88] Both loans were guaranteed by Philex, a Philippine government agency, at the request of Jose C. ("Jolie") Benitez, the minister of human settlements who was close to Imelda Marcos (he was having lunch with her the day Benigno Aquino was shot).[89]

Unfortunately, only about $7 million of these loans ever made it to the Philippines. ARCI used $18 million to buy shares in three Silicon Valley companies whose stockholders were Marcos cronies.[90] Moreover, according to Philippine officials, Credit Suisse-First Boston officers were told in advance by ARCI that this was precisely what it had planned to do with the loans all along. They were warned to keep quiet "because it will upset our plans."[91] Not surprisingly, the California investment funds soon vanished.

Nonetheless, in 1986, Credit Suisse-First Boston shamelessly demanded—with the full support of the Advisory Committee of Foreign Banks—that the Philippines honor all these bogus ARCI loans. At first, the Philippines resisted, arguing that CFSB had "unclean hands" because its officers had known all along that the money would be diverted to California and elsewhere. The negotiation over the ARCI loans became, in the words of MHT's Pflug, "my biggest headache"—it help up a debt restructuring agreement for months.[92] But the banks stuck together, and eventually the Philippines relented. The country was desperate to restore trade credits, which had been on hold since October 1983. As debt negotiator Cesar Virata admitted, "We decided to swallow this bitter pill."[93]

This was only one of several such deals that Credit Suisse had with the Marcos clan. In June 1981, it arranged a $50 million standby facility for Landoil Resources, an oil company that was owned by Ferdinand Marcos, Minister of Trade Roberto Villafuerte, and several other cronies. The company's subsidiaries also received $40 million in loans that were later assumed by Aquino.[94] After Marcos was ousted and his bank records were seized, it became clearer why CSFB had been so friendly. The records revealed a string of transactions with Credit Suisse's Private Banking Department that dated back at least to 1968:

- In March 1968, Ferdinand and Imelda Marcos opened their first four Swiss accounts at Credit Suisse's Zurich branch under the names "William Saunders" and "Jane Ryan," with a deposit of $950,000. The accounts were opened by Credit Suisse director C. Walter Fessler.[95]
- In 1970, these two accounts were closed and the deposits were transferred to two Credit Suisse accounts in the name of a Liechtenstein *stiftung* (foundation). Marcos instructed the bank that "In the event we

would wish to make withdrawals, we will send you a cable with the words 'happy birthday' . . . then you will cause your Hong Kong representative to visit us personally in Manila."

- By 1986, Marcos had set up at least seventeen Liechtenstein *stiftungen* (foundations for the benefit of family members), which, in turn, owned multiple accounts at Credit Suisse. Marcos also controlled four accounts at Credit Suisse's Bahamas subsidiary. As of 1983, the deposits in seven identified Credit Suisse accounts totaled $263.5 million. Credit Suisse only relinquished control over these deposits in 1998.

BEYOND "PEOPLE POWER"

When Corazon Aquino picked up the reigns of power from Ferdinand Marcos in February 1986, many foreign and domestic bankers were a bit nervous about her "People Power" movement. She appeared to be naive and inexperienced, a mild-mannered rich girl and the devout graduate of a Catholic convent who had never even learned to drive a car. She probably would have remained a career housewife forever, if not for the bravery of Benigno Aquino, her husband, and Imelda Marcos's superstitious belief that if Benigno Aquino ever again set foot in the Philippines, her husband's regime would topple. Of course it did anyway, despite his being assassinated as he was descending to the tarmac at Manila Airport—a crime that remains unsolved.

Many feared that Corazon Aquino might soon go the same way. After all, she was flanked on her right by army thugs who were still loyal to Marcos, and on her left by leftist and Islamic insurgencies that were still active in sixty of the country's seventy provinces. She'd also inherited an economy in a deep recession, and a debt that consumed two-fifths of export earnings.[96] Furthermore, relative to the country's size, Marcos had left behind more dirty debt than any other country, except perhaps Argentina under its military junta. And then, after lending more than $1 billion net on average to Marcos and Co. every year of martial law from 1972–86, the foreign banks reduced their new lending to Corazon Aquino to a crawl. In 1986, for example, the Philippines paid out $2.3 billion in interest and amortization and received just $1.3 billion in loans and aid, for a net transfer of −$1 billion. Indeed, during the whole post-Marcos period from 1986–2003, these net transfers have averaged more than −$2 billion a year.[97] Especially given the banks' stinginess, and their long-time involvement with Marcos, there was enormous popular pressure on Corazon Aquino to repudiate this dirty debt entirely. Contrary to the bankers' worst fears, she declared on May Day 1986 that "We will honor all debts . . . as a matter of honor"—even before Citibank CEO John Reed's stern warning about the Philippines honoring its foreign debt that October. Indeed, over the next

decade, the Philippines signed two debt reschedulings and two more IMF letters of intent, its nineteenth and twentieth in twenty-five years. It also paid its
interest bills religiously. Her government and those of her successors, Fidel
Ramos (1992–98), Joseph Estrada (1998–2001), and Gloria Macapagal-
Arroyo (2001–), also embarked on liberalization programa that were as far-
reaching as any outside Pinochet's Chile and the PRI's Mexico. Import quotas were lifted, tariffs were slashed, interest and exchange rates were liberated,
more than two hundred state enterprises and other concessions were privatized, a generous debt-equity swap program was adopted, marginal tax rates
were reduced on higher income taxpayers, marketing monopolies for coconuts and other commodities were abolished, and government spending was
reduced—although not its deficits.

The aim of all this, in the words of Aquino's trade minister, Jose Con-
cepcion, was to become a "newly industrialized country by the year 2000."
That target date soon proved to be a little optimistic, but free-market zealots
at the IMF, the World Bank and private banks could hardly have wished for
more. In the wake of their disastrous cofinancing of the Marcos dictatorship,
they were relieved to be off the hook for the costs of financing the new
democracy. The US, Japan, the World Bank, and the ADB did promise to
restore foreign aid and loans to levels rivalling the peak years of Marcos's rule.
For a while they did, and foreign investment also picked up. Coca-Cola
started building its largest plant in the world in Luzon. During 1988–89, the
economy grew at more than six percent a year, as it recovered from the Marcos trough. By 1989, World Bank president Barber Conable was already
describing the Philippines as "by far the best performer of the seventeen
heavily indebted countries."

But this celebration turned out to be premature. Obviously things might
have turned out worse: Ferdinand Marcos might have lived longer, or one of
his coup attempts might have succeeded, plunging the country into civil war.
Corazon Aquino miraculously survived six coup attempts from 1986 to 1992,
including several that were directed from Marco's hangout in Hawaii. Beyond
that, however, the post-Marcos "Yellow Revolution" turned out to be almost
as overrated as the PCGG's Marcos treasure hunt.

By 1991, the recovery had run out of steam: Real per capita incomes
grew at less than one percent a year from 1991 to 2003, and real incomes for
the vast majority failed to grow at all. This was partly due to unforeseen factors like bad weather, earthquakes, floods, volcanoes, the 1997–98 Asian financial crisis, terrorism, President Estrada's corruption scandals in the late 1990s,
and the fact that from 1992 on, the US, the World Bank, the ADB and private banks, were much less generous than they had been with Marcos.

But it was also due to the country's unreconstructed political economy. Economic liberalization had very mixed blessings. While the Philippines did attract more than $15 billion in foreign direct investment in the 1990s, it also paid out more than $67 billion in debt service. Its experiments with privatization in the power sector proved to be a disaster, aggravating the acute power outages that began to appear in the early 1990s. The benefits of the post-Marcos reforms were also concentrated in a few hands. And the bulk of the population—still dependent on employment in agriculture, low-skilled industrial and service jobs, or overseas employment as maids and construction workers—was rewarded for their struggle against the Marcos dictatorship with power outages, environmental degradation, continuing corruption and insider deals, increased poverty, and mounting social violence. Meanwhile, population growth continued at 2.6 percent a year, one of Asia's highest rates, spurred on by ignorance of birth control methods, Catholicism, and the lowest levels of family planning and contraception in South Asia. By 2025, the Philippines will have more than 125 million people—more than Japan.[98] It could have used MacArthur's Japanese reforms.

To achieve the sustained high growth needed to provide for all these people in an increasingly competitive global economy, many development critics believe that the Philippines must undertake much deeper institutional reforms than its antiquated social structure has so far permitted, and to focus more heavily on agriculture. It would finally have to face up to many of the structural problems that General MacArthur and his staff tackled so successfully in Japan and Korea, but utterly failed to address in the Philippines. Among the key problems that still cry out for solutions are the incompetence and interest-ridden character of the Philippine state, the continuing dependence on foreign debt, and landlessness. As the World Bank's staff stated candidly in a confidential Philippines Country Report:

> The remaining problems go beyond the simple removal of controls and policies that distort factor and commodity prices, or dismantling of inefficient or restrictive government entities. The task before the government is one of reforming basic institutions and structures and tackling fundamental problems, some of which have plagued the growth process for decades.[99]

THE VAMPIRE STATE

Compared with other "Asian tigers" like Korea, Indonesia, Malaysia, and Taiwan, the administrative apparatus of the Philippines state is hopelessly slow and inept. The PCGG's miserable performance is unfortunately typical. One

crucial imperative is simply the ability to enforce the law, developing an efficient, independent judiciary and police force that are not for sale to the highest bidders. These institutions, in turn, would then be better able to protect
private and public property rights, outlaw private armies, and prevent officials
from stealing elections and dipping into the till.

The state's administrative ineptitude is intimately connected to the debt
problem. In the 1990s, one key reason why the Philippines foreign debt continued to grow was the government's inability to collect taxes. It has long
boasted the highest rate of tax evasion in Asia. This problem has also been
compounded by an extraordinary number of tax concessions, which have
precipitated a "race to the bottom" between the Philippines and other Asian
countries competing for foreign investment. The Philippines now has the
lowest tax yield per dollar of national income in Asia, twenty to fifty percent
below the average yields of the "Asian tigers." This belies the simple-minded
"supply-sider" notions of a negative relationship between tax yields and economic development; all of these higher-tax countries have substantially out-
performed the Philippines over the last thirty years. Financing the public
deficit—including the huge interest bill for the public foreign debt—was a
key source of the Philippines's debt troubles; if it had simply achieved the
same average tax yield as, say, Indonesia during this period, the Philippines
debt burden would have been cut by more than half.

This problem of tax administration was compounded by twenty-one
years of dictatorship and a parade of corrupt administrations, most recently
that of President Estrada. By now, tax resistance is deeply engrained in Filipino attitudes. No one expects to go to jail for tax evasion—the fifteen tax
amnesties attempted in the last thirty years have basically been ignored by taxpayers. Tougher tax enforcement also faces enormous political opposition, not
only from the elites, but also from many professional and white-collar workers who have gotten used to skirting taxes. In 1996, when President Fidel
Ramos briefly succeeded in boosting tax collections, his approval rating fell
even lower than those of Marcos in 1986.[100] In 2001, less than sixty percent
of those who were supposed to file income tax returns did so, and businesses
evaded up to forty percent of VAT taxes. All told, the government's annual
losses to evasion now average $5–8 billion—two-thirds more than its entire
budget deficit.[101] As for the Marcos family, as of 2003, they had still not paid
their own substantial tax arrears in an "ill-gotten gains" case where the final
court ruling was issued in 1999.[102] Lucio Tan and other key Marcos cronies
are also facing huge unpaid tax liabilities. This kind of impunity, on top of
decades of mismanagement and corruption, has produced an "ethical deficit"
that conventional neoliberal "reforms" have no way of handling.

DIRTY DEBT

A second basic structural need is to reduce the country's dependence on foreign debt, in order to clear the way for faster sustained growth.[103] Immediately after Marcos fell, one might have thought that it would have been easy for the Philippines to have implemented a selective "dirty debt" repudiation, singling out clear abuses like the Bataan Plant and the Central Bank loans. If Aquino and her successors had also backed that up with domestic reforms and tighter tax enforcement, they might have won international support. Indeed, the overall supply of capital available from abroad might actually have increased, even without more bank loans.

But all this assumed that Marcos's successors and their economic advisors were willing to carry out such an anti-debt program. Like tax enforcement, this has also proved to be impossible. One basic obstacle is that many of these advisors have been close allies of foreign and domestic banking interests. Among Corazon Aquino's worst pro-bank Marcos holdovers were Jose B. Fernandez, Cesar Virata, Ongpin, Villanueva and Vicente Jayme, as well as Fernandez's special assistant and two deputy governors at the Central Bank. She also employed a large contingent of ex-Citibankers, including her Finance Ministry's undersecretary and the chairman of the land bank. Aquino's naive notion was that since these people were from the industry, they must know how to manage the debt. But many of these elite bankers had strong *personal* reasons for honoring the Philippines foreign debt competely, and were also not likely to fight for land or tax reform. Debt repudiation, therefore, was never really seriously considered; instead, Aquino's ministers went off to New York with unlimited discretion to negotiate what turned out to be a very lenient debt restructuring. By 1992, weak-kneed Corazon Aquino had become so unpopular that even Imelda Marcos commanded a larger following in the polls.

The same pro-banker traditions continued throughout the 1990s. The latest example is that of the accidental "People Power 2" administration of Gloria Macapagal-Arroyo was President Estrada's former vice president, who took power in 2001 when he was forced from office on corruption charges. Gloria Macapagal-Arroyo was the daughter of an *illustrado* (elite) family, a PhD economist who attended Georgetown University with Bill Clinton in the 1960s, and became a self-confessed neoliberal admirer of Margaret Thatcher. Her father, Diosdado Macapagal, had also been a key US ally in the early 1960s, winning the presidency with the help of CIA funding in 1962. Her husband, Miguel Arroyo, is a wealthy lawyer, landowner, and businessman from another prominent Filipino family.

Gloria Macapagal-Arroyo, like Corazon Aquino, appeared to have an opportunity to build on the broad coalition that had supported Estrada's ouster and tackle her country's long-standing structural problems. Instead, she surrounded herself with fellow members of the Philippine elite:

- Gloria Macapagal-Arroyo's Central Bank governor was none other than Raphael Buenaventura, who had worked at Citibank from 1965 until 1989, serving as the CEO of Citibank Philippines from 1982 to 1985, and Citibank's senior vice president and division executive for Southern Europe from 1985 to 1989. After Citibank, he returned to the Philippines to become the CEO of the Philippine Commercial International Bank (PCIB)—the Philippines's third largest bank, and the modern-day successor to the Cojuangco's PCB that Tris Beplat first called on in 1950. In December 2000, PCIB's president George Go resigned and fled to Hong Kong, after it was revealed that PCIB had established secret accounts that held up to 3.3 billion pesos ($60 million dollars) in bribes allegedly collected by President Estrada.[104]
- Gloria Macapagal-Arroyo's secretary of trade was Manuel A. Roxas II—a Wharton graduate; a veteran of Dr. Laya's and Ongpin's SGV & Co. accounting firm and New York's investment bank Allen & Co., an heir to the Araneta family fortune by way of his mother, Judy Araneta-Roxas, the son of former Senate President Gerardo Roxas, and the grandson of the country's first president, the Japanese collaborator who had been resurrected by MacArthur in 1946.
- Gloria Macapagal-Arroyo's secretary of finance—the equivalent of treasury secretary—was Jose I. Camacho. From 1999 until his appointment in early 2001, he had been managing director of Deutsche Bank in the Philippines, and before that, the head of all South Asia Investment Banking for Bankers Trust (which was acquired by DB in 1999).[105]
- Gloria Macapagal-Arroyo's first secretary of agrarian reform was Hernani "Nani" Braganza, a former congressman who knew little about land reform, but happened to be the nephew of former President Fidel Ramos. He accomplished little other than antagonizing most peasant groups, and in January 2003, moved over to become Gloria Macapagal-Arroyo's fifth press secretary.

LANDLESSNESS

Of course the other major unresolved problem in the Philippines is land ownership. Every Philippine president since Magsaysay in the early 1950s (under guerilla pressure) has made bold promises about land reform that were later broken. When Marcos declared martial law in 1972, his very first promise was that land reform would become the "cornerstone of our new society." He hired Ray Prosterman, an Oregon University law professor who had designed land tenure programs for the CIA and the US State Department in South Vietnam (1969), Egypt (1970s), and El Salvador (1980). The result was no more successful than these other "partial" land reforms. By the time Marcos left office, only 50,000–70,000 hectares had been redistributed to small farmers, out of 10.3 million hectares of private arable land and 17 million hectares of public land.[106]

Unfortunately President Aquino was not much more successful. In 1986, she also promised that land reform would be the centerpiece of a "genuine economic revolution," and renewed a long-standing commitment by her own family, the Cojuangcos, to make its own 6,431-hectare Hacienda Luisita in Tarlac—the country's largest sugar plantation—"a model of reform." Like Marcos, Aquino hired Ray Prosterman. In 1988, she signed a law that created the "Comprehensive Agrarian Reform Program (CARP), " which subsumed all of Marcos's earlier programs.

Unfortunately, Corazon Aquino's new law was watered down by the landlord-dominated Congress. By the end of Corazon Aquino's first term in 1992, the amount of true land reform was very limited. Her land reform administrators claimed to have transferred nearly a million hectares from 1988 to 1992. But half of this came from less-productive public lands, and less than two percent of it was compulsory. In fact, many landlords seized the chance to sell less-desirable land to the government at inflated valuations. Corazon Aquino's own Agrarian Reform secretary was fired for taking advantage of this loophole.

In other cases, such as Corazon Aquino's own Hacienda Luisita, fancy stock ownerhip schemes and lease-back arrangements left the same big landholders and their families in control. None of the large private holdings, like Eduardo Cojuangco's 4,000-hectare orchard in Negros Occidental his many other holdings on Tarlac, Palawan, Agusan del Sur, Bukidnon and Davao del Sur, Marcos crony Don Antonio Florirendo's 5,212-hectare banana plantation, the huge holdings of former Agricultural Secretary Roberto, or, for that matter, Corazon Aquino's Luisita, were touched. Instead, CARP became a kind of stalking horse for the World Bank's new "market-oriented" approach to land reform.[107] This approach borrowed freely from land reform's romantic rhetoric, like giving "land to the tiller." But what it really boiled down to was a combination of (1) privatizing state land holdings, (2) actually cutting back on the government's budget for private land reform, (3) prolonging the process by making it subject to endless legal challenges, (4) perfecting land titles and the market for real estate, and (5) encouraging voluntary sales of low-valued land that landlords no longer wanted.

Corazon Aquino's revolution proved to be "yellow" indeed. She was no more willing to betray her class by undertaking true, compulsory land redistribution, along the lines followed in Japan, Korea, and Taiwan, than she had been willing to repudiate the foreign debt or clamp down on tax evasion. And all these social problems were joined at the hip—given the debt problem and the tax collection problem, as Corazon Aquino lamented, "We just don't have the money for land compensation."[108]

In 1992, Corazon Aquino's successor, Fidel Ramos, appointed a more serious land reform advocate, Ernesto Garilao, and for a while the program accelerated. However, by the time Estrada succeeded Ramos in 1998, CARP's accomplishments were limited. By then, according to the government, some 4.6 million hectares had been "transferred"—less than half the 10 million-hectare target that had been set for CARP back in 1998. And even these figures were overstated: They included the number of land certifications processed by the government, rather than the actual amount of land received by new owners. Of the total land that was purported to have been redistributed, 2.9 million hectares came from less-valuable public lands. Almost all of the 1.4 million hectares of private land included in the total had been transferred or sold voluntarily. Only four percent was acquired by compulsory purchase.

Thus, the program really didn't touch the most valuable holdings. As of 1998, forty-three percent of all fifteen million Filipino families had at least one member working in agriculture. Of those, sixty-eight percent—four million families and twenty-one million people—still did not own any land other than their own residences (if that), and less than three percent of these farm families had received any land from CARP.[109]

Not only has little progress been made since Corazon Aquino displaced Ferdinand Marcos; there may well have been no progress in the last hundred years. Farm ownership remains highly skewed, but no one is quite sure precisely how much, because land ownership surveys are riddled with errors and many holdings are owned by offshore corporations. However, according to one expert witness, in 1898, when the US first invaded the Philippines, the top 0.8 percent of the Philippine population owned 35 percent of all private agricultural land. By 1998, CARP's tenth anniversary, the top 0.54 percent's share of private land had increased to 48 percent.[110] Today, the best estimate is that more than eighty percent of arable land is owned by just twenty percent of all farms, with the top three percent of farms 10 hectares and larger accounting for thirty percent of arable land, and 5.4 million hectares of forest controlled by just 147 people.

Furthermore, at the very top, the large plantations are still run by the same families that ran them at the end of World War II—the Cojuangcos, Aranetas, Lopezes, Zobel del Ayalas, Laurels, Arroyos, Yulos, Gregorios, Sys, Tys, Sorianos, Sebastians, and Vilars, plus a few Marcos *nouveaus* like Floriendo, Tan, and Enrile, and foreign investors like Guthrie, Firestone, Del Monte, Castle & Cooke, and Sumitomo. At the bottom of the pile are four million landless families—twenty-one million of the country's poorest people, including seventy percent of rural workers, two-thirds of whose families earn less than $150 per month.

Nor did the Philippine's performance on land reform improve under President Joseph Estrada or his successor, Gloria Macapagal-Arroyo. CARP got another six-year extension, but it was on its last legs. The average land transfers in 1999–2002 fell by more than fifty percent, compared with the Ramos admnistration, and under Gloria Macapagal-Arroyo's new administrator Braganza, they hit the lowest level since Marcos. Transfers of public land and voluntary dispositions accounted for more than eighty-five percent of the total. Meanwhile, big landlords like the Cojuangcos, Floriendo, Corazon Aquino, and Gloria Macapagal-Arroyo's husband maintained their positions. As of July 2002, only 3.4 million of the Philippines's 15.9 million families owned land other than their own residences, and of these, only 380,000 families, 2.4 percent of the total, had acquired any of this land through the Philippine government's fifty-three-year-old "land reform" program.[111]

So, after all these years, is there still any hope for genuine, redistributive land reform in the Philippines? Interestingly, the issue is no longer a technical one. After decades of criticizing land reform strategies, even mainstream economists have started to recognize that asset transfers in general, and redistributive land reforms in particular, can have huge social value. First, even on the grounds of economic efficiency, under conditions of capital shortage and surplus labor, farm productivity tends to be inversely proportionate to farm size; in other words, contrary to the traditional defenders of large plantations, small plots can be very efficient, so long as they are supported by market infrastructure and the enforcement of small-owner property rights.[112] Second, as even the World Bank admitted in the late 1980s, "A genuine, widespread land reform could do much to alleviate poverty" by raising the incomes of rural families, usually the poorest in developing countries.[113] Third, it is also now recognized that landlessness has many harmful side effects. It conspires with poverty and ignorance to keep population growth high. And that, in turn, aggravates the land shortage—a vicious cycle. Without private savings, land, or social security programs, large families are one of the few ways that rural workers can provide for their old age—assuming their children support them. The low incomes associated with landlessness also stifle the development of strong domestic markets. By increasing rural incomes, on the other hand, land reform can stimulate both consumption and investments in education and housing.

As in Brazil extreme landlessness also aggravates environmental problems, especially deforestation. Of the seventeen million hectares of public forests in the Philippines, ten million have already been denuded—half by low-intensity agriculture. This starts with the excessive logging of "unclaimed" virgin forest, often for timber exports. It continues with the occupation of logged lands by *kaingineros* (poor families who move in to do slash-and-burn farming), just as in the Amazon, Indonesia, and many parts of Africa. In the 1950s, there were still more than ten million hectares of virgin rain forest in the Philippines; today there are less than a million. Timber exports were supposed to be banned in 1986, but the ban was widely flaunted by Japanese companies and their local contract loggers, many of whom deal with the kaingineros This has also produced massive erosion, endangering coral reefs and coastal fishing.[114] At current reforestation rates, even if overlogging were halted today, it would take a century to replenish the deforested acres.

Yet another harmful side effect of landlessness is the fact that it reduces tenant farmers' incentives to invest in agricultural productivity. Their lack of collateral makes it hard for them to borrow from banks, so they often have to rely on informal moneylenders, who often charge interest rates of one hundred percent or more. There are also the political consequences of "deep" land reform. The anomalous persistence of active insurgencies in the Philippines is due in no small part to landlessness, and the rural poverty and political instability that it engenders.

There are those who argue that land reform would interfere with "free markets." But for decades, large-scale plantations in the Philippines received enormous amounts of government subsidies and low-interest loans, reflecting the political power of the landed elites and their US allies. Most of the proceeds were spent on irrigation systems, imported pesticides, machinery, fertilizer, rural power projects, ports, roads, and aquaculture projects that mainly benefitted the plantations owned by the top fifty agro-industrialists. For example, the foreign-owned Guthrie Plantations received $31 million from Marcos to finance irrigation, plus 40,550 hectares of confiscated land in Agusan del Sur—a case of "negative" land reform. Half of the World Bank's $2.1 billion in Philippine loans from 1965 to 1986 were used to finance eight large irrigation projects, and more than half of the ADB's $2 billion in Philippine loans went to similar projects.

Of course, "deep" land reform alone is no panacea. To succeed, it needs to be implemented quickly, in contrast to the long, drawn-out approach usually taken in the Philippines, a full-employment program for real estate lawyers. It also needs to be supplemented by technical support and investments in soil conservation, storage, roads, and reforestation. For example, it still costs more to deliver yellow corn to Manila from the island of Mindanao than from Houston, Texas—just one indication of how inefficient the Philippine rural delivery system is.

So there is much useful work for technically oriented development organizations like the World Bank to do. But their natural tendency is to attack such problems piecemeal, without recognizing that they are only satellites in the overall political economy. The prospects for serious land reform in the Philippines, as elsewhere, have never really depended on purely abstract economic arguments. Rather, they depend on the actual balance of social forces on the ground. And, apart from a few thousand rebels in the bush, today those forces are stongly aligned behind the preservation of the status quo.

So how does the US now feel about land reform, five decades after General MacArthur, Tris Beplat, and W. I. Ladejinsky missed their chance to create another Japan, Taiwan, or South Korea? As one senior economist at the US Embassy in Manila commented, "Yeah, formally, of course we're still behind it. But frankly we're not sure the government here is up to it—it has very high political costs. And it may be too late now, anyway. Fifty years ago, maybe. But now, you've just got so many people. . . ."

THE LEGACY

Today, nearly two decades after Marcos caught his last flight to Hawaii, the Philippines's democratic trajectory and its economic basis are in deep trouble. The country is still battling all of the same old deep-rooted social problems: debt, tax evasion, landlessness, crime, child labor, sexual exploitation, militarism, and violations of basic human rights. Corruption is still a national sport, if a little more decentralized than it was under Marcos. In January 2001, Joseph Estrada, yet another kleptomaniacal president, had to be removed from office, although his peculations were trivial compared with Ferdinand Marcos'. At least Estrada went off to jail quietly without murdering thousands of political opponents.[115]

Meanwhile, except for its patriarch, the Marcos clan has experienced something of a comeback. Ferdinand Marcos died of a heart attack in Hawaii in September 1989. With the help of US defense attorney Gerry Spence, Imelda Marcos was acquitted in 1990 after a three-month criminal trial in New York. Apparently the jury bought her story that Ferdinand Marcos alone was responsible for all the stealing and repression. Imelda Marcos, her son Ferdinand Marcos Jr., and her two daughters Imee Marcos-Manotoc and Irene Araneta-Marcos, as well as Eduardo Cojuangco, Roberto Benedicto, and other leading cronies, were permitted to return home in the early 1990s, and they have used their wealth to regain substantial political and economic power. In 1998, Imelda Marcos was convicted and sentenced to twelve years in another criminal case in Manila, but that verdict was overturned on technical grounds in October 1998 by the ever-scrupulous Philippines Supreme Court. In May 1999, Imelda Marcos was received warmly by President Estrada at Malacanang Palace, where she received an award as one of the Philippines's "Twelve Outstanding Mothers."

Imelda Marcos still faces numerous criminal and civil lawsuits, and her friend Estrada is gone. But she is determined to clear her name and have Ferdinand Marcos's cryogenically preserved body interred with full honors in Manila's Heroes Cemetery. Until then, it rests at Marcos's ancestral mansion in the province of Illocos Norte, where Ferdinand Marcos Jr. was elected governor in 1998. Imee Marcos-Manotoc, Imelda Marcos's oldest daughter, was elected to represent Illocos Norte in Congress, where she joined Corazon Aquino's son Benigno Aquino III, and Juan Ponce Enrile Jr., the son of Senator Juan Ponce Enrile—Marcos's family lawyer, former defense minister, and Estrada's staunch defender. In September 2001, the schoolchildren in Ilocos Norte celebrated the twenty-second anniversary of Marcos's death by compiling pictures of him and collecting stories from their grandparents on his "greatness," which they presented as a gift to Imelda Marcos. In 2002, she reportedly received a $40 million cash settlement for her equity in just one of more than two dozen crony companies.[116] As of 2003, however, she still claims that she has no money to pay the 9,539 human rights victims who won a $1.97 billion judgment against Ferdinand Marcos's estate in Hawaii in 1995. Indeed, she was still being sued by the estate of tobacco heiress Doris Duke, for a $5 million bail payment that Duke posted in Imelda Marcos's New York trial.[117]

As for the Marcos loot, the family's henchmen have successfully defended almost all of it against the Philippine government's rather clumsy reclamation efforts, aided by a hefty dose of stonewalling from bank regulators in Switzerland, Liechtenstein, and the US. In a fine touch of irony, in 2001–03, the Philippines was placed on a blacklist of "noncooperating countries" by the OECD's Financial Action Task Force, a Paris-based organization that promotes "anti-money-laundering" laws.

Meanwhile, the Philippines is still combating one of Southeast Asia's few remaining left-wing movements, the CPP-NPA, which has had more than nine thousand rebels in the bush for at least twenty-five years and has recently been added to the US's growing list of international "terrorist" organizations. Another 10,000–12,000 rebels are raising hell in southern Sulu's archipelago, fighting for two radical Islamic factions that also have purported ties to "global terrorism"—as well as numerous long-standing grievances.[118]

The Philippine elite—many of whose members had collaborated with the Japanese during World War II, with Marcos until he lost power, and with the US since before World War II—still occupies the country's commanding social and politial heights. Dictators, presidents, and generals come and go, but fortunate families with discreet private bankers last forever.

The country's overall economy has not been so fortunate. It remains subject to episodic outbursts of capital flight, saddled with East Asia's heaviest foreign debt burden, relative to the size of the economy. Already $30 billion when Marcos left, by 2003 it exceeded $55 billion.[119] The country now devotes more than nine percent of national income each year just to service this debt, more than twice what it spends on health care and primary and secondary education.[120] Real per capita incomes are still below their 1982 levels, nearly forty percent of the country's 81 million people are living in absolute poverty (up from thirty-two percent in 1997),[121] and there are more than 716,000 landless, "squatter" families living in Metro Manila—4 million out of the city's 10 million residents. Thirty percent of children below the age of five are malnourished.[122] There are as many people employed in prostitution and the sex industry as in manufacturing. The country's second largest export (next to cheap electronics) is maids, and sixty percent of the rural population still depends heavily on *coconuts* for a living.

Chart 2.1 shows the long-run opportunity costs of the perverse development path that the Philippines has followed. This summarizes relative growth

Real Per Capita Incomes, Five Asian Economies
(1972 = 100)

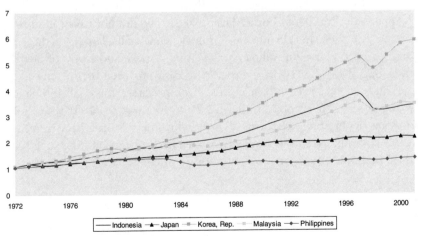

Source: WB (WDI Data), 2003, author's analysis   © JS Henry, 2003

Chart 2.1–Long-Term Development

in real per capita incomes from 1972 to 2001 for five key East Asian countries. Not only has the Philippines's income growth been practically nil, but relative to countries like Korea, Malaysia, and Indonesia, its economy has become almost miniscule.

As for the US, the Philippines's colonial stepfather, throughout the 1990s it agonized over the loss of its two largest military bases outside North America—Clark Air Force Base and Subic Bay—plus some twenty other Philippine bases in the wake of Marcos' ouster. In September 1991, in perhaps the country's most authentic "declaration of independence" ever, the Philippine Senate, responding to overwhelming popular demand, rejected a proposed ten-year extension of these bases. This punished the US not only for decades of unwavering support for Marcos, but also for having secretly quartered hundreds of nuclear weapons at the bases, sanctioning the original creation of the vast "sex-ploitation" industry to service its troops, and refusing to clean up after thousands of tons of toxic waste that had been quietly dumped into Subic Bay.

However, even before the events of September 11, a May 2001 Rand strategy study, authored by a key advisor to President George W. Bush, concluded that the Philippines was still an essential US "forward base."[123] So in May 1999, under great pressure, the Philippine Senate approved a new Visiting Forces Agreement, that permitted the US military to return under certain conditions. In the wake of September 11, the US seized on the opportunity to open a new front in its new global war on terrorism, offering to send troops and $100 million in military aid. This made many Filipinos uncomfortable, not only because of all the past transgressions, but also because it threatened to upset delicate peace negotiations with the rebel groups.[124]

Apparently, President Gloria Macapagal-Arroyo did not have the stomach to say no. After all, the US was her country's oldest ally, largest creditor and trading partner. Her own military was getting restless, and many of her elite friends longed for the "social security" and cash provided by the Americans. So in December 2001, she welcomed back a starter force of 150 Special Forces and 450 other troops. Officially, they came just to "assist" the Philippine Army in fighting "terrorists." Those who knew a little history recalled that the US military and its local constabulary have been hunting such rebels in the Philippines more or less continuously since the late 1890s.[125]

CHAPTER THREE

FUNNY MONEY

If you cannot express it in numbers, your knowledge is of a meager
and unsatisfactory kind.
—Lord Kelvin, 1889

Four years ago a reporter from a German magazine came to talk to
me in Panama, asking questions like the ones you're asking. . . . Two
days later I was having lunch at the German Embassy. I overheard
some fellows talking about how this German reporter had been shot
dead that morning on the streets in Caracas. . . . Are you really sure
you want to pursue this?
—Swiss banker, Miami, 1987

We have ploughed the sea.
—Simon Bolivar, 1830, after resigning from office

VENEZUELA'S FUNNY NUMBERS

*The room's air conditioner sounds like an idling diesel. It's midnight in a lowly
Caracas hotel room that has seen its share of free-lance journalists and one-night
stands, and I'm worn out after an all-day trip from New York. But the tropical warmth
boosts my spirits. At night, during the taxi ride from Maquitea Airport, you can see the
lights of thousands of ranchos clustered on the sides of mountains that surround this
city of four million, lit by power that many people tap for free from La Electricidade,
the local utility. In the daytime, the ranchos return to their invisible role as living quarters for the city's poor, but at night they are a galaxy of little stars. Things haven't
changed very much in these neighborhoods since I first came here in 1980, except that
now there are many more stars.*

*I've returned to Caracas to tackle one of the debt problem's most interesting rid-
dles: How did Venezuela, one of Latin America's oldest and richest democracies, with a
huge oil base and abundant foreign reserves, manage to become completely insolvent in
just one crucial decade? In 1989, it suspended debt payments, called in the army to
shoot rioters, waged a low-intensity war against the opposition, and came close to a military coup. And nearly fifteen years later, in 2003, as a social and political conflict over
the fate of President Hugo Chávez's government brought the country close to econom-*

ic collapse and a civil war, Venezuela was still paying the price for its debacle of the 1980s. When I first visited, the country was widely viewed as a model of development and democracy, and such calamities would have been unthinkable. What happened?

The problem was not really the sheer size of Venezuela's debt—other countries had endured much larger absolute debt burdens without experiencing such consequences. Rather, the mismanagement of Venezuela's foreign debt was one of the main factors responsible for the derailment of its political and social system. And that mismanagement, in turn, was largely due to the avaricious behavior of its "rentier" elite and "Wild West" First World bankers. Those bankers and members of the elite who were quick to blame all Venezuela's troubles on Chávez's "irresponsible" policies and "corrupt policies" really needed to purchase a very large mirror.

On my flight from New York, I sat next to a woman who'd been a close advisor to Carlos Andres Perez, Venezuela's president in the mid-1970s and again in the 1990s. With her help, I was later introduced to several bankers and former officials, including a former Central Banker and a fellow whose job it had been to "audit" Venezuela's foreign debt. By piecing together their stories, with a little sleuthing of my own, I discovered that the advisor had put me on a trail to solving the Venezuelan enigma. Ironically, the trail led right back to her boss. . . .

Venezuela is a unique country in many ways. For decades it was one of the few countries in the world where Pepsi dominated Coke, mainly because of the aggressive tactics of Pepsi's local distributor, which was owned by the powerful Cisneros family. In the late 1940s, before metal cans existed, there was a glass shortage. So Diego Cisneros had his workers buy up all the used Coke bottles in Caracas and toss them in the river.[1] Venezuela also consumes more SPAM than any other country, an average of eight cans a year for each of its twenty-five million citizens, by way of *arepas*, a popular local sandwich. To those who can endure the heat and insects of the Venezuelan Amazon, Angel Falls is the world's tallest waterfall and also perhaps the most beautiful, more subtle and striking than Victoria, Iguacu, or Niagara. Caracas's rush hour is awful, but its Metro system used to be Latin America's finest, a rare exception to the wastefulness of foreign debt-financed projects. Since 1958, Venezuela has held free elections regularly and maintained a fairly free press, docile military, and little social violence. Its presidents were elected for five-year terms and then required to sit out two elections before they were eligible to run again. This encouraged a grab-all-you-can-get attitude toward corruption, but at least it tended to moderate personal authoritarianism—at least until the class wars of the late 1990s erupted, and threatened to make Hugo Chávez a "Bolivarian" in more ways than one.

Venezuela was also one of the few Latin American countries that should have emerged relatively unscathed from the 1980s debt crisis. In the 1930s, unlike all other major debtors, Venezuela had paid off its entire foreign debt.[2] As of 1979, it still had the continent's lowest level of foreign debt service and its second highest per capita income level, with rich farms, great tourism potential, and vast quantities of oil, iron ore, bauxite, hydroelectric power, oil shale, coal, gold, and diamonds. In the 1970s, Venezuela was one of just four Latin American countries officially designated as "upper-middle-income" by the World Bank. It also boasted one of the best income distributions in Latin America.[3] The founder of OPEC was Venezuelan; Venezuela's oil reserves, the sixth largest in the world, have enough oil to last more than a hundred years and still account for more than eighty-five percent of its merchandise exports.[4] Its farms and non-oil industries suffered from the "oil disease;" for decades, they remained heavily protected, not very efficient, and penalized by a strong bolivar. But many Venezuelans believed that the country's natural wealth relieved the country of the need to worry so much about competitiveness in other sectors.

From 1939 until the late 1970s, Venezuela's Central Bank was also relatively independent and well behaved. The bolivar was Latin America's strongest currency, and inflation was held below US levels. For a while in the 1970s, the country was even rich enough to make loans to its neighbors, to help with the cost of importing oil. Beginning with investments by Shell and Standard Oil in the 1920s, Venezuela had also been relatively hospitable to foreign investment. Indeed, for a time back in the 1950s, Venezuela had outpaced Panama as the leading Western Hemisphere tax haven. Multinational companies like Ford and GE set up more than five hundred offshore "base companies" in Caracas to park profits and minimize taxes. A US attorney who specialized in these Venezuelan shell companies recalled that, as of 1956, Venezuela actually had the freest capital markets in Latin America:

> In the mid-1950s Europe was completely dead—still recovering from the war. Latin America was where the action was. And Venezuela was even better than Panama as a tax haven—it had a territorial tax, you could set up shell companies easily, and there were good business facilities because of all the oil. I remember one Caracas newspaper wrote an article about all the haven lawyering I was doing down there. The title was: "Gringo Lawyer Shows How to Beat 'Em and Cheat 'Em."[5]

In the next twenty years, however, Venezuela's attitude toward foreign investors cooled considerably. Oil wealth made it a rentier economy, the "sheikdom of South America." In the 1970s, the government nationalized the steel industry and three oil companies and adopted severe restrictions on foreign investment. Almost everything except oil and loans came to be imported—even food. Under Carlos Andres Perez ("CAP"), who was president from 1973 to 1979, and again from 1989 to 1994, the country went on a spending spree. Its foreign debt grew from $2.8 billion in 1973 to $24 billion in 1979, and then continued rising to more than $38 billion by 1983. The debt's growth funded huge projects like the Guri Dam, the Caracas Metro, and many less sensible ones—including a $3 billion food subsidy program that was riddled with graft, a $1 billion hotel project in the middle of a swamp, and billions of giveaway "loans" to the private sector. The size of the state bureaucracy tripled.[6]

On the other hand, even as it was accumulating its foreign debt, Venezuela also started parking huge amounts of government assets abroad. Thus, in the mid-1970s, it accumulated more than $10 billion in foreign assets in foreign deposits controlled by the Central Bank, Petroleos de Venezuela (PVDSA), the state oil company, and Fundo Investimentos de Venezuela (FIVEN), an institution that Andres Perez created in 1975 to stockpile five percent of oil revenues.[7] Effectively, his government did a massive "back-to-back" loan, investing billions abroad with foreign banks that, in turn, loaned the funds right back to Venezuela's government. Of course, the banks liked this arrangement because the country paid three percent higher interest on all its borrowings than it earned on its own assets. But many observers at the time wondered why the country didn't just reduce its foreign borrowing and use its huge pile of foreign assets to finance its own operations. Defenders of this curious, simultaneous borrow-and-lend policy claimed that it enhanced creditworthiness and controlled misspending. However, this rationale ignored all the misspending that was going on.[8]

So the 'back to back' policy made little sense-unless one credited the more concrete explanation suggested to me by a Panamanian private banker. He had worked at SBC/UBS's Panama City subsidiary in the mid-1970s, just when Venezuela was borrowing heavily and Andres Perez's new Fundo Investimentos de Venezuela (FIVEN) was placing billions of dollars in foreign bank accounts. He explained that the main reason for Venezuela's simultaneous borrow-and-lend policy was really quite simple: It provided magnificent corruption opportunities for Venezuela's senior officials and the handful of influential bankers who serviced them. "You think it's an accident that Andres Perez is the richest politician in Latin America?" he grinned. According to the banker, Fundo Investimentos had invested several hundred million dollars with SBC/UBS in 1976, which loaned the funds right back to Venezuelan government agencies. But not all the interest on these deposits found its way home. According to the banker, he knew personally of a deal where 1/4 percent, or more than $2 million a year, was diverted into the accounts of Cayman Islands companies at SBC's Zurich office, accounts that belonged to senior officials at Fundo Investimentos and Andres Perez himself. Another

SBC-Panama banker confirmed that FIVEN had given SBC/UBS more than $300 million in deposits in the mid-1970s. He also confirmed that the Venezuelan government was SBC/UBS-Panama's leading customer, that "it was common to reward senior officials for such deposits," and that similar games had also been played with PDVSA's idle oil dollars.[9]

SOWING

At the very least, this peculiar borrow-and-lend policy fooled a lot of "debt experts," who believed that the existence of all the foreign assets made Venezuela's net foreign debt quite manageable—even trivial. As late as 1981, Venezuela was still widely regarded as a very low-risk country. The World Bank declared that the country had become too wealthy to be eligible for its concessional "International Development Assistance" loan program. In December 1981, Professor William R. Cline, a noted Johns Hopkins economist and one of America's most prominent debt experts, issued a 135-page study of Venezuela's foreign debt. His key finding was that its estimated $21 billion gross foreign debt was "relatively light"—both Mexico and Brazil had much worse ratings on the "Frank-Cline Rescheduling Risk Indicator." Since Venezuelan agencies owned more than $15 billion in foreign assets, the country's entire *net* foreign debt was supposedly only $6 billion.[10] Cline concluded that the country had "a large, unused capacity for carrying external debt." According to him, it could easily take on an extra $12–20 billion in loans without even flinching.[11]

In December 1982, Arturo Sosa assumed office as Venezuela's new finance minister. An experienced banker in his late fifties, Sosa had also served as finance minister in the "Junta Gobierno" that succeeded Perez Jimenez in 1958. He was a close friend of such prominent international bankers as Morgan's Tony Gebauer, Chase's Francis Mason, and Citibank's William Rhodes.[12] He could sense that an economic crisis was brewing in the whole region. Mexico, Brazil, and Argentina had already experienced credit crunches that year, and investors were raiding Venezuela's Central Bank for up to $100 million a day in flight dollars, anticipating a devaluation. It became critical for Sosa to know the exact size of Venezuela's foreign debt, in order to project how much interest Venezuela would have to pay in the next few months and whether or not he would have to devalue the currency or borrow more money to service it.

Unfortunately, the true size of the debt was completely unknown, notwithstanding Professor Cline's expert study. The debt situation was also a political hot potato. Presidential elections were scheduled for December 1983, and Sosa's party, the Social Christian (COPEI) Party, wasn't eager to devalue the bolivar, which had been stable for many years. Importers, domestic banks, and companies had accumulated heavy private foreign debts as the bolivar had become more and more overvalued, without hedging these bets. They had a strong stake in postponing devaluation as long as possible because their incomes were in bolivars and the interest on the loans had to be paid in dollars. Meanwhile, the political clout of non-oil exporters had been weakened by years of oil wealth. Since 1979 the economy had experienced four years of stagnation, and there was also fear that a devaluation would worsen it. Furthermore, President Luis Herrera Campins, claimed that Venezuela was already mortgaged to the hilt when he took office in 1979, and Luis Ugueto, Sosa's predecessor, maintained that the debt had not really grown at all since then. Andres Perez's Acción Democratica Party ("*el ADecos*") ridiculed these claims, but no one really knew for sure.[13] As the leading newspaper *El Universal* commented: "The Government doesn't know how much each public-sector entity owes to foreign banks; it doesn't know when interest is due, much less amortization. Venezuela's international accounts are in an incredible state of chaos."[14]

Arturo Sosa's first step was to do something that Luis Ugueto had never bothered to do. He telexed the Bank for International Settlements (BIS) in Geneva, which keeps track of international lending, and requested a list of all debts that foreign banks claimed against Venezuelan borrowers. Amazingly, Venezuela didn't have a list of its own public foreign debts or the banks that had supplied them. Or rather, the Central Bank, the Comptroller, and the Treasury each had a different list.

The BIS's response to Sosa's request was shocking—a thirty-seven foot long telex. When Sosa added up the numbers, he discovered to his horror that the banks were claiming $27 billion in loans, one-third more than anyone had anticipated. Even worse, half of them were due in a year, and one-third were due in ninety days. If the banks pulled their credit lines, Venezuela would run out of cash almost over night. Among major debtors, only the Philippines and Mexico could claim anything like this blind dependency on short-term debt.

The irony was that with all its oil wealth, comparative political stability, democratic system, and history of regular payments, Venezuela really should have been Latin America's *best* credit risk. Yet here the country was, funding itself with short-term papers at extraordinary interest rates—the equivalent of going to a loan shark. The interest rates paid to foreign banks by Venezuela in 1981–82 were higher than those paid by any other developing country—at least 20–30 percent above those paid by Argentina, Brazil, or Mexico.

So here we have another example of Venezuela's exceptionalism—apparently Venezuela was unusually inept at negotiating with its foreign bankers. But this was just its own peculiar way of reconciling deeply inconsistent, political-economic imperatives: the desire of its uncontrolled state bureaucracies to spend beyond their means and feather their bank accounts; the eagerness of foreign bankers to finance anything that moved so long as it had a Venezuelan government guarantee; and the desire of Venezuela's president to postpone impolitic changes in economic policy, like the bolivar's value.

Sosa's next step, in December 1982, was to appoint a bright young director general of public finance, Gustavo Galdo. "All I want you to do," Sosa told him, "is to find out exactly how much debt we really owe." Sosa had been a banker long enough not to accept even the BIS numbers at face value. After all, the BIS data relied on data from the foreign banks, which could also easily lose track. During the 1984 debt negotiations, for example, Citibank had overcharged Venezuela by $800 million, billing it twice for two $400 million loans to Sidor, the state-owned steel company. Fortunately, Sidor kept better records than Citibank.[15] Measuring the debt sounded simple, but it took Galdo and a large staff six months just to make a preliminary, yet incomplete, estimate. The basic fact was that Venezuela had completely lost control over its foreign borrowing.

In the public sector, the problem centered on more than four hundred autonomous government agencies, including Venezuela's INOS (the Bureau of Water and Sanitation), CANTV (the state telephone company), CSB (the municipality of Caracas), and CVF (the Venezuelan Development Bank). In the 1970s, they had all started spending wildly beyond their means, wheeling and dealing with foreign bankers, taking advantage of the fact that from the banks' standpoint, all of their borrowing was guaranteed by Venezuela. Under the liberal 1976 Law of Public Credit, the finance minister theoretically had a veto over their borrowing, but there was no central reporting. Privately, the agency heads were actually encouraged by Andres Perez and Herrera Campins to borrow everything they could. In 1979, when Venezuela's attorney general ruled that agencies were borrowing abroad unconstitutionally, Finance Minister Ugueto worked closely with Citibank and Bank of America to circumvent the ruling, substituting four agencies as "pseudo-borrowers" in a $1.8 billion jumbo loan.[16]

At his first meeting with the autonomous agencies in April 1983, Sosa said, "Tell me what you owe the banks, or we won't help you pay." That really hit home—most of them were already flat broke. He hired a consulting firm to design the country's very first foreign debt registration system and ordered the agencies to report all their new loans to him. Most of them had trouble even identifying what their debts were—the controls on borrowing had been unbelievably loose. For example, in 1981, Citibank had accepted and discounted a $300 million promissory note that was nothing more than a handwritten "pay to the order of" on blank stationery, signed by Domingo

Mariani ("*El Bambino de Oro*"), the head of CADAFE, a public utility.[17] Mariani later fled to Europe to avoid corruption charges, because CADAFE was missing hundreds of millions in funds, and the note was simply added to Venezuela's debt. On another occasion, Citibank, CADAFE's lead bank, arranged for a Venezuelan debt syndication to be signed in Hong Kong. Citibank flew in a dozen senior officials, including Domingo Mariani and President Luis Herrera Campins, all at Venezuela's expense.

Another case of loose lending involved Banco de Trabajadores, Venezuela's largest private bank until it failed in October 1982. This event precipitated the financial crisis that led to Sosa's replacement of Ugueto. The bank was owned by CTV, a powerful pro-ADeco union that was rife with corruption. Its lead foreign bank was Bankers Trust (later acquired by Deutsche Bank). In early 1982, the bank had extended a $55 million overdraft to Banco de Trabajadores that simply disappeared into the coffers of the Ministry of Education. When Bankers Trust demanded repayment in 1983, its officers told Minister Sosa that Minister Ugueto had personally assured them that the loan had a government guarantee. Sosa simply pulled out Banco de Trabajadores's bylaws, which the Bankers Trust officers had apparently *never read*. Article Two of the bylaws stated quite clearly that Banco de Trabajadores was not a central government entity. Fortunately for Bankers Trust, the 1983 Presidential election was won by ADeco candidate Dr. Jaime Lusinchi, a pediatrician who had once delivered babies at New York's Bellevue Hospital. He also delivered Bankers Trust and CTV from Banco de Trabajadores's troubles, getting the government to assume its entire $256 million debt. The bank's president, Elias Pinto, later spent two years in jail on fraud charges. The Bankers Trust officers who financed him all received promotions.[18]

Venezuelan lawyers who dealt with foreign banks reported that such lax lending practices were not at all unusual. For example, Bank of America instructed its Caracas lawyers not to worry about such "formalities" as whether express authorizations for loans had been obtained from the boards of government agency, as required by law. Legal limits on rolling over short-term notes were also aggressively ignored. When another Caracas attorney protested the shortcuts, his client—a major US bank—summarily fired him and substituted a more flexible lawyer. Many poorly documented credits were later sold off to unsuspecting US regional banks by the leading international syndicating banks.[19]

The worst abuses involved Venezuela's short-term debt. Under Venezuela's 1976 credit law, agencies were only authorized to borrow for terms of up to a year, unless they got express approval from Venezuela's Congress. Thus, the banks and the agencies simply conspired to sign loan agreements for less than a year—usually ninety days—and rolled them over. The Congress closed this loophole in August 1981, but then the foreign banks simply opened another vein—since the new restrictions didn't apply to state banks like Banco Industrial de Venezuela (BIV), they made loans to these state banks, and the state banks then reloaned the money to other government agencies.

All this loose lending created irresistible opportunities for corruption. Many government officials took "early retirement" in Miami, New York, or Europe. In addition to CADAFE's Domingo Mariani and Banco de Trabajadores's Elias Pinto, the *émigrés* included Guimersindo Rodríguez, Andres Perez's minister of planning; Nerio Neri, the president of CANTV, who reportedly took bribes from Ericsson, the Swedish telephone company; Vinicio Carrera, Herrera Campins's minister of transport; Ali Cordero Vale, BIV's president, who was charged with $45 million in fraud in 1984; John Raphael, Andres Perez's head of CVF, who purchased a refrigerator ship, the "Sierra Nevada," under circumstances that would have put Andres Perez himself in prison, were it not for a one-vote margin in Congress; Diego Arrias, the mayor of Caracas and Andres Perez's head of CSB, who later fled to New York; and Rosario Garcia Serrana, Herrera Campin's managing director of CVF,[20] who fled the country in 1982 under threat of prosecution for corruption. Andres Perez's long-time mistress, personal secretary, and "intermediary" Cecilia Matos, took up residence at 35 Sutton Place in New York City and was a frequent visitor to Geneva, Miami, and the Dominican Republic, where Andres Perez also reportedly owned property. Several leading local bankers also left town with their pockets full.[21] Andres Perez was also repeatedly implicated in many other corrupt deals. Ultimately, in 1993, he would be impeached, removed from office, and then convicted of misappropriating state funds.

One former Bankers Trust officer recalled a typical example of Venezuelan "pirate banking":

It was unforgettable—it was my very first real experience as a lender. Chemical Bank had loaned $5 million to Centro Simon Bolivar (CSB), guaranteed by Venezuela, to buy some buses. One day in 1976, two guys showed up at Bankers Trust. One was a purchasing agent from Centro Simon Bolivar. He had a cashiers check for $5 million that was drawn on Chemical Bank. They wanted to trade the check for two cashiers checks, one made out to the bus company for $3.5 million and the other to some offshore company that clearly belonged to them. I asked my boss, "What's going on here?" He just smiled and approved the checks. After a while, it made you really cynical. You realized that these people were just thoroughly, totally corrupt. And what did that make us?[22]

In late 1982, as the foreign banks started shutting down their credit lines in Latin America, Venezuela's short-term debt—eighty percent of which was owed by "autonomous" agencies—became a transmission belt for the debt crisis. In January 1983, several banks withdrew from Venezuelan syndications when the CVF missed several interest payments. Then Sosa discovered, to his horror, that Banco Industrial de Venezuela owed more than $600 million in short-term notes that had to be rolled over *every night* by the banks. "This is a grenade hanging around my neck," he told President Herrera Campins. "If BIV's foreign creditors won't roll the debt, it will bring down the whole economy." Eventually the "short-term" debt had to be converted into a long-term debt that Venezuela is still servicing in 2003.

The confusion was even worse for Venezuela's private foreign debt. Before 1983, Venezuela had neither exchange controls nor debt registration, so private bankers came and went freely. The country became the world's third-largest flight capital market—courtesy of a bizarre combination of policies that gave investors strong incentives to overstate their foreign debts and take money out of the country. So the true size of Venezuela's legitimate private debt will probably never be known, because of the huge amount of fraud.

What is clear is that there were remarkable incentives to decapitalize the country. Until Sosa devalued the bolivar in February 1983, it had been pegged at 4.3 to the dollar since the early 1970s. After 1979, it had become seriously overvalued—dollars were artificially cheap. So investors and multinational companies began to move huge quantities of dollars abroad, including $890 million during the three weeks just prior to Sosa's February 1983 devaluation.[23] According to a senior Chase Manhattan private banker, part of this moved because of a tip from one of her "very best clients": "I came back from Venezuela knowing that the February 1983 devaluation was coming a week early, because the head of Venezuela's Central Bank was my client. Naturally we told the rest of the bank and other clients. We made a killing."[24] Central Bank governors were not the only ones to engage in such practices. So did many finance ministers, who often maintained bank accounts in New York, London, and Switzerland for just this purpose.

Actually, one of Venezuela's most colorful Central Bank heads at the time, Leopoldo Diaz-Bruzual ("El Bufalo") had long opposed devaluation. In February 1982, just after Mexico's devaluation, he hit the roof when he discovered that Citibank's foreign exchange traders had been mounting speculative attacks against the bolivar, offering Venezuelans twenty-two percent returns if they traded bolivars for dollars. Diaz-Bruzual summoned the manager of Citibank's Caracas branch to his office and threatened to cancel Citibank's banking license. "What are you doing, trying to drain us of money to make a few million dollars for your trading desk?" he raged. For a while the speculation eased.

Diaz-Bruzual later claimed that by the fall of 1982, he had come to favor devaluation and higher interest rates, but was opposed by President Herrera Campins. To be fair, at the time, devaluation was also opposed by the IMF, most bankers, and many leading economists, including Columbia University's eminent Nobel laureate, Professor Robert Mundell, who argued that since most of Venezuela's exports were tied to the dollar, devaluation would only boost inflation. In hindsight, this typical monetarist position overlooked the many beneficial impacts of devaluation on imports, non-oil exports, and capital flight. But as Diaz-Bruzual said, "There are always good prophets for the past. . . . Remember, some foreign banks were still lending to us in December 1982!"[25]

As long as the artificially strong bolivar lasted, there were innumerable ways to profit from it. Combined with CVF loan guarantees, it made foreign loans cheaper and even more abundant than domestic ones.[26] Many dollar loans went directly to the borrowers' offshore accounts, a much safer investment than putting them into bolivar-denominated assets just prior to a devaluation.

Loans made without government guarantees were supposedly more rational, and they had to carry a higher interest rate in order to compensate bankers for this added risk. But after the 1983 devaluation, the cost of repaying these loans in bolivars rose sharply. Even though the banks had already presumably been compensated for this higher risk by the higher interest rate spreads that they received on these non-guaranteed loans, they successfully pressured Venezuela to grant lucrative subsidies and bailouts to cover all these *private* debts, retroactive to the period *before* they were contracted. This turned out to be a rather common practice in developing countries. Following sharp devaluations, similar "socialization" programs for private-elite debts were also implemented under pressure from the banks in Mexico, Chile, Argentina, Indonesia, and several other countries. Even Finance Minister Arturo Sosa caved in on the issue. After all, his own investment bank, FINAVEN, had a $300 million foreign debt that stood to benefit from the government's socialization of private foreign debt.

Throughout 1983, Diaz-Bruzual, who had once been an attorney for SBC/UBS in Geneva, tried to block this government bailout of the private foreign debt. He demanded information from all the banks on the flight assets owned by their Venezuelan "borrowers" abroad—many of whom had just absconded with the loan proceeds, leaving the government stuck with the debts after they were nationalized. All the banks refused. He even got into a fistfight at a Cabinet meeting with Oil Minister Humberto Calderon Berti over Calderon Berti's refusal to relinquish control over the oil company's foreign assets. In March 1984, Diaz-Bruzual refused to resign from the Central Bank and was impeached.

It took Venezuela until 1987 to work out a debt rescheduling agreement with its foreign creditors and private foreign debt issue was one of the key sticking points.[27] At one point, Sosa tried an unorthodox tactic to speed things up. He struck an under-the-table deal with his old friend, Francis Mason, the Chase senior vice president, who had become chairman of the Advisory Committee of Banks in March 1983. Venezuela agreed to pay Chase $300,000 a month under the table, to be reduced to $100,000 a month if the negotiations dragged on past September 1983. When the other banks got wind of this deal, they were fuming, because of the obvious conflict of interest. They insisted that Chase return the $1.5 million it had been paid under the agreement and give up the chairmanship. Francis Mason quickly resigned, so the incident was hushed up. . . .[28]

Arturo Sosa's successor as finance minister, Manual Aizpurua Arreaza, didn't nationalize the private debt outright, but he did agree to sell cheap dollars to the debtors, most of which were multinational companies like Exxon and GE, or companies that belonged to wealthy Venezuelans. By 1986, $14.5 billion in alleged private debt claims were submitted to RECADI, the agency in charge of handing out these foreign exchange subsidies. RECADI was painfully slow to process these claims. One World Bank economist later recalled, "The paperwork was so massive, we feared its office in downtown Caracas would collapse."[29] Eventually, about $7 billion in private debt was subsidized.[30] President Jaime Lusinchi hoped the private sector would repatriate its foreign assets in return for this generous dole—much of the debts were pure "back-to-back" loans. But that didn't happen.[31] As in many other countries, a period of private foreign debt socialization had preceded the fashionable 1990s policy of public sector asset privatization. And much of the "debt" that was socialized had actually ended up in dollar accounts, waiting for the public asset fire-sales to come.

In effect, Venezuela's elite and their bankers made excess profits from foreign debt in at least three ways. First, by having the state borrow abroad to finance the purchase or construction, of public assets, many of which were overpriced; second, by borrowing private dollars abroad, most of which actually stayed in secret dollar accounts, even while the government was persuaded to nationalize the loans that had produced them; and third, following devaluation, by bringing back the dollars associated with these private loans to invest in privatized public assets at bargain prices. Critics like Diaz-Bruzual complained bitterly about this. After all, the elite had already been protected against devaluation by their offshore flight dollars, and exchange risk was just a normal part of international business that they were supposed to anticipate and hedge against, without government insurance. "Why should we subsidize this privileged group? Did workers get subsidies when import prices rose?" Diaz-Bruzual argued.[32] Other leading lawyers and economists also argued that a huge portion of Venezuela's foreign debt was simply *fraudulent* and deserved to be repudiated outright.

Furthermore, in 1990, it was discovered that from 1983 to 1987, leading RECADI officials had sold at least $6 billion in bogus import licenses, at a time when Venezuela was struggling to service its debts. Provided in exchange for bribes, these licenses entitled the holders to buy dollars at artificially cheap prices. Ten senior officials were charged with corruption, including former finance ministers Aizpurua and Hurtado, former Central Bank president Mauricio Garcia, and President Jaime Lusinchi, who fled the country for Costa Rica for five years, until the statute of limitations expired. Senior executives from Ford, Kraft, Kellogg, and Heinz, plus a former director of Born Brothers, an Argentine commodity firm, who happened to be Argentina's finance minister at the time, were also charged with corruption. All told, more than a hundred executives of foreign companies with plants in Venezuela were forced to relocate in order to avoid prosecution. Ford Motors, for example, ran its Venezuelan affiliate out of Aruba for several months.[33]

As for the true size of Venezuela's debt, ultimately it owed more than $32.1 billion in 1981 and $38.3 billion in 1983, including $9 billion in private debt.[34] Compared with Professor Cline's original estimate, this was a fifty-two percent increase. Nor were Venezuela's foreign assets anywhere near as large as he had claimed. The country's net debt was not $6 billion, but nearly four times higher—$22–28 billion. Far from having "unused debt capacity," Venezuela was strapped. The country remained so throughout the 1980s, even while it faithfully continued to pay debt principal as well as interest. In December 1988, during the waning days of Lusinchi's administration, Venezuela finally declared a moratorium on servicing its $20 billion public-sector debt, something it hadn't even done in the 1930s.

CAP'S RETURN—SHOCK THERAPY 101

Just two months after the debt moratorium, one of the key people responsible for the growth of the debt was back in power. On February 2, 1989, President Andres Perez took office for the second time in twenty years, after winning the December 1988 elections with fifty-three percent of the vote—thirteen points more than his main opponent. Despite persistent rumors about his secret wealth and involvement in corruption, most

Venezuelans still associated Andres Perez with good times. Surely, they felt, the wily old social democrat would find a way to bring the boom back.

At his lavish inauguration at Caracas's Teatro Teresa Carreño—constructed during Andres Perez's first term for $500 million, five times the original bid—the audience of 2,400 dignitaries included US vice president Dan Quayle, Spain's Felipe Gonzalez, Nicaragua's Daniel Ortega, Peru's Alan Garcia, Portugal's Mario Soares, Cuba's Fidel Castro, and former US president Jimmy Carter. They listened respectfully as the dapper, ebullient, if not exactly modest, newly elected president characterized his own return to power as nothing less than "a great moment in Latin American history."[35]

Carlos Andres Perez's return to power certainly was a key turning point. In the 1970s, as we saw, Andres Perez was deeply involved in Venezuela's excessive foreign borrowing. By the early 1980s, he was also one of Latin America's wealthiest politicians, after just one term in office. He then retired briefly to his Venezuelan ranch and his homes in the US and the Dominican Republic, continuing to serve as president of the Socialist International, an outspoken proponent of debt relief, and an organizer of aid to Nicaragua, to help it recover from its decade-long civil war. But by the late 1980s, he was ready to run again. He knew that his debt-heavy welfare-state approach to development was no longer feasible. Even with all its oil wealth, Venezuela was tapped out. And it was also more fashionable to join with other late-model Latin American leaders like Mexico's Carlos Salinas de Gortari, Brazil's Fernando Collor de Mello, and Peru's Fujimori and become a born-again neoliberal.

Prior to the election, it would have been politically unwise for Andres Perez to share his full intentions with the public. But as soon as he took office, his belated conversion to neoliberalism was revealed. He quickly concluded an agreement—unprecedented in Venezuelan history—with the IMF. On February 16, 1989, the results were announced in the form of *El Paquete*—an ice-cold neoliberal shower. In exchange for IMF loans and debt rescheduling, Andres Perez agreed to lift Venezuela's moratorium on debt service, launch an aggressive new privatization program, deregulate financial markets, and sharply downsize the Venezuelan state. He also agreed to devalue the bolivar by 150 percent and let it float freely. He eliminated most restrictions on foreign investment—many of which he had pioneered in the 1970s. Finally, effective immediately, Andres Perez removed all price controls for gasoline, public transport, electricity, interest rates, and food.

One can argue that such reforms were directionally correct, in some economist's long-run dream state. But, in typical shock-therapy fashion, Andres Perez introduced them into Venezuela almost overnight, without adequate institutional preparation, as if the country already had adequate bank supervision, security market regulations, and tax enforcement. It did not.

There was also no attempt to cushion the extraordinary social costs of the program. In the short run, where the impoverished majority of Venezuela's inhabitants in the *ranchos* live and die, the results were devastating. Soon after *El Paquete* was introduced, inflation and unemployment reached their highest levels in Venezuela's history. Real incomes for the bottom half of the population dropped by more than twenty percent in six months, and the incidence of poverty soared to more than forty percent. Less than a month after Andres Perez's inauguration, on February 27–28 there was widespread rioting in Caracas—the worst in Venezuela's history. Andres Perez had to declare martial law, suspend civil liberties, and call in Venezuela's long-dormant army to quell the riot. To do so, the army used house-to-house searches without warrants, massive arrests, curfews, press censorship, and summary executions. The "official" death toll of the riot, now remembered as the *Caracazo,* was three hundred. The actual number may have been as high as two thousand, with thousands more injured—a Latin American version of Tiananmen Square. This was by far the worst debt-related riot in any Latin American country, including Argentina's riots in 2001–03.

Despite this inauspicious beginning to his second term, Andres Perez received a warm welcome a year later when he visited the White House and was greeted by President George H. W. Bush. He complimented Andres Perez on his Venezuelan "*Perestroika,*" and commented in rather paternal tones:

> I know this transition, with its difficult, short-term effects, has meant some pain for the people of Venezuela. But it is the kind of new beginning that will lay the foundations for future growth. It isn't an easy path, but we're convinced that it is the only path to prosperity and better lives for all Venezuelans. . . .[36]

AFTERSHOCKS

In fact, the damage done to the fabric of Venezuela's democracy by Andres Perez's neoliberal shock program, on top of the previous decade's excessive borrowing, debt-financed corruption, and debt-induced stagnation, was hardly "short-term" at all. The damage has continued well into the long-term, with Venezuelans, as well as President George W. Bush, still dealing with its side effects more than a decade later.

On February 4, 1992, after two more years of Andres Perez's austere policies, Venezuela experienced its first attempted military coup in thirty years—an effort led by a group of 133 disgruntled young military officers, including an outspoken thirty-eight-year-old Army paratrooper named Hugo Chávez Frías. The son of two school teachers who had sent him to Venezuela's Military Academy, Lt. Col. Chávez and his comrades had founded the

Revolutionary Bolivarian Movement (MRB) in the 1980s, invoking the memory of Venezuela's early nineteenth-century founder and liberator, Simon Bolivar, who was also once an army colonel. They claimed to be disgusted by all the chicanery around them, including rampant corruption at senior levels of the military. They were also angry at the impact that elite policies were having on ordinary Venezuelans. And they had lost all confidence in the capacity of Venezuela's two political parties, the ADecos and the Copeyanos, as well as its legal institutions, to produce solutions for Venezuela's problems.

MRB's first coup attempt took place on February 1992, on the second anniversary of the Caracozco. It failed, after eighteen deaths and sixty wounded. So did a second attempt in November, which Chávez had encouraged with a video tape smuggled out of prison. It took another 230 lives. By December 1992 there were more than three hundred MRB officers in jail. But they attracted a great deal of popular sympathy, given the economic crisis and mounting evidence that the elite—Venezuela's state bureaucrats, business elite, bankers, and members of its two dominant political parties—had basically absconded with much of the country's debt, along with its mineral wealth.

Colonel Chávez and other MRB leaders surrendered and were imprisoned. They might have been executed, but Venezuela's elite realized this would only martyr them and trigger a civil war. So they spent two years in prison and were then pardoned by Andres Perez's successor. Under their influence, Andres Perez did make a few concessions, promising to raise minimum wage and lower interest rates. But he soon had other problems to worry about. In November 1992, one of Venezuela's leading investigative journalists and former presidential candidate on the MAS (Socialist) ticket, José Vicente Rangel, published an article alleging that Andres Perez had been involved in diverting $17.2 million in aid earmarked for Nicaraguan relief to foreign bank accounts. He also suggested that the president had profited from speculating against the bolivar with the help of inside information.[37]

The Venezuelan Congress quickly started impeachment proceedings against the by-now wildly unpopular president. In May 1993, eight months before his term was supposed to end, Venezuela's Supreme Court ruled that there was sufficient evidence to try him for misappropriating state funds, and Andres Perez had to resign. In May 1994, he was sentenced to twenty-eight months in prison and fined by the Supreme Court. By then, he had earned three distinctions: he was the first Venezuelan president to serve two terms, the first one to be impeached, and, to quote President George H.W. Bush, he had indeed found his own "path to prosperity" in becoming one of the world's richest politicians.

Because of his advanced age, Andres Perez was allowed to serve his sentence under house arrest. He was freed in September 1996, but that was not the end of his troubles. In April 1998, Andres Perez was ordered back under house arrest, after being indicted on charges of having diverted $8 million in misappropriated funds to joint accounts that he shared with Cecilia Matos at Citibank, Republic National Bank in New York and Grand Cayman, BNP and American Express Bank in Geneva, and the National Bank of the Philippines.[38] Venezuela's attorney general also started extradition proceedings against Matos in New York.

In December 1998, Andres Perez, seventy-six years old, was elected senator in his home state of Tachira, running on the "Renovation Party" ticket. This freed him from house arrest and earned him a brief period of congressional immunity. However, that was not to last. The forces of instability that his policies had helped to unleash were about to come back to haunt him.

THE NEOLIBERAL PITFALL— VENEZUELA'S BANKING CRISIS

Throughout the 1990s, Venezuela's traditional leaders continued to dribble away the clock. In June 1993, in another nostalgic fling, the country turned to seventy-nine-year-old Rafael Caldera Rodríguez, formerly a member of the Christian Democratic Party (COPEI), who had served as president from 1969 to 1974, just before Andres Perez. This time around, Caldera was elected on the "Convergence Party" ticket, a coalition that was supposed to provide less harsh policies and restore stability, confidence, and morality to the government.

Unfortunately, Caldera's five years in office were marred by instability, soaring capital flight, and even greater corruption scandals than before. In January 1994, just as he was about to take office, Banco Latino (BL)— Venezuela's second largest private bank—collapsed, setting off the largest banking crisis in Venezuelan history. This was almost entirely due to Andres Perez's precipitate shock-therapy program, which had set off a reckless, unregulated banking boom that quickly went bust.

Like most other private banks, Banco Latino had taken advantage of Andres Perez's hasty deregulation of financial markets, the abolition of interest rate controls, and the virtual absence of effective bank supervision to increase lending, bid like crazy for deposits, and diversify into new markets. The decontrol of interest rates fed the speculative mania: at its peak in 1993, Venezuelan banks were offering interest rates of sixty-five percent or more to attract deposits, while lending out at seventy-five percent or more. When the

Central Bank finally raised interest rates to finance a burgeoning budget deficit, the banks were caught out: loan demand slacked off, while they were stuck paying the high rates on deposits. Many banks had also been making dubious loans to their own groups. While Venezuela technically had a bank superintendent, it only had six professional auditors for the entire country, and limited enforcement powers.[39] The larger banks were also effectively protected from oversight by heavyweight political connections. For example, Banco Latino's president and main shareholder was a former head of the Central Bank, Pedro Tinoco. He was also a long-time senior executive with the Cisneros Group, which had very close ties to Andres Perez. Indeed, the Fondo de Garantia de Depositos y Protección, Venezuela's deposit insurance provider (FOGADE), had kept a third of its own deposits in accounts at Banco Latino—for reasons not dissimilar to those involved in the Fondo de Inversiones de Venezuela (FIVEN) case discussed earlier.

The result was a classic capitalist banking crisis, which resembled the many other neoliberal banking crises that have occurred in developing countries with weak bank supervision and wide-open capital markets: Chile in 1982–83, Mexico and Bolivia in 1994–95, Thailand, Indonesia, Korea, and Russia in 1997–98, and Argentina in 2001–02. In Venezuela's case, the main distinction was that almost the entire domestic banking leadership ended up fleeing the country to avoid prosecution, while taking huge quantities of government bailout money with them.

Offering the public high interest rates and its heretofore-impeccable reputation, Banco Latino had attracted more than six million accounts. Allowing for multiple accounts per person, at least ten percent of Venezuelans had money at BL. When it cratered, angry crowds gathered outside the bank's branches, demanding their money back. And since Banco Latino could be at risk, the panic quickly spread to all other domestic private banks, with people closing their accounts and trying desperately to change bolivars into dollars. Soon the country was facing not only a banking crisis, but a foreign exchange crisis. In 1994, capital flight consumed more than a quarter of Venezuela's reserves.

By 1995, FOGADE had nationalized nine of the largest banks and closed seven others. More than half of the domestic banking industry was now in state hands. The cost of bailing out and taking over all these private banks by Venezuela was $10–12 billion, more than half the country's budget and twenty-one percent of GDP.[40] As a result, Venezuela's budget deficit more than doubled, from 2.2 percent of GDP in 1993 to 5.6 percent in 1994.[41]

To finance the bank bailout, Venezuela did not raise taxes on the wealthy. The costs were shouldered by ordinary Venezuelans by way of the inflation tax, with Venezuela's Central Bank simply printing the money. This boosted inflation to 116 percent in 1995–96, the highest rate in Venezuela's history. Meanwhile, the economy shrank by more than two percent, real wages and real per capita incomes plummeted, and many bank depositors lost most of their savings.

Investigations by Venezuelan prosecutors and its controller general later disclosed a series of fraudulent loans, insider loans, and outright theft that involved a large fraction of the $7.5 billion of financial aid that FOGADE and the Central Bank had advanced to the banks in a vain attempt to keep them afloat.[42] There were cases where owners and senior bankers had literally made off with bags of cash in company jets. Prosecutors issued eighty-three warrants for many of Venezuela's most prominent business people, and more than four hundred bankers and corporate directors fled the country.

Among those for whom warrants were issued were Gustavo A. Gómez López, the former Chairman of Banco Latino, plus eleven of his former associates at the bank; Fernando Araujo, President Caldera's son-in-law, and a director of the failed Banco Metropolitano; José Alvarez Stelling, president of Banco Consolidato, part of Venezuela's influential Vollmer Group; Orlando Castro Castro, president of Banco Progresso, who was also later convicted in New York of defrauding a Puerto Rican bank; José Bouza Izquierdo, former president of Banco de Venezuela, who fled to Spain and was briefly detained there; and Ricardo José Cisneros Rendiles, a leading member of the Cisneros family, owners of Venezuela's leading TV network Venevizión, the newspaper *El Nacional*, DirectTV in Venezuela, Telcel, the grocery chain CADA, AOL Latin American, Spaulding Sporting Goods, Spain's Galerias Preciados department store chain, Paternoster Square in London, and Pan-American Beverages, one of the world's top three bottlers, Coca-Cola's key partner in South America.[43]

President Caldera promised that any bankers implicated in fraud would go to jail, but as of 2003, none of these people have served time or paid any fines. In many cases, the country's statute of limitations was permitted to expire before fraud cases were brought; in others, the banks' directors were exonerated for technical reasons. In his 1999 campaign for a Constituent Assembly to rewrite Venezuela's constitution, Hugo Chávez made a huge point of the judiciary's seeming unwillingness to prosecute any of these bankers for fraud. However, it turned out that his administration also played games with justice when cash contributions were at stake. In 2001, thirty-eight bankers were completely absolved of wrongdoing by an appeals court in Caracas.[44] Most of the loans they received from FOGADE were never repaid. In the scandal's wake, in November 1995, the IDB did grant Venezuela a $14 million loan to "strengthen the Superintendency of Banks and . . . correct the weakness of regulatory institutions."[45]

The other players who clearly benefited from this fiasco were the foreign banks. After the crisis, to get rid of the banks that it had just nationalized, Venezuela changed its laws in 1994, and for the first time allowed foreign banks to own up to one hundred percent of domestic banks.[46] Until then, Citibank had been the only foreign bank with domestic operations, a branch in Caracas that it had owned since 1907. In 1994, foreign banks had accounted for just five percent of Venezuela's bank assets. By December 1996, foreign banks had acquired more than *half* of Venezuela's entire banking system. The leading foreign players included ING, ABN-AMRO, Banco Santander, Banco Bilbao Vizcayo, and Chile's Infisa Group, in partnership with JPMorgan Chase.[47] Most observers expected this foreign share of bank ownership to increase, as more and more small, undiversified banks—weakened by the economic crisis—slipped under the wheels of these juggernauts. So the outlook for Venezuela's domestic capital market is one of increasing concentration as well as foreign dominance.

Meanwhile, the banking crisis also undermined almost all the key elements of Andres Perez's neoliberal reform package, except its adverse impacts on price levels and unemployment. To finance the mounting deficits and stem the tide of capital flight, Caldera raised interest rates and suspended currency trading, substituting a "crawling peg" that controlled the rate of devaluation of the "freely floating" bolivar. To cover the gargantuan government deficit, the government raised taxes. To try and recover the assets of the profligate bankers, he suspended the constitution for a year. Finally, in 1996, Caldera, who was elected on a platform that rejected any further dealings with the IMF, returned to the IMF for yet another bailout and another round of tough economic reforms—which at least this time around included recognition of the importance of financial regulation.

All this did not inspire much confidence among ordinary Venezuelans, who had watched previous reform packages come and go and were now paying the price for them. The new reforms failed to rekindle the economy, as Venezuela entered into one of its deepest recessions ever. Unemployment reached eleven percent by 1997 and fifteen percent by 1999, driven by high interest rates, a shortage of new investment, and a continuing slump in world oil prices. The incidence of poverty more than doubled in the 1990s, from thirty percent to sixty-five percent of the population. By 1998, real wages had fallen more than seventy percent since the early 1980s. Real per capita incomes were below their 1970 levels. Given the shortage of jobs in the regular economy, more than half of Venezuelan workers were turning to jobs in the informal economy.[48] While foreign banks were moving in, Venezuela's elite was moving out. The country lost more than $8 billion to flight capital in 1995–98. On top of all this, its foreign debt reached $38 billion, with debt service costing up to 10 percent of income each year.[49]

The only reason there were no more coup attempts under President Caldera was that as soon as Hugo Chávez was released from jail in 1996, he looked around and realized that in two short years there would be another presidential election. Given the absolute mess that the ruling parties had made with all their reforms and social adjustments, a coup was no longer necessary—the masses were eager to throw the bastards out.

THE HARVEST

In the December 1998 presidential elections, former Lt. Colonel Chávez, now the forty-four-year-old candidate of the "Movement of the Fifth Republic" (Movimiento Quinta Republico or MVR), easily defeated seven other candidates, capturing 57.4 percent of the vote. To the horror of the old guard, including the corrupt leadership of the largest trade unions, he was elected on a blatantly populist appeal, attacking "*capitalism sauvage*," decrying the country's "predatory oligarchs," accusing the Catholic Church's hierarchy of "not walking in the path of Christ," and expressing admiration for Cuba's Fidel Castro. He promised to bring about a "Bolivarian revolution, " resist "uni-polar" US dominance, battle the corruption that he claimed was stealing most of the nation's oil wealth, reform the corrupt trade unions, increase tax collections, and help the poor.

This was brave *bonapartiste* rhetoric, if not a very precise platform. Chávez was nothing if not garrulous and personable, "the magician of the emotions," with a call-in radio program every Sunday called *Alo Presidente*, a taste for baseball, red berets, five-hour speeches, and earthy charm; one of his favorite stunts was to parade through Caracas, waving one of Simon Bolivar's swords.[50] His closest advisors were a grab-bag of political malcontents, who'd spent years outside the system looking in. They also happened to include some of the country's best critical minds. Jose Vicente Rangel—a leading investigative journalist, former congressman, and former presidential candidate—became foreign minister, defense minister, and then vice president. Luis Miquilena, an eighty-year-old activist and member of Venezuela's Communist Party, who spent five hard years in prison under the Pérez Jiménez dictatorship in the 1950s, became the minister of the interior and justice, and president of the National Assembly. Manual Quijada, a lawyer who spent time in jail for a coup attempt in the early 1960s, chaired the assembly's effort to restructure the courts. Retired Air Force Lt. Colonel Luis Reyes, who commanded the Air Force squadron that led the November 1992 coup attempt, became infrastructure minister. Another former guerilla, Dr. Ali Rodríguez Araque, "Commandante Fausto," became minister of mines and energy, and later, OPEC's secretary-general and PDVSA's president. Conspicuously missing from this group of jailbirds and left-wing intelligentsia were any "truly distinguished" economists or bankers—although cynics noted that, given the track record of economists and bankers in Venezuela, that concept was ill-defined.

For the moment Chávez decided to leave the Central Bank in the hands of technocrats, to continue servicing the foreign debt, and to welcome foreign investment rather than nationalize it. However, he soon showed a propensity for thumbing his nose at the US, which also happened to be Venezuela's largest trading partner, creditor, and investor. In August 2000, on a tour of OPEC countries, he became the first head of state to visit Iraq since 1991. He also made stops in all the other OPEC countries, including Iran, Qatar, Indonesia, Nigeria, Saudi Arabia, and Libya, where he described Muammar Khadaffi as a "hero." He signed a $1 billion deal to supply oil to Cuba at below-market rates and spent long hours consulting, playing baseball, and singing songs with Fidel. He called for the creation of the South American equivalent of NATO, to defend against *el gringos*. He branded the US air war in Afghanistan as "fighting terrorism with terrorism." His defense minister kicked the US military mission out of its Caracas offices, describing it as a "cold war anachronism." He refused to cooperate in Plan Colombia, the American effort against Colombian drug-trafficking guerrillas, and denied the US access to Venezuelan air space for purposes of conducting the drug war. He was also accused by his increasingly angry opponents in the elite of harboring members of Basque ETA terrorists, Arab terrorists, FARC terrorists, drug dealers, and even al-Qaeda, although none of these charges were substantiated.[51]

In one of his oddest moments, in April 1999, Chávez wrote a letter to fellow Venezuelan Ilych Ramirez Sanchez ("Carlos the Jackal"), who was serving a life sentence for murder in a maximum security jail in France. Chávez's letter addressed him as "Distinguished Compatriot" and expressed solidarity with Ramirez for "the cause and the mission."[52] (Ramirez was the son of Jose Altagracia Ramirez, founder of the Venezuelan Communist Party, who had once shared a cell with Interior Minister Miquilena, Chávez's mentor.) This correspondence certainly did not improve Chávez reputation in conservative circles.

All such gestures must been emotionally satisfying, and they certainly appealed to some of the President's less thoughtful supporters. But they did little to heal the divisions that had characterized Venezuelan politics when Chávez assumed power in February 1999.

A HAVEN FOR MONTESINOS?

In June 2001, Chávez voiced outrage when Peruvian agents, with help from the FBI, located Vladimiro Montesinos, the former head of Peru's national intelligence service (the "SIN"), hiding out in Caracas and fighting to maintain access to an estimated $1 billion in haven deposits that he'd stashed in more than a dozen banks, including Citibank and UBS.[53] What really angered Chávez was that Venezuelan authorities had not been trusted enough to be told in advance—Peruvian agents and the FBI had operated on Venezuelan soil without permission. In an operation called "Checkmate," the Peruvians and the FBI conspired to induce Montesinos's own security guards to turn him in, in return for a promised (but never paid) $5 million reward.

However, in the nick of time, Venezuela's military police showed up, arrested Montesinos, and extradited him to Peru themselves. Miquilena, the aging left-wing interior minister, later denied that the FBI or the Peruvians had played any role in this arrest, claiming it was just sheer coincidence that everyone had found Montesinos at precisely the same time. An FBI spokesperson, on the other hand, claimed the Venezuelans had known Montesino's whereabouts for months. After all, he had been in Venezuela since December 2000, when he flew there from Aruba and Costa Rica for plastic surgery.[54] In protest, Chávez temporarily withdrew his ambassador from Peru, and Peru reciprocated.[55] This incident further polarized Venezuelan opinion about the president. His opponents, including Andres Perez, claimed that Chávez had knowingly harbored a world-class felon, and the FBI agents involved in the case swore that the Venezuelans had been tipped off about their investigation.

Chávez's supporters, on the other hand, pointed out that Montesinos and Andres Perez had actually shared the same Venezuelan doctor, and that several of Montesinos's key bodyguards had held senior positions in the DISIP (Venezuela's domestic intelligence service), as well as other security posts, while Andres Perez, Lusinchi, and Antonio Ledezma, the ADeco mayor of Caracas, were in power. Furthermore, if anyone had aided and abetted Montesinos, it was clearly the US government, which had trained him at its School of the Americas (renamed the "Western Hemisphere Institute for Security Cooperation" in 2000), recruited him as its key agent in Peru, provided technical assistance for his efforts against the guerilla group Shining Path and contributed at least $10 million to his "counternarcotics" unit in the 1990s.[56]

POPULIST SHOCK THERAPY

What really got Venezuelan political juices flowing, however, was Chávez's plan to completely restructure the country's political system. After taking office in February 1999, he moved quickly, exploiting his eighty percent approval rating to push through a referendum that called for a new constitutional assembly. As Chávez said in July 1999, "Our immense responsibility is nothing more and nothing less than to refound the republic. The future of an entire nation is at stake. . . . There can be no middle ground. . . . One is either with God or with the Devil."[57] That month, elections were held for the Assembly. Chávez's supporters emerged with a commanding 120 of 133 seats. The two traditional political parties, AD and COPEI, decided not to participate directly, instead choosing to back opposition candidates who ran as independents. Thus, Andres Perez and most of the other party bosses failed to win seats.

The assembly worked quickly, and by November 1999 it released a new draft of the Constitution to the public, which it proposed as a replacement for the old 1961 Constitution. Just a month later, on December 15, 1999, this new Constitution was approved by an overwhelming majority. The new Constitution called for new congressional and presidential elections in July 2000, giving Chávez a chance to run for another six-year term and still another one after that in 2007. It also gave him the power to dissolve the senate, assume command of the judicial system, and adopt a wide range of measures by decree.

In the July 2000 elections, he was reelected, this time with sixty-one percent of the vote. His MVR party also dominated the new Congress. In December 2000, another national referendum mandated that all existing union leaders be suspended for six months, after which there would be new union elections. Given the widespread perception that Venezuela's union leaders were thoroughly compromised, this was approved with a sixty-five percent rate, although only twenty-two percent of the country's eleven million voters showed up.

Armed with all these new powers, as well as control of the new Congress and judiciary, Chávez started to make fundamental changes, attacking almost every entrenched interest group at once—a populist version of shock therapy. In November 2001, using his "fast track" authority, he announced forty-nine new laws on a wide range of matters, from land reform, ports, and fishing rights to banking and taxation. These measures provoked a hailstorm of criticism from land owners, bankers, and union leaders. One measure, for instance, provided that fifteen percent of all new bank lending had to go to small businesses and farms; another permitted the government to expropriate large estates and unproductive agricultural land, defined as any farm land that was idle more than two years.

Meanwhile, Chávez paid special attention to the needs of his poorer constituents. During its first three years, his administration focused on controlling inflation because it understood that the poor were especially defenseless against it. Until the sharp conflicts of 2002, the Chávez administration also managed to make some progress on cutting unemployment, containing the budget deficit, boosting oil revenues, and maintaining a steady, gradual devaluation of the bolivar. His administration also spent more on programs that benefited the lower classes, like schools and hospital infrastructure, encouraging 1.5 million delinquent kids to attend school, a new microcredit bank for women, vaccinations, road maintenance, 135,000 new homes for low-income people, and small business loans.

At first, many among Venezuela's middle and upper classes—the top twenty percent of the income ladder that received more than half the country's income—had welcomed Chávez as an antidote for corruption and a vigorous alternative to the old moribund parties. Now they began to see him as a threat to their prerogatives and an increasing irritation to Venezuela's northern allies. Whether they liked his policies or not, the objective reality was that the resulting class conflict guaranteed that Venezuela's economy would soon become a battleground.

By the end of 2001, his approval ratings in opinion polls had dropped from eighty percent to less than half. This coincided with the first organized response from the ruling elite to Chávez's reforms. On December 10, 2001, thousands of protesters took to the streets of Caracas, in the first of four general strikes over the following year. They were led by the Venezuelan Workers' Confederation (CTV), the country's largest trade union, and Fedecamaras, Venezuela's powerful Chamber of Commerce.

Meanwhile, there was also a new wave of capital flight, as Venezuelans who still had liquid assets in the country voted with their wallets. From November 2001 to February 2002, the Central Bank spent $7 billion trying to defend the "crawling peg" exchange rate system that it had maintained since 1997. In February, it finally gave up, and the bolivar fell twenty-four percent against the dollar in one month.

But Chávez was determined to press ahead with his agenda. One of his pet structural issues was the country's national oil company, PDVSA. Neoliberal analysts, the World Bank, and the US government, as well as many investment bankers, had long been pressing Venezuela to privatize the oil company. But Chávez had long complained that PDVSA was in fact already a quasi-private fiefdom: a "state within a state" dominated by an avaricious network of overpaid managers, union bosses, board members, and crony contractors at home and abroad who bought and sold from the company on insider terms, greased by hefty payoffs. PDVSA, the world's second largest state oil company, accounted for 80–90 percent of Venezuela's exports, half the government's income, and a third of Venezuela's official GDP. However, until Chávez's government, its executives had been free to decide what projects to fund, who to contract with, what prices to charge, and how much to pay the government each year in royalties. According to Chávez, the result was that more than eighty percent of PDVSA's true profits had simply disappeared into the pockets of the insider network—"the equivalent of fifteen Marshall Plans."[58] Given his ambitious plans for social spending, that was simply no longer acceptable.[59]

Furthermore, while Venezuela had played a key role in organizing OPEC back in the 1960s, more recently it had taken a backseat role, partly to keep the US—its main customer—happy. When Chávez took office in February 1999, crude oil was just nine dollars a barrel—a record low. This was less than half the level, in real terms, of the 1950s oil prices and one-fifth the real level that Venezuela had enjoyed in the early 1980s, before the debt crisis. By September 2000, when Chávez convened a meeting of OPEC oil ministers in Caracas and pushed for tighter quotas on oil production, the price exceeded twenty-nine dollars.[60] Chávez's energy minister Ali Rodríguez become OPEC's new secretary-general, and took the lead in exhorting OPEC members and non-OPEC producers like Russia and Norway to maintain strong price levels.[61]

Meanwhile, Chávez started to gain control over PDVSA. In August 1999, Robert Mandini, PDVSA's president, was forced out after he resisted Chávez's plans to use more of the company's profits for development projects. In the next three years, Chávez changed PDVSA's CEO five more times. In February 2002, as the foreign exchange crisis was mounting, Chávez appointed Gaston Luis Parra Luzardo, a leftist economics professor, as CEO. He wanted to press ahead with new laws that increased the royalty paid by PDVSA to the government on oil exports from sixteen to thirty percent, which required a fifty-one percent government participation in all oil ventures. When PDVSA's existing board resisted the appointment, Chávez fired the entire board of directors, installed his own slate, and then fired nineteen senior executives who had refused the pro-Chávez board's instructions. Later that year, as the social confrontation continued, his latest PDVSA president replaced five thousand of the company's forty thousand workers.

THE COUP . . . NOT

The assault on PDVSA's independence finally caused the pot to boil over. Its senior managers united with leading unions, the Fedecamaras, the hierarchy of the Catholic Church, and Venezuela's dominant TV and newspaper networks to call a national strike in support of the fired managers. Chávez was uncompromising. "Nothing can stop Venezuela," he said, predicting that the strike would be "doomed to fail." On April 9, 2002, a half-million people turned out in Caracas for the strike, and nineteen died in street clashes. With the country heading for civil war, a split developed in the ranks of the military, and for a moment, it looked like this cross-class coalition would push Chávez aside.

On April 11, Chávez was arrested by a rebel military faction, including some of the country's top officers. On April 12, Pedro Carmona Estanga—an economist, president of the *Fedecamaras*, and director of Industrias Venoco CA, a successful Venezuelan petrochemical company that had a direct stake in the coup's outcome—stepped forward as the self-proclaimed head of a purported transitional government. When the smoke cleared, more than a hundred people had died, and Venezuela appeared to have had its first nondemocratic transition since 1958.

Oddly enough, for a country that has lately made so much noise about promoting "democracy and the rule of law" in Latin America and throughout the world, this completely illegal transition was immediately welcomed with open arms by both the US government and leading elements of the US media. On April 12, the State Department issued a press release that—quite falsely—blamed Chávez's government for all the violence and chaos, claiming that he had *first* "fired his vice president and cabinet" *and then* "resigned the presidency." This precise State Department reconstruction of events was no accident. It artfully laid the foundation for the notion that the transition was not a "coup," but entirely legal, since there was no one who could legally take power from Chávez. The US welcomed the resulting "transition" with open arms:

> Yesterday's events in Venezuela resulted in a transitional government until new elections can be held. Though details are still unclear, undemocratic actions committed or encouraged by the Chávez administration provoked yesterday's crisis in Venezuela. The results of these provocations are: Chávez resigned the presidency. . . . Before resigning, he dismissed the vice president and the cabinet. A transition civilian government has promised early elections. We have every expectation that this situation will be resolved peacefully and democratically by the Venezuelan people in accord with the principles of the Inter-American Democratic Charter.[62]

The White House also chimed in, declaring that "The details still are a little unclear, but what we know is that the actions fomented by Chávez caused a crisis."[63] The last time the US was so enthusiastic about a nondemocratic government in Venezuela was in the 1950s, when President Eisenhower stalwart-

ly supported the dictatorship of Marco Perez Jimenez until he was overthrown in 1958.

Embarrassingly, it later emerged that key officials at the White House, the
State Department, NSA, and the Pentagon, plus the AFL-CIO and various
other recipients of US aid, had been very active in the months and weeks
leading up to the 2002 coup, if not quite orchestrating it down to the last
detail, then at least meeting with all its principals and offering them lots of
winks and nods, plus hard cash.[64] After the whole fiasco fell apart, the US also
provided several of the coup's leaders with refuge in Miami.[65] Nor was the
support just limited to hard-line rightists. In an April 13 editorial, the *New
York Times* also celebrated Chávez's departure, asserting that "Venezuelan
democracy is no longer threatened by a would-be dictator . . . [because] the
military intervened and handed power to a respected business leader."[66]

Unfortunately for the coup's supporters, this celebration turned out to be
a bit premature—mainly because the "respected business leader" Carmona
proved to be more of an imperious Al Haig-like figure than a Corazon
Aquino. In just a few hours, Carmona turned his back on the entire broad
coalition that had produced the strike, alienating the unions, most business
people, the Church, and key elements of the military, as well as Chávez's many
critics on the left. Without consulting them, he and an insular band of 10–15
right wingers—later described as the "Taliban of the Right," with close ties
to Opus Dei, the conservative Catholic lay organization—basically tried to
hijack the movement. Their one decree, issued unilaterally, dissolved
Venezuela's Congress and Supreme Court, voided the 1999 Constitution,
cancelled all forty-nine of Chávez's reform laws, ended diplomatic relations
with Cuba, removed "Bolivarian" from the country's title, and announced a
new transitional government that included Andres Perez's former personal
secretary as attorney general. a leading right-wing member of Opus Dei, José
Rodríguez Iturbe, as foreign minister, Hector Ramirez, as the defense minister, and Admiral Mulina Tamayo, who had recently been cashiered, as head of
presidential security. If this were a CIA/US government plot, so the joke
went, the conspirators must have been trying to *keep* Chávez in power.

Meanwhile, Chávez still had many cards to play. He knew that Venezuela's
military, sensitive to its reputation, did not want to be seen as having overthrown an elected government, and certainly was not prepared to "pull a
Pinochet" and murder him in cold blood. So he simply refused to resign.
Many of his key supporters, like the Paratroopers' commander, had also been
left in place, while the generals and admirals were more interested in jockey-
ing for position than in seeing the transition through. Third, Venezuela's new
leaders-for-a-day were almost completely isolated internationally. The coup
was swiftly condemned by the Organization of American States (OAS),

which happened to be holding a summit in Costa Rica for nineteen current and former heads of state, including Mexico's Vicente Fox and Colombia's César Gaviria, its secretary general. The OAS quickly issued a statement condemning "the interruption of Constitutional order in Venezuela" and called a meeting to consider possible sanctions against an "undemocratic country." Indeed, the only countries whose ambassadors showed up to recognize Carmona were the US and Spain, where Jóse Maria Aznar's conservative government was in power, and where Venezuela's dictator Marcos Perez Jimenez had been given refuge ever since his 1958 overthrow, until his death in 2001.

When they heard about the coup, thousands of Chávez's working class supporters poured out of the *ranchos* and headed for Miraflores—the presidential palace—to show support. In contrast, many of Chávez's opponents, especially those in the unions, became disgruntled by Carmona's behavior and went home. Chávez was eventually able to mobilize his military supporters, and by the morning of April 14, he was back in power, even insisting on doing his Sunday radio program. Carmona was put under house arrest, fled to the Colombian embassy, and then escaped to Bogotá. Most of his comrades had long since caught private planes to Miami or Costa Rica.

Over the next year, Chávez continued battling to hold onto power. This time around, the opposition abandoned the *golpista* military coup route to power and collected several million signatures demanding that Chávez hold a national referendum on his presidency in February 2003. But Chávez insisted on sticking to the letter of the Constitution, which provided for a national referendum no earlier than August 2004, halfway through his term. Jimmy Carter showed up in August 2002 to mediate the dispute, but there was little progress. At year's end, Chávez survived another disastrous two-month general strike that started in December 2002 and collapsed in February 2003, without any referendum. As one opposition leader admitted, this last general strike was, in reality, "a stoppage of the middle and upper classes."[67] By then, Chávez's approval ratings in the polls had dropped from eighty to less than thirty percent, but no other national leaders came even close to that level. He was a cat with many lives.

All this had a severe impact on the economy and on the living conditions of the very people Chávez supposedly cared most about. In 2002, mainly because of the unresolved social conflict, Venezuela's GDP shrank another nine percent, unemployment hit seventeen percent, and inflation reached thirty-one percent. In December 2002, during the general strike, oil production fell from 3.2 million barrels a day to less than 200,000. The black market price of gasoline increased up to ten times the normal level; the country was even forced to import gasoline as well as food. In 2002, the bolivar had lost half of its value. By late January 2003, when it became clear that Chávez would survive the strike, the bolivar dropped another twenty-five percent, Venezuela's reserves dropped to less than $11 billion, and the Central Bank was forced to close the exchange market for a week.[68] In December 2002, the State Department warned Americans to leave the country. Companies like Ford, McDonalds, and Microsoft closed their local offices. Per capita income had fallen to *1960* levels, and eighty percent of the population lives below the poverty line, despite having three times the oil reserves of Mexico. Compared with 1999, when Chávez took office, another 3.6 million Venezuelans had fallen below the poverty line. To paraphrase the cynic, "[Chávez] must love poor people; he made so many of them."

Given the importance of Venezuela's oil to the US and its war with Iraq in 2003, the US suddenly tried to encourage a political settlement. But Chávez did not find it easy to compromise. In February 2003, buoyed by the failure of the latest general strike, he ordered the arrest of Carlos Fernandez, Carmona's successor at the Fedecamaras, on treason charges. The economy was in ruins, the political outlook was uncertain, and many of those who could afford to leave the country were doing so.

THE LONG VIEW

Of course there is no shortage of critics who blame this entire mess on Hugo Chávez Frias—the pugnacious *pardo* and career military officer who proved not only to be one of Venezuela's most popular leaders in history, but also, once in power, much more of a *commandante* than a politician. Stubborn and confrontational, hard to bargain with, and even harder to intimidate or buy off, he undoubtedly brought many of his problems onto himself.

There was certainly much to criticize about Chávez's leadership style, even apart from his social programs, which were inevitably controversial, given the country's situation. His foreign policy was needlessly provocative. He did not pay enough attention to fighting corruption in his own ranks, although, as in the Montesinos case, many of the charges turned out to be partisan lies. Unfortunately, personal enrichment is a motive that Venezuelans now ascribe to all their political leaders, but while these charges deserve further investigation, when the dust settles, I suspect that corruption will not turn out to be Chávez's key failing.[69]

His worst failing may be the fact that he has squandered an opportunity to make lasting political and social reforms. Chávez and his supporters bear heavy responsibility for Venezuela's increased polarization and violence, which undermined many of his original goals. He started off by picking fights with almost every interest group at once. This approach may have seemed "revolutionary," but it smacked of adventurism. While Chávez talked a good deal about a democratic alternative to neoliberalism, he also idealized Fidel Castro, who had never won a contested election, and Simon Bolivar, who by the time of his death in 1830 was widely despised and dictatorial, unwelcome in either Colombia or Venezuela (latter-day "Gran Colombia") and was offered a three thousand dollar pension by Congress if he would agree to leave the country. If Chávez really cared about building a progressive political movement, he would have devoted more energy to building a progressive party that had other strong leaders, not just "*un hombre en un caballo blanco*" (man on a white horse). In this respect, the contrast with Brazil's Luis Ignacio da Silva was striking.

Along those lines, perhaps the most intelligent thing for Chávez to have done would have been to step aside. This would have defused the situation, earned the MVR Party credit for avoiding a bloodbath, and helped to build a progressive movement. After all, that was what the most powerful global interests feared most. Saddam and Fidel notwithstanding, these interests are really quite adept at dealing with aging dictators and even with so-called "terrorists." What really threatens the system is a progressive movement with a popular following that is serious about competence, social democracy, and the rule of law.

But whatever becomes of Chávez, his movement at least succeeded in galvanizing millions of Venezuelans on all sides of the political spectrum into civic action. It is too soon to tell, but one can hope Venezuela's corrupt, elitist political infrastructure is at least weakened forever. Whatever else one thinks of Hugo Chávez, that is an achievement. After all, it was that system, not Chávez, that destabilized the country, wasted its wealth, and created the opportunity for him to take power. While he dominated the government for three years, that system dominated the whole society for more than three decades—and not just the executive branch, the Congress, the judiciary, the police, the military, and state enterprises, but all its key business groups, unions, professional societies, and even the church. Together with their First World bankers and other foreign supporters, the members of the elite that composed that system contrived to bankrupt the country and abscond with much of its wealth, long before Hugo Chávez won power.

In short, Venezuela, like many other developing countries, was born rich, yet it has ended up with the vast majority of its people living in dire poverty. To account for this unhappy outcome, it is not necessary to invoke accidents of climate, geography, wars, policy "errors," or even the overall level of Venezuela's foreign debt, much less the actions of subversive radicals or other "enemies." The avaricious behavior of its own elite and their unscrupulous First World allies was more than adequate to accomplish the job.

CHAPTER FOUR

BRAZIL'S FALLEN ANGELS

If you write anything about this, I'll kill you. . . .
—Tony Gebauer, JPMorgan's former senior banker
for Latin America, to the author, February 1986

For what is the crime of burglarizing a bank, compared with the crime of
building one?
—Brecht

Law. What Law? Ain't I got the power?
—J. P. Morgan

*"What have you been up to, Jim? Morgan's going crazy." Jane Amsterdam, Man-
hattan Inc.'s editor at the time, wore her usual elvish grin. "Their ad guys just called.
They said, 'We really like your magazine, but, you see, you're doing this piece on the
bank.' They even sent someone to see the publisher. He has demanded to see the proofs,
but I took them home. You know, we've done stories on some pretty heavy hitters—
Trump, Boesky, Steinberg—but this is the most heat we've ever had."*

*It was the spring of 1987, and I'd just completed an article for Jane's magazine
about Tony Gebauer, a Morgan senior vice president who ran the bank's South American operations during the 1980s debt boom. He'd just been sentenced to 3.5 years in
federal prison for stealing money from several private clients. My investigation had
turned up several interesting puzzles in the case, but at the time I had no idea why
Morgan had anything to fear from my story—it appeared to me to be just a straight-
forward example of "one bad apple gone wrong." When I began to look closer, however,
Morgan bristled. Senior bankers were warned to keep quiet. One Morgan lawyer, an
old friend and neighbor, phoned to tell me that I should call off the hunt. Another Morgan banker who was a friend of Jane Amsterdam's husband told him that the bank was
indeed very nervous about the piece, and its ad agency lobbied hard to get the piece
killed. Naturally, blue-blood institutions like to protect their reputations, but if this case
were really as simple as it seemed, why all the beads of blue-blood sweat?*

*Unfortunately I didn't have time to pursue my research in Brazil before the piece
ran as a cover story that May. But this case turned out to be a very good introduction
to the intricate sociology of bad lending, as well as to the limits of investigating the*

debt/flight story from inside the US. There was indeed much more to Gebauer's story than met the eye. But to get it, I had to do more firsthand research in Brazil, Caracas, London, Miami, Geneva, Panama, and Venezuela, interviewing most of Gebauer's former "clients" in the process. I endured the loss of all my notes and money in a Rio street robbery, and a nerve-racking undercover interview in a heavily guarded Rio penthouse with a leading arms dealer whose personal office was only accessible through a drop-down stairway to the floor below. I also passed several tense days in Bahia, where some of Gebauer's most powerful and unforgiving friends were headquartered. And even after all this, I wasn't able to do the sequel for Jane Amsterdam. Right after my piece ran, her publisher fired her...

In a crowded Manhattan Federal courtroom in January 1987, the occasion is the sentencing of a forty-six-year-old man the judge describes as "Lucifer, a fallen angel from the banking world. . . . An example of the tragedy that results when an ambitious, driven man fails to see the widening chasm between reality and illusion in his own life."[1] Tony Gebauer stands stiffly before the court, a picture-book banker in a dark blue wool suit, tortoiseshell glasses, and, one suspects, maroon suspenders and a monogrammed shirt. Deacons of the Establishment flutter about in the background like the owls of Minerva. Close by sits Morgan's counsel Chris Crowley, from the esteemed Wall Street firm of Davis, Polk, Wardwell. He and his partners worked closely with Gebauer for more than two decades on personal banking and real estate deals. Judge Robert Sweet is a Yale man and a former deputy mayor under John Lindsey, the younger brother of Robert V. Lindsey, Yale '38, Morgan's president until 1986. When Robert V. Lindsey heard the news about Gebauer, he cried.

Tony Gebauer himself is a short Napoleonic Lucifer. A citizen of Venezuela and an "honorary citizen" of Brazil, he was born in Bogotá in 1940, the son of a middle-class Bavarian brewmaster. In 1957 he moved to New York, received his BA and an MBA from Columbia, and acquired great wealth, including an expensive Manhattan co-op, three East Hampton homes, an apartment on Paris's Avenue Hoche, an impressive collection of German Expressionist paintings, pre-Colombian gold and old manuscripts, one-third of a 1,330-acre Bahian coffee farm, a condo on Key Biscayne, a wife who was the daughter of a wealthy Brazilian, another who was the daughter of a former US ambassador to Italy, and three sons. As one of his art dealers explained, "Tony's a collector."

Judge Sweet delivers the sentence. It sounds pretty tough, at least on the surface: 3.5 years in prison and a $100,000 fine, plus $7.9 million in reimbursements to Morgan and $6.9 million to the IRS. Actually he served only 1.5 years at Danbury, one of the nicest "Fat Farms" in the federal prison system, before his release for good behavior in August 1988. But for Gebauer the worst punishment was social excommunication.

After a lengthy investigation by Morgan and careful negotiations with the US attorney, Gebauer pleaded guilty in October 1986 to four felony counts involving bank fraud and tax evasion, on the basis of what prosecutors maintained was the unauthorized diversion of $4.3 million from four wealthy Brazilians. The case seemed straightforward—a talented banker rises to a position of authority and abuses his control over client accounts, a not uncommon example of private bankers turning on their clients. All of the accounts that Gebauer looted were easily mistaken for ordinary flight banking conduits—all were "hold-mail" accounts in the names of haven companies that had never been properly reported to Brazil's Central Bank or the IRS.[2]

From this angle, Gebauer's case was special only because his fall was so steep. By the age of forty, he was already one of only five senior vice presidents in Morgan's International Division. His colleagues and competitors agree that by then he was "Mr. Brazil," by far the best-connected American banker in Brazil, which had the Third World's largest debt. He had played a crucial role in building Morgan's $1.7 billion Brazil loan portfolio and syndicating another $7.2 billion in loans to Brazil. He was also heavily involved in lending to Venezuela, Ecuador, Chile, and Argentina. He advised Brazilian and Venezuelan presidents and ministers, Federal Reserve chairmen, and World Bank and IMF officials on credit policies. In late 1982, when Brazil was no longer able to service its $92 billion debt, Antonio Delfim Neto, Brazil's planning minister, picked Gebauer to restructure it. In 1984, a Morgan spokesman called him "the most highly esteemed banker in Latin America."[3] From 1970 to 1983, Tony Gebauer was Morgan Guaranty's largest single breadwinner and was seriously considered for its presidency.[4]

Meanwhile, despite all this hard work, Gebauer maintained an even more opulent lifestyle than that of his chairman, Lewis T. Preston.[5] The Brazilian press loved to spotlight Gebauer's high living and colorful romances. In the linear world of international banking, this stimulated much jealousy, but so long as Gebauer brought home the bacon, no one in Morgan's higher echelons seemed to mind.

Gebauer was also unusual because he really did fall from bankers' heaven—Morgan, the blue-blooded American bank, "the epitome of solidity and sobriety," "America's classiest bank," the fourth largest and most profitable bank in the US. Until his retirement in 1989, before he left to become president of the World Bank, Morgan's chairman Preston was widely regarded as "the most respected banker in America."[6] The bank was especially proud of the fact that its bankers were, if perhaps not very *alegre*, "fundamentally of good character."[7] Bright young people, hired fresh out of elite schools, they resembled the high-octane candidates recruited by investment banks, which paid higher salaries, but supposedly could not provide, in the words of a Morgan recruiter, "the balance in their lives" of a career at Morgan. Proportionately, Morgan has more lifetime employees than any other bank.[8] Gebauer was its worst scandal since the 1930s, when Richard Whitney, the president of the New York Stock Exchange, " JP Morgan's man on the floor," and the brother of a senior Morgan banker, was sentenced to five years in Sing Sing for filching $800,000 of bonds entrusted to him by Harvard University, the New York Yacht Club, and a Stock Exchange fund for brokers' widows.[9] As a senior banker at a leading competitor remarked, "If a Morgan SVP could be involved in 'tricky business' in Latin America, then *anyone* could be."[10]

Morgan's good name was to some extent in the dock alongside Gebauer's. After all, he'd spent his entire twenty-two-year career at the bank. For most of it he led a dual life—a highly visible one as a dealmaker and socialite and a subterranean one that was equally energetic. When the debt boom ended and his official career stumbled, the criminal side surfaced. At that point, many of his colleagues expressed "complete shock."[11] But in fact the two sides were symbiotic: Gebauer's position at the pinnacle of Latin American lending generated opportunities for crimes almost automatically, and the fact is that his official career would not have been nearly as successful without them.

What is most interesting about this tale is not Gebauer's misconduct, but Morgan's responsibility for it. Even his official crimes were not just a few isolated events. He got Morgan to issue bogus checks averaging $20,000 apiece, 20–40 times a year from 1976 to 1983. He got other Morgan officers to endorse several million dollars in loans to accounts he was tapping and to renew them forty-six times. He also got an officer to prepare twenty-four phony bank statements over a five-year period.[12]

More importantly, there is also evidence, presented here for the first time, that Gebauer's transgressions went considerably beyond those reflected in his guilty plea. His misbehavior did not start in 1976 as the indictment charged, but much earlier. His behavior wasn't unique—he had help from several others inside and outside the bank. He did not have just four Brazilian clients but at least a dozen—including at least one prominent Brazilian official—and his victims were not just his "clients;" several appear to have been his *partners*. Many of Morgan's loans to Brazil were arranged with the help of illegal commissions that Gebauer split with these partners. In some cases, Morgan also made loans to private companies owned by finance ministers and other key officials. Finally, at least two of Gebauer's bosses at Morgan were put on notice about his practices as early as 1981, before he was a senior vice president, but nothing was done.

The Gebauer case thus raises questions about the internal controls and ethical standards at one of the world's most prestigious banks. It also sheds light on a darker side of Third World banking—the practice of cultivating loans with illegal payoffs and insider deals. The fact is that Morgan Guaranty, the world's most profitable bank, depended for a substantial part of its profits in the 1970s and early 1980s on Latin America in general and Brazil in particular, which depended on Gebauer, who depended on such practices.

GEBAUER'S SOCIAL ORIGINS

Gebauer hardly had the usual Morgan profile. He was one of the few Latin Americans ever hired by Morgan, although his indirect ties to the bank were very old. He was the son of a "solid, hardworking, and not very sophisticated" Munich brewmaster, Eugenio Gebauer, who emigrated to Colombia in the late 1920s. In 1946, Eugenio sold his Bogotá maltery to Julio Mario Santo-Domingo, Colombia's richest non-drug entrepreneur. He owned Cervecería Bavaria and Avianca Airlines and was already a Morgan private client. Eugenio moved to Caracas and became brewmaster for Cervecería Nacional, Venezuela's top brewery, owned by Gustavo Vollmer, another long-standing Morgan client. Nacional's chairman was the father of Arturo Sosa, the future Venezuelan finance minister, another close friend of Gebauer's who later became a coinvestor with Morgan in a Venezuelan bank.[13]

Gebauer and his sister Erna grew up in Caracas. The late 1940s were prosperous oil boom years. Even on a brewmaster's salary, Eugenio was able to afford two servants, private schools for his children, and extensive travels. The children attended a German school, where Gebauer met José Alvarez Stelling, another future Morgan client, whose family owned Banco Consolidado and "all the land from Valencia to Caracas."[14] Later, Gebauer enrolled in a Catholic high school and went to summer camp in the US. In the fall of 1957, just as he turned eighteen, Caracas's Central University was closed by riots against the dictator Perez Jimenez. Gebauer moved to New York and enrolled in Columbia University. At first his father wanted him to be a brewmaster, but a Venezuelan broker persuaded him to let his son become a banker. Gebauer then studied economics, earning credits toward an MBA.

Columbia was also where Gebauer met his first wife, Fernandina de Souza Queiroz, in 1962. She was the stepdaughter of João Suplicy Hafers, a coffee broker who represented the Brazilian Coffee Institute in New York. Gebauer had been dating Hafers's sister, but when he met Fernandina, it was love at first sight. They were married in the fall of 1963, after his college graduation. Columbia was also where Gebauer met his first Morgan banker, Charles McVey. He was impressed with Gebauer's international background and outgoing personality. He arranged interviews for him with Heinz Vithzthun and Fred Vinton, two VPs in Morgan's small Latin American group. They liked him, but Walter Page, the head of Morgan's International Division and its future chairman, had doubts: "Do you think this guy will ever sell anything?"[15] Of course "selling" proved to be the very least of Gebauer's problems.

After a brief honeymoon, Gebauer joined Morgan in November 1963 as a trainee in "Latin America—West." He visited Caracas several times in 1964–65, where Morgan's representative let him run the shop.[16] In 1966, he shifted over to the Brazil desk, reporting to John Porges, the head of the Latin American Division.

FOUNDATIONS

One longtime Brazilian banker recalled that at that time Morgan's position in Latin America was "essentially nowhere." Years earlier, it had been one of the first US banks to do international banking. In the 1880s, J. P. Morgan Sr. acquired France's Morgan et Cie and a third of London's Morgan Grenfell, and in 1908 the bank added Guaranty Trust Company, which had French, Belgian, and UK branches. From 1890 to 1930, Morgan floated more Latin American bonds than any other bank. But from the Depression until the 1950s, it had largely neglected Latin America. By 1964, its entire Mexican exposure was only $15 million, and its Brazilian exposure just $50 million. Morgan's Latin American group was run by people who were "not very aggressive . . . bright but not outgoing. . . . [The head] would show up in Rio and wait at his hotel for clients to call on him." Of the group's five bankers, only Fred Vinton, the son of a longtime Citibank rep in Buenos Aires, had ever lived in Latin America. Citibank, Chase, and Bank of Boston all had local branches in Rio and São Paulo, but Morgan did not.[17]

Brazil was a risky place to do banking. Juscelino Kubitschek, Morgan's president from 1955 to 1961, embarked on an ambitious "Fifty Years in Five" program, promoting industrialization and huge projects like Brasilia, the new federal capital in the remote state of Goiás that was aptly described as "the revenge of a Communist architect against bourgeois society."[18] Kubitschek's program produced five years of seven percent growth, unprecedented corruption, and the Third World's largest debt—$2.54 billion by 1960. That may not sound like much nowadays, but it consumed forty percent of Brazil's export earnings. In 1961, Janio da Silva Quadros, Kubitschek's successor, condemned this debt in terms that later generations would fully understand: "All this money, spent with so much publicity, we must now raise bitterly, patiently, dollar by dollar and cruzeiro by cruzeiro. We have spent, drawing on our future to a greater extent than the imagination dares to contemplate."[19]

Kubitschek's excesses led to a conservative reaction. In 1960, Quadros, a former governor of São Paulo, ran for president on an anticorruption platform with a broom as his symbol. He was elected and took office in January 1961. His finance minister, a wealthy banker, quickly signed a tough IMF agreement that agreed to devalue the currency, slash subsidies, and repay the debt. But Janio Quadros soon proved to be one of Brazil's strangest leaders. He tried to ban horse racing, boxing matches, and bikinis on the beach, and when the US pressured him to embargo Castro, he defiantly journeyed to Havana and awarded Che Guevara the Ordem do Cruzeiro do Sul, Brazil's equivalent of the Legion d'Honeur. At one point early in his term, he had been visited by Adolf Berle Jr., President Kennedy's special assistant on Latin America. Kennedy was quietly seeking Quadros's support for the upcoming Bay of Pigs invasion. According to John M. Cabot, the US ambassador at the time, Berle effectively offered "Brazil" a $300 million bribe in return for cooperation. But Quadros became visibly irritated after Berle ignored his third rejection and sent Berle off to the airport unaccompanied. A few months later, in August 1961, Quadros resigned, complaining of being surrounded by "terrible forces," and blamed his downfall on a cabal of "reactionaries" that included Berle, Cabot, and US Treasury Secretary Douglas Dillon.[20]

This allowed the succession of João Goulart, Janio's vice president, a wealthy left-leaning cattle farmer from Rio Grande do Sul. Goulart visited the US in April 1962, addressed a joint session of Congress, and received a ticker tape parade in New York. But he immediately alienated almost every key interest group at once, launching an aggressive land reform, boosting taxes on foreign investors, nationalizing utilities and oil refineries, and even encouraging enlisted men in the army to organize a union. Inflation soared to the unheard-of level of one hundred percent, exhausting four finance ministers in two years. All this was a splendid recipe for counterrevolution. Brazil's usually fractitious military leaders banded together and organized a coup that was supported by businesses, most of the "middle class," and the US government, which spent tens of millions of dollars on a covert anti-Goulart media campaign. In 1963, Goulart's second finance minister visited Washington and asserted that the left-leaning regime's social reforms had been inspired by President Kennedy's own Alliance for Progress. But he received a cold shoulder—the US aid window closed down until April 1964, after the coup. As early as 1962, US intelligence had noted coup preparations and was more than sympathetic. As David Rockefeller, who was the president of his family's bank, Chase Manhattan, told a closed-door conference at West Point in the fall of 1964, "It was decided very early that Goulart was unacceptable . . . and would have to go."[21]

The April 1, 1964 coup that followed—"the worst April Fool's joke ever"—was led by General Humberto de Alencar Castello Branco, commander of the Fourth Army in Recife. During World War II, he had served with Brazil's Expeditionary Force, which fought with the Allies in Italy. His "trench buddy" there was Colonel Vernon A. Walters, the US "military attaché" in Rio from September 20, 1962 to 1967, who would later be promoted to lieutenant general for his accomplishments in Brazil. He went on to serve as a senior CIA officer, the CIA's deputy director from March 1972 to 1976, and Reagan's UN ambassador in the 1980s. Colonel Walters spoke fluent Portuguese and was also very close to General Emílio Garrastazu Médici, head of Brazil's Black Eagles military school during the 1964 coup, military attaché to Washington (1964-65), head of Brazil's CIA, the Serviço Nacional de Informaçoes (SNI) from 1967 to 1969, and then Brazil's president, courtesy of the junta. During the coup, Castello kept both General Walters and US Ambassador Lincoln Gordon "very well informed of pre-coup deliberations," a US Navy "fast" Carrier Task Group was standing by offshore, and six US Air Force C-135 transport planes with 110 tons of arms and ammunition were also available in case there was any resistance.[22] Fortunately, the coup was almost bloodless.

Castello Branco was supposed to step down after a short period of housecleaning, but Brazil's military developed an appetite for power—staying in power from 1964 to 1985. At first, Castello turned the economy over to Octavio Bulhões, an academic-cum-finance minister, and Roberto Campos, a US-educated ex-Jesuit and former head of Brazil's powerful National Development Bank (BNDES), who became planning minister.[23] Their reign from April 1964 to March 1967 was the first in a series of rather disappointing Latin American experiments with monetarism, the notion that controlling the money supply is the *sine qua non* of economic policy. To fight inflation, they reigned in credit, slashed spending (which drove money growth, because the government financed itself by selling bonds to the banking system), and opened the door to imports. They also eased restrictions on foreign investment, eliminated taxes on foreign profits, and outlawed strikes. Dozens of labor leaders were jailed, and wages were frozen, even though inflation was still raging at forty percent a year. But the regime was careful to protect investors against inflation by indexing bonds and bank deposits. A new capital-market law also created Brazil's first investment banks and provided the country with "the most sophisticated company law in Latin America." In 1965, in an attempt to control the money supply, Campos also created Brazil's first Central Bank and a National Monetary Authority.[24]

All these measures went down rather well with bankers and the US government. Regardless of who staged the coup, it soon became quite clear who would pay for it.[25] From 1964 to 1970, Brazil received more than $2 billion in US aid, which made it the third largest aid recipient in the world.[26] About $900 million arrived in the first six months after the coup, and the US Treasury paid seventy percent of the interest due on Brazil's debt. In July 1964, Brazil also signed another IMF agreement, and in the next three years, it received $214 million in IMF loans, which had loaned Brazil nothing from 1959 to 1964. Brazil also suddenly became the World Bank's largest customer, after never receiving any loans from 1950 to 1965, as well as the largest borrower of the IDB and the US EXIM Bank. From 1964 to 1970, direct investment by US companies increased fifty percent.[27] In January 1967, the IMF held its twenty-second convention in Rio, presided over by General Artur Costa de Silva, a former war minister and Castello Branco's successor.

Unfortunately for the majority of Brazilians living in poverty, most of this aid went into paying for budget deficits, planning exercises, and capital-intensive projects. Original Alliance for Progress objectives like "eliminating illiteracy from Latin America by 1970" and "income redistribution" got short shrift.[28] The real value of the minimum wage dropped by one-fourth from 1964 to 1967, and malnutrition and infant mortality rose dramatically. Domestic industry was hit by foreign competition and a recession at once, even as the multinationals were getting cheap finance and lower taxes. Many foreign investors also got "sweetheart" deals: Campos was especially generous to Amforp, a US-owned utility, and in 1965, American billionaire Donald Ludwig was allowed to buy an Amazon forest tract twenty percent larger than Connecticut for $3 million. General Artur Golbery Couto de Silva, the military's "grey eminence," later became president of Dow Chemical do Brasil and a representative of Dow's Banco Cidade. In the early 1960s, Golbery—a top professor at the Escola Superior de Guerra, Brazil's version of the National War College, and the author of the seminal *Geopolitica do Brasil*—had used CIA funding to launch the Institute for Research and Social Studies (Instituto de Pesquisas e Estudos Sociais—IPES), the SNI's precursor. Over the next two decades, the SNI would employ more than fifty thousand people to spy on and otherwise deal with "subversives" at home and abroad. Golbery later served as head of the Casa Civil, and a key aid to President Geisel. Not surprisingly, Dow Chemical got special permission for a new plant in Bahia.[29]

Soon, even nationalist critics started attacking Roberto Campos's program as a "pastoral plan" designed by Americans to eliminate domestic industry. He became widely known as "Bob Fields," "a full-time *entreguista*" (an intermediary for foreigners). In 1964, a popular Rio bumper sticker read, "Enough of intermediaries!—(US Ambassador) Lincoln Gordon for President!" In 1966, the US ambassador complained that US advisors were implicated in "almost every unpopular decision concerning taxes, salaries and prices."[30]

In October 1965, in the last free elections until 1982, the military's candidates for state governorships in Rio de Janeiro and Minas Gerais were defeated. Workers, students, and church organizers turned radical, and several civilian leaders who had supported the coup, including Magalhães Pinto and Carlos Lacerda, also pressed for new elections. There was a sharp increase in capital flight; in 1966, Brazilians sent more money abroad than all the new foreign investment and foreign aid brought in.[31] The nationalists in the military then began to treat the "internationalist" segments of the upper classes harshly. They unleashed a spy operation to catch wealthy Brazilians with foreign accounts. In November 1966—the police, assisted by the SNI and under the command of General Fiuza de Castro—raided the offices of Bernie Cornfeld's Swiss-based IOS flight capital operation in seven cities, arresting thirteen salesmen and seizing files on ten thousand clients.[32]

All this set the stage for a hard-line backlash led by members of the military, who believed that the *castellistas* were selling out to foreigners and were not tough enough on subversives. In late 1966, Castello Branco gave way to the IMF's favorite, General Costa de Silva. Political parties were consolidated into a "majority" party, ARENA, and an official "opposition" party, the PMB—known in the underground as the "yes" and "yes sir" parties. Many opposition politicians, union leaders, and students were stripped of their civil rights. In December 1968, when a federal deputy asked Brazilian women to stop having sex with military officers until political repression ceased, the army demanded that Congress lift the deputy's immunity so he could be prosecuted for "insulting the Armed Forces." When Congress refused to do so, Costa de Silva closed it, disbanded state assemblies and city councils, suspended habeas corpus, and imposed press censorship. Arrests without warrant and torture now became common, while elections were reduced to ratifications of the military's "bionic" candidates.[33]

As for Roberto Campos, in March 1967 he moved over to the private sector, giving way to a more *dirigiste* economic team. He never again exercised much power, although he served as ambassador to England in the mid-1970s. His 1982 diary reads like a "Who's Who" of prominent Brazilians and Americans.[34] Tony Gebauer was listed there, but unlike some of his successors, apparently Roberto Campos didn't do his own private banking at Morgan. The diary lists his accounts at Geneva's Pictet et Cie and Trade Development Bank, whose founder, Edmond Safra, also founded the Republic Bank of New York and Safra Bank, and was an old acquaintance of Campos.[35]

By 1967, Brazil was well on its way to becoming a martial-law state. With the support and guidance of the US government, a left-leaning, though democratically elected, government had been vanquished, and a right-wing dictatorship put in its place. Especially from 1968 until the mid-1970s, the level of repression increased, and the number of political opponents who were murdered or "disappeared" reached the low thousands. This was modest, compared with what went on in Argentina, Chile, and Paraguay, but Brazil's military made up for the body count by teaching the right-wing juntas in these countries all about repression and terror.

DICTATORSHIP OF THE IMAGINATION

While Brazil's military deserved much of the credit for this new system, the US national security apparatus also played a key role. One of its crucial long-term influences was a variation on the so-called "Mighty Wurlitzer" concept that the OSS and the CIA had pioneered with great success in France, Italy, Germany, and Japan in the 1940s and 1950s, and have continued right up to the present in post-Soviet Russia, China, Chile, Pakistan, the Philippines, Nicaragua, and Iraq. This concept was created to develop a nationwide media network that could be used to shape public opinion. In 1964, an energetic, personable young Time-Life executive named Joe Wallach went to work with Roberto Marinho, a Brazilian businessman who was running a newspaper and a local TV station in Rio. Wallach didn't speak Portuguese at the time, but he had a background in TV production and accounting in California, and quickly became Globo's executive director. Time-Life also invested $4–6 million in a joint venture with Globo, which helped Globo buy up concessions and get ahead of its competitors. Time-Life and its close friends at the CIA also encouraged multinationals to direct advertising to Globo, which soon was running a nation-wide advertising cartel.[36] Meanwhile, Globo took a strong pro-military line in its reporting, with cynics referring to it as "The Ministry of Information." Globo also received special licenses for satellite broadcasting, radio, and local stations from the government. It prospered, becoming the world's fourth largest TV network over the next twenty-five years,—under Wallach's leadership. The quid pro quo was simple: Globo provided favorable coverage to its political allies, and they, in turn, helped Globo get TV, satellite broadcasting, radio, and cable concessions that it needed to keep growing. In special cases, the politicians and their families also shared in the ownership of these "goodies."

Over the next three decades, Globo became one of the most politically influential media empires in the developing world. By 1990, it owned seventy-eight stations in Brazil, with fifty million viewers. It had an ad revenue of $600 million a year, eight thousand employees, and more than thirty subsidiaries in Italy, Portugal, Cuba, Japan, and other countries. Globo was also producing and exporting TV programming to 112 countries. After Brazil returned to democracy in 1985, Globo exerted even stronger influence over the selections of many key political leaders, including several Brazilian presidents. To influence elections, it sometimes used blatant propaganda, as in the hard-fought 1989 presidential race between Luis Ignacio ("Lula") da Silva and Fernando Collor.[37]

In 2001–02, long after Joe Wallach had retired and Roberto Marinho had passed the empire on to his sons, Globo's misadventures in Internet and cable investments and crushing foreign debts finally brought it down to earth. This was not unlike the similar fate that befell its original partners at Time-Life, now part of the AOL Time Warner conglomerate. The Marinho family's estimated wealth on the *Forbes's* annual billionaire survey peaked at $6.4 billion in 2000, coinciding with the Internet's peak. By 2002 the Marinhos were down to their last billion, barely eligible for a mention in *Forbes*.[38]

Even then, Globo was still trying to use its political influence as currency. During the 2002 presidential race, in a move that must have made its original partners turn in their graves, Globo for the first time supported the left-wing candidate, who finally won on his fourth try for office. Evidently, having backed the "system" that made Brazil the world's largest debtor, Globo was hoping for some government relief from its own crushing foreign debts.

BANKING ON THE STATE

In addition to military action and media support, the top-down development strategy adopted by Brazil's military and its foreign allies in the 1960s also had a crucial economic component. At first glance, it was hard to reconcile this strategy with free-market principles and democratic rule. But it certainly cleared the way for bankers like Gebauer to earn huge fortunes. These bankers joined forces with a corrupt coalition of officials, industrialists, and agro-exporters to support a new debt-intensive strategy that was designed and implemented by a powerful new minister, Antonio Delfim Neto, who became one of Tony Gebauer's closest friends.

Antonio Delfim Neto was an academic-cum-bureaucrat from a middle-class Italian family in São Paulo. In the 1950s, he wrote a brilliant PhD dissertation on the coffee industry and taught macroeconomics at the University of São Paulo. In the 1960s, he was a consultant to Ralph Rosenberg, whose Ultra Group was the largest private investor in Petrobras; Antonio Carlos de Almeida Braga, the owner of Bradesco, Brazil's largest bank; and Pedro Conde, another bank owner.[39] From 1963 to 1967, Delfim Neto was an advisor to São Paulo governors Carvalho Pinto and Lauro Natel. Then, from 1967 to 1985, Delfim Neto came to wield more influence over Brazil's economy than anyone.

Delfim Neto was as quick-witted as Campos, but most of his success was due to a lack of ideology. As Delfim Neto said in 1969, "I am not going to sacrifice development only to pass into history as someone who defeated inflation at any cost."[40] He was the grand master of bureaucratic infighting, assigning his "Delfim boys"—mostly University of São Paulo-trained economists—to key positions in the government, where they operated a Florentine patronage system, keeping a running tally of favors owed to important people. "I was in the office of [an important banker] when Delfim called. He needed $5 million right away," one banker recalled. "The only argument was how to get it to him. We knew he'd make it up to us."[41] This network of favors and influence earned Delfim Neto unusual longevity. He was Brazil's finance minister in 1969–74, ambassador to France in 1974–78, minister of agriculture in 1979, planning minister in 1979–85, and even after civilian rule returned in 1985, an important behind-the-scenes leader in Congress, where he also enjoyed immunity from prosecution. Among those responsible for Brazil's massive debt burden in the 1980s, only Tony Gebauer enjoyed similar continuity in power.

In August 1969, General Costa de Silva died of a stroke, after learning that his wife had helped deliver Brasilia's telephone exchange contract to Ericsson, a Swedish company that bribed its way all over Latin America.[42] Vernon Walter's friend, General Emilio Médici (1969–74), then took over, and some of Delfim Neto's critics seized the opportunity to accuse Delfim Neto of corruption. But he was so popular with all his other "clients" that Delfim Neto was soon reappointed. He promised Médici, echoing the grandiose Kubitschek in the 1950s, "Give me a year and I will give you a decade."

Meanwhile, from a national security standpoint, Médici was exactly what Brazil's US allies were looking for. He visited Nixon, Kissinger, and General Walters in December 1971. In a meeting just two weeks later with Secretary of State William Rogers, recorded in a transcript released by the National Archives in 2002, Nixon described Médici in glowing terms:

Rogers: "Yeah, I think this Médici thing is a good idea. I had a very good time with him at lunch and he . . ."
Nixon: "He's quite a fellow, isn't he?"
Rogers: "He is. God, I'm glad he's on our side."
Nixon: "Strong and, uh, you know . . . (laughs) . . . you know, I wish he were running the whole continent."
Rogers: "I do, too. We got to help Bolivia. He's concerned about that. We got to be sure to . . ."
Nixon: "Incidentally, the Uruguayan thing, apparently he helped a bit there . . ."[43]

The "Uruguayan thing" was recently clarified when the government declassified the transcript of another Nixon conversation with Britain's prime minister Edward Heath which had taken place that same month. According to Nixon, "The Brazilians helped rig the Uruguayan election. . . . Our position is supported by Brazil, which is after all the key to the future."[44] He was referring to the November 28, 1971 elections in which Uruguay's Frente Amplio, a coalition of left-leaning political parties not unlike Allende's Unidad Popular in Chile, had been defeated by the right-wing Colorado Party. The result was indeed unexpected, and evidently Médici had played a key role in it.

In March, 1972, the Colorado Party's new right-wing president, Bordaberry, gave Uruguay's security forces a green light not only to attack the Tupamaros, Uruguay's urban guerrillas, but also its labor unions, student associations, and political opponents.[45] The military made Bordaberry a puppet in June 1973 and took complete power in 1976, following in Brazil's footsteps. The result was a bloodbath that foreshadowed the thousands of political murders in Chile after Allende's demise in September 1973 and in Argentina after its military seized power in 1976. By then, Uruguay, a country with just three million people that had once been known as "the Switzerland of Latin America," had become a torture chamber, with more political prisoners per capita than any other country in the world. Civilian government did not return to Uruguay until 1985.

According to other newly released documents, General Médici had also assisted the right-wing in Bolivia in August 1971, and Brazil's military—with US support and coordination—played a key role in training and guiding the repressions in Chile, Argentina, Paraguay, and Bolivia in the late 1960s and 1970s. As one scholar noted, "Brazil had a head start on terror."[46] One of the victims may have even been former president Goulart, who died in 1976 of a curious "heart attack" at the age of fifty-eight at his ranch in Paraná. Goulart's family had long suspected that he was murdered by the military. In 2000, Brazil's Congress finally started an official investigation.[47]

In any case, whether or not the "domino theory" ever applied to Communist revolutions, it worked quite well with respect to Latin American right-wing regimes. And their US patron discovered that with only a little nudge to Brazil, the largest domino—as Nixon noted, "the key to the future"—it could wield extraordinary influence on the entire region.

O CÉU DE PORCO (PIG HEAVEN)

Absolute power not only corrupts, but it also often leads to grand visions. With Delfim Neto's help, General Médici unveiled his ambitious 1970 economic plan, whose aim was to make Brazil a "great power . . . constructing a developed, democratic, and sovereign society" in one decade.[48]

To pay for the plan, Delfim Neto's first move was to throw monetarism out the window and ease up on credit. That kicked off the "Brazilian miracle" of 1967–73, when real growth averaged eleven percent a year, the fastest in the world. Because there was so much slack in the economy, inflation held steady, just as Delfim Neto had predicted. There was an incredible wave of optimism. Rio's stock market soared from 100 in 1965 to 4,908 in June 1971, and Citibank's Walter Wriston declared Brazil "the richest country in the world." It soon became "a huge construction camp from north to south," providing the world's largest markets for engineers, power equipment, concrete, and earth-moving equipment.[49] In the long run Delfim Neto's strategy would prove to be a total disaster, but in the short run, he looked like a genius.

Delfim's Brazilian miracle certainly helped foreign bankers. When Delfim Neto took office in 1967, Brazil's foreign debt had been reduced to its 1960 level by the conservative policies of Roberto Campos. By 1972, Delfim Neto had tripled it, and by the peak of Gebauer's career in 1983, it had more than tripled again.[50] The composition of the debt also changed. In 1967, most foreign loans had come from public sources like the World Bank and the IDB, but by 1973, more than two-thirds were from private banks like Citibank and Morgan.[51] At that point, nearly sixty percent of the loans were not going into actual projects, but were simply being added to Brazil's foreign reserves. Since the reserves were managed by the same big banks that made the loans, most of the loans never really left New York. This was the same kind of lucrative "relending" that was used in Venezuela. Even when there were real projects, the procedure was often: "First the loan, *then* the project."[52] In effect, the debt's growth was supply driven and interest-group driven, reflecting Brazil's incestuous involvement with banks and corporate interests, rather than its own objective needs.[53]

Long before OPEC's quadrupling of oil prices in 1973, or any interest rate shocks, therefore the interests and ambitions of Delfim Neto and his banker friends paved the way for Brazil's debt crises. Their choices cannot easily be regarded as "mistakes"—they were simply trying to help themselves. In the energy sector, for example, Delfim Neto's contradictory strategy included subsidizing costly gasohol, nuclear, and hydro projects while maintaining price controls on gasoline and electricity. This did little to reduce Brazil's eighty-percent dependence on oil imports, but it delighted the big sugar farmers, *empreteiras*, the military (which wanted the nuclear program), and industrialists—many of whom liked to consume cheap power and coal.

Delfim Neto's rural policies were also pro-debt. His gasohol program was really an inverted land reform. It greatly increased the concentration of land ownership by favoring crops like coffee, cattle, soya, and sugar produced by the rural elite. Rather than tamper with the south's large farms, the military tried to relocate the country's ten million rural, landless workers to cities or the Amazon through a series of road and railroad projects. The result was an urban explosion. From 1960 to 1970, São Paulo and Rio doubled in size, and the overall urban share of the population increased from forty-five to sixty percent.[54] Crime, congestion, and pollution surged. At the same time, subsidies for huge new power plants in the Amazon, as well as new farms, mines, and roads there resulted in many socially wasteful projects and vast environmental damage.

Delfim Neto's many new subsidies for capital also promoted increased borrowing from the banks. The government provided low-cost loans and tax breaks for industry, promoting the growth of financial conglomerates on the German model. In this model, which has recently also reappeared in the US, there are few local barriers between commercial and investment banking, insurance, brokerages, and other financial services. One result is a capital market that is completely dominated by a handful of big banks.

Indeed, under Delfim Neto, banking became Brazil's most profitable industry. From 1965 to 1980, as the industry consolidated, the number of banks fell from 320 to 92, while the share of deposits captured by the top ten banks rose from one-third to more than half. They were permitted to monopolize corporate finance; Delfim Neto's Central Bank didn't allow companies to issue commercial paper. Under his 1967 Resolution 63, companies also had to do all their foreign borrowing by way of Brazilian banks. By 1982, there was $16 billion in Resolution 63 foreign debt outstanding—a fifth of the total. Equity finance atrophied; laws against insider trading remained weak and courts provided little protection for small investors. The financial conglomerates completely dominated venture capital and the stock market. Brazil's stock market, Latin America's largest, became a speculative casino controlled by only 15–20 wealthy groups.[55]

Meanwhile, Brazil's government financed itself chiefly with short-term debt, which was rolled over every night by the banks. Delfim Neto found it politically safer to borrow than to raise taxes on the elite. As in many other developing countries, its income tax system was very weak—both corporate and personal income taxes were widely evaded. The only other effective tax was the "inflation tax" that hit the poor and unorganized hard. But for the time being, under military rule, their resistance was "manageable." By 1969, Delfim Neto had completely undermined the independence of Campos's Central Bank. This prepared the way for a resurgence of inflation. By 1975, Delfim's inflation rates had surpassed Goulart's. In striking contrast to their attitudes before the 1964 coup, however, the bankers loved Delfim Neto's inflation—everyone just indexed their bank accounts to stay even. There were lots of ways for insiders to make money on Delfim Neto's rigged indexing system, and no one in the government was threatening to raise taxes on corporations or nationalize foreign investment.[56]

The debt financed the explosive growth of the state. By 1982, Brazil's government controlled the flow of two-thirds of Brazil's total savings. The commanding heights of the economy was now occupied by just a dozen huge state-owned enterprises, including Petrobras, the national oil company, Electrobras, Brazil's electric power holding company, and Telebras, the national telephone company. All of these were being financed by good old capitalist banks like JPMorgan, Citibank, Bank of America, Chase, and Midland Bank. Delfim Neto made João Goulart's statism look like child's play. And private foreign banks paid for most of it. In the words of one former Gebauer client, "It was as if Moscow Narodny [the Soviet Union's state-owned foreign bank] had financed the growth of capitalism!"[57]

At the same time, Delfim Neto's policies had harsh effects on the poor. He explicitly embraced inequality as a necessary by-product of growth. Indeed, he believed that growth *required* increased inequality—his motto was "concentrate and grow." From 1960 to 1972, the share of income received by the top ten percent rose from forty percent to fifty-two percent; the share received by the top one percent came to exceed that of the entire bottom half.[58] With the military in firm control, unions became illegal after 1964, and real wages dropped like a stone. As Juan Perón, Argentina's leader, liked to say, "Prices went up by the elevator, wages went up by the stairs." As for government spending, the government preferred accumulating foreign reserves or building dams and highways to investing in teachers, textbooks, or public health; after all, there was no opportunity for politically influential contractors, equipment vendors, banks, and officials to make money on such "social welfare" expenditures. In 1970–73, Brazil's entire education budget was less than half the cost of Tucurui, the disastrous Amazon dam project. Thirty percent of Brazil's population was illiterate, less than half of all children completed high school, only four percent attended college, and there was an acute shortage of skilled labor.[59] It was as if the entire country was being prepared to compete in the 19th century.

Delfim Neto's borrowing binge facilitated a torrent of funny business. (For several other examples, see Chapter I.) For example, the "Relatoria Saraiva" case involved the $100 million Água Vermelha Dam, approved by Delfim Neto personally in November 1972 and syndicated by Banque Credit Commercial de France (BCCF). The affair became public because of intense personal animosity between Campos and Delfim Neto. In 1975, Campos was Brazil's ambassador to the UK, and Delfim Neto was ambassador to France. In an incredible "tale of two embassies," Campos planted his girlfriend, Mariza Tupinambá, as a secretary in Delfim Neto's Paris Embassy. There she overheard a quarrel between Vilar de Queiroz, Delfim Neto's former director of international lending at the Finance Ministry, and Jacques de Brossier, BCCF's manager. When Mariza asked de Brossier about it, he fumed that Delfim Neto had "already been paid $6 million for Vermelha" and was now demanding another $10 million in exchange for BCCF's role as lead syndicator for Tucurui. Mariza reported the affair to Campos, who sent SNI colonel Raimundo Saraiva to question de Brossier. Saraiva repeated the story to his bosses, but all that happened was Mariza was fired and Delfim Neto was warned by the SNI's new boss, future military president João Figueiredo (1979–85), to be a little more discrete.[60]

THE NETWORK

The implication of Delfim Neto's policies for banks like Morgan was clear: "pump it out." One longtime Morgan officer recalls that, "When I was at US AID in 1964, I'd approach banks for piddling loans to Brazil and they'd have nothing to do with it. A few years later, they were just throwing money away down there. The whole thing became a sport."[61]

Alfred "Fred" Vinton Jr. joined Morgan's International Division, right out of Harvard in 1962. He and Tony Gebauer shared a special interest in Latin America. In 1965, they travelled to Brazil together, called on local banks, and wrote an enthusiastic report.[62] Their enthusiasm was shared by Lewis T. Preston, the ex-Marine who took over Morgan's International Division in 1968. In 1967, Morgan had taken a minority position in Finasa, an investment bank owned by Gastal Vidigal, the son of President Vargas's finance minister and owner of Banco Mercantile. In 1968, Morgan published a glowing review of Delfim Neto's policies and opened its first São Paulo office. In 1969, Preston appointed several Brazilians to his new International Council, including Luiz Campello of São Paulo, a close friend of Gebauer's. In 1971, Preston proposed buying a local commercial bank, but was vetoed by Morgan's conservative chairman, John Meyer. In May 1982, just five months before the Mexican debt crunch, Preston fumed that "Citibank publishes its [larger Brazilian debt] figures just to make me mad," and Morgan bought half of Banco Interatlântico SA, a Rio investment bank.[63]

To catch up, Morgan concentrated its lending on state enterprises and multinationals. This strategy had many advantages. The government companies borrowed a lot in one swoop, had federal guarantees, and could easily be marketed out of New York on the basis of high-level connections. Morgan also knew most of the multinationals. Thus, Morgan's Brazilian loans closely tracked Delfim Neto's strategy: More than eighty-four percent of its syndications went to government borrowers, especially Delfim Neto's large projects, including $1.54 billion for Itaipu, $165 million for Siderbrás, $238 million for the Alcominas aluminum project, $300 million for the Carajás iron ore project, and $1.5 billion for gasohol.[64] By 1980, Morgan was the Brazilian government's leading creditor and was second only to Citibank in the whole "public plus private sector" market.

It was not hard to dump money into Brazil during this period. By 1982, eight hundred foreign banks had participated in Brazilian syndications.[65] But Morgan led a disproportionate share of these syndications. This role required a senior banker who understood the language and culture, had a burning desire for deals, and a flair for courting top officials.

Much of Tony Gebauer's success was due to these personal attributes. As one colleague put it, he was a "rainmaker"—an extraordinary dealmaker. "Tony generated an incredible amount of business for the bank. He always had solutions and he worked hard." Another banker, who worked with him for more than five years, said that "He had great esprit with the troops. Everybody loved him. . . ." A banker who'd once interviewed him for a job evaluation recalled that "Tony was attractive, intelligent, hard-working, thoroughly professional—one of the really great performers." Yet another banker wrote Judge Sweet that Gebauer "took a great deal of interest in the welfare of those with whom he worked." A Morgan attorney emphasized his competitiveness. "He would arrive at the office at 7:30 AM, work late, then socialize with clients. If a minister arrived on a Sunday night, Gebauer'd take him to dinner before competitors got to him the next morning." An Argentine banker recalled that his flamboyant style appealed to Latins. "He'd arrive in São Paulo by helicopter, surrounded by the press. After his first marriage, he had an open affair with one of Rio's richest women."[66] Equally important were Gebauer's extraordinary contacts. In the words of one competitor, "Tony had all the quality relationships down there—lots of important people knew and trusted him."[67] Indeed, most of his clients had been his friends for years.

1. Hafers

The earliest contacts were from the family of Gebauer's first wife, Fernandina. His father-in-law, Luiz Suplicy ("Jua") Hafers, was from a well-off family in Paraná, Brazil's coffee-growing center. Hafer's mother's family owned a coffee plantation near São Paulo and Escritoria Suplicy, a leading coffee brokerage. Hafers had served as a pilot in the Brazilian Air Force during World War II, then returned to Santos.[68] His best friend there was Renato Costa Lima, another wealthy coffee farmer, who represented Rockefeller interests in Brazil and was minister of agriculture in the 1950s. It was at Costa Lima's farm in 1952 that Hafers met Fernanda de Souza Queiroz. When Costa Lima became the Brazilian Coffee Institute's (IBC) President in 1957, he asked

Hafers to represent the institute in New York—a very important position, since the IBC was coffee's OPEC at the time, in charge of allocating supplies to importers like Hills Brothers and General Foods.

In late 1957, Hafers moved his wife Fernanda, his two stepchildren, and his sister to a Park Avenue apartment. They were extremely social, giving two or three cocktail parties a week for visiting Brazilians and luminaries like Jackie Onassis, Rockefeller scion Richard Aldridge, and columnist Russell Kirkpatrick.[69] As Hafers's brother said, "Tony traded his whole life on the connections he made in Jua's living room." (And Hafers, in turn, had traded his whole life on the connections he made at Renato's farm.)

2. Borio

Gebauer's most important early client was Leonidas Borio, an engineer from Paraná who succeeded Costa Lima as the IBC's president in 1964. Like Hafers, Borio had been in the Air Force, where he met Colonel Ney Braga, one of the coup's key organizers.[70] In 1962, Braga, Paraná's governor, appointed Borio to run the Paraná Development Bank and promoted him to the IBC after the coup. This was a well-known group of powerful insiders. In June 1963, Braga, Borio, and Roberto Campos met privately with President Kennedy and A. A. Berle Jr. at the White House to discuss "Brazil's future."

Borio's reign at the Coffee Institute was not a happy one. Coffee sales had plummeted, and he was accused by some of behaving like "a gangster."[71] But what mattered to Gebauer was that Borio controlled Paraná Equipamentos SA—one of Brazil's five largest Caterpillar dealerships and the supplier of tractors to the massive Itaipu Dam Project. In the 1970s, Brazil was Caterpillar's largest market in the world, and Caterpillar was the only top one hundred US company that was not a Morgan client. Morgan had lost the relationship in 1935 when it failed to help Caterpillar through the depression. With Borio's help, Gebauer brought Caterpillar back to Morgan.

In 1964, Jua Hafers introduced Borio to Gebauer, who invited him to speak about coffee prices at Morgan. Not long after, Borio transferred IBC's and Paraná Equipamentos's New York accounts to Morgan. In 1968, Borio also introduced Gebauer to his best customer, C. R. Almeida, an engineer who owned one of Brazil's top three construction companies at the time. Almeida was known as "the most powerful businessman in Paraná," a tough customer who carried a gun in his briefcase. He and Gebauer hit it off immediately.[72]

At the time, Almeida and Borio had their hearts set on a new $68 million Paraná railroad. The old line, spanning seven hundred kilometers, carried forty percent of Brazil's coffee across Paraná to the sea. The new one would cut the distance in half. Almeida had been assured by Paraná's governor that he'd be the prime contractor. That meant $19 million in contracts on the first phase alone, and of course it meant Borio would sell more Caterpillars. All that was missing was the finance. But the State of Paraná had never borrowed abroad before, and in the 1960s, foreign banks were reluctant to lend even to Brazil's central government, much less to its states. Caterpillar's lead bank, First Chicago, declined the loan. Then Gebauer, a lowly assistant treasurer at Morgan, had a bright idea: If Caterpillar would give Morgan some business back in the US and if Brazil would guarantee the loan, Morgan would fund it. Borio and Almeida delivered on both counts.[73]

So the mutualities in Gebauer's first big deal were almost perfect. In 1969, Paraná borrowed $50 million, Morgan' largest Third World loan at that time. In the next decade, it loaned Paraná another $160 million.[74] The deal also indirectly led to Morgan loans to Paraná's State Bank ($10 million), electric company ($39 million), Development Bank ($5 million), and several others. It restored Morgan's relationship with Caterpillar, whose Brazilian subsidiary borrowed $10 million. Borio and Almeida also became clients—Almeida borrowed $26 million and Borio $8 million.[75] Morgan later regretted some of these relationships, but at the time they seemed very profitable. For Gebauer's career, the railroad deal was also an inflection point. Morgan had been at the point of firing him, but at the age of thirty, he became assistant vice president and, just two years later, vice president.[76]

As for the railroad, one might well wonder whether a project that satisfied so many special interests could possibly satisfy any public ones? Paraná governor Harold Leon Peres did try to cancel it, but that may have been for selfish reasons. Leon Peres, a former National Assembly deputy who was not part of the Braga-Borio clique, declared war on corruption and froze Almeida's contracts—rather like the young Fernando Collor would do in 1990, during his first year in office, before he discovered the enormous amount of money that could be extracted from "selective prosecution." Within a year, Almeida took a stroll with Leon Peres on Copacabana Beach and used a recorder concealed in a cigarette pack to tape the former deputy demanding a $1 million bribe in exchange for thawing the funds. Much to the relief of Almeida, Braga, Borio, and Gebauer, Médici then fired Leon Peres, who went on to teach at a law school in Curitiba, Paraná's capital.[77]

Borio was also very useful to Gebauer in other deals because of his ties to influential Brazilians. These included Finance Ministers Campos, Mario Enrique Simonsen, Octavio Bulhões, and Karlos Rischbieter. In 1976, when the IDB's annual meeting was held in Rio, Borio gave a dinner for a Morgan delegation that included its Chairman, Ellsmore Patterson, as well as Lewis T. Preston, Robert V. Lindsay, and Tony Gebauer. In May 1986, the very day that

Gebauer's legal problems were publicly disclosed by Morgan, the press tracked down Borio in Rio, to ask about his Morgan accounts. He was at the opera with Mario Enrique Simonsen. "I am going to the opera with my friend," he blustered, and rushed inside.[78]

3. Simonsen

Mario Enrique Simonsen was extremely valuable to Gebauer. In 1969, Simonsen, a thirty-four-year-old economist and partner in the investment bank Banco Bozano Simonsen (BBS), won a trip to New York for his prize essay on inflation. Borio arranged a lunch with Gebauer that sprouted a long-term friendship. From 1974 to 1979, Simonsen served as Brazil's finance minister and then as planning minister. Under Simonsen, Morgan's syndications reached $1.4 billion, compared with only $300 million during Delfim Neto's first term from 1967 to 1972 and $4.4 billion in his second, from 1979 to 1982. This business was not a one-way street. From 1972 to 1983, Simonsen's own BBS received $22 million in Morgan loans, including $11 million while he was finance minister.[79] In the early 1980s, BBS also loaned $1.5 million to an obscure Bahian coffee farm partly owned by Gebauer.[80]

Simonsen also had many other foreign friends. In 1973, BBS bought Maquip, a company representing Westinghouse in the bids for Angra I, the São Paulo Metro, and the Ferrovia de Aço Railroad. Simonsen was accused of helping Maquip and Westinghouse obtain these contracts with overpriced equipment. Shortly after leaving the Planning Ministry, he became a Citibank director.[81]

Simonsen was not the only Brazilian official who received private Morgan loans. While Simonsen was planning minister, Karlos Rischbieter was finance minister. In the 1960s, he had been Borio's chief financial officer at the Coffee Institute. From 1967 to 1972, he was director of Paraná Comercio e Administração SA, which received $1.7 million in Morgan loans.[82] Rischbieter later became chairman of Volvo do Brasil and Bamerindus, Paraná's fourth largest bank, which got $21 million in Morgan loans. He was also Hafers's partner in several ventures, including a consulting company that consumed a $10 million government loan for an ill-fated hotel project in Antigua.

Companies controlled by Roberto Campos also received $3 million in Morgan loans.[83] A company owned by Severo Gomes, another coup plotter and Brazil's minister of industry from 1974 to 1977, received $650,000.[84] Companies belonging to the family of Paulo Maluf, a leading São Paulo politician, received $1.7 million.[85] Rossi-Servix, an engineering company directed by the brother of General Newton de Oliveira Cruz, the SNI's second in command, received $7.6 million.[86] Banco Sul Brasileira, owned by the military, received $7.5 million.[87] And Banco Econômico and other companies associated with Angelo Calmon de Sá, Banco do Brasil's president in 1974–77 and minister of industry in 1977–79, received $51.6 million in Morgan loans. Calmon de Sá was another close friend of Tony Gebauer.

4. Delfim Neto

Delfim Neto was also close to Tony Gebauer. They first met in 1967, soon after Delfim Neto became finance minister. The introduction took place at the Rio apartment of Ruth Almeida Prado, a member of an old São Paulo banking family, who "knew all the important politicians in Brazil," attended school with Gebauer's mother-in-law, and was friends with Borio, Simonsen, and key "Delfim boys" like Carlos Alberto Andrade Pinto, Luis Werneck, and Vilar de Queiroz. Gebauer always called on Delfim Neto when he visited Brazil, and Delfim Neto was often Gebauer's guest in New York. The minister relied on him for personal advice and "showed him all his speeches."[88] He also rewarded Gebauer with huge syndications, like a $1.5 billion gasohol financing in 1979 and the $4.4 billion Brazilian debt rescheduling of October 1982, when Delfim Neto, Galvêas, and Carlos Langoni, the Central Bank president, met privately at Gebauer's apartment to plan the restructuring.[89] Delfim Neto also favored Morgan's multinational clients, who regarded Gebauer as one of the best-connected bankers in Brazil.[90] In 1969, for example, Gebauer facilitated a $20 million sale of GE locomotives and Caterpillar engines to Brazil's National Railway, financed by the US EXIM Bank. Gebauer went directly to Delfim Neto to get the deal approved. It later turned out that GE do Brasil paid a hefty commission for the contract.[91]

5. ACM

In addition to Hafers and the Paraná circle, another crucial Gebauer network involved Bahia, one of Brazil's poorest northeastern states. The network provides an even more striking example of the intricate sociology of pirate banking. It was presided over by another Gebauer crony—Bahia's longtime senator, governor, and minister Antonio Carlos Magalhães ("ACM"). Magalhães is an extraordinary historical figure. His followers have described him as "a figure who opens all doors," "our most prestigious governor," and "an intimate of every Brazilian president from Kubitschek and Castello Branco to Fernando Collor and Fernando Enrique Cardoso." His detractors call him "Toninho Malvadesa," "the Vice Lord of Bahia," and "an octopus who for (thirty) years controlled everyone and everything in his state," who was known to punch journalists and brag that he ran the state of Bahia "with money in one hand and a club in the other."[92]

Born in 1929, the son of a Salvadorian doctor, Magalhães studied medicine and became a professor at Bahia's Federal University in the 1950s. But he was always most interested in politics. By 1958, in his late twenties, he was already a federal deputy and a leader in the right-wing UDN party. He became known as "Juscelino's alarm clock" because he often woke Kubitschek with a 7 AM phone call. In 1964, Magalhães helped plot the coup with military men like Figueiredo and José de Costa Cavalcante. He then became General Castello Branco's chief of staff. The military's official party, ARENA, had its strongest following in Bahia. In 1966, Castello appointed Magalhães mayor of Salvador, and in 1970 General Médici appointed him governor of Bahia. There he remained until 1975, organizing such lucrative projects as the Pedra de Carvalho Dam, the Camaçari Petrochemical Complex, and the Dow Chemical Plant.[93]

Magalhães was certainly no one to trifle with. In 1973, Clemente Mariani, the owner of Banco do Bahia, decided to sell it to Bradesco rather than to Bahia's Banco Econômico, in which Magalhães was rumored to have a hidden interest. Magalhães expropriated Mariani's mansion in Salvador and converted it into a school.[94] In 1975, one of Magalhães's sons-in-law died under suspicious circumstances after quarreling violently with his daughter.[95] In 1976, another son-in-law, Cesar Araujo Pires, founded Constructora OAS Ltd., a Bahian construction company that soon acquired the nickname *Obras Arranjar de Sogro*—"works arranged by father-in-law." Over the next twenty-five years, OAS became a $700 million per year enterprise, with numerous government and private sector projects, especially in Bahia. In the 1990s, part of Constructura OAS's profits were invested with Daniel Dantas, one of Rio's sharpest young investment bankers and privatization mavens, a Bahian who helped to organize the privatization of Companhia Vale do Rio Doce (CVRD). So that was a case where the profits of primitive accumulation acquired through Brazil's raw construction game were later converted into a share of the public sector's "prime filet."

More importantly for Gebauer, General Ernesto Geisel—Brazil's military president (1974–79)—appointed Magalhães to run Electrobras. During his term from 1976 to 1978, Magalhães presided over giant projects like Itaipu and Tucurui, sharing the rewards with old friends like Costa Cavalcante, director of Itaipu Binacional, and Shigeaki Ueki, a Geisel protégé who ran Petrobras and the Ministry of Mines. In 1979, Geisel's successor General Figueiredo then appointed Magalhães as Bahia's governor again, and Magalhães briefly developed presidential aspirations. But his autocratic reputation got in the way. In the 1984 election, Magalhães adroitly decided to back off. Instead he played a kingmaker role, supporting the eventual winners, President Tancredo Neves and Vice President José Sarney.

Magalhães continued to exert great influence, even as the country shifted over to civilian rule. When Neves died of a heart attack, Sarney took over. Magalhães served as Sarney's communications minister from 1985 to 1989, in charge of handing out all radio and TV licenses.[96] Since Magalhães's family controlled TV Bahia, and Banco Econômico owned Cia Satellite de Terreno—a satellite TV company—this was a very useful position. His ministry saw a flurry of licensing activity just before Brazil's new constitution went into effect in October 1988, sharply reducing ministerial powers.[97] Roberto Marinho transferred the lucrative Globo TV affiliate in Bahia to the Magalhães family while Magalhães helped Marinho win a battle for control over the Brazilian subsidiary of NEC, the Japanese electronics giant.[98]

Magalhães's powers of survival were truly amazing. In 1990, he went on to a third term as Bahia's governor, and acted as a kingmaker once again, helping Fernando Collor get elected president of Brazil in 1989. In 1992, when President Collor became involved in a corruption scandal that led to his impeachment, he turned to Magalhães for political support, who as leader of the conservative Liberal Front Party (PFL), had become Brazil's virtual "Prime Minister."[99] But Magalhães detected very early that Collor was spinning out of control, unable to control his appetite for grand larceny. So Magalhães moved on again. In 1994, he was instrumental in building a new alliance between the PFL and Fernando Enrique Cardoso, the Brazilian Social Democratic Party's (PSDB) left-liberal candidate, helping Cardoso defeat da Silva for the presidency in October 1994, with Globo's support as well.

Then, as president of the Brazilian Senate from 1994 to 2001, Magalhães worked hard to get the Constitution amended so that Cardoso could run for a second term in 1998. The quid pro quo was simple. Cardoso and his economic team saw to it that Brazil's privatization program took top priority, and that many of Magalhães's friends, including Dantas and Globo, got ringside seats at closed auctions for key privatization deals. After Cardoso's reelection to a second term in October 1998, however, Magalhães and President Cardoso had a serious falling out. Cardoso was tired of Magalhães's prickly personality and incessant demands. This led to an amazing tale of mutual self-destruction, which contributed greatly to da Silva's triumph in the October 2002 presidential election. In May 2001, Magalhães resigned from the Senate after it was discovered that he had illegally spied on his own colleagues. However, he and his family continue to wield extraordinary power from their Bahian base.[100]

For Gebauer and Morgan, Magalhães was an indispensable friend to have—perhaps more influential over more years than Delfim Neto, Simonsen, Campos, and Geisel combined. During his long career, Magalhães had developed strong ties to many key business players, especially Petrobras, which

based most of its petrochemical plants in Magalhães's state of Bahia, and Odebrecht, the big construction firm that was based in Bahia. Despite having little experience with power dams, Odebrecht won many key contracts in the
1970s: a large part of Itaipu's contracts, a share of Bahia's overdesigned Complexo Pedra do Cavalo water treatment plant (with Constructura OAS), two
hydro dams in the Brazilian states of Rondônia and Goiás, the foundations for
Angra II and III, and Rio's Galeão Airport. The company's inexperience led
to major cost overruns, and in 1977 it nearly failed. Fortunately, Angelo Calmon de Sá, who was both Odebrecht's director and Banco do Brasil's president, bailed the company out with a $400 million government loan.[101]

Odebrecht had the outward demeanor of a tough, hardworking German-
Brazilian firm. Over time, it gained experience and developed a reputation as
"Brazil's Bechtel," one of the more globally competitive construction companies. But it was not adverse to using other methods to win bids. In 1992,
when President Collor de Mello was impeached, it was revealed that one of
his key aids, P. C. Farias, had set up a "consulting firm" to collect millions of
dollars in bribes from Odebrecht, Constructura OAS, and eight other big
empreteiras. Odebrecht was accused of being at the center of a "parallel power
structure," an approach that it may have also tried to export to the US. In
1995–96, it became the largest single donor to the Foundation for Florida's
Future, a nonprofit "public policy center" that raised more than $1.7 million
to fund future Florida Governor Jeb Bush's campaign staff and even published
his book while he was between elections.[102]

Angelo Calmon de Sá was an important intermediary between Magalhães and Gebauer. An engineer by training, Calmon de Sá worked for Norberto Odebrecht Sr. from 1959 to 1966, and then became Magalhães's secretary of industry. His family owned most of Banco Econômico, Brazil's fifth
largest bank at the time, which had investments in satellites, tourism, food,
apparel, petrochemicals, and twenty other industries, including a joint venture
with Petrobras.[103] Together with Odebrecht, the bank owned a third of
Norquisa, a chemical company headed by former President Geisel. From 1971
to 1974, Calmon de Sá was a Banco Econômico executive. Then President
Geisel asked him to run Banco do Brasil. There, he not only bailed out Odebrecht; he also bailed out his family's own Banco Econômico when it refused
to honor its own $19 million cashier's check.[104] In 1977, in the thick of this
incident, Geisel summoned Calmon de Sá to his office, who later reported
that he thought he was going to jail.[105] But Geisel made him minister of
industry. In 1979, Calmon de Sá returned to run Banco Econômico and to
head the National Congress of Banks.

This was an incestuous little network, indeed. Calmon de Sá met
Gebauer through his relative Jorge Eduardo Noronha, a Banco Econômico

director who had worked at Deltec, a New York-based international finance company. Calmon de Sá, in turn, introduced Gebauer to Magalhães and President Geisel, who liked to speak German with Gebauer.[106] During the late 1970s, while Magalhães ran Electrobras and Geisel was Brazil's president, Morgan's loans soared.[107] Gebauer also made numerous loans to Bahian entities, including Bahia State ($100 million) and Cia do Desenvolvimento do Vale do Parag ($14 million). He also loaned $260 million to Petrobras, which was based in Bahia, and $52 million to Banco Econômico's group. Banco Econômico also became a partner in a Bahian military plant with Odebrecht and Engesa, one of Brazil's largest arms exporters, in which Odebrecht was a shareholder. Engesa proved to be one of Gebauer's more interesting clients. Its founder and president, José Luiz Whitaker Ribeiro, was Angelo Calmon de Sá's brother-in-law.[108]

6. Dickie and Turki

The members of Gebauer's other key Brazilian circle had all attended Princeton together in the 1960s. At its center was Richard F. ("Dickie") O'Connell, a Cuban-American whose family had owned copper mines in western Cuba before Castro. Ricardo Sicre, another Cuban-American who joined Morgan right after Princeton and later worked for the bank in Spain, introduced O'Connell to Gebauer in the mid-1960s. O'Connell's roommate was Prince Turki al Faisal bin Abdul Aziz al Saud, the son of Saudi Arabia's King Faisal and the future head of the Saudi Arabian Secret Service, which would later, among many other things, have a great deal to do with introducing Osama bin Laden to Afghanistan. Other Princeton friends of O'Connell were Luis Eduardo Campello Jr., a wealthy Paulista; Fernando Gros, who ran Brazil's Central Bank in 1985 and in 1991–92; Peter Egon Svastiche, who became an international director of Comind, a São Paulo bank; Paul Sorel, a future Morgan attorney; Gustavo de los Reyes, a partner in Venezuela's King Ranch; Percy Steinhardt Jr., the son of Morgan's Venezuela representative; and Sicre. Several of these Princeton alums were eventually involved in deals with Gebauer—which, as a Morgan officer recalled, "brought Tony and Morgan a huge amount of business."[109]

In the 1960s, O'Connell joined Deltec, an early pioneer in international loan syndication, in New York. He became known as a "financial whiz kid" and a kind of adopted son to Deltec's founder, Clarence Dauphinaux. By 1969, he was Deltec's president. He also met Keith McDermott, a South African who joined Morgan in 1965, and Jorge Noronha, who worked with O'Connell in the early 1970s. Gebauer later found O'Connell's sister a job in Morgan's Latin America Department, and O'Connell became godfather to

Gebauer's second son. O'Connell remained at Deltec until 1975, when he formed a joint venture with Turki al-Faisal to build restaurants and housing projects in Saudi Arabia. During that time, O'Connell, Gebauer, and Noronha also became partners in a peculiar little Bahian coffee farm.[110]

Gebauer also came to know many other influential Brazilians during these years. All knew him as "Tony," most of them borrowed money from him, and many set up secret accounts under his control. The group included Luiz Eduardo Campello Jr., a São Paulo investor in Isam and Eluma, two copper companies; Claudio Bardella, of Bardella SA, a joint venture with Brown Boveri that built movable cranes, and Bardella Borriello, an arms company; Interior Minister Mario Andreazza, known by foreign bankers as "Mr. Commissions;" Julio Mesquita, who owned O Estado de São Paulo, one of Brazil's top newspapers; Jorge Paulo Lehman, a former captain of the Harvard tennis team and Vinton classmate, who founded Banco Garantia—a very successful Rio investment bank—and whose stepbrother Alex Hagler ran Credit Suisse's huge Brazil private banking operation; Gilberto Huber Jr., a Deltec partner and '64 coup plotter who ran Listas Telefônicas Brasileiras, which published Rio's yellow pages; Ben Belinki, of Cia Constructora Brasileira de Estradas; Auro "Aurino" Moura Andrade, whose father was president of Brazil's Senate when Janio Quadros resigned, and whose wife owned Wyeth Fontoura, a leading pharmaceutical company; Olavo Monteiro de Carvalho, of Monteiro de Aranha SA, which owned ten percent of Volkswagen do Brasil's Autolatina; Fernando Muniz de Sousa, a São Paulo broker whose father owned Cassio Muniz, a department store, and whose sister married Claudio Bardella; Pedro Conde, Delfim Neto's friend and the owner of BCN; Francisco "Chico" Catão, a debonaire dealmaker and polo enthusiast who was reportedly "worth at least $60 million;" Jorge Wolney Atalla, Brazil's twentieth largest landowner and the head of Copersucar, its largest sugar cooperative; Geraldo Forbes, who owned a São Paulo finance company; and José Luiz Zillo, another landowner who succeeded Atalla at Copersucar in 1981.[111]

When Gebauer's scandal broke in 1986, none of these "friends" were willing to comment. The only exception was Almeida, the outspoken construction magnate. He told the press, "Yes, Tony Gebauer was my friend. As a matter of fact, he was friends with all the presidents of the Republic, and all the Ministers of Finance, and all the presidents of the Central Bank of the country for the last 18 years!"[112]

HOUSE AND GARDEN

Gebauer's colleagues noticed that his lifestyle improved considerably during the early 1970s. Most of them assumed that this was because either his father or his wife was very wealthy. In fact, his wife had no money of her own, and his father was from the middle-class. Yet, by the late 1960s, Gebauer had acquired a very expensive lifestyle. He and Fernandina started out in a rented apartment in New York, but in 1968, after their first son, they bought a larger one. In December 1971, four months before he became a vice president with a salary of less than $25,000, he bought a house in East Hampton for $200,000. He called it "Samambaia," Portugese for "fern," borrowing the name from Campello Jr.'s Santos club. In October 1986, he sold it for $1.9 million. In 1972, after his second son was born, he sold his apartment and used the proceeds "plus a loan from my father" to buy a magnificent two-floor cooperative at 71 East 71st for $157,000. By 1986, it was worth $5.5 million.[113] Not a lot by current standards, but at that time it was a pretty penny.

Throughout the 1970s the acquisitions continued to roll in. In 1978, Gebauer, Noronha, and O'Connell bought a coffee ranch in Bahia, which would play a significant role in the funny business to come. In the late 1970s, he bought a condo in Key Biscayne, close to one owned by O'Connell. In June 1982, he added a second home in East Hampton near Hafer's multi-million dollar estate. In 1984 he acquired a Paris apartment and spent hundreds of thousands redecorating it.[114]

Gebauer also had many other expensive tastes. The *New York Times* claimed that he took the Concorde to London to buy a pair of jodhpurs.[115] That story was not true, but there were many other jodhpur equivalents. He acquired impressive jade and Colombian gold collections, paintings by artists like Paul Klee and Emil Nolde, and first editions of J. P. Morgan Sr.'s two-volume work on Chinese porcelain and William Piso's 1648 natural history of Brazil. He also collected paper pastels by Paul Maze, an eighth century pre-Colombian gold piece, a Louis XVI mahogany desk top, circa 1790, antique dhurrie rugs and pin dot carpets, pencil sketches, pen and inks, and watercolors by Fernando Botero, Nolde, Lyonel Feininger, and Paul Klee.[116]

In 1973, Gebauer hired a live-in Portuguese butler and housekeeper, and a chauffeur for his two new Mercedes and silver Jaguar. He sent his two sons to St. David's, owned a fine ten-meter wooden sailboat, spent hundreds of thousands redesigning his apartment, and made expensive weekly alimony payments to Fernandina after their 1981 divorce. "He always knew what he wanted," said a designer who was involved in four Gebauer redecorations. "He was not a nouveau; he had a sense of quality, which we honed."[117] He also kept a crowded social calendar. In 1970, he joined the Raquet Club, a New York City institution featuring court tennis and squash, and in 1972 he joined the Knickerbocker and Union Clubs, frequented by Edward Finch Cox and Claus von Bulow. Known as a night owl, he often visited New York's "Club A" and Rio's "Hippopotamus." He was the founder of the Brazilian-

American Chamber of Commerce and served as its president, regularly attending its annual Man-of-the-Year dinners, whose winners included friends like Calmon de Sá, Galvêas, and Atalla. He was a member of the Council of the Americas' Advisory Board, president of St. David's board, a member of the Board of Visitors of City University's Graduate School and the East Hampton Village Preservation Society, and a founder of the Brazilian Cultural Foundation.[118] Notwithstanding the barely visible fact that he was stealing millions of dollars and helping others steal much more, Gebauer was a very solid citizen.

How could he afford all this? Certainly not on his Morgan salary alone. In 1976, his salary as a Morgan vice president was only $41,72, one-fourth of his official diversions in July 1976. In 1984, his salary was $153,000, quite a respectable level at the time, but nowhere near his spending needs.[119] To fill the gap, Gebauer had to create his own personal little underground economy.

DIVERSIONS

Gebauer's connections not only made him a successful banker, but they also produced the banking relationships that ultimately led to his downfall. C. R. Almeida opened his first Morgan account in September 1968 as part of the railway deal. By December 1974, it was known as the "Transnational Corporation" account, and from 1976 to 1983, Gebauer diverted at least $800,000 from it. In June 1967, Borio created the shell company Midland Trading Corporation with the help of Morgan's Panama lawyers. In December 1969, Gebauer opened an account under "Midland Trading Corporation," and in November 1975, he opened another one for the Borio company "Four Dimensions." From 1976 to 1983, Gebauer diverted $330,000 from them. Muniz da Souza, a São Paulo broker, opened an account for the Panama shell company "Pendennis" in June 1975. Gebauer drained $833,616 from that account.[120] Francisco Catão—the Rio dealmaker—set up two Morgan accounts: "General Universal Trading Corp." and "Dartois Investments" in 1978–79. From 1979 to 1983, Gebauer diverted $2.3 million from them.[121]

According to the official story, these crimes were simply the result of Gebauer's taking advantage of a normal institutional arrangement. According to Morgan, it allowed its senior officers to handle private accounts on the side, rather than transfer them to the Private Banking Department, if the assets involved were held in corporate names. From August 1976 to July 1983, Gebauer siphoned $1,750 to $75,000 every other week from six accounts under his control, obtaining treasurer's checks made out to himself, family members, art dealers, and other suppliers. There were 210 such checks, including 116 to Gebauer's accounts at Chemical Bank. The withdrawals totaled $566,256 in 1977, $691,408 in 1978, $726,472 in 1979, $663,296 in 1980, and $1,061,534 in 1981. They then declined to $239,000 in 1982, for reasons the official story leaves unclear. The clients he picked on varied. In 1976, it was Muniz; in 1977-78, Almeida; in 1979, Borio, Almeida, and Catão; in l980–82, Catão. After February 1982, there were only three more withdrawals from these accounts—the last one made in July 1983.

Throughout this period, Gebauer's career was soaring. It is interesting to correlate his career with his secret diversions:

- In May 1977, Gebauer assembled a $300 million syndicated loan for CESP, São Paulo's utility. That same month, he drew three checks totaling $32,000 against Muniz's account. Two of these went to his accounts, the third to an art dealer.
- In September 1979, just as he was named a senior vice president, Gebauer wrote four checks against Catão's account for $105,000. Three went to his own accounts, the fourth to Serge Sabarsky, an art dealer.
- In late 1979, Gebauer attended the IMF meetings in Yugoslavia as one of Morgan's key representatives and closed a $1.2 billion gasohol loan to Brazil. That month he drew $112,000 from Catão's account. Three checks went to Gebauer's accounts, three to art galleries.
- In February 1980, Gebauer met Delfim Neto and Galvêas at New York's Westbury Hotel to advise them on a new standby line of credit. That month he wrote two checks totalling $57,000.
- In October 1982, Gebauer met with with Delfim Neto, Galvêas, and Langoni to discuss the debt crisis, and he negotiated the GE locomotive deal. He also withdrew $107,000 from Catão's account.

Gebauer's greed was apparently so great that he drained several of these accounts dry, replenishing them with Morgan loans. In December 1979, he and two other unidentified Morgan officers approved $2.9 million in loans to his four official Brazilian clients. When the loans came up for renewal, Gebauer needed cosignatures from another unnamed Morgan officer to roll them over. From December 1979 to September 1984, these loans were renewed forty-six times. The loans accounted for two-thirds of his diversions.[122]

Unfortunately, the official version propagated by Morgan leaves many questions unanswered about Gebauer's crimes. How was he able to get away with them for so long? Supposedly, his clients rarely checked on their Morgan accounts. There was only one request for a bank statement in a decade, even though each client had several million dollars on deposit.[123] Officially, Morgan also had no warning of Gebauer's misdeeds until Fernando Catão noticed a hole in his accounts in late 1985 after Gebauer had already left Morgan and moved on to Drexel Burnham as senior vice president for its debt restructuring group. But if his crimes were really just embezzlements from innocent clients that Morgan knew nothing about, how could he believe that he'd be able to cover his tracks after leaving Morgan?[124] And why had he stopped diverting money in 1983—two years earlier? From October 1983 on, he actually returned $1.1 million to Catão's accounts and $444,000 to Muniz's over a sixteen-month period. Why did he do this, and where did he get the money?

The official charges fundamentally understated Gebauer's misbehavior and Morgan's involvement and responsibility. His diversions clearly started well before 1976, the start date alleged in the indictment.[125] Moreover, the federal prosecutors ignored many other questionable transactions that were clearly not just "diversions" by one bad apple from innocent clients. But one could learn about these matters by going to Brazil and doing some "archeology" on that country's dirty debt.

ARMING IRAQ

Several of these questionable transactions involved Engesa, a leading Brazilian arms company with very close ties to Brazil's military, Delfim Neto, and Gebauer's Bahian circle, as well as to Iraq and Libya, to whom Engesa sold huge quantities of weapons throughout the 1980s. Engesa was mentioned indirectly in the US attorney's 1987 sentencing memo, but its name was disguised and its transactions with Morgan were entirely omitted from Gebauer's guilty plea. My queries about Engesa met stiff resistance from both the federal prosecutors and Morgan. In retrospect, this wasn't surprising. Unlike Gebauer's official crimes, the Engesa deal was clearly large enough to have required approval from several other senior Morgan officers, and they also showed that some of Gebauer's "clients" were really his partners.

Engesa certainly was a peculiar customer for a leading US bank like JP Morgan to have. It was founded in 1963 by Dr. José Luiz Nolf, a São Paulo dentist, and his brother-in-law, José Luiz Whitaker Ribeiro, a mechanical engineer who had worked at Allis Chalmers in the 1950s. At age thirty, Whitaker developed a new approach to powering heavy vehicles across rough terrain, a "Hummer" precursor that he designed and manufactured for Brazil's Army. Whitaker built the company from scratch. As of 1970, Engesa only had about forty employees at a small plant outside São Paulo, manufacturing power trains and push rods for army trucks.

Then, in the 1970s, Whitaker decided to take Engesa into the Third World arms market. This was an ideal time for such a strategy. Countries like Libya,

Iraq, and Iran were finding it hard to buy arms from First World suppliers, partly because of their own dubious activities. In the 1970s, for example, as the conflict in Northern Ireland escalated and the Provisional IRA sought new sources of advanced arms, most of these weapons not only came from the IRA's traditional sources in New York and Boston, but also from Libya.[126] Especially after the Shah's ouster and the Iran-Iraq War in 1980–88, the Middle East also became a key market for Engesa's arms trucks, accounting for more than half of its exports from 1977 to 1989.

Minister Delfim Neto helped Whitaker develop this new export business. Delfim Neto hoped that the arms business would please his clients in Brazil's military and help Brazil generate new exports. With his help, Whitaker secured a $50 million loan from BNDES to build a new arms factory. BNDES, in turn, borrowed the money from First World banks—a convenient way of concealing the loan's ultimate purpose. In 1973, Whitaker escorted two prototype troop carriers to Libya and demonstrated them personally for Moammar Khaddafi, who ordered four hundred on the spot. This sale helped to establish Whitaker's reputation as someone who could "sell sand in the desert." Until 1980, when Iraq took over the top spot, Libya would be Engesa's single largest customer.

In 1976, Engesa received another 400 million cruzeiro loan from BNDES with the help of Whitaker's brother-in-law, Calmon de Sá, who was on Engesa's board. Calmon de Sá's Banco Econômico also lent heavily to Engesa and invested with Engesa and Odebrecht in an arms factory that made cannons for Iraq. By 1980, Engesa had more than 10,000 employees and produced half the world's armored track vehicles, plus a wide selection of "tropical technology" that included light tanks (built by a Bardella joint venture), short-range missiles, and artillery. Engesa had become Brazil's leading arms exporter, and Brazil, consequently, had become the world's fifth largest arms exporter, supplying more than $5 billion of official arms exports each year. In October 1982, Brazil's military president Figueiredo was so delighted with Whitaker that he appointed him head of IMBEL, a government agency that coordinated all of Brazil's arms exports.[127]

Engesa's success was partly due to its being rather unselective about its customers. In addition to Iraq and Libya, its Third World clients numbered more than forty-two countries, including Peru, Qatar, Algeria, Abu Dhabi, China, Suriname, Bolivia, Indonesia, Colombia, and Chile. But Iraq and Libya alone provided nearly $1 billion a year in orders. Engesa supplied many of the rockets, launchers, armored carriers, and trucks for the Iran-Iraq War. Delfim Neto and Whitaker actually visited Iraq during the war, and Whitaker even went to the war front. In the 1980s, Saddam Hussein selected Engesa to supply all the cars for Baghdad's new subway, for which another Brazilian construction company, Mendes Junior, became the prime contractor. Engesa also worked closely with Iraq on the antiaircraft missile "Piranha." Brazil's leading rocket and nuclear experts also helped out with Saddam Hussein's nuclear weapons and long-range missile projects. Meanwhile, Engesa also represented Casa da Moeda—a company that built national mints for countries—and had a joint venture with a US company that provided the security system for the White House. According to a Chilean military expert, Engesa supplied the very same security system to Saddam Hussein and General Pinochet. When the US objected to Engesa's Libyan sales, Whitaker responded, "I know Khadaffi personally, and I can affirm that he is a highly intelligent and balanced person."[128]

But the program that Whitaker led went far beyond the sale of desert trucks and small arms. In June 1981, when Israel bombed Saddam Hussein's nuclear facilities at Osirak, a large number of Brazilian nuclear experts were killed in the bombing.[129] Throughout the 1980s, Brazil secretly sold Saddam Hussein thousands of kilos of uranium yellow cake. In August 1990, when Saddam Hussein invaded Kuwait, a whole team of Brazilian missile experts were in Baghdad and on the verge of producing a long-range, nuclear-ready missile. Engesa's armored cars, short-range missiles, and light planes were right there, too, leading the very first wave of the Kuwait invasion.[130]

In short, the planners of Brazil's 1964 military coup had succeeded beyond their wildest dreams. Not only had they laid the foundations for a vast, debt-ridden, state-capitalist economy. They also created a first-class, independent, military-industrial empire that wanted nothing more than to sell the world's most lethal technologies to any willing regime whatsoever, no matter its ethical base.

Despite all its future "success," however, as of 1981 Engesa was actually on the verge of bankruptcy, with severe cash flow problems. Most of its Libyan orders had been filled, Iraq was slow to pay, many other Third World countries were short of cash because of the emerging debt crisis, and even the BNDES was tapped out. Fortunately, in this moment of peril, Whitaker was able to call on his friends. These included Tony Gebauer, Delfim Neto, Calmon de Sá, Catão, McDermott, the New York attorney George Bunn Jr., who represented both Engesa and Gebauer, and JPMorgan. Together, they produced an intriguing series of under-the-table deals that saved Engesa from bankruptcy.[131]

In the fall of 1981, Gebauer assembled a syndicate of six banks to lend $35 million to the nearly bankrupt Engesa. At the time, that was Morgan's largest private sector Brazilian loan ever. To do it, Gebauer worked closely with several other Morgan officers, including McDermott, David Walker, I. Bedford, and Maria Fernandez Peña—a former Morgan officer who had moved to

Banco Exterior, which joined the syndicate. Given Engesa's troubled finances, Morgan demanded a guarantee. As one banker recalled, "That was the only way any bank would touch it—the company had a bright red balance sheet."[132] To get the government guarantee, Gebauer turned to his friend Catão.

There's no doubting the strength of Catão's connections. His great-grandfather helped found both the Brazilian Republic and Buenos Aires. His family owned the private docks at Imbituba that handled Tubarão, Brazil's largest coalfield. It also owned companies that controlled twenty percent of Brazil's salt market and thirty-five percent of its chlorox market. Kubitschek and Magalhães Pinto, the influential Minas Gerais governor who helped foment the 1964 coup, were Catão's longtime friends, as were Roberto Campos, João Goulart, President Sarney, General Golbery, and David Rockefeller. According to several sources, Catão was also a leading intermediary in international airplane and arms deals with clients that included Iraq and Nicaragua.[133] I experienced the strength of his connections firsthand in 1987, when Catão arranged interviews for me on very short notice with both General Golbery and General Geisel's former interior minister.[134]

In 1976, Gebauer had met Catão through Hafers, who was once engaged to Catão's sister.[135] When the military expropriated Catão's docks in 1977—the result of a long-running squabble—Gebauer got Brazil's planning minister, Reis Velloso, to pay Catão $15 million and also got permission from Banco do Brasil and the Central Bank to take $12 million out of the country immediately. That money funded Catão's first accounts at Morgan.[136]

Then it was Catão's turn to be helpful. In December 1981, McDermott and Catão met with BNDES's president and secured a government-guaranteed $35 million loan to Engesa. When it defaulted in December 1983, BNDES had to ante up.[137] Favors like this weren't free. In February 1982, Whitaker transferred $45,000 from Credit Suisse to Catão's Morgan account. In March, he added another $1.75 million, and on April 20 and May 28, he added $75,000 and $30,000. Gebauer helped himself to $1.5 million of this, including $700,000 deposited to his father's account at Zurich's Clariden Bank and rerouted to Gebauer's Chemical Bank accounts. Gebauer also relayed $25,000 to a McDermott account at Merrill Lynch. When McDermott suddenly left Morgan in April 1982, he became a paid Engesa consultant. In July 1987, McDermott pleaded guilty to accepting illegal commissions and splitting them with Gebauer.[138] Catão denies any knowledge of these transactions, but that's hard to square with his role at BNDES, Whitaker's transfers to his accounts, and the fact that even the altered bank statements he got from Gebauer reported all these payments. Gebauer may have been cheating his partners, but they were his partners nonetheless.

Gebauer was involved with other Engesa deals. In October l982, Engesa was still having serious cash flow problems, utterly dependent on Iraqi arms sales. Yet that same month, Gebauer signed a "going concern" letter on Morgan stationary that valued Engesa at $130 million. According to a former Engesa director, Whitaker took this letter to BNDES and received another $55 million, part of which was used to pay off Morgan's loan. He also used the letter to persuade Saudi Arabia, through his friend Turki al-Faisal, to invest $5 million. In January 1983, Whitaker showed the Engesa director Gebauer's letter and said, "See this? This cost me $5 million."

According to the director, such commissions were nothing new for Engesa. He claimed that others had been paid to Chile's General Pinochet, by way of his daughter's account at UBS in Switzerland; to Rajiv Gandhi, India's prime minster from 1984 to 89, who was also accused of accepting huge bribes from the Swedish company AB Bofors in the mid-1980s in exchange for howitzer sales by way of Swiss accounts to various Banco Econômico officers (in exchange for a 1981 loan guarantee); to one of Bolivia's presidents; and to Delfim Neto himself, as a reward for all his support. An executive at Mendes Junior, Engesa's contractor on the Iraq subway system, said that Engesa was an "octopus of corruption," and that "Whitaker really got to Delfim."[139]

Even such aggressive tactics couldn't save the company from the fortunes of war, however. In l987, Iraq temporarily stopped payments, while still owing Engesa $50 million, and in 1987 Engesa needed yet another $165 million BNDES loan to stay afloat. In February 1990, after US pressure cost Engesa a huge Saudi tank contract, which went to a US company, Engesa came close once again to bankruptcy and needed another large injection of funds from Fernando Collor's government to stay afloat.

This story suggests solutions for several of the key puzzles in Gebauer's case, especially the apparent dropoff in the "diversions" from his "clients" after 1982. In fact, he may have just been digesting the huge Engesa commissions.[140] Brazil's Central Bank has the right to cancel the repayment of any foreign loan that involves such illegalities, as it did in a 1985 case involving Bank of America. In Engesa's case, however, Brazil has fully repaid Morgan.

O SISTEMA

This was not the only case where Gebauer and his cronies colluded to enrich themselves with foreign loan shenanigans. Not all the allegations are verifiable, but the smoke is thick enough to infer a fire. As one longtime Brazilian banker explained, "Tony had a real system down here. . . . I personally know of two people who split commissions with him in exchange for loans, and their names have never come out."[141]

One deal where the reports are verifiable involved Copersucar, Brazil's largest sugar cooperative. From 1966 to 1981, its director was Jorge Wollney Atalla, a leading beneficiary of the gasohol program and another close friend of Gebauer, Hafers and Delfim Neto. In 1974, Atalla secured an $80 million loan on giveaway terms from the Institute of Sugar and Alcohol to build Paraná's Usina Central, the world's largest sugar mill.[142] Sugar prices then plummeted. In 1976, with Hafers's help and another $50 million loan from Canadian Imperial Bank (guaranteed by Calmon de Sá at Banco do Brasil), he bought Hills Brothers—the US coffee distributor. Coffee prices then fell. By 1979, Hills Brothers was losing $25 million a year, and its net worth was *minus $30 million.* Banco do Brasil ate the loan. In July 1979, again with Hafers's help, Copersucar hired McDermott and Gebauer under-the-table. In March 1982, they provided a $50 million Morgan loan to Reuben Hills to repurchase Hills Brothers from Copersucar. No one told the other six banks in the syndicate, including Bank of America and Citibank, that Gebauer and McDermott had received illegal commissions on the side.[143]

A finance director at a leading Brazilian steel company told a senior Brazilian banker in the early 1980s that Gebauer was going around offering Morgan loans in exchange for commissions. "Is that the way Morgan does business here?" he wondered.[144] A São Paulo banker said that in 1983, Gebauer was soliciting an unusual $8 million loan for Borio. "I've got to help Borio," Gebauer said.[145] A Venezuelan banker at Morgan heard reports from his peers that "loans for commissions" were "common practice," especially in Brazil and Argentina.[146] A Venezuelan financier recalled that in 1984 Gebauer proposed an off-the-record deal that involved selling $25 million worth of Venezuelan Armed Forces notes. The financier said that Gebauer did the deal anyway and also intermediated Banco Industrial de Venezuela's (BIV) debt for his own account.[147] And in 1979, Venezuela's future finance minister Arturo Sosa hired Keith McDermott as an "advisor" in connection with Morgan's acquisition of twenty percent of Sosa's finance company, Finalven. Morgan retained the interest until Sosa became minister in 1982. Fernandina Gebauer recalled that Gebauer and McDermott met Sosa at their apartment to discuss the deal.[148] Finalven ran up a $300 million debt, much of it from Morgan. A senior California banker reported that "a friend paid Gebauer $300,000 to get a loan for a Boston apartment complex."[149] In 1974, McDermott, Gebauer, and O'Connell also arranged a housing project in Saudi Arabia, while McDermott was stationed in Beirut.[150] There were many other such curious cases of Morgan-led funny business; so many, in fact, that it is almost inconceivable that other senior officials at Morgan did not know what its energetic most senior Latin American banker was up to.

Another odd case with Gebauer involved Ecuador. In 1975 Boise Cascade sold Emelec (a utility based in Guayaquil) to Power Engineering (a Miami-based company) in a deal that was financed by a $33 million loan from Morgan and Chase. Two sources familiar with the deal say that Gebauer demanded that his friend O'Connell be hired as a "consultant" by Power Engineering. According to them, they refused.[151]

In 1981, as interest rates were soaring, a São Paulo broker named José Maria Tieppo started offering Brazilians unusually high yields in dollars paid from a New York account at Morgan. Citibank and Chase had declined to give him such an account, but for some reason, Morgan was much more lenient. When $30 million of Tieppo's clients' funds suddenly disappeared in 1982, many of them blamed Morgan for allowing him to use it for credibility. According to one banker who worked for Gebauer at the time, "Tony must have let him have that account."

In February 1986, I called Tony Gebauer at Drexel, where he went to work in August 1985, becoming a senior vice president in charge of Latin American debt swaps, to ask him about Tieppo. That was the first time I'd ever heard of Tony Gebauer, three months before his own scandal erupted. I was still McKinsey's in-house economist, and Gebauer had only been recommended to me as "a Brazil expert who might know something about Tieppo and similar transactions." His response was immediate, heated, and unforgettable: "If you write anything about this, I'll kill you."[152]

There was also an unusually long list of Morgan credits to South American private companies that later folded. A Morgan banker recalled an Argentine deal where Jackson Gilbert, Gebauer's boss at Morgan, had overruled a Morgan Financial Analysis Group recommendation and "virtually ordered" a loan to a very shaky Argentine company. There was also the peculiar case of Argentina's largest private bank, Banco de Intercambio Regional (BIR), which failed in 1980 after its owner, José Rafael Trozzo, looted the bank. Gebauer's group provided extensive credit lines to the bank. [153] Listas Telefônicas Brasileira, the yellow pages company owned by Gilberto Huber, got $22 million in Morgan loans from 1969 to 1978, when it went broke. Two senior Rio bankers said that "Huber had a deal with Tony."[154] Comind, a bank that went bankrupt in 1982, borrowed $14.6 million from Morgan. Svastiche, who'd been at Princeton with O'Connell, was Comind's international director at the time. Morgan also loaned $7.6 million to Rossi-Servix, a construction company owned by generals that got involved in a major scandal at Tucurui and went broke in 1982. In November 1971, Morgan loaned $4.4 million to CCBE, a Rio construction company—a transaction another former Morgan banker in São Paulo called "highly questionable."[155]

Some of the oddest transactions involved Gebauer's Bahian coffee farm—Fazenda Amizade—near Salvador, which was acquired by Gebauer, Noronha, and O'Connell in the 1970s. Morgan client Eduardo Campello Jr., another one of O'Connell's friends from Princeton, was a member of the farm's "Fiscal Council." At the time, it was illegal for an operating farm in Brazil to be majority-owned by foreign nonresidents and to repatriate dividends to them. Yet the farm's records clearly showed that Gebauer and O'Connell were its majority owners. According to Gebauer's former brother-in-law, "This farm was very special—it was the only one in Brazil that was allowed to remit profits abroad, by authority of Brazil's president himself."[156] According to the farm's former general manager, it had only been authorized to operate retrospectively, long after it had been started up, by the minister of agriculture in October 1986, after the alleged payment of a $15,000 bribe.[157] The farm never sold much coffee, but it did receive loans from more than forty Brazilian banks. In early 1987, right after Gebauer was sentenced to jail, the remaining outstanding loan balance was consolidated by a $1.5 million loan from Banco Bozano Simonsen, guaranteed by deposits at the Luxembourg subsidiary of M. M. Warburg, Brickmann, Wirtz & Co.—a leading international private bank in Hamburg that also had offices or representatives in New York, Argentina, and Zurich.

Beginning in 1985 and continuing until Gebauer was jailed in March 1987, there were at least ten suspicious meetings at Salvador's Hotel Enseada, not far from the farm's office. These meetings were attended by Gebauer, O'Connell, Noronha, and several other prominent Brazilians, including Mario Andreazza, Brazil's interior minister; Roberto Shorto, president of Coca-Cola do Brasil; Antonio Dias Leite, a former minister of industry; Luiz Caetano Queiroz, a bank president; and Jua Hafers. Clearly something more than coffee farming was going on. After the last meeting in March 1987, calls were placed from the hotel to M. M. Warburg's Luxembourg office, and eight shell companies suddenly disappeared from the Cayman Islands' company registry.

Finally, from 1972 to 1984, Noronha's had been a director of Banco Econômico, whose group received $52 million in Morgan loans. A prominent Rio banker claimed that in 1984 "Noronha was quietly fired, because he was caught splitting commissions."[158] A Brazilian banker and a construction company executive, who knew Gebauer, both claimed the farm was a "front" for laundering illegal commissions and flight money.[159] Court records also show that Noronha and O'Connell received large personal checks from Gebauer.[160] After leaving Banco Econômico under these questionable circumstances, Noronha went on to Banco Interatlântico, where Morgan had purchased a half-interest in May 1982. By 1985, Banco Interatlântico had obtained $53 million in Morgan loans. Some claim that it was also deeply involved in illegal commissions and back-to-back loans.[161] In any case, in May 1986, shortly after the Gebauer scandal surfaced, William Oullin, a Morgan vice president, made a special visit to its São Paulo office to investigate the case. Not long thereafter, in January 1987, Morgan quietly disposed of its half-interest in the bank.[162]

One of the most striking accusations involved Brazil's 1982 debt rescheduling, when Morgan helped raise $4.4 billion in new loans for the country. According to a former Engesa director, Whitaker told him that "Gebauer split a huge commission with Delfim to roll the debt."[163] In 1984, Helio Fernandez, a Brazilian journalist, also told a Commission of Parliamentary Inquiry that Gebauer and Delfim Neto had split a multi-million dollar commission on the rollover.[164] And three other senior bankers credited similar reports: As one senior Japanese banker in São Paulo said, "It was widely rumored among bankers that Gebauer, Galvêas, and Delfim Neto had carved out a $10–25 million commission for themselves."[165]

Where might such payments have gone? Fernandina Gebauer, Gebauer's wife until 1981, recalled that "around 1973, Tony told me that he had some investments at a European bank." In 1974, he made a hush-hush trip alone to Europe. Fernandina called his hotel in Zurich to find him, and the hotel clerk asked her, "Which Gebauer?" Apparently Tony Gebauer's father was also there. Tony Gebauer later explained to her that he had been on a "secret mission for Morgan." Just before he was sentenced in January 1987, Gebauer made another hurried trip to Zurich. Fernandina said, "He said he was going to see his mother, but she was in Caracas."[166] Part of Engesa's commissions wound up in an account owned by Gebauer's father at Zurich's Clariden Bank, a Credit Suisse subsidiary. And of course, there was also the Luxembourg subsidiary of M. M. Warburg. Knowing Gebauer's appetite for the *hoch bourgeois* lifestyle, wherever the commission went, it would not have been to some dusty Caribbean island.

Gebauer also clearly had many more clients than just the four Brazilians that were disclosed by Morgan.[167] A former Morgan credit officer reported that "Tony managed more than a dozen accounts that were continually running overdrafts."[168] Another Morgan vice president who worked for Gebauer confirmed that "There were not just four clients, but at least a dozen."[169] Almeida claimed that "Morgan was helping a ring of up to forty Brazilians take money out of the country. Many prominent people were involved. To cop a plea, and get Morgan to settle the case, Tony threatened to reveal their names."[170]

A US law enforcement source who was involved in investigating the case provided me with a list of thirteen Panama and Cayman companies whose accounts were under Gebauer's control, in addition to the six accounts that were officially disclosed. I confirmed the identities of eleven of these shell companies in the Panama and Cayman registries. They all had the telltale markings of Morgan-originated shells: They employed the same haven lawyers to set them up, and they had the same corporate officers. Curiously, five of the Cayman companies had been created on the same date—June 30, 1982, not long after the Engesa deals and the Banco Interatlântico purchase. But one of the companies had been created in 1961, two years before Gebauer even joined Morgan. The president of that shell company at the time was none other than Jacques Hentsch, the managing partner of the prestigious Hentsch & Co., one of Geneva's top six private banks. His son Benedict G. F. Hentsch had worked directly for Gebauer and Morgan in Brazil in the 1970s. In 1985, Benedict Hentsch became a partner at Hentsch & Co.; then managing partner at Darier Hentsch & Cie from 1990 until October 2001; president of Switzerland's Private Bankers Association; and vice chairman of Swissair until its bankruptcy that same month. In July 2002, Darier Hentsch merged with Lombard Odier to form Lombard Odier Darier Hentsch & Cie, one of the few remaining "truly private" private banks. In any case, eight of these shell companies had been terminated in March 1987, while Gebauer was entering jail, by someone who took the trouble to visit Grand Cayman's Public Registry in person to avoid leaving a paper trail.

In 1986, following the initial disclosures in the case, Brazil's Central Bank went through the motions of investigating Gebauer's four official clients for tax evasion and exchange control violations, and Brazil's IRS announced that their offshore accounts had not been properly declared. Brazil's government also filed a *letter rogatory* with the US, an official government request for law enforcement assistance, seeking information about any other Morgan clients in Brazil. But none of these efforts went anywhere. Morgan opposed releasing information on anyone other than the four clients it had already named. They were comparative small fries, who were no longer desirable clients anyway. By then, Muniz, Borio, and Almeida were all having financial problems, Catão had been publically implicated in the Engesa payoffs, and none of the four were powerful officials or senators who were able to help Morgan generate business in Brazil or anywhere else.[171]

So who were Gebauer's hidden clients? One former senior Morgan banker identified four more of them—all whose names have been mentioned above.[172] But three other sources said that the real secret was the identity of just two key clients. "Of course you'll never be able to prove it, but they were very powerful Brazilian ministers. I won't say more than that."[173] Among the most likely candidates are Delfim Neto and Magalhães. The key law enforcement agent involved in the case believes it was Delfim Neto: "His name definitely came up in investigation, and we had his checks and accounts. But for some reason [US Attorney Rudy] Giuliani decided not to pursue it." This would not have been the first instance where Giuliani may have cut corners to help his powerful Wall Street allies. A Latin American financier who was close to Gebauer also reported that "Tony once told me Delfim was a private client."[174]

It is also now clear that Morgan had numerous early warnings about Gebauer's misconduct. Three Morgan bankers who worked with him and a half dozen more outside the bank say that by the 1980s, his peculiar practices were common knowledge. As one Brazilian official commented, "In Brasilia, by 1983, Gebauer was well known to be a corrupt banker who took commissions."[175] But Morgan received even more specific warnings. One former Morgan officer who was active in Latin American lending recalled that "In 1975, Tony introduced me to Muniz and described him as his 'partner.' I warned him about taking commissions."[176] In the Siderúgica case mentioned above, a banker passed the information on to Gebauer's superior at the time, Fred Vinton. He said that "A half hour later Gebauer called me, furious. I asked Vinton what he'd done with the information. He said he'd passed it on to Tony's boss, Alex Vagliano, the head of Morgan's International Department, who reported that he'd checked it out and found nothing."[177]

Another very specific warning came from a credit officer in Morgan's Latin American Department. The officer, who retired in 1985 after a thirty-two-year career, said that in early 1981—six months before Gebauer took over as senior vice president for South America from Jackson Gilbert—he had complained to Gilbert that Gebauer was running inexplicable overdrafts in more than a dozen accounts. Only Gebauer handled the accounts. Gilbert— a former Sullivan and Cromwell attorney and the former chief counsel for Adela, an international venture capital firm that was active all over Latin America—certainly knew the law. But according to the officer, "Gilbert's response was very strange and entirely inappropriate. Rather than investigate, he immediately called in Tony to confront me. Gebauer talked his way around it, and for four years, I never got another raise."[178] Asked about this incident, Gilbert, who left Morgan to become the chairman of Riggs National Bank in Washington, DC in 1983, refused to comment, except to say, "I have a good relationship with Morgan. . . . Everything we did was appropriate."[179]

Asked to explain why Gebauer's superiors were so deaf, dumb and blind, the former credit officer hypothesized that "it was because he had such strong supporters." Peter Smith, an executive vice president who became head of Morgan's International Bank in June 1981 and later the head of Morgan's Credit Policy Committee, was another one of Tony's close friends. He was the godfather to Gebauer's first son, and Smith's wife was present at the birth of Gebauer's third son in December 1985.[180] Gebauer reported to Peter Smith during the crucial period from June 1981 to December 1983, when all the deals involving Engesa, Hills, Banco Interatlântico, and Banco Econômico were consummated. Gebauer also had other influential friends at Morgan, including Robert V. Lindsey, Morgan's president from 1980 to January 1987, and Danny Davison, a Morgan executive vice president who became chairman of US Trust in the late 1970s.[181]

How many collaborators did Gebauer have inside Morgan? At first, the bank claimed that he acted alone, but it later admitted that Vice President McDermott and an unnamed assistant treasurer were also involved. Another tantalizing tidbit suggests there may have been others. According to two old acquaintances of Gebauer's, they were both present at a small party in Rio in the 1970s when Gebauer got drunk and boasted that "A guy I work with and me decided we'd never make it to the top at the Bank, so we're gonna get rich." "I forget the guy's name," one of the witnesses said. "But his family owned a European bank."[182] Several of Gebauer's coworkers were from European banking families.

Of course the commission business was not limited to Gebauer and Morgen. As one longtime Citibanker said:

> Everyone offered you commissions in Brazil, it was very common. Even the banks got them! Morgan and Citibank collected 'flats'—illegal premiums— on every public sector loan they made from 1983 to 1986, when money was tight. Until the Central Bank finally clamped down, it was a game: The *empreteiras* paid us by depositing dollars in New York, we loaned to the state companies, and the state companies paid the *empreteiras*. The only difference with Tony was, *he* got the commissions, not Morgan.[183]

THE RECKONING

After the Iranian Revolution in 1979 led to the second oil shock of the 1970s, Brazil's situation deteriorated rapidly. Delfim Neto failed to curtail spending, inflation took off, and foreign reserves sank like a stone. The country borrowed short-term to stay afloat, using state companies like Petrobras and CVRD as fronts for funds that were then "reloaned" to the Central Bank. A few regional banks, like Philadelphia National, saw through this deception and pulled out in 1981, but larger ones like Morgan and Citibank hung on. They were "knee deep in the Big Muddy," and they were afraid to pull the plug.

When Brazil finally ran out of reserves, in September 1982, Delfim Neto appointed Gebauer cochairman of the Advisory Committee. Throughout the fall he conducted key negotiations, such as a November meeting with US Federal Reserve chairman and former Chase strategic planner Paul Volcker, the New York Fed's Anthony Solomon, and Robert Lindsey. Gebauer also appeared on McNeil-Lehrer.[184] In his meetings with the regional banks, Gebauer pressed them very hard to make fresh loans, almost as if he were working for Delfim Neto. They regarded him as a "brow-beating bully."

But the Brazilian elite still loved him. President Figueiredo designated him "an honorary Brazilian" and *Veja Magazine*, the country's leading weekly, featured him as "the High Commissioner of the External Debt." At a Plaza Hotel dinner in May 1983, the Brazilian-American Chamber of Commerce held its fourteenth annual "Man of the Year" dinner. Before a packed ballroom, Brazil's finance minister Ernane Galvêas and US Secretary of State George Schultz shared the award, in recognition of their efforts on the debt. At the end of his speech, Galvêas asked three others in the audience to stand and be recognized as well. The first two were Lewis T. Preston and Walter Wriston; the third was Tony Gebauer.

In retrospect, that was the true peak of Gebauer's career. Regional US banks complained to Volcker about Gebauer's high-handedness, and in June 1983, he was removed from the cochairmanship of the Brazil Foreign Creditors' Steering Committee. Other clouds also gathered, especially after Jackson Gilbert moved from Morgan to Riggs Bank in l983. In a move that may have been an attempt to smoke out his misconduct, Morgan sent Gebauer off to Harvard Business School's Advanced Management Program for three months in January 1984. In May 1984, he was remarried to Aurelia Reinhardt, a former Banker's Trust officer. As usual, family connections had played a role—the couple had been introduced by Aurelia's brother-in-law Wolfgang Traber, a German who had reportedly worked for a Swiss bank, was very close to O'Connell and Deltec, and had known Gebauer for thirty years. The wedding took place in Ercole, Italy, and Catão flew over to attend. On the wedding day, Catão sold Gebauer the first floor of his apartment on Paris's fashionable Avenue Hoche.[185]

Shortly thereafter, Gebauer returned to Morgan as a "Senior Banker," and Gonzalo de los Heras took over as Morgan's senior vice president for South America. Morgan advertised this as a promotion, but Gebauer spent the next year in a holding pattern. In August 1985, he got a "glowing recommendation" from Morgan and moved on to become a senior vice president at Drexel Burham Lambert—the former Morgan partner and junk bond pioneer that Michael Milken was just then piloting to its 1988 peak and 1990 bankruptcy. Having been a principal contributor in the buildup of Brazil's foreign debt, Gebauer's job at Drexel, while it lasted, was to manage debt swaps—exploiting the fact that Latin America's excessive debts now traded at a substantial discount.

In September 1985, soon after the Drexel move, Gebauer's number finally came up. According to the official story, Fernando Catão complained about a "hole" in his accounts at Morgan's Paris office. Gebauer called him on September 25 to reassure him, and tried frantically to cover the shortage. But since he was now at Drexel, Gebauer's formerly malleable assistant treasurer refused to approve any new overdrafts and reported Gebauer's requests to his boss. Morgan also got in touch with Catão. It told him his account balance was not $3 million but $2,877.87. Left to its own devices, then, Morgan would probably never have touched Gebauer. But Catão, perhaps Gebauer's least significant "client," evidently felt betrayed by his arrogant former partner and insisted on some answers.

At that point, Morgan finally decided to ask its former senior banker some hard questions. On October 17, 1985, Gebauer was advised of "discrepancies" in Catão's accounts. On October 29, Gebauer was questioned by five Morgan interrogators, including de los Heras and the chief auditor. Gebauer claimed Catão had authorized him to invest money outside the bank to earn higher interest and that he had unlimited discretion. He also promised to return $2.7 million by November 1.[186] He did so, but Morgan's concerns about a scandal and some of the contradictions in his story prompted an investigation by Morgan's attorney at the Wall Street firm of Davis Polk—Chris Crowley. This was one of the case's many ironies: In 1972–74, Davis Polk had advised C. R. Almeida on setting up his first Morgan account, and Davis Polk was also Gebauer's personal law firm until 1982. One of the checks that Gebauer drained from Catão's account that year was for $10,000, payable to Davis Polk.[187]

Despite the investigation, Gebauer continued his energetic pace. In September 1985, he flew to Brazil to discuss debt swaps with Dilson Funaro, Brazil's finance minister, and Fernão Bacher, president of the Central Bank. He also met with O'Connell, Banco Econômico's Noronha, and former minister Andreazza at the Hotel Enseada in Bahia. In October, between stints with Morgan investigators in New York and Paris, he was off to the IMF annual meetings in Korea, where he heard US Secretary of the Treasury James Baker announce his Baker Plan, which was intended to resolve the Third World debt crisis once and for all. On November 18, 1985, he was back in Brazil to meet with Bracher and Carlos Eduardo de Freitas of the Central Bank, and then O'Connell and Noronha again. In November, Gebauer's new wife Aurelia gave birth to a baby boy, despite having a troubled pregnancy. In December 1985, Gebauer met Catão in Paris, Muniz in New York, and Bracher in Brazil.

Beneath the surface, personal pressures were mounting. In addition to the Morgan investigation and his newborn son's life-threatening condition, Gebauer's father collapsed at his Ft. Lauderdale apartment in August. He developed lymphatic cancer and died a year later. Gebauer's behavior regarding the Tieppo case, in February 1986, was an indication of the stress that he was under. Almeida recalled that when Gebauer and his lawyer, Stanley Arkin, visited him in April 1986 in Curitiba, Gebauer begged him for a backdated power of attorney. "He pleaded with me; he was close to tears. But I refused."[188]

Morgan was also under pressure. The Street expected fast-paced deal makers like Drexel to have scandals, but this was JPMorgan. However, in the course of its history, Morgan had actually experienced more than a few such embarrassing moments:

- In 1982, Ali Kouhestanian, an Iranian car thief imprisoned in the Billerica House of Detention outside Boston had a far-fetched idea: he would call the presidents of major US banks from a prison telephone and pose as "Abdul Aziz Al Quaraishi," the head of Saudi Arabia's Central Bank. He'd say that his poor young nephew was stuck in Billerica, penniless, and could the banker please send money? Ali called fourteen banks, but succeeded in only one case. Robert V. Lindsay, Morgan's president, wired him $43,800. The fiasco was only detected when the real Quaraishi, who had a Morgan account, was charged for the transfer. Unfortunately, the thief had already disposed of $20,000.[189]
- In the late 1970s, Morgan was approached by Honducap, a joint venture between Faiz Sikiffy, a Lebanese-Honduran, and Holderbank AG, a Swiss engineering company owned by the Schmidheiny family, which also owned SBC and Swiss Airlines. Honducap wanted a $60 million loan to expand a cement plant, Cementos de Honduras, located in the north of the country. Morgan knew little about Sikiffy, but Holderbank was an important client, so it assembled a $34 million syndication, including $10 million of its own money. The plant was never finished, the funds disappeared, and in 1985 Faiz Sikiffy pleaded guilty to charges that he had smuggled marijuana and conspired to assassinate Honduras's president.[190] Morgan's only consolation was that Honduras assumed the loan.
- Sam Feuer, a twenty-year employee of Morgan's Custody Department, pleaded guilty in October 1986 to embezzling $1.1 million in 1979–84 by getting Morgan checks deposited to his own brokerage account. Unlike Gebauer, Feuer's crimes were quickly dealt with. After all, he was just an ordinary bank employee who didn't have access to dangerous information about Morgan's top clients and deals.[191]
- In November 2001, just one month before Enron, the Houston-based global energy giant, declared bankruptcy, William Harrison, JPMorgan Chase's CEO, spoke with glee to a group of twenty senior executives in London about his bank's "triumph" at Enron. He declared that

JPMorgan Chase, the new entity formed by the December 2000 merger between JPMorgan and Chase, had won its unique lead role with Enron because "other banks do not have the stomach for such boldness." Only a few weeks later, Harrison's gut was probably feeling a little queasy. It turned out that JPMorgan Chase had indeed loaned Enron more than $2.6 billion, $600 million of it entirely unsecured, and another $1.1 billion that was covered only by "surety bonds" that insurance companies were refusing to honor because of alleged fraud. By 2003, JPMorgan Chase had written off $1.13 billion of this debt, and it had set aside another $900 million to cover additional losses and lawsuits. Meanwhile, an investigation by Enron's board disclosed that JPMorgan Chase had also helped the company design transactions with "special purpose entities" in offshore havens that inflated Enron's profits by more than $1 billion.[192]

To avoid further embarrassments from Tony Gebauer, Morgan started negotiating with him in March 1986. He had already repaid $4.2 million to clients, and he agreed to restore another $3.7 million and keep the names of other clients secret. In return, Morgan agreed not to sue him and to narrow the scope of its criminal complaint.

Even these negotiations proceeded, the Brazilian-American Chamber of Commerce held another Man-of-the-Year Dinner at the Plaza Hotel in May 1986. As usual Gebauer was there, seated among prominent Brazilians like Olavo ("Olavinho") Monteiro de Carvalho, José Luiz Zillo, and Auro Moura Andrade. This time, however, the atmosphere was different. Whispers swept through the hall that Price Waterhouse, Morgan's accountant, and Davis Polk's Chris Crowley had already been down to Brazil, looking into a scandal about missing money. The word was that some *urucubaca*—a Bahian bad-luck spirit—had finally gotten to Tony.[193]

One man who knew more than others about the case was Monteiro de Carvalho, Morgan's coinvestor in Banco Interatlântico. The day after the dinner, Monteiro de Carvalho paid a call on Lewis T. Preston and Boris Berkovitch, Morgan's vice chairman. Worried that the story might leak to the press, Morgan seized the initiative. On May 20, it issued a three-paragraph statement disclosing "irregularities" in Brazil and asked US attorney for the Southern District Rudy Guiliani for help. On May 22, an article appeared in the *New York Times*, entitled "Doubts Emerge about an Elite Banker." The article was based on several internal Morgan sources, who portrayed Gebauer as the lone, overweening, avaricious bad apple. Morgan's partner, Monteiro Aranha, had helped out with the story—his wife was Betsy Hoge, the sister of *Times* reporter Warren Hoge. Six days later the identities of three of the four official "clients" were revealed in *Veja*. Morgan assured its clients that they wouldn't lose any money, and reported that it had found no wrongdoing by anyone else in the bank.

On the tricky issue of private banking, dirty debt, and orchestrating big-ticket flight capital, Morgan stated baldly that the Bank had "a policy of not accepting accounts where it is in any way on notice that the customer of the bank is violating his country's currency laws. The Bank inquires as to the purpose of the account and does not accept accounts where there is not a plausible explanation. It believes that its policy is as strict as any bank's in this country."[194]

Throughout the summer and fall of 1986, Guiliani's team, Morgan, and Gebauer negotiated his plea behind closed doors. Just as in the Parana Railroad deal years earlier, the final plea bargain satisfied many special interests at once. For Gebauer and his attorney, Stanley Arkin, Gebauer's 3.5-year-sentence, with time off for good behavior, in a comfortable Federal minimum security prison in nearby Connecticut, compared very favorably to the twenty-year sentence he might have received for his official offenses alone. Gebauer's resources were more than ample to handle the remaining $9.1 million of his $15 million bill for repayments, taxes, and interest. Even apart from hidden assets, his Manhattan apartment was worth $5.5 million, his Paris apartment $750,000, his East Hampton house $1.9 million, and his paintings, gold, and farm another million or so. The plea also saved him from prosecution for any other offenses or civil liabilities. As Arkin later said, Tony Gebauer got "a very low sentence." And Arkin got his $460,000 fee.

Giuliani and the prosecutors who negotiated the plea bargain were also pleased. It let them nail a prominent white-collar criminal without doing much work. As one investigator said, "There were lots of other leads, but you have to remember that this was just one of four hundred bank fraud cases that my office was pursuing. We also didn't have the resources to spend a lot of time tracking these folks all over the world."[195] Guiliani, a conservative Republican with political ambitions, who would later become New York's mayor, was also glad to have prosecuted the felon without embarrassing one of New York's most hallowed financial institutions and generous political contributors.

The plea also avoided a messy trial where wealthy, influential Brazilians might have to testify in public about their secret accounts—which probably violated, at the very least, Brazilian capital controls and income tax laws. In return, the prosecutors ignored Engesa and all the other dirty deals and clients. Of the half dozen other Morgan bankers who'd been accomplices in Gebauer's deals, the prosecutors only pursued McDermott, who'd left Morgan in 1982. They even let Gebauer put his $2 million home in his wife's name and sell it just two days before his plea.

Davis Polk's lawyers were also happy. Several of them, like senior Davis Polk partner Fritz Link, owed their careers in no small measure to Gebauer's huge Latin American loans, which they'd helped to structure, and Davis Polk also wanted to avoid an embarrassing trial. So did the US Federal Reserve— an entity that is actually not a government institution, but is privately owned by its member banks. So did the US State Department and Brazil's government, not to mention the many officials, generals, and Caterpillar and GE executives who had made use of Gebauer's services. After all, complex matters like commissions, arms traffic, flight money, and "flats" are better discussed with sympathetic cognoscenti behind closed-doors.

And finally there was Morgan Bank. Morgan wanted Gebauer to pay for his crimes—but not too much, since that might lead him to reveal other matters that were best left off the record. The bank didn't want any more clients revealed, and it certainly didn't want Gebauer taking the stand to testify in public about the seamier side of Latin lending. Except where exposure forced its hand, Morgan's role in this case was to ask as few questions as possible of its clients, so long as the clients avoided publicity; of its borrowers, so long as the borrowers had government guarantees for their big projects; and of Tony Gebauer, so long as he made money.

From this standpoint, it is especially interesting to look more closely at the precise charges that Gebauer pled guilty to: (1) tax evasion, (2) bank fraud, and (3) filing false bank statements. To a criminal lawyer, there are two striking omissions: embezzlement and mail fraud. But in order to prove "embezzlement," the government would have to show that the "missing" funds were not the proceeds of other crimes. And, unlike the charges Gebauer pled guilty to, embezzlement and mail fraud are also "predicate acts" under RICO, the federal racketeering statute—offenses that, if established, would open the door to a RICO prosecution of Morgan. By excluding them, US attorney Guiliani thus made it impossible for anyone to sue Morgan under RICO for engaging in an "ongoing criminal enterprise" in Brazil. The bank fraud charge also made Morgan out to be Gebauer's victim, even though it is not clear that he ever really defrauded the bank. But under RICO, the victim of a criminal enterprise can't be made a party to it. The prosecutors also avoided messy topics like the Engesa deals, where Morgan clearly profited from Gebauer's crimes.

Gebauer's fellow bankers at Morgan, who had known him for years and "felt a sense of betrayal" at his actions, were certainly among those most relieved by his plea. As one banker said, "We're trying to put him behind us." They were happy to refocus their energies on Morgan's latest frontier— investment banking for First World corporations, many of which had become rather disenchanted with the Third World by the late 1980s. Indeed, by the late 1980s, Morgan had discontinued almost all of its Latin American operations—just as it had done in the 1930s. It would only restart these operations in the 1990s, in the context of its consolidation with Chase, Chemical, and MHT, from which it emerged as JPMorgan Chase—a global bank with more than $750 billion in assets (the sixth largest), named the "Bank of the Year" in 2001 by the trade press, serving ninety-nine percent of the Fortune 1000. It would survive even its heavy involvement in the Enron scandal.

Finally, there were all those undisclosed clients, delighted to have their identities, foreign bank accounts, and dubious dealings kept hidden from public view. And the official proceedings had indeed protected them, at least for the time being.

EPILOGUE

However, even the darkest chambers of the global underground economy occasionally admit a little light and air, if one is persistent. And years after the events in Judge Sweet's courtroom, thinking back to all those meanderings to the Bahian farm, the public records offices in the Cayman Islands and Panama; the odd meetings at the Hotel Enseada; the unclaimed offshore companies; the inexplicable loans and the transfer to the Hamburg/Luxembourg bank—we remembered . . . that Wolfgang Traber, Gebauer's brother-in-law, had "been a friend for thirty years . . . had known Dickie . . . and had worked for . . . 'some Swiss or German bank.'"

A little more digging revealed that as of 2003, Traber was the chairman of the Hanseatic Corporation, a "private investment" company "with minority equity positions in early and late stage companies in the US and Europe," based in New York City. Apparently the company has a long and colorful German lineage.[196] In 2003, its President was Paul Biddelman, a Columbia lawyer with a Harvard MBA, who had been managing director of corporate finance at Drexel Burnham Lambert during the 1980s, where he might well have met Gebauer. And Biddelman and Traber now sit on the boards of numerous companies in which Hanseatic has invested.

But what really caught the eye were two key facts. One was an obscure footnote in a 1995 SEC filing, which reported that one of the Hanseatic Corporation investments had borrowed $5 million from Hanseatic through "Deltec Asset Management"—O'Connell's old company, which acted as custodian.[197] The other key fact was buried in the back of another SEC document filed in January 2002 for Star Gas, a "diversified home energy distributor" with 850,000 US customers. This document matter-of-factly reported that in December 1999, M. M. Warburg Bank Luxembourg extended a $37.5 million line of credit to Hanseatic Americas Inc. (HAI), and in December 2001, M. M.

Warburg Bank Luxembourg also extended a $20 million line of credit to Hanseatic Corporation and HAI—Traber's companies.[198]

Was it a it coincidence that Deltec's O'Connell traveled from New York to Bahia with Gebauer so many times? Or that the money transfers from Bahia and Banco Econômico went to the very same Luxembourg bank that later loaned the funds to an investment company run by Gebauer's brother-in-law? Or were the numerous high-level past and present Brazilian officials, who met with Gebauer and O'Connell at least four times a year in Bahia, just travelling there for the local coffee and the *candomble* (Brazilian voodoo)?

After all, it turns out that M. M. Warburg was not a complete stranger to handling funny money—even from senior government officials. In September 2000, its Swiss subsidiary was one of six banks disciplined by the Swiss Federal Banking Commission for violating money laundering guidelines and due diligence requirements in connection with more than $660 million that had been diverted to Swiss subsidiaries by Nigeria's former dictator, Sani Abacha, by way of his two sons, Ibrahim and Mohammed. When these findings surfaced, two members of M. M. Warburg's board and a senior manager at the bank were forced to resign.[199]

Luxembourg, one of Europe's most sophisticated tax havens, is also no stranger to funny business. When the money is really dirty, it is said that even Swiss bankers go there to do their washing. In August 2002, Switzerland's own ambassador to Luxembourg was arrested on charges of using several accounts at a Luxembourg bank to launder money for a Spanish drug dealer.[200]

Nor is it obvious what else a convicted Colombian felon—trained by one of the world's most sophisticated banks, with indisputable energy and talent, extraordinary global connections in the First and Third Worlds, and still, presumably, an appetite for the best things that money can buy—was supposed to do with the rest of his life.

But the real story of the underground economy often takes decades to emerge. And so Tony Gebauer's real story has only been understood long after the rather narrow official version was presented in Judge Sweet's courtroom. Back then, Gebauer's sentence concluded, the courtroom emptied quickly, "the most highly esteemed banker in Latin America" slinked away with his eyes on the ground through a side door to jail, and a bevy of pinstriped bankers returned to the hallowed halls of the institution that J. P. Morgan Jr. once described as follows: "There is no place in the world which begins to compare with it for position and dignity—besides which it has the added charm of being profitable."[201]

CHAPTER FIVE

BLEEDING NICARAGUA

Latin American countries face a great paradox. . . . A great volume of capital has flowed constantly from this area to countries that are considerably stronger financially, preventing the use of such funds to finance projects in the countries where the funds originate. The importance of this fact for the social, political, and economic reality of the countries of Latin America has only begun to be appreciated. . . .
> —Key private banker for General Anastasio Somoza de Bayle, 1970

We have no food. The children cry from hunger. There is no work. The coffee growers cannot get money to pay us.
> —Yamileth Dávila, Nicaraguan farm worker, 2001

We've had ten years of war which tried to crush an alternative economic model and now no reconstruction program. What else are thousands of demobilized troops and their families to do? They've been told to "insert themselves into the world economy," so they export cocaine to you . . .
> —Miskito Indian nurse, 1994

The problem here is if you submit to their policies, you're good. When you want to keep your dignity, you're bad. That's the story of Latin American countries and American presence. . . .
> —Daniel Ortega, FSLN presidential candidate, July 15, 2001

NICARAGUAN BLOOD BANKING

It was a torrid summer afternoon in Mexico City, and the traffic and pollution were oppressive, but investigative journalists have strange tastes. I was delighted because I'd finally tracked down a former UN official who'd spent six months auditing the Central Bank of Nicaragua way back in 1979. The audit had given the Sandinistas powerful ammunition in their debt negotiations, but it was kept a state secret. The Sandinistas wanted to restore good relations with the banks, and General Somoza's foreign bankers certainly had no interest in revealing the findings. As in the case of the Philippines, auditing a Central Bank that has been working for a ruthless dictator turns out to be hazardous work. In this case, the UN official had been threatened, one of his coworkers was shot in Managua, and a US investment banker who advised the Sandinistas had his New York City office rifled twice.[1]

A decade later, however, the small restaurant on Paseo de la Reforma seemed like a safe place to finally tell the story. It was also convenient, just across town from the residence of one of General Somoza's key private bankers. So after lunch, my Colombian research assistant and I paid an unscheduled call on the private banker's home in a fashionable Mexico City suburb. . . .

On January 10, 1978, Pedro Joaquín Chamorro Cardenal, the editor of *La Prensa*, Nicaragua's leading newspaper, was murdered in downtown Managua by a gang of four hired thugs. One week later thirty thousand people attended his funeral. It turned into a bloody riot, the most important mass protest ever held against the brutal forty-two year dicatorship of General Anastasio Somoza Debayle and his father General Anastasio Somoza Garcia, who had ruled Nicaragua after the US military ended its twenty-one-year occupation of the country in 1933. Lawrence A. Pezzullo, who served as US ambassador to Nicaragua in 1979–81, later described Chamorro's murder as "the catalytic event that brought together all the opposition groups. . . . It was the beginning of the end for Somoza."[2] The murder also helped to produce a civil war that postponed Nicaragua's return to democracy for more than a decade.

What interests us here are the events that led up to Chamorro's murder. He'd been a thorn in Somoza's side for years, but his fate was sealed by a series of articles that he published in September 1977, describing Somoza's involvement in a peculiar kind of export business.[3] In the mid-1970s, Dr. Pedro Ramos, an enterprising young Cuban-American, had founded a company in partnership with the dictator's son Anastasio ("Tachito") Somoza Portocarrero, popularly known as "the apprentice dictator," who also served as a colonel in Nicaragua's National Guard and the head of its Basic Training School. Their scheme was not original—François ("Papa Doc") Duvalier had tried something similar in Haiti.[4] The company would buy blood from poor Nicaraguans for five dollars a liter, extract the plasma at one of Anastasio Somoza's factories, and export it to the US for twenty-five dollars a liter. Under a 1974 Nicaraguan law, all the profits from this scheme were be tax-free, since the company was deemed to "benefit the country." Received abroad in dollars, they were readily invested in Anastasio Somoza's many foreign holdings, including his Houston Mercedes dealership, Miami restaurants, and bank accounts at Citibank and Southeast Bank.[5] Unfortunately for Anastasio Somoza and Dr. Ramos, one of the four murderers was arrested, and he confessed that Dr. Ramos had paid him $14,285 to do the murder. Dr. Ramos fled to Miami the day before the killing. The crowd at the funeral singled out the blood factory and burned it to the ground.[6]

The resulting mass protests over the death of Pedro Chamorro helped to bring about Somoza's downfall, but it was not the end of Third World blood traffic. In the early 1980s, two Mexican journalists exposed more than five hundred private clinics that had been set up in Mexico to buy blood from poor people and export it to the US, as agents for leading drug companies like Cutter Labs, Parke Davis, Lederle, and Green Cross.[7] Through a process called "plasmapherisis, " the fluid portion of the donors' blood was separated and the red blood cells returned. The plasma was converted to antihemophilic drugs and hepatitis vaccine. The traffic thrived despite an explicit prohibition of blood exportation in the Mexican Sanitary Code (Article 207, Title X) and an acute blood shortage at Mexico's Red Cross.

These drug companies also purchased blood from plasma centers located all along the border from Texas to California, catering to Mexicans who crossed the border to sell their blood. Since the 1980s, coincident with Mexico's economic troubles over the last two decades, every border town has acquired at least one such center. By the 1990s, El Paso had eight, San Antonio four, Fort Worth two, and Brownsville two. Texas had forty-one, California thirty-four, and Florida twenty-two. Traffic was very high—one center in Nogales, Arizona reported an average of five hundred blood sellers a week. The sellers were paid $20–30 per visit. Under US Federal Drug Administration guidelines, they were allowed to sell just twice a week, up to two-thirds of a liter each time. As of 2003, each liter of source plasma is worth $100–110 on the international market, with prices ranging up to $650 per liter for plasma with special antibodies.[8] This blood business can be very profitable, so long as there is a stable flow of donors. To attract donors, the centers have used radio ads in Spanish, cash bonuses for donations on birthdays, and raffles for TV sets. But the real driving force has been Mexico's continuing series of economic crises. With real wages cut to 1960 levels as of the mid-1990s, thousands of businesses failing, increased competition from US exporters under NAFTA, and 15–20 percent underemployment in many parts of the country, regular blood donations can easily double a family's earnings, especially if several members get involved.

Third World blood has thus became a very valuable commodity. Purchasing, reprocessing, and exporting high-valued products like "human source" plasma is now at least a $30–40 billion global business. There is also growing traffic in other human body parts, like kidneys, livers, and corneas.[9] While First World countries have been able to rely more heavily on organizations like the Red Cross, voluntary donors are on the wane, with just five percent of the adult population willing to donate. All told, purchased blood now accounts for more than half of the US blood supply, and over half of the 60–70 million liters of human blood products consumed in First World countries each year. And this share is increasing, because of the increasing value of blood components and the negative impact of the AIDS epidemic on voluntary donations. Furthermore, while the Red Cross is deep in debt, and its blood supply division loses money, private blood collectors have been able to exploit profitable niches of the market, like plasma, Factor VIII, and other valuable blood components.

Third World countries like Mexico and Nicaragua have come to depend on purchased blood for an even larger share of their blood supplies—more than sixty percent of the forty million liters they consume each year, and up to eighty percent in countries with lower per capita incomes, like India and Indonesia.[10] This reliance on purchased blood greatly increases the risk of contamination by HIV/AIDS, hepatitis, and other blood-transmitted diseases, since those who are most willing to sell blood are often from poorer, higher-risk populations, including drug users, alcoholics, and sex workers. In developing countries, the facilities available for screening donors, sterilizing collection instruments, and storing collected blood are also often inadequate. This has already produced several large-scale disasters. For example, in Henan Province in South China, thousands of peasant farmers were induced to sell their blood to government-run health clinics in the mid-1990s. Corrupt local health officials who ran the clinics sold the plasma to private drug companies, and six hundred thousand people contracted HIV/AIDs as a result.[11] Problems like this have scared off voluntary donors, further increasing the global blood collection system's dependence on purchases.[12]

The exposure of this clandestine traffic has led to several attempts by the World Health Organization and "donor" countries to regulate it, especially since the HIV/AIDS epidemic. In France and the UK, the commercial collection of blood is already illegal. Of course there are no magic cures for such traffic; like capital flight, corruption, and drug trafficking, it is deeply rooted in global inequality. But it is important to be aware that "globalization" and "trade" are not just limited to running shoes, handicrafts, and semiconductors.[13] For there, too, the example of global blood traffic also provides a striking parallel to the relationship between rich and poor countries in international capital markets. For there, too, the First World has bled the Third, of the financial and human capital that it desperately needs for growth.

This blood traffic story provides a good introduction to the tragic tale of one of Central America's most troubled economies—Nicaragua. In the last century—under the influence of repeated foreign interventions, a parade of kleptocrats, thoughtless development banks, and unprincipled private bankers—it went from being a small country with natural resources and prospects as good as any of its neighbors, to being one of the poorest, most heavily indebted countries in the world. This chapter provides a telling example of how much trouble developing countries can get into just by being in the wrong neighborhood—and by daring to challenge the system.

SOMOZA'S BANKERS

In July 1979, less than two years after Chamorro's funeral, the Sandinista Army (the Frente Sandinista de Liberación Nacional or FSLN) swept into Managua and ended four decades of Somoza rule. They were a hearty band of courageous, well-meaning, and rather naive young Marxists and social democrats. They had learned quite a lot about guerilla warfare, but had almost no experience managing a small developing country. They could have used it; the real war was just beginning.

When the FSLN took over, Nicaragua's economy was already in trouble. In a country of just 2.9 million people, the civil war had taken 45,000 lives, wounded 100,000, and caused more than $3 billion in property damage. There were critical shortages of food, medicine, and oil, and more than 600,000 people were homeless. In 1979 alone, the last year of the war, national income had fallen by nearly one-fourth. Furthermore, even without the war's damage, the FSLN would have inherited a country with serious social problems. The Somoza legacy was a country where fifty-two percent of the population was illiterate, life expectancy was fifty-three years, infant mortality was 123 per 1,000, and three-fourths of the population was undernourished.

Meanwhile, at the Central Bank, the FSLN discovered that the cupboard was bare. When Somoza fled to Miami on just two days before the FSLN arrived in Managua on July 17, he had taken all but $3 million in Central Bank reserves—nowhere near enough to service the country's $1.5 billion foreign debt. Some foreign aid was available from Venezuela, Mexico, and Cuba, but the US—Nicaragua's key ally, trading partner, and aid donor for more than seventy years—had basically shut off the spigots. On the other hand, Nicaragua's foreign creditors, like First Chicago and Citibank, wasted no time in threatening to completely cut off Nicaragua's trade finance if the debt wasn't honored in full.

The debt situation was one of the top priorities for Nicaragua's new five-member Junta de Gobierno de Reconstrucción Nacional (JGRN), which included the FSLN's José Daniel Ortega Saavedra, Luis Alfonso Robelo Callejas, and Violeta Barrios de Chamorro. Initially it considered repudiating the debt outright. In a September 1979 speech to the UN, Ortega declared that the debt was really the international community's responsibility.[14] Not long after, however, the JGRN decided to accept Fidel Castro's advice and negotiate with the banks. Castro gave Ortega the same advice that he would later give to Venezuela's Hugo Chavéz in 1998: Cuba had made a serious mistake back in 1959 when it renounced all its debts, because the international banks had made Cuba's life miserable ever since.[15]

In late 1979, the JGRN prepared for negotiations with the banks with the help of several debt experts from the UN Conference on Trade and Development (UNCTAD). The experts opened up the Nicaraguan Central Bank's books to see what had become of all the loans. What they found was startling. Out of $1.2 billion in loans that had been disbursed to Somoza's government from 1971 to 1979, more than seventy-five percent had "flown" the country within a few months of their arrival. From 1974 to 1978, Nicaragua's debt had increased by $834 million. At least $585 million of this went into offshore bank accounts, often within a few days of having entered the Central Bank. In a pattern that would later be followed in many other developing countries, Nicaragua was left holding the bag, even though the debts had been poorly invested, while the assets—the dollar loans—had already been "privatized."

There were several different flight patterns. One was by way of the Central Bank. Somoza's government agencies borrowed all the dollars they could and traded them for *cordobas* at the Central Bank, which sold them to the elite. This continuous loop of public borrowing and private decapitalization was facilitated by an overvalued fixed exchange rate. Throughout the 1970s, the Central Bank had fixed the *cordoba* at just seven to the dollar, even though Nicaragua's inflation rate was twice that of the US. The resulting overvaluation hurt exports, but the price for Nicaragua's main export, coffee, was set by the international market. The policy really helped those influential folks who had access to foreign exchange at the Central Bank and who wanted to trade dollars for Miami condos, offshore accounts, arms to fight the rebels, and Mercedes. (Somoza's family also controlled the Managua Mercedes dealership.) Arturo Jose Cruz, the new regime's first Central Bank president, recalled, "It was really quite ingenious—they ran the whole country like a private laundry. . . ."[16]

Nicaragua's leading foreign creditors—First Chicago, Bankers Trust, Citibank, Chase, Lloyds Bank, SBC, Bank of America, Wells Fargo, and the Royal Bank of Canada—had supplied most of these loans that financed elite capital flight. Their private banking departments had helped ferry a great deal of it out of the country to private accounts. These banks had also helped to finance Somoza's mounting government deficits and his arms purchases. Furthermore, all the flight dollars that they gathered from Somoza and his supporters would later provide valuable seed money to the Contras, who took up arms against the revolution after Somoza's departure and helped to produce a civil war that claimed another thirty thousand lives in the 1980s. The Contras were funded not only by the Reagan adminstration, and Oliver

North's illegal Iran-Contra arms scam, but also by General Somoza, and, after his "bullet-proof" Mercedes exploded in Paraguay in 1980, by his family's cronies. It is not surprising that when these banks presented the bill for all this to Nicaragua's new government in early 1980, and then also declined to extend any new loans, the JGRN was a bit disgruntled.

The JGRN soon had even more reason to be unhappy. The UNCTAD auditors discovered that foreign governments, the banks, and even the IMF had provided many loans that lined Somoza's pockets *directly*. For example, a $160 million loan from Spain's Foreign Trade Bank to finance "Spanish buses" had provided the dictator a $28 million commission in 1976. And a $66 million IMF standby loan that had been pushed through by the Carter administration in Somoza's waning hours in May 1979 also wound up in his offshore accounts.[17]

According to two specialists who worked on the Central Bank audit and the 1980 debt negotiations, Somoza also profited from several "roundtrip" transactions that involved illegal behavior by major US banks. The auditors discovered that at least $450 million of Nicaragua's foreign debt—more than half of the country's borrowings from private foreign banks—had arrived in Managua by way of a curious little Panama-based company, Ultramar Banking Corporation.

Ultramar was owned by Eduardo Rodriguez Feliu, a Cuban exile who'd migrated to Mexico City in 1960.[18] By the 1970s, his bank had offices in Mexico City, Miami, the Cayman Islands, and Nicaragua, and it was also advising borrowers in Costa Rica, Venezuela, and Argentina. But the Somoza regime was by far his best customer. Another banker who dealt extensively with Central America recalled, "It was just common knowledge—the way you made loans to the General was through Eddie."[19] Ultramar advised General Somoza's Banco Centroamericano, his other private companies, and many agencies of the Nicaraguan government. Ultramar was an "advisor" to numerous Nicaraguan loans.

Ironically, in October 1970, Rodriguez Feliu had delivered a very perceptive speech on the whole subject of foreign debt and capital flight at the Third Annual Mexican Convention on Foreign Commerce in Mazatlan, where the audience included Mexico's finance minister and many leading businessmen. He offered the following cogent analysis of the debt-flight cycle:

> In financial terms, Latin American countries face a great paradox. . . . A great volume of capital has flowed constantly from this area to countries that are considerably stronger financially, preventing the use of such funds to finance projects in the countries where the funds originate. The importance of this fact for the social, political, and economic reality of the countries of Latin America has only begun to be appreciated. I believe that it is urgent and necessary that progressive countries in our region design a solution to this

problem. . . . It is indispensable to create mechanisms that permit the repatriation of Latin American funds that have been sent abroad.[20]

Rodriguez Feliu went on to say that by the late 1960s, fund transfers from Third World to First World countries already exceeded $10 billion.[21] He concluded that it was time to create a "Latin-American dollar market," to help attract these flight dollars back home.

Three decades later, Rodriguez Feliu's analysis seems remarkably prescient. This might have been due to the fact that Rodriguez Feliu's knowledge of flight banking and debt diversion was not just theoretical. When the UN auditors looked more closely at all the loans that had passed through Ultramar's hands, they discovered that an extra 0.75 percent had been tacked on to the interest rate. One of the auditors described how the system worked:

> It was really pretty clever. Ultramar got all the mandates to arrange loans for the Central Bank or Nicaragua's Development Bank. The mandates were awarded at rich terms, say 1.5 percent over LIBOR, with a 1 percent "flat" fee, at a time when the going rate was only 1 percent. Then Ultramar went to the banks and found some that were willing to lend at, say, 1.25 percent over. Since the mandate was overpriced to begin with, that was easy. Ultramar then went back to Nicaragua and demanded the present value of the difference between the higher rate and the actual rate up front. It also got part of the flat flee from the banks. Even for Central America, this was a very large commission. So Nicaragua started out with only about ninety-four cents for every loan it borrowed. Of course the remaining ninety-four cents weren't used too well, either.[22]

These commissions, worth more than $40 million, were diverted through a complex chain of shell companies that started in the Cayman Islands and Panama and ended up in Switzerland and Miami. According to the debt auditors from UNCTAD, the beneficiaries of the diversion were the Somozas.[23]

Since the US Corrupt Practices Act of 1977 promised stiff sanctions for foreign bribery, and since the Ultramar payoffs were so blatant, Citibank, First Chicago, Bankers Trust, the Royal Bank of Canada, and Nicaragua's other key foreign creditors were understandably a bit nervous when they met with the representatives of Nicaragua's new government for the first time in New York in 1980 to renegotiate Nicaragua's foreign debt. Their chief adversaries were Alfredo Cesar, a Stanford-trained MBA who had managed Nicaragua's largest sugar mill before the Revolution, and Arturo José Cruz, a fifty-six-year old finance specialist who spent ten years at the IDB before taking over the Central Bank for the JGRN.[24]

Cesar, the more hardcore Sandinista, was in charge of the negotiation strategy. At the outset he sounded tough, refusing to accept any IMF monitoring of Nicaragua's economy. However, he decided not to press the question of the illegal commissions. One of Nicaragua's former advisors at the time later recalled Cesar's reasoning:

> "The feeling was, commissions like this were just a normal way of doing business in Nicaragua—Somoza got a cut of everything. And it was common knowledge that he and Eddie were pals. I advised the Sandinistas to press the issue, but the new government didn't want to take it on. The attitude was, "Well, that's history, and besides, we'll never get the money back anyway." But anytime Somoza's name was brought up, the banks started climbing the walls. "We're not dealing with politics," they'd say, "We're dealing with the continuing institution of the Nicaraguan Government." As if they hadn't been financing him for forty years!
>
> Anyway, we did distribute a questionnaire that asked the banks to tell us which loans had been arranged through "intermediaries," just to show we were studying the issue. First Chicago, Nicaragua's largest lender, took a very long time with that questionnaire. At the start, the Advisory Committee was chaired by Steve Thomas, a First Chicago VP. Suddenly, one day he stepped aside, and Citibank's Bill Rhodes took over. You see, Thomas was probably the only guy in the room who'd actually made any of those loans.
>
> Of course, Bill Rhodes later became famous as Citibank's point man on the entire Latin American debt negotiation. But this was how he got his start. . . .
>
> We also asked Bank of New York for help, since it had disbursed all the loans and all the commissions. It never responded.[25]"

In November 1980, Nicaragua concluded an agreement with its 120 creditors that rescheduled more than $600 million of its foreign private bank loans. To outside observers, the terms were surprisingly generous. After all, the Sandinistas were already being attacked as hardcore Communists by Ronald Reagan, who was running for president against Jimmy Carter. But their new regime got twelve years to repay the money, with five years of grace, and even a new $90 million loan. The interest rate on the deal was only a half point above the London Inter-Borrowing Rate (LIBOR), a very low spread, considering the country's situation. Finally, the deal also left the IMF's "policy police" on the sidelines.[26]

All told, this was one of the most lenient debt reschedulings in history, and it had been achieved by the neo-Marxist government of a tiny Central American country, just two months before Ronald Reagan took office. While Nicaragua's debt level stood at $2.2 billion by the end at 1980, a relatively high 1.3 times the level of national income, the deal raised hopes that the worst days of Nicaragua's debt and economic crisis were finally over.[27]

Some observers wondered why the banks, already knowing that Reagan had been elected, didn't just wait for him to take power and strengthen their negotiating position. At the time, commentators attributed the favorable terms to the sheer negotiating skills of Cesar and Arturo Cruz.[28] But Cruz later admitted, "There was really no reason for bragging about what we achieved." Nicaragua's former advisors and the debt auditors from UNCTAD are convinced that the favorable terms were due to the threat of exposing the truth about how the banks and the dictator had really done business in Nicaragua.[29]

COUNTERREVOLUTION

By the end of 1980, with the civil war concluded, Somoza assassinated in Paraguay, and the debt settlement concluded, many Nicaraguans looked forward to rebuilding their economy and finally achieving a more peaceful society. It was not to be. Undoubtedly the Sandinistas deserve part of the blame for the way things turned out, though the odds were clearly stacked against them. As the strongest faction in the winning coalition and "the boys with the guns," at first they commanded overwhelming popular support, having rid the country of the world's oldest family dictatorship outside of Saudi Arabia and Paraguay.

However, like Venezuela's Hugo Chavez in the 1990s, they were torn between leading a social revolution and building a multiparty democracy. Their hero, Augusto Sandino, "the general of free men," had fought the US military and the Nicaraguan Army for six years to a standstill before he was betrayed and murdered by General Anastasio Somoza Garcia in 1934. After a decade of insurgency in the 1970s, the Sandinistas's most important lifetime experiences had been armed struggle, clandestine organizing, and very rough times in Somoza's jails. Unhappily, one of their most accomplished political leaders, Carlos Fonseca, was murdered by the National Guard in 1976.

On the other hand, it is not impossible for committed revolutionaries to lead a fairly peaceful transition to a multiparty democracy. After all, South Africa's African National Congress waged just as long a struggle against a state that was no less repressive than Somoza's. Many of the ANC's supporters were just as radical as the Sandinistas, and they also received most of their weapons and advisors from states like the Soviet Union, East Germany, and Libya.

But South Africa was not as easy for the US to push around. It accounted for two-thirds of sub-Saharan Africa's economy and most of the world's gold, diamonds, platinum, and vanadium. By 1979, with Israel's help, it had acquired nuclear weapons. Compared with Nicaragua, South Africa's economy was also in relatively good shape when the ANC came to power. While there had been a protracted, low-intensity war against apartheid, South Africa managed to avoid the violent full-blown civil war that Nicaragua had to go through in the 1970s to rid itself of the Somazas.

Nicaragua was objectively far less important from a geopolitical stand-point. Unfortunately, to Washington's National Security planners, that made it a much better target for "demonstration." Its population was the same as Iowa's. Its entire economy was smaller than Des Moines's. It had few distinctive natural resources. Its only "weapons of mass destruction" were volcanoes, earthquakes, and hurricanes. It was surrounded by other countries that were also of modest strategic value—except for the symbolic value of repeatedly crushing the rising aspirations of the poorest people in the Hemisphere. During the late nineteenth century, Nicaragua had been selected several times by the US Canal Commissions for a canal across Central America, until Teddy Roosevelt finally opted to *create* Panama and build a canal across it in 1902, for reasons that had more to do with Wall Street than engineering.[30] After that, Nicaragua's canal plans went nowhere. This was especially true after the US Marines landed in 1910 to collect debts owed to British and US banks and to depose a nationalist leader who had made the fatal mistake of seeking European funding for an alternative to the Panama canal.[31]

The ANC also had one other weapon that the Sandinistas lacked. This was the extraordinary wisdom of Nelson Mandela, who had earned everyone's respect during his twenty-seven years in prison. He had learned key survival skills like patience, diplomacy, and the ability to compromise with bitter enemies. Under his influence, the ANC set out to build a mass party. It agreed to hold free elections within two years of his release, and committed itself publicly to a multiparty democracy with proportional representation, a market economy, civil liberties, and peaceful reconciliation.

Most of the Sandinistas's top leaders—the *cupula*—were not really interested in building a mass party, much less a multi-party democracy, at least not at first. They saw themselves as a vanguard party of the left leading the masses toward a social revolution. As Sergio Ramirez, a leading FSLN member who served as Nicaragua's vice president under Daniel Ortega from 1984 to 1990, wrote in *Adios Muchachos*:

> The FSLN was not prepared . . . to assume its role of party of opposition inside a democratic system, because it had never been designed for this. Its vertical structure was the inspiration of Leninist manuals, of the impositions of the war and of *caudillismo*, our oldest cultural heritage.[32]

To be fair, the FSLN leadership believed that the first priority was to attack the country's dire health, literacy, land ownership, and education problems, and to build "direct democracy" through civic organizations, not through party politics and national elections. Given the country's emergency and the need to recover from the civil war, this was entirely understandable. But it did provide cheap shots to the FSLN's opponents and even the mainstream US media, which basically wrote Nicaragua off very early as a reprise of Castro's Cuba.

The Sandinistas were also widely criticized for lacking the soft touch when it came to domestic politics. Among their many ham-handed moves was the May 1980 decision to expand the Council of State to include "mass organizations," the August 1980 decision to postpone elections until 1984, the rough way they dealt with the Miskito Indians, the 1986 decision to shut down *La Prensa* (by then, CIA-subsidized), and Daniel Ortega's various high-visibility trips to Havana, Moscow, and Libya.[33] They were also criticized for implementing a compulsory draft, detaining alleged Contra sympathizers without trial after the Contra War heated up, permitting the FSLN's National Directorate (Daniel Ortega, Tomas Borge, Victor Tirado, Henry Ruiz, and Bayardo Arce) to remain an unelected body until 1991, and seizing a huge amount of property from ex-Somocistas—even from the middle class—for their own use during the *Piñata* period after Ortega lost the 1990 election.

At the same time, they were not given much credit for preserving a mixed economy, reforming the health and education systems, pursuing relations with numerous non-Communist countries in Latin America and Europe, implementing a badly needed land reform, tolerating the virulent *La Prensa* until 1986, holding reasonably free elections in 1984 and 1990, and respecting the outcome, of these elections (. . . and 1996 . . . and 2001 . . .) when they lost.

The reality is that from 1981 on, Nicaragua's new government was operating in an increasingly hostile international environment, where the Western media, the US government, and the Miami-based Somicistas were predisposed to seize upon the slightest departures from Roberts's Rules of Orders to consign them to hell. And if no such departures were evident, to invent them. These hostile attitudes had much less to do with the FSLN's behavior than with the US government's new aggressive stance with respect to the Soviet Union—dating back at least to President Carter's initiation of a Contra-like war against the Soviet-backed government in Afghanistan in July 1979.[34] Despite the FSLN's undeniable missteps, it would have taken divine intervention to save Nicaragua from the wrath of Ronald Reagan, who decided almost immediately upon taking office to single out Nicaragua for a replay of the Carter/Brzezinski strategy in Afghanistan.

STATE-FUNDED TERRORISM—US-STYLE

Former CIA analyst David MacMichael testified at the International Court of the Hague's hearings on a lawsuit brought by Nicaragua against the US in 1986 that from early 1981 on, the US government set out to create a "proxy army" to "provoke cross-border attacks by Nicaraguan forces and demonstrate Nicaragua's aggressive nature," forcing the Sandinistas to "clamp down on civil liberties . . . arresting its opposition (and) demonstrate its allegedly inherent totalitarian nature."[35] In other words, if they were not totalitarian enough to begin with, the US would see to it that they became totalitarian and then blame them for the conversion.

President Reagan offered several different justifications for this bloody-minded policy. In March 1983, in a speech to Congress, he presented his Subversion Theory to Congress, warning that the Sandinistas had already "imposed a new dictatorship . . . supported by weapons and military resources provided by the Communist bloc, [that] represses its own people, refuses to make peace, and sponsors a guerrilla war against El Salvador."[36] At other times he emphasized the Beachhead Theory, in which the Sandinistas provided a "Soviet beachhead . . . only two hours flying time away from our borders . . . with thousands of Cuban advisors . . . camped on our own doorstep . . . close to vital sea-lanes."[37] He offered similar characterizations of the threat posed by left-wing guerillas in El Salvador, Honduras, and Guatemala. In 1982, Jeane J. Kirkpatrick, Reagan's hawkish UN ambassador, also promoted the beachhead theory:

> I believe this area is colossally important to the US national interest. I think we are dealing here not . . . with some sort of remote problem in some far-flung part of the world. We are dealing with our own border when we talk about the Caribbean and Central America and we are dealing with our own vital national interest.[38]

Other elements were sometimes thrown into the mix. On November 6, 1984, just two days after the Sandinistas won a decisive sixty-seven percent victory in the country's freest elections in history, there was a huge media flap in the US press over their alleged attempt to buy Soviet MiGs for air defense. This story later turned out to be a wholesale concoction by the State Department's "Office of Public Diplomacy," Oliver North, Otto Reich, and Robert McFarlane—just one of many US propaganda efforts designed to distract attention from the FSLN's victory in the 1984 elections.[39]

Together, the subversion theory and the beachhead theory revived the timeworn domino theory, transposed from Southeast Asia to Central America. Apparently the notion was that since Nicaragua bordered Honduras and El Salvador, which bordered Guatemala and Belize, which bordered Mexico, the Red Army might just jet in to El Paso in their MiGs from Managua, "only two hours away." The fact that "the Reds" were already ninety miles away in Havana, armed with brand new MiG 23 Flogger bombers and MiG 29s, was not mentioned by Reagan. After all, Cuba had already demonstrated that it could stand up to a US invasion, and the Bay of Pigs was not a happy memory.

The rather strained analysis of Nicaragua's purported threat to US national security was later endorsed, with only slight variations, by the January 1984 Bipartisan National Commission on Central America chaired by Dr. Henry Kissinger. One might have expected him to draw a different conclusion, given his long personal experience with Vietnam, Laos, Cambodia, and China, whose leftist regimes spent most of the 1970s fighting each other. But Kissinger was ingratiating himself with the Republican Party's conservative wing. And unlike the National Commission on Terrorist Attacks, which he resigned from in December 2002, it did not require him to identify his consulting firms' private clients.

In any case, long after there were peace settlements in Nicaragua, El Salvador, and Guatemala and long after the Sandinistas had handed over political power to their opponents, Republicans like Senators John McCain and Jesse Helms were still seeing ghosts in Nicaragua well into the 1990s, trying to make hay out of the Sandinistas' alleged subversive threat. These charges even played a role in Daniel Ortega's defeat in Nicaragua's presidential elections in 2001, even when his running mate was Violeta Chamorro's son-in-law.

Eventually, all the stockpiles of AK47s, landmines, rocket launchers, and surface-to-air missiles acquired by the Sandinistas to defend Nicaragua against the Contras did end up posing a security threat to the US, but it was not the one that the Sandinista's right-wing critics had predicted. In November 2001, Colombia's eleven thousand-strong, right-wing, drug-dealing paramilitary group—the AUC—procured 3,500 AK47s from Nicaragua's military stockpiles by way of Israeli arms merchants based in Panama and Guatemala. The AUC also reportedly purchased arms from army stockpiles in El Salvador and Guatemala. The arms were part of a five-shipment package that included thirteen thousand assault rifles, millions of bullets, grenades, rocket launchers, machine guns, and explosives.[40] The AUC, which was on George W. Bush's official list of terrorist groups, was supported by landlords who wanted to combat Colombia's leftist guerillas—the ELN and the FARC. The AUC was also supposedly fighting Colombia's Army. From 2000 to 2003, Colombia received $2.5 billion in US military aid, plus more than four hundred Special Forces troops, making it the world's third largest recipient of US aid.[41] In 2002, an OAS study also revealed that a Lebanese arms broker with al Qaeda links had tried to purchase twenty SA-7 missiles from Nicaragua's stockpiles.[42] The US started pressuring Nicaragua's President Bolaños, a neoliberal businessman, to reduce these stockpiles, but hopefully not by selling them to the AUC. In the long run, by forcing the comparatively harmless Sandinistas to stockpile all these weapons to defend themselves and by arming the right-wing militaries of El Salvador and Guatemala to the teeth, the US may have set a trap for itself.

In reality, Nicaragua's leftists, even if they were so inclined, were neither necessary nor sufficient to "subvert" their neighbors. Those neighbors with the most serious liberation movements, like El Salvador, Guatemala, and Colombia, had already done a perfectly good job of subverting themselves. Their rebel movements developed over many decades from within, on the basis of incredibly unbalanced social structures. For example, El Salvador's *catorce*—its top fourteen families—controlled 90–95 percent of the country's land and finance capital, while in Guatemala, just 2 percent of the population controlled more than 70 percent of arable land.[43] In Nicaragua, the Somoza family alone laid claim to a quarter of the country's arable land. The resulting social conflicts were also similar. In the 1980s, El Salvador's class war claimed more than eighty thousand lives, while Guatemala's claimed two hundred thousand, with the vast majority due to their own brutal armed forces and paramilitaries. On the other hand, Costa Rica, Nicaragua's good neighbor to the south, had long since inoculated itself against revolution by developing an old-fashioned, middle-class democracy, with numerous small farms and more teachers than police, abolishing its military in 1948.

While the Reagan adminstration asserted over and over again in the early 1980s that the Sandinistas had shipped arms to leftist guerillas in El Salvador, two decades later, these allegations have been shown to be as spurious as the purported MiG purchases.[44] In fact, the Sandinista aid to El Salvador's rebels, the FLMN, was miniscule and was terminated around 1981.[45] The claim that El Salvador's FLMN had acquired several hundred tons of weapons from the East Bloc, Arafat, and Libya was also conjured out of thin air. In fact, the rebel armies in El Salvador and Guatemala were poorly armed, notwithstanding the Galil rifles and rocket launchers they managed to steal or purchase from corrupt army officers. Leading Sandinistas like Tomas Borge explicitly rejected the notion of "exporting revolution," except by way of the FSLN's example. After all, the FSLN had not relied on Soviet or Cuban backing for their own revolution. They had their hands full rebuilding Nicaragua. The last thing they needed was another war with El Salvador or Guatemala, in addition to the Contra War.

Finally, while the Sandinistas were hardly liberal democrats and committed many political blunders, they were scarcely in a position to run a "dictatorship," even within Managua's city limits. To their credit, they had greatly increased the amount of popular involvement in the country's governance. In November 1984, they held national elections that most international

observers, including Latin American scholars and Western European parlia-
ments, agreed were reasonably clean—despite the Reagan administration's
provision of $17 million to opposition candidates, its systematic efforts to dis-
credit the elections, and the fact that Nicaragua was already under steady
assault from US-backed Contras.[46] Certainly by comparison with the rigged
Somoza elections and other countries in postwar situations—El Salvador and
Guatemala in particular—Nicaragua's degree of political freedom was reasonable, if not beyond reproach.

Although seventy-five percent of registered voters turned out for the
November 1984 elections and the FSLN received a commanding sixty-seven
percent of the vote—capturing the presidency and sixty-one of ninety-six
seats in the new National Assembly—Nicaragua was accused by the Reaganites of being a "dictatorship." Former *New York Times* senior editor John B.
Oakes wrote that "The most fraudulent thing about the Nicaraguan election
was the part the Reagan Administration played in it."[47]

Another troubling fact about Reagan's Nicaraguan policy was that the
Soviet Union really did not have any interest in acquiring yet another
dependent, state-socialist backwater like Vietnam, Afghanistan, or Cuba,
which by the early 1980s was already costing the USSR about $3 billion a
year in aid. In hindsight, far from being an expansionist "evil empire," the
USSR was really just hanging on for dear life—a wounded giant, obsessed
with its own serious economic problems, which were even forcing it to
import grain from Argentina's fascist junta. Internationally, it was busy with
trying to stave off an embarrassing defeat in Afghanistan on its southern border. The USSR was also pressing existing clients in Eastern Europe, Africa,
and Southeast Asia to practice self-reliance.

In 1980–81, before the US made it clear that it was basically seeking
"regime change" in Nicaragua, the Sandinistas tried to restore good economic relations and access to World Bank and IDB loans. But for US intervention, this access would have been maintained. That, in turn, might have
significantly reduced Nicaragua's dependence on East-Bloc aid. After all, as a
senior World Bank official noted in 1982, "Project implementation has been
extraordinarily successful in Nicaragua, perhaps better than anywhere else in
the world."[48]

Nicaragua also sought aid from many non-Soviet countries, including
Venezuela, Mexico, and France. It was most successful with Mexico, which
resisted US pressures and became Nicaragua's largest aid provider until
1985.[49] When Nicaragua tried to buy $16 million in arms from France in
early 1982, however, President Reagan got French president Francois Mit-
terand to delay the sale "indefinitely."[50] Only then—under increasing attack

from the Contras—did Nicaragua turn to the Soviet Union and Cuba for arms and advisors.

Many Sandinistas were undoubtedly committed radicals, dedicated to policies like land reform, free health and education, and the seizure of Somocista-owned properties. But these policies were arguably defensible, given Nicaragua's economic conditions and its need to play catch-up with basic social justice. These are, after all, policies that the US itself has supported, or at least tolerated, in many other times and places, when they happened to serve its interests. The Nicaraguans may have been stubborn and full of radical bravado, but they were far from anyone's pawns. These characterizations were '50s-vintage hobgoblins, left over from the days when Ronald Reagan helped to run purported leftists out of the Actors Guild in Los Angeles. At best, they reflected a desire to show the USSR who was boss by making an example of a tiny, weak, left-leaning regime.

From this standpoint, the US government basically succeeded in pushing Nicaragua into relying very heavily on Soviet and Cuban arms and economic aid for its own survival.[51] The US government then used that reliance as an excuse to expand its own provocations into a full-scale war that ultimately claimed thirty thousand lives. This is surely one of the clearest examples of state-funded terrorism ever.

SAYING UNCLE

All these inconvenient little details were brushed aside by the Reaganites when they took office in January 1981, prepared, in President Reagan's words, to make the Sandinistas "say uncle." They never did. In fact, by 1988, they had "whupped" Oliver North's Contras pretty good. But this was not for want of US efforts at subversion.

In March 1981, President Reagan signed an Executive Order that mandated the CIA to undertake covert operations in Central America to interdict arms shipments "by Marxist guerillas." By November 1981, US focus had shifted from "arms interdiction" to regime change. That month, the Reagan administration provided an initial $19 million to mount a fairly transparent "covert" effort to destabilize Nicaragua. The strategy, implemented by a now-famous gang of future presidential pardonees, was the classic scissors tactic employed by the US and its allies in many other twentieth century counter-revolutionary interventions.

On the one hand, the US government tried to cut off Nicaragua's cash flow, reducing access to new loans from the IMF, the World Bank, the IDB, EXIM Bank funding, and OPIC risk insurance. In September 1983, the US slashed Nicaragua's sugar quota. In November 1985, it added a total embargo on all trade with the US, Nicaragua's main trading partner and foreign investor at that time. Given the country's dire economic straits, this had the practical effect of cutting off all US private investment and private bank lending.

Meanwhile, the Reagan administration was stubbornly opposing all efforts to embargo trade or investment with respect to South Africa's apartheid regime. In September 1983, the State Department approved a Westinghouse application to bid on a $50 million ten-year contract to maintain and supply South Africa's two nuclear power stations. The US also continued to support World Bank and IDB loans to right-wing regimes in Guatemala and El Salvador throughout the 1980s.

The other half of the scissors strategy was the US government's creation of an eighteen thousand-person Contra Army—financed by $300 million in taxpayer money, in-kind military assistance, $100–200 million raised from private donors like the Sultan of Brunei, and an untold amount of cocaine proceeds.[52] The main faction, the Frente Democrático Nacional (FDN)—consisted of 3,000 ex-Somocista National Guard members and another 12,000–13,000 assorted mercenaries, anti-Castro Cubans, Israeli trainers, Argentine interrogators, and cocaine traffickers.[53] The Reaganites knew they were not dealing with angels here. As the CIA's inspector general later admitted in 1998, the agency made sure to get a statement from the US Department of Justice in 1982, waiving the CIA's duty to report drug trafficking by any Contra contractors.

From 1982 to 1989, this army stoked a war that ultimately took about 30,000 lives, including 3,346 children and more than 250 public school teachers.[54] Another thirty thousand people were wounded, and eleven thousand kidnapped, according to the National Commission for the Protection and Promotion of Human Rights. Another half million fled the country to avoid the chaos. With the help of Harvard Law School professor Abram Chayes, Nicaragua later successfully sued the US for launching *terrorist* attacks and causing substantial damage. In November 1986, the International Court at the Hague found the US liable for several clear violations of international law—notably, for launching an unprovoked war not justified by any "right of self-defense." The Court suggested that the resulting property damage was on the order of $17 billion. But the Reagan administration declined to appear in court and refused to recognize the judgment.[55]

NICARAGUA'S REAL DEBT CRISIS

Our main interest here is in the war's devastating impact on Nicaragua's economy and its crushing foreign debt burden. Ultimately the FSLN soundly defeated the Contras with a combination of adroit military tactics and a large standing army raised by a national draft. To pay for all this, the FSLN had to boost military spending from five percent of national income in 1980 to eighteen percent in 1988, when the first in a series of armistices was finally signed. By then, more than half of Nicaragua's government budget was devoted to paying for an army that numbered 119,000—seven percent of all Nicaraguans between the ages of eighteen and sixty-five.

Early on, the Sandinistas had made a strong commitment to building new health clinics and schools in the country. These social programs, plus land reform, were among their most important accomplishments. Even in the midst of the war, with the help of 2,500 Cuban doctors, they managed to increase spending on health and education, open hundreds of new medical clinics, and sharply reduce infant mortality, malnutrition, disease, and illiteracy.[56] They also implemented a land reform program that redistributed more than than forty-nine percent of Nicaragua's arable land to small farmers.

But the war made it very hard to sustain these undeniable accomplishments. Despite the FSLN's military "victory," Nicaragua's regular economy took a very direct hit. Trade and investment plummeted, unemployment soared to twenty-five percent and inflation reached an astonishing thirty-six thousand percent by 1988–89.[57] From 1980 to 1990, Nicaragua's average real per capita income fell thirty-five percent, and the incidence of poverty rose to forty-four percent.[58] To deal with shortages in the face of soaring inflation, the FSLN had to implement a rationing system for food and other basic commodities. What the Nixon administration had done to the Allende regime in Chile a decade earlier, the Reaganites were doing to Nicaragua—they were making the economy "scream."

THE WORLD'S HEAVIEST DEBT

By 1990, Nicaragua had displaced Honduras as the poorest country in Central America. It also became the *world's* most heavily indebted country, on a per capita basis. To fund the defense budget and their other commitments in the face of declining tax revenues, trade, investment, and multilateral funding, the FSLN partly relied on inflationary finance, having the Central Bank print more *cordobas*. But for vital foreign purchases, including oil and weapons, it required dollar loans from sympathetic countries—the Soviet Union ($3.3 billion), Mexico ($1.1 billion), Costa Rica, Germany, Spain, Venezuela, Brazil, and Guatemala, plus more than $500 million from the Central American Bank for Economic Integration—one multilateral institution that the US did not control.

When the newly elected government of Violeta Barrios de Chamorro took office in April 1990, the debt stood at $10.74 billion—more than ten times its level in 1980 and nearly eleven times Nicaragua's national income.

This was by far the highest foreign debt burden in the world—thirty times the average debt-income ratio for all developing countries. And it was not derived from technical policy errors, economic accidents, or geographic misfortune. It was partly due to the $1.5 billion in dirty debt left over from the Somoza years, and most of the rest derived from the US's ruthless persecution.

NEOLIBERAL DAWN?

The Reagan/Bush administration did fulfill one of its wishes for Nicaragua. In February 1990, after fifteen years of civil war and a two-year cease-fire that was unevenly unobserved, Violeta Barrios de Chamorro— Pedro Chamorro's widow and the candidate of the centrist National Opposition Union (Unión Nicaragüense Opositora, or UNO), a coalition of fourteen anti-FSLN parties—soundly defeated incumbent president Daniel Ortega by a fifty-five to forty-one percent margin.

This result surprised most pollsters. A *Washington Post*/ABC News survey in December 1989, had estimated that forty-eight percent of Nicaraguan voters favored Ortega, thirty-two percent favored Chamorro, and sixteen percent were undecided. The outcome completely shocked the FSLN, which had made no preparations to transfer power, especially legal control over all the assets that its members had seized from the Somocistas.

However, in retrospect, the outcome made sense. The US was not the only cause of the FSLN's defeat. By the 1990s, people were growing tired of feeding on revolutionary rhetoric. The FSLN was perceived as having lost its revolutionary purity and fervor during its decade in power, becoming arrogant and bureaucratic. Second, many people feared that another FSLN government might bring even more economic hardship. Nicaragua's US lawyer said that "Whatever revolutionary fervor the people once might have had was beaten out of them by the war and the impossibility of putting food in their children's stomachs."[59] The US government, under President George Bush I, sent a clear message: On the one hand, it promised that a new Chamorro administration would receive hundreds of millions of dollars in economic aid. On the other hand, it also strongly suggested that so long as the FSLN was in power, Nicaragua would be fair game for a continued trade embargo, restrictions on multilateral lending, and perhaps even a continuation of "humanitarian" aid to the Contras. Meanwhile, Violeta Chamorro held out the prospect for a free-market economic revival, reform of Nicaragua's inefficient state enterprises, and an end to the Sandinistas's unpopular draft.

To drive these points home, the US did not encourage anti-FSLN candidates to withdraw from the elections, as it had done in 1984. Rather, it spent up to $50 million to influence the election's outcome in UNO's favor—outside interference that is clearly illegal in most democratic countries, including the US.[60] Despite this interference, the mainstream US media loudly celebrated Chamorro's upset victory in February 1990 as the product of a "free election," unlike Ortega's 1984 victory. Among the most vocal celebrants were soft-shelled liberals like *The New Republic*'s Michael Kinsley and *The New York Times*'s Anthony Lewis. They were both enormously relieved to find that somehow, despite all the blood and gore of Reaganite policies on the Right and radical Sandinista extremists on the Left, the "middle" had supposedly triumphed.[61] ABC's Peter Jennings went so far as to declare that Nicaragua was holding its "first free election in a decade." As Noam Chomsky astutely observed, this statement was three times false: It implied that the Somozas had held free elections; it ignored the fact that reasonably free elections had been held by the FSLN in November 1984; and it overlooked the US's ample interference in the 1990 election.[62]

TRANSITION

The Sandanistas handed over power peacefully to President Chamorro in April 1990, the first such peaceful transition in Nicaragua's history and a test of democratic values that the ANC, for example, has never had to face. When President Chamorro took office, however, the mood was much more somber than when the Sandinistas triumphed over Somoza. In June 1990, her supporters tried to inject a little merriment by throwing her a fancy inaugural ball at a former country club in Managua, the first social gathering of Nicaragua's social elites in more than a decade.[63] But the effort felt a little off-key to many observers, given the country's economic troubles. Most Nicaraguans still hoped for a revival of peace and growth, but they had long since learned that this would not be easy in a country riven by deep social and political divisions.

Their worries were justified. Violeta Chamorros's inauguration was the first in a series of neoliberal administrations that had two basic goals: (1) restoring economic growth and (2) reversing almost all the Sandinista's most effective reforms, including land reform, health care, child care, womens' rights, and public education. It succeeded only at the latter.

Her first move was her most popular one—the abolition of compulsory military service. Even though enforcement of the draft had been on hold since 1989, this was a source of enormous relief to most young Nicaraguan males. She then appointed a new education minister, who immediately eliminated the requirement that schoolchildren sing the Sandinista anthem every day, including the words, "We shall fight against the Yankee, the enemy of humanity."

Despite continuing harassment by a few hundred heavily armed Re-Contras, holdovers from the original Contra Army, her administration succeeded in reducing the army to less than seventeen thousand by 1994. At the same time, she resisted US pressure to isolate the Sandinistas completely. In the interests of promoting national reconciliation, she wisely accepted Carlos Andres Perez's advice and appointed Humberto Ortega, Daniel's brother, to the post of defense minister.

Chamorro's economic measures were much less successful. Soon after her inauguration, Chamorro introduced a sweeping package of neoliberal reforms that were worked out with the help of IMF "structural adjustment" experts, who returned to Nicaragua after a twelve-year absence. The package included deep cuts in spending on health and education; layoffs of state workers; the privatization of all state enterprises by June 1991 (except for utilities); reductions in import quotas, duties, and subsidies for food and public utilities; increased tax collections for sales taxes; reduced corporate taxes; and the revival of Nicaragua's "free-trade" zone on the outskirts of Managua, with low taxes, no labor rights, and no customs duties.

The FSLN fought many of these measures, not only in the National Assembly, but also with two national strikes and other protests. They forced Chamorro to slow down some the implementation of some measures, especially with respect to privatizations, but much of her "creeping counterrevolution" was eventually implemented. The most important accomplishments were on the inflation front, which was sharply reduced to less than thirty-five percent. Foreign investment and exports started to pick up a bit after 1994, but the economy continued to grow very slowly because of tight interest rates, budget cutbacks, external factors like the Mexican debt crisis of 1995, and, most importantly, Nicaragua's continuing debt burden.

On the debt front, Chamorro's economic team managed to reduce the foreign debt from $10.7 billion to $6 billion by 1996, mainly with the help of a generous $3 billion debt write-off by the former Soviet Union and a $1 billion write-off by Mexico. The US was far more stingy. It forgave $260 million in bilateral debt, but only after Chamorro quietly agreed not to enforce the World Court judgment. By 1992, this would have been worth almost $23 billion, including interest—almost *twice* Nicaragua's entire foreign debt.[64]

Private foreign bank debt, left over from 1980, totaled about $1.3 billion, including accumulated interest. In December 1995, the World Bank ($40 million), the IDB ($40 million), and the governments of Holland, Sweden, and Switzerland ($8 million) agreed to lend Nicaragua $88 million so that it could buy eighty percent of the debt back from the private banks—a typical case of a (quiet) public bailout for the bankers' 1970s folly of having lent so much money to a dictator. But the price they got was another indicator of the country's sorry situation—just eight cents on the dollar.[65]

Despite these accomplishments, after six years in power, Chamorro and her economic team were basically exhausted, while the country's economy continued to stagnate. Except for the reduction in inflation, her programs had produced few positive results for Nicaraguans, who were now poorer than ever. By 1996, Nicaragua's real national income remained below its 1987 level, underemployment had risen to 50–60 percent in many parts of the country, and the proportion of people living below the poverty line was approaching 50 percent. One might have thought that this situation would have created a golden political opportunity for the FSLN to return to power. But that ignored Daniel Ortega's stunning capacity to snatch defeat from the jaws of victory.

DESIGNER LEFTIES

The FSLN had been largely excluded from the Chamorro government, except for Defense Minister Humberto Ortega. FSLN leaders fell to fighting amongst themselves, ultimately splitting up in February 1996 when former Vice President Sergio Ramirez and several other leaders broke with the Ortegas to form the Sandinista Renewal Movement (MRS), a party that was opposed to the FSLN's growing internal corruption and "new-class" elitism.

One key reason for this split was that some FSLN leaders, including the Ortegas, had apparently decided to cash in on other sorts of "golden opportunities." As noted, the February 1990 electoral defeat caught the FSLN by surprise. Assuming they would stay in power, they had not bothered to legalize their expropriations of Somocista assets during the 1980s—hundreds of millions in land, private homes, cars, TV and radio stations, newspapers, and many other businesses. In the FSLN's last few weeks in office, the lame-duck National Assembly, controlled by the FSLN, rushed through several new laws that granted titles for all this expropriated property to its current possessors—in most cases, FSLN party leaders and their supporters.

These measures became popularly known as the Piñata Laws, named after the candy-filled crepe paper dolls at Latin American birthday parties. The FSLN defended them as necessary to protect their progressive land reform, which was unquestionably one of the regime's most important achievements.[66] Others defended the Piñata as an unavoidable payoff to the FSLN's leaders in return for social peace and support for Chamorro's program. Whatever the justification, there were many abuses, which made use of all the tricks in the private bankers' tool kit. The beneficiaries included former Nicaraguan president Daniel Ortega, who latched onto a beautiful home in the fashionable El Carmen district of Managua that had belonged to a leading Nicaraguan banker, Jaime Morales Carazo. It was already chock-full of Morales family heirlooms, but Ortega and his partner for more than twenty years, Rosario Murillo, former minister of culture, reportedly added more artifacts "liberated" from the National Musuem.[67] Several other prominent Sandinistas also enjoyed the benefits of this golden handshake, including Humberto Ortega, who reportedly became a multimillionaire, and Bayardo Arce, the Sandinista ideologue, who not only invested in Interbanco but also became a partner of Chamorro's son-in-law and future vice presidential candidate, Antonio Lacayo, in a supermarket chain.[68]

During the transition period, the FSLN-controlled Central Bank also printed cordobas like crazy, providing another enrichment opportunity for those with access to dollar accounts—like the days of Somoza. There were also many other stories about FSLN asset grabs during this period. One Nicaraguan sociologist observed that "the problem was not so much with those who "only helped themselves to a house . . . but [those] who also got a second one on the coast, then a third, along with 600 *manzanas* of land and 800 head of cattle."[69]

Tales about Daniel Ortega's expensive tastes, the widely publicized stories about Ortega's alleged sexual abuse of his step-daughter, and the cupula's preferred access to dollar shops, transportation, and foreign bank accounts did not exactly strengthen the FSLN's reputation as the vanguard party of the oppressed.[70] Nor did it help when, in 1994, former FSLN leader Humberto Ortega, acting in his capacity as defense minister, ordered Nicaraguan troops to open fire on demonstrators protesting Chamorro's austere policies in the northern town of Esteli, or when Daniel Ortega chose a wealthy landowner, Juan Manuel Caldera, as his running mate for the November 1996 elections—an unsuccessful attempt to bolster his standing with Nicaragua's business elite.

Despite all the economic woes, when faced with a choice between Ortega and his neoliberal opponents, Nicaraguans repeatedly chose the hard-right neoliberals, who were at least candid about their contempt for social justice. In November 1996, Arnoldo Aleman, the former mayor of Managua, ex-Somocista, and bankers' lawyer, who was jailed by the Sandinistas as a counterrevolutionary for nine months in 1980, defeated Daniel Ortega by a 49 to 38 percent margin. Aleman, whose father had been an official in Somoza's government, ran on the ticket of the Liberal Constitutionalist Party (PLC), a splinter group from Anastasio Somoza Debayle's original National Liberal Party. Despite all his Somocista ties, his victory was greeted enthusiastically by Nicaragua's business community and their US allies. The American Enterprise Institute, the archconservative Washington think-tank, lost no time in declaring that "Aleman's victory . . . represents a desire for a new synthesis. . . . The Nicaraguan electorate has made the right choice."[71]

Furthermore, when Ortega ran for president again in November 2001, Enrique Bolaños, a businessman from a well-known elite family, defeated him by a 56 to 42 percent margin. The PLC also captured a majority of seats in the National Assembly.[72] Bolaños, a former representative of COSEP, a business lobbying group, had also been imprisoned by the FSLN in the 1980s and had served as Aleman's vice president. In many ways he was even more conservative than Aleman—though they had other important character traits in common.

The US government, also the Catholic Church's hierachy, and the Miami hard-right exile community also tried to intervene in these elections. In 1996, President Aleman received a $2.5 million illegal campaign contribution from Jorge Mas Canosa, a far-right member of Miami's Cuban exile community.[73] Several high-ranking Catholic priests also campaigned openly against Ortega in both elections. And on November 1, 2001, just three days before the 2001 elections, Nicaragua's Cardinal Miguel Obando y Bravo held a huge open-air mass in Managua and indicated a strong preference for a "good Catholic" like Bolaños.[74]

Ortega later blamed both these defeats on the US and the Catholic Church. In 2001, he accused the US of waging a "dirty campaign" and creating a "climate of fear." By then, many of the principal architects of the 1980s proxy war—including Otto Reich, John Negroponte, Elliot Abrams, and Admiral Poindexter—were back in power in George W. Bush's adminstration. Ortega and the FSLN had been careful to adopt a moderate, pro-business platform, promising to support the free-market economy, work with the IMF, cooperate with the US on drug enforcement and trade, and strengthen US ties. But he still made the Bushites see red, just as he had the Reaganites. In 2001, US ambassador Oliver Garza and a progression of senior State Department officials rejected Ortega's overtures and went out of their way to suggest that he was still nothing less than a dangerous fanatic, an admirer of Fidel Castro, with "links to terrorists" like Saddam Hussein and Muammar Khaddafi. Violeta Chamorro scoffed that " Everyone's been to Cuba—even Pope John Paul II has been to Cuba. This is not to defend Fidel Castro; it's just to recognize Cuba for what it is—one of today's tourist places!"[75]

When it looked like a candidate from the Nicaragua's Conservative Party might split the Right's vote and permit Ortega to win, Ambassador Garza strongly suggested that he should withdraw—which he promptly did.[76] President Bush also expressed grave misgivings about Ortega, and Jeb Bush, Florida's governor, wrote a vehement denunciation that was reprinted as a full-page ad in *La Prensa* shortly before the election, accusing Ortega of still associating with "terrorists." In late October 2001, three US Senators—including Florida democrat Bob Graham—introduced a resolution that asked President Bush to "reevaluate" his whole policy toward Nicaragua if Daniel Ortega were elected.[77]

Despite all the interference, it really was unbelievable that the FSLN managed to lose both the 1996 and 2001 elections to right-wing neoliberals, given the economic mess the neoliberals had made. The bitter truth for FSLN supporters was that by the 1990s, Daniel Ortega had become the Harold Stassen of Nicaraguan politics, overstaying his welcome and refusing to leave the stage. Many people on the Left and Right alike viewed him as someone vastly more interested in his own political career than anything else and distrusted even by his oldest comrades. Only by exercising tight control over the FSLN's internal selection processes had he managed to assure his three-time candidacy. In 1999, he even worked closely with the corrupt President Aleman on a "pact of governability" that sought to make it much more difficult for third parties to challenge the dominance of the PLC and the FSLN. At a time when the Aleman adminstration was turning out to be thoroughly corrupt, this pact proposed immunity from prosecution for all former presidents and the runners-up in presidential races, which included both Aleman and Ortega.[78]

It is too simple to blame Ortega's third presidential defeat in a row on "outside forces." In many ways, Ortega became the Right's favorite opponent. By clinging to power, excluding his rivals, making a fetish of bourgeois comforts, and forcing people to identify the FSLN's future with his own, Ortega had undermined the credibility of the movement.

ENCORE

President Enrique Bolaños assumed office in January 2002, the third free-market administration in a row, scheduled to remain in power until 2008, the thirty-second anniversary of Carlos Fonseca's death. After twelve years of neoliberal policies, eighteen years of civil wars and "proxy wars," forty-five years of dictatorship, and twenty-one years of US occupation, the Nicaragua that President Bolaños inherited was not in good shape.

In the first place, his former running mate, predecessor, and fellow PLC leader, President Arnoldo Aleman, had been one of the most corrupt politicians in Nicaraguan history. In December 2002, he was stripped of parliamentary immunity, placed under house arrest, and charged with diverting $97.1 million from fifteen state agencies to himself and fourteen of his cronies and family members, as well as defrauding a TV station of $1.5 million. Investigators found $51 million in dirty money in Panamanian and Costa Rican bank accounts under the control of Aleman's treasury minister.[79] Aleman's net worth, which had been $118,000 when he became the mayor of Managua in 1990, increased to an estimated $250 million by the end of his term in 2001.[80]

There were also strong suspicions about the 2001 privatization of ENI-TEL, Nicaragua's telephone company. After failed efforts to sell off forty percent of the company in 1995 and 1999, a consortium formed by Sweden's Telia and Honduras's EMCE—the only bidders—bought the stake for $83 million in August 2001, in the closing days of Aleman's adminstration. The IMF applied intense pressure to the Aleman government to sell the phone company quickly, because it feared that Ortega might win the November 2001 election and then halt the privatization. That, in turn, created an ideal pretext for a "sweetheart" deal. The bid proceeded despite a court order that barred it and strong complaints from Managua's mayor that ENITEL was actually worth at least $450 million. Among the serious charges under investigation was the possibility that Aleman himself was a secret "shadow bidder."[81] In September 2001, the brother of President Aleman's biggest campaign contributor, Jorge Mas Canosa, stepped forward to claim that Aleman had simply pocketed their $2.5 million campaign contribution in 1996. Apparently Jorge Mas Canosa, too, had had his sights on ENITEL.

Despite all the soot, public officials like Aleman could expect special treatment from Nicaragua's hopelessly corrupt, slow-moving court system. As its comptroller general said in 2001, "Illicit enrichment has not been classified as a crime. . . ."[82] Officials under suspicion could simply depart for Miami or NewYork, as more than a dozen of Aleman's cohorts did in 2001–02.[83] The US (Miami and New York in particular) welcomed them and their bank accounts with open arms.

Because of Daniel Ortega's intercession on his behalf, former President Aleman was able to avoid the trek to Miami. He and his family were permitted to stay under house arrest at one of his estates, costing taxpayers a thousand dollars a day for security.[84] Ortega also proposed that Aleman's ultimate fate be decided by a national referendum, but that suggestion did not fly.

President Bolaños was also not beyond corruption charges. In November 2002, Nicaragua's attorney general charged him and Vice President Jose Rizo with electoral crimes and $4.1 million in fraud during their 2001 presidential campaign.[85] By 2003, virtually the entire political establishment of Nicaragua was under suspicion, indictment, or living outside the country—especially the army of neoliberal "reformers" who had promised voters that, unlike the FSLN, they were practical businessmen who really knew how to manage the country.

AS FOR THE DEBT . . .

The furor over all these corruption cases was intertwined with the continuing saga of Nicaragua's foreign debt. Despite many promises, President
Aleman did little to reduce the debt in the late 1990s. His mounting corruption troubles became a serious obstacle to debt restructuring. By 2003,
Nicaragua's foreign debt had increased to more than $7 billion—about 3.2
times the national income and more than three times the average debt-
income ratio in other heavily indebted developing countries, still the world's
highest foreign debt burden.

Aleman's pro-bank regime made a point of continuing to service this foreign debt religiously. Debt service consumed more than half of his government's budgets. In 2000 alone, debt service—interest and principal—
amounted to 12.5 percent of Nicaragua's national income, while foreign
investment brought in just 10.6 percent. Even in the virtual-reality world of
neoliberal economics, this was a losing proposition.

Ordinarily, such a debt burden would have qualified Nicaragua for the
World Bank/IMF's new HIPC ("Heavily Indebted Poor Countries") debt
reduction program. Introduced in the mid-1990s, this program allowed qualified countries to write off up to eighty percent of their foreign loans. However, because of all the corruption in Nicaragua's case, the World Bank/IMF's
Consultative Group for HIPC countries refused to admit it to the program.
Because of the Aleman government's notorious behavior, individual aid
donors like Switzerland, Germany, and Sweden also suspended their assistance.[86]

In December 2002, a year after Aleman left office, the IMF and "Paris
Club" creditors—the providers of bilateral country loans, including export
agencies—agreed on a debt restructuring program to reduce Nicaragua's debt
by at least $2 billion by 2005. One of the IMF's conditions for the deal was
the consummation of several more privatizations, including several hydrodams
and ENITEL, now on its fourth attempt at privatization.[87] Given the economy's sad state, however, observers worried that it would not be easy to attract
foreign investments to Nicaraguan privatizations. After all, several of
Nicaragua's top neoliberals had just been caught reenacting the "Piñata" on
an even larger scale, the kind of "personal privatization program" that one
only expected from dangerous radicals like Daniel Ortega.

THE COFFEE CONNECTION

On top of everything else, an acute coffee market crisis hit Nicaragua in
2000–02. Nicaragua relied on coffee for 25–30 percent of its exports. The cri-

sis was a striking example of the unintended side effects of globalization and of neoliberal development banking at its worst. After all, coffee is grown by millions of small farmers in more than fifty developing countries, including several of the world's most heavily-indebted nations—indeed, it is second only to crude oil as a developing country export. So if you wanted to pick one global commodity market *not* to screw up, this would be it. But that did not stop the World Bank, the IMF, and the ADB from doing so.

Even in the twenty-first century, Nicaragua not only remains at the mercy of intransigent rightists, corrupt elites, and egomaniacal leftists, but also at the mercy of massive screwups by half-baked neoliberal experiments located halfway around the globe—and undertaken by fellow "former socialist countries."[88] In 1986, the Socialist Republic of Vietnam's Communist Party leadership decided to switch from central planning to a liberalization policy called *doi moi* (change and newness). This was partly because Vietnam could no longer depend on the (crumbling) USSR for huge subsidies. It was also because senior economists at the IMF, UNDP, World Bank, and ADB were preaching the glories of free markets and holding out the prospect of billions in aid. The resulting program, designed with extensive assistance from the world's leading development banks, was a controlled version of a standard orthodox adjustment program. It set out a ten-year plan for export-led growth, based on opening up Vietnam's heretofore closed economy to trade and investment, allowing state-owned banks freedom to lend to individual borrowers, de-collectivizing the farm sector, and encouraging small farmers and state-owned companies to develop new cash crops for export.

At the same time, political power was to be kept firmly in the hands of the Communist Party's politburo. Despite that slightly illiberal gracenote, from 1993 on, this *doi moi* economic liberalization package was generously supported with plenty of advice and more than $2 billion a year in foreign loans and grants from the Asian Development Bank, the UNDP, Japan's JIBC, France's Development Fund (AFD), the World Bank, the IMF, and the aid agencies of the US, Sweden, France, and several other Western governments.[89]

Nicaragua's forty-four thousand small coffee farmers, the six million small farmers in forty-nine other countries who collectively produced more than eighty percent of the world's coffee beans, and the one hundred million-plus people whose jobs and livelihoods depended on coffee beans had probably never heard of *doi moi*. But they became one of its first targets. Right from the start, evidently without much thought about collateral damage, Vietnam and the neoliberal wizards decided to embark on a brave new coffee export business.

While coffee had been grown in Vietnam ever since the 1850s, production and exports had been limited. The domestic market was small and there were few facilities to process the raw beans. As of 1990, green bean exports were a mere 1.2 million sixty-kilo bags per year. But Vietnam's central highlands had rich hills, abundant rainfall, and low labor costs—ideal conditions for achieving high yields and low prices. This was especially true for low-grade, easy-to-grow *robusta* beans. From a consumer's standpoint, this species was inferior to the *arabica* beans grown by Nicaragua, most other Central American producers, and big producers like Brazil and Colombia. *Arabica* traditionally accounted for more than three-fourths of the world's coffee production. But *robusta* had twice the caffeine content of *arabica* at half the price, and it could also be used as a cheap filler and blending ingredient by the giant coffee conglomerates.

By the 1990s, bean quality was no longer an absolute barrier to entry in coffee farming. The global market was increasingly dominated by a handful of giant First World coffee processors, roasters, and grinders, including Nestle, Kraft, Sara Lee, P&G, the German company Tchibo, and retail store owners like Starbucks, which generated their own blends. Increasingly, these companies obtained coffee beans from all over the planet, mixing and matching them to produce blends that not only satisfied customer tastes, but also minimized costs. These global buyers worked overtime on new technologies that took the edge off the cheaper *robusta* beans and allowed them to be used for extra punch and fill. With the help of commodity exchanges, they also defined standardized forward and futures contracts that allowed them to hedge against price fluctuations—making for a much more "perfect" global coffee market.

From the standpoint of the small farmers, most of whom did not have easy access to such hedging devices, "market perfection" was in the eyes of the beholder. The changes introduced by the giant buyers amounted to a radical commoditization of the market that they depended on for their livelihoods, and a sharp increase in direct competition. Even as downstream market power became more concentrated in the hands of the First World giants, the farmers' share of value-added plummeted. In 1984, raw coffee beans accounted for more than sixty-four percent of value-added in the US retail coffee market. By 2000, this share dropped to eighteen percent. From 1990 to 2000, while global retail coffee revenues increased from $30 billion to $60 billion, the revenues earned by bean-growing countries dropped from $10 billion to $6 billion. By then, for every $3.50 cafe latte sold by Starbucks, the farmers earned just 3.5 cents.[90]

The farmers' shrinking role was due in part to the basic structure of the global coffee industry. On the supply side, by the 1990s, raw beans were being exported by more than fifty competing countries. But while a few growers like Brazil and Colombia tried to break into foreign markets with their own processed brands, global First World buyers still dominated processing and marketing. Many of the world's leading exporters of processed coffee, like Germany and Italy, grew no coffee at all.

This long-standing First World control over global coffee processing stemmed partly from technical factors. There are economies of scale in processing, but not in coffee farming—production costs don't decline much because farms get bigger. Unlike petroleum or natural gas, which can be stored for free in the ground, coffee beans are costly to store, and aged beans have no incremental value. Furthermore, most small coffee farmers depend on coffee sales for their current incomes. Global coffee demand is not very price-sensitive and has been growing at a modest one percent per year. All this means that prices tend to fluctuate wildly with current production, so there is an incentive for processors to stay out of farming, shifting market risk to millions of poorly diversified producers. The fact that coffee beans can be stored 1–2 years, while roasted or ground products have a much shorter shelf life, favors locating processing facilities close to the final consumer markets.[91] And anyone who has been to France, Italy, or Brazil knows that tastes for particular kinds of coffee vary significantly across countries.

But the coffee industry's international division of labor is not based only on technical factors, many of which are actually eroding. It is also based on long-standing trading patterns and colonial relations; for example, the original sixteenth-century role of the Dutch in smuggling coffee plants out of Yemen to their colony in Java, which fostered Indonesia's coffee industry. First World dominance was reinforced by trade barriers that favor the importation of raw beans over processed coffee. The net result of this would be analogous to France, Italy and California all being compelled to export their grapes to Managua, Nairobi, and Jakarta in order to have them processed into wine.

Given the importance of small coffee farmers in debtor countries and the World Bank's supposed commitment to "poverty alleviation," it may seem surprising that the World Bank, the IMF, and other development lenders devoted no energy in the 1990s in designing a buyers-cartel-breaking strategy for coffee growing countries, to help them break down this division of labor and these trade barriers. Instead, the development bankers did just the opposite, helping Vietnam implement an anti-producer-cartel strategy that ultimately helped to drive the coffee-producing countries' association completely out of business in 2001. Could it be that these First World development banks were not influenced by the fact that the world's leading coffee conglomerates happen to be based in countries like the US, Japan, France, Switzerland, and Germany, not far from the development banks' own headquarters?

COFFEE CONTRAS

Vietnam's decision to push coffee bean exports as a cash generator in the 1990s was not just based on rational economics. Like most critical decisions in economic development, it also had a crucial political motive. Vietnam's best region for growing coffee turns out to be the Central Highlands, along the border with Cambodia and Laos. About four million people inhabit this region, including 500,000–1,000,000 members of non-Buddhist ethnic minorities known collectively as the Montagnard/Dega hill tribes.[92] These fiercely independent peoples have battled the Communist Party and most other central authorities for as long as anyone can remember. In the 1960s, eighteen thousand tribespeople joined the CIA's Village Defense Units and fought hard against the NLF. They also had many run-ins with South Vietnam's various dictators. After the war ended in 1975, some Montagnard tribes continued armed resistance until the late 1980s.

To shore up control over this volatile region, in the early 1980s Vietnam's government embarked on its own version of ethnic cleansing—or at least dilution. It actively encouraged millions of ethnic Kinh—Vietnam's largest ethnic group—plus other non-Montagnard minorities to migrate from the more crowded lowlands to the Central Highlands. At first, the government directly organized these migrations. But by the 1990s, they were being driven by a combination of market forces and government subsidies. On the one hand, the migrants sought to escape the poverty and resource exhaustion of the lowlands. On the other, they were attracted by the prospect of obtaining cheap land and credit to grow coffee, the exciting new cash crop, which became known to the peasants as "the dollar tree."[93]

The result was an influx of up to three million people to the Central Highlands provinces in less than two decades. In 1990–94 alone, three hundred thousand new migrants arrived in the provinces of Dak Lak, Lam Dong, Gia Lai, and Kontum, looking for land. By 2000, these four provinces alone accounted for eighty-five percent of Vietnam's coffee production. This reduced the Montagnard tribes to the status of a minority group in their own homelands. They watched in anguish as their ancestral lands were reassigned to outsiders, including state-owned companies controlled by influential party members in Hanoi with close ties to leading Japanese, American, and Singaporean coffee trading companies. Many of the Montagnards were forced to resettle on smaller plots without compensation. Over time, as the local economy became more vulnerable to fluctuations in world coffee prices, this contributed to explosive social conflicts.

From the standpoint of Nicaragua's farmers, the key impact was on world coffee prices. In Vietnam, migrants and Montagnards turned to coffee for support on increasingly crowded plots. In the early 1990s, coffee still offered greater revenue per unit of land, compared with other cash crops like rice or peppers, and was actively promoted as a cash crop by state banks, trading companies, and the government.

It took three to four years for a new coffee bush to mature, so the real surge in exports did not occur until 1996–2000. Then, in just a four-year period, Vietnamese exports flooded the market. From 1990 to 2002, they increased more than tenfold, from 1.2 million sixty-kilo bags to more than 13.5 million bags.[94] By 2000, Vietnam had become the world's second largest coffee producer, second only to Brazil.[95] In the crucial market segment of cut-rate green *robusta* beans, the blenders' choice, Vietnam became the world leader. While other producers like Brazil also increased their *robusta* exports during this period, Vietnam alone accounted for more than half of all the increased exports, which helped boost *robusta's* share of all coffee exports to forty percent.

In pursuing this strategy, Vietnam did not bother to join coffee's equivalent of OPEC—the Association of Coffee Producing Countries. Indeed, it acted rather like a scab, providing an incremental eight hundred thousand metric tons of low-priced coffee by 2000, about the same amount as the world market's overall surplus. The giant coffee buyers were quite happy to buy up low-priced coffee and swap it into blended products like Maxwell House and Taster's Choice, using it to discipline other leading supplier-countries. At the same time, foreign debt-ridden countries like Indonesia, Brazil, Uganda, Peru, and Guatemala boosted their coffee sales in order to generate more exports. In September 2001, partly because of this beggar-thy-neighbor strategy, the Association of Coffee Producing Countries collapsed and was disbanded.[96]

The resulting export glut caused world coffee prices to tumble to a thirty-three-year low by 2002. According to the World Bank's estimates, this resulted in the loss of at least six hundred thousand jobs in Central America, leaving more than seven hundred thousand people near starvation.[97] Worldwide, the effects of the coffee glut were even more catastrophic, because the world's fifty-odd coffee producing countries included many of the world's poorest, most debt-ridden nations. Ironically, just as they were supporting Vietnam's rapid expansion into exports like coffee, in 1996 the World Bank and the IMF had launched a new program to provide debt relief to the world's most "heavily-indebted poor countries"—the so-called HIPC program. By 2001, the HIPC program had made some progress in debt reduction, cutting the "present value" of the foreign debts for those countries that completed the program by an average of thirty percent. However, of the 28 heavily-indebted poor countries that had signed up for the World Bank's

HIPC program by 2003, 18 of them were coffee growing countries—including not only Nicaragua, but also desperately poor places like Boliva, Honduras, Uganda, the Congo, Cameroon, Rwanda, the Ivory Coast, and Tanzania.

Indeed, for the larger coffee exporters in this group, even when they managed to wend their way through HIPC's complex program and qualify for debt relief, they found that most of its benefits were offset by the coffee crisis! For example, Uganda, the very first country to qualify for HIPC relief, discovered that by 2001, just one year after qualifying for HIPC, its foreign debt was higher than ever—mainly because it had to borrow to offset the impact of the coffee crisis on exports.

Furthermore, many other "not-quite-so-heavily indebted" developing countries that produced coffee, like India, Indonesia, Peru, Guatemala, Kenya, Mexico, and El Salvador, were also badly hurt. Overall, if one had *set out* to create destitution and suffering in as many of the world's developing countries as possible at one fell swoop, one could hardly have devised a better strategy that to encourage Vietnam to thoughtlessly expand its coffee exports.

In Nicaragua's case, the average wholesale price for its Arabica beans fell from $1.44 a pound in 1999 to $0.51 a pound in 2001 and to less than $0.40 a year later, compared with typical production costs of $0.83 a pound.

Among the hardest hit were Nicaragua's forty-four thousand small producers, who accounted for two-thirds of Nicaragua's coffee production and provided jobs that supported another four hundred thousand Nicaraguans, most of them landless farmers in the rural northwest around Matagalpa, north of Managua. They depended upon Nicaragua's annual coffee harvests for most of their employment and income. The resulting crisis in the countryside set off a migration to Managua and other cities of thousands of hungry, landless people crowding into makeshift shacks on the edge of town.

Obviously these developments begged many questions concerning the roles of the World Bank and Vietnam's other international lenders and advisors. After all, Vietnam was a very poor state-socialist country that was undertaking free-market reforms for the first time—after fighting and winning a thirty-year war of its own with the US. The World Bank, IMF, and the ADB were supposed to be the experts, implementing reforms all over the world, backed by billions in loans and hundreds of Ivy-League economists. And Vietnam was intended to be one of their poster stories for desocialization, and for the claim that growth, free markets, and "poverty alleviation" can go hand in hand.

In April 2002, sensitive to NGO charges that the World Bank and other development lenders might actually bear some responsibility for this fiasco, the World Bank went out of its way to issue a press release denying any responsibility for the crisis whatsoever. More precisely, it denied having *directly* provided any financing to expand coffee production in Vietnam. It maintained that its $1.1 billion of loans to Vietnam since 1996 tried—though evidently without much success—to steer farmers away from cyclical crops like coffee. It also argued that its lending to Vietnam's rural sector only started up after 1996, while coffee production had increased since 1994, and that none of its investments were "designed to promote coffee production." The World Bank did identify two projects that "could be linked" to coffee production: a 1996 Rural Finance Project that helped Vietnamese banks lend money to farmers and an Agricultural Diversification Project. But the Bank simply observed that it didn't dictate how such institutions reloaned their funds.[98]

Overall, the World Bank basically washed its hands of the coffee crisis—one of the worst disasters to strike small farmers, their dependents, and debtor countries in modern times. The World Bank did, however, assure the public that it was extremely concerned about the plight of these farmers, promising new lending programs to address their woes.

On closer inspection, this defense had a few holes. Whether or not the World Bank financed any new coffee farms, clearly the World Bank, the IMF, the UNDP, and the ADB were up to their elbows in designing, managing, and financing Vietnam's economic liberalization program. They played a key role in pushing Vietnam to liberalize trade, exchange rates, and banking quickly. To set targets for Vietnam's macroeconomic plans, they must have known which export markets the government planned to go after. After all, coffee was not just another export. After the removal of Vietnam's quotas on coffee and other exports in 1990, partly at the request of the IMF, coffee quickly became the country's second-leading export behind oil. Coffee continued to be a top-ten export even after prices cratered. The ADB and the World Bank worked closely with Vietnam's Rural Development Bank, the country's largest rural lender, to improve management and structure new lending programs.[99] They also advised Vietnam on how to set up a Land Registry, so that rival land claims could be settled and farmers—at least non-Montagnards—could borrow to finance their new crops more easily.

At the same time, far from encouraging Vietnam to work with other coffee producers to stabilize the market or design an overall long-term strategy to break up the coffee buyers' market power, the development banks bitterly opposed any such interference with "free markets"—no matter how concentrated the buyers were or how many artificial restrictions were placed by First World countries on the importation of processed coffee. One senior World Bank economist observed in 2001, during the very depths of the coffee glut:

Vietnam has become a successful [coffee] producer. In general, we consider it to be a huge success. . . . It is a continuous process. It occurs in all countries—the more efficient, lower cost producers expand their production, and the higher cost, less efficient producers decide that it is no longer what they want to do.[100]

Despite its 2002 press release, the World Bank's true attitude about this whole fiasco appears to have been a combination of "not my problem," *sauve qui peut,* and Social Darwinism.

Meanwhile, back in Vietnam, the small farmers of the Central Highlands learned the hard way about the glories of global capitalism. Thousands of them were "deciding that it is no longer what they want to do," but finding few easy ways out. After the 1999–2002 plunge in coffee prices, Vietnam's export earnings from coffee fell by seventy-five percent from their level in 1998–99 to just $260 million in 2001–02. In 2002–03, they fell another thirty percent. In the Central Highlands, thousands of small farmers—low-landers and Montagnards alike—had gone deeply into debt to finance their growth. They were struggling to feed their families and send their children to school, because market prices now covered just sixty percent of their production costs.[101]

Ten thousand miles from Managua, in Vietnam, highland farmers were having to face the same bitter neoliberal truths that the Nicaraguan farmers were facing. They had more in common with each other than with the stone-hearted elites, economists, and bankers who governed their respective societies, designing futures that did not necessarily include them.

In Vietnam, the resulting economic crisis severely aggravated social and political conflicts in the Central Highlands. In February 2001, several thousand Montagnards held mass demonstrations in Dak Lak—demanding the return of their ancestral lands, an end to evictions for indebtedness, a homeland of their own, and religious freedom (since many Dega are evangelical Christians). Vietnam responded with a harsh crackdown, sending thousands of troops and riot police to break up their protests. They made several hundred arrests and then used torture to elicit confessions and statements of remorse. They also destroyed several local churches where the protestors had been meeting. Those protest leaders who did not manage to escape to Cambodia were given prison sentences of up to twelve years.

From one angle, this was the handiwork of a conventional Communist dictatorship. From another, it was actually just another example of the repressive tactics that neoliberalism has often used to implement free-market policies, from Argentina to Zambia. In Vietnam's case, instead of solving its political problems in the Central Highlands, the politburo discovered that their neoliberal reforms had inadvertantly helped to revive the Dega separatist movement.[102] Evidently, economic and political liberty did not always go hand in hand.

The politburo and their foreign advisors did have something to show for the coffee strategy. In 2000–02, the profit margins earned by the five giant companies that dominated the global coffee market were higher than ever. Furthermore, cocaine producers in the Andean region no longer had to worry about farmers substituting coffee for coca. In Colombia's traditional coffee-growing regions, just the opposite started to happen in the late 1990s as many farmers converted coffee fields to coca, in the wake of the coffee glut.[103] From 1995 to 2001, coca cultivation more than tripled in Colombia, including a twenty percent increase in 2000–01 alone. This occurred despite hundreds of millons of dollars spent by the US government on coca eradication efforts—the centerpiece of its "Plan Colombia." In 2000–01, coca production also started to increase in Peru, Bolivia, Ecuador, and Venezuela. There were reports that farmers were even turning away from coffee and towards coca or poppies in areas that had never before produced drugs, like the slopes of Kenya's Mount Kilimanjaro.[104] And unlike coffee, coca and opium were attractive in that both the farming and processing could be done at home.

NEOLIBERAL DUSK

By the late 1990s, after so many years of economic decline and endemic corruption, many Nicaraguans despaired for their country's future. A 1998 nationwide survey found that most adults were very distrustful of public officials, politicians, and judges. They believed that corruption was widespread and that it posed a "serious threat to the system's stability."[105] A nationwide poll of young Nicaraguans in 2000 found that two-thirds of them wanted to emigrate. From 1990 to 2000, even after the FSLN's demise and the end of the Contra War, the number of Nicaraguans living in Miami increased from 50,000 to 125,000. It has continued to grow since then.[106] But most were professionals and elites who could afford to get visas and relocate and whose job prospects were better.

For the vast majority of Nicaraguans who could not afford to emigrate, the situation had been dire enough in 1990, at the end of the contra war. But after thirteen years of neoliberal bloodletting—under Chamorro, Aleman and Bolaños, plus misfortunes like 1998's Hurricane Mitch and the coffee fiasco, the economic situation became nightmarish.[107] In the countryside, where forty percent of Nicaragua's 5.2 million people live, the coffee crisis was compounded by many other chronic problems. As of 2003, four out of five people in rural areas still live without sanitization and one-third lack electricity. Just as the coffee crisis hit, so did another debt crisis. The government responded by cutting back sharply on rural credit programs, health care, and infrastructure spending. The coffee growers had made annual contributions to a government fund that was supposed to protect them against price drops, but the IMF forced Aleman's Central Bank to freeze spending and reserves. This was done not only to contain inflation, but also because the IMF feared that Aleman's *banditos* might abscond with the country's dollar reserves. This meant that the coffee price stabilization fund was placed off-limits just when the growers needed it most.

In April 2001, to protect thousands of coffee growers who were $116 million in debt and on the brink of losing their farms, Nicaragua's National Assembly adopted a bill that suspended all farm foreclosures for a year. However, this bill angered bankers, the IMF, and the IDB, which held up a $50 million loan to Nicaragua, forcing President Aleman to veto the bill. At the same time, subsidies to politically influential owners of large estates, like Presidents Bolaños and Aleman, actually increased in the late 1990s, while the Sandinistas' land reforms came under fierce attack. In 1995, Chamorro had legalized the transfer of two hundred thousand small homes and farms expropriated since 1974, offering their former owners compensation unless they were members of the Somoza family. Since few people had money to pay compensation, after President Aleman was elected, many former owners returned and started to evict tenants aggressively.

By 1997, more than a hundred thousand new occupants were facing eviction proceedings instituted by 5,500 former landlords. The court system was jammed with twenty-four thousand lawsuits, claiming title to two million blocks of land and 4,251 houses. Even Bolaños joined the herd, demanding the return of three farms allegedly taken from him. A new law tried to compensate the old landlords with ENITEL bonds, but few believed they were good substitute for their properties. Aleman even allowed several Somoza family members to return from Miami and sue for their old estates, and appointed one of them to be his ambassador to Argentina.[108] The US government, led by Senator Jesse Helms, found a way to support the property claims of former Somocistas. They simply demanded compensation for US citizens who had been expropriated, whether or not they had been US citizens at the time of the expropriations. Many Somocistas found it lucrative and surprisingly easy to obtain dual citizenship just so they could press such demands.[109]

Meanwhile, along the country's northern border, bands of *recontras* continued to plague locals with armed robberies, extortion, carjackings, and kidnappings. From 1990 to 1998, they were responsible for at least 1,850 killings.[110] Landmines were another continuing Contra War legacy. As of 2003, more than a hundred thousand landmines were still in place along the northern border. In the 1990s, landmines killed 53 people, maimed 558, and caused more than 60 new civilian casualties each year. The country also had to deal with twenty-six thousand people who had been injured in the war— 10–15 percent of whom required prosthestic devices.[111] The Chamorro government sharply reduced the budget for disabled veterans, so many of them ended up begging on the streets.

In Nicaragua's cities, especially after 1995, thousands of small businesses were crushed under the twin juggernauts of economic slowdown and increased imports, after tariff barriers were reduced. Some of the economic slack was taken up by the underground economy, including drug trafficking, car theft, fraudulent tour guides, arms trafficking, kidnapping, extortion, prostitution, tax evasion, child labor, and petty corruption. Violent crimes, including domestic violence, also soared. The overall crime rate increased by an average of ten percent a year in the 1990s, assisted by a lack of resources for law enforcement. As of 2002, there were only about seven thousand (poorly paid) police officers in the whole country. El Salvador, with a slightly larger population, spent up to thirteen times as much on policing. The crime wave was also exacerbated by a growing influx of families from the countryside.

Inadequate policing compelled those who could afford it to "privatize" their own security by hiring guards, buying firearms, and installing alarms, glass-edged high walls, and window bars. The whole society was becoming unstable—everyone scared, armed to the teeth, ready to defend themselves at the drop of a hat. The country was awash with more than 250,000 weapons, innumerable mercenaries and security guards, and hundreds of *Pandillas*, heavily armed youth gangs.[112] As conventional society disintegrated, these violent gangs sprang up to play an increasingly powerful role in daily life, creating a "state of seige" much more frightening to ordinary people than the Contra War.[113] In 2002, one Managua resident described the atmosphere:

> You can't go out anymore, you can't wear rings, bracelets, nice shoes, anything that makes us look a little better than we really are. . . . You never feel safe in the *barrio*, because of the lack of trust. There always had to be somebody in the house, because you can't trust anybody to look out for you, for your things, to help you, nothing. People only look out for themselves— everyone, the rich, the poor, the middle class. . . . Life is hard in Nicaragua, and you've just got to look out for yourself.[114]

The increase in drug trafficking was especially disturbing. In the late 1990s, it became one of the economy's few growth spots. Near Puerto Cabezas, along Nicaragua's unpoliced Caribbean coast, there are a surprising number of fancy new oceanfront homes. In the wake of improvements in Caribbean drug enforcement, Colombian traffickers had stumbled on this area, making it the first stop on the Central American-Mexican corridor and a convenient alternative way station to the US. It was close to Colombia's island of San Andres, where one could trade drugs for arms, and there were several thousand demobilized, underemployed army troops and former Contras in the area who were available for hire.[115]

After 1998, crack cocaine and ecstasy became pervasive in Nicaragua's cities, displacing glue and marijuana as drugs of choice among the *pandillas*. As conventional society disintegrated, these violent gangs assumed an increasingly important role in daily life, more frightening to ordinary people than the *contra* war had ever been. Developments like these underscored an interesting shift that took place in US government policy toward drug trafficking and "terrorism" in the late 1990s. As the CIA finally admitted publicly in 1998–99, the US government had basically turned a blind eye to the involvement of leading Contras and the CIA's own contractors in cocaine smuggling during the 1980s—including Danilo Blandon, a former director of Nicaragua's Foreign Marketing program and a leading Contra supporter, who was widely credited with a pioneering role in creating L.A.'s crack cocaine market.[116] Technically speaking, there were no CIA agents involved in cocaine dealing—limiting "agents" to the Agency's full-time civil servants. But as the CIA's inspector general told a closed-door congressional hearing in May 1999, "In the end, the objective of unseating the Sandinistas appears to have taken precedence over dealing properly with potentially serious allegations against those with whom the agency was working."[117]

By 2002, the new global wars on drugs and "terrorism" had officially replaced anti-Communism as the next big opportunities for the exertion of US government muscle in Central America and Colombia. In 1998–2000, the US government sent 4,700 troops to Nicaragua, the twelfth time US troops had entered the country since the 1850s. Ostensibly, they were sent to provide humanitarian assistance, repairing damage caused by Hurricane Mitch, although no other Central American countries were favored with so many troops. In 2001, the US government also sent DEA agents to Nicaragua to provide drug enforcement training, sweetened by a $3.7 million aid package for Nicaragua's National Police. The US pressed the Aleman and Bolaños governments to amend Nicaragua's 1987 Constitution so that US ships could enter the country's waters in pursuit of drug traffickers or other undesirables.[118] In 2002, for the first time since 1979, the US invited senior Nicaraguan military officers to attend the Western Hemisphere Institute for Security Cooperation, the successor to the infamous School of the Americas

in Fort Benning, Georgia. Cynics described it as one of the world's first terrorist training camps.[119]

Among the supposed beneficiaries of all these new drug enforcement
efforts were the growing number of "dump children" living on the streets of
Managua. By the late 1990s, they numbered more than 14,000, including
about 8,500 who had joined the city's 110 *pandillas*. Many others had joined
more than 250,000 Nicaraguan children under the age of fifteen who, according to Nicaragua's Labor Ministry, were employed in child labor.[120] To handle the daily grind, in the mid-1990s, many turned to sniffing Fuller Glue,
imported from the US for a few *cordobas* per jar. By the late 1990s, glue had
been displaced by crack cocaine, raising the level of murders, assaults, and
armed robberies. As the *pandillas* took over retail distribution, Danilo
Blandon's pioneering role in LA crack cocaine came full circle.

In Las Mercedes Zona Libre, the free-trade zone on the outskirts of
Managua, in a row of hangars surrounded by barbed wire and security
guards, lived thirty-five thousand hard-working Managuans—eighty percent
of whom were women. They worked 12–16 hour shifts, with mandatory
overtime and one 45-minute break, for about $1.50–3.00 per day—one of
Central America's lowest wage rates. They were employed at more than
eighty new foreign-owned, nonunionized shoe and jeans factories. The Zona
Libre had originally been established by the Somoza government in 1976,
attracting a dozen or so US garment companies. The Sandinistas shut it
down and converted the facilities into state-run factories. In 1992, however,
the Chamorro government revitalized the Zona Libre to take advantage
of the new preferential trade access to the US market that was made available for a variety of cheap textiles by the Reagan/Bush adminstration's
Caribbean Basin Initiative (CBI) and its various installments. The new factories, owned by a variety of relatively unknown Taiwanese, Korean, US, and
European manufacturers, had sprung up to make running shoes, denim jeans,
and other low-end merchandise for retailers like Walmart, KMart, Sears,
Kohl's, The Gap, and JC Penney, supplying brands like NO FEAR and High
Sierra. They were competing with a growing number of virtually identical
macquilas, free-trade zones that had sprung up all over the Third World since
the 1980s in countries like Mexico, Honduras, Guatemala, El Salvador,
Burma, the Philippines, South China, Lesotho, and Indonesia. They were
encouraged by zero customs duties, zero income tax for the first ten years of
operation, zero social security, pension, or health benefits, limited saftey or
health restrictions, no minimum wages, no unions, minimal restrictions on
hours and other working conditions, and the Zone's special access to the US
market by way of the CBI's textile quotas.

On paper, the purpose of the Zona Libre, which was very popular with IMF/World Bank economists, was to create jobs, boost exports, diversify Nicaragua's economy away from traditional crops like coffee, and alleviate poverty. In practice, the Zona Libre forced some of the world's poorest people to compete head-to-head on the amount of exploitation that they will tolerate.

In effect, the Zona Libre was the urban workers' equivalent of Vietnam's coffee export program—an organized, global effort to increase the level of direct, cost-based competition among poor people. And while each country that developed a macquila industry could honestly claim to have designed its own local variant, it was no accident that in the background, cheering these "pro-export" policies on and rewarding them with adjustment loans, was the usual cast of First World development experts, banks, governments, and investors. One former Zona Libre worker described what it was like to work there: "You're sitting down all day on a wooden bench with no back. The lighting isn't very good, and by the end of the day, you can't see anything, not even the hole in the needle. But still they don't want you to lose even one minute."[121]

In April 2001, when the workers at Chentex—a company owned by Nien Hsing, a Taiwanese conglomerate and the world's largest jeans maker—demanded a little more than the twenty cents they earned per pair of jeans ($20 retail), their organizers were fired. When hundreds of workers protested, the Aleman government sent in a police squad in riot gear to arrest them. When a Taiwanese journalist accused President Aleman of "dollar diplomacy," since Taiwan had lubricated its business dealings with Nicaragua by paying for Nicaragua's Presidential Palace, several roads, and bridges, Aleman labeled him a "communist."[122] Of course, Aleman had a point; after all, if the workers did not like the jobs they were offered, they could always "decide that it is no longer what they want to do."

Nicaragua's other neoliberal policy experiments also had very mixed results. In the financial sector, a premature attempt to liberalize without adequate bank regulation had resulted in several bank failures, notably the demise of Interbanco in 2000, in which former Sandinista leader Bayardo Arce and other Sandinistas had invested, at a loss of $200 million.[123] Efforts to privatize the country's largest state enterprise—the state telephone company—finally succeeded only with the help of corruption at the country's highest levels.

In March 2000, the Aleman adminstration also tried to please the IMF by following in Chile's footsteps and privatizing Nicaragua's social security system. Most Nicaraguans were skeptical—to qualify for benefits, workers had to be sixty-five years old with a twenty-five-year work record. Since the life expectancy for Nicaraguan males is 66.6 years and only three percent of Nicaraguans make it to over the age of 65, this program is not likely to be a panacea. But at least it may be inexpensive.

BLEEDING NICARAGUA

By 2003, Nicaragua's real per capita income had fallen to $400—its 1951 level. With population growth averaging 2.4 percent a year, the economy would have to grow at 5 percent a year for more than thirty years just to recover its "prerevolutionary" 1977 per capita income level. The actual average growth rate during the 1990s was 1.3 percent. By 2003, underemployment levels exceeded 60–70 percent in many parts of the country, and the overall proportion of people living in poverty was 67 percent, second only to Honduras in Latin America. This means that there are now 1.6 million more Nicaraguans living on the borderline of existence than in 1990.

In the 1980s, the Sandinistas had been justifiably proud of their health, education, and literacy programs. Even in the depths of the *Contra* War, rates of infant and maternal mortality, malnutrition, and illiteracy had declined. Infant mortality fell from 120 per 1,000 live births in 1979 to 61 in 1990, immunization coverage rose, and the share of the population with access to health care increased from 43 to 80 percent.[124] In the 1990s, however, there were sharp increases in all these maladies, aided by Chamorro's seventy-five percent cut in public health and education spending by 1994.[125] By 2000, Nicaragua was spending almost four times as much on debt service than on education and a third more than on public health.[126] The infant mortality rate was still thirty-seven per thousand, and the children-under-five mortality rate was forty-five per thousand, among the highest in Latin America (for comparison, Cuba's equivalent rates were 7 and 9 per thousand.) As of 2000, twelve percent of Nicaraguan children were underweight, and twenty-five percent were below average height.[127] More than twenty-two percent of children under the age of nine—three hundred thousand children—were malnourished.[128] By 2000, thirty-seven percent of children were not enrolled in classes, and illiteracy, which an intense campaign by the Sandinistas in 1980–81 had reduced to fifteen percent, had climbed back up to thirty-four percent, which was even higher in rural areas. Women's rights also suffered acutely, as the church conspired with the conservative governments of the 1990s to ban abortions, even at the cost of higher maternal mortality rates because of botched illegal abortions.[129]

Coincidentally, by 2003, Nicaragua's four hundred dollar per capita income had become almost identical to that of the Socialist Republic of Viet-

nam. In one of history's many ironies, these two formerly "leftist" countries
were now passing each other on the globalization escalator, heading in opposite directions. By 1998, according to the statistics published by the UNDP,
Vietnam's poverty rate had dropped to thirty-seven percent, while adult literacy had reached ninety-four percent, above Nicaragua's (declining) level of
sixty-three percent. Vietnam's average life expectancy equalled Nicaragua's
68.3 years. And far from having a chronic foreign debt problem, Vietnam
became one of the development banks' darlings, receiving $2 billion a year in
concessional finance throughout the decade, plus more than $30 billion in
foreign investments. Yet Vietnam's ratio of debt to national income was just
one-tenth as large as Nicaragua's level.

Furthermore, with all outside help, plus its entry in to the coffee market,
Vietnam's growth rate averaged more than nine percent a year in the 1990s,
while Nicaragua's growth stagnated.[130] In 2001, when Vietnam's Ninth Communist Party Congress adopted its "Tenth Ten-Year Strategy" for 2001–10,

A. World Country Ranks

	1980	1990	2000
Costa Rica	34	44	43
Panama	44	54	57
Belize	46	53	58
El Salvador	66	83	104
Honduras	70	89	116
Guatemala	78	95	120
Nicaragua	68	94	118

B. Relative to Nicaragua

Costa Rica	2.00	2.14	2.74
Panama	1.55	1.74	2.07
Belize	1.48	1.77	2.03
El Salvador	1.03	1.13	1.13
Honduras	0.97	1.06	1.02
Guatemala	0.87	0.99	0.98
Nicaragua	1.00	1.00	1.00

Source: UNDP (2002), JSH analysis   © JS Henry 2003

Table 5.1–Relative to more prosperous (haven) neighbors

the World Bank and the IMF were both on hand in Hanoi to celebrate with yet another generous structural adjustment loan program—carefully shielded from any angry Montagnards who might wish to complain.

By the new millenium, out of 173 nations ranked by the UNDP according to their "human development" metrics, Nicaragua had dropped from 68 in 1980 to 118. Vietnam is now number 101 and rising. The responsibility for Nicaragua's decline can be evenly divided between the *Contra* War of the 1980s and the Neoliberal War of the 1990s. Evidently it wasn't enough to pull off a revolution and defeat a US-backed puppet army, as both Vietnam and Nicaragua had succeeded in doing. Daniel Ortega and his comrades must wonder, "If only we had managed to install a full-fledged, centrally planned Communist dictatorship, as we were often accused of trying to do—perhaps the world would have been as generous to Nicaragua as it has been to Vietnam."

History has not been kind to Nicaragua. And high-minded Americans may be tempted to blame that entirely on its own sorry leaders. Indeed, there have been quite a few domestic culprits. But much deeper forces have also been at work. The most powerful enemy of Nicaragua's development in the long run has been an interlocking global system of institutions and interests. It does not require conspiracies. It is self-organizing. It consists of an amazing array of mutually reinforcing interests. And it takes no prisoners.

In the 1980s, a handful of rather foolhardy Sandinistas challenged this global system. They made many mistakes and required much on-the-job training. But at least they tried to stand up. When they did so, they were attacked, and when they defended themselves, they were portrayed as the aggressors. Ultimately, they won a victory of sorts, but it left their country in shambles. Then their neoliberal successors came to power preaching reform and market freedom, and ended up turning the country into a *bantustan*. Perhaps Nicaragua will need another revolution.

Figure I.1–Chile 1960. Credit: Pierre St. Amand.

Figure 1.1–Angra I and II. Credit: Greenpeace web site/Brazilian Government.

Figure 1.2–Norberto Odebrecht.
Credit: Odebrecht SA.

Figure 1.3–Lago do Balbina. Credit: Solidaritetshuset.

Figure 1.4–Antonio Delfim Neto. Credit: Lula's Campaign.

Figure 1.5–Bataan Nuclear Power Plant. Credit: Ferdinand Escalona.

Figure 1.6–Laguna Verde, Mexico. Credit: BBC.

Figure 1.7–General
Augusto Pinochet and
Dr. Henry Kissinger.
Credit: Universidad
de Alicante.

Figure 1.8–General Jose Efrain Rios Montt.
Credit: AP.

Figure 1.9–Guatemala Exhumations. Credit: Berlin Juarez, PhotoKids
(2002).

Figure 2.1–Ferdinand and
Imelda. Credit: AP.

Figure 2.2–Dr. Batliner and
Helmut Kohl. Credit: Heide
Reiss.

Figure 2.3–Rafael B. Buenaventura, Citibank.
Credit: Central Bank of the Philippines.

Figure 2.4–Jobo Fernandez and
Vicente Jayme. Credit: International Development Review.

Figure 2.5–Gloria Macapagal-Arroyo.
Credit: AP.

Figure 2.6–Joseph Estrada. Credit: Philippine Police.

Figure 3.1–Carlos Andres Perez. Credit:
International Development Review.

Figure 3.2–Hugo Chavez Frias. Credit: AP.

Figure 3.3–Gustavo Cisneros.
Credit: Radio & Television Americana.

Figure 3.4–Vladimiro Montesinos. Credit: Peruvian
Government.

Figure 3.5–Pedro Carmona Estanga.
Credit: PBS.

Figure 3.6–Chavez and Cardoso. Credit:
Fondo de Inversion Social de Venezuela.

Figure 4.1–Tony Gebauer.
Credit: Gebauer Family Picture.

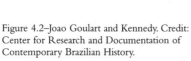

Figure 4.2–Joao Goulart and Kennedy. Credit:
Center for Research and Documentation of
Contemporary Brazilian History.

Figure 4.3–General Vernon A. Walters.
Credit: Televisió de Catalunya.

Figure 4.4–Delfim and Simonsen.
Credit: Editora Politica.

Figure 4.5–Antonio Carlos Magalhaes.
Credit: Mirian Fichtner.

Figure 4.6–Jose Sarney.
Credit: Jornal do Brasil.

Figure 4.7–Gebauer and Finance
Minister Galveas. Credit: UPI (1981).

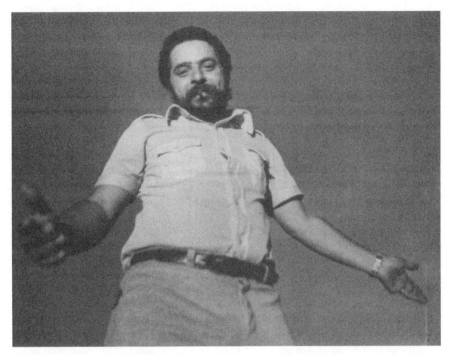

Figure 4.8–The young Lula. Credit: Teodomoro Braga.

Figure 5.1–Pedro Joaquin Chamorro C.
Credit: Confidencial.com.

Figure 6.1–General Leopoldo Galtieri.
Credit: Argentine Military.

Figure 6.2–General Jorge Rafael Videla.
Credit: AP.

Figure 6.3–Domingo Cavallo.
Credit: Telepolis.

Figure 7.1–General Alfredo Stroessner.
Credit: Paraguayan Government.

Figure 7.2–Victor Jara.
Credit: Patria Grande.

Figure 7.3–Professor Milton Friedman.
Credit: University of Chicago News Office.

Figure 7.4–Carlos Salinas de Gortari.
Credit: AP.

Figure 7.5–Cuauhtemoc Cardenos.
Credit: El Mundo.

Figure 7.6–Vicente Fox.
Credit: Mexican Government.

Figure 8.1–President Truman and the Shah 1949. Credit: U.S. Government.

Figure 8.3–T.E. Lawrence and Gertrude Bell. Credit: Gertrude Bell Photographic Archive, Department of Archaeology, University of Newcastle Upon Tyne.

Figure 8.2–Muhammad Mossedegh. Credit: TIME Magazine.

Figure 8.4–King Feisal I of Iraq, "Before and After."
Credit: Buchkritik.at/Encyclopedia of the Orient.

Figure 8.5–Abdul-Karim Qasim.
Credit: Encyclopedia of the Orient.

Figure 8.6–Saddam and
the Shah, Algiers, 1975.
Credit: Iran Government.

Figure 8.7–Persepolis Tent City, 1971. Credit: Persepolis Celebrations, republication of Iran Government photo.

Figure 8.9–George W. Bush and George H.W. Bush. Credit: Austin College.

Figure 8.8–Donald Rumsfeld and Saddam Hussein, December 1983. Credit: CNN.

Figure 8.10–Baghdad Burning, 2003. Credit: CNN.

CHAPTER SIX

ARGENTINA'S LAST TANGO

History in Argentina . . . is a process of forgetting.
                                                    —V. S. Naipaul

[She should] walk a mile in their moccasins.
    —Ronald Reagan, commenting on the Carter administration human
        rights coordinator's criticisms of the Argentine military junta

"Basta con el pasado."
                    —President Raul Alfonsin's campaign slogan, 1983

ARGENTINA'S PUZZLE

To the historian of political and economic development, Argentina certainly presents an interesting set of contradictory tendencies. For decades it was widely regarded as Latin America's most developed country, with the highest per capita income and more skilled European immigrants than anywhere else in the Western Hemisphere except the US. On the basis of its rich farms, substantial early investments in railroads, roads, and ports, and "human capital," Argentina's income level had already reached the world's top ten by the late 1920s, on a par with Canada's and well above Japan's. Argentina was also the most cosmopolitan country in Latin America—many members of its elite spoke English with an Anglo accent, took afternoon tea, played polo, cricket, and golf, and sent their children off to finishing schools in England and Switzerland. World-renowned artists like Juan Luis Borges and Mercedes Sosa are from Buenos Aires. Even now, after three decades of economic upheaval, the city remains a slightly rundown combination of Paris and Madrid, with beautiful wide avenues, cafes, more than twenty theaters, and one of the world's best operas. Unfortunately, the opera also now has other associations—it is located right across the plaza where Argentine death squads in the late 1970s sometimes deposited their victims fresh from meat lockers, frozen solid in grotesque upright positions.

Because its early achievements were so great and its prospects so bright, Argentina's deterioration since the 1970s has been even more striking than that of Venezuela, the Philippines, or Nicaragua. What happened? Many historians have focused almost exclusively on internal factors, especially the prolonged political stalemate between the radical left—the union-based Peronist movement—and the military, landowners, ranchers, and well-protected industrialists on the right. This stalemate was rooted in the country's early success as an agricultural exporter. Originally, commodity exports like beef and grain generated high dollar incomes. These, in turn, stimulated imports and encouraged domestic industry—with support from the unions—to pursue import substitution with protection from import competition behind high government tariffs. Unlike Venezuela, much of the export income was captured initially by just a thousand or so large farmers, who, along with British investors, had provided most of Argentina's industrial capital in the nineteenth and early twentieth centuries. The result was a classic case of "Junker" development, with weak liberal institutions, a militant labor movement, a heavily protected, rather inefficient domestic industry, no impetus for land reform, and social polarization.[1]

However, all these domestic factors were reinforced by Argentina's long-standing, incestuous relationship with foreign capital—especially international banks. While Argentina's restrictions on foreign investment and trade were tighter than in Venezuela or the Philippines, the country was extremely open and hospitable to foreign banks since the beginning. In particular, both the government and its private sector came to rely heavily on foreign debt. The business elite, politicians, and generals also acquired a strong taste for foreign bank accounts, holding a substantial share of their wealth offshore, partly to avoid taxes, but also as a safeguard against political turmoil. On the macroeconomic level, this discouraged the growth of domestic capital markets. It also made it more difficult for the state to finance development by taxing domestic private income or capital.

Without any minerals or oil to export and with a chronically weak tax system, Argentina's developmental state came to rely heavily on a combination of inflationary finance—printing money—and foreign borrowing. When the Peronists were in power during the 1950s, the early 1970s, and the late 1980s, the bankers turned away, and the state relied more heavily on printing money, which boosted inflation. When the Right returned to power during the late 1970s, the early 1980s, and the 1990s under Carlos Menem's "neoliberal Peronism," the foreign bankers warmed up again, and the foreign debt soared. Regardless of who was in power, there was a chronic tendency to export wealth, because everyone expected these recurrent cycles of political instability to continue.

Leading international banks—mainly American and British—contributed mightily to this process of anti-development. They not only provided a huge amount of finance for misguided government spending, but they also provided private tutorials to Argentina's elite on how to move vast amounts of their "rich" country's wealth to New York, Miami, and Switzerland. In the case of the military junta that ruled Argentina from 1976 to 1983, their excessively generous lending not only destabilized the economy and helped to provoke a war, but it also financed a brutal reign of terror that Argentina has still not recovered from. In the case of the neoliberal civilian regime that came to power in the 1990s, their behavior—combined with unbelievable oscillations in IMF policy—eventually contrived to make things even worse.

FINANCING DIRTY WARS

One might have thought the Falkland Islands were scarcely worth fighting over—200 rather inhospitable, widely-dispersed islands, located 300 to 2,000 miles off Argentina's coast in the chilly South Atlantic, with nothing more than 4,000 square miles of steep impassable mountains, windswept treeless fields, seals, wild foxes, 4 kinds of penguins, 65 species of sea birds, an abundant supply of illex squid, a few thousand reindeer, 70,000 sheep, and about two thousand English-speaking "kelpers," most of whom make their living from squid and wool. Occasionally there have been claims that up to sixty billion barrels of oil might be located beneath the sea near the islands, but most of these claims have been made by oil exploration companies seeking investors. After nearly a decade of drilling that started in 1994, no commercial quantities have yet been found.

The Falklands' hardy local residents, who are of British descent, have always firmly supported British sovereignty, which has been in place since Britain first seized the islands in 1833. Argentina asserted its first rival claim in 1920, based on the islands' physical proximity, nationalism, and the 1494 Treaty of Tordesillas, by which Spain and Portugal purported to divvy up the New World—even though there was no recorded landing on the islands until 1690. But Argentina only began to press its claim to the islands seriously at the UN in the mid-1960s, during the heyday of anticolonialism. Negotiations with the UK then dragged on until the 1980s. The British were not eager to make territorial concessions that might encourage embarrassing questions about their more valuable colonial residues, like Gibraltar and Hong Kong. But until Argentina's right-wing military junta seized power in March 1976, no one on either side imagined that it made sense to wage modern war over these desolate rocks and their somewhat daft inhabitants.

Enter Argentina's new military junta, circa 1976. Adopting a policy of harsh repression at home and aggressive chauvinism abroad, the junta spent the next seven years waging a domestic war against purported "subversives," building up its military arsenal, engaging in an arms race with its rival fascists in General Pinochet's Chile, and preparing to grab the Falklands in the interest of Argentine nationalism. Of course none of this behavior was completely unexpected. Argentina's military has had strong fascist traditions ever since the 1930s, and the country not only sympathized strongly with Hitler and Mussolini during World War II, but also provided shelter for more than 150 top-ranking Nazis thereafter.[2] But none of these activities could have been paid for without a great deal of help from foreign banks—mainly American, French, and British. From March 1976 to 1983, the junta increased Argentina's foreign debt from $7.2 billion to nearly $46 billion, raising their country's debt-income ratio from ten to fifty percent and boosting the cost of debt service from two percent of national income to a record seven percent.[3] To pull this off, the junta required the active assistance of numerous major banks, including Bank of Boston, Citibank, Bankers Trust, Bank of America, Morgan, Lloyds, UBS/SBC, Deutsche Bank, Barclays Bank, and BNP.

But its best friend by far was Chase Manhattan's CEO and chairman David Rockefeller Sr. Chase loaned the junta more than $800 million directly and syndicated billions more, becoming the leader in Argentine loan syndications during this period.[4] Moreover, the junta's key economy minister Jose Martinus de Hoz ("Joe, the Wizard of Hoz") was a former senior advisor to Chase and a very close friend of Rockefeller's.

Meanwhile, on the other side of the balance sheet, Chase, Citibank, UBS, and Bank of Boston took the lead in helping key members of the junta and its friends stash billions of their own dollars abroad. According to a former senior Chase private banker, David Rockefeller was personally involved in servicing the Argentine generals' foreign accounts.[5] By the early 1980s, Argentina was Latin America's second largest private banking market, second only to Mexico. This provided the junta with a valuable insurance policy, which did not encourage moderation.

For a while, the junta's neoliberal economic policies appeared to work: inflation declined, growth picked up, and investment recovered. While most of the benefits of the junta's policies were concentrated in the hands of the elite, by 1980, Argentina's real per capita income in dollars was its highest ever—almost $15,000.[6] However, it soon turned out that these achievements were more apparent than real. In 1981, the cumulative effect of Argentina's massive foreign borrowing, the global recession, and the Latin American debt crisis combined to produce a severe economic crisis in the country. Inflation topped 535 percent, per capita incomes fell 13 percent, unemployment soared, and real wages plummeted by more than a fifth.[7] While de Hoz's polices had been enormously profitable for the banks, they completely destroyed Argentina's competitiveness, bankrupted the government, and made the whole economy hostage to a debt crisis.

At the same time, the virulently antileftist junta had killed or "disappeared" 30,000 of its political opponents.[8] The military characterized these victims as subversives, urban guerillas, and terrorists. But the vast majority appear to have been completely innocent people who just happened to fit profiles that the military considered suspicious: students, nuns, social workers, union leaders, members of Argentina's liberal Jewish community, journalists, and university professors.

Of course, Argentina's urban guerillas—the Montoneros and the ERP—were not saints. In the 1970s, they conducted numerous kidnappings, including one that extracted a $60 million ransom from one of David Rockefeller's favorite clients, the family that owned Bunge-Born, a leading commodity trader. They also killed a former foreign minister and several executives from GM, Ford, and Chrysler, blew up an Argentine naval vessel, and detonated a bomb at the Federal Intelligence Department that killed eighteen people. But the Army's own investigations later concluded that even at the peak of guerilla activity in the mid-1970s, the country had less than 1,500 guerillas. Instead of dealing with the threat surgically, the junta unleashed a wholesale campaign of terror and extermination. A senior military officer described the junta's repression strategy: "First we will kill the activists, then the supporters, and then the indifferent."[9] The introduction to the official report prepared by Argentina's National Commission on the "disappeared" in 1983 provides one concise view of how this reign of terror worked:

People were taken off the streets, from their homes at night, or from their workplace in broad daylight and driven blindfolded to detention camps. Their houses were looted and their property stolen. Most of them lived the rest of their lives in the detention centers, hooded or blindfolded, forbidden to talk to one another, hungry, living in filth. The center of their lives—dominating the memories of those who survived—was torture. They were tortured, almost without exception, methodically, sadistically, sexually, with electric shocks and near drowning, some buried to their necks and left in the sun and the rain for days. They were constantly beaten, in the most humiliating possible way, not to discover information—very few had any information to give—but just to break them spiritually as well as physically, and to give pleasure to their torturers. Most of those who survived the torture were killed. Disposing of the bodies presented a tactical problem. First they were burned in mass unmarked pits, but later, a more efficient final solution was discovered. The disappeared were loaded into planes with an open door, flown over the sea, and then thrown out. Most of them were first drugged or killed, but some were alive and conscious when they left the plane.[10]

By early 1982, on top of the economic crisis, all these killings and disappearances of innocent people were undermining the regime's support among many middle-class Argentines. While the junta obviously didn't have to worry about winning elections, the rising discontent was affecting its ability to get cooperation from key unions, business organizations, and the church. It was also hurting the junta's pocketbook—tax collections as a share of national income declined from 15.5 percent in 1979 to an abysmal 8.2 percent in 1982.[11] Many unions and large sectors of the middle classes started to oppose the junta openly. In March 1982, there were mass demonstrations against unemployment, inflation, and repression led by the unions and "*Las Madres de Mayo*," which represented the relatives of the disappeared.

ROSARIO I

To rekindle political support for the regime, the head of the junta, President/Lt. General Leopoldo Fortunato Galtieri, decided quite cynically that it was time to start a war. Analysis of the junta's decision to invade the Falkland Islands later revealed that it was made quite explicitly to divert attention away from all its economic and political woes and unite the country around aggressive nationalism.

Galtieri appeared to be the ideal leader for the job. Fit and good looking, with striking blue eyes, he was the son of Italian immigrants, a hard-drinking 1949 graduate of the US School of the Americas in Panama. He had served as commander of the Second Army Corps in Rosario, Argentina's second largest city in the northeastern province of Santa Fe. He was perhaps best known for having set up a political prison and terror laboratory in an elegant home in Rosario, one of more than 340 secret detention centers opened by the military all over the country during this period. In Rosario, Galtieri had presided over a notorious reign of terror, arresting and torturing people for as little as donating books to the wrong libraries. As he told one female prisoner, "If I say you live, you live; if I say you die, you die. As it happens, you have the same Christian name as my daughter, and so you live."[12] When he became commander in chief of the army, the chain of command for Battalion 601— the intelligence unit that ran the entire "dirty war"—reported directly to him.[13]

In December 1981, Galtieri became the junta's third military president, pushing aside General Roberto Viola, who had proved unable to deal with mounting political opposition and the gathering economic crisis. Galtieri dusted off the military's invasion plan for the Falklands, which was code-named "Rosario." The invasion was originally scheduled for July 9, 1982, Argentina's National Independence Day. This was not just for ceremonial reasons. July was winter in the South Atlantic, with stormy seas that would greatly complicate any British counteroffensive. Britain was also scheduled to retire the HMS Endurance by July, its only military vessel near the Falklands. Furthermore, by theory, Argentina would have received a new, more lethal shipment of Exocet AM-39 missiles that it had ordered from France. Therefore, waiting a few months might well have made a huge difference.[14] However, because of the mounting economic crisis—based, in large part on Argentina's excessive debts—Galtieri made the fateful decision to accelerate the invasion by three months, to April 2. He took this decision not only in the face of these tactical disadvantages, but also despite a clear warning delivered in person by former Deputy CIA director and US ambassador-at-large General Vernon A. Walters. General Walters told a drunken General Galtieri late one night in March 1982 that Galtieri should *"have no doubt the US will side with the UK if you invade."*[15]

Another reason why Galtieri ignored Walter's advice was his firm belief that the UK didn't really care enough about the islands to fight hard for them. As he told a TV interviewer at the time, glass of Black Label Scotch in hand, the UK was "a country governed by two women—Queen Elizabeth and Margaret Thatcher. They would not be willing to sacrifice their children." Galtieri knew that his real war aim was to force the British to the bargaining table as fast as possible and negotiate a settlement. He thought this would happen quickly, without much bloodshed: "I expected them to send four ships, not a Task Force."

Equally important, despite General Walters's warning, Galtieri still firmly believed that the US would stay neutral and help pressure the UK into a quick settlement. This view was based in part on his analysis of US interests. After all, the US had long asserted the Monroe Doctrine with respect to European colonies in the Western Hemisphere. Since the 1960s, it had also developed a close working relationship with right-wing regimes in Latin America, including Argentina, Brazil, Chile, Bolivia, El Salvador, Guatemala, and Uruguay—the so-called "Operation Condor" coalition, designed to combat Latin America's leftists. And influential US banks like Chase and Citibank had far more outstanding loans with the government of Argentina than they did with Britain.

The junta also believed that it had many powerful friends inside the Reagan administration. The junta had worked hard to spruce up Argentina's image in the US after the 1976 coup. In 1976, it hired the leading US public relations firm Burson-Marsteller to work on Argentina's "international image . . . projecting an aura of stability for the nation, its government and its economy."[16] In 1979, the junta had retained the influential DC-based lobbying firm of Deaver and Hannalord—the firm led by Michael Deaver, Reagan's campaign advisor and White House deputy chief of staff from 1981 to 1985. Deaver's other clients included Guatemala and Taiwan, which also had serious image problems in the US. To launder Argentina's image, among other things, Deaver saw to it that Economy Minister de Hoz was referenced on several of President Reagan's national radio broadcasts. In one of them, Reagan described the last six years under the junta as "one of the most remarkable economic recoveries in modern history," and added:

> Today, Argentina is at peace, the terrorist threat nearly eliminated. Martinez de Hoz . . . points out that in the process of bringing stability to a terrorized nation of 25 million, a small number were caught in the cross fire, among them a few innocents. . . . If you ask the average Argentine-in-the-street what he thinks about the state of his country's economy, chances are you'll find him pleased, not seething, about the way things are going.[17]

Apparently all these lobbying efforts were helpful. When General Galtieri and General Roberto Viola visited Washington in early 1981, they got a warm reception from Richard Allen, Reagan's National Security advisor, who called Galtieri a "majestic general." In addition to Deaver's lobbying work, this reception may have been due to Reagan's gratitude for Argentina's kind offer to send trainers to advise the *contras* in Nicaragua and army officers in Guatemala and El Salvador on antiguerilla military tactics and interrogation techniques. In fact, the aid provided by Argentina's junta to the *contras* before 1983—compensated by various favors that the US government and US banks provided to Argentina—may have been an early version of the Iran-Contra gambit used later by the Reagan administration to provide off-the-books aid to the *contras*.

These high-level connections were reinforced by other conversations even closer to the events in question. On March 8, 1982, shortly before the invasion, Galtieri met with US undersecretary of state Thomas O. Enders in Buenos Aires. Enders, a career diplomat, had some military experience, helping to choose bombing targets for the US Air Force in Cambodia in 1973. He assured Galtieri that the US had "no interest in the Malvinas," and would maintain a "hands-off" position.[18]

On April 2, the same day that General Galtieri sent 2,500 troops to storm Port Stanley, the Falklands' main city, UN ambassador Jeane J. Kirkpatrick was the guest of honor at a dinner sponsored by Estaban Takacs—Argentina's ambassador to the US—and attended by several leading members of the Argentine military. From Argentina's standpoint, Kirkpatrick richly deserved the honor. She was a "neocon" professor at Georgetown and a former aide to Senator Henry Jackson, who had lost to Jimmy Carter in his bid for the 1976 Democratic Party presidential nomination. In 1979, she wrote a pugnacious piece that attacked Carter's human rights policy and tried to distinguish "moderately repressive" authoritarian regimes—like the Argentine junta— from "totalitarian" states.[19] This theoretical distinction captured Reagan's attention when he ran against Carter in 1980. In 1981, Kirkpatrick was rewarded with the UN ambassadorship. Once in office, behind-the-scenes, she lobbied hard for a neutral US stance on the Falklands. In her view, it was far more important to work closely with the Argentine junta and the other "Condor coalition" members to defeat global communism than to help Britain defend an obscure, anachronistic colonial outpost.

The April 1982 dinner for Kirkpatrick was attended by US general Richard B. Meyers, US secretary of the army John O. Marsh, and US under-secretary for defense Frank Carlucci. All these senior US officials knew full well that the invasion was in progress while they dined. The night before, the UK's ambassador had addressed the Security Council about the situation, and President Reagan, briefed by British intelligence, had called General Galtieri. The General refused to back off, and the invasion proceeded.

Another interesting guest at the April 1982 Kirkpatrick veneration was her long-time friend, Wenceslao Bunge, an Argentine businessman and Harvard Business School graduate. British intelligence described him as "the unofficial diplomatic representative" of Brigadier General Basilio Lami-Dozo, junta member and commander in chief of the Argentine Air Force. In the next few weeks, Bunge actively pressed Argentina's case with Kirkpatrick, the State Department, the White House, the UN, and the UK. He and General Lami-Dozo hoped for a quick diplomatic victory by getting the US to convince Britain's Margaret Thatcher to accept a truce.[20] As we'll see later, he also continued to play a colorful, influential role in Argentina long after the junta and its fellow travelers were an ugly memory.

The friendly behavior on the part of senior US officials and the top US military brass did not exactly discourage Argentine aggressions. The junta was very surprised to learn, therefore, that when push came to shove, as Argentina's UN ambassador later reported, "Señora Kirkpatrick has good will toward our country, but her capacity for action is very limited because of the promises made to the UK, and her differences with the secretary of state." In the interim, Margaret Thatcher was not at all pleased by Kirkpatrick's behavior. She might call herself a fellow neoconservative, but rather than siding with the UK—the United States' long-time democratic ally—she had chosen to take sides with a country that had not only launched premeditated invasions, but also imprisoned, tortured, and murdered thousands of its political opponents, persecuted Jews, and sheltered top-shelf Nazis.

Immediately after the invasion, all ten European Common Market countries sided with the UK, banning all Argentine imports. The US responded meekly at first, while the policy battle raged between Kirkpatrick, her nominal boss Secretary of State Al Haig, and quietly behind-the-scenes, Michael Deaver. Reagan dispatched Haig to London and Buenos Aires for ten days of shuttle diplomacy. In London, Thatcher told him in no uncertain terms that the war would continue until Britain recovered the islands or Argentina withdrew. US neoconservatives might wink and nod at "authoritarianism," but there would be no appeasement of blatant fascist aggression on her watch. Haig agreed and continued to argue forcefully for a pro-UK stance over the next two months, right up until the war's end. He found his efforts repeatedly undermined by Kirkpatrick and White House deputy chief of staff Deaver, who pushed the *contra* agenda and wanted Argentina's help. On June 25, shortly after the war's conclusion, Haig resigned. The Falklands crisis, on top of differences over Israel's invasion of Lebanon, was one of the key reasons. As Haig said later, "There were contacts made with Argentine officials by the White House which were neither discussed with me nor cleared with me and which had the practical effect of confusing the issue. . . ."[21] On April 3, the UN Security Council passed Resolution 502, which demanded an immediate Argentine withdrawal and cessation of hostilities. Argentina, with the support of most other Latin American countries, refused to withdraw, while Britain refused to cease hostilities. Thus, the war continued until the UK decisively defeated Argentina in June.

For a very brief time, the invasion did produce the political effects that Galtieri had been seeking. In early April, less than two weeks after his police had broken up union protests against the junta's economic policies in the Plaza de Mayo, he stood on the balcony of the Casa Rosada overlooking the same plaza, now filled to capacity, and heard the crowd cheer when he promised to give Thatcher a bloody nose. But this support proved to be as fleeting as the Argentine military's willingness to put up a fight. By June, when the invasion had proved to be a fiasco and the dead and wounded were coming home, the support was replaced by revulsion. On June 17, Galtieri resigned in disgrace. In 1986, he was court-martialed, convicted of "negligence" for mismanagement of the war, and sentenced to twelve years in jail. In December 1989, after serving four years, he was pardoned by President Carlos Menem.

All told, Argentina lost 649 men to Britain's 272, plus 10,000 prisoners, all the islands, more than $2 billion in direct war costs, and many billions more in military preparation costs. The war rattled the nerves of foreign bankers and greatly exacerbated the 1982 Latin American debt panic. But things might easily have been worse—with a little better planning and a delay until summer, most military analysts now agree that Argentina might easily have *won* the war. And that, in turn, would have been a disaster for the demilitarization and democratization efforts of countries like Chile, Brazil, and Argentina.[22] Whether or not any particular regime was "merely authoritarian," what Kirkpatrick had forgotten was much less important than the total amount of democracy generated by the international system over time.

Ironically, the main political beneficiary of the Falklands War was not the junta, but Margaret Thatcher. Until the war, her popularity had plummeted to record lows in the face of rising unemployment. But since March 1982, her approval ratings soared. Most political analysts believed that the Falklands was the key factor in her decisive victory in the June 1983 British general elections, which gave her a large majority and helped her stay in power until 1990. A *New York Times* editor commented that "Had Argentina's invasion . . . not happened, it would have had to have been invented."[23]

As for Argentina, ironically, the junta's invasion and defeat ultimately did help to bring about a return to popular government with increased human rights—in the words of some junta critics, "Margaret Thatcher won us our freedom back." The defeat utterly discredited Argentina's repressive, decadent brand of militarism. After all, in the midst of a deep economic crisis, the junta had launched a costly war for a worthless bunch of islands where, even had it won, Argentina would only have become a detested colonialist. It had completely botched wartime diplomacy. From a technical standpoint, it had also managed to lose a sure thing, despite the fact that the Falklands was virtually undefended and eight thousand miles from Britain, and the junta had had years to prepare a surprise attack. This put an end to the junta's adventures with the *contras* in Nicaragua, as well as its aid to El Salvador and Guatemala. It also forced the US to revise its whole strategy in aiding right-wing allies.

In the wake of the defeat, Galtieri resigned on June 17, 1982. Over the next six months, the junta faced mounting protests from war veterans, unions, and human rights groups. The economic crisis continued to worsen. Demoralized, exhausted, and out of ideas, in February 1983 the military announced that it was relinquishing power and scheduled elections for the fall. In October 1983, in the country's first elections since the 1976 military coup, Dr. Raul Alfonsin, a medical doctor, won an upset victory for the Radical Civic Union (UCR), defeating a Peronist candidate to become the country's first freely elected non-Peronist president since 1916.

By destabilizing the junta's economic base and inducing it to launch a premature invasion that ultimately led to its defeat, Argentina's excessive foreign borrowing had actually helped to restore democracy. But if the banks and the US government had simply refused to coddle the dictators in the first place, this salutary result might have been achieved by a much less circuitous, deadly route.

PEACE CRIMES—THE ANATOMY OF "MODERATE" REPRESSION

In the wake of Argentina's defeat and the junta's demise, Argentina gradually learned about the depths to which its "moderately repressive" rulers had sunk. It is worthwhile to review a few highlights of this sordid record, because of the heavy responsibility that the junta's foreign patrons, especially its private

bankers, bear for it. Twenty years after the junta's fall, while some senior leaders are finally being brought to justice, hundreds of other military officers have
avoided punishment. Moreover, the vital role played by the regime's foreign
sponsors has been largely forgotten. Only with the election of President Nestor
Kirchner in May 2003 is this kind of impunity beginning to be undone.

Waging armed combat with opponents who are not entirely helpless was
perhaps just not the Argentine military's long suit. On April 26, 1982, Alfredo
Astiz, a young Argentine lieutenant, surrendered his entire company to British
commandos on South Georgia, the largest Falkland island, without firing a
single shot. Astiz's profile provides a good example of the kind of "moderately
repressive" regime that David Rockefeller financed and Jeane Kirkpatrick
apologized for in advance. By the late 1970s, Astiz, while not much of a
fighter, had established a solid reputation on other fronts. He was a notorious
military torturer who brutalized young women. At the time of his surrender
to the British, he was wanted by Interpol on charges of kidnapping and murdering two French nuns, Alice Domon and Léonie Duquet. He was also
reportedly involved in the murders of at least eight other women, including
a seventeen-year-old Swedish girl, Dagmar Hagelin, whom, according to the
Swedish extradition request, he shot in the neck from behind while she was
walking down the street.[24]

Because Astiz was a prisoner of war, the British did not hand him over to
the French courts at the war's end, but returned him safe and sound to
Buenos Aires. In 1987, he was arrested and held for five months in Argentina,
and then released under the "Due Obedience" amnesty law signed by President Raúl Alfonsin. The law pardoned all those who had been "following
orders," regardless of what they had done.[25] In 1990, a French court indicted
Astiz in absentia and sentenced him to life in prison. In July 2001, he surrendered to an Argentine court, which considered the extradition requests from
France, Sweden, and Italy. In January 2002, these requests were rejected again,
and he was released in Buenos Aires—the only restriction being his inability
to travel outside the country.[26] One woman who had experienced Astiz's
handiwork firsthand recalled, "He was very brave when all he had to do was
murder unarmed women. . . ."[27]

Many other Argentine military officers also committed serious crimes,
including pushing prisoners out of airplanes, stealing and selling babies taken
from pregnant political prisoners, raiding their victims' bank deposits, and
latching on to their farms and homes. Former army commander general Jorge
Rafael Videla, the junta's first president from 1976 to 1981, was a dapper, mus-
tached, urbane fellow who had a taste for English-tailored suits. He also took
a professional interest in the fine points of torture, particularly in understanding how long different victims could hold out under alternative forms of

punishment. In 1985, General Videla was sentenced to life in prison for his role in the death squads.[28] In 1990, he was pardoned by President Carlos Menem. But in 1998, an Argentine judge ruled that Videla could be charged for infant trafficking. More than five hundred babies had been seized by the military from their imprisoned mothers shortly after delivery, often by forced C-sections. Senior officers like Videla had been directly involved. The children were issued new identities and sold to couples seeking adoptions who had friends in the military. Apparently the motivation for this baby trade—in addition to greed—was political: The junta feared that if the orphans were allowed to grow up knowing what had become of their parents, they would become diehard opponents of the military. So it was not enough for the regime to "disappear" adults—they also needed to rob their children of their identities. Because Videla was over seventy by the time of the baby charges, he was permitted to remain under house arrest. In July 2001, he was indicted again for conspiring to eliminate political opponents in the 1970s, after an Argentine judge invalidated the two amnesty laws adopted in the late 1980s.[29]

In 1985, the junta's second president Roberto Viola, a 1971 graduate of the US military's School of the Americas in Panama, was convicted of murder, kidnapping, and torture. He was sentenced to seventeen years.[30] In 1998–2000, baby-stealing charges were brought against junta members Admiral Emilio Eduardo Massera, General Renaldo Bignone—the junta's fourth and final president—and several other senior officers.[31] In late 1983, shortly before the restoration of democracy, General Bignone ordered the burning of all documents regarding missing persons, condemning their relatives to a lifetime of not knowing what had happened to them. Admiral Massera, who also ran the 1978 World Cup soccer franchise, was convicted in 1985 of murdering three Argentines, including Hector Hidalgo Sola, Argentina's ambassador to Venezuela. He was sentenced to prison, but he was freed by President Menem in 1990. However, he was convicted in the baby-stealing case and confined to house arrest. In October 2001, he was also charged with being part of a ring that had stolen the property of three business people who had disappeared.[32]

Even now, the truth about this period is woefully incomplete. However, bits and pieces of the brutal, bank-sponsored regime's story have continued to surface. In the mid-1990s, Adolfo Scilingo, a former naval officer, decided that he could no longer remain silent. In 1997, he testified in a Spanish court that 1,500 Argentine naval officers under the command of Admiral Massera had participated in "death flights," where more than 4,400 political prisoners were flown out to sea, drugged, and dropped into the ocean. He himself confessed to having pushed thirty prisoners out the door.[33] "I thought that we were fighting a war, but it was a genocide," he said. In 1998, Spanish prosecutors charged four other officers, including Astiz and General Antonio Bussi, governor of Tucumán Province and former head of Argentina's Third Army.[34] In 2000, a court in Italy convicted seven other officers *in absentia* of kidnapping and killing Italian citizens.[35]

As for General Galtieri, in November 1999, a Spanish court indicted him and ninety-five other military officers on charges relating to the disappearances of six hundred Spanish citizens during the 1976–83 "Dirty War."[36] Galtieri had already been court-martialed and sentenced to twelve years in jail in 1986, not for human rights crimes, but for professional negligence. But he was also pardoned by Menem after serving four years. However, in March 2001, in the midst of Argentina's deepest economic crisis, a courageous federal judge, Gabriel Cavallo, finally struck down the amnesty laws that had protected thousands of Argentine military officers and "soldiers" accused of such crimes. In July 2002, another judge charged Galtieri and twenty-eight other senior officers with human rights violations. Galtieri, frail and suffering from pancreatic cancer, was placed under house arrest on charges related to the abductions and killings of nineteen Montoneros members while he was Rosario's regional army commander. In January 2003, awaiting trial on these charges, he died of a heart attack.

In August 1997, President Menem announced that Argentina would issue $3 billion in government bonds in compensation to the relatives of the "disappeared." Many families refused to apply for the payments. As one *Las Madres de Mayo* member who had lost her nineteen-year-old son commented, "Life does not have a price." But more than eight thousand families did apply, at $200,000 of bond face value per victim.[37] Unfortunately, because of its renewed debt crisis, Argentina became virtually bankrupt after 2000, so the market price of the "victim bonds" fell to zero. Like all the junta's other debts, the bonds remain unpaid.

ARGENTINA'S FUNNY NUMBERS

Raul Alfonsin's campaign slogan in the October 1983 elections had been "*Basta con el pasado*" (Let's be done with the past). Unfortunately, another key event that month revealed that the past's burden might not be so easy to escape—the completion of Argentina's first foreign debt survey. To date, this October 1983 survey is the only solid evidence on how much foreign debt the military junta contracted and wasted. Along with the junta's victims, most of Argentina's debt history for the period of 1976–83 had also been "disappeared."

Until Argentina's October 1983 debt survey, the total size of its foreign debt was a closely guarded state secret. Jose Maria Dagnino Pastore, economy minister after Galtieri's fall, admitted in July 1982 that "the debt is now over $35 billion" and declared that "the time has come to explain without hypocrisy what the money was used for." A few weeks later, Domingo Cavallo, the junta's undersecretary of the interior in 1981 and its last governor of the Central Bank in 1982, produced a larger estimate that kicked off a bewildering debate. [38] Then in September 1982, Argentina finally admitted that it was $2 billion behind on interest payments, and asked for the IMF's help.

Throughout the fall of 1982, a team of IMF technicians and bankers poured over the Central Bank's debt records in Buenos Aires to get a handle on the precise size of the foreign debt. One Morgan banker recalled their frustration:

> The Argentines would sit across from us and present different numbers every time we met. And none of the foreign banks knew, either. It took Morgan, which was one of the better-organized banks, four months to know what our loans were. Bank of America and Citibank took a lot longer. Meanwhile, the British and the French bankers were not even talking to each other. They were at each others' throats over the Falkland Islands—we almost had fistfights in Advisory Committee meetings. [39]

There were also recurrent rumors—which ultimately proved to be accurate—that the IMF had found more than $11 billion of debt missing from the official accounts. [40]

The pressures for a more rigorous debt audit were mounting because of political events. In February 1983, the military had scheduled new elections for the fall. Foreign banks and the IMF knew that popular opposition against repaying the junta's huge debts was strong, so they raced to sign a new debt rescheduling agreement with the junta before a new civilian-led government took office. Unfortunately, the military kept missing the IMF's economic targets by a mile, which delayed debt restructuring negotiations and debt audit. [41]

In September 1983, with the foreign banks rushing to conclude a debt settlement, an Argentine judge suddenly ordered Domingo Cavallo jailed on treason charges. The judge, an ardent nationalist, accused Cavallo of striking an unconstitutional deal with foreign banks to nationalize private sector debts and refinance Aerolinas, Argentina's national airline. The judge added that "the debt of all firms is in question until we know its overall size." [42] His ruling was eventually reversed, but it precipitated a sharp run on Argentina's peso.

In the midst of all this chaos, the debt survey finally started in October 1983. Bankers and former officials agree that Argentina's debt numbers were, if anything, in even worse shape than Venezuela's had been. In Argentina, there was no foreign debt registration program for loans to the central government, nor for loans to state companies or the private sector. There was also the problem of the Argentine military's foreign debt. This was kept entirely off-the-books, so there is still no precise estimate of its size. After the junta lost the war, few banks were willing to step forward and admit having helped finance it. But most experts agree that the military had borrowed at least $10–12 billion from foreign banks.[43] Most of this disappeared into arms purchases, and quite a bit also ended up in junta member's personal offshore accounts.

Ironically, because of Argentina's close historical ties to the UK, it turns out that a large chunk of this military debt was actually arranged by British banks. During the year prior to the Falklands invasion, Lloyds, National Westminster, and Barclays Bank had packaged more than $2.4 billion in syndications for Argentina, with much of it financing the Argentine military by way of state-owned conduits like YPF, the state oil company.[44] This unprincipled lending helped to finance arms imports, and, as noted, the economic strains caused by Argentina's unmanaged debts were a key factor behind Galtieri's decision to invade. This was not unique: excessive foreign debts have often played a role in precipitating military interventions.[45]

Argentina's October 1983 debt survey turned up just $2 billion of official unreported military debt. But there really was a great deal more. When Argentina halted debt service in 1982, all these loans were quietly written off, never appearing in any official statistics. Some consisted of supplier credits from French companies like Dassault-Breguet and Aerospatiale for Super Etenard and Mirage fighters and Exocet missiles. Other secret loans were obtained by army-owned companies like SOMISA, a steel company, and Fabricationes Militares, or by state banks and nonmilitary state companies that diverted loans to arms projects. For example, two German submarines were purchased by the Argentine Navy in 1979, funded by a $406 million Deutsche Bank syndication that was "officially" made to Banco de la Nación, a state-owned bank.[46] Other key conduits included Aerolinas Argentina and YPF, which absorbed $6 billion. Aerolinas' lead bank was JPMorgan; YPF's creditors included Chase, Lloyds, Barclays, Deutsche Bank, Citibank, SBC, and Bankers Trust. YPF was a military preserve—its chairman from 1981 to 1983 was Guillermo Suarez Mesa, commander of the First Army Corps, who was later convicted of being personally involved in torturing and "disappearing" people.[47] On March 12, 1982, just two weeks before the invasion, two syndicated loans to YPF totaling $242 million were signed in Paris, led by Chase Manhattan and Bankers Trust. Even while US officials like Secretary Haig and General Walters were trying to deter Argentine aggression, US banks and their UK counterparts were quietly financing it.

As in Venezuela, undisciplined borrowing by Argentina's 350 state companies also financed a great deal of funny money. Nearly $11 billion of foreign loans went to unprofitable state entities whose losses totaled more than $2 billion a year.[48] Another large chunk financed military honey pots like the

July 1978 World Cup championships. The junta spent over $700 million on this little party. And it had other costs. To win the championship, Argentina needed a four-point spread over Peru in the semifinals. It won 6-0. Shortly thereafter, Peru received an entire nuclear research facility, courtesy of Argentina.

A substantial share of Argentina's debt also ended up in the generals' private accounts. One Buenos Aires money manager who had strong ties to the military and got "a piece of the action" during the soccer games recalled the spirit of the times:

> Every General had his pet projects. For Jorge Videla, it was the World Cup; for Roberto Viola it was a huge Argentine power dam at Yacyreta; for Galtieri, it was the Malvinas War contracts. The Navy, under Admiral LaCoste, the minister of Social Security, and Admiral Massera, ran the Soccer Cup franchise. They ran the kickbacks on the construction. It was standard—"The country needs it, but everybody's making a dime, so why not?" We called it "butter on the ceiling"—you throw it up and a little bit sticks.
>
> There used to be a barber in Buenos Aires, "Alfredo," who was famous for introducing people to do these deals. I remember one deal with OSN, the public water works, in 1976. The head of the company was a retired military guy. He wanted a $120 million loan, so he went to Chase, Bank of Boston, and Morgan. The "haircut" was ten percent; Chase got the loan. Alfredo's piece was $50,000.[49]

RIDING BICYCLES

As for Argentina's private debts, while Venezuela had *implicitly* encouraged its private sector to borrow and send money abroad, Argentina's Central Bank, under the leadership of de Hoz, *explicitly* provided strong incentives to do so. De Hoz was a colorful figure: a patrician Eton graduate, cattle breeder, professor of agrarian law, and the chairman of Argentina's largest private steel company. He was a fanatical disciple of Milton Friedman's brand of free-market economics. The generals were a bit less concerned with doctrinal purity, so long as de Hoz took care of their soccer games, salaries, bank accounts, and arms imports. But de Hoz also took care of de Hoz. Within days of his father's death, he abolished death duties, avoiding estate taxes on one of Argentina's largest fortunes.[50]

Of course, one reason why right-wing ideologues rose to power in the first place was that many of their predecessors among the Peronists had been equally mad. De Hoz's inheritance from the Peronists in 1976 included high inflation and huge deficits. He responded with a curious mixture of decontrol and increased intervention. On the one hand, he eliminated ceilings on interest and exchange rates and restrictions on foreign investment. Banks that had been nationalized by the Peronists were quietly returned to their former owners, including Chase and Morgan. On the other hand, de Hoz instituted free insurance for bank deposits. After 1978, he also interfered with the peso's free fall, permitting it to become sharply overvalued. His landowner/monetarist prejudice was that Argentine industry was doomed to noncompetitiveness anyway, and that a strong peso would increase import competition and help curtail inflation. Of course, an overvalued peso also pleased the military—the country's largest single importer and one of its largest exporters of dollars to offshore accounts.

In the state sector, which accounted for almost a third of Argentina's national income, de Hoz privatized a few state enterprises and tried to cut spending. But many of these reforms were blocked by the military or the state bureaucracy. To finance his continuing government and trade deficits, de Hoz relied on bankers like Rockefeller. The resulting combination of high interest rates and guarantees against exchange risk encouraged everyone who knew a friendly foreign banker to borrow abroad.[51] The outcome was a huge surge in foreign debt, interest rates, and imports, on top of a crushing recession in the regular economy. Contrary to President Reagan's glowing appraisal of de Hoz's policies, the only sectors of the Argentine economy that performed well during this period were banking, arms imports, luxury imports, large export-oriented farms, the construction of soccer stadiums, and the market for stolen babies. Imports grew by forty percent in 1979–81, even as domestic bankruptcies and unemployment rose sharply. Meanwhile, strikes were outlawed and wages were forced to lag behind inflation. Despite these antilabor policies and the surge in imports, inflation never fell below eighty percent.

But for the banks, it was party time. The exodus of capital flight from the country raged side by side with all the foreign borrowing. Anyone could see that the junta's economic policies, on top of the repression, were approaching a dead end. Financial deregulation, combined with the new deposit insurance program, provided bankers irresistible opportunities to seek new deposits by promising exorbitant interest rates. Domestic banks levered themselves to the hilt and made risky loans, often to their owners' companies. The whole situation became a merry-go-round, which ignored the elementary fact that even a free-market economy requires honest bank inspectors. But the Argentine Central Bank's poorly paid inspectors were for sale to the highest bidder. One Buenos Aires banker recalled:

> You had a situation where, overnight, our bank would increase its interest rates by, say, fifteen percent. The staff would work until 11 P.M. handing out coffee and biscuits to people who queued up to put their money in. We were

promising eighty-four percent, adjusting our rates once a day. And nobody was looking over our shoulder—or if they did, they got paid to look elsewhere. Everyone was doing it. It was a great time to be a bank inspector.[52]

In March 1980, this Ponzi scheme of high-risk loans, government-insured deposits and astronomical interest rates, finally cratered. The country's largest private bank, Banco de Intercambio Regional (BIR), failed. It had to be taken over by the Central Bank. It turned out that BIR had made numerous loans to Panama shell companies that were controlled by its owner, Jose Rafael Trozzo, who fled to Mexico. He had delayed the day of reckoning by borrowing from foreign banks like JPMorgan, bribing de Hoz's bank inspectors, and losing all his bank's records in a suspicious fire. Asked about his extensive credit lines to Trozzo, Tony Gebauer, Morgan's senior vice president for Latin American, explained, "That was soon stopped despite plenty of outside pressure. We didn't like what was going on at that bank." The next three largest private domestic banks in Argentina went under, and their owners went to jail. Eventually seventy others needed to be propped up. As in Chile, Mexico, and many other countries, the bankruptcy of Argentina's domestic banking system was a leading indicator for the bankruptcy of the country as a whole.

But before the collapse, wealthy Argentine investors and their bankers got caught up in an incredible spiral of debt and flight. From 1979 to 1981, under the Seguro de Cambio program, de Hoz intentionally created a situation where knowledgeable insiders could earn risk- and tax-free returns of more than one percent a month, paid abroad in dollars, through an arbitrage scheme that coupled increased debt with flight. A US banker stationed in Buenos Aires at the time recalled:

> We didn't need any credit analysis to justify those Seguro loans. De Hoz and the Argentine government was guaranteeing high returns to its friends, so why not lend? The idea that Argentina itself might stop paying was just too theoretical. De Hoz wanted the dollars to finance the military—he didn't give a shit who brought the loans in or who took them out so long as the money kept flowing. And, quite frankly, neither did we.[53]

Sophisticated investors took advantage of de Hoz's Seguro de Cambio program to construct *bicicletas* (bicycles). To "ride the bicycle," you simply borrowed dollars abroad, registered your new dollar loan with the Central Bank, and then traded the dollars for pesos. Then the fun began. You repaid the loan to your offshore bank under-the-table, usually from your own account. In fact, most of the "loans" were not true loans, but "back-to-back" transactions that leveraged deposits you had already stashed offshore. But you and your banker conspired to tell Argentina's Central Bank that the loans were genuine.

Once registered with the Central Bank, the bogus loans entitled you to buy dollars at very favorable exchange rates in order to "repay" them under the Seguro de Cambio program. Given soaring inflation, the gap between the peso's value when the loans were registered and when they were due was huge. The program became a license for the insider elite and their private bankers to coin money.

For instance, in 1979, someone who borrowed $1 million could trade it for 130,000 pesos from the Central Bank. Without de Hoz's program, he would have needed 180,000 pesos to repay the loan a year later. The guarantee allowed him to buy $1 million for the original 130,000 pesos. Instead of repaying the loan, he strolled down the street to his neighborhood black market dealer and traded the $1 million for 180,000 pesos—an immediate thirty-eight percent profit. Interest on the loan also qualified for special exchange rates and tax deductions. Furthermore, the "loan" provided a convenient explanation if anyone asked where the dollars came from. With creative back-dating of documents and more borrowing, endless variations of this basic scheme were possible. All of them were out-and-out frauds on Argentina's Treasury that added significantly to the country's foreign debt, even as they simultaneously stimulated capital flight.[54]

Of course, ultimately, Argentina's economic czars were responsible for this horseplay. In fact, most of them profited from it. Roberto F. Alemann, who succeeded de Hoz as economy minister from December 1981 to July 1982, went on to become UBS's private banking representative in Buenos Aires.[55] But none of this bicycle round-tripping would have been possible without the *active* collusion of Argentina's largest creditors, including Citibank, Chase, Morgan, The First National Bank of Boston, the major Swiss banks, and MHT. All these members of the global banking *cupola* were deeply involved in crooked deals, while lending heavily to Argentina's government and delivering patronizing lectures about the need for free market-oriented policies in Argentina. They all sat on Argentina's Advisory Committee of Banks in charge of restructuring its debt. And two of Argentina's largest government-owned banks, Banco de la Nación and Banco de la Provincia de Buenos Aires, were also deeply involved in facilitating bicycle round-tripping.[56]

The foreign debt generated by the Seguro de Cambio program totaled $9.3 billion. Most of this simply disappeared into private pockets. All of it was later assumed by Argentina's government. In December 1983, the Alfonsin government asked major banks like Chase Manhattan to report on whether specific loans under this program had been backed up by "borrower guarantees" (foreign deposits, which would have indicated the existence of back-to-back loans). As in the case of Venezuela, the banks simply refused to answer.

Another $5.5 billion of private foreign debt was also nationalized by the government at the behest of foreign banks and leading multinationals. Among the main beneficiaries of that program were Citibank, the First National Bank of Boston, Deere & Co., Ford, Chase, IBM, and Bank of America. All told, Argentina nationalized nearly $15 billion of private debt, most of which was completely fraudulent.

So in December 1983, on his first day in office, President Raúl Alfonsin received several pieces of bad news. First, he learned that Argentina's generals had absconded with more than $1 billion of the Central Bank's reserves. Argentina's coffers were almost empty when Alfonsin took office—only $200 million remained. Second, the October debt survey had identified $44.8 billion of regular foreign debt and $1.2 billion of interest arrears, for a grand total of $46 billion—twenty-five percent above the highest previous estimate.[57] Relative to exports, as of 1983, Argentina had the highest debt burden of any country in Latin America except Bolivia—whose debt had just been restructured by Argentina's Central Bank—and $20 billion of this Argentine debt was due in less than a year. The new debt survey also told Alfonsin that speculative private borrowing and the junta's arms buildup accounted for nearly half of this debt, including $20 billion that de Hoz had borrowed from 1979 to 1982.

Armed with all this, one might have expected Alfonsin to demand a little leniency from the foreign banks. But over the next five years, his new civilian government stubbornly continued to service the foreign debt, signing IMF agreements and cutting back sharply on spending and growth. Despite all these sacrifices, all of Argentina's leading foreign creditors, including Chase, Morgan, UBS, Bank of Boston, and Citibank, basically stopped lending to the country. They claimed this was because of Latin America's overall debt crisis. But many Argentines knew better—the bankers secretly pined for the generals, who had been much more lucrative to deal with. When David Rockefeller Sr., Chase Manhattan's CEO, visited Buenos Aires in January 1986, he was greeted by thousands of angry demonstrators. They might not know precisely where the bodies were buried or even how many bodies there were, but they certainly knew who had helped to pay for the burials.

As in Venezuela and the Philippines, Argentina's heavy debt burden wasn't simply a question of the absolute size of its debt. The same policies that accounted for the debt had also ruined the economy and fostered a costly war. By 1983, in addition to the debt, the junta's short-term legacy included average incomes that were twenty-five percent below their 1975 levels, a sharp fall in investment, high inflation, and a huge amount of private wealth that was permanently outside the country.

THE SEQUEL

Most of the key foreign patrons of Argentina's junta readily shifted their concerns to other targets once it lost power. Among the key principals, Chase's David Rockefeller, Sr. retired as its chairman in 1981 and then focused his attention on numerous private foundations. With respect to Latin America, his most important roles were as honorary chairman of the Council on Foreign Relations; the chief benefactor of Harvard's David Rockefeller Center for Latin American Studies, which he founded in 1994; and founder and international cochairman of the Americas Society, a post he shared with ex-Citibanker William V. Rhodes.

Jeane J. Kirkpatrick continued to serve as Reagan's UN ambassador and White House cabinet member until 1985, staunchly supporting the administration's other Latin American ventures in countries like Nicaragua, El Salvador, and Guatemala. She then became a professor at Georgetown and a senior fellow at the American Enterprise Institute. Michael Deaver continued to serve as Reagan's deputy chief of staff, played a major role in his 1984 campaign, and then left in 1985 to join the leading D.C. PR firm, Edelman Worldwide, as its vice chairman.

In Argentina, one of the more interesting career paths was that of junta lobbyist and Kirkpatrick friend Wenceslao Bunge. In 1983 he turned up as the founder of an organization called the Argentine-American Forum.[58] By the 1990s, he had become the key advisor, confidant, intermediary, and principal spokesperson for Alfredo Yabrán, a Syrian émigré and Argentine billionaire who was very close to Carlos Menem. In August 1995, Yabrán was described by Finance Minister Domingo Cavallo in testimony before Argentina's Congress as Argentina's "head of the mafia" and "Public Enemy No. 1." According to Cavallo, Yabrán, who ran a huge courier-service business, had benefited greatly from Argentina's privatization program, employing a large number of ex-military officers who were veterans of the "dirty war" as security guards and couriers. Cavallo told a TV interviewer, "Yabrán is no ordinary businessman. He uses front men and is the head of a criminal association that controls the postal service and aims to control the issue of passports and identity documents—everything that has to do with the movement of people and goods."[59]

At the time, Argentina's Congress was voting on a bill to privatize the postal system, and Yabrán was the leading candidate to acquire the entire system. In fact, his companies were among the leading beneficiaries of Argentina's privatization program in the 1990s. Yabrán also reportedly had close ties to former members of the junta, like Admiral Emilio Massera.[60]

Investigative journalists described him as "Menem's P. C. Farias," a busy beaver who allegedly played a key role in arranging a triangular trade in drugs, arms, and money laundering that involved supplying arms and Condor II missile technology to Syria's President Hafez al Assad, Croatia, and Ecuador in the 1990s.[61] Argentine journalists determined that many calls were placed between the Presidential Palace and Yabrán's office telephones during this period.[62]

In July 1996, Domingo Cavallo lost his job for a while over these accusations, and in August 2002, right after his own release from prison, he retracted them, under strong pressure.[63] However, in 1998, an Argentine judge ordered Yabrán's arrest on charges of having ordered the murder of José Luis Cabezas, a photojournalist who had dared to take Yabrán's picture—the first ever published. In May 1998, Yabrán was found dead with a gunshot wound to his head. The case was ruled a "suicide," but Alfredo Castañon, a former aid to Menem, commented, "It is important to know whether he committed suicide himself, or was *forced* to commit suicide."[64]

CAVALLO'S FOLLY—DE HOZ II

Meanwhile, on the economic front, the Alfonsin government labored through its five-year term under the burden of the heavy debts it inherited from the military. With no debt capacity, a weak tax base, little foreign investment, and renewed demands for social spending from Argentina's militant working classes, his government had increasingly relied on the Central Bank to finance its deficit by printing money. By the end of the 1980s, not only was inflation out of control, but most state enterprises were completely starved for finance, long-term credit had disappeared, and most businesses and consumers were living from day-to-day.

To get out of this situation, Argentina chose to follow the global trend toward neoliberalism. The experiment lasted a decade and ultimately ended up in a debt crisis that was even more profound than the one that had developed under the junta. And, sadly enough, it occurred with the help of the very same foreign banks that had been so influential back then—plus the IMF, the World Bank, and the IDB. As before, only the banks made money on the experience.

President Carlos Menem was elected on a Peronist party ticket in May 1989. He took power in the midst of hyperinflation, with prices rising more than one thousand percent a year. To deal with the hyperinflation, Menem took a hard right turn, following in the footsteps of Venezuela's Carlos Andes Perez and Mexico's Salinas. His key appointment on the economic front was

Domingo Cavallo, the junta's last central Bank governor. To everyone's surprise, Menem made Cavallo his foreign minister in 1989–90, and then his
finance minister in 1990–96.

Cavallo, a well-connected Argentine with a Harvard Ph.D. in economics,
proceeded to design a package of neoliberal reforms that included all the
usual elements—take the rapid privatization of state enterprises, sharp budget
cuts, the liberalization of trade and capital markets, privatization of the social
security system, and deregulation. But his most unique contribution was the
ultra-neoliberal April 1991 "Plan de Convertibilidad." The plan was essentially an attempt to put the Central Bank and Argentina's inept political classes
in a monetarist straightjacket, to end hyperinflation once and for all. It created a currency board that pegged the peso's value at one peso per US dollar. Adopted by Argentina's Congress, the plan required another act of Congress to undo it. The purpose of this was to guarantee that anyone who held
pesos could count on being able to convert them to dollars. The idea was that
such a guarantee would encourage people to hold more pesos. Since the Central Bank was required to meet any selling pressure on the peso by automatically selling foreign reserves, and since reserves are a key component of the
money supply, this would automatically cut inflation—which was always the
result, in monetarism's simple-minded view, of "too much money chasing too
few goods." Furthermore, key economic interests, knowing that the peg was
there and that Argentina would collapse if it were abandoned, would supposedly believe the peg would last forever, and be more willing to trade, invest,
lend, and maintain deposits in Argentina.

In effect, the plan was a bootstrap, an attempt to substitute a rigid rule for
good government and for Argentina's total lack of financial credibility. The
plan placed several huge bets: first, that Argentina's economy would be able to
generate enough dollar exports to service all the foreign investment and new
debts encouraged by liberalization and privatization; second, that global credit
markets would finance Argentina until it did so; third, that the dollar would
maintain a stable relationship against the currencies of other key Argentine
trading partners in Europe and Asia, like the euro and the yen; and fourth, that
the process of globalization going on all over the developing world would not
interfere with Argentina's exports or its financing. Unfortunately, all of these
assumptions eventually proved to be problematic.

For the time being, however, Cavallo's jerry-built scheme created the
appearance of success, just as de Hoz's first round of "neoliberal chemother-
apy" had done back in 1970s. From 1991 to 1994, inflation fell sharply,
deposits returned to the banking system, credit markets surged, and foreign
capital rushed in—especially foreign bonds and bank loans, since many privatizations were financed with debt. Buoyed by the surge in investment, cheap

imports, and a return to normalcy after hyperinflation, the economy picked up. Real per capita incomes averaged 2.9 percent a year from 1992 to 1998, and real consumption increased, while inflation fell sharply. The entire economy became "dollarized"—contracts for everything from utility bills to loans and bank accounts were denominated in dollars, as if the peso were almost a functionless appendage. Argentines, never reluctant to spend money and easily persuaded that they lived in a First World country, started to borrow and buy again as if they had already obtained the permanently higher real incomes that they so obviously deserved.

Politically, from Menem's standpoint, the quick fix was a huge success, becoming the main factor in his reelection to a five-year term in May 1994. It commanded widespread support despite the fact that it mostly benefitted the top tier of the wealth distribution and foreign creditors. While all classes benefitted from lower inflation, the harmful effects on unemployment, poverty, social spending, and the country's financial stability took longer to become apparent. Their connection to the "peg" was not transparent to most people. As late as December 2001, the same month that Argentina declared a default on all its debts, opinion polls still showed that a majority of Argentines still supported convertibility. The fact that very few Argentines understood the link between convertibility and the country's collapse only underscored the difficulty of designing complex policies on the basis of opinion polls.

Up to this point, Cavallo's neoliberal adjustment program resembled that of de Hoz. But unlike de Hoz, Cavallo did try harder to attack Argentina's state sector by privatizing Argentina's largest state enterprises, especially during Menem's first term. He sold off most of the crown jewels, including YPF, which CSFB privatized for $3 billion, Latin America's largest privatization at the time; ENTEL, the state telephone company, which was divided in half and sold to a consortium of banks and two state-owned European telephone companies, Telefonica de Espana and France Telecom; Aerolineas Argentina, the national airline; the national railroad system; SOMISA, the steel company; Obras Sanitarias de la Nación (OSN), the military's favorite sanitation company, whose operations in Buenas Aires were bundled into a thirty-year concession awarded to a consortium led by the Belgian-French company Suez Lyonnaise des Eaux, another sanitation company in La Plata and Bahia Blanca, conceded to Azurix Corporation, an affiliate of Enron; toll roads, TV and radio stations, power plants, gas companies, and twenty state-owned banks, acquired by foreign banks like Citigroup, FleetBoston, HSBC, Banco Bilbao, and Lloyds TSB.[65]

Many of these privatization opportunities were state-owned monopolies that just needed capital to succeed. With help from the World Bank/IFC, Cavallo cleaned up their balance sheets and offered them at incredible prices to private investors. The deals also provided opportunities for generous fees and lending to foreign banks, plus enormous corruption payoffs for leading members of the government. All this was wildly popular with the Argentine elite, foreign investors like Telefonica, and the banks that structured and financed most of these deals. By 1994, Menem and Cavallo had become neoliberalism's poster boys, lionized by the IMF, the World Bank, Wall Street, and Argentina's traditional lead banks, now consolidated into JPMorgan Chase, FleetBoston, Citigroup, CSFB, and Bank of America. In the 1990s, these banks issued more than $88 billion in Argentine-backed dollar bonds. By the end of Menem's second term, 154 state enterprises had new private owners.

CUL-DE-SAC

Despite its early successes, by the late 1990s, Cavallo's neoliberal strategy had run into a brick wall. By then Argentina had exhausted all the easy reforms—new sources of revenue, politically acceptable spending cuts, and other quick fixes were getting harder to come by. On the other hand, it seemed that the hard work of genuine product/market innovation, microeconomic strategy, and productivity improvement did not receive nearly as much attention from Argentina's government or its business elite.

On the revenue side, stiffer tax enforcement, which had never been Argentina's strong suit, was bitterly resisted by the elite. While tax collection did increase somewhat from its miserably low level of the 1980s, it remained stuck at a modest 12–13 percent of national income. Indeed, the national tax take was even lower, once the flourishing underground economy is taken into account. And less than a fifth of all tax revenue came from income taxes.

After 1998, economic growth also slowed to a crawl. The economy became increasingly constrained by the need to maintain tight money to support the vaunted peso. The strong peso made imports and foreign loans artificially cheap, even as it stifled exports. Export growth slowed and the trade deficit increased. The country struggled to maintain the dollar peg under the impact of the 1995 Mexico crisis and the sharp 1998–99 devaluations by Asia, Russia, and especially Brazil, Argentina's largest customer and competitor. The dollar—artificially strengthened by the Internet bubble in the US stock market also rose against most other currencies. Since Argentina's peso was tied to it, that made everything Argentina produced more expensive, except for its exports to the US. For the majority of Argentine exports that were sold elsewhere, the combination of the rigid peg and the sharp devaluations by its competitors made its exports much less competitive.

Despite all its reforms, Argentina's competitiveness and productivity did not improve nearly enough to offset the stronger peso. The result was that from 1990 to 2000, exports as a share of GDP averaged just 9.2 percent—about the same as during the 1980s, and well below the 15 percent export share achieved by Latin America as a whole and 24 percent by all developing countries during the 1990s. From 1991 on, Argentina's external balance—exports minus imports—was consistently negative.

Despite mounting evidence that convertibility was a dead-end policy and that the peso was overvalued, Argentina refused to devalue until it was far too late. There were several reasons. For Cavallo and other technocrats, including the IMF's top economists, convertibility had become an *idée fixe*. Given Argentina's peculiar experience with hyperinflation, this obsession was partly understandable. But eventually any such peg needs to have some flexibility. On the contrary, Cavallo and his successors decided to "double down," taking on even more foreign debt on the bizarre assumption that this would somehow make investors more confident that the policy would never be abandoned—because the cost of doing so would be astronomical.

Once again, Argentina had entrusted its future to doctrinaire authoritarian personalities whose egos were wrapped up in half-baked theories. But the convertibility policy was not designed in a vacuum—there were also powerful interests at stake. These included local companies and banks whose revenues were received in pesos, but had borrowed heavily abroad in dollars; anyone who had loaned such companies money; middle-class consumers, who enjoyed artificially cheap imports; those who didn't care, because they traded in commodity markets that were priced in dollars or in markets where demand was not price-sensitive; and private bankers and speculators who made a good living out of moving dollars in and out of Argentina freely, running the same kind of "roundtrip" schemes that had surfaced in the late 1970s. As its elite and bankers speculated against the peg's lifespan, in the late 1990s Argentina once again became a major capital flight supplier, just as the early 1980s. It also became a leading money-laundering center—including among its clients the senior members of Mexico's largest drug cartel in Juarez, who started moving money through Citibank accounts to Argentina.[66]

Argentina's increasingly unsavory financial situation was also complicated by the fact that by the late 1990s, most of the large privatizations had already been completed—there was not much "family silver" left to sell off. And the results had been very mixed. At the microlevel, many privatizations—at least those outside the banking sector—increased efficiency and profits, and reduced government spending by removing loss-making state enterprises from the budget. At the macrolevel, however, by rushing through all the privatizations at once, the government have reduced the average prices obtained for the deals, since the world only had so much demand for Argentine risk. Furthermore, the congestion also increased unemployment levels dramatically. No longer protected by public-sector unions, an average of forty percent of workers at privatized companies lost their jobs. With so many laid off at once, the labor market had trouble absorbing these workers. Not surprisingly, sixty percent of them reported that their earnings fell sharply after dismissal. These factors added significantly to prolonged unemployment and poverty. By 2000, after a decade of neoliberal reforms, only the top ten percent of the population had experienced any increase in their real per capita incomes since the early 1990s.

Many of the gains from privatization were also pocketed by the new owners. In sectors like sanitation and telephony, the acquired virtual private cartels. Since Cavallo's neoliberal government had little patience with antitrust laws, price controls, or other regulations, there was nothing to compel these companies in the absence of effective competition, there was nothing to compel these companies to share their efficiency gains with the public, by way of lower prices or better service. In fact, *regulation*, neoliberal doctrine notwithstanding, was an important pre-condition for successful privatization. Otherwise, privatizations often just raised profits, increased unemployment, and worsened the distribution of income and wealth.

Furthermore, while Argentina's privatizations brought in some foreign investment, many of them were financed by foreign loans, so they actually added to Argentina's foreign debt burden. Except for YPF, the oil company, few privatizations added anything to exports. As in Brazil, Argentina's privatizations also artificially postponed the day of reckoning for its overvalued currency, making the 150 percent real devaluation that ultimately did occur in January 2002 that much more dramatic. Finally, the 1993–94 privatization of its social security system proved to be an absolute disaster. Not only did it aggravate the budget deficit by reducing government revenues, forcing the government to take on more debt, but it also provided a pool of pension fund assets that desperate officials like Cavallo, in the final hours of his struggle to maintain convertibility in 2001, could latch on to and invest in worthless government bonds. When these bonds were declared worthless in 2002, Argentina's hapless working class lost much of its life savings.

Overall, Cavallo's neoliberal program eventually proved to be a maze of contradictions. A postmortem by leading Argentine economists concluded, "It seemed as if the system was overdetermined."[67] Tight money, the strong peso, and high real interest rates conflicted with the need for higher growth, lower unemployment, increased tax collections, and a lower budget deficit. Rapid privatization conflicted with the need for a more competitive exchange rate, an improved trade deficit, and lower unemployment. Social security privatization conflicted with the need for government revenues and a reduced debt. Over time, convertibility conflicted with the need to generate exports, improve the trade balance, and control debt. The rapid liberalization of financial markets ultimately conflicted with the need to generate a stable environment for free trade. And the neoliberal insistence on implementing all these reforms at once meant that they collided in the hallway, and left almost everyone worse off—except the elite, their bankers, and selected government officials.

BAILOUTS AND "SILENT RETREATS"

As the financial noose began to tighten around Argentina's neck in the late 1990s, it came to rely increasingly on two of its most vocal neoliberal cheerleaders, the IMF and the World Bank. The IMF was consistently overoptimistic about the country's policies during this period. In 1998, Argentina arranged a $2.8 billion IMF standby credit. At the time, the IMF predicted that Argentina's economy might dip a little in 1998–99, but would then "recover potential output by 2000"—implying a 3–4 percent real GDP growth. Supposedly unemployment would "decline gradually."[68] In March 2000, the IMF's standby line of credit was expanded to $7.2 billion, and the IMF projected 3.5 percent real GDP growth in 2000, "which would accelerate to 4 percent in subsequent years."[69] In fact, real growth turned out to be −3.4 percent in 1999 and −0.5 percent in 2000, and unemployment soared to 15 percent.

In January 2001, the IMF raised its standby commitment again to $14 billion as part of a $39.7 billion package for Argentina, arranged with help from the World Bank, the IDB, Spain, and private banks. The IMF projected that Argentina's real GDP growth in 2001 would be 2.5 percent. US treasury secretary Lawrence Summers, another strong supporter of Argentina's neoliberal strategy, commented that "Argentina is a country that has a strong record of reform during the 1990s, and that should serve it well."[70] Stanley Fischer, the IMF's acting managing director, was also extremely bullish:

> The new Argentine government has embarked on a strong economic program aimed at promoting the recovery and sustained growth of the economy, with continued price stability, and an external current account maintained within financeable limits. . . . Market reactions to the program have been positive. . . . These developments bode well for a recovery of confidence in the period ahead.[71]

In September 2001, just three months before Argentina defaulted on its entire foreign debt, the IMF expanded its standby credit to $21.6 billion and increased Argentina's actual use of this money to $8.3 billion. The IMF predicted that if neoliberal policies were continued, real growth in 2002 would be 2.5 percent—despite the fact that its own estimates showed Argentina's 2001 growth rate as negative.[72] In fact, Argentina's actual real GDP growth rate turned out to be −3.4 percent in 2001 and an incredible −10.9 percent in 2002—the lowest growth rates in Latin America and Argentina's worst since at least World War II.

Throughout all these overpredictions, the IMF continued to insist that Argentina stick religiously to Cavallo's original neoliberal script. Indeed, the farther Argentina departed from the IMF's rosy projections, the more blood-letting the IMF demanded of it. A secret September 2000 Technical Memorandum of Understanding between the IMF and Pedro Pau, Argentina's Central Bank governor, indicates the kind of harsh regimen that the IMF demanded in exchange for all these credits. Even in the midst of a deep recession, with unemployment and poverty at record levels, the IMF's Memorandum of Understanding demanded that Argentina continue slashing its budget deficit from $5.3 billion to $4.1 billion in 2001, cut emergency unemployment benefits from $200 per month to $160, cut civil servant salaries another 12–15 percent, and slash pension benefits—all the while maintaining Cavallo's rigid peg of the peso to the dollar.[73] The IMF also demanded the privatization of the nation's largest remaining state-owned bank—Banco de la Nación—a move that was especially controversial because Banco de la Nación held the mortgages on more than fourteen million hectares of prime Argentine farm land. In effect, as Argentina's nationalistic farmers quickly noted, this would have amounted to turning over the country's best land to the foreign banks.

So by early 2001, after a decade of high real interest rates, a rigid peso, slow growth, and increased import competition, Argentina's economy was knee-deep in bankruptcies, unemployment, and poverty. Tax collections and export earnings were plummeting, adding to the government's deficit blues. Despite the IMF's generosity, the country was on the brink of exhausting its capacity to take on any new foreign loans to defend the peso. By early 2001, Argentina's $280 billion economy had accumulated a $146.2 billion foreign debt. This was more than twice the $65.2 billion that Cavallo and Menem had started with in 1989, and more than three times the $46 billion debt that was inherited from the junta in 1983. Debt service was by far the largest single item in the government's budget, accounting for more than forty-one percent of all government spending and ten percent of national income. In fact, but for debt service, Argentina's government, having followed the IMF's prescriptions by ruthlessly slashing all noninterest government spending, would have actually run a $10 billion budget surplus in 2001. But its $16 billion debt service bill more than offset this surplus, forcing it back in the red. That year alone, debt service cost the country fifty percent more than it spent on education and almost as much as it earned from all foreign trade.

Meanwhile, even as the IMF and the World Bank were putting more of their public money at risk in Argentina, sophisticated private investors and banks were heading for the exits, insuring themselves against the possibility that Argentina's iron peg policy would fail. This was an odd spectacle, with public money being liberally applied to subsidize a policy that was ostensibly designed to promote free markets, even as private capital was voting with its feet and fleeing the country.

Capital flight, which Cavallo had proudly claimed to have squelched, took off again in the late 1990s. By 2001, an estimated $130 billion had left the country, more than half of it flowing to foreign bank accounts.[74] The cumulative value of all this privately owned "flight wealth" outside the country was almost certainly much greater than the value of Argentina's foreign debt, but there was no way for the government to tax the dollar earnings that it generated. To stem the tide, the government was compelled to bribe foreign bondholders and banks to continue to hold Argentine bonds. Yields surged to more than seventeen points over LIBOR by July 2001, and by November 2001, just before default, to sixty-one percent. At those interest rates, default risk was clearly on everyone's mind. And the high rates implied that every single penny of the $40 billion public bailout arranged by the IMF, the World Bank, and other public lenders effectively went right out the back door to pay interest costs to private lenders and finance private capital flight. The Central Bank's reserves continued to fall throughout the year.

Since Argentine banks owned a large share of Argentine bonds, the growing perception that the government might default spooked many private depositors and eventually led to a run on the banks. Indeed, Argentina's government later blamed small savers for decapitalizing the banks in an attempt to justify the deposit freeze of late November 2001, which barred more than twelve million small depositors from withdrawing more than $1,000 per month from their accounts, forcing many of them into hardship or even bankruptcy.

However, a closer analysis reveals that the worst—and first—"asset strippers" and flight artists were not small savers, but the private foreign banks. From February to November 2001, they quietly reduced their credits to Argentina's financial system by more than $25 billion. During this period, deposits from individuals fell by just $18.6 billion, mostly just after July, by which time most of the "big bank" flight had already occurred.[75] At the same time, the banks also reduced their assets outstanding—mainly loans—by $37.4 billion. More than sixty percent of these reductions were accounted for by Argentina's top ten foreign banks, including Citibank, FleetBoston, BBVA, JPMorgan Chase, and HSBC. These banks also arranged to swap most of the unguaranteed Argentine bonds in their portfolios for $40 billion in government-guaranteed loans and to convert other liabilities back into domestic peso debt at favorable exchange rates.[76] Long before Argentina's small savers decided to take their savings out of the shaky banking system therefore, the world's most sophisticated banks decided it was time to beat an "orderly, silent retreat"—under the cover of the IMF's glowing forecasts and generous loans.[77]

MEGASWAPS AND MEGADEFAULTS

In March 2001, Domingo Cavallo returned to office as economy minister under President Fernando de la Rua. His predecessor, Lopez Murphy, had tried and failed to implement an orthodox program of revenue increases and budget cuts, and he had missed all the IMF's targets. But the global financial community was convinced that Cavallo could work his old magic, at least for them. To get him to return, Argentina's Congress had given him special emergency powers to change economic policy by decree.

Cavallo's return was the occasion for a euphoric celebration on the part of the First World banking establishment. David Rockefeller, Citibank's William Rhodes, CSFB's David Mulford, and former World Bank president Robert McNamara—all members of the Americas Society—travelled to see Cavallo's inauguration in Buenos Aires, where they declared themselves to be in "profound sympathy" with the new economy minister.[78] This was no accident—just like twenty years before, Cavallo's most important priorities were to defend the peso and, barring that, find ways to help foreign banks and bondholders get their money back. On March 20, his first day in office, Cavallo called his old friend Dr. David C. Mulford, who had served as undersecretary and assistant secretary of the US Treasury from 1984 to 1992, under the Bush and Reagan adminstrations. Mulford had managed the US government's entire foreign debt strategy. In the late 1980s, he had been in charge of implementing the Treasury's Baker/Brady Plans for restructuring Third World debt. As we've seen, those plans ultimately did little to reduce Third World debt, which was sixty-six percent higher in the year 2000 than it was when Mulford left public service in 1992.

But at least the contacts and experience that he gained at the US Treasury had permitted Mulford to reduce his own debt burdens. After the Treasury, Mulford became chairman of Credit Suisse First Boston's International Group, in charge of brokering debt swaps and privatization deals for developing countries. As Argentina's debt woes mounted in 2000–01, Mulford saw a golden opportunity. When the anxious Cavallo called him for ideas, he suggested that the time was ripe for an unprecedented debt swap, substituting Argentine bonds that were about to be due for an even more massive amount of new, longer-term foreign debt.

Just a few weeks later, in May 2001, Cavallo announced that Mulford's Credit Suisse First Boston (CSFB) had assembled a syndicate of six other banks, including JPMorgan Chase, Citigroup's Schroder Salomen Smith Barney (SSSB), Hongkong Shanghai Bank (HSBC), and the Spanish banks Banco Santander, Banco Popular/Banco de Galicia, and BBV/Banco Frances. They had agreed to handle what later became known as the *Megacanje* (Megaswap), one of the largest and most irresponsible debt swaps in developing-country history. This was the second of Argentina's record-setting debt swaps. The first, in February 2001, had involved just $4.2 billion. Before that, the previous record was Venezuela's $500 million swap in July 1998, which exchanged shorter-term debt for twenty-year bonds with a fourteen percent yield. In his June 2001 megaswap, Cavallo offered to exchange $29.5 billion of Argentine bonds, including $13 billion maturing between 2001 and 2005, for $63.8 billion of new bonds that would only be due in 2005–13. The swap package also included about $2.3 billion of entirely new debt.

At first glance, almost all Wall Street analysts pronounced this deal a home run, a brilliant scheme that would buy Argentina the time it needed to get itself in order.[79] Cavallo predicted that it would restore growth to six percent or more and eventually reduce Argentina's debt burden. Mulford described it as "essential to long-term success in restoring Argentine growth."[80] The IMF issued a statement saluting "the successful conclusion of the debt swap offer . . . which should permit a substantial reduction of the gross financial requirements through 2005." It was overscribed by eager holders of existing bonds, including many foreign investors, less than six months before Argentina went belly-up.

Whatever the merits of the megaswap for Argentina were, Mulford's syndicate of foreign banks made a killing on it. The seven banks split a 0.55% commission on the deal—$140 million—just for placing the new bonds. They also got a windfall in the form of bonuses that Argentina paid bondholders to convert, including higher interest payments, since most of them had old bonds to exchange. And as was later revealed in charges filed against Cavallo and the banks in Argentina's federal court in 2002, they also pocketed an additional $150 million by secretly revising the terms that had already been approved by Argentina on the eve of the swap.[81]

As several more careful observers noted at the time, the swap's fine print contained much cause for concern. The new debt introduced by the swap carried much higher yields. The trade-off was unusually unfavorable to Argentina—compared with the 12.1 percent yields that Argentine debt maturing in 2010 carried in February 2001, for example, the new debt promised yields of 15–17 percent. It also promised to increase Argentina's long-term debt burden significantly in exchange for a rather modest short-term debt reduction. So by 2005, unless economic growth absolutely exploded in response to the swap, it would dramatically increase Argentina's already astronomical debt-service burden, not lower it.

Argentina's megaswap also sent a strong signal to sophisticated investors that the country was so close to default that its officials were spending all their time worrying about financial cosmetics. From a slight distance, the notion that a country already heavily indebted could fix its problems by going even deeper into hock was counterintuitive. The transaction clearly distracted Cavallo's attention from more serious policy alternatives for debt reduction, like negotiating tougher terms with Argentina's creditors to slash debts to a more sustainable level, or abandoning the IMF's fixed exchange rates and devaluing the peso.

Far from deferring default, as these side effects and complications came to be appreciated, the swap actually made default more likely. This was consistent with the quiet exodus of the big banks from the market. In the wake of the swap, critics started to poke holes in the pro-swap propaganda put out by the IMF, Argentina's government, and the syndicating banks. One leading Columbia finance professor described the results of the transaction as "jumping out of a thirty-story building."[82] Another leading Wall Street banker described it as "a bit of near-term debt service relief for a huge increase in the debt burden. . . . If they weren't insolvent before the swap, they almost certainly will be insolvent in three to four years."[83] Even Michael Mussa, the IMF's former chief economist, later admitted that the megaswap was "an act of desperation by a debtor who can promise anything in the long run, in exchange for relatively modest short-run relief."[84] The leading international credit agencies agreed with these criticisms. On May 6, two days after the debt swap was announced, Standard & Poor's Corp. downgraded Argentina's long-term foreign debt to "B." This was the third downgrade in six months, placing it on the same dismal, subinvestment par level as Nicaragua, Venezuela, and Paraguay.[85] Moody's and Fitch soon followed suit.

In June 2001, just as this swap was unfolding, Cavallo's main political sponsor, former president Carlos Menem, was arrested and charged with leading a conspiracy to ship $100 million of illicit weapons to Croatia in 1991 and Ecuador in 1995, violating international embargoes on arms sales to both countries. According to the charges, Menem had signed three presidential decrees authorizing the sales by Fabricaciones Militares, officially to Panama and Venezuela, but in fact to these other destinations, with the support of the army chief of staff General Martin Balza, defense minister Antonio Erman González, and presidential advisor Emir Yoma.[86] Menem was also being investigated on charges of allegedly taking a $10 million bribe to help cover up Iranian ties to a 1994 bombing that killed eighty-five people at a Jewish com-

munity center in Buenos Aires.[87] In the course of the inquiries, it was determined that Menem had at least $10 million in two Swiss banks accounts at
UBS (Geneva) and Banque du Gotthard (Zurich) in the names of his ex-wife,
his daughter, and Ramon Hernandez, Menem's personal assistant.[88] Eventually, in November 2001, Menem was released, when Argentina's Supreme
Court—several of whose members he had appointed—dismissed the charges.
But the case sent shocks through Argentina's already shaky financial system.

Despite the initial "success" of the megaswap, by July 2001, yields on
Argentine debt had climbed another fifty percent, capital flight was surging
again, and people were beginning to speculate openly about the prospects for
default. At this point, Cavallo persuaded his friends at the IMF to provide one
more bailout, releasing $8 billion from its standby lines in August. He also
appointed Mario Blejer, a senior IMF economist who had worked for the
IMF for twenty years, as Central Bank governor. But these measures failed to
stem the tide. In September 2001, Stanley Fischer—one of Cavallo's best
friends at the IMF—gave his farewell address and left to become vice chairman at one of the few clear beneficiaries of the IMF's lending to Argentina—
Citigroup.

With yields on Argentine bonds soaring above twenty-nine percent, Cavallo grew increasingly desperate. He flailed at academic economists who criticized his debt swap, calling them "mad intellectuals."[89] He tinkered with
taxes and pension fund contributions, introducing a tax on financial transactions—a belated recognition that perhaps financial markets had become a little too perfect. He also tried another megaswap, involving more than $60 bil-
lion in government bonds. Designed by Merrill Lynch's Jacob Frenkel, it
pressured pension funds, banks, and insurance companies to exchange their
existing bonds for new ones backed by future tax revenues, but promised a
maximum yield of only seven percent, with repayment delayed an extra three
years. Cavallo rationalized this last-ditch measure on the grounds of equity
and affordability:

> Any reasonable person knows that Argentina cannot grow if it has to pay
> interest on its debt that ranges between eleven percent to twenty-five per-
> cent—and in the case of some provinces, up to thirty percent a year. [We]
> seek to ensure payment on the basis that Argentina is viable and to stop try-
> ing to pay [interest rates] that only reflect the march of Argentina towards
> default. It's a question of telling the truth.

But banks are not noted for responding to such appeals. From their perspective, given Argentina's incredibly risky situation, the terms of Cavallo's new
swap were perhaps the most easily refusable offer ever made. Conspicuously
absent from the offer was any Brady Plan-like debt guarantee by the US Trea-

sury, the IMF, or the World Bank. By then, the IMF had already decided to cut its Argentine losses. With Stanley Fischer gone and Argentina continuing to miss its IMF targets by a mile, US treasury secretary Paul O'Neil was looking askance at further generosity. Since US bank exposure to Argentina had already been substantially reduced by the 'quiet retreat,' the IMF had no political support for disbursing any more loans. Indeed, there were even reports that it was thinking seriously about recommending that Argentina devalue. In a final plea, Cavallo dispatched President de la Rua to Washington DC to meet with President Bush, who backed the debt swap plan, but didn't offer any financial aid. Credit rating agencies like Fitch viewed this last debt swap rather differently than President Bush; they classified it as a "distressed exchange" that put Argentina in default.[90]

As all these other measures failed to produce results, Cavallo turned his back on his free-market roots. At the end of November, he froze all private bank deposits. The freeze put an end to convertibility by establishing exchange controls. In early December, he confiscated the assets of all pension funds—including those that had been created by his social security reform—and forced them to invest their cash in Argentine bonds. He also tried to slash the salaries of public employees, which had already been sharply reduced over the past decade, by another thirteen percent.[91] As usual, Cavallo, the banks, and economists at the IMF and the World Bank underestimated the popular opposition to such policies. These measures only succeeded in provoking a full-scale uprising, including riots and looting throughout Buenos Aires on December 20–21 that left twenty-seven people dead, one thousand injured, and more than two thousand in jail. Argentina had not seen such popular opposition to its government since June 1982, after the Falklands debacle.

On December 20, Cavallo resigned. President de la Rua followed him into retirement on December 21, fleeing the country in a helicopter. On December 23, his interim replacement, President Adolfo Rodriguez Saa, announced that Argentina would default on $95 billion of commercial foreign debt. This was the largest debt default in developing-country history. It affected more than sixty percent of Argentina's entire foreign debt, which by then had reached $155 billion. Eventually the country also halted debt service on most of the remaining debt for over a year.

On January 1, 2002, Eduardo Duhalde, another Peronist, was sworn in as the fifth president in less than a month. One of his first acts was to officially abolish Cavallo's peg, permitting the peso to float freely for the first time since April 1991. Free to seek its own value, the peso suffered a real depreciation of 150 percent in one month. Trade collapsed and unemployment soared. The depreciation was partly due to an overreaction to all the bad news, but it validated all those who had long maintained that the currency was greatly overvalued. To stem the outflows and prevent even more banks from failing,

Duhalde introduced a policy called "pesofication," which forcibly converted more than $60 billion in dollar deposits in Argentine banks into pesos and further strengthened exchange controls. The forced exchange was mandated at 1.4 pesos per dollar, well below the black market rate. A year later, the peso was trading at 3.15 per dollar.

By the time Cavallo and his clever neoliberal friends in the international banking community were through, Argentina's banking system had collapsed; its pension system was worthless; the political system was in chaos; leading privatized enterprises like YPF, the telephone companies, and domestic banks had been delisted by the stock exchange; free capital markets were out the window; those foreign investors who could move their money had disappeared; and the domestic elite had also moved more of their liquid wealth outside the country. This time around, Argentina had not needed the junta to destroy its economy—its intransigent neoliberals and their allies in the international banking community had been quite sufficient for the task.

ROSARIO II

In the town of Rosario, General Galtieri's hometown, a wig maker in February 2002 advertised that, because of the peso's collapse, he could no longer afford to import raw materials and would buy hair locally. The response was overwhelming. More than four hundred people showed up in two days, including several who peddled twenty miles on bicycles just to collect three to four dollars for their hair. "We paid for some hair of poor quality," the factory owner commented. "But we did it because people were desperate. They didn't have money to buy food, and they even offered us their children's hair." When a truck carrying two dozen cattle to a local meatpacking plant overturned, a crowd of four hundred people quickly gathered and butchered the animals on the spot to feed their hungry families.

By April 2002, official unemployment in Argentina had reached twenty-four percent and Cavallo was (temporarily) in jail, charged with helping President Menem facilitate the illicit arms sales to Croatia and Ecuador in the 1990s. Only half of those still employed had full-time jobs; sixty percent of the population had fallen below Argentina's $110/month poverty line. For those still lucky enough to have jobs, wage cuts and involuntary increases in work hours became standard. Consumption of food and medicines fell sharply, and an estimated twenty percent of Argentine children—2.3 million—were malnourished, with scores dying. In Buenos Aires, it became common to see whole families begging together. Each night, up to a hundred thousand *cartoneros* prowled the streets, searching for food in garbage cans and trying to earn a few dollars by recycling waste materials. Middle-class Argentines were reduced to selling their furniture and other household goods to make ends meet. Aid workers told heartrending stories of fastidious older gentlemen, carefully dressed in suits and ties, waiting patiently in breadlines each morning. In June 2002, Telecom Argentina, one of the privatization program's proudest achievements, announced that its net equity value had fallen to $30 million, less than two percent of its value in January 2002. Apparently most Argentines were having so much trouble affording necessities that basic phone service had become a dispensable luxury.[92] Whoever could afford it either emigrated or moved their money abroad. In 2002–03, Argentina experienced an exodus of both financial capital and skilled labor. In late 2002, the country also defaulted on all its debts to the World Bank and the IMF, joining the ranks of Iraq and Zimbabwe as countries that had also defaulted on loans from these institutions. In March 2003, Argentina's Supreme Court ruled that Duhalde's "pesofication" decree had been illegal and that domestic banks owed Argentina's depositors at least $10 billion in compensation. But there was no money to pay them.[93]

As for the architects of this disaster, from April to June 2002, Domingo Cavallo was jailed on illegal weapon sales charges, but was soon released. In September 2002, to help Cavallo out, New York University's Stern School of Business appointed him distinguished visiting professor. David Mulford and Jacob Frenkel returned to their respective posts at CSFB and Merrill Lynch, and Stanley Fischer joined Citigroup, where he served alongside former Treasury Secretary Robert Rubin, the chairman of Citigroup's Executive Committee. Lawrence Summers became president of Cavallo's alma mater, Harvard University. Released from prison in November 2001, the seventy-year-old Carlos Menem and his thirty-six-year-old beauty-queen wife turned their attention to the April 2003 presidential elections, which he lost to Nestor Kirchner, the progressive governor of a southern province.

All this happened in a country that is still the world's fourth largest food exporter, with fifty million cattle and thirty-seven million people—Latin America's cultural capital, which also once boasted that it was the continent's most developed country. Most observers agree that it may take decades to recover from this latest debacle. Hans Tietmayer, head of Germany's Bundesbank, remarked in 2002 that "Argentina is condemned to insignificance, probably forever."[94] Tietmayer may well be wrong—after all they have been through, Argentines are certainly among the world's most resilient people. But it is true that far from being done with the past, this rich/poor country continues to be haunted by it. And this is not only because of its own leaders' admittedly gargantuan mistakes, but also because of its long-standing incestuous and ultimately quite toxic relationship with people like Rockefeller, Kirkpatrick, Fischer, and Mulford, and institutions like Chase, Citibank, UBS, and CSFB.

CHAPTER SEVEN

BANKING ON DICTATORSHIP

When you cut the tail off a dog, you don't cut it an inch at a time.
—Professor Milton Friedman,
advice to General Pinochet, Santiago, March, 1975

Who knows what political system works best? All we ask is, can they pay
their bills?
—Thomas C. Theobald, Vice Chairman, Citibank, 1981

We would bring in the money every day, and the money would literally go
away the next day.
—Angel Gurria, Mexican Director of Public Credit

TRACKING GENERAL STROESSNER'S LOOT

In 1989, I received a call from a friend who'd been involved in the search for Marcos's assets. General Alfredo Stroessner, Paraguay's long-time dictator, had just been overthrown, and its new attorney general was in New York City looking for help. My research assistant and I agreed to meet with him. We explained that "dictator treasure hunts" usually took years, and they often only recovered a small fraction of the loot. We also explained that unless Stroessner had left behind lots of personal banking records, the search would be almost impossible. But the attorney general was determined, partly because he wanted to expose the regime's numerous crimes.

It turned out that either General Stroessner had really been very careful, or the new government wasn't sharing all its information with us. But after my assistant spent a few weeks in Asunción, we stumbled on an approach to the investigation that yielded surprising new evidence on where Latin America's longest-standing military dictator had done all his private banking. . . .

One of the global debt crisis's few redeeming features is that it helped to rid the world of some noxious dictatorships. In some cases, like Iran, the successor regimes offered little improvement. But in other cases, human rights violations and corruption declined. At least the notion that unelected technocrats who have unfettered discretion will do a better job with economic policy has finally been discredited. General Alfredo Stroessner's regime was one of those that crumbled. The son of a Munich brewmaster and an officer in Paraguay's artillery unit, he seized power in 1954 at the age of forty-two.

With the help of rigged ballots, censorship, a vigilant secret police, and graft, he and his party—the Colorados—proceeded to win the next eight elections with more than ninety percent of the vote. By February 1989, Stroessner had become the world's oldest dictator, well ahead of Indonesia's Suharto and Zaire's president-for-life Mobuto.

Stroessner's longevity was certainly not due to his tolerance and generosity. His opponents faced long prison terms, exile, torture, and death. Paraguay also became a sanctuary for all sorts of right-wing criminals on the lam, including Dr. Josef Mengele, the Auschwitz doctor who holed up there for twenty years and could often be found drinking beer with "*die Alte Kameraden*" in Asunción's German bars; former Gestapo agents Auguste Ricord and Christian David of "French Connection" fame, who made Paraguay a key transit point for heroin; and convicted murderers of General Pinochet's opponents in Chile.[1] Despite such unsavory guests, by all the standards of the dictator's handbook—stability and enrichment, if not geographic expansion—Stroessner was a huge success. Before his regime Paraguay had had 22 Presidents in 27 years. Surrounded by Brazil, Argentina, and Bolivia, with only 3.9 million people to defend its rich cattle, cotton, and soybean farms, it was constantly at war, one of which in the 1870s had cost it four-fifths of its male population. Stroessner's internally-focused brand of fascism brought the country stability, peace and new sources of illicit income, while his German-trained secret police kept the opposition divided and voiceless. He struck profitable deals with his neighbors, including two hydroelectric projects that greatly enriched his own family as well as many Brazilian and Argentine officials. He also made himself useful to his fellow fascist regimes in Brazil, Chile, Argentina, and Bolivia, in projects like Condor. And until the very end, Stroessner was also a master at distributing the fruits of power widely enough to tranquilize potential rivals.

For example, General Andres Rodriguez, a key supporter of the 1954 coup and commander of Paraguay's US-trained First Army Corps, was permitted to acquire Cambio Guarani, Paraguay's largest exchange house; TAGSA, an air taxi service; the Aeroclub of Paraguay, which owned a valuable airstrip near Asunción; several cattle farms; and an immense white-and-yellow mansion that was built as a miniature version of Versailles. His daughter Marta married one of Stroessner's two sons.[2] Asked how he got so rich on a meager army salary of four hundred dollars per week, Rodriguez's answer was simple: "I gave up smoking."[3] In 1976, he was reported to have facilitated drug exports to the US, and in 1984, his chief of staff (and the future police chief) was accused of importing large quantities of chemicals needed to make cocaine.[4]

Under Stroessner's long reign, a growing share of the economy disappeared off the books. Paraguay never quite became the international banking haven that Panama did—it lacked Panama's central location and strong US relationship, which was rooted in the Panama Canal. But Paraguay did master most of Panama's other black arts. Officially its exports in the 1980s and 1990s averaged just $500–800 million a year and consisted mainly of cotton and soy; in fact, they averaged more than $1.5–2 billion, and consisted mainly of contraband: electronics, whiskey, soy, sugar, coffee, gold, perfume, and drugs. A huge market also developed for fraudulent passports, illicit arms, and stolen goods— Brazil's car thieves supplied half of Paraguay's eighty-five thousand cars.[5]

With the help of this invisible economy, up until the Latin American debt crisis in the early 1980s, Paraguay's legitimate economy performed rather well. Incomes grew at an average rate of 1.4 percent from 1955 to 1972 and then accelerated to 3 percent until 1982. The growth spurt took place mainly because of the $20 billion Itaipu Dam. General Stroessner became very close to the project's organizers, especially Brazil's Jose Costa Cavalcanti, the director general of Itaipu Binacional. Brazil loaned Paraguay $400 million and channeled hundreds of millions more to Paraguayan engineering, insurance, and construction companies, including several owned by General Stroessner himself.[6]

Costa Cavalcanti is hard to forget for another reason. In 1982, Chase's International Private Banking department in New York mistakenly mailed several of his bank account statements to the wrong address in Brazil. The recipient happened to be a member of the opposition PMDB Party. In 1986, the statements came into the hands of Dilson Funaro, Jose Sarney's assertive second finance minister, and eventually to me. The statements show that Costa Cavalcanti's Chase accounts contained no less than $138 million— quite a hefty sum for a former general and lifelong public utility executive.[7]

In any case, despite its vibrant underground economy, Paraguay's growth slowed considerably after 1982. Spending on Itaipu and Argentina's massive Yacyreta-Apipe Dam peaked, there were several bad harvests, and the global debt crisis crimped Paraguay's trading partners. The country also started to feel the burden of its own $2.4 billion debt. Much of this had disappeared into poorly conceived projects, like a $500 million French cement plant that failed to work.[8] About $1 billion was owed to Bank of Boston, Citibank, Chase, Lloyds, American Express Bank, Bank of America, and BNP. Another $400 million was owed to Brazil, $416 million to the World Bank, and $400 million to the IDB.[9] By 1984, Paraguay had contracted a serious capital flight problem: its foreign assets came to be worth more than half its debt.

All these problems, plus Stroessner's age and illness, eroded his political base. In the late 1980s, a succession battle erupted between General Rodriguez's traditionalists, who favored a greater role for the Colorado Party, and the "militants" led by Stroessner's oldest son Gustavo, who favored a nepotistic solution to succession. Their rivalry broke out into the open at a contentious party convention in August 1987. In late 1988, the traditionalists were propelled into action by a destabilizing series of events. Stroessner entered the hospital and appeared to be sinking fast. At that point, he appointed Gustavo, who had no piloting experience, as Air Force colonel, and the militants pressured General Rodriguez to cut the defense budget and retire more senior officers. In February 1989, General Rodriguez and the First Army launched an attack on the palace that took 250 lives and forced the Stroessner family dynasty into exile to Brasilia, where Costa Cavalcanti made everyone feel at home."[10]

The long-suffering Paraguayan opposition received the news with mixed feelings. They recalled that an earlier General Rodriguez had seized power in 1814, sealed the country off, and ruled by decree for twenty-six years. But to everyone's surprise, the new General Rodriguez made pro-democratic moves. He freed political prisoners (except those just arrested), ended censorship, invited all exiles home, and announced new elections in May. He also promised to recover Stroessner's foreign assets to "pay the external debt with this fortune."[11] The opposition had little choice but to go along, and the elections took place too soon for them to put up much of a fight. Three months later, Rodriguez won the presidency with sixty-eight percent of the vote, becoming Paraguay's first freely elected president in fifty years, notwithstanding his status as a Class-I drug dealer.[12]

For our purposes, the most interesting thing about all these events is that they opened up a rare window on the private banking behavior of Latin America's oldest dictatorship. The paper trail to Stroessner's assets was thin, but he left one important set of clues: records of all international telephone calls he and other militants made the year before they were exiled. These records aren't absolutely conclusive; we don't know what transpired during the calls. But they do show the overall pattern of the dictator's foreign banking and other foreign relationships. They also challenge the conventional wisdom about where General Stroessner did his banking.

Most observers had assumed it was Switzerland or Austria, given his German origins and his occasional public conflicts with the US. But these phone data reveal that his bankers were in fact employed by Paraguay's largest US "creditors"—a striking example of the debt-flight cycle in action.

In the year before the 1989 coup, the records show that Gustavo Stroessner placed numerous calls to Citibank International Private Banking's Miami office, specifically to the account officer in charge of Paraguayan clients. He also called the private banking departments of Banco Exterior, Riggs National, Bank of Boston, Credit Suisse, Florida governor Jeb Bush's Private Bank and Trust Company in Miami, SBC, Republic National, Hong Kong and Shanghai Bank in New York, and Arias, Fabrica, and Fabrica—Panama's leading law firm. Other members of Stroessner's inner circle made similar contacts. Cesar Romeo Costa, Paraguay's Central Bank president, apparently made numerous calls to the banker handling Paraguayan clients at American Express Bank's

International Private Banking Group in New York. Manuel Gonzalez Llamas, the husband of Graciela Stroessner (the General's daughter) and a leading shareholder in Gustavo's Bancopar, placed many calls to the Miami offices of Citibank's International Private Banking Group and Credit Suisse. Jose Alberto Planas was Gustavo's former schoolmate and an investor in his Alfa Beta Construction Company. He placed calls to the New York office of Chase's International Private Banking in New York and the Miami offices of Lloyd Bank's International Private Banking, Credit Suisse, and Total Bank. Juan Enrique Nogues, the son of Stroessner's former personal secretary and an investor with Gustavo in Vipar S.A., which operated gambling casinos, placed calls to Miami's Florida National Bank. Mario Abdo Benitez, the General's personal secretary and the owner of CIE, which bought Itaipu's turbines, made calls to Bank of Boston, Lloyds, Sudameris, and Chase. He later admitted to having accounts at all of them. Delfin Ugarte Centurion, Stroessner's minister of industry, placed calls to Lloyds and Citibank and admitted to having accounts there. He was also apparently a client of Arias, Fabrica, and Fabrica.

The phone data also reveals interesting patterns in Paraguay's overall haven banking relationships. The following table, based on data obtained from Paraguay's attorney general, summarizes the destinations of 2,753 calls by seven of Stroessner's closest cronies during the year before the 1989 coup:

Destination	# of Calls	% of Total
Florida	805	29%
No. Virginia	287	10%
New York	80	3%
Wash. D.C.	67	2.5%
Missouri	52	2%
Pennsylvania	43	2%
Texas	42	2%
New Jersey	38	2%
Other US	197	7%
(Total US):	1661	61%
Switzerland	434	16%
U.K.	190	7%
Spain	155	6%
France	85	3%
W. Germany	82	3%
Other non US	146	5%
(Total Non US):	1092	39%
Grand Total	2753	100%

Table 8.1

Overall, this evidence provides clear support for the hypothesis that the US—Miami in particular—was the Stroessner clique's main banking haven and trading post. We also note the unusually large number of calls placed to northern Virginia, a place not usually regarded as an international banking center. Was that just another kind of haven relationship?

CHILE'S "MIRACLE"

I remember the Chilean coup of September 1973 very clearly. I was attending a graduate economics course at Harvard taught by a protégé of Professor Milton Friedman. One of my fellow students, Sebastian Pinera, a member of one of Chile's oldest families and the future owner of the airline LanChile, got word halfway through the class that Allende had been ousted. He was ecstatic—"We won!" he cheered. The professor shared in his delight. Like many other US economists, he saw the overthrow as a victory for the neoliberal doctrines preached by leading University of Chicago economists like Friedman and Arnold Harberger, who both later consulted directly for Pinochet's junta. Over the next twenty years, "Los Chicago Boys" came to exert a strong influence on Chilean economic policy. The label was a little unfair to Chicago—there were also many Ivy League disciples of hard-shell free market doctrines. Dr. Jose Pinera, my classmate's brother, was also Harvard trained. He later became one of the main architects of Pinochet's labor policies, which banned strikes, closed union shops, privatized pension funds, and sharply cut real wages, jobs, and unemployment benefits. In hindsight, Pinochet conducted the first in a series of experiments by the New Right that culminated in the neoliberal programs of Margaret Thatcher, Ronald Reagan, and a lengthy list of Third World imitators. In First World democracies, their programs were moderated somewhat by the need for popular support. In countries like Chile, Mexico, and Argentina, however, where the lines between rich and poor were starker and the political systems were rigged, much less time was wasted on democratic niceties. To their credit, a few principled conservatives were bothered by the resulting alliance between dictatorship and liberal economic reform. But many others got lost in bogus distinctions between "authoritarian" and "totalitarian" regimes. In Chile's case, the resulting repression produced more than four thousand disappearances and extrajudicial killings, thousands of secret arrests and tortures, and sixteen long years without free elections, in a country that had previously been one of Latin America's most democratic countries. As Herr Friedman reportedly told General Pinochet at a Santiago audience in 1975, "When you cut the tail off a dog you don't cut it off inch by inch. You cut it off at the root."

But these points are very general, and repression is very concrete. I remember a 1974 lecture by Chilean economist Orlando Letelier, who was killed in 1976 by a car bomb planted by the DINA, Pinochet's secret police, in Washington D.C. And I remember Victor Jara, a talented Chilean folk singer and guitarist whose music I greatly

admired. When the junta seized power, he was arrested and transported to a soccer sta-
dium in Santiago where "political" prisoners were held. The police took him out in front
of the crowd and they cut off his hands. . . .

The overthrow of Salvador Allende's elected Popular Unity government in September 1973 was greeted with jubilation by Chile's propertied classes. He'd been elected with a thirty-six percent plurality in 1970, and the Popular Unity coalition's support increased to forty-four percent in the March 1973 congressional elections. But the elite was eager for a change by any means. From 1968 to 1973, at first under Christian Democrat Eduardo Frei Montalva and then Salvador Allende, government spending as a share of GNP had increased from fifteen to forty percent. A third of large farms and many private companies had been nationalized at low prices. There was seven hundred percent inflation and frequent shortages of consumer goods, and Chile's foreign debt had reached the unprecedented level of $2.5 billion. Foreign investment dried up and flight capital was pouring into accounts at Bankers Trust, Chase, and JPMorgan—Chile's leading creditors.

The CIA, multinationals like ITT, and the US government certainly played a prominent role—with a hefty dose of financial chicanery—in the 1970–73 coup activity that followed. But intervention had not started there. According to former CIA agent Philip Agee, who had been stationed in Uruguay in the early 1960s, John M. Hennessy—chairman of Credit Suisse First Boston (CSFB) from 1989 to 1996—had been assistant manager at Citibank's Montevideo branch in 1964 and reportedly helped transfer substantial funding to the campaign of Eduardo Frei Montalva, who was running for president against Allende. Frei won the election and served as Chile's president from 1964 to 1970. In the early 1970s, Hennessy became assistant secretary of the treasury for international affairs in the Nixon adminstration, in charge of coordinating economic pressures against Allende's government.[13] In 1974, Hennessy returned to Wall Street, where he became managing director of First Boston Corp., which was later acquired by Credit Suisse.

Despite the CIA's involvement, the sufficient conditions for the 1973 coup against Allende were provided by a Franco-like alliance of military officers, the Catholic Church's hierarchy, the top ten percent of landowners and industrialists, and the next twenty percent in the income distribution—the middle class. Immediately after the coup, they began to get what they thought they wanted.

The junta turned to a small band of inexperienced but supremely self-righteous economists—Los Chicago Boys—who had been mentored by University of Chicago economist and future Nobel laureate Professor Milton Friedman and Professor Arnold Harberger. After Pinochet took power, there was actually a prolonged period when several different economic camps competed for the junta's favor. But Friedman and Harberger, dean of the University of Chicago's Economics Department, tipped the balance when they visited Chile in March 1975. Since the 1950s, with help from the Rockefeller and Ford Foundations, Harberger had developed a close relationship between the University of Chicago and Chile's Catholic University, where he had taught as a visiting professor. With support from the Rockefeller and Ford Foundations, scholarships were provided for bright young Chileans who wanted to study economics. Many of these Chicago-trained economists returned to Catholic University to teach, and they later served in Pinochet's government. Their trip was sponsored by Javier Vial—head of the business group BHC, one of Chile's largest conglomerates, and the eventual owner of Banco de Chile, the country's largest private bank at the time, and sixty other companies. He was also a very strong supporter of Pinochet's dictatorship, on personal terms with the General.[14] Friedman reportedly received $30,000 for the three-day trip. His wife Rose objected to the visit because Pinochet's hard right regime and the goose-stepping Chilean military reminded her of Nazi Germany. Professor Friedman tried to assuage her guilt by requesting the release of two Jewish political prisoners in the custody of Pinochet's police. Unfortunately, the two Jewish prisoners were never located.

Just one month after the visit, in April 1975, the junta introduced an orthodox, monetarist "shock plan," along the lines that Friedman and Harberger had recommended. Professor Friedman's Chicago-trained protégé Sergio de Castro replaced Fernando Leniz as minister of the economy. Other key neoliberals on Pinochet's economic team included Pablo Baraona, president of the Central Bank, Alvaro Bardon and Jorge Cauas Lama at Treasury, Rolf Lüders as treasury minister and minister of the economy, and Juan Carlos Mendez as director of the budget.

This tiny band's shared vision of Chile's future was one that later became common among neoliberal Third World governments—a Latin version of a low-wage, export-oriented Asian tiger, with weak unions, low inflation, privatized pension funds, and a minimal state—apart from the police, the military, and the national copper company, most of whose income went to the military. To pursue this anti-Marxist utopia, they started out with a sharp, recessionary shock. They banned strikes, abolished price controls for food and housing, and slashed tariffs from a hundred to ten percent in just two years.

The junta also introduced Latin America's most radical privatization program ever. In 1973–74, more than 250 nationalized companies were returned to their former owners, and 200 more were sold off at bargain prices. These were not the middle-class privatizations of France, Japan, or the UK, where the buyers included millions of small investors. Like other developing countries, Chile had a very thin capital market, and hard times had made it even thinner. The big buyers at this fire-sale were a handful of closely held groups like Javier Vial's and Cruzat-Larrain's, which owned most of the local banks and had very strong ties with foreign banks.[15]

All these changes set the stage for the dictatorship's 1977–81 phase, which was described at the time by *The Wall Street Journal's* neoconservative editorial page—in even more glowing terms than it had reserved for the Argentine junta—as "the Chilean economic miracle." Indeed, during this brief period, when the economy was recovering from the sharp recession that Los Chicago Boys had engineered, growth averaged 5–8 percent a year. But what was perhaps most miraculous was the regime's inability to foresee that its economic policies—in addition to increasing poverty and inequality—were about to cave in on each other, completely bankrupting the country and forcing the nationalization of the entire private sector.

By 1977, the junta had wiped out any organized political opposition and achieved most of its early economic goals. But the neoliberal ideologues pushed it to new extremes. Under Dr. José Pinera's radical 1979 Plan Laboral, the government abolished closed shops for unions and tried to privatize everything from health care and pensions to education. The 1980–81 pension fund privatization substituted a "fully funded" system administered by privately managed pension funds owned by institutions like Citigroup and Aetna. They came to dominate the new, highly concentrated private system that replaced the old "pay-as-you-go" government system. But this pension reform was probably the most successful of the neoliberal reforms.[16] Others succeeded only in cutting social spending, while military spending and sacred cows like the nationalized copper company were spared. The copper company was famous because of the uproar it provoked when Allende seized it from Anaconda in 1971. But Pinochet kept it nationalized—a secret law gave the military ten percent of its profits. So even under the junta, Chile's largest enterprise and exporter remained "socialist."

In any case, the junta's most important neoliberal experiments—and worst mistakes—concerned macroeconomic policy. The point man was Dr. Sergio de Castro, a Los Chicago Boy who became Pinochet's second finance minister in 1979. Like Argentina's de Hoz, de Castro was a strict believer in the monetarist view that the best way to fight inflation in small economies like Chile was by eliminating tariffs, deregulating capital and trade, and maintaining a fixed exchange rate. So he fixed Chile's peso at thirty-nine to the dollar and held it there from July 1979 until June 1982. With copper prices in a slump and the size of the state sector shrinking, this was only possible because foreign banks were willing to lend money hand-over-fist to Chile's private sector. Foreign banks were sympathetic to Pinochet's conservative economists, much as they had been to Argentina's, and they were flush with cash and very competitive, given Chile's high real domestic interest rates.

So, just as in Argentina, many domestic borrowers took advantage of fixed exchange rates and the temporary generosity of foreign bankers to make lucrative back-to-back deals. Javier Vial, the sponsor of Friedman's 1975 visit and Chile's richest man by 1978, acquired control over Banco de Chile in the late 1970s and used it as a front to borrow heavily from foreign banks like Bankers Trust and Chase. When he was its president, Banco de Chile, in turn, reloaned the dollars to Vial's other private companies, including several based in Panama, like Banco Andino. All these shenanigans became public after Vial's empire cracked in 1983. In 1997, after a 14-year investigation, he was sentenced to 4.5 years in jail for bank fraud, and former Economy and Treasury Minister Rolf Lüders, who had owned ten percent of BHC, was sentenced to 4 years.[17] Chile was stuck with Vial's debts when the bank failed and had to be nationalized. All this was no surprise to his foreign bankers. One former Bankers Trust officer, who had personally handled Vial's Panama accounts, told me, "We knew he was lending to himself, but no one wanted to pull the plug."[18]

As a result of de Castro's policies, Chile's private foreign debt boomed during the "miracle" years. In 1981 alone, $6 billion in new credits was issued by foreign banks, mainly to leading domestic private banks like Banco de Chile, Banco de Santiago, Banco Internacional, and Banco Colocadora, whose groups owned a huge equity stake in Chile's private sector. From 1980 to 1982, private foreign debt doubled; by 1982 the total foreign debt had approached $20 billion—two-thirds of it private. The Central Bank repeatedly warned that it was not responsible for the private debt, but it allowed the spree to continue. Given all the "cheap" dollars and low tariffs, imports also soared—luxury imports became Chile's equivalent of flight capital.

The whole situation finally began to unravel in May 1981 when Crav, a leading sugar company, failed. The real crunch came in the summer of 1982 when the Latin American debt panic dried up new loans, forcing Chile to devalue and tighten interest rates—a lethal combination. By January 1983, unemployment was thirty percent, and the six top private banks and the country's two largest private groups, Vial and Cruzat-Larrain, had folded.

At this point Finance Minister de Castro began to get intense pressure from foreign banks like Chase and Bankers Trust to "nationalize" the private foreign debt. For a while, he stuck to his free-market principles, reminding them of his earlier warnings that such a move would be no more justified than Allende's nationalizations and that this was, after all, private foreign debt, freely contracted, presumably with compensation for the risks of default built into the interest rates.

But the banks were not concerned with such abstract principles. In January 1983, they quietly cut off Chile's foreign trade credit lines, to the point where oil tankers en route to Santiago started to turn around and head home. De Castro was forced to resign, and his replacement quickly declared that the junta would assume responsibility for the private foreign debt (though not its offshore flight assets.) In the words of one Chilean banker, "Pinochet achieved what Allende only dreamed of—the complete socialization of our private sector."[19]

Nor was this the end of the story. When Pinochet's fourth finance minister, de Castro protégé Hernan Buchi, took office in 1985, he had to embark on yet another, even larger round of privatizations simply to rid the government of all the debt-ridden companies that had been acquired through forced nationalization. Subsequently, foreign bankers, the World Bank, Wall Street, and the IMF all gave Buchi and the Pinochet regime rave reviews for their brilliant privatization strategy, designed to attract foreign investment, boost savings, and downsize Chile's state. But they never acknowledged why his privatization program had been necessary and possible in the first place, because in 1983, neoliberal policies had produced a disaster, and the junta had been forced by its foreign creditors to take the fall for so many bad debts.

Finally, who were the main beneficiaries of Chile's latest round of privatizations? To avoid the insider-trading outrages that had characterized many of the 1970s privatizations and helped groups like Vial and Cruzat grow quickly, Buchi offered low-cost loans to workers and pension funds to help them buy stock. By 1988, worker-owned funds comprised fourteen percent of privatized shares, not a bad achievement in worker control for an ostensibly right-wing regime. But two other kinds of investors became even more important. The first were foreign investors, especially the foreign banks. In 1986, under the Central Bank's "Chapter 19" program, foreign investors were allowed to swap their (dubious) nationalized loans for equity in state-owned companies that were privatized on very favorable terms. As a result, Bankers Trust obtained forty percent of Provida (the country's largest pension fund), plus the Pilmaiquen Power Plant for half its book value; Aetna Insurance bought the country's second largest pension fund; Chase, MHT, and Citibank also acquired major local interests. By 1990, a handful of foreign-managed pension funds controlled seventy percent of Chile's pension system, its largest pool of capital. Alan Bond, the erratic Australian investor whose financial empire later collapsed, was even permitted to buy the famous telephone company that ITT had fought Allende so hard for. COPEC, the Chilean oil company that had been privatized cheaply by Grupo Cruzat-Larrain in 1976, had since turned into a debt-ridden conglomeration of fishing, mining, forestry, and finance companies, including half of Banco de Santiago. When Cruzat-Larrain cratered in 1983, Chile's government reacquired ownership of the now-heavily indebted COPEC, which was Chile's largest private enterprise.

Four years later, it reprivatized COPEC to Grupo Angelini, another leading
Chilean private conglomerate, again at cheap prices, continuing the cycle.[20]
This "Chapter 19" debt-equity swap program was credited by its supporters—especially the banks—with reducing Chile's debt by more than $2
billion. It was ironic for the banks to be praising this achievement. Many others saw the program as a dead giveaway. By assuming all private foreign debt
in the first place, Chile had rewarded bad lending. After a decade of tightfisted
government, many of the privatized assets had actually been in pretty good
shape. Except for the copper company and a few military suppliers, the only
ones the government retained were assets no one else wanted. It made little
sense to let foreigners trade dubious loans for such valuable assets at rock-bot-
tom prices. It seems that Chile hadn't really eliminated state intervention; it
had merely inverted its class bias.

The other key investor in Buchi's privatizations was the Chilean elite.
While the government nationalized private debts, it didn't touch private foreign assets. And Buchi now offered flight capitalists a generous tax amnesty if
they brought their money home. His "Chapter 18" program allowed them to
buy debt from banks and swap it for government bonds or equity in state
companies at very favorable prices. By 1990, this program had brought in
another $2 billion. Again, the banks and their clients naturally sang Chapter
18's praises. However, it rewarded tax evasion and effectively swapped foreign
for domestic debt that may well prove more costly to service in the long run.
Such criticism meant little to officials in charge of the program, and some
even benefitted from it personally. Soon after he left government, Dr. Jose
Pinera became president of an electric utility company that had been privatized. Moreover, his brother ended up owning the privatized national airline,
which he proceeded to turn into quite a profitable enterprise, even while
serving in Chile's Senate.

So the circle was complete: having been bailed out of their foreign debts
by the government, Chile's elite and the foreign banks now bought back their
assets at 50–60 cents on the dollar or less, often with the same flight dollars
that the original loans had financed. Here we have one of the purest examples of abusive banking, one that poses the question of the foreign banks'
responsibility very clearly. Chile's 1983 debt crisis obviously had little to do
with inefficient public enterprises, excessive public debts, Marxists, welfare-
state liberals, or all the other usual suspects blamed by neoliberals. At that
point, two-thirds of Chile's foreign debt was private, and the Pinochet administration had long since eliminated much of the state's inefficiency, not to
mention the political opposition. Yet by the end of 1983, Chile had ended up
with one of the highest per capita *public* foreign debts in the world, as well as

one of the developing world's largest state sectors. This "Chicago road to socialism" was taken in part because there was no political opposition, no accountability, and no one to stop the foreign banks, the domestic elites, their unregulated domestic banks, and the generals. So perhaps democracy has its uses, after all; perhaps "free markets" alone are not sufficient.

MEXICO—COMING INTO THE PICTURE

Mexico not only became the world's largest flight market in the 1970s and 1980s, but it also housed some of the world's most corrupt senior officials. Largely because of its highly organized system of corruption, it remained a ruthless one-party dictatorship until the election of Vicente Fox in July 2000—the first opposition presidential candidate to be elected in seventy-one years. Until then it had stubbornly resisted the democratization that had already occurred in Eastern Europe, the Soviet Union, South Africa, and the rest of Latin America. The debt crisis had forced Mexico to liberalize its economy in the early 1990s. But even after that, elections were still routinely stolen; political opponents and independent journalists feared for their jobs and lives; and the police and Army remained riddled with trafficantes, torturers, and death squads. More than three dozen journalists were murdered from 1989 to 2003.[21]

Of course the world has many other brutal dictatorships, but in my experience this long-suffering US neighbor is one of the most distressing, if only because it is right next door, and in so many ways, a dependent variable with respect to "Yanqui" behavior. Once, after my research assistant interviewed a leading Mexico City economist for an article, he called in absolute terror, afraid that someone in the "ruthless" PRI government would make it impossible for him to work if he were quoted.

The case of Mexico is also important for us to understand because foreign and domestic banks have had at least as much deleterious influence there as anywhere. It also clearly presents the question of the relationship between political and economic development.

MEXICO'S 1982 CRISIS

The Mexican crisis of August 1982 was the high water market of the 1980's Third World "debt crisis," but to insiders, it not much of a surprise at all. Indeed, it had actually been greatly *over-predicted* by, as one banker put it, by "All the froggy little economists at the Fed and the Treasury," as well as by many bankers. By early 1981, it didn't take much foresight to see that a crunch was coming—interest rates were soaring, the global economy was slipping into a recession, and Poland and Turkey had already stopped paying interest on their debts. The Fed was most concerned about Mexico and

Brazil, because that was where US banks had most of their loans. Mexico, in particular, accounted for more that a third of all US loans to Latin America, and its foreign debt was already $75 billion and soaring. The Fed also had private evidence that much of Mexico's debt money was taking flight, ending up in New York, Houston, and Miami.

So in February 1981, the New York Federal Reserve assigned one of its best economists to look closely at Mexico's debt situation. In September 1981, after a careful eight-month review, he presented his findings to the US Interagency Cross-border Exposure Review Committee (ICERC), a secretive panel of federal banking experts, including three apiece from the Federal Reserve, the Comptroller of the Currency, and the Federal Deposit Insurance Corporation. Their job was to rate the creditworthiness of specific countries, as Moody's does for private borrowers. Based on the economist's work, the New York Fed recommended that ICERC downgrade Mexico's credit rating. If this recommendation had been followed, it might have slowed lending to Latin America dramatically in 1981–82. Even though debt levels were already very high, the eventual August 1982 extreme crunch might have been avoided.

But the Fed's proposal was defeated—according to this Fed economist, because of high-level political shenanigans. The problem was the President Ronald Reagan was about to meet Mexico's President Lopez Portillo in Cancun for an official state visit, and the State Department—especially Secretary of State Alexander Haig—didn't want any embarrassments. So, on the very eve of the ICERC vote, at least two members of the nine-member committee got late-night calls from the White House. The word was, "It is not in the foreign policy interest of the US to reclassify Mexico's loans at this point." Two ICERC members switched their votes and the proposal was defeated 5 to 4.

This may have had very far-reaching consequences. From October 1981 to August 1982, Mexico's debt increased by $1 billion a month, and Latin America's debt increased by $40 billion—almost twenty percent. In August 1982, Mexico's Finance Minister, Jesus Silva Herzog, was compelled to deliver his famous line to US Treasury Secretary Donald Regan: "*No, with great respect sir, I believe* we *have a problem.*" Two weeks later, Mexican officials discovered to their horror that they actually owed foreign banks more that $26 billion of *90-day paper*, including $6 billion that Mexican banks had borrowed surreptitiously. This discovery—and not Silva Herzog's warning—marked the true crisis. It wasn't revealed at the time, but if the Fed had not secretly intervened to underwrite two New York banks in September 1982, the entire global interbank loan market might have come crashing down. When the dust cleared, Mexico's 90-day paper had become *30-year* paper, debt that it is still servicing to this day.

DE LA MADRID

Mexico was in its worst economic crisis since the 1930s when President Miguel de la Madrid took office in December 1982. He'd never before held elective office. A life-long bureaucrat with a Mexican law degree and a Masters in Public Administration from Harvard, he was appointed President by Jose Lopez Portillo, his predecessor and law professor. But until the late 1990s, it was not at all unusual for Mexican Presidents, much less senior Mexican officials, to have never held elective office. From 1929 on, the country was governed by the "revolutionary" PRI, sort of a cross between the Teamster's Union, the Mafia, and Chicago's political machine in the 1960s, under Mayor Richard Daley. Decisions about who governed the country were routinely taken behind closed doors and enforced ruthlessly. As Fidel Velazquez Sanchez, for forty years the boss of the Confederation of Mexican Workers, the PRI's largest and most loyal union, once warned an opponent, "Just remember: if you *move*, you might not come out in the *picture*."

At least de la Madrid must have known something about the country's $85 billion debt problem when he took office. After all, as Portillo's planning minister from 1976 to 1982, when the debt increased fourfold, he had been one of its main architects. Now de la Madrid lectured his countrymen on the need for "belt tightening," and in 1983, he and Planning Minister Carlos Salinas de Gortari implemented a tough IMF-type stabilization. For the already-slim-waisted "shirtless ones," this belt-tightening just meant higher unemployment and declining real wages. De la Madrid's other declared priority was a "moral renovation," an attack on the country's soaring corruption problem. The only difficulty was that much of the corruption originated right at the top of the political system: since Porfirio Diaz from 1876 to 1911, right on down through Miguel Aleman in the 1940s, and since every Mexican President has emerged from office vastly richer than when he entered. After the 1970s oil price rise, Mexico's increased oil wealth had compounded the problem, because there was now so much more to steal. De la Madrid was not eager to stray away from this tradition. So he granted his predecessor immunity, allowing former President Lopez Portillo to retire to a palatial compound just outside Mexico City. Informed observers estimate that Lopez Portillo walked away with at least $1 billion—as ordinary folks said, *"La Revolución le hizo justicia"* (The Revolution brought him justice).[22] But Lopez Portillo didn't get off completely—he was never permitted to forget his vow in February 1982 to "defend the peso like a dog," just two weeks before he devalued it sharply. After that, his compound became known as "Dog Hill," and whenever he appeared in public, someone was sure to start barking. The only other consolation was that under Mexican law, Lopez Portillo was limited to just one term. As Lopez Portillo said of Mexico's banks when he nationalized them in September 1982 for their involvement in capital flight, "They've robbed us once . . . They shall not rob us again."

De la Madrid did try to punish a few of Lopez Portillo's cronies. He booted out Arturo Durazo Moreno, Mexico City's former police chief and leading dope dealer at the time, whose house—like Imelda Marcos's film center—was a full-scale replica of the Parthenon, complete with five hundred marble statues. Jorge Diaz Serrano was George H. W. Bush's former business partner in Zapata Oil and the head of Pemex—Mexico's national oil company—under Lopez Portillo. In addition to other properties, Diaz Serrano owned a mansion right on the golf course in Vail, Colorado. He was later charged with pocketing a $34 million commission on two oil tankers—actually a rather modest sum, considering the fact that up to 300 million barrels of oil were *missing* from the country's accounts during his six-year term. He only served five years in prison, which works out to be an average "salary" of $7 million a year for the tanker fee.

Apart from these two sacrifices, most other PRI magnates avoided prosecution under the de la Madrid regime. Those overlooked included Carlos "Hank" Gonzalez, the Mexico City mayor who used his position to acquire a vast business empire, an estate in New Canaan, Connecticut, and a private zoo; Fidel Velazquez, the union boss, who sold labor peace for a hefty sum to the PRI's business allies; and most interesting to us here, Joaquin Hernandez Galicia ("La Quina"), the "Director of Revolutionary Works" for Pemex's powerful oil union in the 1980s.

Hernandez Galicia, a former welder from the Gulf town of Ciudad Maderos, had been the oil workers' boss since 1961 and a personal advisor to four Mexican presidents. He was so certain of his power that in February 1982 he warned de la Madrid, "You will have to become a friend of the oil workers whether you like it or not."[23] Hernandez Galicia also had close friends who were foreign bankers, as we'll see.

Unfortunately for de la Madrid, several episodes in the early days of his administration undercut his rhetoric about "moral renovation." In May 1984, the day de la Madrid arrived in Washington DC on his first official visit, Jack Anderson leaked a CIA report estimating that de la Madrid had already accumulated $162 million abroad. Apparently some of the funds had been wired to a Cayman Islands bank and the National Security Agency was listening. Mexican diplomats labeled the story a lie, but the State Department only responded that the "US Government applauds President de la Madrid's commitment to address the issue of honesty in government."[24]

Next, in September 1985, an earthquake devastated Mexico City. Shoddy high-rise apartments built by friends of senior government officials tumbled like card houses, with thousands of people buried in the rubble and thousands more forced to camp out for weeks in squalid shelters and abandoned offices. The quake did uncover a secret burial site for political prisoners at the offices of Mexico's Attorney General.

A few months later, wealthy Mexicans got a different kind of shock. In February 1986, the US Treasury, which requires banks to identify people who deposit more than $10,000 in cash, fined the Texas Commerce Bank of Houston $1.9 million for failing to file seven thousand such reports, mainly for Mexicans. Hundreds feared their names would be revealed and started shifting their funds elsewhere. In March 1986, the Mexican periodical *Jueves de Excelsior* published a list of 575 people who had at least $1 million in US banks. De la Madrid was trying to reschedule the debt for the second time since 1982, and he'd just declared that foreign banks should "shoulder a greater part of Mexico's debt burden." The disclosure of all these *sacadolares*—"people who take out dollars"—showed that Mexico's elite wasn't any more willing to finance the country than the banks were.

Two years later, during the run up to Mexico's July 1988 presidential elections, the debt was being restructured for a third time, and a similar list of big-league flight capitalists appeared.[25] This time, the run was inspired by a candid statement from Augustin Legorreta, a Mexican banker who was very close to President de la Madrid. In a meeting of businessmen closed to the press, Legorreta admitted that despite the PRI's seventy years of revolutionary rhetoric, "Mexico is still a country run by only three hundred families."

Despite such embarrassments, de la Madrid did make some progress toward economic recovery. By the time he picked his successor in 1987, bankers were citing Mexico as proof that the one-on-one "negotiated" approach to the debt problem was working—at least for them. Off the record, they also liked Mexico's compliant debt policy, compared with other (more democratic) debtors.

THE PRECOCIOUS SALINAS

De la Madrid's anointed successor was Carlos Salinas de Gortari, a fortyish Harvard technocrat. Like his mentor, Salinas was a member of the PRI's hereditary revolutionary family. His grandfather was a prominent Monterrey businessman, and his father, Raul Salinas Lozano, also Harvard educated, had been a minister of commerce in the 1960s. Salinas was not only wellborn, but also precocious: at age four, he had picked up a pistol and shot his maid dead. He finished his Harvard Ph.D. in political science in 1978 (his dissertation was on the "impact of government spending on elections"), and by 1982, he was already minister of planning—the youngest Cabinet member ever at thirty-five.

Like de la Madrid and many other US-educated elite/technocrats in the PRI's "reform" wing, Salinas believed that Mexico's main problem was its own bloated government. He favored downsizing the state, deregulating the economy, and, if anything, *increasing* the role of foreign banks and investors. Despite a dearth of new loans, he and de la Madrid continued to pay all of Mexico's foreign interest bills on time, repeatedly restructured the debt, and experimented with almost every idea on the bankers' wish list, including debt swaps, securitization, debt conversions, and privatization. Mexico's debt emissaries spent a fortune on innumerable junkets to Paris, London, Washington, DC, and New York. Meanwhile, the country staunchly refused to be drawn into a debtors' coalition with Brazil, Argentina, and Peru.

By the end of de la Madrid's term in 1988, however, there was precious little to show for his deference to foreign bankers.[26] The debt cost more to service than Mexico earned from oil exports—tantamount to Pemex being handed over lock, stock, and barrel to the banks. From 1982 to 1988, Mexico paid over $40 billion in interest and got back only $14 billion in new loans, half of them from the IMF and the World Bank. The country transferred more than a third of its savings abroad each year. In fact, taking flight capital into account, Mexico was actually a net lender to the outside world—more than $50 billion throughout the 1980s. By 1985, the market value of its flight assets already exceeded the value of its entire foreign debt. And most of these flight capital outflows were captured by its major "creditors." One Citibank private banker—operating surreptitiously out of the fourteenth floor of Citi's office tower in Mexico City—bragged, "We could easily repay our loans to Mexico with the flight capital that we've collected here—you know, there really are quite a few fabulously rich Mexicans!"[27]

Given the banks' unwillingness to provide Mexico's government with any more loans, the skepticism that foreign investors had toward the country, and the government's reluctance to get tougher with foreign banks and its own domestic elite, Mexico had little choice but to rely on its own resources to finance investment. Since Salinas and de la Madrid wanted to shrink public spending and budget deficits and were unwilling to tax the elite, they raised interest rates to stimulate private savings. That reduced growth and unemployment, which was anathema to workers, *campesinos*, and "protected" business sectors. But the de la Madrid-Salinas program was supported enthusiastically by Mexico's top families, bankers, the bureaucratic elite, union bosses, oil workers, police chiefs, and Army officers. Given the one-party system, these were the only constituencies that really counted. The economic program turned out to be very unpopular, and Salinas's detractors in the PRI worried that it might be a mistake to bet on an uncharismatic technocrat in a period of rising political ferment. But this argument carried little weight with de la Madrid, who'd once been an uncharismatic planning minister himself. So in September 1987, Salinas was nominated the PRI's candidate for president.

Almost immediately, the regime's policies began to misfire. The global stock crash that took place in October 1987 actually started in Mexico City, when the Central Bank suddenly lifted restrictions on investments in debt instruments, causing the Mexican stock market to lose three-fourths of its value in one week. Capital flight resumed, the government missed its budget targets, the peso sank like a stone, and by year's end, inflation was at fifteen percent a month and rising. De la Madrid was forced to implement yet another round of "belt tightening," squeezing credit and freezing wages and prices. Since 1981, Mexico had experienced seven years of negative growth. Real incomes for everyone but the elite had fallen by a quarter, and there were incipient signs of social unrest all over the country. The country stagnated under the weight of its foreign debt, which totaled $101 billion by 1988.[28]

THE 1988 "ELECTION"

The July 1988 presidential elections were the greatest challenge to the PRI's hegemony in its history—at least until Vicente Fox won in 2000. In the party's first deep split since 1929, Cuauhtemoc Cardenas, the PRI's governor of Michoacan State and the son of President Lazaro Cardenas, who nationalized the oil industry in the 1930s, joined forces with disenchanted leftists and nationalists to form the "National Democratic Front." The Front's radical rhetoric gave voice to widespread discontent. It also claimed to support democracy, but had a few strange bedfellows of its own, including Luis Echeverria Alvarez—Mexico's president in the 1970s and one of Mexico's wealthiest men—and Hernandez Galicia . But at least it supported a popular job creation program, which it intended to pay for with a repudiation, or radical restructuring, of Mexico's foreign debt.

Just a few weeks before the 1988 election, Cuauhtemoc Cardenas had been doing very well in the polls. Salinas, on the other hand, would have nothing to do with such irresponsible policies. The consummate planning bureaucrat-turned-free marketeer, he saw himself as continuing the tradition of authoritarian top-down reforms begun by Porfirio Diaz—the tough nineteenth-century dictator who ruled Mexico for thirty-five years with the support of the landowning elite, foreign bankers and investors, and his own well-heeled entourage.

Evidently many Mexicans did not share Salinas's enthusiasm for Porfirio Diaz or for the neoliberal agenda. To them, he was still just another in a long series of little-known, remote members of the *Priista* technocracy who came down from the temple every six years and went through the motions of seeking their mandate. Despite massive advertising on his behalf by the PRI's machine (with help from Hill and Knowlton, the renowned PR firm whose clients had also included Duvalier and BCCI), as of election eve, non-government polls found that he and Cardenas were still running neck and neck. Of course many voters viewed all Mexican elections with skepticism, because of the PRI's long history of election fraud. But Salinas and his predecessor, Miguel de la Madrid, had sworn this time would be different.

On July 6, 1988, when the polls closed and the government started tallying the count at its central computing office in Mexico City, the country eagerly awaited the results. There was much disappointment when Manual Bartlett, the PRI's interior minister in charge of administering the vote, announced the next morning that the Federal Election Commission's computer system had crashed and that the results would be delayed. When they finally emerged a week later, Salinas was declared the victor by a wide margin. Officially, the PRI received fifty-two percent of the vote, compared with the PRD's thirty-one percent, and the business party PAN's seventeen percent.

Opposition leaders have claimed that the computer crash was contrived to buy time for rigging the vote once it became clear that Cardenas was winning. Despite widespread rumors, these claims were not easily confirmed. Many of those on the inside were too scared to talk, and Salinas's foreign supporters, including leading newspapers like *The Wall Street Journal* (whose parent company, Dow Jones, added President Salinas to its corporate board, where he remained until April 1997) and *The New York Times* did not investigate too deeply. They believed that a compliant, technically-competent neoliberal would serve the mutual interests of Mexico and its trading partners better than Cardenas.[29]

In June 1994, before Mexico's August 1994 Presidential election, *Computing*, a UK magazine that focuses on technology, became interested in the computer failure aspect of the 1988 elections. It tracked down several data entry operators who had worked on the election and obtained the following eyewitness account of what had actually happened in July 1988:

> We arrived at work on the morning of July 6, election day, at the central computer and statistic official. When we got there we discovered that the rooms were empty and our computers weren't there. We were ordered into a

minibus and taken to the Government House (in Mexico City), to a room with blacked-out windows. Our computers had been set up there, complete with the voter database. We started to enter the data. As the supervisors saw that Salinas was losing, they ordered us to leave aside votes for the PRI and only enter opposition votes. Then, at about 3 A.M. on July 7, the supervisor called a halt, and with tears in his eyes, he told us: "If you care for your families, your jobs, and your lives, enter all votes from now on in favor of the PRI. I went back to work and did as I was told. I wanted to cry, but I had to do it.

They kept us there until five or six in the evening the following day. When I'd finished my work, I called up the voting record for my uncle, and to my astonishment the computer record showed that he, an opposition supporter, had voted for Salinas. That was when I realized why we had been told only to enter opposition votes in the beginning. While we were away from the computers, they had reversed all the data from the first session of data capture so all those votes showed up as Salinas votes.[30]

To the consternation of the Salinas government, these details were confirmed in July 1994 by a former director of Mexico's Federal Electoral Institute. But when *Computing* tried to verify them with Unisys, the US multinational that had supplied the computers used in the election, it responded that the 1988 "fault reports" for its Mexico subsidiary had been destroyed and that Unisys had "not been involved in the electoral process."

In December 1994, Adolfo Onofre, the courageous computer consultant who had cooperated with the investigation of the Unisys computer "failure," was arrested and badly beaten by Mexico's Federal Police when he returned to Mexico City from Britain, where he had sought political asylum.[31]

LA QUINA'S PRIVATE ARMY

Salinas not only lost Mexico City by a landslide in 1988, but most independent observers now believe that he also lost the whole country. Without an army of its own, most members of the opposition decided to recognize his "victory," which the Reagan Administration and the domestic and foreign business community lost no time in doing.

A few powerful dissidents like Hernandez Galicia refused to do so, however. Hernandez Galicia had already battled Salinas over the Pemex union's contract, and there was much more to fight about. For forty years, oil workers had been Mexico's best-paid workers. Under a 1947 agreement that was still in force, they received 2.5 percent of all drilling contracts as "dues," plus 10 percent for the union's Fund for Social Works, which Hernandez Galicia happened to administer. Under a 1977 agreement with Lopez Portillo, the union also controlled forty percent of all drilling contracts and half of all other Pemex contracts. The standard gambit was for union bosses to set up intermediary companies, subcontract work, and pocket 10–25 percent spreads. The union even had its own contractors, owning a whole fleet of oil tankers and two drilling platforms that employed *pelones* (nonunion workers). At Salinas's insistence, the bidding reservation was abolished for onshore bids in 1985, but offshore work remained with the union. There was also rampant overmanning. The contracts gave the union exclusive power over hiring, and Hernandez Galicia openly sold the jobs. There were also thousands of "ghost workers" on the payroll. Not surprisingly, Pemex's output per worker was only a third as high as that of PDVSA, Venezuela's state oil company.[32] When oil prices plummeted in the mid-1980s, the company chose to cut exploration rather than take on the union. By the late 1980s, Pemex was pumping four times as much oil as it was finding, and Mexico's reserves had fallen below Venezuela's.[33]

By then, Hernandez Galicia 's union really became a state within a state, with more than nine hundred full-time officials and three thousand "enforcers" on call. In addition to the tankers and drilling companies, his Fund for Social Works controlled movie theaters, service stations, a watch factory, 130 supermarkets, a fleet of airplanes, the Alameda Hotel in Mexico City, the Emiliano Zapata Ranch in Tamaulipas (with three thousand cattle), and at least five other ranches. Hernandez Galicia also owned a stake in the Continental Performation and Construction Company, a Texas drilling company and Pemex subcontractor. In 1983, he estimated the value of all these assets at $670 million.[34] They were managed for him by Sergio Bolaños, a Mexican businessman. Collectively, they were known as Grupo Serba.

Despite all the corruption, while Hernandez Galicia was powerful, foreign bankers were quite happy to support him. In the 1970s, for example, Bank of America, Pemex's leading creditor, had loaned nearly $500 million to Grupo Serba, Bolaños, and Hernandez Galicia . The loans were arranged by Bank of America's influential Mexico City representative Pepe Carral, a former schoolmate and close friend of Presidents Luis Echeverria and Lopez Portillo. Bank of America was also Pemex's largest lender. And after he retired from Bank of America, Carral set up an investment fund that managed assets for several of these friends.

So even after Salinas took office in late 1988, he still had very powerful enemies. On the eve of his inauguration, Hernandez Galicia tried to embarrass Salinas, charging that Mario Ramon Beteta, de la Madrid's Pemex director, had pocketed a commission on a tanker deal just like Diaz Serrano, his predecessor.[35] Hernandez Galicia also warned Salinas that his union would strike if the government disposed of "even one millimeter of the petroleum industry to the private sector." And the union secretly started to buy automatic weapons. That was serious—Hernandez Galicia really did have his own private army. His union's 210,000 members were disbursed all over the country, and they outnumbered the Mexican Army by two to one. The upshot was that in January 1989, just a few days after Hernandez Galicia visited the National Palace to pay his respects to Salinas, a bazooka blew down his door in Cuidad Madero at 9 A.M. in the morning, and Mexican Army troops dragged him off to jail in his underwear. Hernandez Galicia, Bolaños, and forty-three other union officials were charged with crimes that ranged from murder and arms trafficking to "gangsterism." The police confiscated several hundred Uzi machine guns and fifty thousand rounds of ammunition. A week later, Mexico's attorney general asked the US Federal Reserve to freeze all US bank deposits owned by these union officials. They turned up more than *$3.2 billion* stashed in accounts at Citibank, Chase, MHT, and Bank of America.[36]

So it was not only could Mexico's capitalists and corrupt officials who could employ private bankers, but "Directors of Revolutionary Works" as well. If Salinas hadn't acted as quickly as he did, Hernandez Galicia 's stash might have bankrolled a second Mexican revolution. This was by no means the only union leader jailed by Salinas. He also jailed the head of Aeromexico's union, the head of the social security system's union, and the heads of a Mexico City bus line's union—all of whom were protesting the privatization of their respective enterprises.

Salinas wasted no time with amenities when it came to civil liberties. In 1994, Amnesty International described some of the methods used by Mexican security forces against the Indians in Chiapas who were protesting the extraordinary concentration of land ownership:

> Hundreds of people were tortured and ill-treated by the army and other security forces in Chiapas. In other parts of the country the frequent use of torture by law enforcement agents, particularly the state judicial police, continues to be reported. Torture methods included beatings; near-asphyxiation with plastic bags; forcing peppered water into the nose; electric shocks and burning. Some detainees died as a result. Confessions extracted under duress continued to be admitted as evidence in courts, and medical treatment for detainees who suffered torture was frequently not available. By the end of the year none of those responsible for any of the hundreds of cases of torture reported in Chiapas and throughout the country had been brought to justice.[37]

LA CONTRA-REVOLUCIÓN

Having stolen the election and demolished his remaining political opponents with brute force, Salinas proceeded with what opposition leaders called his "neo-Porfirista" reforms. Porfirio Diaz had been overthrown by *La Revolución* in 1912. Now, from 1989 to 1994, Salinas introduced a dramatic neoliberal *Contra-Revolución*.

His first step was to undertake Mexico's fourth foreign debt restructuring since 1982. In March 1989, when US Treasury secretary and former investment banker Nicholas Brady announced the "Brady Plan," Mexico volunteered to be its first guinea pig. Unlike the 1985 Baker Plan, the Brady Plan seemed to recognize the need for debt reduction, underwritten with aid from First World governments.

The basic idea was that banks would trade their Mexican loans in for new government-backed bonds that were issued at steep discounts from face value, backed by US Treasury bonds. But it soon became clear that the actual aid available was small. After all, the US government had debt problems of its own. Furthermore, by 1989–90, many foreign private banks were too worried about their shaky domestic portfolios to put much new money into Mexico—Citibank, for example, came within a hairsbreadth of having to be bailed out by the Federal Reserve.

So the July 1989 Mexican rescheduling—concluded only after great pressure from the US Treasury—merely reduced Mexico's debt by $7 billion, enough to cut its interest bill just ten percent. Like all such "voluntary" approaches to the debt problem, the Brady approach ended up being mainly a complex, time-consuming substitute for a real solution—although it generated nice fees for investment bankers!

Partly because this "free market-based" approach to debt reduction produced such meager results, Salinas had to redouble his strategy of liberalizing the economy while holding on tight to the reigns of power. Given his reluctance to raise taxes, he turned to relying on attracting foreign investment and flight capital back to Mexico with a major privatization and liberalization program.

Soon Salinas became one of Latin America's most vocal advocates in the neoliberal movement that swept through Latin America's elites in the aftermath of the 1980s debt crisis. Following in the footsteps of Pinochet's Los Chicago Boys, its followers professed an almost religious faith in the virtues of unfettered private markets and free trade. Their agenda included the sharp retrenchment of government borrowing and social spending, the rejection of state intervention in favor of privatization and lower taxes, and the deregulation of markets for capital, labor, land, traded goods, and even environmental rights. Support for this agenda soon became almost as prevalent among the elites and their business and banking friends as their dizzy optimism about state-led development had been in the 1970s. Indeed, its supporters included many who had dined heartily on the debt-heavy meals of that period.

The result was a proliferation of free-market reforms in the early 1990s. Under Salinas, Mexico became a vanguard and a policy laboratory for the whole global neoliberal movement, as Marcos' Philippines had been for development planning. This was a crucial conquest. While Chile's free-market experiments had been interesting, that country was, at best, an industrious copper exporter with thirteen million inhabitants located at the ends of the earth. Mexico was a real player—it boasted a $250 billion diversified economy, fabulous oil and mineral wealth, the world's third largest metropolis, and ninety-two million poor people who shared a two thousand-mile border with the world's richest country. Depending on how this relationship was managed, Mexico could be a very useful neighbor—a supplier of low-cost labor, goods, and energy, and a major market for First World loans, investments, and exports. Or it could be a time bomb.

As we saw, even before his "election," Salinas was already the favorite son not only of Mexico's oligarchs and party bosses, but also of multinational investors like GE, Allied Signal, Alcoa, and GM; commercial banks like Citibank and JPMorgan; investment banks like Goldman Sachs and Morgan Stanley; the US media; press; and, the US government and its financial acolytes—the IMF and World Bank. During the two years before the 1988 elections, the IMF and the World Bank had provided Mexico with $4 billion in new credits, and private banks had helped out by rescheduling $43 billion of Mexico's outstanding debt.[38] Before and after the election, a parade of First World leaders, including George Bush Sr. (a friend of Salinas's father, Raul Sr.), Paul Volcker, Citibank chairman John Reed, newly elected World Bank president Lewis B. Preston (formerly of JPMorgan), IMF director Michel Camdessus, and many lesser officials and bankers descended on Mexico to encourage its newfound passion for free markets. They praised the quality of the PRI's Ivy League-educated economists and touted Mexico as a model of stability and growth—much as they had done with the Philippines two decades earlier.

After the election, foreign investors also stepped forward to ratify Salinas's agenda. From 1988 to 1994, Mexico became the darling of the international investment community, attracting more foreign investment than any other developing country except China. It accounted for nearly half of the $175 billion in new foreign direct and portfolio investment that poured into Latin America during this period.[39] In the wake of the debt crisis, "foreign" investors—including members of the domestic elite who secretly repatriated their flight capital to avoid taxes and conceal their investments—replaced foreign bankers as the leading suppliers of finance to Mexico and other "emerging markets," providing more than three-fourths of Mexico's entire capital budget. Much of this capital was attracted by Salinas' privatization program, one of the most aggressive in Latin America. It involved selling public assets in key sectors like telecommunications, steel, airlines, and banking, including the reprivatization of all the banks that Lopez Portillo had nationalized in the early 1980s, and then using the proceeds to finance the budget. By 1994, this fire-sale had raised $24 billion, more than any other Latin American country.[40]

Salinas introduced many other sweeping changes, like a new investment law that opened many sectors to foreigners and a tax amnesty for returning flight capitalists. He slashed government spending as a share of GDP and opened up Mexico's capital markets to foreign banks, brokerages, and insurance companies. He sanctioned an amendment to Mexico's constitution that effectively put an end to restrictions on private landholding, an attempt to undermine the communal farms that had been the cornerstone of Lazaro Cardenas's agrarian reform in the 1930s and 1940s. With the help of high real interest rates, he reduced inflation from 130 percent to around 20 percent in two years and strengthened Mexico's peso. In 1989, he also declared that drug trafficking was a threat to the nation, presided over the seizure of a record amount of cocaine, and signed a new drug enforcement cooperation treaty with the US. Finally, he negotiated the NAFTA treaty, a new "free trade" zone with his powerful neighbors—the US and Canada—that opened doors to their markets, exports, and investors. For good measure, he even had Mexico join the GATT and the OECD. Porfirio Diaz himself could not have designed a more complete deconstruction of the PRI's statist heritage.

All these moves were greeted enthusiastically by Salinas's allies, especially the three hundred top families, the US government, the banks, foreign investors, and the neoliberal intelligentsia. Combined with the 1990 oil price rise, this helped set off a foreign investment boomlet from 1991 to 1995.

The result was a vast feeding frenzy on the part of the private elite. Far from simply opening up the economy, this actually consolidated their hold on many sectors. Sweeping privatizations of the banking, telecommunications, media, mining, agriculture, and airline industries provided numerous sweetheart deals, especially for a dozen or so key insiders, like Carlos Slim, Carlos Hank Gonzalez, and Roberto Gonzalez Barrera—all of whom were close to the President and his family. Other private groups that held dominant positions in export industries like glass, beer, cement, tourism, and mining or were able to offer investment opportunities and partnerships to foreigners, also benefited immensely from NAFTA, which was concluded by Salinas and President George H. W. Bush in late 1992 and strong-armed through the US Congress by President Bill Clinton in late 1993.

So it is not really surprising that inequalities of wealth and income in Mexico rose dramatically from 1988 to 1994. The number of Mexicans on

Forbes Magazine's annual survey of the world's billionaires increased from one in 1988 to twenty-four in 1994, placing Mexico in fourth place, just ahead of France and the UK.[41] It also earned Salinas de Gortari many personal tributes. As noted, he became a member of Dow Jones' corporate board. On December 7, 1994, he was treated to a $400 per plate testimonial dinner in his honor at the Jeane J. Kirkpatrick's American Enterprise Institute in Washington, DC, for his "contribution to improved public policy and social welfare."[42] In 1995, just before the scandals involving his brother Raul broke, his name was briefly put forward by the Clinton adminstration as a candidate for the new head of the World Trade Organization.

Salinas's political opponents complained that all these tributes overlooked the huge surge in corruption and drug dealing that had also accompanied his liberalization programs, as well as his "unelected" status. They saw his policies as basically returning Mexico to its old role as an appendage of the US economy, a place where labor was cheap and "anything goes," and where domestic farmers and industry would be wiped out by cheap US imports. After seventy years of "revolutionary" government, the country still didn't accord its workers basic labor rights like effectively enforced maximum hours, minimum wages, child labor laws, or occupational health and safety. Despite all the excitement about free trade, there were no free trade unions. Despite Salinas's new environmental law, Mexico's environment was poorly protected. And despite high nominal taxes, private income and wealth went largely untaxed.

Most importantly, the PRI was still unwilling to allow free elections except when it served its own interests. It had permitted some candidates from the right-wing PAN party to win state governorships for decorative purposes, but when Cardenas had threatened to win, the elections were stolen in plain view. When workers at Mexico's largest copper mine protested their privatization, Salinas sent in the Army. Critical journalists were routinely intimidated, fired, or assassinated. And senior members of the Salinas family had been cultivating some interesting sidelines of their own, which made Hernandez Galicia 's business practices look clean by comparison.

FREE TRADE—IN "BADS"

The other side of liberalization was that it really unleashed Mexico's burgeoning underground economy, especially drug trafficking. For the first time, Mexico acquired a world-class international drug cartel in the 1990s, complete with accounts at Citibank's Swiss subsidiary and personal protectors in the office of the presidency. Mexico's role in drug exports had been growing ever since the mid-1980s, when Colombia's traditional supply routes through

Florida were pressured, Colombia cracked down on its own crime bosses, and new Mexican gangs developed their own supply routes and political connections. Like all other exporters to the US, the dealers were aided by NAFTA's increasingly open borders. As the traffickers' wealth grew, so did the opportunities for official corruption. One investigation showed that in 1994–95, more than thirty tons of cocaine confiscated by Mexico's Federal Police simply disappeared.[43] According to a report by a former senior Mexican drug enforcement official, the traffickers were simply given a green light by President Salinas to generate foreign exchange.[44] The crisis in the legal economy increased the supply of human "mules" willing to risk border crossings, even as Mexico's enforcement efforts suffered budget cutbacks. So it is not surprising that during the 1990s, illegal drugs and illegal immigrants became the country's largest exports, next to oil and debt service payments.

But for corrupt PRI officials, neoliberalism had an entirely new meaning—more opportunities to make money quickly, launder it, and stash it. Among the chief beneficiaries was the president's brother, Raul Salinas Jr. In late 1995, his primary bank accounts at Citibank New York, Citibank's Swiss subsidiary, Pictet, Rothschild, Julius Baer, Banque Genevoise de Gestion, Bank Cremi, and a network of dozens of other banks in Mexico, the Cayman Islands, London, New York, Germany, and Luxembourg were revealed to be involved in laundering and concealing $130 million to $400 million of unexplained wealth.[45] Paulina Castañon, Raul's wife, was halted by Swiss authorities on November 15, 1998, when she tried to withdraw $84 million from an account at Bank Pictet in Geneva. A Swiss prosecutor who worked on the investigation for seven years concluded that at least $70 million had come from drug deals.[46] Raul Salinas claimed that the money came from undocumented loans or investment funds that he was given to manage by wealthy Mexican businessmen, like Carlos Hank Rhon, Gonzalez's son.

But Swiss authorities found his explanation dubious. They uncovered evidence of payments by Juan García Abrego, the head of the Gulf cartel, whom other witnesses claimed had met with both Carlos and Raul at a Salinas family ranch.[47] There were also many other allegations of high-level drug dealing and money laundering. Furthermore, both the Bush and Clinton administrations were probably aware of some of these links to organized crime, but did nothing, because they were concerned it might jeopardize Salinas's support for the NAFTA treaty. The head of the US Drug Enforcement Agency's Dallas office from 1984 to 1994 said, "The intelligence on corruption, especially by drug traffickers, has always been there. But we were under instructions not to say anything negative about Mexico—it was a no-no since NAFTA was a hot political football."[48]

Eventually, in January 1999, after a four-year trial, Raul Salinas was sentenced to fifty years in prison—later reduced to twenty-seven years—for his role in the 1994 murder of his brother-in-law, the PRI's general secretary Jose Francisco Ruiz Massieu.[49] Carlos Salinas, afraid that he might be murdered or prosecuted if he remained in Mexico, fled to Ireland, which had no extradition treaty with Mexico, until the late 1990s. The US Department of Justice briefly launched a money laundering investigation of Citigroup, based on the fact that it handled more than $100 million in the scheme; Raul had claimed that Amy Eliot, a vice president in Citigroup's International Private Banking Group, had "'devised the whole strategy.'"[50] However, the Clinton adminstration never brought money-laundering charges against Citibank. By 2000, the five-year statute of limitations on this offense had probably expired. It was pure coincidence that former US Treasury secretary Robert Rubin joined Citigroup as its vice chairman after October 1999 and that Citigroup also hired the Federal Reserve's top expert on money laundering, Richard Small, as its director of Global Anti-Money Laundering.

TEQUILA SUNRISE

In August 1994, Ernesto Zedillo, a Yale economist and another lifelong PRI bureaucrat who had never before held elective office, was elected to succeed Carlos with 50.2% of the official vote. Zedillo was nominated only after Salinas's first choice, Luis Donoldo Colosio, was mysteriously assassinated in March 1994 in Baja, Zedillo's home state. The PRI had its work cut out for them to make Zedillo—theretofore Colosio's campaign manager—a credible candidate in just four months. But the PRI succeeded with the help of a massive advertising campaign, which featured the slogan, "Welfare for your family!" The curious appearance of the "guerrilla" movement in Chiapas in January 1994 and an epidemic of political violence probably also convinced some voters to support the "stable" PRI.

Because the PRI had generously renounced paying for elections with government money in 1994, it had to find its campaign funding in other ways. But since it was the ruling party, that was no problem. Salinas simply invited thirty of Mexico's top business moguls to dinner at a private mansion in Mexico City's fashionable Polanco district—including Carlos Slim, who owned a significant part of Telmex, the formerly state-owned telephone company; Robert Hernandez, owner of Banamex, which had been privatized in 1991; Emilio ("El Tigre") Azcarraga, a TV and media czar; and Lorenzo Zambrano, owner of Cemex, which controlled sixty-five percent of Mexico's cement market.[51] It was "payback" time: everyone in the room had benefit-

ted enormously from Salinas's reforms in the last six years, especially from privatization, and they were about to profit even more from the liberalization of
trade. As Don Emilio Azcarraga reportedly told them,

> I, and all of you, have earned so much money over the past six years that I
> think we have a big debt of gratitude to this government. I'm ready to more
> than double what has been pledged so far, and I hope that most in this room
> will join me. We owe it to the president, and to the country.[52]

Evidently this sentiment was widely shared. At the end of the evening, the
PRI had reportedly collected pledges of $25 million a head, for a grand total
of $750 million. Since these business moguls were not in the habit of giving
away so much money for nothing, the amount raised was also an indication
of how much they expected to benefit from government favors that would
flow from a PRI victory.

Another factor that aided Zedillo's 1994 victory was an economic "card
trick." As of mid-1994, the country was riding the crest of a temporary economic boom, created by the policy of opening the doors to foreign investors.
Their willingness to provide a substitute for bank loans meant that the whole
issue of Mexico's foreign debt appeared to have long since passed. Moreover,
Salinas's economic team decided to defer an overdue but unpopular devaluation of the peso until after the 1994 elections, because it would have boosted
inflation. The team also secretly boosted government spending by more than
was disclosed in official statistics. These politically-motivated policies were
maintained, despite numerous warnings from independent economists, the
US Treasury, and even the IMF.

To sustain the pre-election spending, Mexico had to take on a huge
amount of short-term debt—mainly in the form of interbank loans and new
issues of Mexican bonds sold to US investors through Wall Street investment
banks. The debts of Mexico's domestic banks to international banks nearly
doubled from 1991 to 1994 (from $8 billion to $15.5 billion)—all of it
denominated in dollars. And the Mexican banks, also newly privatized, rapidly expanded their loans to Mexico's private sector. Many of these bank loans
were wasted on poor projects or on "loans" to their owners' other companies.
Bank of Mexico's former vice governor Francisco Gil-Diaz wrote later that
many of the private investors who took over banks in the 1989–92 privatizations were political insiders with little banking experience. They took on
credit risks they did not understand.[53] Also at work was something economists call "moral hazard," a fancy way of saying that—in the absence of effective bank regulation, the presence of insider influence, and the likelihood of
a government bailout for their lending errors—the "novice" Mexican bankers
had discovered that they could essentially write themselves blank checks.

Once again, hasty privatization and weak banking regulation, the twin Achilles' heels of neoliberal finance, were influential. Since it was clear that Mexico could not sustain this level of borrowing, investors started to speculate that the pegged value of the peso had to give. But until it did, the Central Bank continued dishing out reserves, delaying the inevitable.

Another key component of Mexico's $100 billion foreign debt was short-term Mexican dollar bonds, or *Tesobonos*. By 1994, these had increased from almost nothing in 1988 to $28 billion, more than a quarter of Mexico's total foreign debt.[54] About $18 billion of the $28 billion had been sold through Wall Street firms to their favorite big-ticket investors, and the other $10 billion was held by wealthy Mexicans. All of them had been well compensated for inducing investors to bear the risk of holding Mexican debt with high yields. Combined with Mexico's weak non-oil exports and its high propensity for imports, this policy of depending heavily on short-term foreign finance and then delaying the necessary adjustments brought the chickens home to roost. But in the short run, it basically allowed the PRI to manipulate its way to another electoral victory. Indeed, in August 1994, the threat from the left temporarily evaporated. Cardenas's PRD splintered, managing just seventeen percent of the official vote. The conservative PAN party got twenty-six percent. And this time the computer system was supplied by IBM and Booz Allen Hamilton, not Unisys.

THE TEQUILA CRISIS

Not long after the 1994 elections, however, these macro-economic policies came completely unglued. In December, there was a disastrous attempt by Zedillo's finance minister and Yale economist Jaime Serra to make up for lost time, finally devaluing the peso. The problem was that it did not stabilize—it kept falling. Its value fell by more than fifty percent in one week, precipitating a massive wave of capital flight that caused it to sink even lower.

The crisis marked the return of capital flight and foreign borrowing. Large capital outflows had been reported in the months since the assassination of presidential candidate Colosio in March 1994 and just before the December peso float. Apparently some high-level domestic investors had had advance warning.[55] Foreign investors trailed behind a little, but they also quickly lost confidence. The devaluation then triggered the largest wave of capital flight since 1982. About $8 billion in reserves had already fled the country from March 1994 to the end of October. In the following two months, Mexico lost the rest of the $25 billion in reserves that Salinas had carefully accumulated during the previous five years. Even as real wages were plummeting, the government was compelled to boost real interest rates—the "wages" of capital—to more than thirty percent a year in a desperate effort to woo investment capital. Just like the 1920s, however, when Mexican and Argentine bonds experienced a similar loss of confidence, Mexico learned the hard way that foreign bondholders can be even more fickle than foreign bankers.

Mexico's capital flight problem marked the beginning of its deepest economic crisis since the 1930s. Over the next year, as the new Zedillo government took office, there was no bailout for ordinary Mexicans. Unemployment tripled to twenty-eight percent and real national income fell by more than seven percent. At a time when the labor force grew at the rate of a million new workers each year, 1.6 million jobs were lost. Real wages—already below their 1980 levels—fell by another twenty-five percent. Taking the government's claims about continued prosperity at its word, many people had gone heavily into debt. Forty percent of Mexico's eighty-six thousand small businesses, several hundred thousand individual debtors, and several large industrial companies now went bankrupt.[56] Two million small farmers lost everything and were forced to migrate to find work. Meanwhile, to help pay for this fiasco and satisfy the IMF's demands for lower deficits, the government raised sales taxes and prices for gasoline, electricity, and foodstuffs by fifty percent.

For those in the bottom eighty-five percent of the income distribution who still produced mainly for the domestic market, the consequences of all this were catastrophic: an unprecedented combination of soaring inflation, interest rates, and job losses, yielding, in turn, a sharp rise in suicides, divorces, malnutrition, "voluntary" blood sales, kidnappings, political murders, land conflicts, homelessness, and day-to-day street violence. NAFTA may well have helped to generate $250 billion in cross-border trade since its adoption in 1993. But given the economic crisis, the vast majority of Mexicans were seeing very few of its benefits. By the year 2000, more than half the country's population was surviving on less than four dollars per day, and the traditional "middle class" had been emptied out, as inequality and poverty both soared.[57] If this was "conservative reform," many ordinary Mexicans wondered how radical alternatives could possibly have been any worse.

And this was not Chile's distant little laboratory. There were ninety-nine million potential Mexican immigrants right on the US border. Mass unemployment and the plunge in real wages, combined with the adjacent US boom, encouraged Mexican laborers to leave the country in droves. The years 1995–2003 proved to be record years for illegal emigration. Detentions by the US Border Patrol increased by sixty-six percent, despite a quadrupling of patrols, the adoption of harsher penalties for US employers who hire illegal immigrants, sophisticated new detection technologies, and the enactment of tough new anti-immigrant legislation, like California's Proposition 187.[58]

More than one out of every seventeen professional class workers had left Mexico since 1980.[59]

THE BAILOUT ... AND THE BUYBACK

In the ensuing 1995 Tequila Crisis, all of the country's top ten private banks, which had stoked the borrowing spree with careless loans and excessive foreign borrowing, might have failed, were it not for the $50 billion bailout provided to them and to the holders of Mexican bonds by former Goldman Sachs investment banker and US Treasury Secretary Robert Rubin and the IMF.[60] Of course, these were the very same banks that had been nationalized by President Portillo back in 1982. Among them were Mexico's largest private bank, Bancomer, which had been acquired by Eugenio Garza Lagüera, and the second largest, Banamex, which had been sold to well-connected non-bankers Roberto Hernández Ramírez and Alfredo Harp Helú in 1991 for $1 billion. The source of all this investment was not clear. But within a year, the bank had registered a $500 million profit, enough to pay back half the investment.[61] Banco Serfin, Mexico's third largest commercial bank, had been sold to non-banker Adrián Sada González. All told, Salinas had sold all these banks back to the private elite for only $12 billion.

Now, in effect, their loan portfolios had to be renationalized. The "cleanup" cost to taxpayers turned out to be at least a whopping twenty-two percent of Mexico's GDP, or $80 billion, payable at the rate of $15–20 billion a year plus interest.[62] The ultimate amount will probably be even greater, since it depends on the "recoverability" of assets used to secure the loans. Interestingly, FOBAPROA, Mexico's deposit insurance agency, refused to identify the precise list of funds that would be paid to reimburse the banks for uncollected debts. In 1999, Michael Mackey, a Canadian auditor hired by the Mexican Congress to examine precisely what had become of all the bank loans that FOBAPROA insured, discovered that at least $7.7 billion in loans absorbed by the bailout involved "highly irregular or plainly illegal" conduct, where bank executives had made billion-dollar loans to themselves that they never repaid, loaned millions of dollars to investors to buy shares in their banks, or made huge "loans" to their friends and family without credit analysis.[63]

It turned out that the holders of $29 billion in Mexican bonds were also "not without influence." After all, these bonds were issued with the help of leading investment banks like Goldman Sachs, Morgan Stanley, and Citibank. Just as in the 1920s, these banks had helped organize the bond issues and place them with private clients and institutional investors. When the peso crisis struck in December 1994—reportedly aggravated when Salinas's family started moving their capital into dollars in the wake of the growing scandal involving Raul Salinas—Mexico ran out of reserves to preserve the peso and service its bonds. About a third of them were owned by wealthy Mexicans. The other two-thirds were owned by the clients of Wall Street firms like Rubin's old employer, Goldman Sachs. Clearly, Rubin understood what was at stake—he was Goldman Sachs's vice chairman from 1989 to 1992, in charge of international currency operations. He was also reportedly involved with Carlos Slim's Telmex financings. And Goldman Sachs was one of a handful of Wall Street firms that had dealt heavily in Mexican bonds. From 1992 to 1994, it had purchased $5.2 billion of Mexican bonds on behalf of its clients or its own portfolio, one-fifth of the total. These were the very bonds that Rubin's bailout was about to salvage.[64]

This time around, *unlike* during the 1920s, the banks worked closely with the Mexican government, mounting a successful lobbying campaign to get the Clinton administration and the IMF to bail out all these wealthy bondholders and Mexico's private banks, *in full*. One investment banker said that Mexico's elite "pulled its usual act, pointing a gun to its head and threatening to pull the trigger," unless it got another bailout.[65]

Against the opposition of most Americans, President Clinton decided to bail out his friends on Wall Street and in Mexico. This was the fourth Mexican bailout since 1982. To do so, Clinton had to behave in a somewhat extrademocratic way. To circumvent Congress, Secretary of the Treasury Robert Rubin drew on a US Treasury Emergency Stabilization Fund (ESF) that had originally been intended to support the US dollar. Clinton argued that the dollar might somehow be vulnerable to a speculative run on the peso. The argument was strained at best, but it is not surprising that Rubin was sympathetic.

The result was a $50 billion injection of First World taxpayer money, almost all of which went directly into the pockets of wealthy bondholders and the banks. About $20 billion came from the IMF, $20 billion from the special US Treasury's ESF, and $10 billion from Europe's Bank for International Settlements. At the end of the day, however, these lenders all demanded their money back, with interest, from the Mexican government. So the costs ended up being borne by Mexico's taxpayers—mainly the millions of ordinary Mexicans who bear the brunt of the country's taxes.

For a select few, therefore, the economic crisis that followed the peso collapse was not without its compensations. In fact, there was never a better time to be a speculator, a buyer of undervalued government assets, or a flight banker. The elite were effectively insured against the effects of the crisis they had helped to create. With the help of the US, the Mexican government relieved the largest banks of many bad loans. The US also bailed out wealthy foreign and domestic investors who had bought Mexican bonds. Finally, the elite had their own life preserver. Even after Salinas's reforms, most of them had still kept at least half their private wealth outside the country in dollars, much of it in secret trust and foreign bank accounts. So it was no accident that in 1995–96, even as the peso was losing half its value, new sales of Mercedes and other luxury cars in Mexico City's affluent neighborhoods set new records.

At the time, there were many in the financial community, including Citibank's former CEO Walter Wriston and many European bankers, who disagreed with the position taken by Clinton and Rubin. They argued that this "crisis" was very different from 1982—since no major international banks (e.g., Citibank) were at risk this time. The public interest in bailing out this crowd of relatively sophisticated, well-healed owners of Mexican bonds and banks was negligible.[66] Moreover, there were serious questions about what the Mexican banks had done with all their "loans" the first place. Despite all their promotional rhetoric about free markets, when their own pocketbooks were at stake, these powerful transnational interests decided to opt for state intervention—just as Chile's bankers had done in 1983. One is reminded of the line from Auden: "When there was peace, he was for peace. When there was war, he went."

In less than a month, the resulting bailout added $50 billion to Mexico's public foreign debt, undoing a whole decade of tedious debt restructuring. By the end of 1995, Mexico's foreign debt had ballooned to more than $160 billion—the highest of any developing country, higher in real terms by fifty percent and larger relative to GDP than it had been the year of Mexico's first debt restructuring in 1997. To service this debt, Mexico had pay more than $56 billion in interest and principle in 1995 alone, and very high continuing debt service costs. After a decade of "reform," it was the worst year ever for the growth of Mexico's foreign debt and capital flight.

At the same time, nearly half a million Mexican individual debtors and small businesses managed to organize their own nationwide union, El Barzon, seeking relief from the extraordinary interest rates that Mexican banks were charging. They had some success, but ultimately the government and banks responded harshly, breaking up their demonstrations and throwing several of their leaders in jail.[67] In 2000, over their stalwart protests, the new Mexican president Vicente Fox decided to both honor the FOBAPROA obligations to the banks and to keep the list of government bailout recipients a secret. Like many other things in Mexico, debt relief was distributed in inverse proportion to need and in direct proportion to influence.

Despite all the bailouts for the elite and bondholders, the peso's value hit an all-time low in November 1995, and the government raised interest rates again, prolonging the crisis. As its domestic banking industry cratered, for a while it appeared that Mexico might even need another increase in its credit line with the US and the IMF. But in December 1995, it received a stay of execution from the Federal Reserve, which lowered US interest rates to prevent the US economy from sinking into its own recession.

Yet, the turbulence continued for quite a while. One day the peso fell five percent on rumors of a military coup against Zedillo; another it tumbled four percent on reports that peace talks with the ELZN guerrillas had been called off; the next, it was roiled by the discovery of Raul Salinas's foreign accounts. Because of Mexico's heavy dependence on foreign finance, the economy remained hostage to events and expectations beyond its control. Meanwhile, in addition to bondholders and Mexican bank owners, there was at least one other group that profited from the Mexican crisis. In the aftermath of the crisis, to reduce FOBAPROA's costs of repairing the damage to Mexico's banking system, Mexico decided to open up its banking system to foreign ownership. Prior to the crisis, there had been severe restrictions on the rights of foreign banks to own a controlling position in Mexican banks. In fact, Citigroup was the only bank in Mexico City—having opened early in the twentieth century—that was "grandfathered" in. But now this barrier was dropped, and the buyers wasted no time in capitalizing on the opportunity. By 2001, Citigroup was the proud owner of Banamex. Banco Bilbao, Spain's largest financial group, purchased Bancomer; and Banco Santander, another leading Spanish bank, purchased Banco Serfin.

In 2003, Mexico's economy is stalled again, waiting for the US to recover. When the US does so, Mexico's economy undoubtedly will also rebound in the next few years. After all, it has one of the world's richest endowments of human and natural resources, and its labor costs are relatively low. But more than twenty years after the so-called "Third World debt crisis" began and more than a decade after it was supposed to have ended, Mexico is far from healthy, NAFTA and neoliberal reforms notwithstanding. It has massive, unsolved corruption and narco-trafficking problems, a huge supply of surplus labor, and a gargantuan foreign debt. While technical policy errors, bad luck, and local conditions all played a role in this outcome, it is hard to place the systemic blame anywhere but on authoritarian neoliberalism and its correlates: overborrowing, capital flight, corruption, money laundering, and dependent development.

In the last twenty years, Mexico ceded more and more control over its economic destiny to global markets, international bankers and their internal collaborators. Like other countries that have allowed themselves to become too far dependent on these transnational interests, Mexico still lacks a coherent, long-term economic strategy and an authentic democratic culture. It also lacks a solution to the basic problem of generating the five percent growth— or the one million plus new jobs—that it needs each year to lift its people out of poverty and become something more than a servants' quarters, oil reserve, illicit drug store, and vacation spot for its more affluent northern neighbors.

...

CHAPTER EIGHT

IT'S NOT ABOUT THE OIL

The Shah is expected to remain actively in power over the next ten years.
—US Defense Intelligence Agency, October 1978,
three months before the Shah left Iran

We ask, why does one group of people have to live in such poverty while another group spends $5 million just for decorating their villas?....They take this nation's oil and its other sources of wealth, they plunder this nation so that they can live like this while others live in poverty. We are shouting that we won't be plundered in this way...
—Ayatollah Khomeini, Speech # 38, Paris, October 1978

The problem is the future. The tribes don't want to form part of a unified state; the towns can't do without it. How are we going to support and protect the elements of stability and at the same time conform to the just demand for economy from home? . . . It's very significant that there are so few "wise" people in Baghdad—i.e., people who want a British mandate. No one knows exactly what they do want, least of all themselves, except that they don't want us.
—Gertrude Bell, British agent, describing the situation in Iraq under British occupation, September 5, 1920

PROLOGUE—THE "COALITION"

In March 2003, a US-led coalition launched "Operation Iraqi Freedom," invading Iraq with a force of 255,000 US troops, 45,000 British, 2,000 Australians, 400 Czechs and Slovaks, and 200 Poles.[1] Its official aims were to "liberate Iraq" from Saddam Hussein, "disarm" the country, eliminate its "weapons of mass destructions," and "restore democracy."[2] Skeptics recalled the speech by General Sir Frederick Stanley Maude, the British commander who seized Baghdad from the Turks in March 1917 and stayed on until 1932: "Our armies do not come into your cities and lands as conquerors or enemies, but as liberators."[3] But many others embraced the action as a sign that after supporting dictatorship and monarchy in the Middle East for decades, the US and the UK had finally decided to right some of their past wrongs.

Indeed, the US and the UK were deeply involved in creating a disastrous twenty five-year dictatorship in Iran and helped to bring Saddam Hussein's Ba'athist's regime to power in Iraq in the 1960s. In the 1970s, they also helped Saddam Hussein broker a deal with the Shah that undercut his Kurdish opponents. In the 1980s, they cynically encouraged Saddam Hussein to invade Iran, then financed and armed him to do so. After the war, they stood by and watched while his debt-ridden country, out of desperation and resentment, prepared quite publicly to invade Kuwait. After the invasion, they destroyed much of the military might that they had sold Saddam Hussein, but permitted him to regain power. Finally, during the 1990s, while they were enjoying unprecedented prosperity, they cynically permitted his people to be tortured by sanctions and repression for over a decade at a cost of thousands of lives, hoping that Iraq's people would rise up and bear the costs of overthrowing him. From this angle, it is not only Iraq that is debt-ridden. The First World has an enormous moral debt to both Iraq and Iran. The only question is, what is the best way to repay it?

The invasion was the easiest part of the war. After a rocky start, it proceeded very quickly. In twenty-one days of combat, the Coalition flew 41,000 air sorties, dropped 43 million leaflets and 27,718 bombs (sixty-seven percent of which were precision guided), fired 955 cruise missiles and 908 guided cluster bombs, killed several thousand Iraqi troops and several thousand more Iraqi civilians, and captured 7,500 prisoners. Through the end of April 2003, the coalition's official loss was just 157 troops—one-fourth by accidents and "friendly fire." After three weeks, it had overwhelmed Iraq's 350,000-person army, which the US Defense Intelligence Agency had once ranked as the fourth most powerful in the world. But after a decade of UN sanctions and "no fly" bombing, apparently Iraq's military was much less powerful than it had been when Saddam Hussein invaded Kuwait in August 1990. It was ill-equipped, underfed, reluctant to die for a lost cause, and unable or unwilling to launch even a single plane, scud missile, or any of its "weapons of mass destruction" that it was supposed to be hoarding. When leading members of Saddam Hussein's vaunted Republican Guard were offered an opportunity to surrender, many of them did so.

On the other hand, contrary to their own expectations, the invaders were not exactly greeted as liberating heroes. Throughout the summer of 2003, low-level guerilla attacks took a steady toll of that came to exceed the coalition's losses in the initial invasion. And in the first few months of liberation, much of the "liberating" done was of rare artifacts, office equipment, government cars, hospital generators, and almost anything else that was not tied down. The victorious US Marines stood by and watched Baghdad's residents celebrate Saddam Hussein's departure with an orgy of criminality and destruction. But when ordinary Iraqis managed to take a break from defending against the looting and other postwar traumas, most seemed glad to be rid of Saddam Hussein, who had brought them little besides war, economic hardship, disgrace, and repression.

However, many of them did not, at least initially, feel grateful to the coalition or eager to have the US and the UK settle into a long-term presence in their country. Throughout the summer of 2003, there were continuing guerilla attacks against US and UK forces, claiming more casualties than the invasion. There were also widespread demonstrations against the new occupants, even by Iraqis who had no sympathy for Saddam. After all, as many Iraqis knew, US relations with Saddam Hussein dated back to the late 1950s, when he was a Ba'athist Party errand boy without a high school degree, living in an apartment rented for him by an Egyptian military attaché. Many Iraqis were also aware of the shifting policies that the US and its allies had followed in the region ever since: first courting, and then double-crossing "allies" like the Kurds, the Shi'a, and devotees of Wahabi' Islam; encouraging Saddam Hussein to launch aggressive wars, and then denouncing him for it; sometimes being indifferent to his regime's brutality, and sometimes denouncing Iraq as part of the "axis of evil"; encouraging his opponents to rise up, and then standing by idly while he fed those who did into giant paper shredders. They had seen the US turn on a dime and abandon him, then turn again and permit him to regain power. Even though most believed that Saddam Hussein was now gone for good, they feared that the US might once again decide that popular rule threatened its "vital interests," and find them yet another brutal errand boy.

Of course, all these concerns arise even before we reach the really tough questions regarding oil, the Shiites, the Kurds, unresolved territorial disputes with Kuwait, Turkey, and Iran, and global terrorism. Like all imperial powers, the US has acquired a reputation for tricky, duplicitous behavior—viewed not just as a "liberator," but as one of the architects of the prison.

The invasion might soon turn out to be one of the more thankless quests in history. The US had already paid a heavy price in terms of global relationships. Officially, the invasion was supported by a "coalition" of forty-five countries. But only five provided troops, and eight preferred not to be publicly identified. Morocco did provide two thousand monkeys to help clear land mines. Unlike the 1991 Gulf War, the coalition's members did not agree to share the cost of the war or its aftermath.[4] That was not surprising, since the supporters included such heavily indebted countries as Nicaragua, the Philippines, Uganda, Rwanda, Eritrea, and Honduras, all of which depend on institutions like the World Bank and IMF, and would probably have even support a US invasion of Canada. The coalition also included such long-time "defenders" of democracy and human rights as Singapore, Bulgaria, Uzbekistan, Azerbaijan, Georgia, El Salvador, Albania, Romania, Mongolia, Turkey, Panama, and the Ukraine. In September 2002, the Ukraine's autocratic leader Leonid Kuchma was revealed to have sold a $100 million radar system to Iraq, violating the UN weapons embargo. He was also facing mounting domestic opposition over his role in the death of a leading Ukrainian journalist. Evidently Kuchma was trying to recover the good graces of the US, which had already reprogrammed $54 million of aid because of the radar sale.[5]

On the other hand, there were some interesting omissions from the official list of coalition supporters.[6] Kazakhstan was left out, even though it had strongly endorsed the coalition's goals.[7] But the US had other reasons for not being too vocal about Kazakhstan's support. On April 4, 2003, James H. Giffen, a leading New York merchant banker, was arrested by federal authorities at JFK International Airport on his way to Kazakhstan, on charges of sixty counts of bribery, money laundering, fraud, false income tax returns, and violations of the US Federal Corrupt Practices Act. This was in connection with funneling at least $78 million in kickbacks to Kazakhstani officials, including President Nursultan Nazarbayev, former Prime Minister Akezhan Kazhedgeldin, and Balgimbayev, the head of the state oil company. The purpose of the payoffs was to win oil concessions. J. Bryan Williams III—former director and senior vice president of Mobil Oil Corp. (now ExxonMobil), responsible for negotiating more than half of Mobil's global crude oil requirements in the 1990s, was also charged with receiving $2 million in kickbacks from Giffen. The bribes, paid from May 1997 to September 1998, were reportedly channeled from ExxonMobil, Amoco Oil (now BPAmoco), and Phillips Petroleum to DeutscheBank/Bankers Trust in New York, then on to the accounts of several British Virgin Islands, Liechtenstein, and Swiss shell companies and trusts at four Swiss banks—Credit Suisse First Boston (CSFB), Credit Agricole Indozuez (CAI), Pictet, and United European Bank. A Swiss investigation in 2001 unearthed a massive amount of similar US/UK oil company-funded corruption all over Central Asia. Another grand jury was also investigating Giffen's arrangement of illegal oil swaps for ExxonMobil with Iran, violating the 1996 US Iran Trade Sanctions Act.[8]

One of the most intriguing details in the case was that until recently, Williams, a former Wall Street lawyer and general counsel in Mobil's Saudi office in Jeddah from 1979 to 1984, had also served as the US government's sole UN overseer on the Iraq Sanctions Committee, in charge of making sure Saddam Hussein did not obtain any illicit offshore income from oil sales.

One approach to solving First World oil supply problems was simply to buy off local officials. This has long been the preferred route, beginning with the original design of whole new countries by the Allied Powers in the 1920s in Kuwait, Iraq, Saudi Arabia, and the other Gulf States. Apparently Saddam Hussein was beyond the point of requiring such intermediaries.

Also conspicuously missing from the list of supporters for the Iraq invasion were all the other permanent members of the UN Security Council (France, Russia, and China), eight out of the world's ten largest countries, longtime US allies such as Canada, Mexico, Germany, Saudi Arabia, and Kuwait, leading African countries like Nigeria and South Africa, every Muslim country, and every country in Latin America except Colombia where the US has deployed several hundred troops to help protect Occidental Petroleum's five hundred-mile oil pipeline and combat the growing left-wing insurgency. The Iraq invasion was also condemned by Pope John Paul II, the Archbishop of Canterbury, the Dalai Lama, most US and UK Catholic bishops, the Methodist Church, the Patriarch of Russia, many leaders of the Greek Orthodox Church, thirteen mainstream US Christian churches, many liberal rabbis, and most of the moderate Muslim clerics who had condemned the September 11 attack. The Southern Baptist Convention did support the invasion, at least unofficially, as did Pat Robertson, Chuck Colson, Billy Graham's son Franklin, who called Islam an "evil and wicked religion," and Jerry Falwell, who called the Prophet Mohammed a "terrorist."[9]

The invasion was condemned as illegal by most international legal scholars, on the grounds that it was not undertaken in response to an Iraqi attack or an imminent threat, as required by the UN Charter, and that its "approval" by the UN Security Council was doubtful at best.[10] The week before the invasion, there were unprecedented antiwar protests in almost every major capital around the world. Public opinion polls showed that, except in the US, the concept of a preventive invasion was very unpopular—even in the case of coalition members like Spain, the UK, Italy, Japan, and South Korea—especially if pursued without a UN mandate. None of this made any difference to President George W. Bush. His critics noted that foreign policy and war making were not exactly his long suits—he was a "C+" student at Yale, Harvard MBA, failed oil company executive, former baseball club owner, devout ex-alcoholic Christian, and one-term Texas governor who had dodged military service. He had traveled outside the US three times in his life before his presidency, including twice to Mexico, and devoted only forty-five words to foreign policy in his 2001 inaugural address. But in this regard, perhaps the key point is that he was not all that different from the average American: only twenty-one percent have a passport, just thirteen percent of college-age Americans can find Iraq on a map, a third cannot find the Pacific Ocean, and the median-aged American was just 2 years old during the Vietnam War's peak and 6 years old during Watergate.[11]

But even US public opinion may have been irrelevant to the Bush's decision to go to war. As *New York Times* editorialist Thomas Friedman observed in an April 2003 interview with Ha'aretz, the leading Israeli newspaper:

> [This] is the war the neoconservatives wanted . . . [and] marketed. Those people had an idea to sell when September 11th came, and they sold it. Oh boy, how they sold it. This is not a war that the masses demanded. This is a war of an elite. I could give you the names of 25 people (all of whom sit within a 5-block radius of my Washington D.C.) office, who, if you had exiled them to a desert island a year and a half ago, the Iraq war would not have happened.[12]

As President Bush said in early March, "We don't need anyone's permission." Clearly, President Bush did have the power—at least enough to start the war and commit the US to increased involvement in the Middle East and a more radical experiment in "nation building" than ever before. But despite the coalition's swift military victory in Iraq, the real war may only be beginning. Whether or not President Bush's invasion ultimately makes the world a safer place, or the Middle East more peaceful and democratic and at what cost, is far from certain. At this point, our focus is not on such questions, which will take years to sort out. As the social history Barrington Moore, Jr., once said, however, "Those who would break the chains of the past must understand the conditions that forged them." It is possible to provide a useful perspective on recent events by examining the historical roots of the conflict. From our particular vantage point, this means examining the role that excessive debts, misguided lending, and leading First World financial institutions, banks and multinationals played in setting the table for this debacle. For it turns out that our old friends, the global banks and multinationals, as well as various leading intelligence services, have been hard at work in this region at least since World War I, exerting decisive influence at key turning points.

ORIGINS

In 1951, Iran's constitutional government, led by nationalist prime minister Muhammad Mossadegh, nationalized the Anglo-Iranian Oil Company, the forerunner of BP. That was enough to motivate the British Secret Intelligence Service (BSIS, or MI6 as it is more widely known) to suggest to the CIA that it was time for a coup. President Truman opposed the idea, but in November 1952, a new, more hard-line Republican administration took office under President Dwight D. Eisenhower.

In March 1953, Eisenhower authorized CIA director Allen Dulles to overthrow Mossadegh. In August 1953, the CIA and MI-6 organized a coup, code-named TP-AJAX.[13] They provided the detailed plan; recruited, selected, and paid $5 million to Fazolla Zahedi, the prime minister who would replace Mossadegh, and dispatched General H. Norman Schwarzkopf, father of the 1991 Desert Storm commander, to persuade the skittish thirty-six-year-old Muhammad Reza Shah Pahlavi to go along. And when the original coup attempt failed and the Shah fled to Rome, CIA operatives stepped in, mobilizing paid demonstrators and sending Iranian hirelings to arrest Mossadegh. In 1958, Kermit Roosevelt Jr., one of Theodore Roosevelt grandsons who helped to orchestrate these events, left the CIA to become president of Gulf Oil, which had a major oil concession in Kuwait. Roosevelt's other grandson, Archibald Roosevelt Jr., remained with the agency until 1974, when he left to become vice president of International Relations for Chase Manhattan, a position he retained until 1990.[14] Over the next three decades, it was common for leading such global banks and multinationals to work closely with intelligence agencies, sharing information, strategies, contacts, and personnel.

Meanwhile, in Iraq, foreign influence was also being wielded to great effect in the interests of sympathetic monarchies. To understand the roots of Saddam Hussein's rise, it is necessary to go back a bit farther. The phrase "Hashemite monarchy" sounds like a venerable institution, but in fact—like the Saudi Royal Family, Jordan's monarchy, and every other "royal family" in the Gulf States—it was a modern invention. It was just one of several extended family dictatorships created by the British, the French, and the US—the world's largest oil consumers—out of the remains of the moribund Ottoman Empire at the end of World War I to maintain order, grant oil concessions, and facilitate military buildups. One of the Ottoman Turks many fateful mistakes was that they sided with Germany. In 1919, Britain was designated the mandatory power for "Mesopotamia," and it proceeded to cobble together a new country out of three Ottoman provinces: Mosul, Baghdad, and Basra, including the Ottoman subprovince later known as "Kuwait."

"Iraq's" original boundaries were arbitrary—a fact that would have profound consequences. They were roughed out on tracing paper by Gertrude Bell—the "uncrowned queen of Iraq," a close friend of Feisal Hussein's, and the only female intelligence agent in Britain's Arab Bureau—and T. E. Lawrence—another Arab Bureau member who had incited Sherif Hussein of Mecca and his Hashemite tribes to revolt against the Ottoman Empire. After the war, Sherif Hussein's son Feisal, who was very close to Lawrence of Arabia, wanted to rule over Syria, but it was a French mandate. When the French booted Feisal Hussein out in 1920, Lawrence and Bell lobbied the British to give him another sinecure, which became "Iraq." They promised the Allies to make sure this idea was acceptable to the locals. And, indeed, it was: In 1921,

Feisal Hussein's new monarchy received a stunning ninety-six percent approval in a rigged national plebiscite.[15]

The formation of Iraq left the Kurds out in the cold, creating yet another prolonged conflict marked "made in the UK." The Kurds were a collection of eight hundred northern tribes whose main tie was not necessarily religion, ethnicity, or even language, but the fact that they all lived in "Kurdistan," a mountainous region that spans Turkey, northern Iraq, Syria, and Iran. In 1919, a US-sponsored study, the King-Crane Commission, had recommended an independent state for the Kurds.[16] But this would have included the northern province of Mosul, where British explorers were uncovering huge oil finds around Kirkuk. Since large oil fields were not discovered yet in "Iraq's" other two provinces, the British feared that a Kurdish state would deprive Feisal Hussein's new kingdom—and themselves—of its principle source of income. And since the UK was already subsidizing Feisal Hussein's entourage to the tune of $750,000 per month, income was a key requirement.[17] The Kurds were not pleased by this betrayal—the first of many. But when they resisted, the British supplied "King Feisal" with troops and the Royal Air Force (RAF) to crush their revolt.

In fact, the use of aerial bombardment against Kurdish villages by the RAF in the 1920s and early 1930s was perhaps the first case of warfare conducted against civilians in the twentieth century. It predated Hitler's bombing of the Spanish village of Guernica in April 1937, and probably exceeded Guernica's 1,600 fatalities several times over. Winston Churchill, who was then colonial secretary, even urged the RAF to experiment with mustard gas on the Kurds, because it might prove more efficient. On February 19, 1920, he wrote to Sir Hugh Trenchard, the RAF's pioneer of air warfare: "I do not understand this squeamishness about the use of gas. I am strongly in favor of using poison gas against uncivilized tribes."[18] The RAF did not drop gas bombs in Iraq because of technical difficulties, but the British Army did use poison gas shells "with excellent moral effect" against Iraqi tribesmen in the Euphrates river basin who resisted the British mandate.[19] Throughout the 1920s, the RAF waged a steady "police bombing" campaign against Kurdish villagers, and also against similar local tribes in Aden (south Yemen), the southern Sudan, north-west India, and Transjordan. Arthur ("Bomber") Harris, commander of the UK's bomber offensive against Germany during World War II, reported in 1924:

> [The Arab and Kurd] now know what real bombing means, in casualties and damage; they now know that within forty-five minutes a full-sized village can be practically wiped out and a third of its inhabitants killed or injured by four or five machines, which offers them no real target, no opportunity for glory as warriors, no effective means of escape.[20]

In 1932, when the British mandate ended, the RAF turned the bombing over to the Iraqi Air Force, which the RAF recruited, trained and armed.

QASIM'S DEMISE

Given the divergent tribal and religious composition of the provinces that Iraq was awarded, Feisal Hussein I and his descendents did not have much success in providing a stable government. By 1958, the country had seen more than fifty cabinets come and go. It also had one of the most unequal distributions of land and oil wealth in the Middle East. In July 1958, King Feisal Hussein II was assassinated, and the corrupt Iraqi branch of the Hashemite monarchy was overthrown. The new president, Abdul-Karim Qasim, resembled Mossadegh in several respects. Even though he was anti-Communist, he was also nationalistic, left-leaning, and probably one of the more popular nonsectarian leaders in modern Iraqi history. He tried to introduce a progressive land reform to break up Iraq's many large holdings. He also tried to admit Kurds into his first government, threatened to nationalize the foreign oil concessions, and, later, refused to recognize Kuwait's independence in 1961. All this earned him many powerful enemies. But what really sealed Qasim's fate was his attempt to nationalize the oil concession owned by the Iraq Petroleum Company. This joint venture had been formed in 1928 by the Anglo-Iranian Oil/BP, Royal Dutch Shell (the predecessors of ExxonMobil), and CFP (a leading French oil company), with an exclusive concession from the grateful Feisal for almost the entire country.[21]

Qasim also did not make many friends in the US and the UK with his decision—six days after "Kuwait" obtained formal independence from its British mandate in June 1961—to reject the move. He declared that "Iraq and Kuwait remained one indivisible whole until 1913. Since then the people have been fighting imperialists. . . . There exists no boundary between Iraq and Kuwait. If anyone claims that there are boundaries then let him prove it."[22] Qasim's UN ambassador in 1961, Adnan Pachachi—who in 2003 became one of the US State Department's leading candidates to head a postwar caretaker government—declared at the time that "Kuwait is not more than a small coastal town on the Gulf."[23] This move also threatened BP, which had also played a seminal role, with the US company Gulf Oil, in the discovery of oil in Kuwait, and the organization of the Kuwaiti Oil Company in the early 1930s.

The whole notion of "Kuwait" as an independent nation was an even more recent invention than "Iraq," and no less dependent on British midwifery. The Ottoman Empire, knowing nothing of Kuwait's oil wealth, had regarded it as a remote subprovince of Basra that was too poor to tax. The proposed Anglo-Ottoman Convention of 1913 described it as "an

autonomous *qada* [subprovince] of the Ottoman Empire."[24] In 1932, as part
of the deal to grant Iraq independence and relax Britain's control, Iraq's prime
minister did acknowledge Kuwait's existence, but the 120-mile boundary was
never properly specified. In 1934, Kuwait's new monarch granted a generous
oil concession to BP/Gulf's Kuwaiti Oil Company. In any case, clearly the
British were not just innocent bystanders or disinterested observers.

In 1961, when Qasim threatened Kuwait's existence, the British immediately sent troops to the country to deter an invasion, supported by yet another
"pseudo-coalition" of troops from Saudi Arabia and Egypt that represented
the "Arab League." This crisis foreshadowed Saddam Hussein's 1990 invasion
of Kuwait and provided an example of how such an invasion might easily
have been deterred. It also showed that Saddam Hussein's claim to Kuwait was
not based only on his own evil territorial ambitions—many other Iraqi leaders of various political persuasions had reached the same conclusion.

In any case, as in Iran, the CIA and MI-6 did not sit idly by when Qasim
threatened what they considered to be vital US and UK (*viz*, oil) interests. By
the late 1950s, the CIA and Egyptian intelligence had developed a close relationship with key members of Iraq's Ba'athist Party. At the time, this party,
which had sister organizations in Syria and Egypt, was actually viewed by the
US as a "secular, progressive, democratic" alternative to the dangerously pro-
Soviet tendencies that were emerging throughout the region, particularly
Iraq's powerful Communist Party. This was despite the fact that the Ba'athist's
ideology was more accurately described—by another pungent phrase—
"national socialism."

One of the agents the CIA and MI-6 recruited to assist in their efforts
against Qasim was twenty-two-year-old Saddam Hussein, a tough young
Ba'athist Party sympathizer who had not yet graduated from high school. He
was reportedly recruited by Captain Abdel Maquid Farid, an assistant military
attaché at the Egyptian Embassy in Baghdad, who obtained an apartment for
Saddam Hussein located right across the street from Qasim's office. Fortunately for Qasim, the young Saddam Hussein was not much of a shot. When
he tried to assassinate Qasim in October 1959, he lost his nerve and only
wounded Qasim in the shoulder. With help from his Egyptian handlers, Saddam Hussein then escaped by way of Syria and Beirut to Cairo, where he was
given another apartment. He spent the next four years finishing high school,
studying law at the University of Cairo and making numerous trips to the US
Embassy, prompting Egyptian security officials to warn him to be more discrete.[25]

Finally, in February 1963, the CIA, the US military, and MI-6 succeeded
in organizing a coup that overthrew Qasim—who was executed on live TV
by a firing squad—and brought the Ba'athists to power for the first time in

Iraq. William Lakeland, a US military attaché in Baghdad, had coordinated the coup with Ba'athist Party leaders. William McHale, officially a member of Time Magazine's "Beirut bureau," compiled lists of suspected Iraqi Communists. About five thousand were rounded up and summarily executed following the "death squad orchestration" approach that the CIA employed to similar effect in Indonesia, Uruguay, Chile, Argentina, Brazil, and Guatemala.[26] One might have called this Iraq's first experience with mass terror and repression, but James Critchfield, head of the CIA's Middle East Desk, later hailed the coup as "a great victory." Ali Saleh Sa'adi, the new Ba'athist minister of the interior, admitted that "We came to power on a CIA train."[27] One of those who caught the train—returning from Cairo with a high school degree, a half-finished law degree, and unbridled ambition—was the twenty-six-year old Ba'athist Party activist Saddam Hussein.

There were many other twists and turns along the way, including a November 1963 military coup that briefly tossed the Ba'athists out and sent Saddam Hussein to jail, and another CIA-assisted coup in 1968 that concentrated power in the hands of a Ba'athist faction that originated in the region around the northern Sunni city of Tikrit. This faction was led by President Ahmed Hasan al-Bakr and his second cousin, Saddam Hussein, who become his vice president and head of security.

From the standpoint of foreign influence, another key episode took place in 1975, when Henry Kissinger and David Rockefeller helped to arrange the Algiers Accord between the Shah of Iran and the heretofore hostile Iraqi regime represented by Saddam Hussein.[28] This accord tried to settle the long-standing territorial dispute involving the Shatt al Arab outlet at the mouth of the Tigres-Euphrates River, including several islands that the Shah had seized by force in 1971. Like Mossadegh and Qasim, Iraq's Ahmed al-Bakr had antagonized the US and the UK by nationalizing Iraqi oil in 1972. As a response to this move and a favor to the Shah, President Nixon and Henry Kissinger got the CIA to provide more than $16 million in arms and aid to the Kurds in northern Iraq, who were now fighting the Ba'athists for independence.

By now, however, the Ba'athists had consolidated power, with the help of Saddam Hussein's deft touch as head of security. He was too entrenched to be overthrown by Kermit Roosevelt's methods, which the Ba'athists had learned about firsthand. At the time, the Ba'athists also showed that they were adept at cutting deals and compromising territorial disputes with their neighboring rivals—a fact that undercuts those who portray Saddam Hussein as an evil maniac intrinsically bent on world domination.

Henry Kissinger dealt with Saddam Hussein extensively. At Algiers, Saddam seized the chance to call off the Kurds by compromising Iraq's territo-

rial claims with Iran, and both parties agreed that each country would hence-
forth be free to deal with its internal problems as it saw fit. In practice, this
deal gave the Shah's secret police, the Savak, a free hand to crack down on
Shi'ite fundamentalists, who had a strong base in southern Iraq as well as Iran.
Over the next three years, under this Kissinger-arranged accord, more than
fifteen thousand of the Shah's opponents were eliminated. In 1978, at the
Shah's request, Saddam Hussein also expelled Shi'ite leader Ayatollah Ruhol-
lah Khomeini from southern Iraq, where he'd lived in exile for fifteen years.
The expulsion actually backfired on the Shah, when Khomeini was permitted by the French to take refuge in Paris, which gave him a worldwide platform and set the stage for the following year's revolution.

The Algiers Accord also ended, for the time being, the support given by
the Shah, the US, and Israel to the Kurds. This promptly led to a new wave
of repression by Saddam Hussein and the flight of two hundred thousand
Kurds to Iran. A heart-rending March 1975 letter from Mustafa Barzani,
leader of the Kurdish Democratic Party since 1945, to Henry Kissinger read:
"Our movement and people are being destroyed in an unbelievable way, with
silence from everyone. We feel, Your Excellency, that the US has a moral and
political responsibility towards our people, who have committed themselves
to your country's policy."[29] This provided the occasion for Kissinger's famous
rejoinder: "Covert action should not be confused with missionary work." This
was just one in a long series of betrayals of the Kurds by the US and the UK,
harkening back to the UK and France's double-dealing at the 1919 Paris
Peace Conference, and the RAF bombings. In 1979, Mustafa died of cancer
and heartbreak in the US. His son Massoud took over the KDP.

In any case, by the mid-1970s, the Ba'athist Party was firmly in control
of Iraq, and the Shah and the US had healed their rifts with al-Bakr and Saddam Hussein. It is fair to say that at this point, the US and the UK really could
claim to have birthed both these brutal regimes. Iraq and Iran both faced similar "internal problems" from the Communists, and the Shah's radical Shi'ite
problem was complemented by Saddam Hussein's own problems with radical
Shi'ites in the south and Kurds in the north. When this neat balance was upset
by the Shah's sudden demise in 1979, it created aftershocks that are still being
felt today.

THE SHAH'S PRIVATE BANKER

First World banks cultivated important relationships with both Iran and
Iraq during this period. Since at least the 1950s, the Shah was one of Chase
Manhattan's most important private banking clients. There was literally noth-
ing the bank wouldn't do for him. David and Nelson Rockefeller both vis-

ited Iran frequently, as did John J. McCloy, the influential US diplomat, German high commissioner, and World Bank president who served as an advisor to every US president from FDR to Ronald Reagan, and Chase Manhattan's chairman from 1953 to 1960.

In October 1971, David Rockefeller was a guest of honor at the Shah's elaborate three-day commemoration in Persepolis of the Persian conquest of Babylon in 539 B.C., 2,510 years of monarchy in Iran, and his own "White Revolution." The cost of the festival was variously estimated at $22 million to $200 million. Rockefeller was flown in along with 69 heads of state and 450 other dignitaries, including Ferdinand and Imelda Marcos, Ethiopia's emperor Haile Selassie, Romania's president Ceaucescu, Princess Grace, Orson Welles, and US vice president Spiro Agnew. A nineteen-square mile area in the middle of the desert was cleared of snakes, lizards, and scorpions, and an exotic Tent City was constructed. For months the Iranian Air Force shuttled back and forth from Paris, carrying Italian drapes, Baccarat crystal, Limoges china, Porthault linens, and more than five thousand bottles of wine. Two top Paris hairdressers were hired to attend to the female guests, and a staff of 159 French chefs and bakers prepared the menu. The guests were also treated to an elaborate parade that featured 1,700 soldiers in costumes and fake beards, riding hundreds of horses and camels that harkened back to the sixth century. Ten acres of top soil were brought in so that George Truffaut, the gardens manager at Versailles, could create a perfumed garden with roses and cypresses. An international congress of 250 Persian scholars was also convened.[30] Meanwhile, the Ayatollah Khomeini, in exile at the sacred Shi'ite city of Najaf, Iraq, found out about the ceremony and issued a scathing denunciation, calling it an "evil celebration." This prompted General Nematollah Nassiri, head of the SAVAK, to arrest 1,500 people. There was no terrorism during the event, which Iranians who were not in jail got to watch on their black and white TV sets.

The commemoration was by no means the Shah's only extravagance. From 1970 to 1978, his arms purchases totaled more than $20 billion. Especially after the 1973 OPEC oil price increase, the Shah's weapons purchases soared from less than $400 million in 1972 to $4.3 billion in 1974 and $5.7 billion in 1977.[31] The increased arms purchases coincided nicely with oil price increases, which the Shah and Saudi Arabia supported vigorously. Iran's oil revenues increased to more than $20 billion a year by 1977, as its exports surpassed 5.2 million barrels per day. Arms purchases made the Shah the largest single purchaser of US weapons during this period, accounting for more than a quarter of all US arms exports. However, all this new income and arms purchases destabilized Iran's economy, and inflated the Shah's sense of security. During the same period, he initiated $34 billion of grandiose construction projects that were immediately cancelled by the new Khomeini government when it took power in 1979.[32]

Despite the fact that the US government had to approve the export of all the weapons and that the US was the main ally, export market, and banker for the two leading proponents of oil price increases—the Shah and Saudi Arabia—the US failed to exert any leverage over them. Some observers speculated that the price increases were secretly welcomed by senior US policymakers like Henry Kissinger, and key interest groups. From a narrow corporate perspective, the increased oil revenues certainly funded an enormous amount of new arms sales, construction projects, bank deposits, and country loans. And most of the resulting surge in oil dollars flowed through just a handful of influential banks, oil companies, and contractors. They financed, in turn, an enormous increase in Third World borrowing and capital flight, for which the same major banks were the dominant players. Furthermore, while the price increases had negative effects on growth and productivity in the US, Europe and Japan (the United States' main competitors), as well as many Third World countries, were relatively disadvantaged by them. Conspiracy theorists have not yet produced much direct evidence for this explanation of the US' extraordinary passivity, but the apparent powerlessness of the West to resist the increases remains an interesting anomaly.

Whatever this theory's merits, however, it is clear that mismanagement of all the largesse that resulted from the oil price surge contributed greatly to destabilizing the Shah's regime. Apparently, no one at the State Department or the intelligence agencies foresaw this rather obvious developmental risk. Indeed, in the short run, the Shah behaved as though he had the upper hand in the relationship. As Henry Kissinger noted during the January 1977 address at an Iranian Embassy banquet in Washington, DC, "The US is counting on Iran . . . as a stabilizing force in the Middle East."[33] The US did not want to see the Shah lean towards the Soviet Union—with whom he maintained good relations in the 1970s, supplying the Soviets with natural gas. US corporate interests also did not want to see him shift his borrowing, investing, buying, and selling elsewhere.

In any case, rather than being channeled into social development, most of Iran's increased oil revenues were wasted on arms, white elephant projects, and huge commissions wired straight to the Shah's cronies' and generals' offshore bank accounts. There were also many dubious foreign investments, such as the Pahlavi Foundation's investments in New York City real estate, Krupp, the failing German industrial company, and dozens of hotels, restaurants, casinos, and nightclubs. And there was a surge in high-end imports. By 1977, Iran was importing goods from 129 countries.[34] It even managed to live beyond its income during this period, greatly increasing foreign debt aid to $12 billion by the end of 1978.[35]

All this did little for most Iranians, except to increase their costs of living and create glaring inequalities between the new, Westernized urban elite and the masses, most of whom continued to be rural peasants. The Shah made much of his efforts to "modernize" the country, asserting on French TV in 1977 that "in 10–12 years, we shall reach the quality of life enjoyed by you Europeans."[36] Indeed, he did make an effort to urbanize and industrialize. He attempted a poorly planned land reform that ended up driving many people into the cities. Against the grain of an intensely religious culture, he also tried to introduce women's rights and promote secular education. But even the best of his reforms got stuck in the unresolved contradictions between his own imperial tendencies, the country's conservative religious traditions, and the massive corruption and wasteful spending generated by the sudden increase in oil revenues and debts. In short order, Iran was anything but a stabilizing force in the Middle East; it became a vortex.

The Shah's economic development problems provided ample grist for Khomeini's opposition movement. Khomeini has often been simply portrayed as a religious zealot, but a great deal of his support was derived from his pointed criticisms of the Shah's economics. As Khomeini said in Paris on October 20, 1978, three months before the Shah's ouster:

> Wherever you look, you see there is something wrong. The economy is in ruins. According to experts, agricultural production in Iran now is only sufficient to meet the needs of the nation for thirty-three days a year. . . . The result of the gentleman's "Land Reform Program" was to turn Iran into a consumer market for America. . . . They are taking our oil now in such a way that in thirty years' time, the reserves will run dry. . . . In return, the Americans sell us the arms that they want for their military bases that they have set up in Iran to confront the Soviet Union. . . . They take our oil and in return they sell us planes worth $350 million [each]. . . . The Soviet Union, too, must announce its support, because they are taking the country's gas. . . .
>
> . . . If we had an honest government which sold the oil in a proper way and spent the revenues from it on the people, then this nation would not be in the state it is today.
>
> That is why we are shouting. We ask, why does one group of people have to live in such poverty while another group spends $5 million just for decorating their villas? . . . Their wealth comes from the people. . . . They take this nation's oil and its other sources of wealth, they plunder this nation so that they can live like this while others live in poverty. We are shouting that we won't be plundered in this way, that this regime must be replaced . . . .[37]

Despite such criticisms, the Shah made no significant changes in his strategy. One key reason was that so many insiders were profiting from the system. In particular, foreign banks like Chase and Citibank benefitted immensely from the simultaneous surge in oil payments, deposits, and foreign debts. Chase

Manhattan became the Shah's largest single creditor, lending more than $2.7 billion in 1977–79, right before his collapse.[38] As of 1979, Chase also managed more than $6 billion of Iranian government deposits and substantial private banking assets for the Shah and his family. Henry Kissinger, David Rockefeller's close friend and the chairman of Chase's International Advisory Committee, supported the sharp increase in US arms sales while he was US secretary of state from 1973–76. A close relationship with the Shah was also promoted by Zbigniew Brzezinski, President Jimmy Carter's National Security advisor from 1977 to 1981, who was appointed the first director of David Rockefeller's Trilateral Commission in 1973. Indeed, in the early 1970s, Carter first caught David Rockefeller's eye by way of Brzezinski, who introduced him as the thoughtful governor of Georgia who had opened trade missions for his state in Brussels and Tokyo. In 1973, David Rockefeller and Brzezinski recruited Carter to serve on the Trilateral Commission, providing him valuable name recognition.[39]

Such relationships were also cemented by a strong network of private banking transactions. In the waning days of the Shah's regime, Chase Manhattan became involved in several highly questionable loans to Iran. In late 1978 it loaned $90 million to a subsidiary of the Iranian National Oil Company (INOC). According to an Iranian insider who was involved in the transaction, on instructions from the Shah's oil minister, Chase transferred the funds provided by this loan to a company that was owned by the Shah's sister, ostensibly for "services" to INOC. Actually, the money never left New York. Since his sister had private accounts at Chase, everything was accomplished with a few offsetting bookkeeping entries at the bank's headquarters in lower Manhattan.

In November 1979, during the hostage crisis, the US government froze $12 billion of Iran's deposits at US banks. Chase, Citibank, and MHT—the main US beneficiaries of the Shah's government accounts and his family's personal accounts—controlled more than eighty percent of these deposits, and also accounted for the lion's share of his foreign loans. Acting unilaterally, they immediately seized all Iranian government deposits at their disposal and used them to pay off outstanding loans. This was done, despite the fact that the loans were not yet due, that Iran's new government had been servicing them scrupulously, and that the seizure violated conventional banking practices, in which all possible steps are usually taken to avoid defaults.

This seizure outraged Iranians—especially moderates who were just then struggling against religious zealots. It also outraged many foreign banks and smaller US banks that also had loans outstanding to Iran, but few Iranian deposits to grab. Interestingly, no other country followed the US banks' lead of seizing Iranian government assets, or the trade embargo that the US tried to impose on Iran. Several European banks continued to lend money to Khomeini's regime. While the asset freeze and the resulting boycott may have generated surplus profits for Chase and Citibank, it probably hurt the US trade balance, smaller US banks, and the overall US-Iran relationship.[40]

In Chase's case, the egregious opportunism went even further. The $90 million "loaned" to the Shah and diverted to his sister was one of the loans that Chase paid off with the deposits that it seized. So in the end, Chase was paid back its $90 million, the Shah's sister was $90 million richer, and the Iranian government was stuck with a $90 million reduction in its liquid assets.[41] This kind of sharp practice was not likely to win much of a following for the US in Iran.

When the Shah fell in January 1979, all these cosy relationships were disrupted, along with the United States' entire Middle East strategy. In the short run, the US National Security Agency lost its invaluable secret TACKSMAN signals bases in the Elbourz Mountains, where it monitored the USSR's missile test ranges. But the US and Israel lost a loyal ally, a huge market, and a role model for the secular development of Islamic countries. Overall, the Shah's demise was one of the greatest setbacks to US foreign policy in the entire post-World War II era, almost as embarrassing as the Vietnam War, and with far more profound long-term consequences.

Apparently the US was caught completely off guard by the Shah's rapid demise—despite the fact that in 1976, Iran was already labelled by Amnesty International as the "world's most repressive regime." The first CIA memo warning that he might be in trouble was dated October 1978, just three months before he fled. CIA director Stansfield Turner later commented, "What we had not predicted was that a 78 year-old man, an Ayatollah who had spent 14 years in exile, could forge together these forces and turn all of these volcanoes into one immense volcano, into a national and real revolution." The US Defense Intelligence Agency (DIA) fared just as bad, declaring on September 28, 1978, that the Shah "is expected to remain actively in power over the next ten years." As one Kennedy School postmortem on the Shah's demise concluded, "Less than a year [before his fall], no analyst, inside or outside government, came close to predicting that the Shah was in such trouble."[42] That is not quite true. But those who had correctly predicted his demise were not working for second-rate intelligence agencies.

The real failure rested not with middle-level intelligence analysts, but with the senior policy architects who had winked at all the arms trafficking, bad projects, and loans. Among the worst offenders was David Rockefeller's advisor, Henry Kissinger, who had not only exerted a strong influence on US policy toward the Shah since 1968, but also knew a great deal about Iran's inner financial workings through his Chase relationships. While Khomeini was returning to Iran in February 1979, Kissinger tried to blame the Shah's demise on the Carter administration's "hollow pursuit of the defense of human rights."[43] He suggested that a more repressive approach, along the lines of the one that he had employed in early 1970s Chile, might have saved the day. In fact by the time the US government realized the Shah was in trouble, it was much too late. Kissinger's view simply reflected his own deep cynicism and his inability to accept his own responsibility—and that of his friends and former employers—for their indulgent, short-sighted policies.

The rapid disintegration of one of the US's most critical alliances in the Middle East, based on an untenable development strategy, and coupled with the agonizing hostage crisis that began in November 1979, was extraordinarily traumatic for US policymakers. It was also cataclysmic for key US allies like Saudi Arabia, Kuwait, and Iraq, which all took careful note of Khomeini's February 1979 threat to "export the Islamic revolution" to his corrupt neighbors. The Shah's demise and the subsequent rise of Khomeini's most extreme followers to power were not inevitable. But time after time, the US and its allies opted for elitist, short-sighted, antidemocratic policies that foreclosed other alternatives. At the end of this long road was the 2003 US invasion of Iraq.

THE BANKERS AND THE HOSTAGES

One of the most fateful choices was made in 1979, right after the Shah's overthrow. As soon as he left the country for Cairo in mid-January, Chase's inner circle began a vigorous lobbying campaign to win asylum for him in the US. David Rockefeller, the consummate private banker, assigned his personal aid Joseph V. Reed—a Chase vice president and future US ambassador to Morocco under President Reagan—to look after the Shah's personal finances. He also asked his close friend, New York Hospital's Dr. Benjamin H. Kean, to look after the Shah's health, and David Armao, a PR consultant who had worked for David Rockefeller's brother Nelson, to help improve the Shah's image. Henry Kissinger, David Rockefeller, and former Chase chairman John J. McCloy all started lobbying the Carter administration relentlessly over the next ten months to get the Shah asylum. This effort included at least five private approaches by Kissinger to President Carter, a visit by David Rockefeller to the White House, innumerable handwritten notes from McCloy to Carter's press secretary Hamilton Jordan, and many calls from other supporters. Former undersecretary of state George Ball later described the lobbying effort as "obnoxious," and asserted that, but for their efforts, the Shah would never have been admitted.[44]

At first, the Carter administration had no problem with asylum. Nor, for that matter, did Khomeini—who was not yet firmly in control in Tehran and actually wanted the Shah as far away as possible, because he feared a possible counterrevolution. However, the Shah vacillated, wasting six weeks in Egypt and Morocco, hoping for counterrevolution that never came. Incredibly, the Carter administration also flirted seriously with the idea of fomenting yet another coup. In January, it dispatched General Robert Huyser as a special envoy to Iran for a month, where he held intense meetings with key commanders in the Shah's army—most of whom the US military had trained. His orders were to see if such a plan could be devised.

But the situation moved too fast for the US to replay its 1953 restoration. On February 11, 1979, as Iran's armed forces were losing control to what was clearly a very popular uprising, Carter gathered his closest advisors at Camp David to consider his options. National Security advisor Brzezinski still favored a 1953-like coup and was on the verge of getting Carter's approval. But when Brzezinski called General Huyser in Tehran to ask about its feasibility, the General replied that it would only be possible "with the direct support of the US military," including ten thousand soldiers from elite units and an unlimited budget. That was too much even for Zbigniew.[45]

Having missed the opportunity for a military coup, President Carter decided to focus on trying to establish relations with the new, hopefully moderate government of Prime Minister Mehdi Barzargan. On February 14, 1979, a group of militants seized the US Embassy in Tehran for three hours, providing a clear example of what might happen if there were further US provocations. Fearing such reprisals, US ambassador William Sullivan and other key Embassy staff wrote to the State Department, expressing strong opposition to giving the Shah asylum.[46] By then, in the words of one Iranian newspaper, the vast majority of Iranians were celebrating "the end of 2,500 years of imperial dictatorship."[47]

On February 23, 1979, the Carter administration—over the opposition of Brzezinski—informed the despondent Shah that both the coup and the asylum offer were off the table. For the next nine months, while Kissinger, Rockefeller, and McCloy tried hard to reverse this decision, the Shah and his family wandered from Cairo to Morocco to the Bahamas, to Cuernavaca, to Panama, and finally to Egypt, where he eventually died of cancer in July 1980. All this meandering prompted Kissinger—who may have felt a pang of guilt about the Shah's situation—to complain in May 1979 that he was being treated like a "Flying Dutchman who cannot find a port of call."

Kissinger, Rockefeller, and McCloy were not people who were used to being turned down. In October 1979, they tried a new gambit, with David

Armao and Joseph V. Reed floating reports that the medical condition of the Shah, who was then in Cuernavaca, was critical, and that only New York City doctors could save him. In fact, Dr. Kean, the only US physician who actually performed a detailed physical on the Shah during this period, was more relaxed. While the Shah had contracted lymphoma as early as 1974, his condition in 1979 was not yet dire. For years he had been under the care of the same French physicians who attended to him in Mexico, and Dr. Kean believed there were at least nine other countries willing to take him that had adequate medical facilities, including Mexico. The real problem seems to have been the Shah's taste for fine living. He simply wanted to spend his last years in New York City, close to friends like Kissinger and Rockefeller and more accessible to all his royal friends passing through.

On October 21, 1979, after ten months of pestering, President Carter gave in to the medical ploy and decided to admit the Shah "temporarily" for treatment. An election year was approaching, and Carter may have feared that if the Shah died without being admitted to the US, Kissinger and his influential friends would scapegoat him for both his downfall and his death. Apparently, Carter made the decision without asking for a second opinion from an independent doctor, over the continuing vocal objections from the US Embassy's remaining staff in Tehran. They saw the moderate Barzargan's grip on power slipping and wanted to avoid any incidents that might provoke Khomeini's militants.

Why the US Embassy neglected to take more security precautions during this period is unclear. Its staff had already been reduced from 1,400 (the world's largest) to less than 65 by the time of the occupation. The remaining Embassy staff members were also committed to rebuilding relations with Iran's new government. In the fall of 1979, before the Embassy takeover, they reported that relations were improving. There were also reportedly more than a few valued "intelligence assets" among the remaining staffers.[48] However, just as the Embassy staff predicted only two weeks after it was announced that the Shah was headed for New York, on November 4, 1979, the US Embassy was occupied by militant students. Fifty-two US hostages were seized. They would not regain their freedom for 444 days. Brzezinski advised President Carter to respond immediately with military force. But Carter waited, trying to rely on weaker methods such as the seizure of Iranian bank deposits. After four months of stasis, with Senator Kennedy challenging him in the spring primaries and an election coming up in November, Carter gave in to his National Security advisor's hair-brained scheme for a long-distance night raid. The raid ended in the Iranian desert with eight US soldiers dead in a helicopter crash, Secretary of State Cyrus Vance resigning in protest, and Khomeini's supporters more furious than ever at the US and President Carter.

The fifty-two hostages were finally freed by Khomeini in January 1981, the day President Ronald Reagan took office. Former President Carter flew to Germany on Air Force One to meet them. Several greeted him coolly. They could not believe that he not only launched the "Hail Mary" rescue attempt, which might easily have killed half of them, but ignored their advice and risked their lives for the sake of providing a few days of nonessential medical care for the Shah. They did not understand the influence that leading Wall Street bankers and their proxies can bring to bear on indecisive, well-intentioned presidents, especially during an election year.

To explain Carter's failure to win the hostages' release during the last eight months of his term and his loss to Reagan in the November 1980 presidential elections, some journalists and former Democratic policy advisors later developed the "October Surprise" theory. This was the notion that future CIA director William J. Casey, former CIA director George H. W. Bush, and other operatives in the Reagan campaign had negotiated a secret deal with Khomeini's representatives in Madrid and Paris during the summer and fall of 1980, promising an end to the asset freeze and US weapons in return for a delay in the hostages' release until after the November elections. This theory was most eagerly advanced by former Carter NSC staffer and Columbia University professor Gary Sick.[49] In 1992, a year-long investigation was conducted by a US Congressional Task Force chaired by Democratic congressman Lee H. Hamilton. On January 13, 1993, it issued a report concluding that there was "no credible evidence" supporting the theory.

However, the task force's investigation was complicated by the fact that several alleged direct witnesses were either dead (Casey and Iranian arms dealer Cyrus Hashemi) or had serious credibility problems. The theory did have a certain logic. By the end of October 1980, most opinion polls showed that Reagan was likely to win unless Carter were able to perform a miracle, like a hostage release.[50] Under these conditions, with the presidency within reach, Reagan's staff might well have wanted to buy some insurance by cutting a deal. It also made sense for the Iranians because, even though Carter may have also been willing at this point to trade arms and frozen bank assets for the hostages, the arms transfers would take time, and he might not be reelected even with a release. But all this assumed that the Iranians trusted the Reaganites to keep their promises and that it would take at least until November to get the arms.

There were also some tantalizing leads that the task force failed to track down. A six-page October 1992 cable was found in 1995 by investigative journalist Robert Parry in a box of task-force records in a storage room at the Rayburn Building. The cable, addressed to Congressman Hamilton, was from Sergei Stepashin, chairman of the Supreme Soviet's Committee on Defense and Security Issues. Based on Soviet intelligence, the cable alleged that key European meetings between Casey and Bush had indeed taken place and that the quid pro quo for delaying the hostage release had been spare parts for F-14s, Lance-class surface-to-surface missiles, and other US weapons that Iran's US-trained army depended on. These were to be shipped with US approval by way of Israel and private arms dealers. According to Parry, the Committee received this cable from the Russians on January 11, 1993, two days before its final report, and ten days before President Clinton's inauguration. Incredibly, the Committee decided not to investigate the allegations further.[51]

There was also another curious incident that involved Rockefeller's close aid and the Shah's personal banker, Joseph V. Reed. In December 1992, Charles G. Cogan, a senior Middle East specialist at the CIA, gave a classified deposition to Hamilton's Task Force. He reported that in September 1981, he happened to be in CIA director William J. Casey's new seventh floor office in Langley, Virginia when Reed suddenly appeared. Cogan testified under oath that he had a "definite memory" that he overheard Reed remark to Casey, "We really fucked up Carter's October Surprise." Questioned later about the incident by FBI agents at his fifty-acre estate in Greenwich, Connecticut, Reed admitted that as the newly-appointed US ambassador to Morocco, he had called on Bill Casey to "pay his respects." But he denied even knowing what "October Surprise" referred to. He also denied having visited Casey in 1980, during the run up to the elections, even though a sign-up sheet at Reagan-Bush Headquarters in Arlington revealed that he and Archibald B. Roosevelt Jr., one of the 1953 coup architects and a Chase vice president had indeed both called on Casey on September 11, 1980.[52] Without more new evidence, however these allegations were just interesting curiosities. The October Surprise theory is likely to remain yet another unproven conspiracy theory, attracting those who like to believe that history is just one cabal after another.

Moreover, as interesting as it was, the October Surprise theory basically missed the big picture. The far more important "cabal" was out in plain view: the small group of Chase bankers and fellow-travelers whose lobbying efforts helped to precipitate the hostage crisis and all the desperate rescue attempts that followed. Furthermore, through all their unquestioning support of the Shah's strategy, they had also helped to create an opportunity for the Ayatollah Khomeini to return by popular acclamation and take control of the country. Long before the Shah's downfall, it was this unquestioning support—lubricated with arms, aid, loans, bribes, kickbacks, money laundering services, spying skills and technologies, plus the 1953 coup—that fed his arrogance and encouraged his unbalanced development strategy. This did not require a conscious conspiracies. It merely required this self-organizing network of interests that was basically out for itself.

In the end, the Shah and his supporters in foreign governments and banks had helped "develop" Iran. However, sixty-one million Iranian citizens were not consulted about the design. The resulting animosity directed towards the US—reflected in Khomeini's description of the US as the "Great Satan" and in mass demonstrations held in Tehran that still chant "Death to America" to this day—has often been attributed to Khomeini's version of Islamic fundamentalism. But this hostility had nothing to do with intrinsic religious doctrines or atavistic mullahs. It had much more to do with the First World's own *decades* of unsavory behavior. Pogo, meet the enemy.[53]

SEEDING THE WIND

The Shah's demise had many costly side effects. To begin with, in its aftermath, the US decided that it had to take strong action in the Middle East, not only to reassure shaky oil monarchies like Saudi Arabia, the UAE, and Kuwait that they would not be next in line for Islamic revolutions, but also to prevent the Soviets from exploiting Iran's instability. To keep the Soviets preoccupied and away from the Gulf, in May–June 1979 the Carter administration, under Brezinski's guidance, initiated covert operations in Afghanistan in collaboration with Saudi Arabia and Pakistan. The aim was to destabilize Afghanistan's pro-Soviet dictator and lure the Soviet Army into a costly occupation. On July 3, 1979, President Carter signed a National Security directive that approved a limited amount of secret funding for the formation of an anti-Soviet Afghan insurgency. Brzezinski told President Carter that "In my opinion, this aid was going to induce a Soviet military intervention."

In December 1979, the Soviet Army did invade Afghanistan—their "Mexico," an impoverished, unstable, drug-ridden autocracy right on their southern border—with a force that ultimately reached 115,000 troops. It replaced one dictator with another hand-picked stooge. President Carter responded by calling Pakistan's military dictator, General Zia-ul-Haq, and offering him hundreds of millions in aid to help foment a large "Afghan-Arab" rebel insurgency. This effort, which was considerably expanded by the CIA's William J. Casey during the Reagan administration, amounted to a sharp reversal of US policy toward General Zia.

Over Brzezinski's objections, the vacillating Carter had cut US aid to General Zia off in 1977. At the time, Carter's decision to boycott the dictator—who was developing nuclear weapons and long-range missiles, exporting terrorists to Kashmir, and murdering his political opponents—had been greeted with harsh criticism by geopolitical "realists" like Kissinger, William Safire, and Jeane J. Kirkpatrick, who portrayed Carter as weak-kneed.[54] Decades later, with both Pakistan and India having acquired nuclear weapons, Pakistan's dictatorship barely clinging to power against growing anti-Americanism, and the country now a favorite hiding place for global terrorists, these critics may have second thoughts. In the 1980s, Pakistan led the way in recruiting, training, and arming thousands of militant young Muslims— "Afghan Arabs"—from Saudi Arabia, Egypt, Yemen, and other Sunni Islamic countries. These included the young Saudi construction magnate, Osama bin Laden, as well as militant veterans of the anti-Soviet struggle like Gulbuddin Hekmatyr, who in 2003 urged a new *jihad* against US troops in Afghanistan, and Abdul Haq, who was greeted by Ronald Reagan as a "freedom fighter" despite taking credit for terrorist attacks, like a 1984 bomb blast at Kabul's airport that killed twenty-eight people.

Under the immediate direction of Pakistan's ISI, its British-trained imitation of MI-6, with funding and arms provided by the US and Saudi Arabia, the rebels' role was to harass the Soviet occupiers from bases in Pakistan and Afghan's mountainous regions. From 1980 to 1988, the US government provided more than $2 billion in military aid to these *mujahideen* terrorists, including (after 1985) hundreds of handheld Stinger missiles, which proved invaluable against Soviet helicopters. As a leading military journal noted, "The trainers were mainly from Pakistan's ISI, who learned their craft from American Green Beret commandos and Navy SEALS in various US training establishments."[55] These "freedom fighters" also financed their efforts through the opium and heroin trade, using their new skills and international connections to develop new markets, buy arms, and launder the proceeds. Indeed, Soviet troops provided one of the best markets for heroin, much like US soldiers had done in Vietnam. The whole Afghan drug industry really began during this period. Twenty years later, the trade is still booming. In the mid-1990s, the Taliban tried to control it, but after their overthrow by the US in 2001, it surged again. It now provides the main source of income for regional warlords that threaten Afghanistan's weak central government. It has also spread HIV/AIDS widely in Russia and Central Asian countries, since thousands of returning war veterans contracted the virus from dirty needles.

By the time the Soviets withdrew in February 1989, the resulting decade-long war had indeed become what Brzezinski proudly referred to as "the Soviet Vietnam," with 15,000 Soviet soldiers killed or missing and an incredible 470,000 other Soviet casualties, mainly from disease. It really is more accurate, however, to describe the war as "Afghanistan's Vietnam," since the main victims of this artifically-induced conflict were the Afghan people. Because of its one-sided nature and the savage tactics employed by the Soviets—including the widespread use of land mines, aerial bombardments, and strafing of villages by helicopter gun ships—the war produced more than 1.3 million Afghan casualties and 5.5 million refugees, over a third of the country's population.[56]

At the war's conclusion, one might have expected the US and Pakistan to implement a "demilitarization" program for the "freedom fighters"—to whom people like Brzezinski sometimes credited the ultimate demise of the whole Soviet Empire. But as in the case of the Kurds, the US quickly lost interest in the "Afghan-Arabs" after they had served their purpose. They quickly went from being "freedom fighters" to "terrorists." The Bush administration ignored them, focusing its energies elsewhere, like the overthrow of Manuel Noriega, political change in Eastern Europe, and arms and finance for Saddam Hussein. All this left Afghanistan, as *The Economist* reported, "awash with weapons, warlords and extreme religious zealotry," and, it might have added, opium. The country then quickly reverted to another warlord dictatorship, which was overthrown in 1994–95 by the Taliban—mostly young Afghans who had been schooled by radical Islamic clerics in Pakistani refugee camps during the 1980s. In 1996, the Taliban, in turn, offered safe haven to Bin Laden and thousands of his sympathizers who were also veterans of the US-sponsored war.

As noted, Brzezinski, George H. W. Bush, and other supporters of the Afghan insurgency liked to credit this violent policy for the relatively peaceful collapse of the Soviet Empire and the Cold War. Perhaps the Afghan fighters and people like bin Laden and Hekmatyr deserve some of the credit. Perhaps the Polish unions also deserve a mention, as do Gorbachev, Yeltsin, and other Soviet reformers, who finally saw the economic handwriting on the wall in the late 1980s. Khomeini may even deserve some credit, because he toppled the Shah and helped to provoke the US response in Afghanistan. Short-term "successes" always have many fathers; long-term failures usually go unclaimed. What is clear now is that by seeding this particular Islamic wind, the First World has inherited a whirlwind, and a global, low-intensity "Hot War" that may last even longer than the Cold one.

SADDAM HUSSEIN'S PREVENTIVE WAR

The other tributary that sprang from the Shah's sudden fall involved Iraq. As noted, on February 11, 1979, Khomeini had threatened to "export our revolution to the four corners of the world," especially to countries that he viewed as the corrupt clients of foreign powers like the US and the Soviet Union. This made many countries in the Middle East nervous, especially those that were close to Iran and had large Shi'a populations: Iraq (60–65 percent of the population, and 85 percent of the army), Saudi Arabia (at least five hundred thousand Shi'a citizens), Kuwait (30 percent), Bahrain (70 percent), and Soviet-occupied Afghanistan (15–20 percent). So with tacit US support, Saudi Arabia, Kuwait, Jordan, and the Gulf States started to rebuild relationships with their new best friend in the region—Iraq's Saddam Hussein.

By the late 1970s, Saddam Hussein had already ruthlessly consolidated his power base. In July 1979, he pushed aside President Ahmed al-Bakr "for health reasons" and purged sixty-eight members of Iraq's Revolutionary Council, accusing them of conspiring with Syria's Ba'athists.[57] He then turned his attention to Iran. His motives were partly defensive. Not only had Khomeini promised to export revolution, but he also singled out secular states like Iraq, Egypt, and Jordan, promising to "eradicate or subjugate" Arab nationalism to achieve "the higher unity of Islam."[58] In June 1979, he exhorted Iraqis to "rise up and overthrow the Saddam Husseinite regime." Apparently Khomeini hoped that Iraqi Shi'as (albeit Arabs, not Persians, unlike most Iranians) might rise up spontaneously. Most did not, and those who did were easily suppressed. But from Saddam Hussein's perspective, it was the thought that counted.[59]

Saddam Hussein feared that once Khomeini consolidated his grip on Iran, the country might become a serious strategic threat right on Iraq's doorstep. After all, Iran had a population three times greater than Iraq, a far more modern military, a capital city that was farther from the border and easier to defend, a long coastline, and a longer history as a unified country under its Persian Shiite majority.[60] While Iraq was also an oil exporter with a large standing army, and had even tried to acquire nuclear weapons in the 1970s, it had not spent anywhere near what the Shah did on jet fighters, a navy, tactical missiles, or air defense. With the Shah gone, Saddam Hussein also saw signs that Khomeini was resuming aid to the Kurds, who constituted fifteen percent of Iraq's population.

On the offensive side, Saddam may have seen an opportunity to reverse the concessions that he had been forced into by the Shah at Algiers, to get Iran to call off the Kurds. This included half of the Shatt-al-Arab waterway, Iraq's only outlet to the Persian Gulf. It is unlikely that Saddam intended to conquer all of Iran, or kill Khomeini, which would have exacerbated his political problems with Iraq's Shi'a majority. But depending on how the war went, he may have hoped to seize oil-rich Khuzestan, Iran's key oil province in the southwest. A third of its 3.5 million people were not Persians but Arabs. Finally, he may have also viewed the invasion as a way to enhance his clout in the region, in the wake of Sadat's ejection from the Arab League after Egypt's 1979 peace treaty with Israel. In this regard, he may have hoped not only to impress countries like Saudi Arabia and Kuwait, but also the US, filling the void left by the Shah.

At first Saddam experimented with diplomacy. Iraq was one of the first countries to recognize the new Islamic Republic of Iran in early 1979. In August 1979, it invited Mehdi Barzargan, Iran's moderate first president, for a visit. But Barzargan's government fell apart during the early days of the hostage crisis and was replaced by that of President Abol Hassan Bani-Sadr, which was more hostile. Khomeini's followers had also started to incite revolt among Iraq's Shi'as. In February 1979, after Khomeini's threat to export revolution, Saddam Hussein dispatched troops to suppress demonstrations incited by Iranian radicals in the southern Shi'a holy cities of Najaf and Karbala. These demonstrations were strong enough to compel Saddam to institute martial law and to arrest Ayatollah Sadr, a leading Shi'a cleric and Khomeini ally. After the execution of ninety-seven of their supporters in April 1980, the militant Shi'a group Ad Dawah, with Iranian support, tried to kill Iraq's deputy premier Tariq Aziz. The assassination attempt prompted Saddam to get even tougher: He ordered Sadr's execution, closed Iraq's border to Shi'a pilgrims, expelled up to a hundred thousand Shi'as, and put relations with Iran on hold.[61] By April 1980, Saddam had given up on the diplomatic alternative and was focused on preparing an invasion—in George W. Bush's terms, a "preventive war."

With Iran in turmoil, its entire officer class purged after unsuccessful coup attempts in May and July 1980, and the hostage crisis still unresolved, Saddam believed the time was right to strike early and dismember Iran's regime. If he waited, he feared that the Islamic Republic would only grow stronger. It might even strike a covert arms deal with the US to release hostages, trading improved relations for spare parts. He was right to suspect these possibilities—from 1981 on, the Reagan administration did all of these things, taking the first steps toward "Iran-Contra."

Like Argentina's junta on the brink of the Falklands invasion, Saddam initially expected the war to last only a couple of weeks. Among other things, he hoped that Khuzestan's Arabs would greet him as a liberator and support the formation of a "Free Republic of Iran," with the Shah's deposed former premier Shahpour Bakhtiar as its head. His financial resources were adequate for a short war. Partly because of the Iran Crisis, oil prices in 1979–80 had skyrocketed and Iraq's coffers were full. Indeed, Saddam had already ordered major new weapons systems, like French Mirage jet fighters, for delivery in 1981. But since training on these systems would take time, he decided not to wait. His impatience proved very costly.

All that was missing was international support. Ordinarily one would have expected Saddam to turn to the Soviets. Since the 1972 Treaty of Friendship with Iraq, the Soviet Union had been one of Iraq's largest oil buyers and its largest arms supplier, along with France, Poland, China, Czechoslovakia, and Brazil. But the Soviets already had their hands full in

Afghanistan. They feared that Khomeini's revolution might well spread to their own Muslim-majority republics in Central Asia. They also wanted to make sure that Iran's new regime would not support any Afghan rebels of its own. It did not; in fact, long before the US discovered the Northern Alliance in Afghanistan, the Soviet Union and Iran were both aiding the Alliance against the Taliban.

It is not clear how much warning Saddam Hussein even gave the Soviets about the invasion. He seems to have been most interested in using the Soviets as a bargaining chip, to get more support from the US and its allies. When Iraq invaded Iran in September 1980, the Soviet Union acted completely surprised. Indeed, it actually condemned the invasion, imposed a two-year weapons embargo on both Iraq and Iran, and halted some of its own weapons shipments that were already on the way to Iraq.[62] When Iraq's deputy premier, Tariq Aziz, showed up in Moscow on September 22, 1980, the day of the invasion, he was greeted at the airport by lower-level officials and unceremoniously sent home.[63]

Oddly enough, the "totalitarian" Saddam Hussein turned not to the Soviets, but to the liberal democracies—the US, the UK, France, Italy, and Germany—plus their client monarchies, for political support and a stunning amount of arms and aid. In January 1980, the US had already declared its "Carter Policy" after the Soviet invasion of Afghanistan, designating the Persian Gulf a "vital interest" and threatening to repel any attempts by outside powers to gain control. It was important for Saddam Hussein to clarify his intentions to the US. Given the Soviet position, he may have also wanted a friend on the UN Security Council to prevent condemnation or an extension of the Soviet arms embargo.

With help from the Ba'athists' long history of CIA contacts, he already had such a friend in waiting.[64] There are many indications that the US had an early warning of Saddam Hussein's 1980 invasion from its allies, its own intelligence sources, and even Iraq itself. Yet it did absolutely nothing to stop it. As we'll see, this curious passivity was repeated again in the buildup to Saddam's August 1990 invasion of Kuwait.

Despite the official line that the US was just a bystander in the events leading up to the Iran-Iraq War, there is increasing evidence that it actively encouraged it.[65] Certainly when the war started, there was no "this will not stand" statement from President Carter like the one issued by President George H. W. Bush almost immediately after Saddam invasion of Kuwait in 1991. When the Iran invasion occurred on September 22, UN deliberations were delayed for several days, which allowed Iraq's forces to gain ground. Even when the UN finally met on September 28, there was no condemnation. Resolution 479, adopted by the UN Security Council that day, simply called for an "end to the fighting," not even for a withdrawal of forces. Back then, Iraq still had friends in high places—or at least more friends than Iran had.

In April 1980, Brzezinski signaled that the US was open to a warmer relationship with Iraq.[66] In June 1980, Iranian students disclosed a copy of a secret shredded memo found at the US Embassy in Tehran, addressed from Brzezinski to Secretary of State Vance. It recommended that the US enlist Iran's neighbors to "destabilize" Iran's new regime, much as the US was doing in Soviet-occupied Afghanistan.[67] Iran's president after Barzargan, Bani-Sadr, later charged that Brzezinski had met with Saddam Hussein in Jordan just two months before the invasion, reportedly informing him that the US would not oppose the separation of Iran's oil-rich province of Khuzestan from the rest of the country. The US government also may have shared a confidential memo on Iran's internal situation with Saddam that suggested—quite falsely—that Khomeini's regime was crumbling.[68] Other reports indicate that by mid-1980, the US was already considering the restoration of diplomatic relations with Iraq, which had been suspended since the 1967 Six-Day War. But it delayed the move to avoid the appearance of an explicit link to the invasion. By December 1980, a Miami-based arms dealer, Sarki Soghanalian, had informed the US government—reportedly without any objection—of his efforts to supply Saddam Hussein with advanced weaponry, including Austrian 155mm artillery and East Bloc weaponry that Saddam was having trouble slipping past the Russian embargo.[69] An April 1981 briefing by Al Haig, summarizing the highlights of his visit to the Middle East that month, reported that "It was interesting to confirm that President Carter gave the Iraqis a green light to launch a war against Iran through Fahd."[70]

Whatever pre-war encouragement Saddam Hussein received from the US, it is quite clear that he received even more from US client states in the region. In May 1980, Saddam traveled to Amman to visit Jordan's King Hussein—another long-time recipient of CIA largesse—and discuss his plans to invade Iran. The King was reportedly very receptive.[71] On September 5, 1980, Saddam Hussein—on his very first visit to Riyadh—conveyed the same message to Saudi's King Fahd, who promised to support the move with finance and arms purchases. He also reportedly obtained similar encouragement from Kuwait's Emir, Morocco's King Hasan, and Egypt's Sadat.[72]

Encouraged by all this support, on September 17, Saddam Hussein abrogated his Algiers treaty with Iran. On September 22 he attacked with five of his twelve divisions across the Shatt-al-Arab and launched air strikes on ten Iranian airfields, modeling his attack on the "Lightning Strike" tactics used by the Israelis during the 1967 Six-Day War. Unfortunately for Saddam, he did not have the expertise of Israeli pilots, US jets, or much strategic imagination. Most of Iran's Air Force survived and then retaliated almost immediately with crippling counterstrikes on his oil facilities in Basra. The siege tactics that he employed against four Iranian cities in Khuzestan also failed to win much support among the locals Arabs.

THE LONGEST WAR

By October 1980, having failed to achieve a decisive knockout, Saddam was already trying to sue for peace and withdraw from the conflict. Like Hitler and Stalin, he was an arrogant brutal dictator who often ignored his own generals in planning an invasion. Unlike Hitler and Stalin, he was no strategic genius and he was also a bit of a fraidy-cat.

But Khomeini would hear nothing about a ceasefire. The conflict quickly escalated from a two-week incursion into an eight-year war, the largest land battle since World War II, "fought with 1980s weapons, the tactics of World War II, and the passion of the Crusades."[73] It was the first war in history where both sides attacked each other with ballistic missiles, and the first since World War I in which chemical weapons—mainly mustard gas and nerve gas—were used extensively. Until its own horrific battle losses finally stopped it, Iran was settling for nothing less than total victory, including "regime change" in Iraq. Saddam had messed with the wrong mullahs.

In the aftermath of Saddam Hussein's failure to achieve a quick victory in 1980, Iran's new Islamic republic mounted a strong defense, which included destroying most of his oil exporting terminals in the Gulf. The result was a $20 billion decline in Iraqi oil revenues by 1982 and a serious cash flow problem. In March 1982, Iran launched "Operation Undeniable Victory," a massive counterattack that included thousands of young "Pasdaran" zealots, who attacked across minefields in human waves. The offensive drove Saddam out of Iran. But Khomeini didn't stop there. He invaded Iraq and laid siege to Basra. For a while, it appeared that Saddam's regime would crumble. Fortunately for him, by then he had already deepened his relationship with the US, Saudi Arabia, Kuwait, and other Gulf states, to the point where they started to supply him with many of the advanced arms and all the funding that he needed to continue the war.

The Reagan administration took office in January 1981 and basically continued to improve US-Iraq relations. Reagan issued a codicil to the Carter doctrine, promising that "the US would not permit Saudi Arabia to become an Iran." In March 1981, Haig testified before the Senate Foreign Relations Committee that Iraq, like the US, was "concerned by the behavior of Soviet imperialism in the area." In April, the US approved the sale of five Boeing commercial airliners to Iraq and dispatched Deputy Assistant Secretary of State Morris Draper to Baghdad for talks with Iraq's foreign minister—the highest level State Department contact with Iraq since 1977. He expressed strong interest in increasing US trade with Iraq and assured the Iraqis—falsely—that the US would not sell any arms to Iran.[74] In May 1981, senior State Department officer Thomas Eagleton also met with Tariq Aziz, reiterating the administration's desire for warmer business relations.

When Israel used sixteen F-16s to bomb Iraq's French-supplied Osirak nuclear reactor in June 1981 without US permission, the White House advised Congress that this was a "substantial" violation of the Arms Export Control Act and reduced Israeli access to US satellite intelligence of its neighbors for a while.[75] By the end of 1981, according to former US senator D'Amato, the US had "State Department" people coming out from Baghdad to monitor Iraq's front lines and provide tactical intelligence.[76] On the other hand, the US wasn't ready for a public tilt in Iraq's direction. That would have greatly alarmed its other key ally in the region, Israel, which had nuclear weapons, had demonstrated its capacity to act independently if threatened, and had a much stronger political lobby. Nor did the US really want Iraq to win the war—for example, it intervened with the Saudis and others to block the use of air bases in the Gulf by Iraq. The cynical objective, as a CIA agent who supplied intelligence to both sides during the war said, was to "keep the war even."[77]

As Iraq's military and financial position deteriorated and Iran's soldiers crossed the border in 1982, however, the US leaned farther and farther in Saddam Hussein's direction. In February 1982, Reagan removed Iraq from the State Department's list of countries that allegedly supported "state-backed terrorism." Iraq had been one of the top four countries on the list since 1979, along with Syria, South Yemen, and Libya. It was still harboring legendary terrorists like Abu Abbas and Abu Nidal—although Saddam Hussein briefly expelled Nidal in 1983 to gain better US relations.[78] The reclassification made Iraq eligible to buy dual-use technologies from the US, like helicopters and heavy trucks, and also allowed it to obtain US EXIM Bank credits and other US government-guaranteed loans.[79]

The relationship continued to build in 1983, with an informal meeting between Secretary of State George P. Schultz and Tariq Aziz in May 1983, and a secret July 1983 National Security policy directive by Reagan, declaring it US policy to prevent Iraq from losing the war.[80] In October 1983, the US supported the adoption of UN Resolution 540, which called for an immediate cease-fire and negotiations. Iraq supported the resolution and was grateful to the US for its support. Iran voted against it, because its goal was regime change.[81] In the face of increased Iranian attacks on Iraqi oil tankers, Reagan approved another directive in November 1983 that called on the US government to undertake "whatever measures may be necessary to keep the Straits of Hormuz open to international shipping."[82] That eventually led the US to undertake air strikes against Iranian ships and oil facilities.

THE HIGHEST LEVEL

To prepare the way for even closer relations, in December 1983, Reagan dispatched Donald H. Rumsfeld—the former (and future) secretary of defense under President Ford and CEO of the pharmaceutical company G.D. Searle & Co.—to meet with Saddam Hussein and Tariq Aziz in Baghdad, as well as with King Fahd in Saudi Arabia, King Hussein in London, and King Hasan in Morocco. At the December meetings in Iraq, Rumsfeld emphasized that the US was ready for a resumption of diplomatic relations, and that Iraq and the US had many shared interests. These included "keeping Syria and Iran off balance and less influential," restoring Iraqi-US business relationships, and preventing arms sales by Third World countries to Iran. Indeed, since 1983, in an operation called "Staunch," the US lobbied allies like the UK, France, Germany, and Israel to squelch their own arms sales to Iran. Of course it was later revealed that the "other hand" of the Reagan administration and Israel had been secretly conspiring to sell arms missiles and spare parts to Iran throughout this period, as part of the double-dealing that eventually mushroomed into the 1985–86 Iran-Contra arms scandal.

Another top priority for the US was to help Iraq's oil exports recover. They had fallen to less than 500,000 barrels per day in the wake of Iran's bombing campaigns, interference with Iraq's oil tankers, and Syria's March 1982 decision to close its 1.2 million barrel per day pipeline from Iraq.[83] To solve the oil problem, in both of his meetings with Saddam Hussein and Tariq Aziz, Rumsfeld underscored a proposal by the US construction company Bechtel (where Secretary of State George P. Schultz had been CEO from 1974 to 1982 and a board member after he left office in 1989, and where Defense Secretary Caspar W. Weinberger was vice president and general counsel from 1975 to 1980) to build a new $2 billion pipeline to carry one million barrels of oil a day across Jordan to Aqaba through the Red Sea. The Iraqis listened with interest, but raised the obvious concern that a pipeline through Jordan might be especially vulnerable to an attack by Israel—after all, Israel had already demonstrated its willingness to attack Iraqi facilities. Still, in June 1984, with encouragement from Secretary of State Schultz, the EXIM Bank approved $485 million in loan guarantees for the $1 billion first stage of this project, with another $85 million in project guarantees from OPIC. Eventually, in late 1985, Iraq and Jordan dropped the proposal, partly because it required Bechtel to pay Israel "protection" money by way of an unusual side deal with Israel's prime minister Shimon Peres and Swiss billionaire and Bank of New York investor Bruce Rappaport.[84]

In any case, the head of the US interests section in Iraq later commented that Ambassador Rumsfeld's visit had "elevated US-Iraqi relations to a new level," describing this as "both symbolically important and practically helpful. . . . [T]he Iraqi leadership was extremely pleased with Ambassador Rumsfeld's visit. Tariq Aziz had gone out of his way to praise Rumsfeld as a person. . . ."[85] On January 1, 1984, it was reported that "the US has informed friendly Persian Gulf nations that 'the defeat of Iraq in the three-year-old war with Iran would be contrary to US interests' and has made several moves to prevent that result."[86]

Among the topics conspicuously missing from Rumsfeld's discussions were Iraq's repeated use of chemical weapons and its many programs to develop nuclear weapons, biological weapons, long-range missiles, and other "weapons of mass destruction." In Rumsfeld's ninety-minute discussion with Saddam Hussein on December 20, 1983, these subjects were not mentioned once. In his two and one-half hour meeting the following day with Tariq Aziz, there was a one-sentence mention, one of several matters like "human rights" and a "possible escalation in the Gulf" that might "inhibit US efforts" to assist Iraq. Nor were these contentious subjects even mentioned in Rumsfeld's follow-up meetings with Aziz in Baghdad in March 1984.[87] The Bechtel pipeline matter, however, featured prominently in all these discussions.

Inattention to chemical weapons and other "WMD" issues was certainly not due to US ignorance. The CIA had concluded just before Rumsfeld's visit that even after Israeli bombing of the Osirak reactors, Saddam's nuclear efforts had continued.[88] As for chemical weapons, Tehran Radio broadcast allegations that Iraq had already used chemical bombs in November 1980 at the town of Susangerd, clearly violating the 1925 Geneva Protocol, which both Iran and Iraq had signed. But the real surge in Iraq's chemical weapons use came after May 1982, when Iran's advances and its "human wave" tactics forced Iraq to search for tougher anti-personnel weapons. In the next two years, Iraq used CS and mustard gas at least fifty times, and also experimented with tabun, a nerve gas. It continued to use chemical weapons throughout the war, adding the nerve gases sarin and VX to its arsenal in 1988. However, the US and the UN never placed any sanctions on Iraq during this period. Iraqi documents obtained by UNSCOM, the UN weapons inspectors in the 1990s later showed that between 1983 and 1988, the Iraqi Air Force dropped 13,000–19,500 chemical bombs.[89] "Bomber" Harris would have been proud.

In November 1983, two State Department memos to Secretary Schultz and Undersecretary of State for Political Affairs Lawrence S. Eagleburger, more than a month before Ambassador Rumsfeld's visit, called attention to the fact that Iraq had been using tear gas, skin irritants, and lethal gas "quite effectively" against Iran as early as July 1982; that Iraq had used them again in October 1982, August 1983, September 1983, and was now using them "almost daily"; that Iran had complained to the UN about Iraq, and that Iraq had also acquired "a CW production capability, primarily from Western firms, including possibly an (unnamed) US foreign subsidiary."[90] In February 1984, just after Rumsfeld's first visit to Baghdad, an Iraqi military spokesperson acknowledged their existence, warning that "The invaders should know that for every harmful insect, there is an insecticide capable of annihilating it . . . and Iraq possesses this annihilation insecticide."[91] On March 5, 1984, with the UN about to issue a report confirming Iran's allegations, the State Department issued a statement acknowledging that Iraq had used chemical weapons. But this was a mere footnote, compared to all the friendly private discussions with Iraq's dictatorship about restoring diplomatic relations, building pipelines, and helping Iraq secure new sources of finance. Indeed, on March 23, 1984, the day before Rumsfeld had a follow-up meeting with Aziz in Baghdad, Iran's news agency reported that Iraq launched yet another chemical weapons attack, injuring six hundred soldiers. The very day of Rumsfeld's visit, UPI reported that the UN had substantiated Iran's allegations.[92] So this must have felt a little like sitting down with Hitler and von Ribbentropp in the Bertesgarten in 1943, and pitching a new pipeline to Rumania.

Given the fact that about half of US oil came from the Middle East and an even higher share for its First World trading partners in Europe and Japan, the US government was focused primarily on what it considered essential for the security of its oil suppliers in the region, not such distracting "moral" issues. At the time, the chemical weapons issue was viewed as a public relations annoyance to be managed, not a priority concern. Privately, from a technical standpoint, the US was even sympathetic to the viewpoint that Iraq needed weapons like chemical weapons and cluster bombs to respond effectively to Iran's human waves—with thousands of children sent forth in groups of twenty, roped together to prevent them from losing courage, human versions of Morocco's mine-detecting monkeys. CIA director William J. Casey viewed cluster bombs as an ideal "force multiplier" for Iraq under these conditions.[93] In the words of one US Defense Intelligence Agency officer who assisted Iraq with detailed battle planning, "The use of gas on the battlefield was not a matter of deep strategic concern. . . . It was just another way of killing people. The Pentagon was not so horrified by the Iraqi's use of gas."[94] An Iraqi general later described the effects of chemical weapons on the Iranian waves: "We harvested them."

In 1986, when it looked like Iran might be regaining the initiative again, the US vetoed a UN Security Council resolution condemning Iraq for the use of mustard gas against Iran's troops. That year, Vice President Bush also reportedly advised Saddam Hussein to increase his air strikes on Iran, even as the Reagan administration was busy selling anti-aircraft missiles to Iran—a case of supply creating its own demand.[95]

In 1987–88, when it became clear that Saddam Hussein's military was using chemical weapons in a "scorched earth" strategy against Kurdish villages in northern Iraq, some members of the US Congress started to demand sanctions against Iraq. But the Bush administration rejected sanctions out-of-hand, even after the widely publicized use of mustard gas and nerve gas on thousands of Kurdish civilians by Iraq in the northern city of Halabja in March 1988 caused up to five thousand deaths.[96] Ironically, in 2002–3, George W. Bush and Tony Blair would cite this episode as a key example of Saddam Hussein's inhumanity. At the time, however, the elder Bush's administration, European governments, and the UN let it pass in silence—just one of many appeasements that may have encouraged Saddam Hussein to believe that he would be permitted to go even further. UN Security Council Resolution 620, passed in August 1988, did not even mention Iraq by name, but simply condemned the use of chemical weapons in the war and called on all states to strengthen their controls on chemical weapons supplies.[97] And Richard W. Murphy, the assistant secretary of state, wrote a memo in September 1988 saying that "The US-Iraqi relationship is . . . important to our long-term political and economic objectives. We believe that economic sanctions will be useless or counterproductive to influence the Iraqis."[98] Not only was there no public outcry from the US government, but it actually increased its aid to Iraq, joining in attacks on Iranian ships and oil rigs, expanding the illicit BNL financing scheme through the Department of Agriculture, and increasing US export approvals for Iraq. Former assistant secretary of defense and deputy secretary of state Richard Armitage commented on the policy in 1990, "It was a cold calculation of national security."[99] And John Kelly, US assistant secretary of state for Near Eastern Affairs, paid a call on Saddam Hussein in Baghdad at the end of the Iran-Iraq War and told him, "You are a force for moderation in the region, and the US wants to broaden her relationship with Iraq."

Overall, in contrast to Iran's leaders, who were portrayed as mad mullahs who were sacrificing their children, Saddam Hussein was generally portrayed back then as "ruthless but pragmatic" as a 1984 US DIA analysis put it.[100] Until the 1990s, after the invasion of Kuwait, he was not viewed as evil incarnate, the "Butcher of Baghdad," or even territorially aggressive, but as rational and serious, with no particular religious or political agenda—a useful counterweight to Syria's conniving President Assad and Iran's zealots. Even in the face of mounting evidence of Saddam's appetite for brutality and aggression, produced at first by a handful of journalists like the *Financial Times*'s Alan Friedman and by Congressman Henry Gonzalez, chairman of the US House Banking Committee—the conservative establishment of the period preferred to regard him as someone we could do business with, "moderate" . . ., in a word, appease. In April 1990, US senators Robert Dole, Howard W. Metzenbaum, Alan Simpson, and former senator Howard H. Baker Jr.—who had also served as Reagan's chief of staff, majority leader in the US Senate, and a member of the Foreign Intelligence Board—visited Saddam Hussein in Baghdad. On April 12, 1990, Senator Simpson told him, "I believe your problem is with the Western media, not the US Government. . . . The press is spoiled and conceited. My advice to you is to allow those bastards to come here and see things for themselves." Or, as Senator Metzenbaum put it, just four months before the invasion of Kuwait, with no dissent from any of the other senators present, "I believe your Excellency can be a very effective force for peace in the Middle East."

Of course, the US recognized that Saddam Hussein had axes to grind, like a Palestinian state, which he favored, and Kurdish independence, which he opposed. But these were not issues that threatened the basic US-Iraq relationship. As FDR once remarked about Nicaragua's General Anastasio Somoza Garcia, "He may be a sonafabitch, but he is *our* sonafabitch." In Saddam Hussein's case, he was never quite "our sonafabitch," but we had as strong a claim to paternity as anyone.

THE FLOODGATES

The Rumsfeld visit in December 1983 was widely viewed, not just as an incidental house call, but as a real icebreaker. It established a direct channel between Saddam Hussein and the White House and laid the foundations for the restoration of full diplomatic relations, which followed in November 1984. Soon after that, the US business community joined in, eager to capitalize on commercial opportunities. That same month, the US-Iraq Business Forum was founded by Marshall Wiley, a former State Department officer who had been stationed in Baghdad. It was chaired by A. Robert Abboud, the former chairman of First Chicago Bank from 1975 to 1980, who in 1988 had taken over Houston's failing First City Bank with the help of a $1 billion capital injection from the Federal Deposit Insurance Corporation (FDIC).[101] Its members included leading US companies such as HP, ITT, GM, Westinghouse and AT&T. Collectively, they accounted for one hundred of the eight hundred export licenses that the US Commerce Department granted for exports to Iraq in the 1980s.[102] Over the next few years, their lobbying efforts paved the way for a dramatic increase in US exports to Iraq, much of it financed by government loans. Abboud's First City Bank extended several loans to Iraq, including $38 million by way of the US Commodity Credit Corporation program and a $49.9 million credit in February 1989 to Rafidain, Iraq's Central Bank, which defaulted on the loan after the invasion of Kuwait.[103] Abboud was also very close to the Bush family. On August 7, 1990, just a few days after Saddam Hussein's invasion of Kuwait, he attended an invitation-only event at the White House, and ten days later, he repaid the Bush administration in spades for the FDIC's support: First City bailed out "Dubya's" nearly bankrupt Harken Energy oil company, refinancing its $20 million debt at a time when banks like Bank of Boston were calling in their loans.[104]

There were many other indicators that pointed in the direction of a growing Iraqi relationship with Western suppliers and governments in these years. From 1981 until the invasion of Kuwait, the Iran-Iraq War and its aftermath produced a bonanza for all the world's leading arms suppliers, including the Soviet Union, the US, the UK, France, Germany, Brazil, and Chile. They all made a fortune off the World War I–like stalemate that developed between the two belligerents. During this period, Iraq and Iran beat the Shah's record by a mile for having the largest Third World arms market. Iran alone reportedly spent more than $80 billion during the decade, with much of its arms coming from eclectic sources like Israel (retransferring US arms and spares), China, and North Korea. Iraq spent more than $100 billion on imported military hardware to counter Khomeini's more labor-intensive approach to the war, plus another $20 billion on related services and technology.

Despite its brief embargo, the Soviet Union remained Iraq's largest supplier of military hardware. It ended the embargo in 1982, not only because it feared an Iranian victory, but also because it didn't want to lose the growing Iraqi market to the West. The Soviet Union accounted for about fifty-one percent of the $34 billion in official "complete weapons systems" that Iraq imported from 1980 to 1990.[105] Officially, France and China were tied for second, with about $5.2 billion each, followed by Czechoslovakia, Poland, and Brazil. But these data probably understate the role of First World suppliers like the US, Israel, the UK, France and Germany in Iraq's arms-related acquisitions during this period.[106]

For sophisticated technology, Iraq had to rely on the First World. From the French, it bought Exocet missiles, Mirage jets, and howitzers; from the UK, advanced tanks, missile parts, artillery, sophisticated machine tools, and specially-milled gun barrels; from Germany and the Netherlands, nerve and mustard gas manufacturing capability; from the US, helicopters, supercomputers, surveillance systems, biological seed stocks, pesticides, armored ambulances, engineered components, and many other dual-use supplies.

Most of the US-sponsored arms deals with Iraq at first went through the back door, by way of allies like Egypt, which sent Iraq its old Soviet T-62 tanks and replaced them with US M-60s, and Jordan, which retransferred US artillery.[107] Similarly, Saudi Arabia retransferred TOW missiles and MK-84 2,000-pound MK-84 bombs to Iraq, in violation of the US Arms Control Export Act, using the overseas subsidiaries of US companies.[108] Another route was through arms dealers like Carlos Cardoen, a Chilean arms manufacturer and dealer who, with William J. Casey's support, got US permission in 1983 to license cluster bomb technology from International Signal and Control, a Pennsylvania company. He not only sold cluster bombs to Iraq, but an entire cluster bomb plant—later destroyed by a US bomb during the Gulf War. To help with his relations in Washington D.C., Cardoen hired former US ambassador to Chile James Theberge, who also continued to serve on a CIA senior review panel.[109] Teledyne Industries, a leading US conglomerate, was later convicted of criminal conspiracy and violating the Arms Control Act for selling Cardoen 130 tons of zirconium for bomb fuses.[110] Miami-based Sarki Soghanalian packaged a $500 million helicopter deal and a $1.6 billion deal for 155-millimeter howitzers. Working with a D.C.-based company, Global Research International, in 1983 he also arranged to sell Iraq $183 million in military uniforms that were actually manufactured in Romania, then under the control of the Communist dictator Ceaucescu. GRI was reportedly run by Lt. Colonel John Brennan, a former aid to President Nixon; GRI had Nixon, John Mitchell, and Spiro Agnew on its board.[111] In another case, an Iraqi-born engineer who had designed a chemical weapons plant in Libya settled in Florida, where he sourced chemical weapons components for Iraq.[112]

Meanwhile, in December 1982, the Reagan administration approved the export of sixty Hughes MD 500 Defender helicopters to Iraq, which had been advertised as an antitank killer.[113] They were delivered in 1983, along with ten Bell helicopters, officially for "crop spraying" by Iraq's Agricultural Aviation Department, but easily modified to handle chemical weapons. In February 1984, Bell Textron's Italian subsidiary sold Iraq eight AB 212 military helicopters, worth $164 million, for antisubmarine warfare, and with Soghenalian's help, its US division sold them another forty-eight Bell 214ST helicopters, worth $200 million. Some of these helicopters, including those modified by Cardoen to fly long distances, later turned up in Saddam Hussein's March 1988 gas attack on Halabja.[114]

In August 1984, the CIA set up a direct Washington D.C.-to-Baghdad intelligence link, permitting Saddam Hussein access to satellite photos and other intelligence. Over the next six years, a team of sixty US DIA officers secretly provided Iraq with detailed information on Iranian troop and ship deployments, tactical planning, and plans for air strikes—information that Iraq used to improve its bombing raids. It also used this information to "calibrate" the effects of mustard gas attacks on Iranian troops—a case of US forces collaborating directly with Iraq in violation of the 1925 Geneva treaty barring the use of chemical weapons.[115] General Fawzi al-Shamari, who defected to the US in 1986 to run a sweetshop in Northern Virginia, reported that he had indeed fired chemical weapons from howitzers with devastating impact. Since he had no satellites of his own and was miles from the target, how did he do the targeting? "We got the information from American satellites."[116]

After the March 1982 relevation by *New York Times* reporter Leslie Gelb that Israel had established a lucrative weapons trade with Iran, re-selling US-made weapons and spare parts, and especially after a small Lebanese newspaper with close ties to Iran, *Al-Shiraa*, exposed the Iran-Contra arms scandal in November 1986—Iraq became more suspicious of its US allies.[117] It suspected that all the "free" intelligence may have had a price. In February 1986, when Iran captured the Fao Peninsula near Basra, Iraq blamed the defeat on US government manipulation of intelligence: "They kept telling us that the Iranian attack was not aimed against Fao."[118] Nevertheless, Iraq maintained relations with the US, double-checking information whenever possible with other sources, including the Soviets. The whole enterprise became a hall of mirrors, with only battlefield outcomes able to decide who was lying or selling what to whom.

Meanwhile, with Western help, Iraq was able to establish a first-rate supply chain for chemical weapons. Here the real market leaders were the West Europeans. The German company Preussag supplied Saddam Hussein with tons of raw materials required for manufacturing nerve gas, and helped build production facilities. Hoechst reportedly supplied at least ten tons of phosphorus oxychloride to make sarin, and Karl Kolb helped Iraq build chemical weapons manufacturing facilities. The Dutch firm KBS supplied Iraq with three thousand tons of precursor chemicals from 1982 to 1984.[119] By 1985, with the help of German and UK technology, Iraq was able to produce about fifty tons a year of mustard gas at a factory in Sammara. However, the process it used depended on importing large quantities of a chemical called thiodyglycol. In April 1988, US Customs discovered that a Baltimore company, Alcolac International, was shipping 538 tons of thiodyglycol to Iraq by way of a shell company in Brooklyn.[120]

In 1988, the State Department approved the sale to Iraq of a million atropine injectors, an antidote to nerve gas, ostensibly for "defensive" purposes—even though Iran only had cyanide gas, not nerve gas. Their real purpose was to handle "blowback" accidents caused by Iraq's own gases when they were used on offense. A huge stockpile of these US- and European-supplied injectors was discovered by US troops when they invaded Iraq in 2003.

In December 1988, long after the incidents at Halabja, the US Commerce Department approved Dow Chemical's sale of $1.5 million in pesticides to Iraq, financed by the US EXIM Bank. The bank found "no reason" to stop the sale, despite the fact that the pesticides were highly toxic to humans, capable of causing asphyxiation.[121] Other US companies provided chemical analysis equipment for Iraq's Atomic Energy Commission.[122] And while Bechtel may not have won the Jordan pipeline, it was listed in Iraq's December 2002 report to UN weapons inspectors as one of the key companies that supplied Saddam Hussein with equipment and know-how for producing chemical weapons, as the prime contractor on PC 1 and 2—two petrochemical plants that it built in Iraq during the 1980s with dual-use capacity.

By 1990, with all this help, Iraq had produced at least a hundred thousand unfilled and forty-six thousand filled chemical munitions.[123] But Saddam Hussein also wanted to develop biological weapons in his arsenal to offset Iran's population advantage. From 1984 to 1990, not long after Iraq began a secret biological weapons development program in 1985, the US and other First World countries supplied Saddam Hussein with seed stock, growth media, fermentation equipment, atomizers, and other supplies needed to make biological weapons in quantity. Between 1984 and 1989, the US Center for Disease Control sent Iraq at least eighty agents, including botulinum toxoid, Yersinia pestis, dengue virus, and the West Nile antigen and antibody. The American Type Culture Collection (ATCC), a nonprofit organization based in Rockville, Maryland, that supplies biological products to scientists, also made numerous shipments to Iraq. Between 1985 and 1989, ATCC sent Iraq seventy shipments with twenty-one strains of anthrax, including three strains of the virulent "vollum" variety, plus fifteen Class III pathogens, including E. coli, Salmonella cholerasuis, Clostridium botulinum, Brucella meliteusis, and Clostidium perfringens. Other suppliers of biological weapons materials and equipment included France, Germany, Russia, and the UK.[124]

By 1989, Saddam Hussein had been able to assemble the technical expertise required to have a stockpile of biological weapons munitions that included 150 aerial bombs, at least 25 special chemical/biological Al-Hussein ballistic missile warheads, biological weapons sprayers for the Mirage F-1 aircraft, and mobile production facilities that could produce "dry" biological agents.[125] Iraq admitted to UNSCOM that it had produced at least 8,500 liters of anthrax in the 1980s, but the actual number may have been higher. It also admitted to having produced 19,000 liters of botulinum toxin.[126]

With a seemingly inexhaustible appetite for advanced weapons, Saddam's regime continued to pursue the development of nuclear weapons and other more exotic weapons, such as fuel-air bombs, long-range missiles, and the "supergun," designed by the eccentric Canadian engineer Gerald Bull.[127] In fact, very little was denied to Saddam Hussein during this period, despite the fact that helping him to develop such weapons was often a clear violation of international law. In the five years leading up to the invasion of Kuwait in August 1990, the US Department of Commerce licensed more than $1.5 billion in US equipment exports to Iraq, including many delivered directly to his weapons labs.[128]

THE LIST

In December 2002, when Iraq responded to the demands of UN weapons inspectors for an itemized declaration of all their "weapons of mass destruction," Iraq surprised the Security Council with an 11,800-page document that included data on the sources of weapons procurements that they had never been asked to provide. The US reportedly obtained an advanced copy of the full document from its friends in Colombia, which was temporarily presiding over the Security Council. It then prepared a three thousand-page version of the document that omitted all the details on weapons suppliers, and distributed the document to the ten nonpermanent members of the Security Council, including Germany.[129] The ever-circumspect Kofi Annan, the UN secretary general, said only that it was "unfortunate" that his organization had allowed the US to take the only complete dossier and edit it. However, the German newspaper *Die Tageszeitung* managed to obtain the full version of the report.[130]

The original version included more than two hundred companies from twenty-one countries that, according to Iraq, had supplied them with parts, material, training, or other assistance relevant to their "weapons of mass destruction" programs from 1980 to 1998—most of which dated from the 1980s. The list included 86 German, 24 US, 18 UK, 17 Austrian, 16 French, 12 Italian, 11 Swiss, 7 Belgian, 6 Russian, 4 Japanese, 3 Chinese, 3 Dutch, 3 Spanish, 3 Argentine, and 2 Swedish companies. While Germany led the way in sheer numbers, fifty-five of the companies were US subsidiaries of foreign companies, indicating the importance of the US as a source for Iraq's advanced weapons efforts. Many companies on the 2002 list had in fact already been included in a 1990 compilation of press reports assembled by the Simon Wiesenthal Center.[131] The resulting supply network was a hit parade of leading Western multinationals. In addition to those already mentioned, it included the following companies: ABB, AEG, Aerospatiale, Alcolac, Astra Holdings PLC, Bechtel, Bofors, Carl Zeiss, Cerberus, Consarc, Creusot-Loire, Data General, Daimler Benz, Dassault, Dresser Industries (later acquired by Halliburton), Dupont, Eastman Kodak, Fanuc, Fiat, Gerber Systems, GM, Hochtief, Interchem Inc., International Computer Systems, HP, Hoechst, Honeywell, KWU, Leybold Vacuum, Lummus Crest, Mack Truck, Mannesmann, Matrix Churchill (75% owned by Iraq), M.W. Kellog, MBB(Messerschmidt Bolkow Blohm), Minolta, NEC, Osaka, Philips Petroleum, Perkin-

Elmer, Preussag, Rockwell International, Semetex, Scientific Atlanta, Siemens, Snecma, SNPE, Spectra Physics, Sperry Corp., Tektronix, Thomson CSF, Thyssen, Saab-Scania, Unisys, United Technologies (Pratt & Whitney), US Steel, Voelst-Alpine, Volvo and Waida. Also included on the list of suppliers were the CDC, the US Departments of Energy, Commerce, Defense, and Agriculture, and the US government laboratories at Sandia, Los Alamos, and Lawrence Livermore.[132] Many other foreign companies also provided arms and infrastructure to Iraq during this period, including Brazil's Engesa; South Korea's Hyundai, which built more than $4 billion in fertilizer plants, power stations, roads, and housing; Japan's leading trading houses Marubeni, Mitsubishi, and Sumitomo; and China's Wanbao Engineering Company and State Missile Company.[133]

These relationships were not concealed from Western governments. They actively encouraged them—not only during the Iran-Iraq War, but even after it, when US and European exports to Iraq surged to record levels. By then, it seems, the market had simply become irresistible. In the rush to take advantage of Iraq's seemingly insatiable arms demand, the US overlooked the country's dire debt situation, its burgeoning military muscle, and of course its form of government. By the late 1980s, in the wake of the Iran-Iraq War, many First World policymakers viewed Iraq as a perfect substitute for the Shah's Iran—not only as an important short-term ally, but as a strategic long-run partner.

Richard Murphy, the US State Department's top Middle East diplomat, said in 1988 that Iraq was seen as a "very valuable market . . . once it got out from under the load of war debt. Most experts predicted that would happen in three to five years."[134] That year, William Waldegrave, the UK's minister of state at the Foreign Office, observed glowingly, "I doubt if there is any future market on such a scale anywhere where the UK is potentially so well placed, if we play our diplomatic hand correctly, nor can I think of any major market where the importance of diplomacy is so great to our commercial position."[135] Peter Allen, sales director for Matrix Churchill, a UK/US firm that supplied Iraq with machine tools for its nuclear program, said, "We were actively encouraged to go there" by Britain's Overseas Trade Board.[136]

At the end of all this mercenary activity, Saddam Hussein had indeed emerged as a force, all right. But it was hardly a force for peace. By August 1988, his new military had become strong enough to achieve the upper hand over Iran, finally persuading Khomeini to agree to a cease-fire. But by then, Iraq had developed into a military state, with the world's fourth largest standing army, a modern air force, extensive experience in ground warfare and chemical weapons, more than eight hundred long-range Scud missiles, and a growing ability to manufacture a complete arsenal, including artillery shells, aircraft bombs, rocket-propelled grenades, rockets, tube-launched rockets, short-range missiles, and a wide variety of chemical and biological weapons. According to the UN's weapons inspectors, by the time of the Gulf War in February 1991, Iraq was just a few years away from enriching uranium to nuclear bomb-grade levels.[137] To destroy this war machine, it would take two full-scale invasions by the US and its allies. And this Frankenstein could not have been built without this extraordinary foreign assistance—and finance.

BANKING ON SADDAM

One necessary condition for all these arms was the cash to pay for it. One might have expected an oil-and-gas rich country like Iraq to have no need for loans to finance its war effort. Depending on the estimates, Iraq has at least 110–200 billion of economically feasible oil reserves, the world's second or third largest, and among the least costly to produce. However, when Iraq suffered severe damage to its oil exports early in the war and the war dragged on, this led to a cash crunch. Therefore, the supply of foreign loans, not weapons, became the really scarce resource. On the spending side, from October 1980 through 1988, Iraq's military imports averaged $6–12 billion a year, while other imports, mostly food grains and durable goods, averaged $6 billion.[138] The size of its armed forces increased from 222,000 full-time military, 250,000 active-duty reserves, and 80,000 paramilitary in 1979 to 520,000 military, 480,000 reserves, and more than 655,000 paramilitary in 1987. In an economy where nearly half the population was under the age of eighteen, that was the equivalent of almost twenty percent of all able-bodied males.[139]

Meanwhile, Iraq's oil revenues, which accounted for at least ninety percent of its export earnings and almost all its government's foreign exchange income, plummeted.[140] Before the war, Iraq's oil production had peaked at 3.5 million barrels per day, of which about 3.2 million were exported. In the wake of the Shah's demise and the invasion of Iran, crude oil prices had more than doubled, from $15 a barrel in 1978 to nearly $35 in 1981. This permitted Iraq to assemble a $31 billion "war chest" of foreign reserves by the start of the Iran-Iraq War. However, Iran's air force survived Iraq's initial attack. It then proceeded to bomb Iraq's two main oil export terminals in the Persian Gulf, Mina al Bakr and Khawr al Amayah, as well as one of its key refineries at Basra, all of which remained closed until 1988. And while most other Arab states had closed their Tehran embassies in 1979, the ruling Ba'athists in Syria decided to side with Iran. The Syrians assisted Iran's efforts to aid the Hizbollah, a militant Shi'ite group that occupied Lebanon in the 1980s, and shut down a key Iraqi pipeline.

Chart 8.1. Key Oil Price Trends and Events, 1973-81

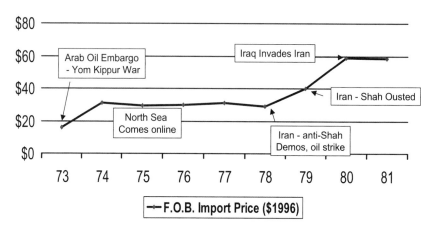

Source: WTRG Econ (1998), analysis by James S. Henry

Chart 8.1–Key Oil Price Trends and Events, 1973–81

Iraq's oil exports fell from 3.2 million barrels per day in 1979 to less than 600,000 barrels per day in 1982–83, and world oil prices also declined because of the global debt crisis and recession. The result was that Iraq's oil revenues declined from a peak of $27 billion in 1980 to less than $10 billion a year in 1981–84. After 1983, Iraq gradually restored oil exports to a million barrels per day by 1985 and 1.7 million by 1987, using a combination of new channels, including tanker-truck convoys through Turkey and Jordan, expansion of its pipeline through Turkey, and a $2.2 billion add-on to its Saudi pipeline to the Red Sea port of Yanbu, built by a consortium of Japanese, South Korean, French, and Italian companies (another 500,000 barrels per day by 1986 and 1.2 million more by 1989). With Soviet help, it also undertook to develop new oil fields in West Al Qurnah's Mishrif reservoir. By 1990, Iraq had restored its export capacity to pre-war levels, but without having to depend on Persian Gulf shipping.

Despite all these developments, Iraq was barely able to recover half the oil revenues that it had achieved in the late 1970s. In 1986, just as all these new channels were coming on stream, Saudi Arabia and Kuwait decided to increase oil production by more than forty percent. It is still not clear why this move was taken. Some argue that it was simply to restore these oil kingdoms' own oil revenues, which had also slumped. But the increased output

Chart 8.2. Key Oil Price Trends and Events, 1981-2003

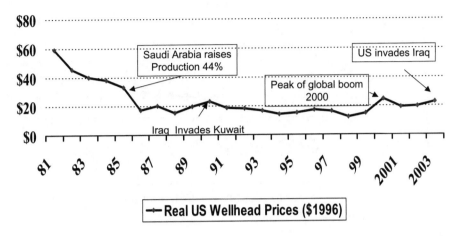

Source: WTRG Econ (1998), analysis by James S. Henry

Chart 8.2–Key Oil Price Trends and Events, 1981– 2003

caused spot oil prices to plummet back to thirteen dollars a barrel, less than half the level when the war started and the lowest real level since 1973. They remained very low until Iraq's 1990 invasion of Kuwait.

As a result, from 1981 on, Iraq experienced mounting trade deficits, as oil revenues plummeted while Iran's fierce counterattacks necessitated increased military spending. While Saddam was able to cut back on imports for the civilian sector to some extent, there were limits to his ability to do so without provoking a popular revolt. By September 1984, Iraq's foreign reserves had fallen from $31 billion at the start of the war to less than $3 billion, and Iraq was tapped out.[141] To finance the gap and pay for the war once his own reserves were exhausted, Saddam borrowed money from almost everyone—the wealthy kingdoms he was protecting, the First World export credit agencies that financed his imports, arms suppliers, First World banks, and special under-the-table financing arrangements made by the US government and its allies.

Estimates vary widely for Iraq's foreign debt, partly because different measuring rods and time periods are often used. But by all measures, Iraq's accumulated debt burden was very heavy by the end of the 1980s. Iraq's official estimate of its foreign debt as of December 31, 1990 was $42.1 billion. But this left out a large amount of "quasi-loans" that it obtained from its

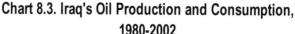

Chart 8.3. Iraq's Oil Production and Consumption, 1980-2002

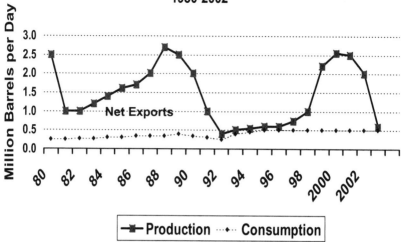

Source: WTRG Econ (1998), analysis by James S. Henry

Chart 8.3–Iraq's Oil Production and Exports, 1980–2002   WTRG Economics © 1998

neighbors, a crucial issue in the events leading up to the Kuwaiti invasion. Since the country was embargoed throughout the 1990s, except for UN-approved "Oil-for-Food" transactions, it did not contract any new loans after 1990. The World Bank/Bank of International Settlements estimate (2001) is that as of 1998, Iraq's foreign debt totaled $127.7 billion, but this included $47 billion in interest that had accrued in the 1990s. Since this was a period when Iraq was subject to sanctions that interfered with debt restructuring, it is questionable whether it is fair to charge Iraq for all this imputed interest (calculated by the World Bank at seven percent yield). In any case, these numbers imply that Iraq's foreign debt was $80.7 billion by 1990, just before the Gulf War—including all the disputed finance from the Gulf States. This gave Iraq a debt-to-national income ratio of 1.1, or $4,600 of foreign debt per capita, which clearly made it a "heavily indebted country."[142]

Of this, about $47 billion was provided by the Arab kingdoms, including $17 billion from Kuwait (not including its claims for interest) another $30 billion from the Gulf States and Saudi Arabia, and $300 million from Jordan and Morocco. Most of this was provided during the first three years of the war, when these countries were most afraid that Iraq might lose. The US Defense Intelligence Agency estimated that Kuwait and the Gulf emirates provided Iraq $1 billion a month from October 1980 through the end of 1984.[143] Another $13.5 billion was provided by the Soviet Bloc, including $12 billion from the USSR ($7 billion for arms), $1 billion from Bulgaria, and $500 million from Poland, mainly for export credits. Another $800 million was loaned by Iraq's good neighbor to the north, Turkey. Iraq also received $50 million in foreign aid from the Soviets and Western Europe during this period.

Finally, $19 billion of Iraq's foreign debt came from First World sources. This included $13.5 billion of Western bilateral and government-guaranteed export credits from sixteen countries in the Paris Club, financing Iraq's imports of goods and "bads." The leaders were France's COFACE, which loaned $3.75 billion in export credits for arms and $4.3 billion for other goods; Japan's JEXIM and leading trading houses, which loaned Iraq 700 billion yen ($5.8 billion); the UK's ECGD, which provided more than $1 billion in credits and became Iraq's "paramount favored creditor"; Germany's HERMES, and several more.[144]

Many private foreign banks got involved in delivering these guaranteed credits, and some also provided other credits to Iraq. Among the most important private banks involved were Commerzbank, JPMorgan, Chase, Gironzentrale (Austria), First City Bank of Houston, and Gulf International Bank (Bahrain). As we saw in Chapter IV, in 1981, Morgan also made several rather unusual, life-saving loans to the Brazilian arms company, Engesa, one of Iraqi's principal arms suppliers. In the late 1990s, former secretary of state and former Bechtel CEO George P. Schultz became the chairman of JPMorgan Chase's International Council.

Iraq's heavy debts at the end of the war in 1988 must have been apparent to Saddam Hussein's foreign creditors. So why didn't they force him to reschedule? Indeed, by 1986, there were mutterings among Paris Club members that it was time for such a move. But Saddam Hussein resisted, because it would have forced him to tighten up on new foreign borrowing, and slowed his reconstruction plans. The eight-year Iran-Iraq War had taken at least four hundred thousand Iraqi lives and caused several hundred thousand more casualties. It also caused $200 billion in damage to infrastructure, leaving Iraq with a struggling economy. There were a million men under arms, with few jobs available outside the military. With oil revenues still depressed by increased production from Saudi Arabia and the Gulf States and with an economy that was still heavily dependent on oil exports and largely closed to foreign investment, the fact was that Saddam Hussein was *entirely* dependent on foreign loans.

So Saddam Hussein preferred to hold off debt rescheduling and keep the export credits flowing as long as possible. To do so, he played on the competitive rivalries of individual countries and suppliers, promising more new orders to those who played along and to those who lobbied for his demands.

For a while the plan worked. Even by the fall of 1989, when most international banks finally stopped lending to Iraq, he found ways to continue borrowing—with the help of the US EXIM Bank, the US Department of Agriculture, and a peculiar giant state-owned Italian bank.

HONEYPOTS

The most important US involvement in Iraqi lending was by way of the US EXIM Bank and the US Department of Agriculture's Commodity Credit Corporation. As Iraq's debts increased, its aid from the Gulf States tapered off and its credit-worthiness declined, government-insured credits became increasingly important. Many were extended after Iraq had already defeated Iran, and after its extensive use of chemical weapons had become public.

As we saw earlier, President Reagan had cleared the way for such lending by removing Iraq from its list of terrorism-sponsoring states in 1982. But EXIM's director William M. Draper III still had reservations about Iraq's credit-worthiness, and had to be lobbied hard by the State Department and the White House to start lending. In December 1983, Undersecretary of State Lawrence Eagleburger wrote to Draper, recommending that EXIM consider financing for Iraq. Vice President George H. W. Bush and National Security advisor Robert McFarlane also weighed in to support the loan.[145]

In June 1984, as noted, the US EXIM Bank approved $485 million in funding for Bechtel's proposed pipeline project. In 1985, it started to advance short-term trade credits and insurance for companies that were selling other goods to Iraq. In March 1986, Iraq went "off cover," because its economic situation had deteriorated to the point where it was almost out of reserves, and it started to default on some of its loans. However, in May 1987, Vice President Bush intervened once again with EXIM, against the advice of its professional staff, which argued that Iraq was deeply in debt and had already defaulted on $1 billion of Western credits. EXIM's Board overruled its staff and extended Saddam Hussein another $200 million credit line.[146]

In January 1990, when Congress was threatening to cut off EXIM Bank loan guarantees for Iraq because of concerns about human rights violations and Saddam Hussein's use of gas against Kurdish villages, a presidential waiver was drafted by Baker and signed by President George H. W. Bush, stating that the sanctions were not "in the national interest of the United States." By August 1990, EXIM had provided $267 million of credits to finance 187 US export sales to Iraq, including 250 armored ambulances, portable communications gear, and Dow's pesticides.

More importantly, in December 1982, the US Department of Agriculture (USDA) approved Iraq's participation in its Commodity Credit Corporation

(CCC) GSM-102 export credit program. Under the program, the CCC underwrites private credit extended by American banks to foreign banks or US exporters. In 1983, it granted Iraq $385 million in credits to import US grain. This was the first in a long series of such credits. By 1990, they were being extended at the rate of $1 billion per year, and accounted for more than twenty percent of the CCC's entire program. These loans were made, not to feed Iraq's people and support US farmers, but as part of an effort to continue the arming of Iraq, when noone else would pay for it.

In June 1989, US secretary of state James A. Baker III wrote to US secretary of agriculture Clayton Yeuter, asking him to boost the CCC's loan guarantee program to Iraq to $1 billion a year, which the USDA soon did. Even after the scandal involving Banco Nacional del Lavoro (BNL) surfaced in September 1989, Baker lobbied hard to continue the lending, and the State Department commented in February 1990 that "the CCC program is a key component of the relationship. . . . We need to move quickly to repair the damage to the US-Iraqi relationship by getting this critical program on track."[147]

Many prominent banks helped to arrange Iraqi credits under the CCC program, including BNL, JPMorgan, Midland Bank, Chase, First City Bank of Houston, the Bank of New York, Bank of America, Gulf International Bank (Bahrain), and Girozentrale (Austria). From 1983 to 1990, the USDA's CCC program extended more than $5.5 billion in credits to Iraq—of which $2 billion was still outstanding when it invaded Kuwait. For a country of seventeen million people, this was an enormous amount of credit. And much of the grain that it was supposed to have purchased did not even reach Iraq, but was traded by Saddam Hussein's intermediaries in Jordan, Turkey, and the Soviet Union for munitions, spare parts, chemical and other military supplies.

One key route for the grain/arms trade with Iraq was through Wafai Dajani, a close associate of King Hussein, the CIA's long-time designated "king" of Jordan.[148] His Jordanian companies—Amman Resources, Wafai Dajani & Sons, Arab Holdings and Aqaba Packing—accounted for more than eighty percent of the CCC grain, mainly rice and wheat, that was supposed to be shipped to Iraq. His companies had also reportedly helped Iraq procure arms abroad in Portugal and Cyprus. The USDA did not even bother to confirm that the grain actually reached its destination. An October 1989 USDA audit of the program concluded that "It appears more and more likely that CCC guaranteed funds or commodities may have been diverted from Iraq to third parties in exchange for military hardware."[149] Another reported grain/arms conduit and CCC credits beneficiary was the New York-based commodity firm Entrade, an affiliate of Enka, one of Turkey's largest multinationals and an arms manufacturer. Entrade reportedly participated in at least fifty-two CCC-financed transactions, all of them by way of the prolific

Atlanta branch of BNL—the same one that Dajani used. Clearly something was afoot.[150]

THE BNL SCANDAL

By far, the most important player in the CCC program was the Georgia-regulated Atlanta branch of Italy's largest bank, ninety-eight percent state-owned, Rome-based BNL. BNL was not unknown to US banking authorities. It had assets of more than $100 billion, and by the time its Atlanta branch was raided by the FBI in August 1989, it also had branches in Chicago, Los Angeles, Miami, and New York.

BNL also had an influential US clique. In addition to his duties on Chase's International Council, Henry Kissinger served as a member of BNL's Consulting Board on International Policy from 1985 until the summer of 1991. Chase's David Rockefeller was a member of BNL's Consulting Board.[151] Alan Stoga, Kissinger's partner at Kissinger Associates, who had also been chief economist at Abboud's First Chicago Bank, met with Saddam Hussein in Baghdad in June 1989 to discuss potential commercial relationships. Many Kissinger Associates clients not only got export licenses for Iraq from the Commerce Department, but BNL loans as well.[152] Brent Scowcroft—Kissinger Associates' vice chairman and the key National Security advisor to Presidents Reagan and Bush—briefed BNL's board on several occasions and was heavily involved in lobbying for the continuation of the CCC's programs for Iraq even after the BNL scandal broke in September 1989.[153] From 1986 to 1989, Kissinger's former executive assistant, undersecretary and deputy secretary of state Lawrence Eagleburger, who was Kissinger Associates' president (and CEO of an ITT subsidiary) from 1984 to 1989, was on the board of LBS Bank—a New York State-chartered subsidiary of Yugoslavia's largest bank, Ljubljanska Banka. During this period, LBS Bank did about twenty-five percent of its business with BNL, including the purchase of many BNL loans to Iraq.[154] When Eagleburger left the LBS Bank's board in 1989 to return to the State Department, Renato Guadagnini—who worked at BNL for thirty-nine years and was BNL's regional manager of its Atlanta operations when most of its illicit Iraqi loans were contracted—took over.[155] LBS Bank's parent company, Ljubljanska Banka, also became involved in a $1 billion promissory note fraud in the late 1980s that rocked the entire Yugoslav banking system. With yet another Kissinger Associates consultant, former Brazilian ambassador Sergio da Costa, heading up BCCI's activities in Brazil during this period, Kissinger Associates' collective exposure to major international bank scandals during this period must have provided for interesting partner meetings.

BNL's Atlanta branch had experienced very unusual growth in its loans and letters of credit in the late 1980s. In early August 1989, the FBI was tipped off by two BNL employees. When it raided the Atlanta office, it found that the branch had made more than $5 billion in unauthorized loans to Iraq, including $900 million that had been guaranteed by the USDA's CCC program, plus about $3 billion in loans and letters of credit to Rafidain, Iraq's Central Bank, secured only by BNL's say-so.[156] The US EXIM Bank had also insured fifty-one BNL loan transactions that were worth another $47 million.[157]

All this made BNL the CCC's largest relender, as well as Iraq's single largest source of private loans in the late 1980s, a period when most other banks had stopped lending. Most of these loans were not reported to the Federal Reserve or even to BNL's own management in the US and Rome. At least half—$2.2 billion—had gone to Iraq's Central bank and its Ministry of Industry and Military Industrialization (MIMI) to finance the military procurement network managed by Saddam Hussein's son-in-law, Hussein Kamil. The funds were used to procure equipment for Iraq's Scud missile upgrades, short-range rockets, 155mm and 210mm howitzers, the supergun project, its Condor II long-range ballistic missile project and others. This procurement network operated with amazing efficiency and mendacity. In the case of the most sensitive materials, Saddam Hussein's operatives went to great lengths to conceal the ultimate destination and what the materials would be used for, laundering orders through a hierarchy of offshore holding companies in London, the Isle of Man, the Cayman Islands, and other leading havens. BNL was the key link in the supply chain—suppliers were routinely directed to Atlanta for payment.

Even though the Atlanta branch had supposedly concealed all this activity from banking authorities, from 1986 to 1990, BNL had sent more three thousand telexes to Iraq. Since the National Security Agency routinely monitors such communications, the US government must have known about the branch's unusual activities. (The US government spends $20–30 billion a year on the National Security Agency's signal interception services.)

Most of the suppliers in MIMI's network had been selected for their raw technical acumen. But political connections also counted. Servass, Inc., another BNL client, was headquartered in Indianapolis, in Vice President Dan Quayle's home state. It was owned by Dr. Beurt Servass, a leading Republican who, together with his wife Cory, was the owner and publisher of the *Saturday Evening Post*. Dr. Servass also had other interesting conservative credentials. In 1976, at the height of South Africa's apartheid regime, he had assisted the apartheid government's efforts to launch *The Citizen*, a new right-wing English language daily newspaper based in Johannesburg. It was later revealed to have been a front organization for the apartheid government, receiving more than 64 million rand of secret funding from South Africa's Ministry of Information.[158] In the 1990s, Servass served as president of the Indianapolis City Council.

In November 1988, Servass Inc.'s subsidiary, Bridgeport Brass, received a $40.6 million letter of credit from BNL for the construction of a "copper scrap refining factory" in Baghdad. The factory was designed to produce brass from spent shell casings for the State Armament Directorate's Al-Shaheed military complex. In his April 1991 testimony before the House Banking Committee, Dr. Servass claimed that he thought the brass was only for civilian applications. But documents obtained by the committee showed that most of its production was intended for artillery shells, cartridges, and fuses for Saddam Hussein's army.

On July 16, 1988, Dr. Servass was reported to have met with Dr. Safa Al-Habobi—chairman of TMG Engineering and Matrix Churchill Ltd. and head of all procurement for Iraq's nuclear, biological, chemical weapons and missile programs—in Pittsburgh to negotiate the deal. To prepare for any possible US arms embargo on Iraq, Servass Inc. had also taken care to transfer its contracts with Iraq to IZANE, an offshore company registered in the Isle of Man. By the time Iraq invaded Kuwait in August 1990, the plant was not yet finished. But Servass Inc. was paid in full for the plant out of $1.3 billion in Iraqi assets that were seized by the US government after the Kuwait invasion.[159]

Such revelations, and subsequent investigations of the CCC program and BNL, unearthed a wealth of similar revelations on dubious behavior, including grain diversions to Soviet bloc countries in exchange for arms and kickbacks paid to US companies that had Iraqi connections, and Iraqi officials. George H. W. Bush administration's response was to try and bury this embarrassing problem and continue with business as usual. For one thing, it proceeded with the strong relationship already established with Iraq's military. In September 1989, just as the BNL story was breaking, the US military—including the Office of Naval Research, the Air Force Armament Laboratory, and representatives from the Sandia, Livermore, and Los Alamos Labs—sponsored the attendance of several leading Iraqi technicians at its Ninth Symposium (International) on Detonation at the Red Lion Inn in Portland, Oregon. One of the main topics was the detonation of nuclear weapons. As Dr. Khidir Hamza, a senior Iraqi nuclear scientist who defected in the early 1990s, later recalled at the conference: "[We] got anything that was current in the field about how to make top-notch [high-explosive] lenses" vital for this process.[160]

On October 4, 1989, even after learning of the BNL mishaps and other problems with the CCC program, the USDA, under strong pressure from senior members of the Bush adminstration, approved another $400 million line of credit for Iraq for FY 1990. At this point, Iraq rejected the aid offer as insulting, complaining to Secretary of State Baker that they had received $1.1 billion the previous year. Baker promised Tariq Aziz that he would "look into the matter immediately." On October 2, 1989, President Bush signed National Security Directive 26 on US Policy Toward the Persian Gulf, which mandated a policy of providing "economic and political incentives for Iraq to moderate its behavior. . . . [W]e should pursue, and seek to facilitate, opportunities for US firms to participate in the reconstruction of the Iraqi economy. . . ." On October 26, the State Department cited this directive in recommending a new $1 billion CCC program for Iraq in FY 1990. Baker and Eagleburger intervened with Agriculture Secretary Yeutter to support this recommendation, which was accepted in November 1989. The CCC program was finally halted in May 1990, only three months before the invasion of Kuwait, because of all the controversies surrounding the BNL investigation. By then, however, half of Iraq's $1 billion allocation for FY 1990 had already been used.

Meanwhile, the lower-level professional civil servants at the Department of Justice and the FBI pursued a lengthy investigation of the BNL matter. But the administration responded with a full-scale cover-up of almost Nixonian proportions. A US Senate investigation revealed that the US Commerce Department, charged with providing export licenses for US companies supplying dual-use products to Iraq, sped up the process and even changed the data recorded on at least 68 of the 771 export licenses for sales to Iraq from 1985 to 1990 to conceal their military purposes. This was reportedly done on orders from Paul Freedenberg and Dennis Kloske, two successive directors of the US Commerce Department's Bureau of Export Administration in the late 1980s.[161] Moreover, according to House Banking Committee chairman Henry B. Gonzalez, top State Department and CCC officials repeatedly lied to Congress about the Iraq program.[162]

In February 1990, Attorney General Richard Thornburgh prevented Department of Justice investigators from traveling to Rome and Istanbul to interview senior people at BNL and pursue other leads.[163] He also squelched all efforts to establish what intelligence agencies in the US, the UK, and the Italian government really knew about BNL's Atlanta branch. And even after Iraq's invasion, in September 1990, he wrote to Congressman Gonzalez, appealing to him to call off his House Banking Committee investigation of the BNL saga on grounds of "national security."[164]

In the end, the US Justice Department waited a whole year, until the culmination of the Gulf War in February 1991, to issue a draft indictment. It tried to pin all the blame on Chris Drogoul, BNL's Atlanta branch manager, and a few lower-level associates. The initial indictment charged Drogoul with 347 counts of money laundering, tax evasion, and a multibillion dollar bank fraud, as if it were a rogue operation. This permitted BNL to avoid being indicted for fraud against the US government. The fraud claim also meant that *BNL* could later claim $400 million from the Clinton administration in 1995, as compensation for Iraq's failure to honor its loans.[165]

However, this "rogue operation" assumption ignored the substantial body of evidence that BNL-Rome, the Italian government, the UK government, and the US government had all known about BNL's Iraqi procurement network right from the start. Judge Marvin Shoob, the highly-regarded US Federal District Court judge who presided over Drogoul's prosecution in 1991–93, observed at the sentencing of five lower-level BNL bank officials who had been charged with bank fraud:

> The Court concludes that officials at BNL-Rome were aware of and approved Mr. Drogoul's activities. . . . BNL-Rome was an extremely political organization, operating more as an agency of the Italian government than as a bank. . . . Morgan Guaranty and the Bank of New York, and confidential CIA reports, concluded that it was well known in international banking circles that BNL-Atlanta provided substantial financing for Iraq's purchases of agricultural, military and non-military products. . . . The Italian Parliament's extensive report on the "BNL scandal" concludes that Mr. Drogoul was not a "lone wolf." . . . Mr. Drogoul's chief mentor at BNL retired in 1987 and became a consultant at Entrade . . . a participant in the scheme. . . . High-level officials in the Justice Department and the State Department met with the Italian ambassador to discuss the case. They appeared to help steer this case, and gave support to BNL-Rome's position that it was a victim in this matter. . . .
>
> The Justice Department cancelled investigators' necessary trip to Italy and Turkey. . . . The Italian ambassador met with Attorney General Richard Thornburgh in Spring 1990, and told him that incriminating BNL-Rome would be "a slap in the face." The local prosecutor in this matter received one or more highly unusual and inappropriate calls from the White House Office of Legal Counsel about this case. . . . The Government . . . made no effort to bring in any knowledgeable bank officials from Rome. . . . The Government failed to interview Wafai Dajani, despite evidence of his substantial involvement with the scheme, when he was in Atlanta and had agreed to meet with the prosecution. . . . The Government has provided no credible explanation for its failure to indict Wafai Dajani, Matrix Churchill, Enka, and the Central Bank of Iraq. . . . The CIA did not respond to repeated requests from the Court concerning knowledge and involvement in the

activities of the Atlanta branch. . . . The raw intelligence reports indicate an awareness of extensive funding of Iraq by BNL-Atlanta. . . . This Court again strongly recommends that an independent prosecutor be named to investigate this matter. . . .[166]

However, the US government did not take Judge Shoob's advice. In fact, on August 23, 1992, John Hogan, the chief of staff for President Clinton's new attorney general Janet Reno, informed Shoob that his own four-month investigation of the case had concluded that: "The people in Atlanta were not working . . . at the direction of, with the knowledge of, or under the auspices of the bank in Rome. . . . [W]e did not find compelling evidence there was a conspiracy."[167] The incredulous Shoob responded by sentencing the five indicted BNL officials to probation or home detention, reiterating that in his view:

> [The five defendants] were pawns or bit players in a far larger and wider-ranging conspiracy that involved BNL-Rome and possibly large American and foreign corporations and the governments of the US, England, Italy and Iraq. . . . It would be the height of hypocrisy to sentence these defendants as if this were a simple case of wrongdoing by a branch's employees.[168]

Following this sentence hearing, the Justice Department got Judge Shoob removed from the case. His more compliant replacement refused to entertain any allegations by Drogoul's defense team of a wider conspiracy. In September 1993, Drogoul, who had already been in jail for seventeen months, pled guilty to three minor charges involving wire fraud and filing false reports with the Federal Reserve. He was released with credit for time served.[169]

In January 1995, the Justice Department's Janet Reno issued an enhanced version of John Hogan's earlier findings, declaring that there was no evidence

Bank	Origin	CCC Payments ($MM)
Arab Banking Corp	Bahrain	$146.1
BNL	Italy	$400.0
National Bank for Cooperatives (Cobank)	US – Denver	$111.2
DG Bank	Germany	$15.3
First City Bank	US – Houston	$37.9
Gulf International Bank	Bahrain	$457.3
Girozentrale	Vienna	$110.7
JP Morgan	US	$125.3
National Bank of Kuwait	Kuwait	$150.5
UBAF-Arab America Bank	US (Arab owned)	$195.4
TOTAL		$1749.7

Table 8.1–USDA CCC Program—Reimbursements for Iraqi Defaults (1990–2003)

that "US agencies or officials illegally armed Iraq."[170] Three weeks later, the Clinton administration announced that the CCC would pay BNL $400 million in compensation for the loans that Iraq had defaulted on.[171] This was in addition to the $1.35 billion that the CCC had already paid out to ten other banks, including four Middle Eastern ones—one of which, Gulf International Bank, was partly owned by Iraq. (See Table 8.1.)[172]

For students of the 1992 Clinton-Gore campaign, this was quite an about-face. After all, during the fall 1992 election campaign, Democratic vice presidential candidate Al Gore had claimed that "Iraqgate" was "worse than Watergate," and Bill Clinton had promised that if he were elected, an independent prosecutor would be appointed to investigate the matter. He appeared to have George H. W. Bush on the spot. President Bush had asserted in his third debate with Clinton and Ross Perot that "there isn't any evidence that those grain credits were diverted into weaponry—none, none whatsoever."[173] And in October 1992, just two weeks before the election, Acting Secretary of State Eagleburger had written a letter to *The New York Times*, denying that any investigation of the CCC program had shown that Iraq had used it to obtain weapons, that BNL had obtained any credit guarantees, that US technology had made any significant contribution to the Iraqi military, or that there was anything secret about US policy toward Iraq.[174]

In the UK, the Labor Party had also made hay out of the scandal, coming within a single vote of unseating Prime Minister John Major over the issue in February 1996, when Sir Richard Scott delivered the results of a three-year investigation of "the arming of Iraq" to Parliament. The investigation revealed that UK senior government officials had misled Parliament in 1989–90 about the government's policy on exports to Iraq, though it "did not find their actions duplicitous in the sense of a cover-up."[175]

Once in office, the Clinton administration never mounted anything like Sir Richard Scott's three-year independent investigation. Perhaps it was the electorate's fleeting attention span, or the Democrats' loss of a majority in the House of Representative in the fall 1994 elections, or the fact that "Iraqgate" had already served the Democrat's political purposes. There was also the uncomfortable fact that to really pursue the investigation, it would have to take on the National Security establishment. Indeed, Hogan's report had made curious references to "compartmentalized information" and "specialized agencies" within the CIA that even the agency's own guide dogs had not known about. Moreover, a cross section of leading US businesses and banks had profited from the policy, including some leading Democrats. Among the largest beneficiaries of the USDA's CCC program for Iraq in the late 1980s were Arkansas rice farmers, who accounted for more than half of all CCC "rice" exported to Iraq. Former Arkansas governor Clinton had always been one of their strongest supporters.[176]

PYRRHIC VICTORY

In the wake of Iraq's victory at Kharbala V in 1987–88, the Ayatollah Khomeini finally became convinced that the war was unwinnable. In August 1988, he agreed to accept the UN cease-fire that had been offered a year earlier under Resolution 598. The result was essentially a return to existing borders. The two sides had fought the largest land war since World War II to a deadlock after eight years, with neither one gaining an inch of territory. Despite all the costs to both sides, the US government considered this to be a great success. A classified State Department document reported in 1988: "The outward thrust of the Iranian revolution has been stopped. Iraq's interests in development, modernity, and regional balance should compel it in our direction."[177]

But from Iraq's standpoint it was at best a Pyrrhic victory. The war had cost Iraq at least three hundred thousand dead and more than five hundred thousand other casualties, plus $100–200 billion in damage to infrastructure. The Iraqi economy was in ruins. By 1989, there were still more than 1 million men under arms, out of a population of 17 million. They could not be demobilized; there were no jobs.

The situation was not aided by Iraq's "allies" in the region, Kuwait and Saudi Arabia. The day after Iraq's cease-fire with Iran, Kuwait announced plans to increase oil production beyond its OPEC quota, even while Iraq respected its own quota. In June 1989, Kuwait boosted increased oil production again, despite Iraq's appeals to stop. Each dollar-per-barrel change in prices cost Iraq about $1 billion in lost revenues. By 1990, the situation was critical. In the run up to the Kuwaiti invasion, one of Saddam Hussein's main grievances concerned oil. According to him, "certain Gulf States" were flooding the market with oil, pushing down prices. And Kuwait, he alleged, was also "slant drilling" in the rich oil field of North Rumaila, a region that had long been claimed by Iraq. But Kuwait rejected these complaints out-of-hand. As one senior Bush official noted, "When the Iraqis came and said, 'Can't you do something about it?' the Kuwaitis said, 'Sit on it.' And they didn't even say it nicely. They were arrogant . . . they were terrible."[178]

In addition to the oil price slump, Iraq's ability to restart its economy was severely constrained by its huge foreign debt. By the Iran-Iraq War's end, Iraq had one of the world's highest per capita debt burdens. And most of it had been incurred, not to build weapons of mass destruction, but for conventional weapons that were essential to prevent Khomeini's troops from overrunning the country, as well as for basic imports like food-grains. Meanwhile, Saudi Arabia and Kuwait halted new funding for Iraq completely after 1988. They also started to reclassify their previous funding as "loans," not grants, even as they boosted oil production. With no new loans forthcoming and little to show for all the past loans except the fact that it had saved its wealthy neighbors, Iraq was facing a prolonged period of stagnation and rising discontent among its people. This was an extremely volatile situation, whether or not the country was ruled by "The Butcher of Baghdad," a representative democracy, or Adenoid Hynkel of Tomania.[179]

BEAR TRAP?

By the early 1990s, all the supply-side conditions needed to motivate Saddam Hussein to launch his second major war in a decade were in place—not only his intrinsic aggressions, but also his country's huge debts, social crisis, and the substantial "excess capacity" in military might that he'd been encouraged to acquire. But all this just constituted a necessary but insufficient cause for the war that followed. To account for the war, we also have to acknowledge the role played by the international community.

The most notorious example of appeasement was US ambassador April Glaspie's interview with Saddam Hussein in Baghdad on July 25, 1991, just a week before the invasion. Glaspie was an experienced professional diplomat and Middle East expert who was the first female US ambassador posted to an Arab country. She had been stationed in Baghdad since 1987. Summoned on short notice to meet with Saddam Hussein, who rarely met with ambassadors, she knew that he had already moved thousands of troops close to the border with Kuwait and had been complaining loudly about Kuwait's overproduction of oil and its role in Iraq's foreign debt. But rather than present Saddam Hussein with a flashing red light about invading Kuwait, she gave him the following indulgence:

> Glaspie: I have direct instructions from President Bush to improve our relations with Iraq. We have considerable sympathy with your quest for higher oil prices, the immediate cause of your confrontation with Kuwait. As you know, I have lived here for years and admire your extraordinary efforts to rebuild your country. We know you need funds. . . . I have received an instruction to ask you, in the spirit of friendship—not confrontation—regarding your intentions: Why are your troops massed so very close to Kuwait's borders?

Saddam Hussein: As you know, for years now I have made every effort to reach a settlement on our dispute with Kuwait. There is to be a meeting in two days; I am prepared to give negotiations one more brief chance. When we meet and we see there is hope, then nothing will happen. But if we are unable to find a solution, then it will be natural that Iraq will not accept death.

Glaspie: What solutions would be acceptable?

Saddam Hussein: If we could keep the whole of the Shatt al Arab—our strategic goal in our war with Iran—we will make concessions. But if we are forced to choose between keeping half of the Shatt and the whole of Iraq, then we will give up all of the Shatt to defend our claims on Kuwait to keep the whole of Iraq in the shape we wish it to be. What is the United States' opinion on this?

Glaspie: We have no opinion on your Arab-Arab conflicts, such as your dispute with Kuwait. Secretary Baker has directed me to emphasize the instruction, first given to Iraq in the 1960s, that the Kuwait issue is not associated with America.[180]

Glaspie later became the Bush administration's scapegoat for this Munich-like response. The State Department disavowed her statement, and never gave her another senior post. In 1993, when she was serving at the UN Mission in New York, Madeleine Albright, the new US ambassador to the UN and future secretary of state, ordered her to clear out her office by the end of the day.[181]

However, Glaspie was by no means the only senior First World official who sent Saddam Hussein mixed signals. In the UK, in July 1990, a cabinet meeting chaired by Foreign Secretary Douglas Hurd agreed to scrap all the UK's remaining restrictions on arms sales to Iraq. On July 24, 1990, Margaret Tutweiller, the State Department's spokesperson told an audience of journalists that "We do not have any defense treaties with Kuwait, and there are no special defense or security commitments to Kuwait." On July 26, when asked by journalists whether the US government had filed any protest with Iraq over its movement of thirty thousand troops to the Kuwaiti border, she replied that she was "unaware of any such protest," and let the matter drop. On July 31, the same day that the US DIA detected Iraqi forces moving military supplies to the border, John Kelly, assistant secretary of state for Near Eastern Affairs, testified before Congressman Lee Hamilton's House Subcommittee on Europe and the Middle East that "We have no defense treaty relationships with any of those countries [in the Gulf]. We have historically avoided taking a position on border disputes or on internal OPEC deliberations." Hamilton then questioned him explicitly:

Hamilton: If Iraq, for example, charged across the border into Kuwait, for whatever reason, what would be our position with regard to the use of US forces? . . . In that circumstance, is it correct to say . . . that we do not have a treaty commitment which would oblige us to engage US forces? Kelly: That is correct.[182]

That same day, in a last ditch effort to broker a settlement and avoid a war, leading Arab countries held a summit at Jeddah, Saudi Arabia. According to King Hussein, the Al-Saud (Saudi) and Al-Sabah (Kuwait) families also held a preliminary meeting before the summit where they agreed to boost oil prices, forgive the sums that Iraq had received from them, and contribute $10 billion each toward paying off Iraq's other debts. But at roughly the same time, Sabeh Ahmed al-Jaber al-Sabah, Kuwait's foreign minister and the Emir's brother, ridiculed the threat of an Iraqi invasion to Jordanian diplomats and reportedly told them, "If they don't like it, let them occupy our territory. . . . We are going to bring in the Americans." At the summit, he informed Iraq's vice chairman Izzat Ibrahim al-Duri that he would only offer Saddam Hussein $500,000.[183] The Iraqi delegation walked out furious at the insults. At midnight on August 1, 1990, Iraq crossed into Kuwait with a hundred thousand troops and three hundred tanks, and Saddam Hussein embarked on his "project to rewrite history."

To his evident surprise, the Bush administration responded quickly with great hostility, embargoing oil imports from Iraq, freezing Iraqi assets in the United States, and moving naval reinforcements to the Persian Gulf. The US flatly rejected an offer by Saddam Hussein on August 5 to withdraw his troops. On August 6, the UN Security Council passed Resolution 660, unanimously condemning the Iraqi invasion and calling for an immediate and unconditional withdrawal. The contrast with the UN's tepid response to Iraq's 1980 invasion of Iran was striking.

In retrospect, some have argued that all this must have been an elaborate "bear trap" contrived to lure Saddam Hussein into invading Kuwait so that the US could turn on him and destroy him. After all, Iran's menace had now been contained. In the process, however, Saddam Hussein's power had been enhanced to the point where he was beginning to worry his neighbors—not only Israel, but also the oil kingdoms. With the demise of the Soviet Union in 1989–90, he could no longer rely on it for defense. The Bear Trap theory also makes sense of US indifference to the risk of a Kuwait invasion. It was certainly not out of the question for the US to sell out its partners and change sides quickly once it perceived a new balance of power: As the diplomat's almanac says, "No permanent friends, no permanent enemies, just permanent interests." If independent journalists are to be believed, there is even some hard evidence that points in this direction.[184]

However, the Bear Trap argument may give too little credit to Saddam Hussein's own tendency to underestimate his enemies and make incredible strategic blunders. Of course, it was not helpful that senior diplomats in the US and the UK sent Saddam Hussein so many ambiguous messages. Once he went over the line, the Bush administration may well have seized the opportunity to contain this increasingly problematic dictator. The CIA or DIA would probably love to take credit for luring him into the trap. However, given the intelligence agencies' abysmal track record at forecasting, as well as their generally conservative view of Saddam Hussein at that time, they may have been as amazed by his behavior as everyone else. As the hapless DIA predicted in September 1984, in a classified analysis of likely trends after the war with Iran:

> In the longer term . . . it is unlikely that Hussein will dismantle his military machine to any great extent. This will leave Iraq with a large seasoned military force, one that likely will continue to develop its formidable conventional and chemical capability, and probably pursue nuclear weapons. Nonetheless, it is unlikely that Baghdad will display any enthusiasm for engaging its military in new adventures. . . . [N]either Iraqi military nor subversive activity against Arab moderates is likely over the next few years.[185]

THE COSTS

Compared with the enormous costs of the 1991 Gulf War, the $27 billion deal with Iraq that Kuwait rejected in July 1990 must now seem like a bargain to all sides. The costs of the Gulf War alone include an estimated $100 billion in damage to non-oil infrastructure in Kuwait and $50 billion in Iraq; $61 billion in direct military expenses for the coalition forces; up to $600 billion in long-term reductions of the region's gross domestic product; about 2,500–3,500 civilians, 50,000–100,000 Iraqi soldiers, and 350 coalition forces killed; up to 111,000 indirect civilian deaths, including 70,000 children, due to the subsequent breakdown in sanitation and the spread of infectious diseases; up to 25,000 coalition troops who complained of Gulf War syndrome, a mysterious "illness," that many believed might have been caused by exposure to chemical weapons; nearly 700 oil wells that were set afire, costing another $20 billion; and 11 million barrels of oil that were released into the Arabian Gulf, twenty times the size of the 1989 Exxon Valdez spill.[186]

In addition to its $81–150 billion foreign debt, postwar Iraq was also saddled with UN sanctions and an extra $320 billion in claims for damage compensation, which it was mandated to pay out of oil revenues, channeled through the UN under terms imposed by the coalition.[187] The claims included $117 billion claimed by Kuwait's Public Authority for Assessment of Compensation. By 2003, $148 billion of those claims had been settled for thirty cents on the dollar, or $43 billion. The remaining claims may be worth $30–40 billion. At that rate, if these claims were honored, Iraq would ultimately have paid at least $80 billion in Gulf War compensation—the same as its entire Iran-Iraq War debt. In the wake of the 2003 US invasion, Kuwait indicated that it might be willing to exchange a portion of Kuwait's claims and unpaid loans for a stake in Iraq's new oil concessions. Throughout the 1990s, Iraq protested to no avail that many of Kuwait's claims were spurious, amounting to yet another forced transfer of Iraq's oil revenues to wealthy Kuwaitis, while its own citizens were going hungry. For example, one wealthy Kuwaiti received $4 million from the UN in compensation for his lost thoroughbreds, jewelry, and art collection.[188]

There was also the enormous cost of the trade sanctions, which banned all imports of Iraqi goods. Imposed by the UN four days after the invasion, this was one of the most comprehensive economic blockades ever. It failed to get Saddam Hussein out of Kuwait, topple him from power, or reveal what he'd done with all his "weapons of mass destruction," which the UN inspectors continued to pursue with mixed success from 1991 until October 1998 and again in 2002–03. However, the sanctions did succeed in interrupting Iraq's supply of basic medicines and hospital equipment, chlorine and pipes for water treatment plants, pollution control gear for the country's oil refineries, and many other imported necessities. All this imposed a frightful cost on ordinary Iraqis. UNICEF estimates that these 1990s UN sanctions boosted infant mortality in Iraq from 25 per 1,000 births in 1990 to 92 per 1,000 in 1995, and reduced per capita caloric intake by one-third. In 1996 the UN Oil-for-Food program was introduced to moderate these effects, but humanitarian organizations estimated that for the decade as a whole, sanctions claimed 60,000–100,000 victims per year—half of them children.[189]

When asked by reporter Leslie Stahl in 1996 about whether the sanctions on Iraq were worth the deaths of five hundred thousand Iraqi children, Secretary of State Madeleine Albright replied, "I think this is a very hard choice, but we think the price is worth it." Others did not agree. Two successive senior UN humanitarian program coordinators and the head of the World Food Program resigned from the program in 1998 and 2000, describing what was being done to the people of Iraq as "intolerable." One commented, "How long should the civilian population of Iraq be exposed to such punishment for something they have never done?"[190] The Clinton administration's answer was that, from the standpoint of its own interests, this policy was preferable to the full-scale invasion that would be needed to take Saddam Hussein out. Only after September 2001, when most Americans woke up to find out that the world's nastiness had landed on their own shores, and wanted to blame someone, was there an appetite for such a move.

Meanwhile, the Iraqis *least* affected by sanctions were of course the regime's leaders. A 2002 study by the US General Accounting Office found that, while the UN Oil-for-Food program was handling $51 billion of Iraq's oil revenues from 1997 to 2001, another $6 billion of illicit income was generated through illegal oil exports and surcharges levied by key officials in exchange for purchasing contracts.[191] Much of this income ended up in dollar accounts in offshore banking havens like Switzerland, Lebanon, and Cyprus, controlled by Saddam Hussein and his cronies.

Even before taking into account the costs of the 2003 US-led invasion and the subsequent reconstruction, Saddam Hussein's attempt to solve his "debt and oil" problems by invading Kuwait in August 1990 easily had a price tag—even apart from all the suffering it caused—of at least $500 billion. And that decision derived from his original October 1980 decision to invade Iran, which derived from the Shah's restoration and demise. By the summer of 2003, when the "Operation Iraqi Freedom" liberators were finally done with the initial heavy fighting, they discovered that a majority of the long-repressed people they had just liberated were devout Shi'as, just as in Iran. The first thing they did was to hold mass demonstrations, demanding that the US leave their country. Perhaps Khomeini and his supporters had really won the Iran-Iraq War after all.

BEYOND SADDAM HUSSEIN?

After the Kuwait invasion, many Western leaders tried to make sense of this complex story by demonizing Saddam Hussein, accepting the long-standing hawkish view of the "neocon" intelligentsia that he was evil incarnate. As Daniel Pipes wrote in 1991, Saddam Hussein's invasions of Iran and Kuwait must have been motivated by "greed and revenge," with "brutality and aggression" tossed in for good measure.[192] In this view, his invasions of Iran and Kuwait were just part of long-standing plans for expansion. They were inevitable once Saddam Hussein had enough military power. He was viewed as impetuous and undeterrable, so there was no alternative but to remove him from power. After waiting twelve years for his own people to do that, the US and its "coalition" finally decided to do it themselves.

Of course, Hussein's regime was indefensible. But it is interesting to contrast the Manichean view of his behavior with the perspective that many First World observers had of him in the 1980s—even after the invasion of Iran, the poison gas incidents, and of course, the repression of his own people. For example, in 1990, a detailed history of the Iran-Iraq War was written by the Strategic Studies Institute of the US Army War College. On the subject of why Saddam Hussein invaded Kuwait, it concluded:

> Conventional wisdom maintains that Iraq always was covetous of Kuwait, and that, indeed, the nature of the Ba'athists is to be expansionists; in invading, the Iraqis were merely following their instincts. This explanation does not hold water. Why, for example, if they desired territory, didn't they seize Khuzestan at the end of the war when Iran was prostrate? Why did they not at least insure themselves control of the Shatt Al Arab? By withdrawing completely from Iran, and turning the issue over to the UN for settlement, the Iraqis behaved as a responsible member of the world community.
>
> Nor does it seem reasonable to argue that Iraq invaded Kuwait because it thought it could get away with it. Throughout the war, the Iraqis had ample evidence of the importance of Kuwait to the superpowers. . . . It seems obvious that Iraq invaded its neighbors because it was desperate. It had a million man army that it could not demobilize, because it had no jobs to send the men home to. It had no jobs because its economy had been ruined by the war. . . . Thus the Iraqi leadership saw itself in a vicious dilemma. . . . In the end, although it emerged "victorious," it practically bankrupted itself.[193]

In this view, Saddam Hussein was less a madman bent on territorial domination or revenge against his neighbors and Israel than a bungler, driven into a corner by his country's economic crisis and isolation.

Decades ago, in response to the loss of the Shah, the "calculators" in the national security establishment tried to create a neat perpetual stalemate between two nasty regimes by helping the slightly lesser-of-two evils. In the process, they created three monsters. The first, in Iran, became the Shah's ruthless, corrupt secular autocracy. Twenty-five years later, Iran is still struggling to find a balance between democracy, theocracy, and peaceful relations with its neighbors and the US. The second, in Afghanistan, ultimately became an al-Qaeda training camp, an opium farm, and a hunting ground for warlords. The third, Saddam Hussein's Iraq, was courted, seduced, and exploited as a blunt instrument by its "allies" when it suited their purposes. Then it was abandoned. When Saddam Hussein appealed to First World banks, Kuwait, and Saudi Arabia to reschedule his debts and share the costs of the war that he had fought partly on their behalf, they declined, and cut him off. Evil instincts notwithstanding, this policy was not calculated to encourage him to be a good neighbor.

But for this war, it is hard to imagine the 2003 invasion of Iraq—regardless of how repressive Saddam was to his own people. Ultimately, the First

World's policy toward Iraq was reminiscent of the Allies' policy toward Germany's war debts and reparations after World War I. In that case, the resulting economic burden contributed mightily to the rise of Hitler, and to the "second war" that Hitler launched.

And so it was that by summer 2003, Saddam Hussein was finally gone—or, at least, on the run. The coalition forces continued to be harassed by guerilla actions, but they tried to turn their attention to searching for weapons of mass destruction and reestablishing law and order—just a little too late to prevent rampant footing at Baghdad's renowned Museum of Antiquities and National Library. They did, however, manage to secure the premises of six hundred oil wells and the Iraqi National Oil Company. But it was not about oil. Within weeks, Schultz' Bechtel was selected for a $600 million reconstruction project, and Halliburton, where Vice President Cheney had been CEO and Lawrence Eagleburger served as a director, was selected as a subcontractor for others that were worth more than $700 million.[194] L. Paul Bremer, the former Managing Director of Kissinger Associates, was selected by President Bush to head the new Office of Reconstruction in Baghdad. He and Assistant Secretary of Defense Paul Wolfowitz—a key aid to Secretary of Defense Donald Rumsfeld—appealed to France, Russia, and Iraq's other major creditors to forgive all their Iraqi loans as soon as possible, so that the country could have a fresh start.

Those who take the most from the table
teach contentment.
Those for whom the taxes are destined
demand sacrifices.
Those who eat their fill
speak to the hungry
of the wonderful times to come.
Those who lead the country
into the abyss
call ruling too difficult
for ordinary men.

Bertolt Brecht

. . . Let the history we lived
be taught in the schools,
so that it is never forgotten,
so our children may know it.

**Mayan Indian, Testimony before Guatemala's
Commission for Historical Clarification, 1999**

ENDNOTES

NOTES TO INTRODUCTION

1. For more about the Chilean earthquake of May 22, 1960, see US Geological Survey, "Surviving a Tsunami – Lessons From Chile, Hawaii, and Japan, Circular 1187," Washington, DC, US Department of the Interior, US Geological Survey, 1999.

2. For a recent global opinion poll, see The Pew Research Center, "What the World Thinks in 2002: How Global Publics View Their Lives, Their Countries, The World, America, December 4, 2002, available at *http://people-press.org/reports/files/report165topline.pdf*. See also British Broadcasting Corporation, "Global Anger at US Growing," December 4, 2002.

3. For a description of this anomalous "golden age" from 1947 to 1973, see Prof. E. J. Hobsbaum, *The Age of Extremes*, New York, Vintage Press, 1996, pp. 6, 8, 257-286.

4. World Bank World Development Indicators, online database (2002). See also Giovanni Andrea Cornia (2002), "Sources of Child Poverty Changes During the Globalization Era," Chapter 4, Harnessing Globalization for Children: A Report to UNICEF, pp. 5–6. Available at *http://www.unicef-icdc.org/research/ESP/globalization/chapter4.pdf*.

5. For more on China's recent development experience, see Yao and Zhang (August 2000); Shujie Yao (2000), "Economic Development and Poverty Reduction in China Over 20 Years of Reform," *Economic Development and Cultural Change*, vol. 48, pp. 447–74 Bjorn Gustafsson and Wei Zhong, "Why Are Some People in Rural China Poor While Others Are Not?," International Conference on the Chinese Economy, "Achieving Growth with Equity," (July 2001). (*www.econs.ecel.uwa.edu.au/economics/Links/papers/aces_Gustafsson_B.pdf.*)

6. World Bank Online Data, World Debt Tables; International Financial Statistics.

7. *Reuters*, September 4, 2002, "Earth Summit Disappoints Poor on Farm Subsidies;" *Chicago Tribune*, August 27, 2002: "Third World Leaders Demand an End to US Farm Subsidies." *The Wall Street Journal* (Sept. 16, 2002, A10). See OECD comments on the May 2002 US farm bill, *http://www.europa.eu.int/comm/trade/pdf/farmbill_qa.pdf* (May 2002). See *http://www.europa.eu.int/comm/trade/pdf/farmbill_qa.pdf* (May 2002).

8. See *http://editors.sipri.se/pubs/yb02/highlights.html*. See UN Conference on Trade and Development (UNTAD), *The Least Developed Countries Report* (June 2002), Statistical Appendix, Table 19. For the rich countries' commitments to spend .7% of GDP on official aid at the 1992 Rio Earth Summit, see *The Guardian*, "The Monterrey Poverty Summit," March 18, 2002.

9. World Bank, Online Data (2002). See also UNCTAD, supra. See *Financial Times*, "US to Create Agency That Will deliver Additional Aid," November 27, 2002, p. 2.

10. See Asian Development Bank, "Report and Recommendations of the President to the Board of Directors on Proposed Loans to the Republic of Indonesia for Power Sector Reform," RRP:INO 31604, Manila: Asian Development Bank, March 1999.

11. Friedman, Thomas, *The Lexus and the Olive Tree*, New York: Farrar, Straus, May 2000.

12. See Paul Hare, "Trade Policy During Transition—Lessons from the 1990s," VI World Congress for Central and East European Studies, Tampere, Finland, July 29–August 3, 2000.

13. For the World Bank's 1990 forecast and its 2000 revision, see World Bank Online Data, "World Development Report, "2000/1, Washington, DC, The World Bank, 2001. For the measurement problems, see Sanjay G. Reddy and Thomas W. Pogge (Columbia University), "How Not to Count the Poor," *www.socialanalysis.org*, June 14, 2002, *passim*; Reddy and Pogge, "Unknown—The Extent, Distribution, and Trend of Global Poverty," August 2002, *www.socialanalysis.org*.

14. For a typical example of numerical development goals, see *www.oecd.org/dac/indicators*. Also see Jan Vandemoortele, "Are the MDGs Feasible?" July 2002, to be published as *Targeting development: Critical perspectives on the Millennium Development Goals and International Development Targets*, edited by Richard Black and Howard White, Routledge (forthcoming).

15. For a recent summary of economic trends affecting the world's 49 "least developed countries" that underscores their plight, see UN Council on Trade and Development, "The Least Developed Countries Report—Escaping the Poverty Trap," New York, UNCTAD, June 2002. "Millennium Development Goals," New York, UN Development Program, September 2000; International Conference for Financing for Development, New York/Monterrey, UN Development Program, March 2002.

16. See Shigemitsu Sugisaki, Deputy Managing Director, IMF, "Ensuring a Sustained Asian Recovery," *Asiaweek*, December 15, 2000. Data from World Bank Online, and Asian Economic Monitor, November 2002, *http://www.aric.adb.org/aem/ind_oct.pdf*.

17. See *www.InQ7.net*, June 27, 2002; August 5, 2002. See also the UNDP, "Human Development Report," 2002.

18. For very longrun trends in income disparaties among countries and regions, see Andre Gunder Frank, *Global Economy in the Asian Age*, University of California Press, April, 1998, excerpt at *http://www.eh.net/lists/archives/eh.res/nov-1997/0052.php*. See also Paul Bairoch and Maurice Levy-Leboyer, eds., *Disparities in Economic Development Since The Industrial Revolution*, London: MacMillan, 1981.

19. Data on billionaires and their estimated wealth are from *Forbes.com*, "The World's Billionaires," February 28, 2002. See also World Bank Online, 2002. See also Cornia (2001), *op. cit.*

20. See Jubilee 2000, November 2002, " HIPC Debt Relief to 42 Countries," *http://www.jubileeresearch. org/hipc/progress_report/tables.htm*. See Anne Krueger, "A New Approach to Sovereign Debt Restructuring," National Economists' Club Annual Members' Dinner, Washington DC, November 26, 2001. *http://www. imf.org/external/np/speeches/2001/112601.htm*.

21. World Bank Online Data, 2002.

22. For examples of the rather antiseptic "policy error/natural catastrophe" interpretation of the 1980s debt crisis, see William E. Cline, *International Debt: Systemic Risk and Policy Response*, M.I.T., 1984; John H. Makin, *The Global Debt Crisis*, Basic Books, 1984; Gordon W. Smith and John T. Cuddington, *International Debt and the Developing Countries*, World Bank, 1985; and Pedro-Pablo Kucynski, *Latin American Debt*, Johns Hopkins Press, 1988.

23. SIPRI (2000–02 Annual Yearbooks available at *http://www.sipri.se*). All estimates relied on here are in constant 1985 dollars, and are from US Arms Control and Development Agency, "World Military Expenditures and Arms Transfers" (US State Department, various dates). Congressional Research Service study, *New York Times*, August 11, 1991.

24. The BIS governor quote is from an interview with "Miami Banker #5," December 5, 1987.

25. See John Maynard Keynes, *The Economic Consequences of the Peace*, New York, Harcourt, Brace, and Howe, 1920, p. 270.

26. For the prevalence of second languages among non-Hispanic Americans, see Gallup, May 1, 2001," available at *http://www.gallup.com/poll*. For the polls about American ignorance of world geography, see *Miami Herald*, "US Geographic Literacy No Better After September 11," December 1, 2002.

NOTES TO CHAPTER ONE

1. Paul Drake, "Debt and Democracy in Latin America, 1920-1980s," an article in Barbara Stallings and Robert Kaufman, *Debt and Democracy in Latin America*, Boulder, Westview Press, 1989, p. 43.

2. For the leak story, see *Epoca*, September 2001, summarized at *www.edie.net/news/Archive/4735.cfm*. For other details about Angra I, II and III, and Brazil's nuclear power program and recent energy crisis, see *Bulletin of Atomic Scientists*, September/October 2001; *WiseNews*, October 18 1996; September 1, 2001; *The New York Times*, August 1, 2000; *China News*, September 9, 2001; *Siemens* Standpunkt, August 1996; *Inter Press Service*, October 18, 2000.

3. *Movimento*, 11.20.78; *Veja*, 11.5.86; 5.20.87; "Senior Official," Rio, 2.14.89; "SP Attorney," Sao Paulo, 2.21.89. *Veja*, 5.20.87.

4. See *www.angra-dois-reis.com*.

5. Luis Pinguilli Rosa, Vice Director of the Engineering School at Rio's Federal University, *Bulletin of Atomic Scientists*, September/October 2001.

6. *ISE News Service*, September 12, 2001.

7. *The New York Times*, October 9, 1990, p. 1. *The New York Times*, July 29, 1990, p. 19.

8. For more about Valarie Giscard d'Estaing's and his relatives dealings in Third World countries, see Jonathan Kwinty, *The Wall Street Journal*, April 23, 1981. See Telegraph, November 5, 1996; *www.eu.observer.com*.

9. International Rivers Network, *Greenhouse Gas Emissions from Dams*. (Berkeley: International Rivers, June 2002), 14. See also British Broadcasting Corporation, "Water Power Fuels Climate Change," May 31, 2000.

10. *Jornal do Brasil*, 10.27.87, 8. Catherine Caufield, "The World Vs. The World Bank," *IDR*, V. 1, N. 1, Fall 1988, pp. 6-13. *Jornal do Brasil*, 5.10.87.

11. See also Ricardo Canese, *La dueda ilicita de Itaipu: el mas nefasto negociado contra el Paraguay*, Asunción, Editorial Generacion, 1999; Paulo Schilling and Richardo Canese, *Itaipu: Geopolítica e Corrupção*, São Paulo, CEDI, 1991. For Juan Carlos Wasmosy, see Ultima Hora, "Paraguay: ex presidente Wasmosy condenado a 4 años de cárcel," April 12, 2002; La República en la Red, August 26, 1999: "Justicia paraguaya procesó a Wasmosy por corrupción; *The New York Times*, April 16, 2002; Clarin, April 12, 2002. The August 30, 2001 account in *La Nación* of Wasmosy's alleged Cayman accounts was also reported in *La Prensa*, September 1, 2001.

12. Tucurui's cost estimates are from *Folha do Sao Paulo*, 8.2.75.

13. See the "1984 Hearings on Relatoria Saraiva, Brazilian Congress," April-May 1984. Tucurui's environmental problems are described in *Veja*, 10.10.84, and by "SP Attorney," Sao Paulo, 2.21.89.

14. *O Estado de Sao Paulo*, March 21, 1987. See also the World Commission on Dams Report, November 16, 2000.

15. See Normal Gall, "Blackout in Energy Policy," Ferdinand Braudel Institute Paper #31, 2002. *http://www.braudel.org.br/paping31a.htm*).

16. For the origins of the project, see Claudio Antonion Scarpinella, "*Porto Primavera: O Paradigm de Analise e Os Processor Decisao de Implantacao*," Thesis, University of Sao Paulo, December 1999, pp. 95-141, available at *www.iee.usp.br/biblioteca/producao/1999/teses/Scarpinel.pdf*.

17. See *Istoe*, "Electric Confusion," February 5, 2001.

18. Scarpinella, *op. cit.*, p. 101.

19. Scarpinelli, *op. cit.*, p. 104.

20. Istoe, "Electric Confusion," February 5, 2001.

21. Mieceslau Kudlavicz, Pastoral Land Commission, Testimony. World Commission on Dams, Regional Consultations on Brazil, August 1999. (Available at *http://www.dams.org/kbase/consultations/latin/abs_p5_en.htm*) O Estado de Sao Paulo, May 13, 1996; Normal Gall, "Blackout in Energy Policy," Ferdinand Braudel Institute Paper # 31, 2002. *http://www.braudel.org.br/paping31a.htm*). See also the environmentalist viewpoint, at *http://www.socioambiental.org/website/noticias/english/brazil/2001-09-26-11-14AM.html*

22. British Broadcasting Corporation, "Brazil's Unsustainable Amazon scheme," August 12, 2002.

23. *Istoe' Senhor*, 2.22.89.

24. Tubarao's horrific economics were described by "Energy Expert," London, 2.09.89. Acominas's miserable economics were described by "NY Banker #19," 1.6.88, NYC, and the aluminum, steel, and electricity subsidies by Robert Penteado, "Eletronorte: subsidio ao aluminio trara prejuizo," *O Estado de Sao Paulo*, 4.21.87.

25. Marcelo Pinho and Maricio Ribeiro de Valle, "Changes in Profitability of the Brazilian Steel Industry After Privatization—The Impact of Exogenous Events," (Sao Paulo: USP, March 2000). *http://www. wifo.ac.at/~luger/pinho_ribeirodovalle.pdf*.

26. For a detailed treatment of the gasohol project, see Barbara Nunberg, "Structural Change and State Policy: The Politics of Sugar in Brazil Since 1964," *Latin American Research Review*, Vol. XXI, #2, 1986, pp. 53-93. For more about the smaller Brazilian white elephants, see *Veja*, 5.20.87; and 11.5.86.

27. For more details, see Parry, "Lost History: Marcos, Money, and Treason" (1996), and "October Surprise: Finally, Time for The Truth," (1997), at *www.consortiumnews.com*. See also Hong Kong Deposit and Guar. Co. Ltd. v. Hibdon, 602 F. Supp. 1378, 1383 (S.D.N.Y. 1985), and Tetra Finance (HK) Ltd. v. Shaheen, 584 F.Supp. 847, 848 (S.D.N.Y. 1984).

28. *Inquirer News Service* (Manila), May 15, 2002 article about the Phliippines' private purchase agreements for electricity.

29. For the history of the Bataan nuclear power plant, see *TG*, "Philippines to Scrap Nuclear Albatross," Sept. 7, 1999; *FEER*, June 10, 1993; *WISE News Communique*, October 1, 1998; inQ7.net, "PPA the bitter fruit, BNPP the rotten root," July 22, 2002. For Enron's two power projects at Batangas and Subic Bay in the Philippines, and the failed IPP program in general, see Inter Press Service (1995 report on Enron power plants in the Philippines); British Broadcasting Corporation, "Sparks Fly Over Philippine Electricity," June 12, 2002; *Philippine Center for Investigative Journalism*, "Trail of Power Mess Leads to Ramos," August 5-8, 2002.

30. For Yacyreta's history, see "World Commission on Dams, Damming the Rivers: The World Bank's Lending for Large Dams," (1994); World Bank press conference, James Wolfensohn, World Bank President, Press Conference, April 15, 1998; "World Bank Discusses Report of Advisory Panel on Yacyreta Hydroelectric Project," World Bank press release, January 14, 2000; Elias Diaz Pena and Ella Stancich. *No Mas Danos en Yacyreta* (2000.) See also *http://www.redlisted.com/paraguay_yacyreta.html*, and the case study of Yacyreta at American University's Trade and Environment Database, at *http://www.american.edu/TED/ted.htm*. See also the IDB's 1999 evaluation of the project: "Management's Status Report on the Yacyreta Hydroelectric Pro-

ject (Loan 760/OC-RG), June 14, 1999. The World Bank audit is reported in UK House of Commons, "International Development—Appendix to Minutes of the Evidence," March 22, 2001, available at *http://www.parliament.the-stationery-office.co.uk/pa/cm200001/cmselect/cmintdev/39/39ap01.htm*.

31. For an analysis of the structure, trends, and sources of growth of agricultural productivity in Peru, see Jackeline Velazco, "Agricultural Production in Peru (1950-1995): Sources of Growth," *www.fao.org/DOCREP/003/X9447E/x9447e08.htm*.

32. For Andres Perez's public toilet employment program, see Tyler Bridges, "Down the Toilet: Where Did Venezuela's Debt Go?," *Washington Monthly*, December 1986.

33. Bolivia's unusual acquisitions of C-130s was described by "Chilean Military Analyst," Sao Paulo, 2.18.89.

34. For more about El Cajon, see *http://www.csuchico.edu/anth/loker/index.htm*.

35. See Witness for Peace, "A People Dammed: The World Bank-Funded Chixoy Hydroelectric Project and its Devastating Impacts on the People and Economy of Guatemala." (Washington, DC, May 1996). For more gruesome details on specific actions by Guatemala's military against Mayan villages in the central highlands during the early 1980s, see the UN Comisión para el Esclarecimiento Histórico (CEH), *Guatemala Memoria del Silencio*. (UN, June, 1999), available at *http://shr.aaas.org/guatemala/ceh/gmds_pdf/indice.pdf*. See also article on the Commissions's report in *The Washington Post*, February 26,1999, and the May 3, 2000 June 2001 legal complaints against the military high command of former General Romeo Lucas García and General Jose Efrain Rios Montt that were submitted by Guatemala's Association for Justice and Reconciliation to the Guatemalan Public Ministry (available at *www.justiceforgenocide.org/garcia.html*.)

36. From the May 3, 2000 AJR complaint against Lucas Garcia.

37. See The Rome Treaty of the International Court articulated by the UN and opened for signature and ratification in 1998.

38. For a transcript of the conversation between Wolfensohn, Fischer and Ladner captured at the April 13 2000 day long conference on globalization at American University, see *www.nisgua.org/articles/AU.html*.

39. For the World Bank's dam-oriented lending, see Leonard Sklar and Patrick McCully, "Damming the Rivers: The World Bank's Lending for Large Dams." International Rivers Network Working Paper 5. (November 1994.) The 1991 World Bank quote is from World Bank Online Data, "Project Completion Report, Guatemala: Chixoy Hydroelectric Power Project," Washington, DC, December 31, 1991. Wolfensohn's 1996 quote is from his June 18, 1996 letter to Paul Scire, Executive Director, Witness for Peace, available at *http://www.irn.org/programs/finance/chixoy960618.html*. See also Christopher L.Bryson, "Guatemala: A Development Dream Turns into a Repayment Nightmare." *The Christian Science Monitor*, May 1, 1987. For more about the Chixoy debacle, see The World Commission on Dams, "Chixoy Dam Case," at *http://www.dams.org/kbase/submissions/showsub.php?rec=soc073*; International Rivers Network, "Letter to Wolfensohn," June 28, 1996; Karyn Levy, "Life Submerged—The Environmental Impacts of Guatemala's Chixoy Dam," International Rivers Network, April 2002, available at *http://www.irn.org/programs/latamerica/index.html*. For the Woodrow Wilson report, see The Working Group on Multilateral Institutional Accountabiity, Graduate Policy Workshop, Woodrow Wilson School, "The Chixoy Dam and the Massacres at Río Negro, Agua Fria, and Los Encuentros," Princeton, 2000, available at *www.advocacynet.org*. The $350 million to $500 million estimate from losses due to corruption is from Cronica, "Las Miserias de Chixoy no Son Solamente de los Guatemaltecos," May 4, 1990. See also *www.irn.org*, Press Release, August 2, 1999. The Bolanos quote is from Witness for Peace, "A People Dammed: The World Bank-Funded Chixoy Hydroelectric Project and its Devastating Impacts on the People and Economy of Guatemala." (Washington, DC, May 1996). See also Fundación de Antropología Forense de Guatemala, *"Las masacres de Rabinal.* (1997); Inter-American Development Bank. "Guatemala: Project Report. Additional Funding for the Pueblo Viejo-Quixal Hydroelectric Project on the Chixoy River," September 1985. The original 1974 cost estimate of $270 million is from Witness for Peace, *op. cit.*, citing an unpublished study by Matthew E. Davidson (1987). The original cost Consorcio Lami. *"Proyecto Hidroelectrico Pueblo Viejo-Quixal: Informacion Sobre el Proyecto,"* (December 1982). The IDB's 1975 cost estimate was $341 million, and may be found in "Chixoy: Obra de Infrastructura sin Precedentes en Guatemala." Inforpress Centroamericana, No. 176. (January 22, 1976). For the Chulac dam, see M. Davidson (unpublished m.s.), "Hydro Frustration in Guatemala," Guatemala City, June 18, 1987; Cornerhouse (2002), "The Record of Twelve European Dam Companies," *op. cit.*

40. See World Bank Online Data (2002). See also World News Service, "Facts on File—Mobutu, May 22, 1997." For a more detailed description of Mobutu's career as a kleptocrat, client of leading Western intelligence agencies, and brutal dictator, see Michela Wrong, *In the Footsteps of Mr. Kurtz: Living on the Brink of Disaster in Mobutu's Congo*, London, Fourth Estate Ltd., 2000.

41. See British Broadcasting Corporation, "Nigerian Road Trip: Abuja," December 21, 2001.

42. See *www.freeafrica.org/looting3.html*, p. 5. The quotation is from Mr. Achim Katz, EC Commissioner to Kenya, Report to the EC, March 1986, reported in *Index on Censorship*, August 1990, p. 19. See also *Financial Times*, November. 27, 1991, and *www.freeafrica.org/looting3.html*, pp. 5-7. For more on the Turkwell Gorge Dam saga, see Patrick McCully, *Silenced Rivers: The Ecology and Politics of Large Dams*, London: Zed Books, 1996; *Financial Times*, "Mr. Biwott the Businessman: A Look at the Former Kenyan Minister's Road to Riches," November 27, 1991.

43. For reports of the scandal, and the Kenyan press' reaction to them, see UK House of Parliament, March 22, 2001, Committee on International Development ( ) Appendix 1: Recent Cases of Corruption Involving UK Companies and UK-Backed International Financial Institutions, Turkwell, Kenya; available at *http://www.parliament.the-stationery-office.co.uk/pa/cm200001/cmselect/cmintdev/39/39ap06.htm*; Patrick McCully, *Silenced Rivers- The Ecology and Politics of Large Dams*, London: Zed Books, 1996, p. 262. For the aid freeze to Kenya, see *People's Daily*, "No Major Progress on Aid Talks Between WB, IMF Chiefs, Kenyan President," February 26, 2001; British Broadcasting Corporation, "New Brooms for Graft-Ridden Kenya," December 29, 2002.

44. See Smith Hempstone, *Rogue Ambassador.: An African Memoir*, University of the South Press, 1997; British Broadcasting Corporation, "Moi sues ex-US Ambassador," July 31, 2001. For more on the Ouko case see *Africa Today*, September 2001.

45. *Financial Times*, November 27, 1991.

46. British Broadcasting Corporation, "Moi sues ex-US Ambassador," July 31, 2001.

47. See note 46 above.

48. *The New York Times*, October 21, 1991.

49. For the "list of shame," see British Broadcasting Corporation, May 10, 2000, CNN, July 19, 2000; *Boston Globe*, July 17, 2000. The Citibank tale about Nicholas Biwott is reported in *The New York Times*, October 21, 1991.

50. For a discussion of these effects, see Korinna Horta, "Making the Earth Rumble—The Lesotho-South African Water Connection," *Multinational Monitor*, May 1996 Vol 17, No. 5, available at *http://www.irn.org/programs/lesotho/mm0596.05.html*.

51. James Wolfensohn, Address, 1996 Annual World Bank Meetings, Washington, DC, October 1996. See the US Foreign Corrupt Practices Act of 1977 ("FCPA"), 15 USC §§ 78dd-1, et seq. For the World Bank's anti-corruption guidelines, see its 1996 Guidelines for Procurement Under IBRD Loans and IDA Credits, Sections 1.15. "Fraud and Corruption," and its 1997 Guidelines for Selection and Employment of Consultants, Section 1.25. "Fraud and Corruption." See also Shang-Jin Wei, Harvard University and NBER, "How Taxing is Corruption on International Investors," Eighth International Anti-Corruption Conference, Lima, Peru. (September 1997) available at *http://www.transparency.org/iacc/8th_iacc/papers/jinwei.html*.

52. *La Prensa*, "Dos sociedades panameñas están relacionadas en uno de los escándalos más importantes de soborno," July 9, 2000; *The Guardian*, "Blacklisting threat to UK firm in dam cash scandal," July 6, 2002.

53. See British Broadcasting Corporation, "Corporate Bribery Verdict in Lesotho," May 20, 2002.

54. See British Broadcasting Corporation, "Bribery firm protests its innocence," October 29, 2002; ENS, "Canadian Firm Paid Bribes to Win Lesotho Dam Job," September 18, 2002.

55. Lesotho's Attorney General Fine Maema, quoted in Karen McGregor, "Lesotho's—a small country is showing big heart in combating corruption," *Business Ethics Direct*, Fall 2002. Available at *www.ethicsa.org*.

56. See *Folha do Sao Paulo*, Interview with ABB CEO Goran Lindahl, August 22, 1999. For more about the Lesotho Highlands Water Project story, see Korinna Horta, "Making the Earth Rumble—The Lesotho-South African Water Connection," *Multinational Monitor*, May 1996 Vol 17, No. 5, available at *http://www.irn.org/programs/lesotho/mm0596.05.html.*; *The Cornerhouse*, "The Record of Twelve European Dam Building Companies," Stockholm: The Swedish Society for Nature Conservation, February 2000, available at *http://www.ern.org/general/dams/dams_inc.zip*; Environmental News Service, "Canadian Firm Paid Bribes to Win Lesotho Dam Job," September 18, 2002; *La Prensa*, "*Dos sociedades panameñas están relacionadas en uno de los escándalos más importantes de soborno*," July 9, 2000. The details regarding company payoffs are from David Grebe, *Business Day*, "Official Faces charge over R12 million bribe," July 29, 1999; BD, "Corrupt Firms Face Blacklist," July 30,1999; *The Washington Post*, "Big Firms Accused of Bribery in African Dam Project," August 13, 1999. The allegations of corruption against Balfour Beatty are reported in International Rivers Network, "The Lesotho Highland Water Development Project. Part II—What Went Wrong," presentation to Chatham House, July 10, 2000. available at *http://www.irn.org/programs/lesotho/index.asp?id=/programs/lesotho/chatham.01.html*.

57. The US Bureau of Reclamation official quote is from an interview reported by Probe International's Patricia Adams, September 23, 1993. in Margaret Barber and G. Ryder, editors, *Daming the Three Gorges—What Dam Builders Don't Want You to Know*, Toronto, Probe International, 1993.

58. See International Rivers Network, "Citizens Guide to the World Commission on Dams," Berkeley: 2002, p. 32.

59. See World Bank Online Data (2003), "Statistics on the World Bank's Dam Portfolio," available at *www.worldbank.org.*

60. See the organization sponsored by George Soros and 40 NGOs that proposes precisely this: *www.publishwhatyoupay.org.*

61. See Philip Gray, "Private Participation in Infrastructure: A Review of the Evidence," Kennedy School MS, October 2001.

62. See Vasquez, *op. cit.*

63. For more about EXIM's loans to Halliburton and the SEC investigation, see *Los Angeles Times,* "State Department Eases Deals for Halliburton," October 27, 2000; British Broadcasting Corporation, "Cheney accused of corporate fraud," July 10, 2002.

64. See US EXIM Bank, "EXIM's Role in Greenhouse Gas Emissions and Climate Change," August, 1999.

65. For more data about lending by export credit agencies, see *www.eca-watch.org.*

NOTES TO CHAPTER TWO

1. "USAID Official," interview with the author, Manila, April 22, 1989.

2. Interviews with "Keo," Manila, April 24-26, 1989; *Associated Press,* January 19, 1982; *Financial Times,* February 20, 1982; *The New York Times,* February 7, 1982; *Los Angeles Times,* October 9, 1990.

3. *Los Angeles Times,* October 9, 1990.

4. See *http://nsarchive.chadwyck.com/phintro.htm.*

5. See *Washington Post,* May 4, 1991, p. A20.

6. David Chaikin, "Tracking the Proceeds of Organized Crime—The Marcos Case," Paper for the Transational Crime Confrence, Australian Institute of Crimology, March 9, 2000.

7. See *www.Inq7.net,* August 2, 2002.

8. Marites N. Sison, "Recovering the Marcos Wealth: Show Us the Money," *www.filipinasmag.com,* May 2000; "Long recovery for Marcos crony assets," *www.abs-cbn.com* June 22, 1999; Raul Dancel, "Marcos Legacy Special Report—Foreign Debt: The Price of Greed?," *Inquirer News Service,* September 21, 2002. See also *Reuters,* 12.9.90; *Los Angeles Times,* 11.24.90; Jonathan Greenberg, "Dry Those Tears, Imelda." *Forbes,* 7.9.90.

9. See *www.philstar.com,* January 17, 2003. Also see *The Manila Times,* October 18, 2002.

10. See Donna S. Cueto, "Probe sought on mysterious P2B Imelda Marcos Settlement," *Inquirer News Service,* November 9, 2002. See the account of the allegations in *The Philippines Daily Inquirer,* "Four Hackers Break Into Swiss Bank," December 10, 1999. See Lucy Komisar, "Marcos's Missing Millions," *In These Times,* August 2, 2002; Donna S. Cueto, *The Philippines Daily Inquirer,* "PCCG Willing to Hear Witness in Marcos Funds Transfer," July 3, 2002. See *Financial Times,* "KPMG Accused of Ignoring Xerox Warnings," January 30, 2003, p. 15. See Komisar, *op. cit.* See *http://www.vatican.va/roman_curia/pontifical_academies/acdscien/documents/miscellanea2.pdf.* For more about the doctor, see David Pallister, Owen Bowcott and Alex Bellos, "Lawyer, Art Lover, and Trusted Fixer," and "King Fahd Is Moving Large Sums Through Liechtenstein," *The Guardian,* July 17, 2002; Conal Walsh, "Trouble in Banking Paradise as Uncle Sam's Sheriffs Ride In," *The Observer,* November 6, 2002; *Financial Times,* "G7 Cracks Down on Hot Money," September 20, 2000; *Tax-news.com,* September 4, 2000. See Stacy Mosher, "Laundry Probe Hangs Over Financier," *www.thedailydeal.com,* July 22, 2000. For Batliner's involvement in the Habibie case, Kohl, the Philippines, and Brazilian soccer, see "CBF Uses Laundry of Kohl and Dealers," *www.Abknet.de,* December 27, 2001. See also Philip Sherwell, "Liechtenstein: A Magnet for Money Launderers," *Die Tageszeitung,* January 23, 2000.

11. See Blanche Rivera, "Marcos Cases Over in 2 years—PCGG," *The Philippines Daily Inquirer,* July 11, 2001.

12. See Donna S. Cueto, "Seized Marcos Assets Slowly Disappearing," *The Philippines Daily Inquirer,* September 21, 2002.

13. *Financial Times,* September 22, 1988.

14. For the doubts about Jacobi, see Curtiss Waters, "I never met with Aranetas," *Inquirer News Service,* March 19, 2001.

15. See *The Philippines Daily Inquirer,* "Irene's Account," July 8, 2001.

16. See Article 305 of the Swiss Penal Code.

17. John Authers and Richard Wolffe, *The Victim's Fortune: Inside the Epic Battle Over The Debts of the Holocaust,* New York, HarperCollins, 2003. See *http://www.swissbankclaims.com/index.asp.* See also Itamar

Levin, *The Last Deposit: Swiss Banks and Holocaust Victims' Accounts*, New York, Praeger, 1999. See Jacobi's website, *www.marcosbillions.com*.

18. See "PCGG's Swiss lawyer has brod in bank with Irene," *www.philstar.com*, September 12, 2002; Curtiss Waters, "I Never Met with Aranetas," *Inquirer News Daily*, March 19, 2001.

19. See *The Philippines Daily Inquirer*, "Irene Araneta Swiss Deposits Feared Gone," July 9, 2001.

20. For Imelda's statements regarding her wealth, see *The Philippines Daily Inquirer*, "Interviews with Imelda Marcos," December 5-9, 1998.

21. See endnote 3 above.

22. The Yamashita story was revived by Sterling Seagrave in *The Marcos Dynasty*, New York, Harper & Row, 1988, pp. 351-352. See "Yamashita Treasure a Myth," *The Philippines Daily Inquirer*, April 17, 1989, p. 8.

23. For more details on the sources and extent of the Marcos's criminal wealth, see the 100 page RICO action that was filed against them in California in 1989: Republic of the Philippines vs. Ferdinand E. Marcos, Imelda R. Marcos, et al. (US District Court, Central District of California, Case No. CV 86-3859-MRP (Gx), 1986), and The Central Bank of the Philippines v. Ferdinand E. Marcos, et al,(US District Court for the District of Hawaii, Case No. 86-0213, 1986). See also the Special Committee on Public Accountability, Report on the Inquiry on Operation Big Bird, Philippines House of Representatives (1991); W. Scott Malone (1987), "Ferdinand E. Marcos: A Trail of Corruption," Investigative Report for PBS (1987); J. Crewson, "Marcos Graft Staggering," *Chicago Tribune*, March 23, 1986; Ricardo Manapat, *Some Are Smarter Than Others: The History of Marcos's Crony Capitalism*, New York: Aletheia, 1991, Chapter 1.

24. For a report on the geological survey of the Philippines, see *Financial Times*, March 21, 1989.

25. Interview with Ms. Margaret Beplat, March 28, 1989; Tris Beplat, March 30, 1989.

26. Barrington Moore Jr. *Social Origins of Dictatorship and Democracy*, Boston: Beacon Press, 1966, pg. v. The "Initial Post-Surrender Policy" is described in Robert E. Ward, *Japan's Political System*, Englewood Cliffs, NJ, Prentice-Hall, 1967, pp. 7-21.

27. Calculated from Kazushi Ohkawa and Henry Rosovsky, *Japanese Economic Growth: Trend Acceleration in the Twentieth Century*, London: Stanford University Press, 1973, Appendix.

28. Alfred Maizels, *Industrial Growth and World Trade*, Cambridge, Cambridge University Press, 1963.

29. Yoshio Suzuki, *Money and Banking in Contemporary Japan*, New Haven, Yale University Press, 1980, p. 9.

30. Interview with Tris Beplat, March 30, 1989.

31. For more on the evolution of MacArthur's policies in light of Cold War politics, see Walter Lafeber, *America, Russia, and The Cold War, 1945-46*, New York: John Wiley & Sons, 1967, Chapters 2-3.

32. Tristan E. Belplat, quoted in Norman Gall, "US and the World Economy—Dinheiro, Ganacia, e tecnologia, Part 2—Japan, Russia, Brazil," Braudel Papers, No. 21, 1998.

33. See Ladejinsky's article "The Plow Outbids the Sword in Asia: How General MacArthur Stole Communist Thunder with Democratic Land Reforms, Our Most Potent Weapon for Peace," *Farm Journal*, June 1951. See also Louis J. Walinsky, ed., *Agrarian Reform as Unfinished Business: The Selected Papers of Wolf Ladejinsky*, New York, published for the World Bank by Oxford University Press, 1977. William Manchester, *American Caesar: Douglas MacArthur, 1880-1964*, Boston, Little, Brown, 1978, pp. 506, 508.

34. For more background, see Putzel (1992), *op. cit.*, Chapter 3.

35. See Putzel (1992), *op. cit.*; Bellow and de Guzman, *op. cit.*

36. This quote from Wolf Ladejinsky is from *Reforma Agraria, http://www.fppm.org/2001-reforma%20 agraria.htm.*

37. See the case for a "trend acceleration" in Japan's GNP growth rate after World War II in Kazushi Ohkawa and Henry Rosovsky, *Japanese Economic Growth: Trend Acceleration in the Twentieth Century*, London, Stanford Univeristy Press, 1973.

38. See Bank of Japan, Quarterly Bullet: Japan's Non-Performing Loan Problem, November 2002. See "Japan's Banks Get Another Mr. Fix-It," *Business Week*, October 14, 2002.

39. After 1946, Japan's capital account with the rest of the world was consistently positive—reflecting its current account surpluses. See Ohkawa and Rosovsky, *op. cit.*, Table 11, p. 302.

40. Interview with the author, Margaret Beplat, March 28, 1989.

41. Stanley Karnow, *America's Empire in the Philippines*, New York: Random House, 1989, pp. 326-28; 346-54; 362-63.

42. See Michael McClintock, *Instruments of Statecraft: US Guerilla Warfare, Counterinsurgency, Counterterrorism, 1940-1990*, New York, Pantheon, 1992, pp. 83-85.

43. See Victor Nebrida, "The Balangiga Massacre: Getting Even," available at the Philippines History Group of L.A., *http://www.bibingka.com/phg/menu.htm.*

44. Jose David Lapuz, Philippine political scientist, quoted in *Asiaweek*, June 6, 1998.

45. For the US inteventions in these postwar Philippines elections, McClintock, *op. cit.*, pp. 82-138,

46. For more about the Bell Act's provisions, see Karnow, *op. cit.*, pp. 260, 325-27. See also Cheryl Payer, *The Debt Trap.* (New York: Monthly Review, 1974), pp. 50-54. See also Alan Berlow, "The Independence Day That Wasn't," NPR, July 4, 1996, transcript available at *http://www.bibingka.com/phg/misc/july4not.htm.*

47. See "Ladejinsky Firing Protested," 104:35,398, December 24, 1954, p. 12, Letter. See Ladejinsky, "Land Reform in Indonesia," 1964.

48. Tris Beplat, March 30, 1989.

49. See endnote 48 above.

50. "NY Banker #7," December 22–23, 1988, NYC; "NY Banker #13," NYC, 1.17.89. *Euromoney,* "The Philippines—A Survey," Supplement. April 1982, p. 25.

51. "London Banker #5," 1.26.89.

52. Severina Rivera, PCCG counsel, 4.1.89.

53. Margaret Beplat, 3.28.89. Severina Rivera, PCCG counsel, 4.1.89.

54. "NY Banker #1," 4. 10-21.86; Severina Rivera, 4.1.89.

55. See Asian Development Bank, *Key Indicators of Developing Member Countries,* Manila: Asian Development Bank, 1989.

56. World Bank, *The Philippines: A Review of External Debt,* Report No. 4912-PH, Washington, DC, 1984, p. 42.

57. *Euromoney,* April 1984.

58. Quoted in Robert Shaplen, "The Philippines, Part II," *New Yorker,* September 1986, p. 61.

59. *Rundt's Weekly,* January 31, 1983.

60. See description of the Binondo Central Bank in Aurora Javate-De Dios, et al, *Dictatorship and Revolution: Roots of People's Power,* Manila, Conspectus Foundation, 1988, pp. 111-115.

61. Fox Butterfield, *New York Times,* January 14, 1978. For the "powder keg," see the *New York Times* story by this title, September 24, 1979.

62. *The Wall Street Journal,* January 5, 1981.

63. According to the World Bank, private foreign creditors arranged commitments in 1982 totaling $1.073 billion, compared with $1.039 billion in 1981, the previous record year. *Euromoney,* April 1984. See also *Rundts' Weekly,* January 31, 1983; *Manila Chronicle,* November 4, 1986, p. 5.

64. "NY Banker # 17," January 25, 1989.

65. "NY Banker #15," 1.18.89. The Advisory Committee's Economic Subcommittee that made the visit was chaired by Gordon Nelson of Morgan, and included Sacho Kojima of Bank of Tokyo and William Nedereider of Dresdner Bank.

66. "NY Banker # 17," January 25, 1989; *The Wall Street Journal,* December 19, 1983.

67. "NY Banker #15," NYC, January 18, 1989.

68. *Euromoney,* April, 1984, p. 50.

69. For more details on all these gold flights, see W. Scott Malone, "Ferdinand E. Marcos—A Trail of Corruption," unpublished notes for PBH-Frontline, 1987.

70. *Philippine Central Bank Review,* "Clearing the Doubts," May 1986.

71. For more details on all these gold flights, see W. Scott Malone, "Ferdinand E. Marcos—A Trail of Corruption," unpublished notes for PBH-Frontline, 1987.

72. The KLM Cargo Air Waybill, #074-9184-8212, *Central Bank Review,* op cit.

73. W. Scott Malone, "The Golden Fleece," in *Regardie's Magazine,* October 1988, pp. 116–140, 121.

74. Malone, op cit., pp. 129–130.

75. Interview with Richard Hirschfield, 2.6.89. See also Hirschfield's account in Malone, *op. cit.,* p. 137.

76. Marcos's Washington law firm was Anderson Hibey. Richard Hirschfield, 2.6.89. "NY Banker #17," January 25, 1989.

77. "NY Banker #7," January 19, 1989; December 22–23, 1988.

78. Dimitri Belatsos, 1.17.89 "NY Banker #14, January 17, 1989, January 18, 1989; "NY Banker #18," January 25, 1989.

79. "NY Banker #18," January 25, 1989.

80. *Business Day's* Annual Corporate Profiles and Yoshihara Kunio, *Philippine Industrialization: Foreign and Domestic Capital,* New York, Oxford University Press, 1985.

81. Lucy Komisar, *Corazon Aquino,* New York, George Braziller, 1988, p. 127.

82. Interview with the author, Walter W. Wriston, February 19, 1988. Other observers are much less sure about Marcos's war record. See Stanley Karnow, *op. cit.*

83. Interview with the author, Fox Butterfield, March 31, 1988.

84. Fox Butterfield, March 31, 1988. EXIM Bank Credit # 6122, Philippine Nuclear Power Station #1, "Summary of Direct Loans," US Export-Import Bank, January 26, 1976. *New York Times,* January 14, 1978; Gary Southern, former MHT project financing, January 26, 1989; Tony Constant, former MHT Ltd, January 26, 1989.

85. "NY Banker #14," January 18, 1989; Professor James Boyce, February 3, 1989.

86. *Asia Banking*, September 1986.

87. This included the debts assumed for PDCP. See endnote 86 above.

88. Malone, Memo # 3, *op. cit.*, p. 30.

89. Sandra Burton, *Impossible Dream: The Marcoses, The Aquinos, and the Unfinished Revolution*, New York, Warner Books, 1989, p. 124.

90. *Manila Times*, March 30, 1986; February 13, 1985; *Business Day*, March 24, 1986; Professor James Boyce, University of Massachusetts at Amherst, March 28, 1989.

91. Boyce, *op. cit.*, quoting a January 1989 interview with Cesar Virata.

92. David L. Pflug, MHT, 1.24.89.

93. Cesar Virata, "Testimony," Congress of the Philippines, Committee on Ways and Means, August 17, 1987.

94. See Rosendo D. Bondoc, former head of Philex, "Testimony," Philippine National Assembly, Sub-committee on Monetary, Credit and Financial Matters, October 2, 1987, pp. VII-2.

95. Malone, Memo # 3, *op. cit.*

96. The World Bank, *Philippines: Toward Sustaining the Economic Recovery. Country Economic Memorandum Report No. 7438-PH*, Washington, DC, January 30, 1989; and Asian Development Bank, *Key Indicators of Developing Member Countries*, Manila, ADB, July 1988.

97. Source: World Bank (WDI Online data), 2003.

98. See "Philippine Population Trends," US Department of Commerce, Bureau of the Census, February 1996.

99. World Bank, *op. cit.*, 1.

100. See "Taxing Their Patience," *Time International*, February 26, 1996.

101. See *Inquirer News Service*, "Government Lost P242 Billion Yearly Due to Tax Evasion," November 21, 2001. For more about the scale of tax evasion in the Philippines, see "Filipino Taxpayers and Tax Evaders," *www.inqy.net*, December 7, 2002; Dave L. Llorito, *The Manila Times*, "Bad Timing for Implementing Tax Reforms," December 3, 2002; *The Manila Times*, "More Tax Incentives Mean More Losses for RP," December 4, 2002; "RP Seen as Haven for Tax Evaders," *Inquirer News Service*, March 30, 2001. For the Marcos's tax arrears, see "It's War," *The Economist*, October 3, 2002.

102. For the Marcos's tax arrears, see "It's War," *The Economist*, October 3, 2002.

103. World Bank, Country Report on the Philippines, January, 1989, *op. cit.*, pp. 45–46.

104. For Buenaventura's biogrpahy, see *http://www.pdic.gov.ph/board%20of%20directors/rbuenaventura.asp*.

105. For Jose I. Camacho's biography, see *http://www.op.gov.ph/profiles_camacho.asp*.

106. Interview with Dr. James Putzel, Manila, April 22, 1989. See also Dr Putzel's superb book: *A Captive Land: The Politics of Agrarian Reform in the Philippines*, London, Catholic Institute for International Relations; New York, Monthly Review Press, 1992.

107. For an early version of the World Bank's "market-oriented" agrarian reform policy, see World Bank Online Data, Policy "Paper on Land Reform," Washington, DC, World Bank, 1975.

108. Figures on the Aquino land reform are from Saturnino M. Borras Jr. "Stuck in the Mud: CARP in Its 14th Year," Institute for Popular Democracy, "Political Briefs," May 2002, available at *http://www.ipd.ph/pub/polbrief/2002/may/carp14.shtml#4*. See also the excellent biography of Aquino by Lucy Komisar, *Corazon Aquino: The Story of a Revolution*, New York, George Braziller, 1987–88, pp. 181.

109. Philippines National Statistical Office, Annual Poverty Indicators Survey (1998), at *http://www.census.gov.ph/data*.

110. Estimates by Zen Soriano, Amihan, a national federation of women peasant groups, quoted in *Philippine Tribune*, June 16, 1998.

111. See Philippines National Statistical Office, *Annual Poverty Indicators Survey* (July 2002), available at *http://www.census.gov.ph/data/pressrelease/2003/ap0207ptx.html*, released January 8, 2003. For more details about the the relative performance of the Aquino, Ramos, Estrada, and Macagapal—Arroyo administrations with respect to land reform, see Saturnino M. Borras Jr. "Stuck in the Mud: CARP in Its 14th Year," Institute for Popular Democracy, Political Briefs, May 2002, available at *http://www.ipd.ph/pub/polbrief/2002/may/carp14.shtml#4*.

112. For a useful introduction to the "revisionist" literature on land reform, see Dr. James Putzel, "Land Reforms in Asia: Lessons From the Past for the 21st Century," LSE Development Studies Institute, Working Papers Series No. 00-04, January 2000.

113. World Bank, *op. cit.*, p. 98.

114. Asian Development Bank, "Report and Recommendations of the President to the Board of Directors on Proposed Loan and Technical Assistance to the Republic of the Philippines for a Forestry Sector Program," Manila, ADB, May, 1988, unpublished.

115. See ADB, Plan for the Philippines, 1989, Manila, ADB, 1989, ii.

116. See Donna S. Cueto, "Probe Sought on Mysterius P2B Imelda Marcos Settlement," *Inquirer News Servcice*, November 9, 2002; "Levy Celerio's songs fail to console Imelda," *Inquirer News Service*, November 18, 2002.

117. See Final Judgment, Celsa Hilao, et al., v. Estate of Ferdinand E. Marcos, US District Court (Hawaii), MDL No. 840, C.A. No. 86-0390 (1995). For the Duke estate case, see *The Philippines Daily Inquirer*, "Doris Duke Estate Sues Imelda Marcos," March 5, 2000. For the Hawaii lawsuit, and the continuing stalemate over it, see "Marcos Renege on Word to Pay HR Victims," *www.philstar.com*, October 4, 2001; *www.inquirer.net*, October 26, 2000.

118. See *The Manila Times*, "Peace Process in Limbo," August 13, 2002. See VOA News, January 17,2003. See *Associated Press*, June 22, 2002.

119. See *Inquirer News Service*, "Foreign Debt Rises by $4B," September 20, 2002.

120. These conclusions are based on estimates for spending on debt service, health care, and primary and secondary education are from WB (WDI online database), 2003.

121. See *http://www.panasia.org.sg/mimapph/v830901c.htm*.

122. See *http://www.da.gov.ph/NNC/summary.html*.

123. See Rand Corporation, "The US and Asia: Toward a New US Strategy and Force Structure," Santa Monica, Rand Corporation, May 2001.

124. British Broadcasting Corporation, "US Troops Land in South Philippines," December 14, 2001; *Associated Press*, June 18-22, 2002.

125. See Madge Kho (Jolo, Philippines), "Jolo—Chronology of the Moro Resistance (2003)" available at *http://www.waltokon.com/Jolo16.html*.

NOTES TO CHAPTER THREE

1. For the origins of the Cisneros's Pepsi franchise, "Venezuelan Consultant," Caracas, February 1987; "Miami Banker #8," Miami, April 21, 1988. Pepsi's dominance in Venezuela was confirmed by Brandt Davis, Corporation Communications, Coca-Cola, October 10, 1990.

2. Economic Commission on Latin America, *Integración, Sector Externo y Desarrollo Economico de American Latina*, ECLA: Santiago, l966.

3. World Bank Online Data, 2003.

4. See BP, "Statistical Review of World Energy (2002)," available at *http://www.bp.com/centres/energy2002/oil/reserves.asp*.

5. "Beat 'em," William J. Gibbons, Baker & McKenzie, February 17, 1988.

6. For the bathroom attendant requirement, see Tyler Bridges, "Down the Toilet," *The Washington Monthly*, December 1986, p. 21.

7. See William R. Cline, "Venezuela's External Debt," Johns Hopkins and Institute for International Economics, unpublished, December 1981, p. 8.

8. Cline, *op. cit.*, p. 51.

9. For the foreign accounts at SBC, "Swiss Banker #1," Panama City, October 9, 1987. Confirmation for the SBC role in FIVEN finance was provided by another former SBC banker, "Miami Banker # 5," Miami, December 15, 1987.

10. Cline, *op. cit.*, pp. i, 9, 36, 92. See Charles R. Frank Jr., and William R. Cline, "Measurement of Debt Servicing Capacity: An Application of Discriminant Analysis," *Journal of International Economics*. Vol. 1 (3), l971, pp. 327–344.

11. Cline, "Venezuela's External Debt," *op. cit.*, pp. iii, v.

12. The tale about Sosa's takeover as Finance Minister was related to the author by Beatrice Rangel, an advisor to Carlos Andres Perez, Caracas, 2.7.88. It was confirmed by Galdo.

13. Alfredo Pena, *Lusinchi Fracaso: Acusa Luis Herrera*, Caracas, Editorial Ateneo de Caracas, 1987, pp. 119–121.

14. "State of Chaos," *El Universal*, August 17, 1983.

15. For the Citibank overcharge for loans to Sidor, Gustavo Galdo, former Director General of Public Credit, Caracas, February 8, 1988; "NY Banker # 8," January 4, 1989.

16. *Euromoney*, Ocotober 1980, p. 207.

17. For the story about Citibank's discounting of CADAFE $300 million note: Galdo, *op. cit.*, February 8, 1988.

18. For the CADAFE Hong Kong signing and the Banco de Trajabadores case, John Sweeney, *VE*, Caracas, February 1988; Beatrice Rangel, Caracas, February 1988.

19. For the procedural short-cuts taken by US banks in Caracas, "Venezuelan Attorney," NYC, February 1988.

20. *VE*, June 20, 1980.

21. "Former Official," February 11, 1988, Caracas; *VE*, March 1985, p. 30. For Celia Matos, Carlos Andres Perez's mistress, see *VE*, May 14, 1980, p. 1; *Resumen*, May 1980.

22. "Totally corrupt:" "Don Reilly," Miami, December 10, 1987. Galdo, *op. cit.*, February 8, 1988.

23. *Rundt's Weekly*, January 24, 1983, p. 20. For the $890 million outflow in February 1983, *Rundt's Weekly*, February 28, 1983.

24. "Miami Banker #6," April 21, 1988.

25. The story about the threatened withdrawal of Citibank's license is from Leopoldo Diaz-Bruzual, former Venezuelan Central Bank President, Caracas, February 11, 1988. See also Leopoldo Diaz-Bruzual, *Crisis y Recuperación*, Caracas, 1984, p. 57. Pedro Palma, Caracas, February 1988.

26. See Pena, *Lusinchi Fracaso, op. cit.*, appendix.

27. Pedro Palma, economist, February 8, 1988, Caracas.

28. "NY Banker #9," January 5, 1989; "NY Banker #8," January 4, 1989.

29. "Feared Collapse," Paul Beckermann, country economist, The World Bank, December 22, 1988.

30. See IMF, Exchange Arrangements and Exchange Restrictions, 1988, p. 510.

31. *VE*, July 1986, p. 8.

32. "Did Workers Get Subsidies?" Diaz-Bruzual, Caracas, February 11, 1988. See also *VE*, March 1986, 12. Jim Nash, Morgan Guaranty, July 11, 1988, NYC.

33. See *Financial Times*, July 20, 1989, p. 3; *New York Times*, August 19, 1989, pp. D1–D5.

34. "Appendix to Venezuelan Debt Restructuring Principles," July 25, 1984, unpublished.

35. See the description of the inauguration in *Financial Times*, February–March 1989 (various issues).

36. President George H. W. Bush, "Remarks at the Welcoming Ceremony for President Carlos Andres Perez," April 26, 1990, available at *http://bushlibrary.tamu.edu/papers/1990/90042600.html.*

37. Jose Vincente Rangel, *El Universal*, November 8, 1992. See Patrick Tierney, *Darkness in El Dorado*, New York, W.W. Norton, 2000.

38. See Angel Bermúdez, "*Cecilia Matos tenia cuatro cuentas in el Republic National Bank*," *El Universal*, February 8, 1998.

39. For more details, see Berend Roosen, "Supervision is the Key to Strengthening Banks," *Economic Reform Today*, November 1, 1995, available at *http://www.cipe.org/publications/fs/ert/e15/case.htm.*

40. For the cost of the crisis, see *The Washington Times*, July 15, 1999. See *El Universal*, March 24, 1999.

41. For Venezuela's overall budget deficit as a share of GDP, see World Bank Online Data, 2003.

42. See *El Universal*, March 24, 1999.

43. See the OAS, Report # 82/981, Case 11.703—Gustavo Gomez Lopez, September 28, 1998, available at *http://www.cidh.oas.org/annualrep/98eng/Inadmissible/Venezuela%2011703.htm*; *El Universal*, "*Gobierno traumata 45 extraditions*," March 25, 1998. For the extradition of Fernando Araujo, son-in-law of President Caldera and director of Banco Metropolitano, see *El Universal*, "*Caldera informado por el MRE*," March 25, 1998. For Orlando Castro Castro's 1997 conviction on bank fraud charges in New York, see *El Universal*, "*Semana en Noticias*," April 28, 1997. See "*José Bouza Izquierdo recupera su libertad*," *El Universal*, May 23, 1998.

44. Marbelys Maváre, "*La pesadilla del Banco Latino regresó: La justicia decidió que nadie tuvo responsabilidad*," *Tal Cual Lunes*, July 16, 2001, available at *http://www.talcualdigital.com/ediciones/2001/07/16/p13s1.htm*; "*Banqueros de rapina*," "*Capitulo 7/La corrupcion en tiempo de Chávez*," (2003), available at *http://es.geocities.com/malversacion/cap07_02.htm.*; *El Universal*, "*TSS libró a ex director del Barinas*," January 22, 1999. For charges that Chávez' administration was taking illegal political contributions in return for weak enforcement against the bankers involved in the 1994 crisis, see *El Nacional*, "*Gobierno blanquea deudas a cambio de contribuciones ilegales*," September 2, 2002.

45. For the $14 million IDB loan, see IDB Press Releases, "IDB Approves $14 Million Loan to Strengthen Venezuela's Financial System," October 11, 1995, NR-218/95.

46. US State Department, Bureau of Public Affairs, November 1994, "Background Note: Venezuela."

47. *The Washington Times*, "New Market Conditions Boost Credibility of Banking Sector," July 15, 1999.

48. "Caracas Is Clearing Its Peddlers . . . But Will It Take Aim at Pirates?" *Business Weekly* (international edition), February 19, 2001.

49. See Jose Ignacio Silva and Reinier Schliesser, "Evolution of poverty in Venezuela," Central Bank of Venezuela, Caracas, 1998.

50. See Luis Jose Uzcátegui, *Chavez: Mago de las Emociones*, Caracas, 2000.

51. See British Broadcasting Corporation, "*España elogia a Venezuela*," March 18, 2002; for the FARC charge, see *The Washington Times*, December 25, 2002.

52. *Time*, "Dear Ilich: I Am Fine. How Are You? Sincerely, President" May 10, 1999.

53. See *http://www.derechos.org/wi/2/america.html*, July 1998. See Craig Mauro, "US, Peru Spy Relations Disclosed," *Associated Press*, January 8, 2001.

54. See Nancy San Martin and Carol Rosenberg, "Cash-Poor Spy Chief Sent E-Mail Threats," *Miami Herals*, June 28, 2001.

55. "*Vladimiro Montesinos fue capturado en Venezuela*," *Agenciaperu*, June 24, 2001; British Broadcasting Corporation, "Chavez Outraged Over Montesinos Grab," British Broadcasting Corporation, "Venezuela 'did not shelter' Montesinos," July 17, 2001; "Peru's Fugitive Ex-Spy Shief Taken to Air Base," CNN, June 24, 2001; British Broadcasting Corporation, "How Montesinos Was Betrayed," June 26, 2001, Andres Oppenheimer, "Go-Between Was Arrested in Miami, Peruvian Special Prosecutor Says," *Miami Herald*, June 26, 2001.

56. For the CIA's aid to Montesinos, see Angel Paez, "CIA Gave $10 Million to Peru's Ex-Spymaster," *The Public I*, Center for Public Integrity, July 3, 2001, available at *http://www.alternet.org/story.html? StoryID=11131*.

57. The Chavez quote is from CNN, "Venezuela's president Says National Assembly Will Have Broad Powers: Opposition Fears Breakdown in the Rule of Law," July 25, 1999.

58. For Chavez' analysis of PDVSA's diversions, see Hugo Chavez Frias, *The Fascist Coup Against Venezuela*, Havana, 2003.

59. See Chavez's Bolivar 2000 Plan.

60. US Energy Information Administration (2003), available at *http://www.eia.doe.gov/emeu/international/ prices.html#Crude*.

61. See "OPEC Secretary General Calls on Russia and Norway Not to Increase Oil Exports," *Pravda*, June 6, 2002.

62. See Philip T. Reeker, Deputy Spokesman, US State Department, "Press Statement: Venezuela: Change of Government," April 12, 2002, available at *http://www.state.gov/r/pa/prs/ps/2002/9316.htm*.

63. White House spokesperson Ari Fleischer, quoted in "Coup D'etat in Venezuela," *www.terra.com*, April 12, 2002.

64. See Katherine Hoyt, "Concerns Over Possible AFL-CIO Involvement in Venezuela Coup Led to February Picket," *Labor Notes*, May 20, 2002, available at *http://www.labornotes.org/archives/2002/05/b.html*. See Christian Marquix, "Washington Channeled Funds to Groups That Opposed Chavez," *New York Times*, April 26, 2002.

65. See "Venezuelan Coup Plotter 'in Miami,'" *The Times*, April 24, 2002. See Edición Imprensa (Chile), "*El desconocido empresario que organizó el golpe contra Chávez*," April 18, 2002. See "Venezuelans Linked to Coup Attempt Said to be in Miami," *Miami Herald*, April 26, 2002.

66. *New York Times*, April 13, 2002, late edition, p. A16, column 1, editorial desk "Hugo Chávez Departs."

67. Teodoro Petkoff, journalist and political commentator, quoted in Chris Harman, "Venezuela: Workers Organize to Halt Right Wing Coup," *Socialist Worker*, December 21, 2002, available at *http://www. socialistworker.co.uk/1831/IX.HTM*.

68. "Venezuela closes foreign exchange market," *The Guardian*, January 23, 2003.

69. For some of the many corruption charges that have been made against Chavez' administration, see "*La corrupción en tiempo de Chavez*," available at *http://es.geocities.com/malversacion*. See also *www.Militares Democraticos.com*.

NOTES TO CHAPTER FOUR

1. Judge Robert Sweet, January 30, 1987.

2. Carlos Eduardo Tavares de Andrade, Brasilian Central Bank, July 1, 1987; February 22, 1989, Brasilia. Gilberto Nobre, Foreign Exchange Department, Central Bank, and Jose Coelho, Legal Department, Central Bank, July 1, 1987.

3. *O Estado de Sao Paulo*, January 24, 1984.

4. Heinz Vithzthun, former Morgan Latin American group banker, 1958-1970, September 19, 1989.

5. See *Veja*, November 28, 1979; March 5, 1980 (interview); December 29, 1982 (photo); January 5, 1983; June 1, 1983 (cover story); May 28, 1986 (cover) and October 15, 1986. He was also a guest on Mac-Neil-Lehrer in October 1982, for a discussion of the debt crisis.

6. *Euromoney*, "Morgan's International Shakeup," May 1982; *Financial Times*, December 3, 1990, p. 34; Anatole Kaletsky, "The Debt Owed to Lewis Preston," *Financial Times*, September 25, 1989, p. 21.

7. Jack Morris, Morgan Public Relations, May 1987.

8. *Fortune*, "Why the Blue Chips Bank on Morgan," July 13, 1981; *Euromoney*, "Morgan's International Shakeup," *op. cit.*, p. 52.

9. *Rendezvous with Destiny: 1932-41*, "Portrait of an American: Stockbroker Richard Whitney," pp. 145–47. See also Louis Auchincloss, *The Embezzle*.

10. William Hayes, former Bankers Trust loan officer in Brazil, January 1988.

11. See the sympathetic reactions to Gebauer's indictment by Carlos Eduardo de Freitas, Director of the Foreign Area for Brasil's Central Bank, and Carlos Langoni, former Central Bank President, in *Veja*, May 28, 1986, p. 85.

12. Government's Sentencing Memorandum, US v. Gebauer, (86 Crim. 884), January 30, 1987.

13. Fernandina Gebauer, May 7, 1987; "Senior Morgan Banker," April 21, 1988.

14. "Senior Morgan Banker," April 21, 1988.

15. Heinze Vithzthun, former Morgan banker, September 14, 1989.

16. "Senior Morgan Banker," April 21, 1988.

17. Robert Blocker, Chase's Banco Lar Brasileira, February 25, 1987. Alexandre Vagliano, head of Morgan's International Banking Division from 1976 to August 1981, March 18, 1987. Heinz Vithzthun, September 14, 1989.

18. See *The Economist*, September 2, 1972, p. 36. "Construction Executive, "Rio de Janeiro, June 10, 1987; February 14, 1989. BNDES quickly became the world's third largest development bank, after the World Bank and the IDB. As of 1962, a study of Brasilian industry showed that more than half of capital belonged to foreign investors. See *Revista do Instituto de Ciências Sociais*, Rio, January–December 1965. For Kubitschek's motivations for building Brasilia, see Jose William Vesentini, *A Capital Da Geopolitica*, Sao Paulo, Editora Atica, 1986, p. 101.

19. Thomas E. Skidmore, *Politics in Brasil, 1930-64*, New York, Oxford University Press, 1967, p. 194.

20. For more about the 1964 coup, see Jan Knippers Black, *United States Penetration of Brazil*, Philadelphia, University of Pennsylvania Press, 1977; William Blum, *Brazil 1961-64, in Killing Hope: US Military and CIA Interventions Since World War II*, Maine, Common Courage Press, 1995.

21. For the coup, see Rene Armand Dreifuss, *1964: A Conquista Do Estado*, Sao Paulo, Vozes, 1981. See also Jan Knippers Black, *United States Penetration of Brasil*, Philadelphia, University of Pennsylvania Press, 1977, p. 78 (Rockefeller quote); and Phyllis R. Parker, *Brasil and the Quite Revolution, 1964*, Austin, Texas, University of Texas Press, 1974, p. 11 (early warnings).

22. Moura, Rio, February 1987. For the carrier task force, see Parker, *op. cit.*, pp. 75–76.

23. República Federativa do Brasil, *Assembléia Nacional Constituinte—1987*, Brasilia, 1987, p. 197.

24. See Campos's Plan of Economic Action of the Government, 1964. For a critical study see J. Carlos de Assis, *A Chave Do Tesouro*, Sao Paulo, Editora Paz e Terra, 1984.

25. Thomas E. Skidmore, *Brasil de Castelo a Tancredo*, Rio, Editora Paz e Terra, 1988, 85.

26. Black, *op. cit.*, p. 61.

27. Black, *op. cit.*, p. 266, citing Ronald A. Krieger, *Brasil: An Economic Survey by First National City Bank*, March 1971.

28. See the objectives for the Alliance for Progress described at Punta del Este, August 1961, in Parker, *op. cit.*

29. Gary S. Hartshorn, "Daniel K. Ludwig's Amazing Gamble," Institute of Current World Affairs, September 1979, in Jordan M. Young, *Brasil: Emerging World Power*, Malabar, Florida, Robert E. Krieger Publishing Co., 1982, pp. 137–39.

30. Skidmore, *op. cit.*, p. 141. See Werner Baer and Mario Henrique Simonsen, "American Capital and Brasilian Nationalism," *The Yale Review*, Vol. LIII, No. 2, Winter 1964. See the attack on Campos in the right-wing journal *A Tribuna*, 6.14.66, p. 11. Mariza Tupinamba, *Eu Fui Testemunha*, Sao Paulo, Vozes, 1983, p. 13. Skidmore, *op. cit.*, p. 89. (US AID workers). See also Black, *op. cit.*, pp. 62–63.

31. IMF, International Financial Statistics (1989).

32. See Robert A. Hutchinson, *Vesco*, Washington, DC, Praeger, 1974, p. 70.

33. Archidiocese of Sao Paulo, *Torture in Brasil*, New York, Random House, 1986.

34. Source: copy of the Robert Campos diary in the author's possession.

35. Campos diary, *op. cit.*

36. For more details about Globo's deal with Time Life, see Daniel Herz, *The Secret Life of Rede Globo*, Brazil, 1989; Bill Hinchberger, "Brazil's Media Monopoly, http://multinationalmonitor.org/hyper/issues/1991/01/mm0191_12.html.

37. See James Brooke, "Looting Brazil," *New York Times Sunday Magazine*, Novemer 8, 1992.

38. See *Forbes.com*, for the annual billionaire rankings.

39. Antonio Delfim Neto's biographical sketch in República Federativa do Brasil, *Assembléia Nacional Constituinte—1987*, Brasilia, 1987, p. 197. See *1972 Who's Who in Brasil*, Sao Paulo: Who's Who Ltd., 1972, p. xxv; Nicholson, *op. cit.*

40. *O Estado do Sao Paulo*, November 11, 1969.
41. "Senior Brasilian Banker," June 22, 1987.
42. See the report on L. M. Ericsson in Venezuela's *El Tiempo*, November 1, 1986.
43. For the conversation about General Medici, see Nixon Presidential Materials, Conversation 16–36, National Archives. December 7, 1971, 6:51 pm: Conversation between President Richard Nixon and Secretary of State William Rogers, available at *http://www.gwu.edu/~nsarchiv/NSAEBB/NSAEBB71*.
44. For the conversation between Nixon and Heath, see VIP Visits boxes 910-954, Nixon National Security Council Materials, National Archives December 20, 1971: Secret memcon from Henry Kissinger on a meeting between the US President and British Prime Minister Edward Heath, available at *http://www.gwu.edu/~nsarchiv/NSAEBB/NSAEBB71/*,
45. See Secret Information Memorandum to Henry Kissinger on The Uruguayan Elections, November 27, 1971, Department of State Subject Numeric Files 1970–73, National Archives, available at *http://www.gwu.edu/~nsarchiv/NSAEBB/NSAEBB71/doc8.pdf*.
46. See *Jornal do Brasil*, May 9, 2000. See the State Department cable from US ambassador to Paraguay Robert White to Secretary of State Cyrus Vance, October 13, 1978. *New York Times*, March 6, 2000.
47. See *Miami Herald*, "Death Deepens Mystery in Brazil, June 29, 2000.
48. *Programa de Metas e Bases*, 1970.
49. Walter Wriston, interview with the author, February 1, 1988, New York. Brasil's 1986 measured GDP, in real 1980 dollars, was $279 billion, 47 percent of South American GDP. Chase Econometrics, Latin America Forecasts and Analysis, 1987.
50. IMF, International Financial Statistics, 1989.
51. Paulo Nogueira Batista Jr., "International Financial Flows to Brasil Since the Late 1960s," *World Bank Discussion Papers No. 7*, Washington, DC, The World Bank, 1987.
52. Raimundo Perreira, February 1989; Jose Carlos Freire, Former Minister-Secretary, DESP, Rio, June 29, 1987.
53. Nogueira Batista, *op. cit.*, p. 12.
54. Oxford Analytica Ltd., "Confidential Brasil Environmental Assessment," October 1980, Chapter III: "Energy Resources." "A Survey of Brasil," *The Economist*, September 2, 1972, p. 16. See Eduardo Matarazzo Suplicy, *Da Distribuição da renda e dos direitos a cidadania*, Sao Paulo, Editora Brasiliense, 1988. William Ellis, IDB senior officer, Rio, June 14, 1987. Teodomiro Braga, *Jornal do Brasil*, February 1989; Brasilia. Eduardo Suplicy Matarazzo, July, 1987; February 1989.
55. Teresa Barger, IFC, March 11, 1987.
56. Ary Cesar Minella, *Banqueiros: Organizaçao e Poder Político No Brasil*, Rio, Editora Espaço e Tempo Ltd, 1988, pp. 134, 150. *Visão: Quem e Quem na Economia Brasileira?* 1984, p. 384.
57. Francisco Catão, Rio, June 27, 1987.
58. Eduardo M. Suplicy, *Da Distribucao da Renda e Dos Direitos a Cidadania*, Sao Paulo, Editora Brasiliense, 1988, pp. 13–14.
59. Helio Jaquaribe, et al. *Brasil: Reforma ou Caos*, Rio, Editora Paz e Terra, 1989. Business International, *Brasilian Roundtable*, Rio, Business International, October 25–29, 1979, p. 60.
60. Mariza Tupinamba, June 1987.
61. William G. Tucker, February 8, 1987. Alexandre Vagliano, former head of Morgan's International Banking Division, March 18, 1987.
62. Willy Casteneira, former Banco Econômico officer, Sao Paulo, June 22, 1987.
63. *Montreal Gazette* (World Financial Markets [JPMorgan]), 1968; *Euromoney*, May 1982, pp. 82, 52.
64. *Diârio Oficial* data base (author).
65. *Euromoney*, "How They Tried to Rescue Brasil," October 1983, p. 79.
66. Jack Morris, Morgan, March 3, 1987; William G. Tucker, February 1987; "Morgan Banker," February 1988; John Hogan, former Morgan banker, February 5, 1987; Alexandre Vagliano, 3.18.87; Letter of Thomas Keesee III to Judge Sweet, reported in GSO, *op. cit.*, p. 61; Tjarda Clagett, former Morgan banker, September 12, 1989; *Fortune*, "The War Among Brasil's Bankers," July 11, 1983, p.53; Chris Crowley, February 27, 1987; Osvaldo R. Agatiello, Argentine Central Bank, March 17, 1987; Frederico de Sousa Queiroz, Sao Paulo, June 1987.
67. Gerald Finneran, February 10, 1987.
68. Helio Guerrero, Brasilian Coffee Institute's New York office, Febraury 19, 1987.
69. Luis Hafers, Sao Paulo, June 1987. Don Nicholson II, NYC, September 1989; Fernandina Gebauer, May 1987; Frederico de Sousa Queiroz, Sao Paulo, February 1987; Leonidas Borio, Rio, February 1989; Rio, June 1987; Robert Blocker, February 25, 1987.
70. Dreifuss, *op. cit.*, p. 116.
71. *Tribuna da Imprensa*, January 13, 1965.

72. Ruth Almeida Prado, friend of Borio's, Rio, July 13, 1987. *Veja*, November 4, 1971. *Manchete*, October 21, 1972. Almeida Deposition, GSO, *op. cit.*, Appendix; "Construction Official," Sao Paulo, February 1989.

73. Leonidas Borio, February 24, 1989.

74. The Parana loan estimates are from my *Diário Oficial* data base.

75. *Diário Oficial* data base.

76. Heinz Vithzthun, September 1989. GSO, *op. cit.*; Gebauer, February 20, 1987; *Brasilian Playboy* December 1986; *O Estada de Sao Paulo*, December 21, 1986.

77. *Veja*, November 4, 1971–December 1, 1971.

78. Leonidas Borio, February 24, 1989.

79. *Diário Oficial* data base.

80. Walter Cerqueira, Gebauer's Bahian farm manager, Salvador, July 1987.

81. *O Estada de Sao Paulo*, October 6, 1978; *Folha do Sao Paulo*, September 26, 1978; *Movimento*, November 20, 1978. Mario Enrique Simonsen, Fundaçao Getulio Vargas, Rio de Janeiro, February 14, 1989.

82. *Diário Oficial* data base.

83. Morgan's loans to Investbanco, of which Campos was President, were as follows: 9.70: $500,000; 5.71-8.71: $650,000. Two other loans totaling $400,000 also went to Banco Irmão Guimaraes in 1972, part of the conglomerate run by Campos, and $700,000 went to Univest, which bought Banco Irmão in 1971. Two other loans to Campos-related companies went to Supergel S.A., registered in 7.71 ($400,000) and 10.71 ($400,000). *Diário Oficial* data base. Supergel S.A. and Investbanco both went bankrupt in the 1970s. Mariza Tupinamba, *Eu Fui Testemunha*. (Sao Paulo: Vozes, 1983), p. 13.

84. Severo Gomes' company was Tecelagem Parahyba S.A. The Morgan loan, $650,000, was registered in 7.71. *Diário Oficial* data base.

85. *Diário Oficial* data base. *Movimento*, November 20, 1978.

86. *Diário Oficial* data base. J. Carloss de Assis, *Os Mandarins da República*, Sao Paulo, Paz e Terra, 1984.

87. *Diário Oficial* data base.

88. Keith McDermott, 9.6.89.

89. The gasohol financing was a case of "disguised balance of payments financing" that "stayed in the market until mid-April 1980." Robert Barbour, former Morgan banker, 1.6.88.

90. Tony's multinational projects included a petroleum project for National Distillers in southern Brasil, Siemens' sales of electrical equipment, Boeing's sales of 747s to Varig, and General Motor's $1.5 billion expansion. Charles Sheehan, GE, 3.87; D. Mediale, former Treasurer of General Motors, March 1987. Morgan loaned to MNC subsidiaries or by way of equipment importers with EX-IM guarantees. For example, Morgan provided EX-IM-guaranteed loans of $212 million to Centrais Elétricas (CESP), the electric utility in Sao Paulo, $42.5 million to Petrobras, and $25 million to Companhia Siderurgica Paulista. Morgan Presentation to GE Trading Company, October 1982. (Unpublished file copy in my possession), p. 7.

91. *Mare de Lama*, November 26, 1978; Tony Gebauer, March 4, 1987.

92. These descriptions are from former aides to Geisel and Figueiredo, "O Vice Rei da Bahia," December 6, 1978. "Sao Paulo Attorney," February 7, 1989 ("octopus"); *Veja*, February 21, 1989; Gilberto Dimenstern, *A República Dos Padriinhos*, Sao Paulo, Editora Brasiliense, 1988, p. 135. Dimenstern, *op. cit.*, p. 135, quoting *Jornal do Brasil*'s Ricardo Noblat. "Senior Executive," Rio de Janeiro, June 1987; February 14, 1989. "SP Construction Executive," Sao Paulo, February 21, 1989.

93. *O Estada de Sao Paulo*, September 14, 1986.

94. "Sao Paulo Attorney," February 7, 1989; February 21, 1989; *Veja*, December 6, 1978.

95. Dimenstern, *op. cit.*, p. 139.

96. *Veja*, December 6, 1978, quoting an aide to Geisel; Nelson Marchezan, aide to President João Figueiredo, *Veja*, December 6, 1978; *Afinal*, December 2, 1986, p. 24.

97. Daniel Herz, *A Historia Secreta da Rede Globo*, Sao Paulo, Tche Editora, 1987, pp. 32–63. "Senior Executive," June 1987; 2.14.89.

98. See Hinchberger, *op. cit.*

99. See *New York Times*, August 17, 1992, p. 3.

100. For ACM's resignation and the details leading up to it, see British Broadcasting Corporation, "Brazilian kingmaker resigns from Senate," May 21, 2001.

101. "Mare de Lama," *Movimiento*, November 20, 1978. "Sao Paulo Attorney/Construction Executive," New York, Sao Paulo, February 7, 1989; February 21, 1989; "Senior Executive," Rio de Janeiro, June 1987; February 14, 1989.

102. For Odebrecht's $70,000 donations to Jeb Bush's "Foundation for Florida's Future" in 1995, see *Campaign Eye Newsletter*, Vol. 6, No. 1, "Campaign Was Built on Solid Foundations," January 1999, available at *http://www.opensecrets.org/newsletter/ce61/07bush.htm*.

103. *Visão: Quem e Quem na Economica Brasileira*, August 31, 1984, p. 384.

104. See *O Estado do Sao Paulo*, October 6, 1987. See also the testimony by the Brasilian journalist Helio Fernandes, *1985 Commission of Parliamentary Inquiry on the Brasilian Foreign Debt*, p. 198; and A Chave do Tesouro, *op. cit.*, "O caso Econômico."

105. Helio Fernandes, testimony, 1985 Commission of Parliamentary Inquiry on the Brasilian Foreign Debt, p. 198.

106. "Senior Construction Official," Sao Paulo, February 21, 1989. Donald Nicholson II, 9.89; Jorge Eduardo Noronha, June 28, 1987.

107. Tony Gebauer, March 4, 1987.

108. Whitaker was married to Anoca, Angelo Calmon da Sa's sister. "Senior Executive," Rio, February 14, 1989; Dun & Bradstreet Company Report on Engesa Especializados S.A., May 1987.

109. "Senior Morgan Banker," Miami, April 21, 1988.

110. Fernando de Sousa Queiroz, Sao Paulo, June 1987; "NY Banker #16," January 25, 1989. Eduardo Suplicy Matarazzo, July 4, 1987. "Senior Brasilian Banker," June 22, 1987. Tony Gebauer, February 26, 1987; Robert Blocker, February 25, 1987; Paulo Sotero, *Gazeta Mercantil*, February 5, 1987. Keith McDermott, September 6, 1989; *Who's Who in Brasil*, 1972.

111. ???????

112. C. R. Almeida, quoted in *O Estado de Sao Paulo*, November 15, 1986.

113. Tony Gebauer, February 19, 1987; Registrar of Deeds, Suffolk County, Riverhead, New York: Deed 6853172, dated December 10, 1971.

114. The purchase date for the farm is from Gebauer, February 19, 1987; Registrar of Deeds, Suffolk Country, Purchase of Dr. Ricardo Bisi's estate in East Hampton for $286,179, Deed 9201277, dated June 23, 1982.

115. The jodhpur story appeared in Erik Berg's *New York Times* story about Gebauer, May 22, 1986.

116. The Piso possession is mentioned in the GSO, *op. cit.*, p. 23.

117. Glenn Lawson, Elizabeth Draper, Inc., 3.3.87; GSO, *op. cit.*; Owner, Coecles Harbour Marine, Shelter Island, March 3, 1987; *Brasilian Playboy*, *op. cit.*; Fernandina Gebauer, May 1987.

118. Tony Gebauer, March 4, 1987. Receptionist, Larama Corporation (Club A and Hippopotamus, March 3, 1987).

119. For Gebauer's salaries see GSO, 1.87, *op. cit.*

120. US Attorney, February 1987.

121. "Senior Morgan Officer," Miami, April 1988; Almeida Deposition, *op. cit.*

122. GSO, *op. cit.*, pp. 27, 28–31, 40–41.

123. Linda Imes, US Attorney, March 1987; GSO, *op. cit.*

124. GSO, *op. cit.*, p. 44–45. The distribution of loans to the accounts is curious.

125. GSO, *op. cit.*, p. 4. Peter Briger, attorney for Almeida, January 5, 1988, New York.

126. Many of the details of Libya's assistance to the Provisional IRA in the 1970s and 1980s are provided in Ed Moloney, *The Secret History of the IRA*, London, Penguin, 2002.

127. For Engesa, see *Veja*, October 17, 1984, pp. 52–54; October 27, 1982, p. 37; Jurandir de Freitas, director of Special Operations, Engesa, June 23, 1987; Frederico de Sousa Queiroz, June 12, 1987, Sao Paulo. See also John Hoyt Williams, "ENGESA—A New Giant," The Atlantic, August 1984. Inter Press Service, February 11, 1988; *Latin American Political Report*, March 4, 1977, p. 66; "Third World Weapons," *World-Paper*, June 1987, p. 4. Dun & Bradstreet, Company Report on Engesa, May 1987. (Company # 89-869-3841).

128. *L.A. Times*, March 23, 1986, p. 12.

129. Teodomiro Braga, interview with the author, January 2003.

130. *Reuters*, August 6, 1990.

131. Jurandir de Freitas, February 1989, Sao Paulo. Satori Namura, ENGESA Financial Department, May 1987. Dun & Bradstreet Company Report, *op. cit.*; *Veja*, November 27, 1982, p. 37. Frederico de Sousa Queiroz, June 12, 1987, Sao Paulo.

132. "Senior Brasilian Banker," interview with the author, Sao Paulo, June 22, 1987. Isaac Zaqury, BNDES officer, June 5, 1987, Rio.

133. Ruth Almeida Prada, July 13, 1987, Rio. Jurandir de Freitas, former director of Special Operations at Engesa from 1981–85, June 23, 1987; July 4, 1987; February 21, 1989.

134. See also Catão's biography in *Who's Who in Brasil*, Vol. II, 1983; Keith McDermott, 6, 1989.

135. Ruth Almeida Prado, Rio, July 13, 1989. Gebauer, *O Estada de Sao Paulo*, December 12, 1986.

136. Gebauer, *O Estada de Sao Paulo*, *op. cit.*

137. Keith McDermott, September 6, 1989; Isaac Zaqury, BNDES, Rio, June 4, 1987.

138. GSO, *op. cit.*, pp. 35–36.

139. "Construction Executive," June 1987, Rio.
140. See GSO, *op. cit.*, p. 42, and US v Gebauer, Memorandum of Understanding, October 8, 1986.
141. "Senior Brasilian Banker," Sao Paulo, June 22, 1987.
142. Chave do Tesouro, *op. cit.*, appendix on Atalla.
143. Frederico de Souza Queiroz, July 3, 1987.
144. "Investment Banker," June 5, 1987.
145. "Brasilian Banker #1," June 10, 1987; February 25, 1987, New York; February 11, 1989, New York; February 22, 1989.
146. "Senior Morgan Banker," interview with the author, Miami, March 1987.
147. "Caracas Financier," January 1991.
148. Fernandina Gebauer, May 1987; "New York Banker #9," January 5, 1988.
149. Luiz Carlos Gastal, Bank of California, June 7, 1987.
150. Frederico de Sousa Queiroz, June 1987.
151. Carlos Ulloa, former Deltec/Power Engineering, January 8, 1987.; John Scopetta Jr., September 6, 1989.
152. Robert Blocker, former head of Chase-Brasil, February 25, 1987; William G. Tucker, former Morgan banker, February 8, 1987. Antonio Gebauer, February 1986.
153. "Caracas Financier," January 1991; "Morgan Officer," Mexico City, June 1988.
154. "Brasilian Banker #2," June 22, 1987. "Investment Banker," June 5, 1987.
155. "NY Banker #19," January 6, 1988.
156. Frederico de Souza Queiroz, June 6, 1987.
157. Sr. Cerqueira, Salvador, Bahia, June 20, 1987.
158. "Investment Banker," June 6, 1987.
159. "Sao Paulo Executive," Sao Paulo, February 7, 1989; February 21, 1989. "Senior Brasilian Banker," June 22, 1987.
160. GSO, *op. cit.*, pp. pp. 18, 40.
161. "Sao Paulo Executive," Sao Paulo, February 7, 1989; February 21, 1989.
162. The transaction was briefly mention in Morgan's Fourth Quarter 1986 report, p. 4.
163. Jurandir de Freitas, June 23, 1987.
164. Helio Fernandez, *Brasilian Commission of Parliamentary Inquiry on the Debt,* January 1984.
165. Luiz Carlos Gastal, Bank of California, Rio, June 7, 1987; "NY Banker #19," March 20, 1987; January 6, 1988; Kobayashi, Bank of Tokyo, June 11, 1987.
166. Fernandina Gebauer, May 7, 1987.
167. "Morgan Credit Officer," March 18, 1987; January 1989; "Investigator," September 6, 1989; "Senior Morgan Banker," Miami, April 21, 1988. For Gebauer's assertions about the role of his clients' accounts in capital flight, see his December 1986 interview in *Brasilian Playboy.*
168. "Morgan Creditor Officer," March 1988.
169. William Tucker, February 8, 1987.
170. C. R. Almeida, February 2, 1989, New York.
171. Carlos Eduardo Tavares de Andrade, Brasilian Central Bank, July 1, 1987; February 22, 1989; Brasilia.
172. "Executive," February 7, 1989.
173. "Senior Morgan Banker," April 21, 1988, "Crony's Father," November 1987.
174. "Law Enforcement," January 1988; "Financier," January 1991.
175. Celso Pinto, a leading journalist who worked in Ministry of Finance in 1983, June 22, 1987.
176. Heinze Vithzhun, September 19, 1989.
177. Jorge Paulo Lehman, Banco Garantia, June 5, 1987.
178. "Morgan Credit Officer," March 18, 1987; February 1989.
179. Jackson Gilbert, former Morgan SVP, Washington, DC, November 17, 1989.
180. "Morgan Credit Officer," March 18, 1987; February 1989.
181. Fernandina Gebauer, May 1987.
182. Luiz Carlos Gastal, June 7, 1987, Rio; Ruth Almeida Prado, Rio, June 7, 1987.
183. Peter von Mutius, Chase Manhattan Bank, June 26, 1987.
184. Gebauer, *Brasilian Playboy, op. cit.*; Gebauer, New York, January 1987.
185. Fernandina de Sousa Queiroz, May 5, 1987.
186. GSO, *op. cit.*
187. GSO, January 1987, *op. cit.*, p. 40.
188. Cecilio Rego do Almeida, February 2, 1989, New York.
189. *The Wall Street Journal,* May 20, 1982, p. 23.
190. Ed Hoyt, former president of Morgan's Miami Edge Act, August 1986.

191. Assistant US attorney Chip Lowenson, March 3, 1987.

192. For JPMorgan CEO's William J. Harrison's speech to the UK executives in November 2001, see *Financial Times*, "JP Morgan Bosses Feel the Heat After Enron," January 29, 2002. For JPMorgan Chase's $900 million reserves against additional Enron costs, see *HC*, "J. P. Morgan Settles Enron Lawsuit," January 3, 2003. For JPMorgan Chase's role in the LJM2 partnership, see JPMorgan Chase Letter of May 8, 2002, responding to Congressman Henry A. Waxman's Inquiry of April 12, 2002; Report of the Investigation by the Special Investigative Committee of the Board of Directors of Enron, February 1, 2002, pp. 8–9.

193. "*O tombo de Tony*," *Veja*, May 28, 1987.

194. *New York Times*, May 23, 1986, p. D3.

195. "Gebauer Investigator," May, 1987, New York.

196. See Interagency Working Group, Records of the FBI, Case Files (1923–69): Box: file 65-5247: "Franz von Papen," available at *www.archives.gov*.

197. Located in a June 7, 1995 SEC 8-K filing by Instituform Technologies, Inc. one of the Hanseatic's investments (SEC File # 0-10786).

198. Reported in a January 7, 2002 SEC 8-K filing by Star Gas Partners L.P., another Hanseatic investment. (SEC # 33-98490).

199. For the Abacha scandal at M. M. Warburg and other leading European and US banks, see Peter Capella, *The Guardian*," British Banks: The Soruce of Dictator's Corrupt Pounds," September 5, 2000.

200. See *Reuters*, "Swiss Drug Money Probe Closes in on Diplomat," August 9, 2002.

201. J.D. Forbes, *J. P. Morgan Jr., 1867–1943*, Charlottesville, University of North Carolina, 1981.

NOTES TO CHAPTER FIVE

1. "Debt Advisor 1," Mexico City, June 24, 1988: NY Banker #16," January 25, 1989.

2. Lawrence Pezzulo, former US Ambassador to Nicaragua, July 5, 1988.

3. *La Prensa*, back issues, September–December 1977, Yale University Library, New Haven, Connecticut.

4. James Ferguson, *Papa Doc, Baby Doc: Haiti and the Duvaliers*, London, Basil Blackwell, 1987, p. 70.

5. "NY Banker #11," January 6, 1989.

6. *New York Times*, January 14, 1978; p. 2; Bernard Diederich, *Somoza*, New York, E. P. Dutton, 1981, p. 157.

7. Victoria Azurday and Miguel Cepeda, "*Aguda Escasez de sangre en Mexico, pero esta permitido exportarla*," *Proceso*, March 23, 1981, pp. 18–21.

8. See *International Blood Plasma News*, Vol. 19, Issue II, June 2002, p. 153, citing The Market Bureau, available at *http://.home.earthlink.net/~mrb_ibpn/jun_02.pdf*.

9. For a description of traffic in kidney donations among the poor in Egypt, see *New York Times*, September 22, 1991. See *New York Times*, February 24, 1998 and March 7, 1998. See also Nancy Scheper-Hughes, "The Global Traffic in Human Organs," *Current Anthropology*, Vol. 41, Number 2, April 2000.

10. See *www.bloodbook.com/* html, "Blood Around the World," (2003); "Blood donation policies around the world," (2001) available at *www.geocities.com/humanoffal/section* 10.

11. See BBD, "Bad Blood Spreads AIDs in China," May 30, 2001.

12. See "Blood Supplies Could Be Halved," *The Guardian*, October 2, 2001.

13. *Proceso, op. cit.*; American Blood Resources Association, Arlington, Va., 6.4.88. See Richard Titmuss, *The Gift Relationship: From Human Blood to Social Policy*, New York, Random House, 1972. *AMA Medical News*, February 6, 1987, p. 9. Norm Selby, New York Blood Bank, May 25, 1988.

14. *New York Times*, September 28, 1979.

15. "Debt Advisor 1," Mexico City, June 24, 1988.

16. Diederich, *op. cit.*, p. 325. Pezzulo, *op. cit.*; Diederich, *op. cit.*, pp. 93, 132.

17. *Facts on File*, 1979, pp. 373, 909. James Ferguson, *Papa Doc, Baby Doc, op. cit.*, p. 70.

18. Eddie Rodriguez Feliu's daughter and secretary, Mexico City, July 1, 1988.

19. "NY Banker #16," January 25, 1989.

20. Rodriguez Feliu, "Nuevos Instumentos Financieros Latinamericanos," address to the Third Annual Mexican Convention on Foreign Commerce, Mazatlan, Mexico. October 3, 1970, pp. 8–9, unpublished.

21. UN, Report of the Secretary General, "The External Finance of Developing Countries," September 1970, p. 67.

22. "NY Banker # 16," January 25, 1989.

23. "Debt Advisor 1," *op. cit.*; "NY Banker # 16," January 25, 1989.

24. *Euromoney*, December 1980, p. 127.

25. "NY Banker # 16," January 25, 1989.

26. *FF*, 1980, p. 698.

27. Foreign debt and national income estimates for Nicaragua in 1980 are from World Bank Online Data, 2003.

28. *Euromoney*, December 1980, p. 125.

29. "Debt Advisor 1," *op. cit.*

30. For more details, see Ovidio Diaz Espino, *How Wall Street Created a Nation*, New York, Four Walls, Eight Windows, 2001, p. 27, passim; David McCullough, *The Path Between the Seas: The Creation of the Panama Canal*, New York, Simon and Schuster, 1977.

31. See Arthur D. Howden Smith, *Commodore Vanderbilt*, New York, 1927, pp. 161 ff, 178–81, 201 ff, 217; Rafael de Nogales, *The Looting of Nicaragua*, New York, 1928, pp. 38–39. See also Charles A. Beard, *The Idea of National Interest*, New York, 1934, pp. 170–182. "Honduras The Expanded Role of the United States" (2001), available at *http://www.workmall.com/wfb2001/honduras/honduras_history_the_expanded_role_of_the_united_states.html.*

32. Sergio Ramirez, *Adios Muchachos*, Madrid, Aguilar M. Editor, 1999.

33. For more about this period's overall history, see Daniel Ortega Saavedra, *Fundacao Cidob* (2003), available at *www.cidob.org.*

34. See John Prados, "Notes on the CIA's Secret War in Afghanistan," *American Journal of History*, September 2002. See Oleg Sarin and Lev Dvoretsky, *The Afghan Syndrome: The Soviet Union's Vietnam*, Novato, 1993, p. 53.

35. McMichael's testimony is quoted in Noam Chomsky, *Culture of Terrorism*, Boston, South End Press, 1994, p. 121.

36. See Ronald Reagan, Address Before a Joint Session of the Congress on Central America, April 27, 1983, available at *http://www.reagan.utexas.edu/resources/speeches/1983/42783d.htm.*

37. See Reagan's "Address to the Nation on the Situation in Nicaragua," March 16, 1986, available at *http://www.reagan.utexas.edu/resource/speeches/1986/31686a.htm.*

38. See Ambassador Jeane J. Kirkpatrick. Testimony, US Congress, Senate Committee on Foreign Relations. Subcommittee on Western Hemisphere Affairs. Human rights in Nicaragua, 1982, p. 77.

39. For the role of the NSC's Oliver North and Robert McFarlane, and the State Department's Otto Reich in this and other dissembling with respect to Nicaragua, see Jane Franklin, "Otto Reich's Distinguished Career," February 22, 2001, available at *http://ourworld.compuserve.com/homepages/jbfranklins.*

40. See *The Panama Times*, July 28–August 10, 2002.

41. See "More US Troops Seek Colombia Hostages, *Associated Press*, February 22, 2003.

42. For more about the AUC arms story and these other incidents, see "Mystery Deepens Over Diverted AK-47s," *Miami Herald*, June 14, 2002; Marcela Sanchez, "Nicaragua's Arsenal and the War on Terrorism," *The Washington Post*, February 23, 2003.

43. See Jonathan Treat, "Guatemala's Landless Movement," July 25, 2002, available at *www.americas policy.org/pdf/focus/0211landless.pdf.*

44. For more details, see the outstanding analysis of this period by Doug Stokes, "Countering the Soviet Threat? An Analysis of the Justifications for US Military Assistance to El Salvador, 1979-92," Political Science Department, Bristol University, in Cold War History (2003, forthcoming.), available at *http://www.aprl52.dsl.pipex.com/elsal.htm.*

45. See the discussion of the alleged shipments to El Salvador in "Summaries of the Decisions Military and Paramilitary Activities in and against Nicaragua," Nicaragua v. USA, Judgment of the Court of June 27, 1986, available at *http://www.mpiv-hd.mpg.de/en/wcd/dec0102.cfm.*

46. For an assessment of the fairness of the November 1984 elections in Nicaragua, see "Report of the Latin American Studies Association Delegation to Observe the Nicaraguan General Elections of November 4, 1984."

47. John Oakes, *New York Times* Op Ed piece on the Nicaraguan elections, November 15, 1984.

48. World Bank official, quoted in Walden Bello, "Disciplining the Third World: the Role of the World Bank in US Foreign Policy." *Covert Action*, no. 39, winter 1991–92.

49. See Robert Armstrong, Marc Edelman, and Robert Matthews, *Sandinista Foreign Policy: Strategies for Survival. NACLA Report on the Americas*, May/June 1985, p. 36.

50. See George Black and Robert Matthews, "Arms from the USSR—Or Nobody," *The Nation*, August 31, 1985.

51. For the US role in pushing Cuba into Soviet arms, see Stokes (2003), *op. cit.*

52. For evidence that drug trafficking provided millions of dollars to the Contras, see Robert Parry, "CIA Admits Tolerating Contra-Cocaine Trafficking in 1980's," *Consortiumnews.com*, June 8, 2000.

53. See "Israel and El Salvador," Third World Traveler, available at *http://www.thirdworldtraveler.com/Middle_East/Israel_ElSalvador.html.*

54. See Oxfam (1985), "Threat of a good example."

55. For the $17 billion judgment, see Mark Uhlig, "US Urges Nicaragua to Forgive Legal Claim," *New York Times*, September 30, 1990. For the Nicaraguan court case, see "Summaries of the Decisions Military and Paramilitary Activities in and against Nicaragua," Nicaragua v. USA, Judgment of the Court of June 27, 1986, available at *http://www.mpiv-hd.mpg.de/en/wcd/dec0102.cfm*.

56. See Emma Curtis, "Child Health and the international monetary fund: the Nicaraguan experience," Jubilee 2000 Coalition, available at *www.jubilee2000uk.org*.

57. See Oxfam International, "Debt Relief for Nicaragua," Position Paper (1998), available at *www.caa.org.au*.

58. UN Children's Fund estimates of poverty rates in 1989 in Nicaragua, reported in *Nicanet*, June 14, 1999.

59. Paul Reichler, US attorney for Nicaragua, quoted in *L.A. Weekly*, March 9–15, 1990.

60. For US efforts to influence the February 25, 1990 Nicaraguan elections, see Jacqueline Sharkey, "Anatomy of An Election: How US Money Affected the Outcome in Nicaragua," *Common Cause Magazine*, May/June 1990; S. Brian Wilson, "How the US Purchased the 1990 Nicaragua Elections," available at *http://www.brianwillson.com/awolnicelection.html*.

61. For a summary and critique of liberal commentators on the 1990 Nicaraguan election, see Noam Chomsky, *Deterring Dissent*, Boston, South End Press, 1991, Chapter 10.

62. Peter Jennings, ABC Nightly News, February 20, 1990.

63. For an account of Chamorro's June 1990 inaugural ball, see O. Pilarte, *Associated Press*, June 8, 1990.

64. See *Reuters*, "US Writes Off Nicaragua's Debt," September 26, 1990, p. 13; "Nicaragua Drops Suit Against US," *Boston Globe*, September 18, 1990, p. 70; Mark Uhlig, "US Urges Nicaragua to Forgive Legal Claim," *New York Times*, September 30, 1990.

65. For the December 1995 Nicaraguan debt buyback, see The World Bank Group, *Transition Newsletter* (1995), at *http://www.worldbank.org/transitionnewsletter/n&d95/agenda.htm*.

66. See Gary Prevost, "Political Policy: The Sandinista Revolution and Democratization," *International Journal of Economic Development*, vol. 2 (2000), pp. 275–302, at 283, 285.

67. See *La Prensa*, "La Casa de Jaime Morales, August 24, 2001.

68. For more about the *Piñata*, see "*Le Nicaragua tenté par un retour au passé*," *Le Monde Diplomatique*, October 1996; David Hirschmann, "Nicaragua's Failed Coup: The Slow Pace of Reform," The World & I Online, November 1991, vol. 6, p. 116.

69. Oscar Antonio Vargas, quoted in *Le Monde Diplomatique, op. cit.*

70. For the "Zoilagate" scandal involving the allegations against Daniel Ortega by his thirty-three-year old stepdaughter Zoilamerica Narvaez, see *Nica News* 14 (June 1998), available at *http://www.nicanews.com.ni/nn14/zoilagate.html*; British Broadcasting Corporation, "The Sins of Nicaragua's Fathers," March 19, 1999. See *El Nuevo Diario* (Managua).

71. See Mark Falcoff, "Nicaragua: Opening a New Chapter," *Latin American Outlook*, American Enterprise Institute, November 1996.

72. For the 2001 election results, see European Union, Election Observation Missions to Nicaragua. Presidential and Parliamentary Elections—4 November 2001, available at *http://www.europa.eu.int/comm/external_relations/human_rights/eu_election_ass_observ/Nicaragua/rep01.pdf*, 2002.

73. For Jorge Mas Canosa's reported contributions to Arnoldo Aleman's campaign, see Mark Caster, "The Return of Somocismo? The Rise of Arnoldo Aleman," *NACLA Report on the Americas*, September/October 1996; Granma Online, "*Anuncian pruebas de que Presidente de Nicaragua se adueñó de $2,5 millones entregados por la FNCA para su campaña*," September 11, 2001.

74. For Catholic Church interference in the 2001 election, see European Union, Election Observation Missions to Nicaragua. Presidential and Parliamentary Elections—4 November 2001, *op. cit.*

75. Chamorro, quoted in "Nicaragua: US Officials Declare Opposition to Possible Ortega Victory," *Central America/Mexico Report*, July 2001.

76. For the US-encouraged withdrawal of Conservative Party candidate Noel Vidaurre from the race on July 18, 2001, see "US Intervenes in Election," *Latin American Weekly Report*, July 3, 2001; "Sandinista Lead Worries US," *La Prensa*, May 26, 2001.

77. For the State Department's "terrorist links" about Ortega, remarks, see British Broadcasting Corporation, "Nicaragua Poll Winner Gets US Vote," November 6, 2001. See Duncan Campbell, "Getting the Right Result," *The Guardian*, November 7, 2001.

78. See Christian Elton, "Ortega Sheds Rebel Past, Dons Pastels," *Christian Science Monitor*, November 2, 2001, *http://www.csmonitor.com/2001/1102/p1s2-woam.html*.

79. For Arnoldo Aleman's charges and arrest, and the $51 million in Panama accounts, see "Nicaraguan Leader Charged with Corruption," British Broadcasting Corporation, August 8, 2002; *Miami Herald*,

August 10, 2002; *Newsday*, December 13, 2002; *Nicaraguan Network Hotline*, "Aleman Indicted and Under House Arrest," January 2, 2003; *New York Times*, August 8, 2002.

80. For Aleman's net worth, see *Centr-Am News*, February 14, 1999; *Proceso*, February 17, 1999; *Nicanet*, February 15, 1999, February 22, 1999. See also *www.pronica.org*.

81. For the ENITEL case, see *La Prensa*, "*Venta 'secreta' de Enitel*," September 1, 2001; *Nicaraguan Network Hotline*, August 5, 2002; "Last Call," *LatinTrade.com*, December 2002; *Financial Times*, September 4, 2001; *Miami Herald*, September 8, 2001.

82. Quoted in *El Nuevo Diario*, October 1, 2001.

83. See "Former Officials Linked to Corruption Scandal Have Left Nicaragua," *EFE*, April 25, 2002.

84. See *Nicaraguan Network Hotline*, January 2, 2003.

85. For the charges against President Bolaños, see *Reuters*, November 7, 2002; *Agence France Presse*, November 9, 2002; *Miami Herald*, November 8, 2002.

86. For the HIPC hiccups and the foreign aid suspension, see *Noticen*, December 23, 1999; July 27, 2000.

87. *La Prensa*, December 5, 2002.

88. For more about Vietnam's liberalization program and the role of Western advisors and lenders, see Asian Development Bank, Program Perfomance Audit Report, Agriculture Sector Program (September 2002), PPQ:VIE 25325, available at *www.adb.org*; "IMF Approves Second Annual ESAF Loan for Vietnam," IMF Press Release, March 1, 1996; IMF/World Bank, numerous country reviews and statistical appendices with respect to Vietnam (1996-2003), available at the IMF and World Bank websites.

89. See Project CVN 1025, *http://www.afd.fr/projets/projet_view.cfm?id=430*.

90. For more details about the coffee value chain, see Oxfam, *Mugged* (2002), *op. cit.*, pp. 18–20.

91. International Coffee Organization data, available at *www.ico.org*.

92. For the conflict with these Montagnard tribes, see Clare Arthurs, "Vietnam Hill Tribe Men Jailed," British Broadcasting Corporation, December 12, 2002; "New Vietnamese school attack," British Broadcasting Corporation, April 16, 2001; "Repression of Montagnards—Conflict Over Land and Religion in Vietnam's Central Highlands," *Hydro Review Worldwide*, April, 2002, available at *http://www.hrw.org/reports/2002/vietnam/index.htm#TopOfPage*; UNHCR Centre for Documentation and Research, "Vietnam: Indigenous Minority Groups in the Central Highlands," Writenet Paper No. 05/2001, January, 2002; available at *http://www.unhcr.ch/cgi-bin/texis/vtx/rsd?search=coi&source=WRITENET*

93. Quoted in Gerard Greenfield, "Vietnam and the World Coffee Crisis: Local Coffee Riots in a Global Context," December 2001, available at *www.focusweb.org/publications/2002*.

94. The data on Vietnam's coffee exports is from the International Coffee Organization, available at *www.ico.org*.

95. Ibid.

96. See "Coffee Cartel Shuts Shop," British Broadcasting Corporation, October 19, 2001.

97. Gerard Greenfield (2002), *op. cit.*; Oxfam, "Mugged: Poverty in Your Coffee Cup," (2002 Report). For more about the economic plight of Nicaragua's coffee growers after 1999 and the factors responsible for the situation, see *http://www.nicanet.org/coffee.html*; Ivan Castro, "Exodus of rural coffee workers alarms Nicaragua," *Reuters*, July 16, 2001; David Gonzalez, "A Coffee Crisis' Devastating Domino Effect in Nicaragua," *New York Times*, August 25, 2001; Catherine Elton, "The world's other food crisis: Central America," *Christian Science Monitor*, October 30, 2002.

98. See "No World Bank Role in Vietnam's Expansion of Coffee Production," March 18, 2002, The World Bank Group, News Release No: 2002/244/S.

99. Asian Development Bank (2003), *op. cit.*

100. Don Mitchell, World Bank economist, quoted in Robert Collier, "Mourning Coffee—World's Leading Java Companies Are Raking In High Profits But Growers Worldwide Face Ruin As Prices Sink To Historic Lows," *San Francisco Chronicle*, May 20, 2001.

101. See "Bitter Harvest for Vietnam Coffee Farmers," British Broadcasting Corporation, October 25, 2002; "Vietnam's Coffee Farmers in Crisis," British Broadcasting Corporation, September 18, 2002.

102. See *Hydro Review Worldwide*, *op. cit.*; Amnesty International, "Vietnam: Harsh Sentences for Montagnards," ASA News Service, September 28, 2001.

103. See Scott Wilson, "Coca Invades Colombia's Coffee Fields—Falling Prices Push Farmers to Plant Illegal Crops, Threatening US Drug War," *The Washington Post*, October 30, 2001.

104. For trends in Andean region coca and cocaine production, and the "centerpiece" characterization of the role of coca eradication, see US DEA, "Drug Intelligence Brief—Changing Dynamics of Cocaine Production in the Andean Region," (June 2002), available at *http://www.usdoj.gov/dea/pubs/intel/02033/02033.html*. For the reports of coca being grown in Kenya, on Mount Kilimanjaro, see "Plan Colombia Criticism Leads to Increased Spending on Andean Initiative," March 13, 2001, available at

http://www.nadir.org/nadir/initiativ/agp/free/colombia/txt/2001/0525Criticism.htm. See also "Coca Production Rose In Colombia, According To US," *The Wall Street Journal,* March 8, 2002.

105. See Mitchell A. Seligson, "Nicaraguans Talk About Corruption: A Follow-Up Study of Public Opinion," Norwegian Agency for Development Cooperation, March 1999, available at *http://www.norad.no.*

106. For an estimate of Nicaraguan migration to Miami, see *Migration News,* August 1999, vol. 6, no. 8.

107. See Alejandro Bendaña, "The Politics of Hurricane Mitch in Nicaragua," *The Post—Parkland Institute,* vol. III, no. 1, Winter 1999, available at *http://www.ualberta.ca/~parkland/Post/Vol3_No1/Bendana-Nicaragua.html.*

108. See *Noticen,* May 11, 2000.

109. See Stephen Marks, "Land Reform at Stake in Nicaragua" (1996), available at *www.cislac.org.au/nicaragua.*

110. For the armed "Re-Contra" groups in the north, see *Noticen,* June 11, 2000. See also "*Una guerra de 1,850 muertos en 10 años,*" *La Prensa,* August 29, 2001.

111. See Dr. William J. Boyce, "Central American Land Mine Survivors—The Need for Action in Nicaragua," *Journal of Mine Action,* version 4.2, June, 2000, available at *http://maic.jmu.edu/journal/4.2/Features/Nicaragua/nicaragua.htm;* Nicaraguan 1993 disabilities survey, Social Information System SIS, Inter-American Development Bank.

112. For the proliferation of weapons in Nicaragua, see Elvira Cuadra Lira, "*Proliferación y control de armas en Nicaragua,*" Fundacion Arias para la Paz y El Progreso, July 29, 2000.

113. Adilia, Managua (2002), quoted in Rogers (2002), *op. cit.,* p. 3.

114. Dona Yolanda, Managua, 2002, quoted in Dr. Dennis Rodgers, "We Live in a State of Siege: Violence, Crime, and Gangs in Post-Conflict Nicaragua," Development Studies Institute, The London School of Economics, September 2002.

115. See Chris Parenti, "King Cocaine in Nicaragua," *www.zmag.com,* January 1994.

116. For Blandon's role, see Webb, *op. cit.;* see also Professor Alfred McCoy (Yale), "CIA Covert Actions and Drug Trafficking," testimony, Special Seminar on CIA drug trafficking convened by the Congressional Black Caucus, February 13, 1997.

117. CIA Inspector General Britt Snider, classified testimony before the US House of Representatives, House Intelligence Commitee, May 25, 1999, quoted by Robert Parry, ""CIA Admits Tolerating Contra-Cocaine Trafficking in the 1980s," *consortiumnews.com,* June 8, 2000.

118. For the return of US troops to Nicaragua and the requested hot pursuit policy, see "US Troops Aid Cradle of Nicaraguan Nationalism," CNN, February 10, 1999.

119. See *Nicaraguan Network Hotline,* February 24, 2003.

120. For the Labor Ministry's estimates of child labor, see Mariela Fernandez, *La Prensa,* July 17, 2001.

121. Auxiliadora Abarca—ex-Fortex worker at Las Mercedes Free Trade Zone—quoted at *http://www.maquilasolidarity.org/resources/maquilas/nicaragua.htm,* 2003.

122. For more about Nicaragua's maquiladoras, see Andrew Bound, "Nicaragua's textile battle zone," *Financial Times,* November 28, 2000.

123. For Interbanco's default and takeover by the Nicaraguan Superintendency of Banks (SIB), see *Noticen,* September 28, 2000.

124. See Emma Curtis, "Child Health and the IMF: the Nicaraguan Experience," *www.jubilee2000uk.org,* 2000.

125. See UNDP, HDI (2002).

126. World Bank Data Online, 2003; UNDP, Human Development Indicators, 2002.

127. UNDP (HDI), 2002.

128. See the 1996 study of child malnutrition in Nicaragua by the UN's Food and Agriculture Organization (1996), summarized in *Nicanet,* July 29, 1996; see also the UN's Children Fund's study of poverty, malnutrition, and infant mortality in Nicaragua, summarized in *Nicanet,* June 14, 1999. See also IMF Press Release #00/78, December 21, 2000.

129. See *Nicaraguan Network Hotline,* September 5, 2000. See also "UN Threatens Nicaragua With Aid Reduction Over Abortion," *Catholic World News,* February 29, 2000.

130. For more details on Vietnam's track record in the 1990s, see Asian Development Bank, Program Performance Audit Report on the Agricultural Sector Program in the Socialist Republic of Vietnam. PPA:VIE 25325, September 2002, available at *http://www.adb.org/Documents/PERs/ppa_vie25325.pdf.*

NOTES TO CHAPTER SIX

1. For the classic study of comparative political development, see Barrington Moore, *Social Origins of Dictatorship and Democracy,* Boston, Beacon Press, 1965.

2. See "Argentina 'Sorry' Over Nazis," British Broadcasting Corporation, June 13, 2000; "Red Cross Admits It Helped Mengele and Other Nazis Flee," British Broadcasting Corporation, February 17, 1999.

3. World Bank Online Data, 2003.

4. Chase Annual Report, 1983.

5. Josephine Hunolt, Chase private banker, May 1989, Miami.

6. For a comparison of Argentina's real per capita incomes over time, and its 1980 peak at $15,000, see Sebastian Galliani, Daniel Heymann, and Mariano Tommasi, "Missed Expectations: The Argentine Convertibility," Argentina, Universidad de Buenos Aires/CEPAL, November 2002.

7. World Bank Online Data, 2003.

8. See Professor Ronald Dworkin, *Nunca Mas*, New York, Faber & Faber, December 1986, Introduction. See "How Many *Desaparecidos* Were There?" available at *http://www.yendor.com/vanished/index.html*.

9. See the account of Galtieri by Andrew Graham-Yooll, "The Look of Utter Hatred in Galtieri's Blue Eyes Seemed to Say 'I'll Get the Lot of You,'" *Daily Telegraph*, January 1, 2003.

10. See Professor Ronald Dworkin, *op. cit.*

11. World Bank Data Online, 2003.

12. See Andrew Graham-Yooll, *op. cit.*

13. For Galtieri's career, see "Leopoldo Galtieri," *The Guardian*, January 13, 2003.

14. See the analysis of these critical logistical problems by Ignacio Fernandez, "The Falklands War," January, 1999, available at *http://guest.xinet.com/ignacio/polsi342/falklands.html*.

15. "US Officer," Rio, February 14, 1989. See also Gladys D. Ganley and Oswald H. Ganley," Unexpected War in the Information Age. Communications and Information in the Falklands Conflict." Harvard University Publication, P-84–3, 1984, p. 105.

16. For the Burson-Marsteller relationship with the Argentine junta, see "What's Wrong with: Burson-Marsteller?" *Corporate Watch Magazine*, issue 2, winter 1996.

17. Quoted in Jonathan Marshall, Peter Dale Scott, and Jane Hunter, *The Iran-Contra Connection*, Boston, South End Press, 1987, excerpt available at *http://www.thirdworldtraveler.com/Ronald_Reagan/ReaganContra Commit_TICC.html*.

18. For Ender's March 8, 1982 assurances, see Argentina's *Informe Rattenbach*, December 1982, available at *http://www.nuncamas.org/document/militar/rattenbach/rattenbach12.htm*.

19. See Jeane J. Kirkpatrick, "Dictatorships and Double Standards," *Commentary*, November 1979.

20. For more about Wenceslao Bunge's role during this period, see *www.nuncamas.org/document/militar/rattenbach/rattenbach33.htm—59k*. For Bunge, see King's College—London: Liddell Hart Centre for Military Archives: Woolly Al Walks the Kitty Back television documentary archive, archive 3/2/1991, available at *http://www.kcl.ac.uk/lhcma/cats/woollyal/xw77-01-.htm#xw77S05*.

21. Haig, quoted in Jonathan Marshall, Peter Dale Scott, and Jane Hunter, *op. cit.*

22. "Chilean Military Analyst," Sao Paulo, February 21, 1989.

23. R. A. ("Johnny") Apple, May 2, 1982. See the post-hoc analysis of the factors responsible for Thatcher's June 1983 victory in I. Crew, "How to Win a Landslide Without Really Trying: Why the Conservatives Won in 1983," in A. Ranney, ed., *Britain at the Polls 1983*, New York, Duke University Press, 1985. See also Patrick Dunleavy and Cristopher T. Husbands, *British Democracy at the Crossroads: Voting and Party Competition in the 1980s*, London, George Allen & Unwin, 1985.

24. For a Swedish report on the case, see Social Democratic Students Organization, "*Argentina måste utlämna Alfredo Astiz*," Pressmeddelande January 14, 2002, *http://studentforbundet.com/ssf/media/press meddelanden/hagelin.asp*.

25. See *Reuters*, "The Promotion of Captain Alfredo Astiz," May 7, 1995.

26. See *Agence France Presse*, "*Remise en liberté d'Alfredo Astiz, ancien militaire de la dictature*," January 30, 2002.

27. See *http://www.yendor.com/vanished/junta.html#astiz*.

28. For Videla, see *San Francisco Chronicle*, June 10, 1998, p. A10; July 15, 1998, C12.

29. For Videla's 2001 indictment, see *San Francisco Chronicle*, July 11, 2001, p. A8.

30. *New York Times*, October 8, 1989.

31. For the baby-selling case, see *The Wall Street Journal*, November 25, 1998, p. A1; *San Francisco Chronicle*, January 21, 1999, p. A14; *San Francisco Chronicle*, March 17, 2000, p. D2.

32. See BBC Mundo, "*Massera Dice Que Es Persequido*," September 7, 2001.

33. For Adolfo Scilingo's testimony, see *San Francisco Chronicle*, January 1, 1998, p. A18. See Horatio Verbitsky, *El Vuelo*, Buenos Aires, Planeta, 1995.

34. For the Argentine military bank accounts case, see *San Francisco Chronicle*, February 24, 1998, p. A11.

35. See *San Francisco Chronicle*, October 10, 1997, p. D2; *San Francisco Chronicle*, July 1, 1998, p. A8; *Wall Street Journal*, December 7, 2000, p. A1.

36. For Galtieri's indictment, see *San Francisco Chronicle*, January 23, 1999; October 3, 1999, p. C3.

37. For the Argentine bond compensation program, see Axel Bugge, "Argentina to compensate 'Dirty War' victims with bonds," *Reuters*, August 19, 1997; Jack Epstein, "Argentina's 'Dirty War' Laundry May Get a Public Airing," *The Christian Science Monitor*, December 4, 1997.

38. Jose Maria Dagnino Pastore, *El Cronista Comercial*, July 6, 1982. See *The Economist*, Economic Intelligence Unit, "Argentina Report," December 6, 1983, p. 16. See also *The Wall Street Journal*, August 9, 1982; and Argentine Central Bank, "External Debt as of December 31, 1982," unpublished 1983 circular.

39. "NY Banker # 10," January 5, 1989, New York.

40. For the missing $11 billion, see Clovis Rossi, "*Instabilidade Politica, um Obstaculo*," *Folha do Sao Paulo*, November 9, 1982, p. 15.

41. *New York Times*, October 4, 1983.

42. *New York Times*, October 4, 1983. For the run on the peso, US Department of Commerce, "Foreign Economic Trends: Argentina," March 1984, pp. 6–7.

43. The $10 billion for missing debt was supported by "Argentine Central Banker," New York, June 6, 1988, and by Jim Nash and Alma Conte, *op. cit.*

44. The data on UK syndications to Argentina are from *Euromoney*.

45. See Raoul Contreras, "Why We Celebrate Cinco de Mayo," North Country Times, May 4, 2002, available at *http://www.nctimes.net/news/2002/20020504/62153.html*.

46. "NY Banker #7," *op. cit.* For the informal write-offs of military debt, see Paul Beckermann, The World Bank, December 22, 1988. The conduit loans to the military were described by "NY Banker # 10," January 5, 1989, NYC, and "NY Banker # 7," *op. cit.*

47. For the YPF funnel role, Peter Beckermann, The World Bank, December 22, 1988.

48. William R. Cline and Riordan Roett, *Latin American Economic Outlook*, Washington, IEA, Inc., 1986, p. 21.

49. "Argentine Businessmen," December 2, 1987, New York.

50. For de Hoz's tax avoidance gambit, see John Simpson and Jana Bennett, *The Disappeared: Voices from a Secret War*, London, Robson Books, 1985.

51. Europa Statistical Survey, 1983, p. 1128.

52. *Euromoney*, "The Amazing Career of Jose Rafael Trozzo," June 1980, pp. 14–15, 21 (Gebauer's comments).

53. "NY Banker #7," *op. cit.*

54. For Minister Roberto F. Alemann's later role as a UBS private banker, see "Argentine Central Banker," June 6, 1988. "NY Banker #7," *op. cit.*; "Argentine Businessmen," December 2, 1987, New York.

55. "NY Banker #7," *op. cit.*

56. Rundt's Weekly, October 10, 1983, p. 6.

57. Alejandro Debat and Luis Lorenzano, *Argentina: The Malvinas and the End of Military Rule*, London, Verso Press, 1983, p. 80.

58. For Bunge's Argentine-American Forum, see *San Francisco Chronicle*, February 28, 1998, p. A7.

59. Uki Goñi, *op. cit.* See also *San Francisco Chronicle*, October 2, 1997, p. A13, and February 28, 1998, p. A7 (regarding Cavallo's accumations).

60. See the study of Yabrán by Jesus Antonio Serrano Sanchez, *Expediente Yabran!* Universidad Nacional Autonoma de Mexico, Facultad de Ciencias Políticas y Sociales, June 1998, p. 8.

61. For Alfredo Yabrán, and Bunge's role as his advisor and spokesperson in the 1990s, see *San Francisco Chronicle*, February 28, 1998, p. A7; Uki Goñi, "Cavallo's Crusade," December 8, 1996, at *ukinet.com/media/text/cavallo.htm*, *http://www.coha.org/opeds/111397.html*; Martín Kanenguiser, "*Como um rato acuado—Alfred Yabrán, amigo de Carlos e suspeito de mandar matar jornalista, suicida-se para não ser preso*," Isto É, May 27, 1998;

62. For the telephone calls by Yabrán to the Presidential Palace, see "*Yabrán al desnudo*," *Que Pasa*, May 14, 2000.

63. See "*Cavallo pidio disculpas a un juez federal*," *Clarin*, August 27, 2002. See Miguel Bonosso, *Don Alfredo*, Editorial Planeta, 2000.

64. "*Martín Kanenguiser, Como um rato acuado—Alfred Yabrán, amigo de Carlos e suspeito de mandar matar jornalista, suicida-se para não ser preso*," Isto É, May 27, 1998.

65. For more details on Argentina's 1990s privatization program, see Sebastián Galiani, et al, "The Benefits and Costs of Privatization in Argentina: A Microeconomic Analysis," University de San Andrés, December 2001, available at *http://www.utdt.edu/~fsturzen/ArgentinePrivatization.pdf*.

66. See Andres Oppenheimer, "Argentina Linked to Mexican Drug Cash," *Miami Herald*, March 1, 2000.

67. This quote is from Sebastian Galliani, et al, *op. cit.*

68. See IMF Press Release 98/1, February 4, 1998.

69. See IMF Press Release 00/17, March 10, 2000.

70. Lawrence Summers, US Secretary of the Treasury, quoted in Jane Bussey, "A Tale of Two Bailouts," *Miami Herald*, October 20, 2002.

71. Stanley Fischer, quoted in IMF Press Release 01/3, January 12, 2001.

72. See IMF Press Release, 01/37, September 7, 2001.

73. See the IMF Technical Memorandum of Understanding with Argentina, September 5, 2000, summarized in Greg Palast, "Who Shot Argentina?," *The Guardian*, August 12, 2001. For the controversy over Banco de la Nación's privatization, see Maria Soledad Casasola, "Producers Defend Argentina's National Banks," Agriculture Online, October 3, 2002., available at *http://www.agriculture.com.*

74. For the $130 billion capital flight estimate, see *The Guardian*, January 15, 2002.

75. For the details on the composition of these changes in the banking system's assets and liabilities during this period, see Javier Llorens and Mario Cafiero, "*El vaciamiento del sistema financiero Argentino en el 2001*," April 2002.

76. See Llorens and Cafiero, *op. cit.*, pp. 18–23.

77. The term "silent retreat" was used by Llorens and Cafiero (2002), *op. cit.*

78. See "*Rockefeller & Cia están eufóricos con Cavallo*," *Página 12*, March 23, 2001.

79. One notable exception was Bloomberg's Thomas Vogel Jr. See his "Don't Cheer for the Argentine Bond Swap." *Bloomberg*, June 4, 2001, available at *http://quote.bloomberg.com.*

80. Mulford is quoted in *Financial Times*, May 17, 2001.

81. See Jules Evans, "Bankers accused of dirty tricks in Argentina," *Euromoney*, January 28, 2002.

82. Professor Charles W. Calomiris of Colombia University's Business School is quoted in "Argentina Buys Some Breathing Room," May 5, 2001.

83. Michael Pettis, former head of Capital Markets, Bear, Stearns, quoted in *Vogel, op. cit.*

84. See Michael Mussa, *Argentina and the IMF: From Triumph to Tragedy*, 2002.

85. See Bloomberg, May 8, 2001.

86. For Menem's 2001 arrest, see *Clarin*, June 7, 2001; *La Nación*, June 5, 2001.

87. See "Swiss to Probe Alleged Menem Bribe," *www.swissinfo.ch*, November 8, 2002.

88. See "Menem's Swiss Accounts 'Hold $10 million," British Broadcasting Corporation, January 21, 2002; "*Des documents bancaires suisses pourraient être remis á la justice argentine avant avril*," *www.lecourrier.ch*, January 24, 2003.

89. See Thomas Vogel Jr. "Don't Cheer for the Argentine Bond Swap." *Bloomberg*, June 4, 2001. available at *http://quote.bloomberg.com.*

90. See Thomas Catán, "Bush Backs Debt Restructuring Plan," *Financial Times*, November 12, 2001; "Argentine Debt Swap 'Constitutes Default,'" *Financial Times*, November 6, 2001.

91. British Broadcasting Corporation, December 19, 2001.

92. See "IMF praises Argentina reforms," British Broadcasting Corporation, June 6, 2002.

93. See Paul Waldie, "Argentina's Top Court Rules Forced 'Pesofication' Illegal," *Toronto Globe and Mail*, March 6, 2003.

94. The Hans Tietmeyer quote is from *Die Welt*, Sept. 16, 2002. For more about social reality in Argentina during the 2001-2002 economic crisis, see Marcela Valente, "Argentina: Images of a Shipwrecked Nation," March 27, 2002 (IPS News Service); *The Guardian*, "Child hunger deaths shock Argentina," November 25, 2002; *Reuters*, "Poor Eat Garbage as Argentina Descends Into Hell," June 20, 2002; Anthony Faiola, "Despair in Once-Proud Argentina," *The Washington Post*, August 6, 2002. For the cartoteros of Buenos Aires, see Rafael Azul, "The Social Costs of Argentina's Crisis," August 2002, *www.wsws.org.* For poverty estimates, see *Agence France Presse*, May 11, 2002. For an analysis of the sources of increases in poverty in Argentina since the 1990s, see Alicia Menendez and Martin Gonzalez-Rozada, *Why Have Poverty and Inequality Increased So Much? Argentina 1991–2002*. Princeton, August 2002, available at *http://www.grade.org.pe/eventos/nip_conference/papers/Gonzalez%20Rozada-ineqpov2.pdf.* For Argentina's immigration history, see Arthur P. Whitaker, *Argentina*, New Jersey, Prentice Hall, Inc., 1964, pp. 54–55.

NOTES TO CHAPTER SEVEN

1. For Paraguay's role in the Ricord story, see Nathan M. Adams, "The Hunt for Andre," *Readers Digest*, May 1973, pp. 225–59; Alfred W. McCoy, *The Politics of Heroin in Southeast Asia*, New York, Harper & Row, 1972, p. 216; James Mills, *The Underground Empire*, New York, Dell, 1986, pp. 554–55; Henrik Kruger, *The Great Heroin Coup*, Boston, South End Press, 1980, pp. 83–86. For Paraguay's role in "Operation Condor"

and its role as a refuge for General Viaux, see John Dinges and Saul Landau, *Assassination on Embassy Row*, New York, McGraw-Hill, 1980, pp. 181–87; Taylor Branch and Eugene M. Propper, *Labyrinth*, New York, Viking/Penguin, 1982.

2. "Colombian Journalist," May 21, 1989; *Financial Times*, February 6, 1989; Nathan M. Adams, "The Hunt for Andre," *op. cit.*, pp. 238–42.

3. *Financial Times*, February 4, 1989.

4. Nathan M. Adams, "The Hunt for Andre," *op. cit.*; James Brooke, *New York Times*, May 1, 1989, p. A3.

5. *Financial Times*, February 8, 1989.

6. *ABC Color*, April 5, 1989; Paraguayan Attorney General's depositions of Mario Abdo Benitez and Juan Martin Villalba de los Rios, May 1989.

7. This episode was outlined in *Jorno do Brazil*, August 28, 1988. Teodomiro Braga, April 14, 1989.

8. *ABC Color*, April 31, 1989.

9. The World Bank, World Debt Tables (1989). IDB, Statement of Loans (1986).

10. *Financial Times*, February 4, 1989, February 8, 1989; Roett, *op. cit.*; *New York Times*, May 1, 1989.

11. Judge Eladio Duarte Carballo was quoted in *ABC Color*, "*US $40 million en el exterior*," April 15, 1989.

12. *New York Times*, May 1, 1989.

13. See Morton Halperin, Jerry Berman, Robert Borosage, and Christine Marwick, *The Lawless State. The crimes of the US Intelligence Agencies*, New York, Penguin Books, 1976, p. 16.

14. For more about Vial, see "La Nueva Derrota," *Que Pasa*, November 10, 1997; S. Rosenfed and J.L. Marre, "Chile's Rich," *NACLA Report on the Americas*, May/June 1997.

15. See "*Milton Friedman: Gurú a regañadientes*," *Revista Qué Pasa*, February 28, 1998. For the account of the 1973-78 period, see Paul E. Sigmund, "Chile: Privatization, Reprivatization, Hyperprivatization," Princeton University, unpublished, July 1989.

16. See Rodrigo Acuña R. and Augusto Iglesias P., "Chile's Pension Reform After 20 Years," The World Bank—Social Protection Discussion Paper No. 0129, December 2001.

17. For Vial's and Lüder's October 28, 1997 sentences, see "*La Nueva Derrota*," *Que Pasa*, November 10, 1997, available at *www.quepasa.cl/revista/1386/18.html*.

18. "Chile Military Analyst," Sao Paulo, February 21, 1989; "Miami Banker," May 1991.

19. Raul Fernandez, former director of Public Credit for Costa Rica, International Bank of Miami, April 22, 1988.

20. See S. Rosenfeld and J. L. Marre, "Chile's Rich," *NACLA Report on the Americas*, May/June 1997.

21. See The Inter American Press Association, "IAPA welcomes study of putting crimes against journalists under federal jurisdiction," February 20, 2003, *http://www.impunidad.com/pressreleases/iapa_news2_20_03E.html*.

22. Jack Anderson, *The Washington Post*, June 5, 1984.

23. Alan Riding, *Distant Neighbors*, New York, Alfred A. Knopf, 1985, p. 176.

24. Jack Anderson, *The Washington Post*, May 15, 1984, p. C15.

25. *Proceso*, April 1988.

26. Banco de Mexico, The Mexican Economy—1988, p. 144.

27. "Mexican Banker #1," July 7, 1988.

28. The World Bank, World Debt Tables, 1991, v. II, p. 264.

29. "The Overselling of Carlos Salinas," *New York Times*, February 24, 1996, p. 20.

30. *Computing*, July 7, 1994.

31. *Computing*, December 8, 1994.

32. Dan La Botz, *The Crisis of Mexican Labor*. (New York: Praeger, 1988), pp. 146-148; Francisco Ortiz, "A cambio de contratos, el STPRM cede su exclusividad en la perforacion de pozos," *Proceso*, 10. 24. 77; Alan Riding, *op. cit.*

33. *Business Week*, October 17, 1988, p. 102.

34. Alan Riding, *op. cit.*, p. 173; *Financial Times*, January 11, 1989; "Mexican Banker #1," March 21, 1989.

35. *Financial Times*, January 12, 1989; October 31, 1989.

36. *Financial Times*, January 18, 1989, repeating the article by *Excelsior*, January 17, 1989.

37. Amnesty International (1994), quoted by The Irish Mexico Group, February 1997, available at *http://flag.blackened.net/revolt/mexico/img/salinas_state.html*.

38. World Debt Tables, *op. cit.*

39. World Bank, World Debt Tables, 1995; ECLA; author's calculations, including gross portfolio, direct, and bondholding investments for 198–94.

40. *Reuters*, January 23, 1996.

41. *Forbes Magazine*, July 8, 1994.

42. See "Heritage of a Thief," *Counterpunch*, vol. 1, no. 24, December 1, 1994.

43. *El Financiero*, February 9, 1996.

44. Eduardo Valle Espinosa quoted by *Spotlight Magazine*, April 17, 1995.

45. *Reuters*, December 2, 1995.

46. See Juan Gasparini, "Switzerland Delegates to Mexico the Task of Finishing the Salinas Investigation," IPI Agency, May 15, 2002.

47. See the article on the alleged meeting by Andreas Oppenheimer, *Miami Herald*, February 17, 1997.

48. See the Dallas Morning News, February 26, 1997.

49. See Agathe Duparc, "Salinas: End of the Criminal Saga in Geneva," *L'Hebdo*, May 15, 2002.

50. See "Citi and the Mexican Millions," *Euromoney*, May 1997, p. 12; *New York Times*, October 31, 1997, p. A1.

51. See the detailed description of this invent in Andres Oppenheimer, *Bordering on Chaos—Guerrillas, Stockbrokers, Politicians and Mexico's Road to Prosperity*, New York, Little, Brown and Company, 1996.

52. Ibid.

53. See Francisco Gil-Diaz, "The Origin of Mexico's 1994 Financial Crisis," *Cato Journal*, vol. 17, no. 3, 1998.

54. See Trond Gabrielsen, "Case Study: Banking Crisis in Mexico," Institute for Policy Dialogue (2003), available at *http://www-1.gsb.columbia.edu/ipd/j_bankingMXN.html*.

55. *The Independent*, August 22, 1995.

56. For the plight of Mexico's small businesses in the crisis, see the statement by Canacintra in the *L.A. Times*, November 16, 1995.

57. See Ginger Thomson, "Free-Market Upheaval Grinds Mexico's Middle Class," *New York Times*, September 4, 2002.

58. *La Jornada*, February 6, 1996.

59. Ginger Thomson, *New York Times, op. cit.*

60. *La Jornada*, February 1996.

61. See *www.narconews.com/fraud1994.html*, 1994.

62. The 22 percent of GDP estimate for the cost of the Mexican bailout is from World Bank Online Data, "Crisis Management Mexico, 1994–1995," June 2001. See *Financial Times*, January 23, 1996; *Reuters*, December 15, 1995.

63. See Julia Preston, "Bailout Audit in Mexico Cites \$7.7 Billion in Dubious Loans," *New York Times*, July 20, 1999.

64. For the role of Rubin and Goldman's stake in Mexican bonds, see SourceMex—Economic News & Analysis on Mexico, March 8, 1995, available at *http://ssdc.ucsd.edu/news/smex/h95/smex.19950308.html SourceMex*.

65. Investment banker from Morgan Grenfall, quoted by *Reuters*, October 13, 1995.

66. See Walter Wriston, *Stern Business Magazine*, Spring 1995.

67. For the crackdown on El Barzon leaders, see *La Jornada*, December 24, 1995.

NOTES TO CHAPTER EIGHT

1. US Central Command, April 7, 2003.

2. See US State Department, "Negroponte Says Coalition Aspires to Liberate, Not Occupy, Iraq," March 27, 2003.

3. General Sir Frederick Stanley Maude, 1917, Baghdad, quoted in "Future Task of Defining When Allies Have Won," *New York Times*, April 6, 2003.

4. See US Department of State, "Statement of Support from Coaltion," March 26, 2003, available at *http://usinfo.state.gov/regional/nea/iraq/text2003/0327coalition-goal.htm*.

5. See British Broadcasting Corporation, "Ukraine Under Pressure Over Iraq," September 26, 2002; Matthew Lee, "US to sanction Ukraine over banned arms sales to Iraq," *Agence France Presse*, January 31, 2003. See Tom Mangold, "Killing the story," British Broadcasting Corporation, April 18, 2002.

6. See US Department of State, "Statements of Support from Coalition Members," March 20, 2003.

7. See US Department of State, "Kazakhstan Said Committed to Partnership with US," March 18, 2003.

8. For more about the Giffen and Williams story, see "Kazakstan: US Investigates Possible Payments to Government Officials From Oil Firm Funds," *The Wall Street Journal*, June 30, 2002; "Prosecutor Says US Oil Giant Is Subject of Investigation In Kazakstan Corruption Probe," EurasiaNet.Org, April 4, 2003; "Ex-Mobil Exec Indicted in Bribery Case," *Associated Press*, April 2, 2003; Tim O'Connor, "Indictments Handed Up Against Mamaroneck Man in Oil Deals," The Journal *News.com*, April 3, 2003; Seymour M. Hersh, "What Was Mobil Up To In Kazakhstan and Russia?," *The New Yorker*, July 9, 2001.

9. See Fawaz A. Gerges, "The Winter of Arab Discontent," ABC News, March 21, 2003. See James Ridgeway, "Southern Baptists OK Dancing (on War Victims' Graves)," *Village Voice*, April 1, 2003.

10. For a summary of legal scholars' views on the legality of the invasion, see Richard Norton-Taylor, "Law Unto Themselves," *The Guardian*, March 14, 2003; "As the Attack Begins, the Question Remains—Is it Legal?," *The Christian Science Monitor*, March 21, 2003.

11. See The National Geographic-Roper Global Geographic Literacy Survey of 3,000 adults, ages 18–24, in Canada, France, Germany, Great Britain, Italy, Japan, Mexico, Sweden and the United States, November 20, 2002, available at *http://www.nationalgeographic.co.uk/press_roperstudy.shtml*.

12. Thomas Friedman, interviewed by Ari Shavit, "White Man's Burden," *Ha'aretz*, April 5, 2003.

13. See James Risen, "Secret History—the CIA in Iran," *New York Times*, April 16, 2000, available at *http://www.nytimes.com/library/world/mideast/041600iran-cia-index.html*.

14. See the biography of Archibald B. Roosevelt Jr., available at *http://www.fas.org/irp/congress/1990_cr/h900607-tribute.htm*.

15. See Eric Davis, "Taking Democracy Seriously in Iraq," Foreign Policy Research Institute, March 27, 2003.

16. See "II. Kurdestan," in The King-Crane Commission Report, Report of [the] American section of Inter-allied Commission of mandates in Turkey. An official United States government report by the Inter-allied Commission on Mandates in Turkey. American Section. August 28, 1919, available at *http://www.cc.ukans.edu/~kansite/ww_one/docs/kncr.htm*.

17. See "Confidential Appendix—The Emir Feisal's Position," in The King-Crane Commission Report, *op. cit.*

18. Geoff Simons, *Iraq: From Sumer to Saddam Hussein*, St. Martins Press, 1994, pp. 179–81.

19. See David Omissi, "Baghdad and British Bombers," *The Guardian*, January 19, 1991.

20. Arthur Harris, quoted in *Omissi, op. cit.*

21. See James A. Paul, "Great Power Conflict over Iraqi Oil: the World War I Era," *Global Policy Forum*, October, 2002.

22. For Qasim's remarks, see British Broadcasting Corporation, "Monitoring Service, Summary of World Broadcasts, Part 4: The Middle East, Africa and Latin America," Caversham Park, June 27, 1961, ME/675/A.

23. For Adnan Pachachi's 1961 remarks on Kuwait, see UN, Security Council Official Records, New York: United Nations, 1961, 957th meeting, July 2, 1961. For his potential role in a post-Saddam Hussein Iraq, see "Who's Who in Post-Saddam Hussein Iraq," British Broadcasting Corporation, April 15, 2003.

24. For Kuwait's description in the 1913 Convention, see J. C. Hurewitz, *The Middle East and North Africa in World Politics*, New Haven, Yale University Press, 1975, vol. 1, pp. 567–70.

25. See Richard Sale, "Exclusive: Saddam Hussein Key in Early CIA Plot," *United Press International*, April 4, 2003; Abdel Darwish and Gregory Alexander, *Unholy Babylon*, New York, St. Martin's Press, 1991; Said K. Abureish, interview, Frontline, March 3, 2003. Miles Copeland, *The Game Player: Confessions of the CIA's Original Political Operative*, London, Aurum Press, 1989.

26. See Said K. Aburish, *A Brutal Friendship: The West and the Arab Elite* (1997); Aburish, interview with Frontline, March, 2003; Said Arburish, "Saddam Hussein, The Politics of Revenge," Bloomsbury, 2000, p. 58.

27. See Andrew and Patrick Cockburn, *Out of the Ashes: The Resurrection of Saddam Hussein*, London, Verso, 2000.

28. See United States Interests Section in Iraq Cable from William L. Eagleton Jr. to Department of State. "Meeting with Tariq Aziz," May 28, 1981.

29. Dan Schorr, "Ten Days That Shook the White House," *Columbia Journalism Review*, July/August 1991.

30. This account of the 1971 festivities at Persepolis draws heavily on an interview with Abdolreza Ansari, published by Cyrus Kadivar, "We Are Awake," *The Iranian*, January 25, 2002, available at *www.iranian.com/CyrusKadivar/2002/January/2500*.

31. See Gabriel Kolko, *Confronting the Third World—US Foreign Policy, 1945–80*, New York, Pantheon Books, 1988, p. 268.

32. See William Branigin, "Iran Set to Scrap $34 Billion Worth of Civilian Proejcts," *The Washington Post*, May 30, 1979, p. A22.

33. Henry Kissinger, January 13, 1977, quoted at *www.iranian.com/history/Feb98/Revolution*.

34. *Kayhan*, Tehran, September 16, 1977.

35. World Bank Data Online.

36. The Shah, quoted in a roundtable discussion with French TV, January 28, 1977, available at *www.iranian.com/history/Feb98/Revolution*.

37. Ayatollah Khomeini, "Speech # 38," October 20, 1978, Neauphle-le-Chateau, France, available at *www.irib.com*.

38. *Euromoney*, January 1980.

39. See Laurence H. Shoup, *Jimmy Carter and the Trilateralists: Presidential Roots*, Boston, Southend Press, 1980.

40. Mark Hulbert, "Chase Helped, US Hurt by Iranian Funds Freeze," *In These Times*, July 2–15, 1980, p. 16. The Chase asset freeze episode is described in "Why Did Chase Move So Fast," *Euromoney*, February 1980, pp. 10–25.

41. "Strategist," February 1986. See also *New York Times*, May 20, 1980.

42. See Richard Haas, "The Fall of the Shah," Harvard Kennedy School of Government Case Studies in Public Policy and Management, #797, Cambridge, January 1988.

43. Henry Kissinger, February 5, 1979, quoted at *www.iranian.com*.

44. William J. Daugherty, "Jimmy Carter and the 1979 Decision to Admit the Shah to the United States," *www.americandiplomacy.org*, March 16, 2003. See also Lawrence Altman, "The Shah's Health: A Political Gamble," *New York Times*, May 17, 1981; Terrence Smith, "Why the US Admitted the Shah," *New York Times*, May 7, 1981.

45. This account of events on February 11, 1979 is based on a summary presented at *www.iranian.com/history/Feb98/revolution*.

46. William J. Daugherty, *op. cit.*

47. *Kayhan*, Tehran, February 11, 1979.

48. See Leslie Woodhead (Director). "444 Days." Antelope/The History Channel, British Broadcasting Corporation, International Télé Images, 1998.

49. See Gary Sick, *October Surprise: America's Hostages in Iran and the Election of Ronald Reagan*, New York, Random House/New York Times Books, 1991. For a review and critique, see Warren Cohen, "October Surprise-Review," *Fletcher Forum of World Affairs*, Summer 1992.

50. See Warren J. Mitofsky, CBS News, "The 1980 Pre-Election Polls: A Review of Disparate Methods and Results," November 1981, available at *www.amstat.org/sections/SRMS/proceedings/papers/1981_011.pdf*.

51. See Robert Parry, "October Surprise X-Files: Part I: Russia's Report," December 11, 1995, available at *http://www.webcom.com/~lpease/collections/denied/octsurprise.htm*.

52. See Robert Parry, "October Surprise X-Files: The Money Trail," January 1, 1996, available at *http://www.Consortiumnews.com/archive/xfile4.htm*.

53. For more about the character of Khomeini's Iran, see Ervand Abrahamian, Khomeinism: Essays on the Islamic Republic. (October 1993), available at *http://ark.cdlib.org/ark:/13030/ft6c6006wp/*; William Shawcross, *The Shah's Last Ride: The Fate of an Ally*, New York, Simon and Schuster, 1988, p. 154.

54. See Steve Galster, "Afghanistan: The Making of US Policy, 1973–90," National Security Archive, 1990.

55. The quote is from Janes' Defense Journal.

56. See Gen. Mohammad Yahya Nawroz, Army of Afghanistan, and LTC (Ret) Lester W. Grau, US Army, "The Soviet Army in Afghanistan" US Army, Foreign Military Studies (1996), available at *http://leav-www.army.mil/fmso*.

57. See Hiro, *op. cit.*, p. 29.

58. See Dilip Hiro, *The Longest War—The Iran-Iraq Military Conflict*, New York, Routledge, 1991, pp. 32–34.

59. For Khomeini's appeals to Iraqi Shi'as to revolt, see Efraim Karsh and Inari Rautsi, *Saddam Hussein: A Political Biography*, New York, Free Press/MacMillan, 1991, p. 138; see also S. Pelletiere, *The Iran-Iraq War: Chaos in a Vacuum*, New York, Praeger, 1992.

60. See Lt. Col. Mark Buckhan and Frank Esuivel, "Saddam Hussein and the Iran-Iraq War," National Defense University, National War College (2001), available at *http://www.ndu.edu/nwc/writing/AY01/5602/SeminarC5602BestPaper.pdf*

61. See American Federation of Scientists, "Iran-Iraq War, 1980-88," available at *http://www.fas.org/man/dod-101/ops/war/iran-iraq.htm*.

62. See Stephen C. Pelletiere, *The Iran-Iraq War: Chaos in a Vacuum*, New York, Praeger, 1992, p. 44.

63. See Jonathan Soverow, "Weapons Dumping and Senseless Slaughter in the Iran-Iraq War, 1999 Princeton memo, available at *www.princeton.edu*.

64. Said K. Aburish, interview with Frontline, March 3, 2003, available at *www.pbs.org/wgbh/pages/frontline*.

65. For the "by-stander" characterization of the US stance during this period, see Michael Dobbs, "US Had Key Role in Iraq Buildup," *The Washington Post*, December 30, 2002.

66. See Larry Everest, "Fueling the Iran-Iraq Slaughter," Znet, September 5, 2002, available at *www.zmag.org*.

67. See Everest, *op. cit.*

68. Aburish, *op. cit.*

69. See "The Iran-Iraq War: Serving American Interests," Aspects of Indian Economy, #33-#34, *www.rupe-india.org*, December 2002. See Frontline, "The Arming of Iraq," September 11, 1990, available at *www.pbs.org*. See also Ted Koppel, ABC NEWS Nightline Show #2690—Air Date: September 13, 1991.

70. See Robert Parry, "Saddam Hussein's Green Light," *www.consortiumnews.com* (1996), p. 2.

71. Said K. Aburish, *Brutal Friendship: The West and the Arab Elite*, London, St. Martin's Press, 1998; Aburish, interview with Frontline/PBS, March 2003.

72. Ibid., 1.

73. See Christopher C. Joyner, *The Persian Gulf War: Lessons for Strategy, Law, and Diplomacy*, Greenwood Press, 1990, p. 66.

74. See Letter from Foreign Minister Sadoon Hammodi to Secretary of State Alexander Haig, April 13, 1981.

75. See Donald Neff, "Israel Bombs Iraq's Osirak Nuclear Research Facility," *Washington Report on Middle East Affairs*, June 1995, pp. 81–82, available at *www.wrmea.com*.

76. Senator Alphonse D'Amato, Frontline, "The Arming of Iraq," *op. cit.*

77. See Memo from Nicholas A. Veliotes and Jonathan Howe to Undersecretary of State for Political Affairs Lawrence S. Eagleberger, "Iran-Iraq War: Analysis of Possible US Shift form Position of Strict Neutrality," Department of State, October 7, 1983, available at *www.gwu.edu/~nsarchiv/NSAEBB/NSAEBB82/iraq22.pdf*. See Bill Herman's 1991 interview with The Age, quoted in Jonathan Soverow, 'Trankenstein of the Desert," *www.princeton.edu*.

78. *New York Times*, February 28, 1982.

79. Digital National Security Archive, "Iraqgate: Saddam Hussein: US Policy and the Prelude to the Persian Gulf War, 1980–94," 2003, available at *http://nsarchive.chadwyck.com*.

80. National Security Directive 99, July 12, 1983. See testimony of Howard Teicher, *In These Times*, March 6, 1995, which, I believe, incorrectly dated it at June 1982.

81. See UN Resolution 540, October 31, 1983; *Washington Report on the Middle East*, "Iran-Iraq: New Dangers," May 28, 1984.

82. See National Security Directive 114, November 26, 1983.

83. See US Embassy in UK cable from Charles H. Price II to the Department of State, "Rumsfeld Mission: December 20 Meeting with Iraqi President Saddam Hussein," December 21, 1983; "Rumsfeld One-on-One Meeting with Iraqi Deputy Prime Minister," December 21, 1983, available at *http://www.gwu.edu/~nsarchiv/NSAEBB/NSAEBB82/iraq32.pdf*.

84. See Institute for Policy Studies, "Rumsfeld Ignored Weapons of Mass Destruction in Pursuit of Oil Pipeline," March 24, 2003, available at *http://ips-dc.org/crudevision/index.htm*.

85. See US Interests Section in Iraq Cable from William L. Eagleton Jr. to the Department of State. "[Excised] Iraqi Pipeline through Jordan," January 10, 1984; "Meeting With Tariq Aziz: Expanding Iraq's Oil Export Facilities," January 3, 1984 *http://www.gwu.edu/~nsarchiv/NSAEBB/NSAEBB82*.

86. *The Washington Post*, January 1, 1984.

87. See US Embassy in United Kingdom Cable from Charles H. Price II to the Department of State. "Rumsfeld Mission: December 20 Meeting with Iraqi President Saddam Hussein," December 21, 1983; US Embassy in the United Kingdom Cable from Charles H. Price II to the Department of State. "Rumsfeld One-on-One Meeting with Iraqi Deputy Prime Minister," December 21, 1983 available at *http://www.gwu.edu/~nsarchiv/NSAEBB/NSAEBB82/index.htm*.

88. See Central Intelligence Agency, Directorate of Intelligence Appraisal, "The Iraqi Nuclear Program: Progress Despite Setbacks," June 1983, available at *http://www.gwu.edu/~nsarchiv/NSAEBB/NSAEBB82/index.htm*.

89. Dr. Hans Blix, "Update on Inspection," UN Security Council, January 27, 2003.

90. See US Department of State, Bureau of Politico-Military Affairs Information Memorandum from Jonathan T. Howe to George P. Shultz. "Iraq Use of Chemical Weapons," November 1, 1983; US Department of State, Office of the Assistant Secretary for Near Eastern and South Asian Affairs Action Memorandum from Jonathan T. Howe to Lawrence S. Eagleburger. "Iraqi Use of Chemical Weapons" (includes Cables Entitled "Deterring Iraqi Use of Chemical Weapons" and "Background of Iraqi Use of Chemical Weapons"), November 21, 1983, available at *http://www.gwu.edu/~nsarchiv/NSAEBB/NSAEBB82/index.htm*.

91. See Michael Dobbs, "US Had Key Role In Iraqi Weapons Buildup," *The Washington Post*, December 30, 2002.

92. See Jeremy Scahill, "The Saddam Hussein in Rumsfeld's Closet," CommonDreams.org, April 8, 2003.

93. See the report on Howard Teicher's deposition *In These Times*, March 6, 1995.

94. Colonel Walter P. Lang, Senior DIA officer, *New York Times*, August 18, 2002.

95. *New York Times*, November 2, 1992.

96. See Christine Gosden, "Why I Went, What I Saw," *The Washington Post*, March 11, 1998.

97. See UN Resolution 620, October 26, 1988.

98. Michael Dobbs, *The Washington Post*, *op. cit.*

99. PBS, "The Arming of Iraq," (1990), *op. cit.*

100. See Defense Intelligence Agency Intelligence Report. "Defense Estimative Brief: Prospects for Iraq," September 25, 1984, available at *http://www.gwu.edu/~nsarchiv/NSAEBB/NSAEBB82/index.htm.*

101. For Abboud's 1988 takeover of First City Bank, see Skip Hollandsworth, "The Killing of Alydar," Texas Monthly, June 2001.

102. Rep. Henry Gonzalez, Congressional Record, April 25, 1991.

103. See First City vs. Rafidain Bank, US Court of Appeals For the Second Circuit, Docket No. 97-7532, July 16, 1998.

104. For the Harken transaction by First City, see Glenn R. Simpson, "Harvard Was Unlikely Savior of Bush Energy Firm Harken," *The Wall Street Journal*, October 9, 2002.

105. See Stockholm Institute for Peace Research, Arms Transfer Data Base, March 5, 2003, author's analysis.

106. SIPRI, *op. cit.*

107. Ted Koppel, Nightline, September 13, 1991.

108. *Newsweek*, September 23, 2002.

109. For Cardoen, see the report on Howard Teicher's deposition *In These Times*, March 6, 1995.

110. See Robert Schoonmaker and Bill Sargent, "Enforcement Case Histories: Anatomy of a Successful Investigation," US Department of Commerce, 1995, available at *www.bis.doc.gov/enforcement.*

111. See PBS/Frontline, "The Arming of Iraq," 1990, *op. cit.*

112. For Cardoen, see the report on Howard Teicher's deposition *In These Times*, March 6, 1995.

113. Kenneth R. Timmerman, "US Export Policy Toward Iraq: An Agenda for Tomorrow," Testimony, Senate Committee on Banking, Housing, and Urban Affairs, Tuesday, October 27, 1992.

114. Mark Pythian, *How the US and Britain Secretly Built Saddam Hussein's War Machine*, Boston, Northeastern University Press, 1997, p. 38. For the claims that Iranian gas was also involved at Halabja, see Adel Darwish, "Halabja: Whom Does the Truth Hurt?, *www.opendemocracy.com*, March 17, 2003. See also Stephen Pelletiere, *The Iran-Iraq War: Chaos in a Vacuum.*

115. See Bob Woodward, *The Washington Post*, December 15, 1986.

116. See *Newsweek*, "Iraq in the Balance," March 19, 2002.

117. See Gelb's column, *New York Times*, March 9, 1982.

118. *New York Times*, January 1, 1987.

119. See Maxim Kniazkov, "Gulf War veterans accuse European firms over supplies to Iraq," *Agence France Presse*, December 24, 2002.

120. PBS (1990), *op. cit.*

121. Michael Dobbs, *The Washington Post*, *op. cit.*

122. *Newsweek*, September 23, 2002.

123. See Arms Control Reporter, February 1991.

124. See US Senate Report 103-900, May 25, 1994, p. 264; *Agence France Presse*, February 26, 1998. Times of India, February 10, 2002; Michael White, "UK Anthrax Strains 'Sold to Iraq'," *The Guardian*, April 3, 1998, p. 10; Martin Hickman, "Britain Exported Anthrax to Iraq Says Lib Dem," *Press Association*, April 2, 1998; Keith Bradsher, "Senator Says US Let Iraq Get Lethal Viruses," *New York Times*, February 10, 1994, p. A9; Kevin Merida and John Mintz, "Rockville Firm Shipped Germ Agents to Iraq, Riegle Says," *The Washington Post*, February 10, 1994, p. A8; William Blum, "Anthrax for Export: US Companies Sold Iraq the Ingredients for a Witch's Brew," *The Progressive*, April 1998, p. 18; Jim Abrams, "US Firms Sold Possible Biological warfare Agents to Iraq," *Associated Press*, February 10, 1994; "Conflict Alleged for Head of Study on Gulf War Illness," *Baltimore Sun*, November 29, 1996, p. 20A. Tim Butcher, "Britain Sent Anthrax Agent to Saddam Hussein," *Electronic Telegraph*, February 14, 1998, *http://www.telegraph.co.uk*; Jeffrey Smith, "Did Russia Sell Iraq Germ Warfare Equipment?," *The Washington Post*, February 12, 1998, p. A1. "Russia Denies Report It Helped Iraq Develop Biological Weapon," *Baltimore Sun*, February 13, 1998, p. 14. A. R. Jeffery Smith, "Iraq's Drive for a Biological Arsenal: U.N. Pursuing 25 Germ Warheads It Believes Are Still Loaded with Deadly Toxin," *The Washington Post*, November 21, 1997, p. A1. J. Venter, "UNSCOM Odyssey: The Search for Saddam Hussein's Biological Arsenal," *Jane's Intelligence Review*, March 1998, p. 1.

125. See US Central Intelligence Agency (CIA), "Unclassified Report to Congress on the Acquisition of Technology Relating to Weapons of Mass Destruction and Advanced Conventional Munitions, 1 July Through 31 December 2000," September 7, 2001, available at *http://www.cia.gov/cia/publications/bian/*

bian_sep_2001.htm; Ali Javed, spring 2001, "Chemical Weapons and the Iran-Iraq War: A Case Study in Noncompliance," Nonproliferation Review 8 (1): pp. 43–58; Physicians for Human Rights, "Winds of Death: Iraq's Use of Poison Gas Against its Kurdish Population," Boston, Physicians for Human Rights, February 1989, pp. 1–2.

126. Dr. Hans Blix, Update, January 27, 2003, *op. cit.*

127. For the "MI6" theory see *De Morgen*, April 15, 1998.

128. See Dennis Bernstein, "Gulf War Syndrome Cover-Up," Covert Action Quarterly, winter 1998.

129. See James Cusick and Felicity Arbuthnot, "America tore out 8000 pages of Iraq dossier," *Scottish Sunday Herald*, December 22, 2002, available at *http://www.sundayherald.com/30195.*

130. See Andreas Zumach, "List of Companies Named in the Iraqi WMD Declaration," *Die Tageszeitung*, December 18, 2002, at *www.taz.de/pt/2002/12/19/a0080nf.test.*

131. See Kenneth R. Timmerman, *The Poison Gas Connection. Western Suppliers of Unconventional Weapons and Technologies to Iraq and Libya*, Los Angeles/Paris, The Simon Wiesenthal Center, 1990.

132. See Andreas Zumach, "List of Companies Named in the Iraqi WMD Declaration," *Die Tageszeitung*, December 18, 2002, at *www.taz.de/pt/2002/12/19/a0080nf.test.* See also Gary Milhollin and Diana Edensword, "Iraq's Bomb, Chip by Chip," *New York Times*, April 24, 1992, p. A35.

133. See Jay Solomon, Jess Bravin, and Jeanne Whalen, "Global Creditors Chase Iraqi Debts of $166 billion," *Dow Jones Newswire*, March 29, 2003.

134. Ibid.

135. *The Guardian*, November 2, 1998.

136. Frontline, March 2003, *op. cit.*

137. See SIPRI (2003), "Iraq and Arms Control."

138. See Veliotes and Howe, "Iran-Iraq War," *op. cit.*

139. See Strategic Studies, *The Military Balance*, 1987–88, London, 1987.

140. See Iraq Ministry of Planning, Central Statistical Organization. Annual Abstract of Statistics, Baghdad, 1985, p. 164.

141. DIA, "Prospects for Iraq," Defense Estimative [sic] Brief, September 25, 1984, available at *http://www.gwu.edu/~nsarchiv/NSAEBB/NSAEBB82/index.htm.*

142. See World Bank/BIS (2001) estimates for Iraq's foreign debt cited in Cavid Chance, "Regime Change Could Benefit Iraqi Creditors," *Reuters*, September 13, 2002; Center for Strategic and International Studies, "A Wiser Peace: An Action Strategy for a Post-Conflict Iraq. Supplement I: Background Information on Iraq's Financial Obligations," January 23, 2003, available at *http://www.csis.org.* Iraq's 1989 GDP is from UN< "Report on the Current Humanitarian Situation in Iraq," March 30, 1999, available at *http://www.un.org/depts/oip/panelrep.html.*

143. DIA, *op. cit.*

144. See Jay Solomon, Jess Bravin, and Jeanne Whalen, "Global Creditors Chase Iraqi Debts of $166 billion," *Dow Jones Newswire*, March 29, 2003; "Japan Not to Write Off Iraqi Debts Reaching $6 Billion," *ITAR-TASS*, April 17, 2003. US EXIM Bank, Country Risk Analysis Division, "Iraqi Payments Situation Deteriorates Further," January 23, 1989.

145. See Action Memorandum from Richard W. Murphy to Eagleburger, "EXIM Financing for Iraq," December 22, 1983, available at *http://www.gwu.edu/~nsarchiv/NSAEBB/NSAEBB81/index.htm*; Henry B. Gonzalez, "The Case of Iraq and the EXIM Bank," Congressional Record, February 24, 2002.

146. See Rep. Henry Gonzalez *op. cit.*, February 24, 1992; Charles Hammond, financial economist, Country Risk Analysis, "Memorandum to the Board of Directors—Country Limitation Schedule Recommendation: Iraq," May 4, 1987, US EXIM Bank.

147. Letter from James A. Baker III to Clayton Yeuter, June 9, 1989; "Status of Iraq CCC Program," US State Department Memorandum, February 28, 1990, available at *http://www.gwu.edu/~nsarchiv/NSAEBB/NSAEBB82/index.htm.*

148. See Rep. Henry Gonzalez, *op. cit.*, February 24, 1992; March 30, 1992; Digital National Security Archive, "Iraqgate, 1980–94," available at *http://www.gwu.edu/~nsarchiv/NSAEBB/NSAEBB82/index.htm*; Russ W. Baker, "Iraqgate: The Big One That (Almost) Got Away, *Columbia Journalism Review*, March/April 1993.

149. See USDA Memo, October 13, 1989, summarized in Rep. Henry Gonzalez, Congressional Record, April 28, 1992. See also George Lardner Jr., "Well-Connected Jordanian Avoided Indictment," *The Washington Post*, April 9, 1992.

150. See Rep. Henry Gonzalez, Congressional Record, March 30, 1992.

151. Rep. Henry Gonzalez, Congressional Record, April 28, 1992.

152. Rep. Henry Gonzalez, *op. cit.*, February 24, 1992; Alan Friedman and Lionel Barber, "Kissinger's Firm Linked to BNL," *Financial Times*, April 26, 1991.

153. Rep. Henry Gonzalez, Congressional Record, April 28, 1992.

154. Rep. Henry Gonzalez, Congressional Record, April 25, 1991.

155. Ibid.

156. See George Lardner Jr., "Well-Connected Jordanian Avoided Indictment," *The Washington Post*, April 9, 1992.

157. Rep. Henry Gonzalez, *op. cit.*, February 24, 1992.

158. See M. Res and C. Day, *Muldergate: The Story of an Info Scandal*, Macmillan South Africa, Johannesburg, 1980; Adam Jones, "From Rightist to "Brightest? The Strange Tale of South Africa's Citizen," *Journal of Southern African Studies*, 24:2, June 1998, pp. 325–45.

159. See Rep. Henry B. Gonzalez, "Iraq's Military Plans," Congressional Record, July 25, 1992.

160. See "Merchants of Death, Activists for Peace," *www.ThePortlandAlliance.org*, April 2003.

161. For the Commerce Department's role, see See Russ W. Baker, "Iraqgate," *op. cit.*; Kenneth W. Timmerman, *The Death Lobby: How the West Armed Iraq*, New York, Houghton Mifflin, 1991.

162. See Rep. Henry B. Gonzalez, Congressional Record, March 30, 1992.

163. See Russ W. Baker, "Iraqgate," *op. cit.*

164. See Rep. Henry B. Gonzalez, Congressional Record, March 30, 1992.

165. See R. Jeffrey Smith, "US to Pay $400 Million to Cover Iraq's Bad Debt," *The Washington Post*, February 17, 1995.

166. See Judge Marvin Shoob, "Judicial Order in the BNL Case," October 5, 1992, US District Court, Northern District of Georgia, US v. Christopher P. Drogoul. Criminal Action 1:91-CR-078-MHS.

167. John Hogan, US prosecutor, to Judge Marvin Shoob, August 27, 1993, quoted in "Decision Brief," *The Center for Security Policy*, August 27, 1993.

168. Ibid.

169. See Kenneth H. Bacon, "Former Official in BNL Case Pleads Guilty, Avoids Trial," *The Wall Street Journal*, September 3, 1993.

170. See Kenneth R. Timmerman, "Whatever Happened to Iraqgate?," *American Spectator*, November 1, 1996.

171. See R. Jeffrey Smith, "US to Pay $400 Million to Cover Iraq's Bad Debt," *The Washington Post*, February 17, 1995.

172. See The Center for Security Policy, "The CCC Fiasco Continues," August 7, 1992; "US Role Questioned on Bad Iraqi Loan," *L.A. Times*, March 31, 1992.

173. George H.W. Bush, Third Presidential Debate, East Lansing, Michigan, October 19, 1992, transcript, available at *www.Geocities.com/CapitalHill/Senate/7891/perot_glaspie.html*.

174. See Russel Dybvik, "Allegations on Communications With Iraq Denied," US Information Agency, October 20, 1992.

175. See Stephanie Strom, "British Report on Iraq Arms Deal Declares Parliament Was Misled," *New York Times*, February 16, 1996, pp. A1, A4 (N).

176. For Arkansas's role as a rice producer and exporter since the 1980s, see USDA, "Rice—Background Issues and Farm Legislation," July 2001, RCS-0601-01.

177. See PBS (1990), "The Arming of Iraq," *op. cit.*

178. Unidentified "senior Bush Administration official," quoted in *Newsday*, January 21, 1991.

179. Charlie Chaplin, *The Great Dictator*.

180. See the transcript of the July 25, 1990 meeting at *http://home.achilles.net/~sal/greenlight.htm*. See also the transcript in James Ridgeway, "The March to War," *op. cit.*

181. See Andrew I. Killgore, "Tales of the Foreign Service: In Defense of April Glaspie," Washington Report on the Middle East, August 2002.

182. See Testimony of US Assistant Secretary of State for Near Eastern Affairs John Kelly, "Developments in the Middle East," July 31, 1990, Report of the Subcommittee on Europe and the Middle East, US House of Representatives, Washington, DC, US GPO, 1990.

183. See the interview with Jordan's King Hussein, *Village Voice*, March 5, 1991.

184. See William Blum, *Killing Hope: US Military and CIA Interventions Since World War II*, Monroe, ME, Common Courage Press, 1995. See also Ramsey Clark, *The Fire This Time*, International Action Center, 1991. See John Pilger, *Distant Voices*, New York, Vintage: 1991/1994. See also Michael T. Klare, *Rogue States and Nuclear Outlaws*, New York, Hill and Wang, 1985.

185. See US Defense Intelligence Agency, "Defense Estimate Brief—Prospects for Iraq," September 25, 1984, DEB-85-85.

186. For the costs of the 1991 Gulf War, see John T. Haldane, "Rebuilding Kuwait," Trade and Finance, April 1991, available at *www.washington-report.org/backissues/0491/9104081.htm*; Mervat Tallawy, UN Social and Economic Commission, "UN Agency: Iraq war losses expected to top $400 billion," *abs-cbn.com*, April

15, 2003; Dr. Eric Hoskins, "Public Health and the Gulf War," in Dr. Victor Sidel and Dr. Barry Levy, ed., International Physicians for the Prevention of Nuclear War, *War and Public Health*, Cambridge, Oxford University Press, 2000; Melissa Krupa, "Environmental and Economic Repercussions of the Persian Gulf War on Kuwait," ICE Case Studies #9, May 1997, available at *www.american.edu/projects*.

187. For a summary of compensation claims against Iraq, see Center for Strategic and International Studies, "A Wiser Peace: An Action Strategy for a Post-Conflict Iraq, Supplement I: Background Information on Iraq's Financial Obligations," January 23, 2003, available at *www.csis.org*.

188. See "UN Pays $863.7 Million in Claims Against Iraq," *Reuters*, April 8, 2003.

189. See Bruce Bartlett, "Sanctions Don't Work," *National Review*, March 19, 2003; "Iraqi Refiners Say Pollution Cost of UN Sanctions is 'Astronomical,'" *News and Observer*, April 27, 1998; Mary Deibel, "Administration Takes on Rebuilding Iraq's Economy," *www.knoxnews.com*, April 10, 2003; Rahul Mahajan, "The Unending War in Iraq," *Resist*, September 2000, available at *www.thirdworldtraveler.com*.

190. Hans von Sponeck, former UN Humanitarian Program Coordinator for Iraq, February 13, 2000.

191. See US Government Accounting Office, "Weapons of Mass Destruction: UN Confronts Significant Challenges in Implementing Sanctions in Iraq," Washington, DC, GAO, May 2002.

192. See the review of Efraim Karsh and Inari Rautsi, *Saddam Hussein: A Political Biography*, London, Brassey's, 1991 by the US neoconservative Daniel Pipes, *Times Literary Supplement*, August 9, 1991.

193. See Dr. Stephen C. Pelletiere and Lt. Col. Douglas V. Johnson II, "Epilogue: Iraq and Kuwait," in *Lessons Learned: The Iran-Iraq War*, vol. 1, Fleet Marine Force Reference Publication (FMFRP 3-203), Quantico, Virginia, US Marine Corps Combat Development Command, December 10, 1990. See also Efrain Karsh and Inari Rautsi, *Saddam Hussein: A Political Biograpphy*, London, Brassey's, 1991.

194. See *The Wall Street Journal*, April 2, 2003.

ACRONYMS/ABREVIATIONS

ABB—Asea Brown Boveri
ADB—Asian Development Bank
AEB—American Express Bank
AFD—Agence Française de Développement
AFD—French Development Fund
AFDB—African Development Bank
ARCI—Asia Reliability Co. Inc.
ATCC—American Type Culture Collection
BBV—Banco Bilbao Vizcaya
BBVA—Banco Bilbao Vizcaya Argentina
BCCF—Banque Credit Commercial de France
BIR—Banco de Intercambio Regional
BNDES—Banco Nacional de Desenvolvimento Economico e Social
BNL—Banco Nacional del Lavoro
CDC—Commonwealth Development Corporation (UK)
CESP—Companhia Energetica de Sao Paolo
CFP—Cie Française des Petroles
COFACE—French export credit agency
CSFB—Credit Suisse-First Boston
CVRD—Companhia Vale do Rio Doce
DIA—US Defense Intelligence Agency
EBY—Entidad Binacional Yacyreta (Paraguay and Argentina)
ECAs—Export Credit Agencies
ECGD—Export Credits Guarantee Department, Britain's export credit agency
Edelca—Electrificacion del Caroni (Venezuela)
EDF—Electricité de France
EIB—European Investment Bank
EX-IM Bank—The US Export-Import Bank
FEBTC—Far East Bank and Trust Co.
FCPA—Foreign Corrupt Practices Act
FDIC—US Federal Deposit Insurance Corporation
FIVEN—Fundo Investimentos de Venezuela
FOGADE—Fonda de Garantia de Depositas y Protección
FSLN—Frente Sandinista de Liberación Nacional
GE—General Electric
HERMES—Hermes Kreditversicherung-AG, Germany's export credit agency
HIPC—Highly- Indebted Poor Countries initiative of the IMF and World Bank
HP—Hewlett Packard
HSBC—Hong Kong and Shanghai Bank
IBJ—Industrial Bank of Japan

IBRD—International Bank for Reconstruction and Development (World Bank)
IDB—InterAmerican Development Bank
IFC—International Finance Corporation (World Bank)
IMF—International Monetary Fund
IMPSA—Industrias Metalurgicas Pescarmona SA
INDE—National Institute of Electrification (Guatemala)
INTERPOL—International Criminal Police Organization
IPP—Independent Power Producer
JGRN—Junto de Gobierno de Reconstrucción Nacional
JIBC—Japan Bank of International Cooperation
KKN—*Korupsi, Kolusi, Nepotisme* (Corruption, Collusion, Nepotism—Indonesian term of art)
KWU—Kraftwerk Union (Siemens Power Generation Group)
LHWP—Lesotho Highlands Water Development Project
MBB—Messer Schmidt Bolkow Blohm
MHT—Monthly Hign Income
MW—megawatts
NAFTA—North American Free Trade Area
NGO—non-governmental organization
OECD—Organization for Economic Cooperation and Development (30 developed countries)
OPIC—Overseas Private Investment Corporation (US)
OSN—Obras Sanitarias de la Nación
PCGG—Presidential Commission on Good Government
PDCP—Private Development Corporation of the Philippines
PLDT—Philippine Long Distance Telephone Co.
PVDSA—Petroleos de Venezuela
SACE—Sezione Speciale Per l'Assicurazione Del Credito All'Esportazione—Italian export credit agency
SBC—Swiss Bank Corp.
SGS—Sociéte Générale de Surveillance Holding SA, the leading Swiss inspection company
SGV & Co.—SyCip, Gorres, Velayo
SIPRI—Stockhold International Peace Research Institute
SOMISA—Sociedad Mixta Siderurgica Argentina
TDB—Trade Development Bank
UBS—Union Bank of Switzerland
UCPB—United Coconut Planters Bank
UNCTAD—UN Council on Trade and Development
UNDP—HDI—United Nations Development Program—Human Development Indicators
UNICEF—United Nations International Childrens' Emergency Fund
USAID—United States Agency for International Development
USDA—US Department of Agriculture
WB—The World Bank
WCD—World Commission on Dams
WHO—World Health Organization
WTO—World Trade Organization
YPF—Yacimientoa Petroliferos Fiscales

ACKNOWLEDGMENTS

I first began to write about the global underground economy in the late 1970s in publications such as *The New Republic*, *The Washington Post*, and *The Washington Monthly*. A series of investigative articles in the 1980s started me out on what became more than a decade of field research in most of the world's leading havens—the Netherlands Antilles, the Bahamas, B.V.I., the Cayman Islands, Geneva, Zurich, Panama, Monaco, Cyprus, and of course New York, Houston, London, Frankfurt, Vienna, and Miami. In addition, I visited many other key pit stops on the global development circuit, including Mexico City, Tokyo, Vienna, Milan, Bogota, Santiago, Caracas, Port au Prince, Sao Paulo, Buenos Aires, Johannesburg, Manila, Beijing, Moscow, and Berlin. This was an extremely time-consuming task, but the stories that I tackled required a transnational perspective. Indeed, investigative journalism now demands a global perspective. The individual nation-state is no longer the most important locus, because its role has been compromised by the global mobility of skills and capital, the existence of a new breed of sophisticated transnational criminals, and of course the haven network, whose tenacles now span the globe, protecting and concealing ill-gotten gains.

Along the way, I've been assisted in my research by literally hundreds of friends all over the globe. Unfortunately, many of them have to remain anonymous. In Brazil, Teodomiro Braga, Eduardo Matarazzo Suplicy, Luis Carlos Bresser Perreira, Donald D. Pearson, Raimundo Perreira, Robert Blocker, J. Carlos de Assis, José Farias, Mariza Tupinamba, Celso Pinto, Octavio and Sylvia Alvarenga, and Frederico de Souza Queiroz provided valuable leads. So did Dr. James Putzel, Severina Rivera, Nick Perlas, and Robin Broad in the Philippines; Dr. Ramirez de la O and Adolfo Lupke in Mexico; Dr. Pedro Palma, Gustavo Galdo, Phil Gunson, and John Sweeney in Venezuela; Stan Kahn, Halton Cheadle, Desiree Markgraaf, and Denis Beckett in South Africa; Fernando Arias, Tomas Cabal, Mai Eisemann, and Rodrigo Miranda in Panama; Senator Fernando Flores in Chile; Santiago Pombo and Maria Theresa Barajas in Bogota, Colombia; Marcella Garcia in Ecuador; Robert Levinson, Norman Casper, John Cummings, Robert Hudson, Ross Gaffney, and Josephina Hunold in Miami; Marshall Langer in Neuchatel, Michael Kinsley, Jodie Allen, and Dr. James Boyce. My tenacious research assistants Kathleen Madigan and Silvana Paternostro, now a distinguished author in her own right, provided invaluable help in Miami, Mexico, Panama, Paraguay, and Sag Harbor, and also rescued me from a nasty encounter with Noriega's police. In Russia, Igor Kondratyin, Sergei Glaziev, and Dmitri Kuvalin were extremely helpful. Thanks are also due more generally to The Fund for Investigative Journalism, Joshua Mailman, Eileen McGinnis, Laura Pearson, Marshall Pomer, and especially to *Tercer Mundo Editores*'s Santiago Pombo and Maria Theresa Barajas Sandoval for taking an interest in a Spanish language "prequel" of the book in 1996. And special thanks are also due to John G. H. Oakes and John Bae at Four Walls Eight Windows, who have been delightful to work with, showing infinite care and patience. I'm also grateful to Barrington Moore Jr., Alex Gerschenkron, and Evsey Domar for stimulating a lifelong interest in comparative history.

Finally, Priscilla Star, Daniel Salcedo, Jim Manzi, Senator Bill Bradley, my father and mother Evan and Evelyn, and my children Alexander and Claire Henry have all provided invaluable encouragement and good humor at crucial points along the way. Investigative journalism is a long, costly, often thankless endeavor, taxing on friends and family. As Bertrand Russell once said, "What is missing is not the will to believe, but the will to find out!"

James S. Henry
Sag Harbor, New York
September 2003

INDEX